PLUTARCH'S
MORALIA
IV

PLUTARCH'S
MORALIA

IN FIFTEEN VOLUMES

IV

263 D—351 B

WITH AN ENGLISH TRANSLATION BY
FRANK COLE BABBITT
TRINITY COLLEGE, HARTFORD, CONNECTICUT

CAMBRIDGE, MASSACHUSETTS
HARVARD UNIVERSITY PRESS
LONDON
WILLIAM HEINEMANN LTD
MCMLXII

First printed 1936
Reprinted 1957, 1962

Printed in Great Britain

CONTENTS OF VOLUME IV

CONTENTS

vi

EDITORS' PREFACE

EDITORS' PREFACE

FRANK COLE BABBITT, the editor and translator of
the first five volumes of the *Moral Essays* of Plutarch,
laid down his task and departed this life on the 21st
of September 1935, in his sixty-eighth year. There
was no appreciable gap between the one act and
the other, for almost to the end he continued to
attend promptly and with his habitual scholarly
acumen to the proofs of the present volume, having
already finished with those of Volume V., which
chanced to come first into the printer's hands. He
foresaw his approaching end and carefully prepared
for the continuation of his Plutarchean work, as his
own preface indicates.

Professor Babbitt graduated from Harvard College in 1890, and received the degree of Doctor
of Philosophy from Harvard University five years
later. The last thirty-seven years of his life he
devoted to the teaching of Greek at Trinity College,
Hartford, Connecticut. Having received his early
training in the ancient classics under such men as
Goodwin, Lane, White, Greenough and Wright, he
was not only an accomplished grammarian but possessed a broad and intimate knowledge of the classical
literatures, history, and institutions, to which he
added, as Fellow of the American School of Classical

Studies at Athens, and later as Professor there, two fruitful years of travel and study in Greece. He had always found in Plutarch a congenial spirit, and from the time when he consented to edit the *Moralia* for the Loeb Classical Library he devoted all his leisure to intensive studies in that field. The five volumes which he was permitted to finish reveal his steady attainment of mastery in all the varied and difficult problems which confront the student of Plutarch; and in particular Volume V., which perhaps of the whole series of these *Essays* presents the most baffling problems of text and interpretation, best reveals his scholarly competence, resourcefulness, and judgement.

The Editors of the Loeb Classical Library not only found in Professor Babbitt a collaborator with whom it was always a pleasure to work, but also conceived for him a lasting friendship.

THE EDITORS.

PREFACE

THE title-page of this volume, like its predecessors, bears but one name, but another might well have been added. The first draft of the translation was prepared by Mr William Helmbold, of Trinity College, Hartford. This was then harmonized somewhat with the preceding volumes, typed, discussed, and harmonized again, so it is to be hoped that no great departures from the style of the other volumes may be noticed. Mr Helmbold provided also the greater part of the references.

The text was prepared from such information as was available in the editions of Wyttenbach, Hutten, and Bernardakis, with occasional consultation of facsimiles, and was sent to the printer before copies of the text of Vol. II. of the new Teubner edition (ed. W. Nachstädt—J. B. Titchener. Leipzig, 1934) had reached this country. Consequently, any additions based on the critical notes or the references in that edition had to be added in the proof. Fortunately these were not very numerous.[a]

There remains the pleasant duty of recording the gracious generosity of Mr F. H. Sandbach of Trinity

[a] For further details and a somewhat adverse criticism see the editor's review of this edition to appear in *Classical Philology*, 1937.

PREFACE

College, Cambridge, who has kindly put at the disposal of the Editors of the Loeb Library the results of his work on Plutarch's *Moralia*, preferring that these should be incorporated here rather than published separately. Much of his work concerns the essays *De Stoicorum repugnantiis* and *De communibus notitiis*, but there are included also notes on other essays, and some facsimiles of MSS., for all of which due acknowledgement should be made.

F. C. B.

TRINITY COLLEGE,
HARTFORD, CONN.
January 1935.

Mr Helmbold must state his great obligation to Professor L. C. Barret of Trinity College for reading Volumes IV. and V. in proof, correcting a number of errors, and making numerous improvements of many kinds. Any errors which remain, however, must not be ascribed to him.

THE TRADITIONAL ORDER OF THE BOOKS of
the *Moralia* as they appear since the edition of
Stephanus (1572), and their division into volumes
in this edition.

THE TRADITIONAL ORDER

THE TRADITIONAL ORDER

THE TRADITIONAL ORDER

THE ROMAN QUESTIONS
(QUAESTIONES ROMANAE)

INTRODUCTION

THE *Roman Questions* is an attempt to explain one
hundred and thirteen Roman customs, the majority
of which deal with religious matters. The treatise
is one of three similar compilations of which two
have been preserved and one, the *Quaestiones Bar-
baricae* (No. 139 in Lamprias's list), has been lost.
Plutarch possessed a great desire to know the
reason why : besides the many discussions of a
similar sort contained in the *Symposiacs* (*Table Talk*),
there is extant a discussion of *Physical Causes*, and
the titles of other writings of the same sort have
been preserved for us in Lamprias's list of Plutarch's
writings.[a]

The Greek title, which means " causes ", is twice
mentioned by Plutarch himself in the *Lives*,[b] and
we might call it " The Reasons Why." In nearly
every case at least two and often more reasons are
given ; of these presumably not more than one can
be right. Thus the other explanations will embody
the results of Plutarch's researches on the matter
or his own quaint speculations. Consequently the
book, which is an important source for Roman

---

[a] (149) Αἰτίαι τῶν περιφερομένων Στωικῶν; (160) Αἰτίαι καὶ
τόποι; (161) Αἰτίαι ἀλλαγῶν; (167) Αἰτίαι γυναικῶν.
[b] *Life of Romulus*, chap. xv. (26 E) ; *Life of Camillus*,
chap. xix. (138 E).

customs, especially for religious customs, has been of the greatest service to students of early Roman religion, a field in which so little is certain and which provides (even as it provided for Plutarch) such glorious opportunities for speculation that it has been somewhat overtilled in recent years. Anyone interested in such matters may observe the trend of this scholarship if he will examine F. B. Jevons' reprint of Holland's translation of the *Roman Questions* (London, 1892); or better, H. J. Rose, *The Roman Questions of Plutarch, a New Translation with Introductory Essays and a Running Commentary* (Oxford, 1924). Professor Rose might, indeed, have improved his translation by consulting some good Greek lexicon; but the essays and the commentary are very valuable, for they contain, among other matters of interest, a discussion of Plutarch's sources and of early Roman religion; the commentary is fortified with abundant references to ancient writers and to modern scholars. It is a scholarly work and the most important contribution to the study of the *Roman Questions* since Wyttenbach.

This treatise could hardly have been written by a person ignorant of Latin. Plutarch in his *Life of Demosthenes*, chap. ii., modestly disavows any profound knowledge of Latin; yet he had read a considerable amount in the language and had spent some time in Rome. Hence he was quite able to use Latin works in compiling the *Roman Questions*. Some Roman writers he mentions by name, especially Varro, and Verrius Flaccus, an antiquarian of the Augustan age. Livy is specifically cited but twice in the *Moralia*, once in the present work and once in *De Fortuna Romanorum*; yet he is referred

3

to no less than twelve times in the *Lives*, most of these citations being in the *Marcellus* and the *Camillus*. Perhaps Plutarch's more exact acquaintance with Livy, if he ever acquired this, dates from a time later than the period during which he was engaged in the compilation of the *Roman Questions*.

Other Roman authorities are mentioned occasionally, such as Cato the Elder, Nigidius Figulus, Antistius Labeo, Ateius Capito, and Fenestella ; but no doubt they and others are used in accounts introduced by such expressions as " they say," " some say," " the story is told," and the like. Some of these references have, in fact, been traced by scholars to their originals. It has been remarked of Cicero that any statement found in that author's works appears, or has appeared, elsewhere. The same affirmation might be made of Plutarch with some confidence. Unless he specifically testifies to oral tradition or hearsay, we may be certain that his facts, like Cicero's, are drawn from his extensive reading.

Critics lay stress on a few mistakes which Plutarch made in interpreting Latin (these will be found noted in Rose and in Hartman), but against them must be set the unnumbered instances in which he is right. He did not, however, have to depend wholly on Latin writers, for he undoubtedly had at hand the *Roman Antiquities* of Dionysius of Halicarnassus (1st cent. B.C.) and the works of Juba,[a] the scholarly king of Mauretania, who as a youth had been brought to Rome in 46 B.C. to grace the triumph of Julius Caesar. Juba became greatly interested in Roman

---

[a] Müller, *Frag. Hist. Graec.* iii. 465-484.

customs, and wrote a book in which he paralleled them with the customs of other peoples.

Many of the matters discussed in the *Roman Questions* are to be found treated elsewhere in Plutarch's work, particularly in the Roman *Lives*. The Lives of *Romulus* and of *Numa* are especially rich in parallel passages ; for very many of the Roman customs were thought to go back to the earliest period of Roman history.

The book was probably published after the death of Domitian in A.D. 96, though this is a not quite certain inference from the text (276 E). The work is No. 138 in Lamprias's catalogue of Plutarch's works. The MS. tradition (on which see J. B. Titchener, *University of Illinois Studies*, ix., 1924) is good.

5

ΑΙΤΙΑ ΡΩΜΑΙΚΑ

1. '' Διὰ τί τὴν γαμουμένην ἅπτεσθαι πυρὸς καὶ
E ὕδατος κελεύουσι; ''

Πότερον τούτων ὡς ἐν στοιχείοις καὶ ἀρχαῖς τὸ
μὲν ἄρρεν ἐστὶ τὸ δὲ θῆλυ, καὶ τὸ μὲν ἀρχὰς κινήσεως ἐνίησι τὸ δ' ὑποκειμένου καὶ ὕλης δύναμιν.

Ἢ διότι τὸ πῦρ καθαίρει καὶ τὸ ὕδωρ ἁγνίζει,
δεῖ δὲ καθαρὰν καὶ ἁγνὴν διαμένειν τὴν γαμη-
θεῖσαν;

Ἢ ὅτι, καθάπερ τὸ πῦρ χωρὶς ὑγρότητος ἄ-
τροφόν ἐστι καὶ ξηρὸν τὸ δὲ ὕδωρ ἄνευ θερμότητος
ἄγονον καὶ ἀργόν, οὕτω καὶ τὸ ἄρρεν ἀδρανὲς καὶ
τὸ θῆλυ χωρὶς ἀλλήλων, ἡ δὲ σύνοδος ἀμφοῖν
ἐπιτελεῖ τοῖς γήμασι τὴν συμβίωσιν;

Ἢ¹ οὐκ ἀπολειπτέον καὶ κοινωνητέον ἁπάσης
F τύχης, κἂν ἄλλου² μηδενὸς ἢ πυρὸς καὶ ὕδατος
μέλλωσι κοινωνεῖν ἀλλήλοις;

2. '' Διὰ τί οὐ πλείονας οὐδ' ἐλάττονας ἀλλὰ
πέντε λαμπάδας ἅπτουσιν ἐν τοῖς γάμοις, ἃς
κηρίωνας³ ὀνομάζουσιν; ''

---

¹ ἤ] some mss. read ἦν, which may be right.
² ἄλλου Toup : καλοῦ.
³ κηρίωνας] κηρίους (*i.e.* cereos) Helmbold ; κηρινοὺς
Wyttenbach.   In 280 E and 288 F also the mss. accuse
Plutarch of making a mistake in his Latin inflexions.

6

THE ROMAN QUESTIONS

1. WHY do they bid the bride touch fire and water ?

Is it that of these two, being reckoned as elements or first principles, fire is masculine and water feminine,[a] and fire supplies the beginnings of motion and water the function of the subsistent element or the material ?

Or is it because fire purifies and water cleanses, and a married woman must remain pure and clean ?

Or is it that, just as fire without moisture is unsustaining and arid, and water without heat is unproductive and inactive,[b] so also male and female apart from each other are inert, but their union in marriage produces the perfection of their life together ?

Or is it that they must not desert each other, but must share together every sort of fortune, even if they are destined to have nothing other than fire and water to share with each other ?

2. WHY in the marriage rites do they light five torches, neither more nor less, which they call *cereones* ?

[a] *Cf.* Varro, *De Lingua Latina*, v. 61. The genders are those of *ignis* and *aqua*, not those of the Greek words.
[b] *Cf. Moralia*, 650 B; Servius on *Virgil, Aeneid*, iv. 167 ; Lactantius, *Institutiones Divinae*, ii. 9. 21.

Πότερον, ὡς Βάρρων ἔλεγεν, ὅτι τῶν στρατηγῶν
τρισὶ χρωμένων, εἰσὶ[1] τοῖς ἀγορανόμοις πλείονες,[2]
παρὰ δὲ τῶν ἀγορανόμων ἅπτουσι τὸ πῦρ οἱ
γαμοῦντες;

264 Ἢ διότι πλείοσι χρωμένων ἀριθμοῖς, πρός τε τὰ
ἄλλα βελτίων καὶ τελειότερος ὁ περιττὸς ἐνομίζετο
καὶ πρὸς γάμον ἁρμοδιώτερος; ὁ γὰρ ἄρτιος διά-
στασίν τε δέχεται καὶ τὸ ἴσον αὐτοῦ μάχιμόν ἐστι
καὶ ἀντίπαλον, ὁ δὲ περιττὸς οὐ δύναται δια-
σχισθῆναι παντάπασιν, ἀλλ᾽ ὑπολείπει τι κοινὸν ἀεὶ
μεριζόμενος. τοῦ δὲ περιττοῦ μάλιστα γαμήλιος
ἡ πεντάς ἐστι· τὰ γὰρ τρία πρῶτος περιττὸς καὶ
τὰ δύο πρῶτος ἄρτιος· ἐκ δὲ τούτων ὥσπερ ἄρρενος
καὶ θήλεος ἡ πεντὰς μέμεικται.

B Ἢ μᾶλλον, ἐπεὶ τὸ φῶς γενέσεώς ἐστι σημεῖον,
γυνὴ δ᾽ ἄχρι πέντε τίκτειν ὁμοῦ τὰ πλεῖστα πέφυκε,
τοσαύταις χρῶνται λαμπάσιν;

Ἢ ὅτι πέντε δεῖσθαι θεῶν τοὺς γαμοῦντας
οἴονται, Διὸς τελείου καὶ Ἥρας τελείας καὶ
Ἀφροδίτης καὶ Πειθοῦς, ἐπὶ πᾶσι δ᾽ Ἀρτέμιδος,
ἣν ταῖς λοχείαις καὶ ταῖς ὠδῖσιν αἱ γυναῖκες
ἐπικαλοῦνται;

C 3. "Διὰ τί, πολλῶν ὄντων ἐν Ῥώμῃ ναῶν
Ἀρτέμιδος, εἰς μόνον τὸν ἐν τῷ καλουμένῳ
Πατρικίῳ στενωπῷ ἄνδρες οὐκ εἰσίασιν;"

---

[1] εἰσὶ F.C.B.: σὺν.
[2] πλείονες F.C.B.: πλείονας (omitted by E).

---

[a] Cf. the Lex Coloniae Genetivae, column 62 (C.I.L. i.[2] 594
=ii. 5439), where it is specified that the aediles shall have the
right and power to possess, among other things, "cereos".

[b] Cf. Moralia, 288 D-E, infra, 374 A, 429 A, and 388 A
with the note on the last passage; Lydus, De Mensibus,
ii. 4.

Is it, as Varro has stated, that while the praetors use three, the aediles have a right [a] to more, and it is from the aediles that the wedding party light their torches ?

Or is it because in their use of several numbers the odd number was considered better and more perfect for various purposes and also better adapted to marriage ? For the even number admits division and its equality of division suggests strife and opposition ; the odd number, however, cannot be divided into equal parts at all, but whenever it is divided it always leaves behind a remainder of the same nature as itself. Now, of the odd numbers, five is above all the nuptial number ; for three is the first odd number, and two is the first even number, and five is composed of the union of these two, as it were of male and female.[b]

Or is it rather that, since light is the symbol of birth, and women in general are enabled by nature to bear, at the most, five children at one birth,[c] the wedding company makes use of exactly that number of torches ?

Or is it because they think that the nuptial pair has need of five deities : Zeus Teleios, Hera Teleia, Aphrodite, Peitho, and finally Artemis, whom women in child-birth and travail are wont to invoke ?

3. Why is it that, although there are many shrines of Diana in Rome, the only one into which men may not enter is the shrine in the so-called Vicus Patricius ?

---

[c] Cf. *Moralia*, 429 F. A few authenticated cases of sextuplets have occurred since Plutarch's day. See also the passages of Aulus Gellius and Aristotle quoted in *Classical Journal*, xxx. p. 493.

(264) "Ἦ[1] διὰ τὸν λεγόμενον μῦθον; γυναῖκα γὰρ
αὐτόθι τὴν θεὸν σεβομένην βιαζόμενός τις ὑπὸ τῶν
κυνῶν διεσπάσθη, καὶ ἀπὸ τούτου δεισιδαιμονίας
γενομένης ἄνδρες οὐκ εἰσίασιν.

4. "Διὰ τί τοῖς ἄλλοις Ἀρτεμισίοις ἐπιεικῶς
ἐλάφων κέρατα προσπατταλεύουσι, τῷ δ' ἐν
Ἀβεντίνῳ βοῶν; "

"Ἦ[1] τοῦ παλαιοῦ συμπτώματος ἀπομνημονεύον-
τες; λέγεται γὰρ ἐν Σαβίνοις Ἄντρωνι Κορατίῳ
βοῦς ἐκπρεπὴς ὄψει καὶ μεγέθει διαφέρουσα τῶν
ἄλλων γενέσθαι· μάντεως δέ τινος αὐτῷ φράσαντος,
ὅτι τοῦ καθιερεύσαντος Ἀρτέμιδι τὴν βοῦν ἐκείνην
ἐν Ἀβεντίνῳ πέπρωται μεγίστην γενέσθαι καὶ
βασιλεῦσαι τῆς Ἰταλίας ἁπάσης τὴν πόλιν, ἐλθεῖν
D μὲν εἰς Ῥώμην τὸν ἄνθρωπον ὡς θύσοντα τὴν βοῦν·
οἰκέτου δὲ κρύφα τῷ βασιλεῖ Σερουίῳ τὸ μάντευμα
φράσαντος, ἐκείνου δὲ Κορνηλίῳ τῷ ἱερεῖ, προσ-
τάξαι τὸν Κορνήλιον τῷ Ἄντρωνι λούσασθαι πρὸ
τῆς θυσίας ἀπὸ τοῦ Θύμβρεως· νενομίσθαι γὰρ
οὕτω τοὺς καλλιεροῦντας. ἐκεῖνον μὲν οὖν ἀπ-
ελθόντα λούεσθαι,[2] τὸν δὲ Σερούιον φθάσαντα
θῦσαι τῇ θεῷ τὴν βοῦν καὶ τῷ ἱερῷ τὰ κέρατα
προσπατταλεῦσαι. ταῦτα καὶ ὁ Ἰόβας ἱστόρηκε
καὶ Βάρρων, πλὴν ὅτι τοὔνομα τοῦ Ἄντρωνος
Βάρρων οὐ γέγραφεν, οὐδ' ὑπὸ Κορνηλίου φησὶ
τοῦ ἱερέως ἀλλ' ὑπὸ τοῦ νεωκόρου παρακρουσθῆναι
τὸν Σαβῖνον.

5. "Διὰ τί τοὺς τεθνάναι φημισθέντας ἐπὶ ξένης

____

[1] ἦ] Dübner would read ἦ here and elsewhere at the
beginning of the first interrogation.
[2] λούεσθαι] λούσασθαι Basel ed. of 1574.

10

Is it because of the current legend? For a man attempted to violate a woman who was here worshipping the goddess, and was torn to pieces by the dogs; and men do not enter because of the superstitious fear that arose from this occurrence.

4. WHY do they, as might be expected, nail up stags' horns in all the other shrines of Diana, but in the shrine on the Aventine nail up horns of cattle?

Is it because they remember the ancient occurrence?[a] For the tale is told that among the Sabines in the herds of Antro Curiatius was born a heifer excelling all the others in appearance and size. When a certain soothsayer told him that the city of the man who should sacrifice that heifer to Diana on the Aventine was destined to become the mightiest city and to rule all Italy, the man came to Rome with intent to sacrifice his heifer. But a servant of his secretly told the prophecy to the king Servius, who told Cornelius the priest, and Cornelius gave instructions to Antro to bathe in the Tiber before the sacrifice; for this, said he, was the custom of those whose sacrifice was to be acceptable. Accordingly Antro went away and bathed, but Servius sacrificed the heifer to Diana before Antro could return, and nailed the horns to the shrine. This tale both Juba[b] and Varro have recorded, except that Varro has not noted the name of Antro; and he says that the Sabine was cozened, not by Cornelius the priest, but by the keeper of the temple.

5. WHY is it that those who are falsely reported to

[a] *Cf.* Livy, i. 45; Valerius Maximus, vii. 3. 1.
[b] Müller, *Frag. Hist. Graec.* iii. p. 470.

11

E ψευδῶς, κἂν ἐπανέλθωσιν, οὐ δέχονται κατὰ θύρας,
ἀλλὰ τῷ κεράμῳ προσβαίνοντες εἴσω καθιᾶσιν[1]
αὑτούς· ''

'Ο μὲν γὰρ Βάρρων αἰτίαν μυθικὴν ὅλως ἀπο-
δίδωσι. φησὶ γάρ, ἐν τῷ περὶ Σικελίαν πολέμῳ
ναυμαχίας μεγάλης γενομένης καὶ κατὰ πολλῶν
φήμης οὐκ ἀληθοῦς ὡς ἀπολωλότων ῥυείσης, ἐπαν-
ελθόντας αὐτοὺς ὀλίγῳ χρόνῳ πάντας τελευτῆσαι,
ἑνὶ δ' εἰσιόντι τὰς θύρας ἀπαντῆσαι κλειομένας ἀπ'
αὐτομάτου καὶ μὴ χαλᾶν ἐπιχειροῦντος[2] ἀνοίγειν.
τὸν δ' ἄνθρωπον αὐτοῦ καταδαρθόντα πρὸ τῶν
θυρῶν ἰδεῖν κατὰ τοὺς ὕπνους ὄψιν ὑφηγουμένην
F αὐτῷ τὴν ὑπὲρ τὸ τέγος εἰς τὴν οἰκίαν καθίμησιν·
ποιήσαντα δ' οὕτως εὐτυχῆ γενέσθαι καὶ γηραιόν·
ἐκ δὲ τούτου τὸ ἔθος καταστῆναι τοῖς ὕστερον.

"Ορα δὲ μὴ καὶ ταῦτα τρόπον τινὰ τοῖς Ἑλληνικοῖς ἔοικεν· οὐ γὰρ ἐνόμιζον ἁγνοὺς οὐδὲ
κατεμείγνυσαν ἑαυτοῖς οὐδ' εἴων ἱεροῖς πλησιάζειν,
οἷς ἐκφορὰ γεγόνει καὶ τάφος ὡς τεθνηκόσι. λέγεται δέ τινα τῶν ἐνόχων ταύτῃ τῇ δεισιδαιμονίᾳ
γεγονότων Ἀριστῖνον εἰς Δελφοὺς ἀποστείλαντα
δεῖσθαι τοῦ θεοῦ καὶ παραιτεῖσθαι τὰς παρούσας
αὐτῷ διὰ τὸν νόμον ἀπορίας· τὴν δὲ Πυθίαν εἰπεῖν

265 ὅσσαπερ ἐν λεχέεσσι γυνὴ τίκτουσα τελεῖται,
ταῦτα πάλιν τελέσαντα θύειν μακάρεσσι θεοῖσιν.

τὸν οὖν Ἀριστῖνον εὖ φρονήσαντα παρασχεῖν ἑαυτὸν

---

[1] καθιᾶσι] καθιμῶσι Abresch, from καθίμησιν, infra.
[2] ἐπιχειροῦντος Helmbold: ἐπιχειρούντων.

have died in a foreign country, even if they return, men do not admit by the door, but mount upon the roof-tiles and let them down inside ?

Varro gives an explanation of the cause that is quite fabulous. For he says that in the Sicilian war there was a great naval battle, and in the case of many men a false report spread that they were dead. But, when they had returned home, in a short time they all came to their end except one who, when he tried to enter, found the doors shutting against him of their own accord, nor did they yield when he strove to open them. The man fell asleep there before his threshold and in his sleep saw a vision, which instructed him to climb upon the roof and let himself down into the house. When he had done so, he prospered and lived to an advanced age ; and from this occurrence the custom became established for succeeding generations.

But consider if this be not in some wise similar to Greek customs ; for the Greeks did not consider pure, nor admit to familiar intercourse, nor suffer to approach the temples any person for whom a funeral had been held and a tomb constructed on the assumption that they were dead. The tale is told that Aristinus, a victim of this superstition, sent to Delphi and besought the god to release him from the difficulties in which he was involved because of the custom ; and the prophetic priestess gave response :

All that a woman in childbed does at the birth of her baby,
When this again thou hast done, to the blessed gods sacrifice offer.

Aristinus, accordingly, chose the part of wisdom and

13

(265) ὥσπερ ἐξ ἀρχῆς τικτόμενον ταῖς γυναιξὶν ἀπολοῦσαι
καὶ σπαργανῶσαι καὶ θηλὴν ἐπισχεῖν, οὕτω τε δρᾶν
καὶ τοὺς ἄλλους ἅπαντας, ὑστεροπότμους προσ-
αγορευομένους. ἔνιοι δὲ καὶ πρὸ τοῦ Ἀριστίνου
ταῦτα γενέσθαι περὶ τοὺς ὑστεροπότμους καὶ τὸ
ἔθος εἶναι παλαιόν. οὐδὲν οὖν θαυμαστὸν εἰ καὶ
Ῥωμαῖοι τοῖς[1] δοκοῦσιν ἅπαξ τεθάφθαι καὶ γεγονέναι
τῆς τῶν φθιτῶν μερίδος οὐκ ᾤοντο δεῖν παριέναι τὴν
B αὔλειον, ᾗ θύσοντες ἐξίασι καὶ θύσαντες εἰσίασιν,
ἀλλ' ἄνωθεν ἐκέλευον εἰς τὰ ὕπαιθρα καταβαίνειν
ἐκ τοῦ περιέχοντος· καὶ γὰρ τοὺς καθαρμοὺς ἐπιεικῶς πάντας ἐν ὑπαίθρῳ τελοῦσιν.

6. "Διὰ τί τοὺς συγγενεῖς τῷ στόματι φιλοῦσιν
αἱ γυναῖκες;"

Πότερον, ὡς οἱ πλεῖστοι νομίζουσιν, ἀπειρημένον
ἦν πίνειν οἶνον ταῖς γυναιξίν· ὅπως οὖν αἱ πιοῦσαι
μὴ λανθάνωσιν ἀλλ' ἐλέγχωνται περιτυγχάνουσαι
τοῖς οἰκείοις, ἐνομίσθη καταφιλεῖν;

"Ἢ δι' ἣν Ἀριστοτέλης ὁ φιλόσοφος αἰτίαν
ἱστόρηκε; τὸ γὰρ πολυθρύλητον ἐκεῖνο καὶ πολ-
C λαχοῦ[2] γενέσθαι λεγόμενον ὡς ἔοικεν ἐτολμήθη ταῖς
Τρῳάσι καὶ περὶ τὴν Ἰταλίαν. τῶν γὰρ ἀνδρῶν,
ὡς προσέπλευσαν, ἀποβάντων ἐνέπρησαν τὰ πλοῖα,
πάντως ἀπαλλαγῆναι τῆς πλάνης δεόμεναι καὶ τῆς

---

[1] τοῖς] all mss except E have τότε.
[2] πολλαχοῦ Wyttenbach: πολλοῦ.

---

[a] Cf. *Comparison of Lycurgus and Numa*, chap. iii.
(77 B) ; Polybius, vi. 11a. 4 ; Dionysius of Halicarnassus,
Roman Antiquities, ii. 25. 6 ; Cicero, *De Republica*, iv. 6 ;
Valerius Maximus, ii. 1. 5 ; vi. 3.9 ; Pliny, *Natural History*,
xiv. 13 (89) ; Aulus Gellius, x. 23. 1 ; Tertullian, *Apol.* vi.
[b] Frag. 609 (ed. V. Rose).

delivered himself like a new-born babe into the hands of women to be washed, and to be wrapped in swaddling-clothes, and to be suckled ; and all other men in such plight do likewise and they are called " Men of Later Fate." But some will have it that this was done in the case of such persons even before Aristinus, and that the custom is ancient. Hence it is nothing surprising if the Romans also did not think it right to admit by the door, through which they go out to sacrifice and come in from sacrificing, those who are thought to have been buried once and for all and to belong to the company of the departed, but bade them descend from the open air above into that portion of the house which is exposed to the sky. And with good reason, for, naturally, they perform all their rites of purification under the open sky.

6. WHY do the women kiss their kinsmen on the lips ?

Is it, as most authorities believe, that the drinking of wine was forbidden to women,[a] and therefore, so that women who had drunk wine should not escape detection, but should be detected when they chanced to meet men of their household, the custom of kissing was established ?

Or is it for the reason which Aristotle [b] the philosopher has recorded ? For that far-famed deed, the scene of which is laid in many different places,[c] was dared, it appears, by the Trojan women, even on the very shores of Italy. For when they had reached the coast, and the men had disembarked, the women set fire to the ships, since, at all hazards, they desired to be quit of their wanderings and their sea-faring.

[c] Cf. *Moralia*, 243 E and the note *ad loc.* (Vol. III. p. 480).

(265) θαλάττης· φοβηθεῖσαι δὲ τοὺς ἄνδρας ἠσπάζοντο
τῶν συγγενῶν καὶ οἰκείων μετὰ τοῦ καταφιλεῖν
καὶ περιπλέκεσθαι τοὺς προστυγχάνοντας. παυσα-
μένων δὲ τῆς ὀργῆς καὶ διαλλαγέντων, ἐχρῶντο
καὶ τὸ λοιπὸν ταύτῃ τῇ φιλοφροσύνῃ πρὸς αὐτούς.
D "Η μᾶλλον ἐδόθη τοῦτο ταῖς γυναιξὶν ὡς τιμὴν
ἅμα καὶ δύναμιν αὐταῖς φέρον, εἰ φαίνοιντο πολλοὺς καὶ ἀγαθοὺς ἔχουσαι συγγενεῖς καὶ οἰκείους;
"Η, μὴ νενομισμένου συγγενίδας γαμεῖν, ἄχρι
φιλήματος ἡ φιλοφροσύνη προῆλθεν καὶ τοῦτο
μόνον ἀπελείφθη σύμβολον καὶ κοινώνημα τῆς
συγγενείας; πρότερον γὰρ οὐκ ἐγάμουν τὰς ἀφ'
αἵματος, ὥσπερ οὐδὲ νῦν τηθίδας[1] οὐδ' ἀδελφὰς[2]
γαμοῦσιν, ἀλλ' ὀψὲ συνεχώρησαν ἀνεψιαῖς συνοικεῖν
ἐκ τοιαύτης αἰτίας· ἀνὴρ χρημάτων ἐνδεὴς τὰ δ'
ἄλλα χρηστὸς καὶ παρ' ὁντινοῦν τῷ δήμῳ τῶν
πολιτευομένων ἀρέσκων, ἐπίκληρον ἀνεψιὰν ἔχων[3]
E ἔδοξε καὶ πλουτεῖν ἀπ' αὐτῆς· ἐπὶ τούτῳ δὲ γενομένης αὐτοῦ κατηγορίας, ὁ δῆμος ἀφεὶς τὴν αἰτίαν
ἐλέγχειν ἔλυσε τὸ ἔγκλημα, ψηφισάμενος πᾶσιν
ἐξεῖναι γαμεῖν ἄχρι ἀνεψιῶν, τὰ[4] δ' ἀνωτέρω
κεκωλῦσθαι.

7. " Διὰ τί δὲ δῶρον λαβεῖν ἀνδρὶ παρὰ γυναικὸς
καὶ γυναικὶ παρ' ἀνδρὸς ἀπείρηται; "

---

[1] τηθίδας Cobet: τιτθίδας.
[2] ἀδελφὰς] ἀδελφιδὰς S. A. Naber (cf. Suetonius, Claudius,
26).
[3] ἔχων F.C.B.: ἔχειν.   [4] τὰ] τὰς E.

---

[a] Hatzidakis objects to the form συγγενίδας; but the very
fact that Pollux, iii. 30, characterizes it as ἐσχάτως βάρβαρον
proves (as do inscriptions also) that it was in use.
[b] Cf. Tacitus, Annals, xii. 5-7.

But they were afraid of their husbands, and greeted with a kiss and a warm embrace such of their kinsmen and members of their household as they encountered; and when the men had ceased from their wrath and had become reconciled, the women continued thereafter as well to employ this mark of affection towards them.

Or was this rather bestowed upon the women as a privilege that should bring them both honour and power if they should be seen to have many good men among their kinsmen and in their household?

Or is it that, since it is not the custom for men to marry blood relations,[a] affection proceeded only so far as a kiss, and this alone remained as a token of kinship and a participation therein? For formerly men did not marry women related to them by ties of blood, just as even now they do not marry their aunts or their sisters[b]; but after a long time they made the concession of allowing wedlock with cousins for the following reason: a man possessed of no property, but otherwise of excellent character and more satisfactory to the people than other public men, had as wife his cousin, an heiress, and was thought to be growing rich from her estate. He was accused on this ground, but the people would not even try the case and dismissed the charge, enacting a decree that all might marry cousins or more distant relatives; but marriage with nearer kin was prohibited.

7. Why is it forbidden for a man to receive a gift from his wife or a wife to receive a gift from her husband?[c]

[c] Cf. Moralia, 143 A.

Πότερον, ὡς Σόλων γράψας τὰς δόσεις κυρίας
εἶναι τῶν τελευτώντων, πλὴν εἰ μή τις ἀνάγκῃ
συνεχόμενος ἢ γυναικὶ πειθόμενος τὴν μὲν ἀνάγκην
F ὡς βιαζομένην ὑπεξείλετο, τὴν δ' ἡδονὴν ὡς παρα-
λογιζομένην, οὕτως ὑπενοήθησαν αἱ γυναικῶν καὶ
ἀνδρῶν δόσεις;

Ἢ φαυλότατον ἡγούμενοι σημεῖον εὐνοίας τὸ δι-
δόναι (διδόασι γὰρ καὶ ἀλλότριοι καὶ μὴ φιλοῦντες)
ἐκ τοῦ γάμου τὴν τοιαύτην ἀρέσκειαν ἀν-
είλον, ὅπως ἄμισθον ᾖ καὶ προῖκα καὶ δι' αὐτὸ μὴ
δι' ἄλλο τὸ φιλεῖσθαι καὶ φιλεῖν;

Ἤ, ὅτι τῷ λαμβάνειν διαφθειρόμεναι μάλιστα
προσίενται τοὺς ἀλλοτρίους, σεμνὸν ἐφάνη τὸ μὴ
διδόντας ἀγαπᾶν τοὺς ἰδίους;

Ἢ μᾶλλον ὅτι δεῖ καὶ γυναιξὶ κοινὰ τὰ ἀνδρῶν
266 εἶναι καὶ ἀνδράσι τὰ γυναικῶν; μανθάνει γὰρ ὁ
λαβὼν τὸ δοθὲν ἀλλότριον ἡγεῖσθαι τὸ μὴ δοθέν,
ὥστ' ὀλίγον διδόντες ἀλλήλοις τὸ πᾶν ἀφαιροῦνται.

8. " Διὰ τί δὲ παρὰ γαμβροῦ καὶ παρὰ πενθεροῦ
λαβεῖν ἐκείνοις κεκώλυται δῶρον; "

Ἢ παρὰ γαμβροῦ μέν, ἵνα μὴ δόξῃ διὰ τοῦ
πατρὸς εἰς τὴν γυναῖκα περιχωρεῖν τὸ δῶρον· παρὰ
πενθεροῦ δέ, ὅτι τὸν μὴ διδόντα δίκαιον ἐφάνη
μηδὲ λαμβάνειν;

---

[a] Cf. *Life of Solon*, chap. xxi. (90 A); [Demosthenes]
xlvi. 14 ; Hypereides, *Against Athenogenes*, 17, 18.
18

Is it that, Solon having promulgated a law ^a that
the bequests of the deceased should be valid unless
a man were constrained by force or persuaded by his
wife, whereby he excepted force as overriding the
free will, and pleasure as misleading the judgement,
in this way the bequests of wives and husbands
became suspect ?

Or did they regard giving as an utterly worthless
token of affection (for even strangers and persons
with no kindly feelings give gifts), and so deprived
the marriage relationship of this mode of giving
pleasure, that mutual affection might be unbought
and free, existing for its own sake and for no other
reason ?

Or is it that women are most likely to be seduced
and welcome strangers because of gifts they receive
from them ; and thus it is seen to be dignified for
them to love their own husbands even though their
husbands give them no gifts ?

Or is it rather that both the husbands' property
should be held in common with their wives and
the wives' with their husbands ? For anyone who
accepts what is given learns to regard what is not
given to him as belonging to another, with the
result that by giving a little to each other they
deprive each other of all else that they own.

8. WHY among the Romans is it forbidden to receive
a gift from a son-in-law or from a father-in-law ?

Is the father-in-law prevented from receiving a
gift from his son-in-law, in order that the gift may
not appear ultimately to reach the wife through her
father ? And is the son-in-law similarly prevented,
since it is obviously just that he who may not give
shall also not receive ?

B 9. " Διὰ τί, κἂν ἐξ ἀγροῦ κἂν ἀπὸ ξένης ἐπ-
(266) ανίωσιν, ἔχοντες οἴκοι γυναῖκας προπέμπουσι
δηλοῦντες αὐταῖς ὅτι παραγίγνονται; "

Πότερον ὅτι τοῦτο πιστεύοντός ἐστι τὴν γυναῖκα
μηδὲν ῥᾳδιουργεῖν, τὸ δ᾽ ἐξαίφνης καὶ ἀπροσδοκήτως
οἷον ἐνέδρᾳ καὶ παρατηρήσει, καὶ¹ σπεύδουσιν ὡς
ποθούσαις καὶ προσδεχομέναις εὐαγγελίζεσθαι περὶ
αὐτῶν²;

Ἢ μᾶλλον αὐτοὶ περὶ ἐκείνων πυθέσθαι ποθοῦσιν,
εἰ σωζομένας καὶ ποθούσας ἐπὶ τῆς οἰκίας κατα-
λαμβάνουσιν;

Ἢ πλείονες ταῖς γυναιξὶν οἰκονομίαι καὶ
ἀσχολίαι, τῶν ἀνδρῶν ἀπόντων, τυγχάνουσι καὶ
διαφοραὶ καὶ ὁρμαὶ³ πρὸς τοὺς ἔνδον· ἵν᾽ οὖν ἀπ-
αλλαγεῖσα τούτων ἀθόρυβον τῷ ἀνδρὶ παρέχῃ τὴν
ὑποδοχὴν καὶ ἡδεῖαν, ἡ προδήλωσις γίγνεται;

C 10. " Διὰ τί τοὺς θεοὺς προσκυνοῦντες ἐπικαλύπτονται τὴν κεφαλήν, τῶν δ᾽ ἀνθρώπων τοῖς ἀξίοις
τιμῆς ἀπαντῶντες, κἂν τύχωσιν ἐπὶ τῆς κεφαλῆς
ἔχοντες τὸ ἱμάτιον, ἀποκαλύπτονται; "

Τοῦτο γὰρ ἔοικε κἀκείνην ἐπιτείνειν τὴν ἀπορίαν.
εἰ μὲν οὖν ὁ περὶ Αἰνείου λεγόμενος λόγος ἀληθής
ἐστιν, ὅτι⁴ τοῦ Διομήδους παρεξιόντος ἐπικαλυψά-
μενος τὴν θυσίαν ἐπετέλεσε, λόγον ἔχει καὶ ἀκο-
λουθεῖ τῷ συγκαλύπτεσθαι πρὸς τοὺς πολεμίους τὸ

---

¹ καὶ added by F.C.B.
² αὐτῶν Bernardakis: αὐτῶν.
³ ὁρμαὶ] ὀργαὶ Wyttenbach.
⁴ ὅτι in E only; καὶ in other mss.

ᵃ Cf. Pliny, *Natural History*, xxviii. 17 (60).

9. WHY is it that, when men who have wives at home are returning either from the country or from abroad, they send ahead to tell their wives that they are coming ?

Is it because this is the mark of a man who is confident that his wife is not up to any mischief, whereas coming suddenly and unexpectedly is, as it were, an arrival by stratagem and unfair vigilance ; and are they eager to send good tidings about themselves to their wives as if they felt certain that their wives would be longing for them and expecting them ?

Or is it rather that the men themselves long to hear news of their wives, if they shall find them safe at home and longing for their husbands ?

Or is it because during their husbands' absence the wives have more household duties and occupations, and also dissensions and outbursts against those of the household ? Therefore the notice is given in advance that the wife may rid herself of these matters and make for her husband his welcome home undisturbed and pleasant.

10. WHY is it that when they worship the gods, they cover their heads, but when they meet any of their fellow-men worthy of honour, if they happen to have the toga over the head, they uncover ? [a]

This second fact seems to intensify the difficulty of the first. If, then, the tale told of Aeneas [b] is true, that, when Diomedes passed by, he covered his head and completed the sacrifice, it is reasonable and consistent with the covering of one's head in the presence of an enemy that men who meet good

[b] *Cf.* Dionysius of Halicarnassus, *Roman Antiquities*, xii. 16.

21

(266) τοῖς φίλοις καὶ ἀγαθοῖς ἐντυγχάνοντας ἀποκαλύ-
πτεσθαι· τὸ γὰρ πρὸς τοὺς θεοὺς οὐκ ἴδιόν ἐστιν
ἀλλὰ κατὰ συμβεβηκός, καὶ ἀπ᾽ ἐκείνου μεμένηκε
τηρούμενον.

Εἰ δ᾽ ἄλλο τι λέγειν χρή, σκόπει μὴ μόνον ἐκεῖνο
δεῖ ζητεῖν, δι᾽ ὃ τοὺς θεοὺς προσκυνοῦντες ἐπικαλύπτονται, θάτερον δ᾽ ἀκόλουθόν ἐστι. τῶν γὰρ
D ἀνθρώπων ἀποκαλύπτονται τοῖς δυνατωτέροις, οὐ
τιμὴν αὐτοῖς προστιθέντες, ἀλλὰ τὸν φθόνον αὐτῶν
μᾶλλον ἀφαιροῦντες, ἵνα μὴ δόξωσι τὰς αὐτὰς τοῖς
θεοῖς τιμὰς ἀπαιτεῖν μηδ᾽ ὑπομένειν μηδὲ χαίρειν
θεραπευόμενοι παραπλησίως ἐκείνοις. τοὺς δὲ
θεοὺς οὕτω προσεκύνουν ἢ ταπεινοῦντες ἑαυτοὺς
τῇ ἐπικρύψει τῆς κεφαλῆς, ἢ μᾶλλον εὐλαβούμενοί
τινα φωνὴν προσπεσεῖν αὐτοῖς ἔξωθεν εὐχομένοις
ἀπαίσιον καὶ δύσφημον ἄχρι τῶν ὤτων ἀνελάμβανον τὸ ἱμάτιον· ὅτι γὰρ ἰσχυρῶς ἐφυλάττοντο ταῦτα,
δῆλόν ἐστι τῷ προσιόντας ἐπὶ μαντείαν χαλκω-
μάτων πατάγῳ περιψοφεῖσθαι.

E ῍Η ὡς Κάστωρ λέγει τὰ ῾Ρωμαϊκὰ τοῖς Πυθα-
γορικοῖς συνοικειῶν, τὸν ἐν ἡμῖν δαίμονα δεῖσθαι
τῶν ἐκτὸς θεῶν καὶ ἱκετεύειν, τῇ τῆς κεφαλῆς
ἐπικαλύψει τὴν τῆς ψυχῆς αἰνιττόμενος[1] ὑπὸ τοῦ
σώματος ἐγκάλυψιν καὶ ἀπόκρυψιν.

11. " Διὰ τί τῷ Κρόνῳ θύουσιν ἀπαρακαλύπτῳ
τῇ κεφαλῇ; "

---

[1] αἰνιττόμενος F.C.B. : αἰνιττόμενον.

a Cf. Jacoby, *Frag. der griech. Hist.* 250, Frag. 15.

22

men and their friends should uncover. In fact, the behaviour in regard to the gods is not properly related to this custom, but accidentally resembles it ; and its observance has persisted since the days of Aeneas.

But if there is anything else to be said, consider whether it be not true that there is only one matter that needs investigation : why men cover their heads when they worship the gods ; and the other follows from this. For they uncover their heads in the presence of men more influential than they : it is not to invest these men with additional honour, but rather to avert from them the jealousy of the gods, that these men may not seem to demand the same honours as the gods, nor to tolerate an attention like that bestowed on the gods, nor to rejoice therein. But they thus worshipped the gods, either humbling themselves by concealing the head, or rather by pulling the toga over their ears as a precaution lest any ill-omened and baleful sound from without should reach them while they were praying. That they were mightily vigilant in this matter is obvious from the fact that when they went forth for purposes of divination, they surrounded themselves with the clashing of bronze.

Or, as Castor [a] states when he is trying to bring Roman customs into relation with Pythagorean doctrines : the Spirit within us entreats and supplicates the gods without, and thus he symbolizes by the covering of the head the covering and concealment of the soul by the body.

11. Why do they sacrifice to Saturn with the head uncovered ?

23

Πότερον ὅτι τὴν ἐγκάλυψιν Αἰνείας παρέδωκεν,
ἢ δὲ τοῦ Κρόνου θυσία παμπάλαιός ἐστιν;
"Η ὅτι τοῖς οὐρανίοις ἐπικαλύπτονται, τὸν δὲ
Κρόνον ἡγοῦνται θεὸν ὑπουδαῖον καὶ χθόνιον; ἢ
ὅτι τῆς ἀληθείας οὐδὲν ἀπόκρυφον[1] ἢ ἐπίσκιον,
ἀληθείας δὲ νομίζουσι Ῥωμαῖοι πατέρα τὸν Κρόνον
εἶναι;

12. " Διὰ τί δὲ τὸν Κρόνον πατέρα τῆς ἀληθείας
νομίζουσι; "

Πότερον, ὥσπερ ἔνιοι τῶν φιλοσόφων, χρόνον
F οἴονται τὸν Κρόνον εἶναι, τὸ δ' ἀληθὲς εὑρίσκει
χρόνος· ἢ τὸν μυθολογούμενον ἐπὶ Κρόνου βίον,
εἰ δικαιότατος ἦν, εἰκός ἐστι μάλιστα μετέχειν
ἀληθείας;

13. " Διὰ τί καὶ τῷ λεγομένῳ Ὀνώρει θύουσιν
ἀπαρακαλύπτῳ[2] τῇ κεφαλῇ; τὸν δὲ Ὀνῶρεμ δόξαν
ἄν τις ἢ τιμὴν μεθερμηνεύσειε."

Πότερον διότι[3] λαμπρὸν ἡ δόξα καὶ περιφανὲς καὶ
ἀναπεπταμένον, δι' ἣν αἰτίαν τοῖς ἀγαθοῖς καὶ
267 τιμωμένοις ἀνδράσιν ἀποκαλύπτονται, διὰ ταύτην
καὶ τὸν ἐπώνυμον τῆς τιμῆς θεὸν οὕτω προσ-
κυνοῦσιν;

14. " Διὰ τί τοὺς γονεῖς ἐκκομίζουσιν οἱ μὲν
υἱοὶ συγκεκαλυμμένοι,[4] αἱ δὲ θυγατέρες γυμναῖς ταῖς
κεφαλαῖς καὶ ταῖς κόμαις λελυμέναις; "

Πότερον ὅτι τιμᾶσθαι μὲν ὑπὸ τῶν ἀρρένων δεῖ

[1] ἀπόκρυφον] all mss. but one have ἐπίκρυφον.
[2] ἀπαρακαλύπτῳ E, as above at the beginning of no. 11:
ἀκαλύπτῳ.
[3] διότι Wyttenbach: δὲ ὅτι.
[4] συγκεκαλυμμένοι some mss., as Petavius had conjectured:
συγκεκαλυμμέναις.

24

Is it because Aeneas instituted the custom of covering the head, and the sacrifice to Saturn dates from long before that time ?

Or is it that they cover the head before the heavenly deities, but they consider Saturn a god whose realm is beneath the earth ? Or is it that no part of Truth is covered or overshadowed, and the Romans consider Saturn father of Truth ?

12. And why do they consider Saturn father of Truth ?

Is it that they think, as do certain philosophers,[a] that Saturn (Kronos) is Time (Chronos), and Time discovers the truth ? Or because it is likely that the fabled Age of Saturn, if it was an age of the greatest righteousness, participated most largely in truth ?

13. Why do they also sacrifice to the god called " Honor " with the head uncovered ? One might translate Honor as " renown " or " honour."

Is it because renown is a brilliant thing, conspicuous, and widespread, and for the reason that they uncover in the presence of good and honoured men, is it for this same reason that they also worship the god who is named for " honour " ?

14. Why do sons cover their heads when they escort their parents to the grave, while daughters go with uncovered heads and hair unbound ?

Is it because fathers should be honoured as gods

---

[a] Cf. Moralia, 363 D ; Aristotle, De Mundo, chap. vii. ad init. (401 a 15) ; Cornutus, chap. vi. (p. 7 ed. Lang) ; Macrobius, Saturnalia, i. 8. 7.

(267) τοὺς πατέρας ὡς θεούς, πενθεῖσθαι δ' ὑπὸ τῶν
θυγατέρων ὡς τεθνηκότας, ἑκατέρῳ τὸ οἰκεῖον ὁ
νόμος ἀποδοὺς ἐξ ἀμφοτέρων ἐποίησε τὸ ἁρμόττον;

"Η πένθους μὲν οἰκεῖον τὸ μὴ σύνηθες, συνηθέ-
στερον δὲ ταῖς μὲν γυναιξὶν ἐγκεκαλυμμέναις, τοῖς
B δ' ἀνδράσιν ἀκαλύπτοις εἰς τὸ δημόσιον προϊέναι;
καὶ γὰρ παρ' Ἕλλησιν ὅταν δυστυχία τις γένηται,
κείρονται μὲν αἱ γυναῖκες κομῶσι δ' οἱ ἄνδρες, ὅτι
τοῖς μὲν τὸ κείρεσθαι ταῖς δὲ τὸ κομᾶν σύνηθές
ἐστιν.

"Η τοὺς μὲν υἱοὺς ἐπικαλύπτεσθαι δι' ἣν εἰρή-
καμεν αἰτίαν ἐνομίσθη; καὶ γὰρ ἐπὶ τῶν τάφων,
ὥς φησι Βάρρων, περιστρέφονται, καθάπερ θεῶν
ἱερὰ τιμῶντες τὰ τῶν πατέρων μνήματα, καὶ
καύσαντες τοὺς γονεῖς, ὅταν ὀστέῳ πρῶτον ἐντύχωσι, θεὸν γεγονέναι τὸν τεθνηκότα λέγουσι.

Ταῖς δὲ γυναιξὶν οὐδ' ὅλως ἐξῆν ἐπικαλύπτεσθαι τὴν κεφαλήν· ἱστορεῖται γοῦν ὅτι πρῶτος μὲν
C ἐξέβαλε γυναῖκα Σπόριος Καρβίλιος[1] ἐπ' ἀτεκνίᾳ,
δεύτερος δὲ Σουλπίκιος Γάλλος ἐφελκυσαμένην
ἰδὼν κατὰ κεφαλῆς τὸ ἱμάτιον, τρίτος δὲ Πόπλιος
Σεμπρώνιος ἀγῶνα θεωρήσασαν ἐπιτάφιον.

15. " Διὰ τί τὸν Τέρμινον, ᾧ τὰ Τερμινάλια
ποιοῦσι, θεὸν νομίζοντες οὐδὲν ἔθυον αὐτῷ ζῷον; "

[1] Καρβίλιος Reiske : Καρβήλιος.

---

[a] The first reason above : The father should be honoured
as a god.

[b] Cf. Cicero, De Legibus, ii. 22 (57).

[c] Cf. 278 E, infra ; Comparison of Lycurgus and Numa,
iii. (77 c) ; Comparison of Theseus and Romulus, vi. (39 B) ;
Dionysius of Halicarnassus, Roman Antiquities, ii. 25. 7 ;
Valerius Maximus, ii. 1. 4 ; Aulus Gellius, iv. 3. 2 ; xvii.
21. 44 ; Tertullian, Apol. vi., De Monogamia, ix.

by their male offspring, but mourned as dead by their daughters, that custom has assigned to each sex its proper part and has produced a fitting result from both ?

Or is it that the unusual is proper in mourning, and it is more usual for women to go forth in public with their heads covered and men with their heads un-covered ? So in Greece, whenever any misfortune comes, the women cut off their hair and the men let it grow, for it is usual for men to have their hair cut and for women to let it grow.

Or is it that it has become customary for sons to cover their heads for the reason already given ? [a] For they turn about at the graves, as Varro relates, thus honouring the tombs of their fathers even as they do the shrines of the gods ; and when they have cremated their parents, they declare that the dead person has become a god at the moment when first they find a bone.[b]

But formerly women were not allowed to cover the head at all. At least it is recorded that Spurius Carvilius [c] was the first man to divorce his wife and the reason was her barrenness ; the second was Sulpicius Gallus, because he saw his wife pull her cloak over her head ; and the third was Publius Sempronius, because his wife had been present as a spectator at funeral games.[d]

15. Why is it that they were wont to sacrifice no living creature to Terminus,[e] in whose honour they held the Terminalia, although they regard him as a god ?

[a] *Cf.* Valerius Maximus, vi. 3. 10.

[e] This is certainly not true of later times : *cf.* for example, Horace, *Epodes*, 2. 59.

(267) Ἡ Ῥωμύλος μὲν ὅρους οὐκ ἔθηκε τῆς χώρας,
ὅπως ἐξῇ προϊέναι καὶ ἀποτέμνεσθαι καὶ νομίζειν
πᾶσαν ἰδίαν, ὥσπερ ὁ Λάκων εἶπεν, ἧς ἂν τὸ δόρυ
ἐφικνῆται, Νομᾶς[1] δὲ Πομπίλιος, ἀνὴρ δίκαιος καὶ
πολιτικὸς ὢν καὶ φιλόσοφος γενόμενος, τήν τε
χώραν ὡρίσατο πρὸς τοὺς γειτνιῶντας καὶ τοῖς
ὅροις ἐπιφημίσας τὸν Τέρμινον ὡς ἐπίσκοπον καὶ
φύλακα φιλίας καὶ εἰρήνης ᾤετο δεῖν αἵματος καὶ
φόνου καθαρὸν καὶ ἀμίαντον διαφυλάττειν;

D 16. '' Διὰ τί δούλαις τὸ τῆς Λευκοθέας ἱερὸν
ἄβατόν ἐστι, μίαν δὲ μόνην αἱ γυναῖκες εἰσάγουσαι
παίουσιν ἐπὶ κόρρης καὶ ῥαπίζουσιν; ''

Ἡ τὸ μὲν ταύτην ῥαπίζεσθαι σύμβολόν ἐστι τοῦ
μὴ ἐξεῖναι, κωλύουσι δὲ τὰς ἄλλας διὰ τὸν μῦθον;
ἡ γὰρ Ἰνὼ ζηλοτυπήσασα δούλην ἐπὶ τῷ ἀνδρὶ
λέγεται περὶ τὸν υἱὸν ἐκμανῆναι· τὴν δὲ δούλην
Ἕλληνες Αἰτωλίδα γένει φασὶν εἶναι, καλεῖσθαι δ'
Ἀντιφέραν. διὸ καὶ παρ' ἡμῖν ἐν Χαιρωνείᾳ πρὸ
τοῦ σηκοῦ τῆς Λευκοθέας ὁ νεωκόρος λαβὼν
μάστιγα κηρύττει, '' μὴ δοῦλον εἰσιέναι μὴ δούλαν,
μὴ Αἰτωλὸν μὴ Αἰτωλάν.''

E 17. '' Διὰ τί παρὰ τῇ θεῷ ταύτῃ τοῖς μὲν ἰδίοις
τέκνοις οὐκ εὔχονται τἀγαθὰ τοῖς δὲ τῶν
ἀδελφῶν; ''

----

[1] Νομᾶς] Νουμᾶς in some mss.

----

[a] Cf. Moralia, 210 E with the note (Vol. III. p. 257).
[b] Cf. Life of Numa, xvi. (70 F); Dionysius of Halicarnassus, Roman Antiquities, ii. 74. 2 ff.
[c] Cf. Life of Camillus, v. (131 B-C); Ovid, Fasti, vi. 551
ff. wth Frazer's note.
[d] Ino is the Greek name for the Greek goddess Leucothea

Is it that Romulus placed no boundary-stones for his country, so that Romans might go forth, seize land, and regard all as theirs, as the Spartan said,[a] which their spears could reach; whereas Numa Pompilius,[b] a just man and a statesman, who had become versed in philosophy, marked out the boundaries between Rome and her neighbours, and, when on the boundary-stones he had formally installed Terminus as overseer and guardian of friendship and peace, he thought that Terminus should be kept pure and undefiled from blood and gore?

16. WHY is it that it is forbidden to slave-women to set foot in the shrine of Matuta, and why do the women bring in one slave-woman only and slap her on the head and beat her?[c]

Is the beating of this slave but a symbol of the prohibition, and do they prevent the others from entering because of the legend? For Ino[d] is said to have become madly jealous of a slave-woman on her husband's account, and to have vented her madness on her son. The Greeks relate that the slave was an Aetolian by birth and that her name was Antiphera. Wherefore also in my native town, Chaeroneia, the temple-guardian stands before the precinct of Leucothea and, taking a whip in his hand, makes proclamation : " Let no slave enter, nor any Aetolian, man or woman ! "

17. WHY is it that in the shrine of this goddess they do not pray for blessings on their own children, but only on their sisters' children?[e]

before her violent death and deification ; Matuta is the supposed Roman equivalent of both Greek names.
   [e] Cf. Moralia, 492 D.

29

Πότερον ὅτι φιλάδελφος μέν τις ἡ Ἰνὼ καὶ τὸν
ἐκ τῆς ἀδελφῆς ἐτιθηνήσατο, αὐτὴ[1] δὲ περὶ τοὺς
ἑαυτῆς παῖδας ἐδυστύχησεν· ἢ καὶ ἄλλως ἠθικὸν
καὶ καλὸν τὸ ἔθος καὶ πολλὴν παρασκευάζον εὔνοιαν ταῖς οἰκειότησι;

18. '' Διὰ τί τῷ Ἡρακλεῖ πολλοὶ τῶν πλουσίων
ἐδεκάτευον τὰς οὐσίας; ''

Πότερον ὅτι κἀκεῖνος ἐν Ῥώμῃ τῶν Γηρυόνου
F βοῶν ἀπέθυσε τὴν δεκάτην, ἢ ὅτι Ῥωμαίους ὑπὸ
Τυρρηνῶν δεκατευομένους ἀπήλλαξεν;

Ἢ ταῦτα μὲν οὐκ ἔχει[2] τὴν ἱστορίαν ἀξιόπιστον,
ὡς δ' ἀδηφάγῳ τινὶ τῷ Ἡρακλεῖ καὶ εὐθοίνῳ
δαψιλῶς καὶ ἀφθόνως ἀπέθυον;

Ἢ μᾶλλον ὡς ἐπαχθῆ τοῖς πολίταις τὸν ὑπερβάλ-
λοντα πλοῦτον κολούοντες καὶ καθάπερ εὐεξίας ἐπ'
ἄκρον εὐσωματούσης ἀφαιροῦντες, ᾤοντο μάλιστα
τιμᾶσθαι τὸν Ἡρακλέα καὶ χαίρειν ταῖς τοιαύταις
ἀποχρήσεσι καὶ συστολαῖς τῶν περιττῶν, εὐτελῆ
καὶ αὐτάρκη καὶ ἀπέριττον τῷ βίῳ γενόμενον;

19. '' Διὰ τί τὸν Ἰανουάριον μῆνα νέου ἔτους
ἀρχὴν λαμβάνουσι; ''

268   Τὸ γὰρ παλαιὸν ὁ Μάρτιος ἠριθμεῖτο πρότερος,
ὡς ἄλλοις τε πολλοῖς δῆλόν ἐστι τεκμηρίοις καὶ
μάλιστα τῷ τὸν πέμπτον ἀπὸ τοῦ Μαρτίου Πέμπτον καὶ τὸν ἕκτον Ἕκτον ὀνομάζεσθαι, καὶ τοὺς

---

[1] αὐτὴ Patzig : ἡ.   [2] ἔχει] εἶχε in some mss.

---

[a] Cf. *Life of Sulla*, chap. xxxv. (474 A) ; *Life of Crassus*,
ii. (543 D), xii. (550 D).

Is it because Ino was fond of her sister and suckled her sister's son also, but was herself unfortunate in her own children? Or is it that, quite apart from this reason, the custom is morally excellent and produces much goodwill among kindred?

18. WHY was it the custom for many of the wealthy to give a tithe of their property to Hercules? [a]

Is it because he also sacrificed a tithe of Geryon's cattle in Rome? Or because he freed the Romans from paying a tithe to the Etruscans?

Or have these tales no historical foundation worthy of credence, but the Romans were wont to sacrifice lavishly and abundantly to Hercules as to an insatiable eater and a good trencher-man?

Or was it rather in curtailing their excessive wealth, since it was odious to their fellow-citizens, and in doing away with some of it, as from a lusty bodily vigour that had reached its culmination,[b] did they think that thus Hercules would be especially honoured and pleased by such a way of using up and reducing overabundance, since in his own life he was frugal, self-sufficient, and free from extravagance?

19. WHY do they adopt the month of January as the beginning of the new year? [c]

The fact is that, in ancient days, March was counted before January, as is clear from many different proofs, and particularly from the fact that the fifth month from March is called Quintilis, the sixth Sextilis, and

---

[b] Probably an allusion to the Hippocratic maxim quoted in *Moralia*, 682 E, 1090 B, and often by Galen.

[c] Cf. *Life of Numa*, xviii., xix. (71 E ff.); Lucian, *Pseudologista*, 8; Varro, *De Lingua Latina*, vi. 33; Ovid, *Fasti*, iii. 99-166.

(268) ἄλλους ἐφεξῆς ἄχρι τοῦ τελευταίου, ὃν Δεκέμβριον
καλοῦσιν ἀπὸ τοῦ Μαρτίου δέκατον ἀριθμούμενον.
ἐξ οὗ δὴ καὶ παρέστη τισὶν οἴεσθαι καὶ λέγειν ὡς
οὐ δώδεκα μησὶν ἀλλὰ δέκα συνεπλήρουν οἱ τότε
Ῥωμαῖοι τὸν ἐνιαυτὸν ἐνίοις[1] τῶν μηνῶν ἡμέρας
B πλείονας τῶν τριάκοντα προστιθέντες.   ἄλλοι δ'
ἱστοροῦσι τὸν μὲν Δεκέμβριον ἀπὸ τοῦ Μαρτίου
δέκατον εἶναι, τὸν δ' Ἰανουάριον ἑνδέκατον, τὸν
δὲ Φεβρουάριον δωδέκατον, ἐν ᾧ καθαρμοῖς τε
χρῶνται καὶ τοῖς φθιμένοις ἐναγίζουσι τοῦ ἐνιαυτοῦ
τελευτῶντος. μετατεθῆναι δὲ τούτους καὶ γενέσθαι
τὸν Ἰανουάριον πρῶτον, ὅτι τῇ νουμηνίᾳ τούτου τοῦ
μηνός, ἣν ἡμέραν καλάνδας Ἰανουαρίας καλοῦσιν,
οἱ πρῶτοι κατεστάθησαν ὕπατοι, τῶν βασιλέων
ἐκπεσόντων.

Πιθανώτεροι δ' εἰσὶν οἱ λέγοντες ὅτι τὸν μὲν
Μάρτιον ὁ Ῥωμύλος πολεμικὸς καὶ ἀρειμάνιος ὢν
καὶ δοκῶν ἐξ Ἄρεος γεγονέναι προέταξε τῶν μηνῶν
ἐπώνυμον ὄντα τοῦ Ἄρεος· Νομᾶς[2] δ' αὖθις εἰ-
C ρηνικὸς γενόμενος καὶ πρὸς ἔργα τῆς γῆς φιλο-
τιμούμενος τρέψαι τὴν πόλιν ἀποστῆσαι δὲ τῶν
πολεμικῶν, τῷ Ἰανουαρίῳ τὴν ἡγεμονίαν ἔδωκε
καὶ τὸν Ἰανὸν εἰς τιμὰς προήγαγε μεγάλας, ὡς
πολιτικὸν καὶ γεωργικὸν μᾶλλον ἢ πολεμικὸν γενόμενον. ὅρα δὲ μὴ μᾶλλον ὁ Νομᾶς[2] τῇ φύσει
προσήκουσαν ἀρχὴν ἔλαβε τοῦ ἔτους ὡς πρὸς ἡμᾶς.
καθόλου μὲν γὰρ οὐδέν ἐστι φύσει τῶν ἐν κύκλῳ
περιφερομένων οὔτ' ἔσχατον οὔτε πρῶτον, νόμῳ
D δ' ἄλλην ἄλλοι τοῦ χρόνου λαμβάνουσιν ἀρχήν·
ἄριστα δ' οἱ τὴν μετὰ τροπὰς χειμερινὰς λαμ-

[1] ἐνίοις Wyttenbach: ἐνίας.
[2] Νομᾶς the better spelling (cf. 267 c): νουμᾶς.

so on to the last, which they call December, since it is the tenth in order from March. Wherefore it has also naturally occurred to some to believe and to maintain that the ancient Romans completed their year, not in twelve months, but in ten, by adding more days than thirty to some of the months. Others state that December is the tenth from March, January the eleventh, and February the twelfth ; and in this month they perform rites of purification and make offerings to the dead, since it is the end of the year. But the order of these months was altered, so they say, and January was put first because in this month on the day of the new moon, which they call the Kalends of January, the first consuls entered office after the kings had been expelled.

But more worthy of credence are they who maintain that it was because Romulus was a warrior and a lover of battle, and was thought to be a son of Mars, that he placed first the month which bore Mars' name. But Numa, in turn, who was a lover of peace, and whose ambition it was to turn the city towards husbandry and to divert it from war, gave the precedence to January and advanced the god Janus to great honours, since Janus [a] was a statesman and a husbandman rather than a warrior. But consider whether Numa may not have adopted as the beginning of the year that which conforms to our conception of the natural beginning. Speaking generally, to be sure, there is not naturally either last or first in a cycle ; and it is by custom that some adopt one beginning of this period and others another. They do best, however, who adopt the beginning

[a] *Cf.* 269 A, *infra.*

(268) βάνοντες, ὁπηνίκα τοῦ πρόσω βαδίζειν πεπαυμένος
ὁ ἥλιος ἐπιστρέφει καὶ ἀνακάμπτει πάλιν πρὸς
ἡμᾶς· γίγνεται γὰρ ἀνθρώποις[1] τρόπον τινὰ κατὰ
φύσιν[2] τὸν μὲν τοῦ φωτὸς αὔξουσα χρόνον ἡμῖν,
μειοῦσα δὲ τὸν τοῦ σκότους, ἐγγυτέρω δὲ ποιοῦσα
τὸν κύριον καὶ ἡγεμόνα τῆς ῥευστῆς οὐσίας ἁπάσης.

20. " Διὰ τί τῇ γυναικείᾳ θεῷ, ἣν Ἀγαθὴν
καλοῦσιν, κοσμοῦσαι σηκὸν αἱ γυναῖκες οἴκοι μυρ-
σίνας οὐκ εἰσφέρουσι, καίτοι πᾶσι φιλοτιμούμεναι
χρῆσθαι τοῖς βλαστάνουσι καὶ ἀνθοῦσι; "

Πότερον, ὡς οἱ μυθολογοῦντες ἱστοροῦσι, Φαύνου[3] μὲν ἦν γυνὴ τοῦ μάντεως, οἴνῳ δὲ χρησαμένη
E κρύφα καὶ μὴ λαθοῦσα ῥάβδοις ὑπὸ τοῦ ἀνδρὸς
ἐκολάσθη μυρσίνης, ὅθεν μυρσίνην μὲν οὐκ εἰσ-
φέρουσιν, οἶνον δ' αὐτῇ σπένδουσι, γάλα προσ-
αγορεύουσαι;

Ἢ πολλῶν μὲν ἁγναὶ μάλιστα δ' ἀφροδισίων τὴν
ἱερουργίαν ἐκείνην ἐπιτελοῦσιν; οὐ γὰρ μόνον
ἐξοικίζουσι τοὺς ἄνδρας, ἀλλὰ καὶ πᾶν ἄρρεν
ἐξελαύνουσι τῆς οἰκίας, ὅταν τὰ νενομισμένα τῇ
θεῷ ποιῶσι. τὴν οὖν μυρσίνην ὡς ἱερὰν Ἀφροδίτης[4]
ἀφοσιοῦνται· καὶ γὰρ ἦν νῦν Μουρκίαν Ἀφροδίτην
καλοῦσι, Μυρτίαν τὸ παλαιὸν ὡς ἔοικεν ὠνόμαζον.

21. " Διὰ τί τὸν δρυοκολάπτην οἱ Λατῖνοι σέβονται, καὶ ἀπέχονται πάντες ἰσχυρῶς τοῦ ὄρνιθος; "

---

[1] ἀνθρώποις F.C.B. (αὕτη Helmbold): αὑτοῖς.
[2] κατὰ φύσιν F.C.B.: καὶ φύσει.
[3] Φαύνου Meziriacus: φαυλίου.
[4] Ἀφροδίτης Schellens: ἀφροδίτῃ.

---

[a] Cf. Macrobius, Saturnalia, i. 12. 21-28.
[b] Cf. 265 B, supra.

after the winter solstice, when the sun has ceased to advance, and turns about and retraces his course toward us. For this beginning of the year is in a certain way natural to mankind, since it increases the amount of light that we receive and decreases the amount of darkness, and brings nearer to us the lord and leader of all mobile matter.

20. WHY is it that the women, when they adorn in their houses a shrine to the women's goddess, whom they call Bona Dea,[a] bring in no myrtle, although they are very eager to make use of all manner of growing and blooming plants ?

Was this goddess, as the mythologists relate, the wife of the seer Faunus; and was she secretly addicted to wine,[b] but did not escape detection and was beaten by her husband with myrtle rods, and is this the reason why they do not bring in myrtle and, when they make libations of wine to her, call it milk ?

Or is it because they remain pure from many things, particularly from venery, when they perform this holy service ? For they not only exclude their husbands, but they also drive everything male out of the house [c] whenever they conduct the customary ceremonies in honour of the goddess. So, because the myrtle is sacred to Venus, they religiously exclude it. For she whom they now call Venus Murcia, in ancient days, it seems, they styled Myrtia.

21. WHY do the Latins revere the woodpecker and all strictly abstain [d] from it ?

[c] *Cf. Life of Caesar*, ix. (711 E), *Life of Cicero*, xix. (870 B); Juvenal, vi. 339.
[d] No doubt this means " from eating it " since they used to eat all small birds.

F Πότερον ὅτι τὸν Πῖκον λέγουσιν ὑπὸ φαρμάκων
τῆς γυναικὸς μεταβαλεῖν τὴν φύσιν καὶ γενόμενον
δρυοκολάπτην ἀποφθέγγεσθαι λόγια καὶ χρησμῳ-
δεῖν τοῖς ἐρωτῶσιν;

"Η τοῦτο μὲν ἄπιστόν ἐστιν ὅλως καὶ τερατῶδες,
ἅτερος δὲ τῶν μύθων πιθανώτερος, ὡς ἄρα τοῖς
περὶ Ῥωμύλον καὶ Ῥῶμον ἐκτεθεῖσιν οὐ μόνον
λύκαινα θηλὴν ἐπεῖχεν, ἀλλὰ καὶ δρυοκολάπτης τις
ἐπιφοιτῶν ἐψώμιζεν; ἐπιεικῶς γὰρ ἔτι καὶ νῦν ἐν[1]
τοῖς ὑπωρείοις καὶ δρυμώδεσι τόποις ὅπου φαίνεται
δρυοκολάπτης, ἐκεῖ καὶ λύκος, ὡς Νιγίδιος[2] ἱστορεῖ.
"Η μᾶλλον, ὡς ἄλλον ἄλλου θεοῦ, καὶ τοῦτον
"Αρεος ἱερὸν νομίζουσι τὸν ὄρνιν; καὶ γὰρ εὐ-
269 θαρσὴς καὶ γαῦρός ἐστι καὶ τὸ ῥύγχος οὕτως ἔχει
κραταιόν, ὥστε δρῦς ἀνατρέπειν, ὅταν κόπτων πρὸς
τὴν ἐντεριώνην ἐξίκηται.

22. " Διὰ τί τὸν Ἰανὸν διπρόσωπον οἴονται γεγονέναι καὶ γράφουσιν οὕτω καὶ πλάττουσιν; "

Πότερον ὅτι τῷ μὲν γένει Ἕλλην ἐκ Περραιβίας
ἦν, ὡς ἱστοροῦσιν, διαβὰς δ' εἰς Ἰταλίαν καὶ
συνοικήσας τοῖς αὐτόθι βαρβάροις μετέβαλε καὶ
γλῶτταν καὶ δίαιταν· ἢ μᾶλλον ὅτι τοὺς περὶ τὴν
Ἰταλίαν φυτοῖς[3] ἀγρίοις καὶ ἀνόμοις χρωμένους
ἔθεσιν εἰς ἕτερον βίου σχῆμα, πείσας γεωργεῖν καὶ
πολιτεύεσθαι, μετέβαλε καὶ μετεκόσμησεν;

---

[1] ἐν added by Bernardakis.
[2] Νιγίδιος Xylander: νίγιδος.
[3] φυτοῖς F.C.B. (σίτοις or σιτίοις Kronenberg; ἀνθρώπους
Abresch): αὐτός.

---

[a] Cf. Ovid, Metamorphoses, xiv. 320 ff.

Is it because, as they tell the tale, Picus,[a] transformed by his wife's magic drugs, became a woodpecker and in that form gives oracles and prophecies to those who consult him?

Or is this wholly incredible and monstrous, and is that other tale [b] more credible which relates that when Romulus and Remus were exposed, not only did a she-wolf suckle them, but also a certain woodpecker came continually to visit them and bring them scraps of food? For generally, even to this day, in foot-hills and thickly wooded places where the woodpecker is found, there also is found the wolf, as Nigidius records.

Or is it rather because they regard this bird as sacred to Mars, even as other birds to other gods? For it is a courageous and spirited bird and has a beak so strong that it can overturn oaks by pecking them until it has reached the inmost part of the tree.

22. Why do they suppose Janus to have been two-faced and so represent him in painting and sculpture?

Is it because, as they relate, he was by birth a Greek from Perrhaebia, and, when he had crossed to Italy and had settled among the savages there, he changed both his speech and his habits? Or is it rather because he changed the people of Italy to another manner and form of life by persuading a people which had formerly made use of wild plants and lawless customs to till the soil and to live under organized government? [c]

---

[b] Cf. 278 c, 320 D, infra; Life of Romulus, iv. (19 E), vii (21 c).

[c] Cf. 274 F, infra; Life of Numa, xix. (72 F); Athenaeus, 692 D; Lydus, De Mensibus, iv. 2; Macrobius, Saturnalia i. 7. 21, and i. 9.

(269) 23. " Διὰ τί τὰ πρὸς[1] τὰς ταφὰς πιπράσκουσιν ἐν
B τῷ τεμένει τῷ Λιβιτίνης νομίζοντες Ἀφροδίτην
εἶναι τὴν Λιβιτίνην; "

Πότερον καὶ τοῦτο τῶν Νομᾶ τοῦ βασιλέως
φιλοσοφημάτων ἕν ἐστιν, ὅπως μανθάνωσι μὴ
δυσχεραίνειν τὰ τοιαῦτα μηδὲ φεύγειν ὡς μιασμόν;
Ἢ μᾶλλον ὑπόμνησίς ἐστι τοῦ φθαρτὸν εἶναι
τὸ γεννητόν, ὡς μιᾶς θεοῦ τὰς γενέσεις καὶ τὰς
τελευτὰς ἐπισκοπούσης; καὶ γὰρ ἐν Δελφοῖς
Ἀφροδίτης ἐπιτυμβίας ἀγαλμάτιόν ἐστι πρὸς ὃ[2]
τοὺς κατοιχομένους ἐπὶ τὰς χοὰς ἀνακαλοῦνται.

24. " Διὰ τί τρεῖς τοῦ μηνὸς ἀρχὰς καὶ προθεσμίας ἔχουσιν, οὐ ταὐτὸ διάστημα τῶν ἡμερῶν
μεταξὺ λαμβάνοντες; "

C Πότερον, ὡς οἱ περὶ τὸν Ἰόβαν ἱστοροῦσιν, ὅτι
ταῖς καλάνδαις ἐκάλουν τὸν δῆμον οἱ ἄρχοντες καὶ
κατήγγελλον εἰς πέμπτην τὰς νώνας,[3] εἰδοὺς δ'
ἡμέραν ἱερὰν ἐνόμιζον;

Ἢ μᾶλλον ὅτι ταῖς τῆς σελήνης διαφοραῖς ὁρί-
ζοντες τὸν χρόνον, ἑώρων ἐν τρισὶ γιγνομένην
διαφοραῖς τὴν σελήνην κατὰ μῆνα ταῖς μεγίσταις,
πρώτῃ μὲν ὅτε κρύπτεται σύνοδον ποιησαμένη
πρὸς ἥλιον, δευτέρᾳ[4] δ' ὅταν ἐκφυγοῦσα τὰς αὐγὰς
τοῦ ἡλίου καταφανὴς πρῶτον ἐπὶ δυσμῶν γένηται,
τρίτῃ δὲ τῇ περὶ τὴν πλήρωσιν αὐτῆς πανσελήνου
D γενομένης[5]; ὀνομάζουσι δὲ τὸν μὲν ἀφανισμὸν
αὐτῆς καὶ τὴν κρύψιν " καλάνδας," ὅτι πᾶν τὸ

---

[1] πρὸς] περὶ in the *Life of Numa*, chap. xxii.
[2] ὃ] ᾧ E. Kurtz.
[3] νώνας, etc., here and elsewhere; the mss. often have νόννας, etc.
[4] πρώτῃ . . . δευτέρᾳ Bernardakis: πρώτη . . . δευτέρα.

23. WHY do they sell articles for funerals in the precinct of Libitina, whom they identify with Venus?[a]

Is this also one of the philosophic devices of king Numa, that they should learn not to feel repugnance at such things nor shun them as a pollution?

Or is it rather a reminder that whatever is born must die, since one goddess presides over births and deaths? For in Delphi there is a little statue of Aphrodite of the Tomb, to which they summon the departed to come forth for the libations.

24. WHY have they in the month three beginnings or fixed points, and do not adopt the same interval of days between them?

Is it, as Juba[b] and his followers relate, that on the Kalends the officials used to call[c] the people and announce the Nones for the fifth day thereafter, regarding the Ides as a holy day?[5]

Or is it rather because, since they measured time by the phases of the moon, they observed that in each month the moon undergoes three very important changes: first, when she is hidden by her conjunction with the sun; second, when she has escaped the sun's rays and becomes visible for the first time at sunset; and third, at the full moon, when her orb is completely round? The disappearance and concealment of the moon they call *Kalendae*, for every-

---

[a] Cf. *Life of Numa*, xii. (67 E): Dionysius of Halicarnassus, *Roman Antiquities*, iv. 15. 5; Varro, *De Lingua Latina*, vi. 47.

[b] Müller, *Frag. Hist. Graec.* iii. p. 470.

[c] Cf. Old Latin *calare*, equated with Greek καλεῖν by Plutarch and by other writers.

---

[5] γενομένης Madvig: γινομένης.

(269) κρύφα καὶ λάθρα " κλάμ " καὶ " κηλάρι[1] " τὸ
λανθάνειν· τὴν δὲ πρώτην φάσιν[2] " νώνας[3] " τῷ
δικαιοτάτῳ τῶν ὀνομάτων, νουμηνίαν οὖσαν· καὶ
γὰρ αὐτοὶ τὸ νέον καὶ καινὸν ὥσπερ ἡμεῖς προσ-
αγορεύουσι· τὰς δ' " εἰδούς " ἢ διὰ τὸ κάλλος καὶ
τὸ εἶδος ὁλοκλήρου καθισταμένης τῆς σελήνης ἢ
τῷ Διὶ τὴν ἐπωνυμίαν ἀποδιδόντες.[4] οὐ δεῖ δὲ τῶν
ἡμερῶν τὸν ἀκριβέστατον ἀριθμὸν διώκειν οὐδὲ τὸ[5]
παρ' ὀλίγον συκοφαντεῖν, ὅπου καὶ νῦν ἐπίδοσιν
τοσαύτην ἀστρολογίας ἐχούσης, περιγίγνεται τῆς
ἐμπειρίας τῶν μαθηματικῶν ἡ τῆς κινήσεως ἀν-
ωμαλία διαφεύγουσα τὸν λόγον.

E   25. " Διὰ τί τὴν μετὰ καλάνδας ἡμέραν καὶ
νώνας[3] καὶ εἰδοὺς ἀνέξοδον καὶ ἀνεκδήμητον
τίθενται; "

Πότερον, ὡς οἱ πλεῖστοι νομίζουσι καὶ Λίβιος
ἱστορεῖ, ὅτι[6] μετὰ τὰς Κυιντιλίας εἰδούς, ἃς νῦν
Ἰουλίας καλοῦσιν, ἐξάγοντες[7] οἱ χιλίαρχοι τὸ
στράτευμα περὶ τὸν Ἀλίαν[8] ποταμὸν ἐκρατήθησαν
ὑπὸ Κελτῶν μάχῃ καὶ τὴν πόλιν ἀπώλεσαν; νομι-
σθείσης δὲ τῆς[9] μετὰ τὰς εἰδοὺς ἀποφράδος προήγαγεν[10] ὥσπερ φιλεῖ πορρωτέρω τὸ ἔθος ἡ δεισι-

---

[1] κηλάρι an obvious correction, first adopted by H. J. Rose :
κήλαρε or κηλάρε (E).
[2] φάσιν Polus and Leonicus : φασὶ.
[3] νώνας, etc., here and elsewhere ; the mss. often have
νόννας, etc.
[4] ἀποδιδόντες] ἐπιδιδόντες in all mss. but E.
[5] τὸ E. Kurtz : τῷ.
[6] ὅτι omitted in most mss., but found in E.
[7] ἐξάγοντες] ἐξαγαγόντες Helmbold.
[8] Ἀλίαν the usual spelling : Ἀλλίαν.
[9] τῆς added by Meziriacus.
[10] προήγαγεν Wyttenbach : προσταγέν.

thing concealed or secret is *clam*, and " to be concealed " is *celari*.[a] The first appearance of the moon they call Nones, the most accurate since it is the new moon : for their word for " new " and " novel " is the same as ours.[b] They name the Ides as they do either because of the beauty and form (*eidos*) of the full-orbed moon, or by derivation from a title of Jupiter.[c] But we must not follow out the most exact calculation of the number of days nor cast aspersions on approximate reckoning ; since even now, when astronomy has made so much progress, the irregularity of the moon's movements is still beyond the skill of mathematicians, and continues to elude their calculations.[d]

25. WHY do they reckon the day that follows the Kalends, the Nones, or the Ides as unsuitable for leaving home or for travel ?

Is it, as most authorities think and as Livy[e] records, that on the day after the Ides of Quintilis, which they now call July, the military tribunes led out the army, and were vanquished in battle by the Gauls at the river Allia and lost the City ? But when the day after the Ides had come to be regarded as ill-omened, did superstition, as is its wont, extend the custom

---

[a] Much is made of Plutarch's mistake in equating *celare* (MSS.) with λανθάνειν rather than with κρύπτειν, but the mistake is more likely that of a scribe.

[b] This is true etymologically ; but is Plutarch thinking of the syllable *nou* in νουμηνία and *nouus* ?

[c] *Cf.* Macrobius, *Saturnalia*, i. 15. 14, where it is stated that *Idus* is derived from the Etruscan *Itis*, said to mean " Iovis fiducia."

[d] *Cf. Life of Aristides*, chap. xix. (331 A).

[e] Livy, v. 37 ; and vi. 1. 11.

δαιμονία καὶ κατέστησεν εἰς τὴν αὐτὴν εὐλάβειαν
τήν τε μετὰ νώνας καὶ τὴν μετὰ καλάνδας;

F ῝Η τοῦτο μὲν ἔχει πολλὰς ἀλογίας[1]· ἄλλῃ τε γὰρ
ἡμέρᾳ τὴν μάχην ἡττήθησαν, ἣν Ἀλιάδα[2] διὰ τὸν
ποταμὸν καλοῦντες ἀφοσιοῦνται, καὶ πολλῶν ἀπο-
φράδων οὐσῶν οὐκ ἐν παντὶ μηνὶ τὰς ὁμωνύμους
παραφυλάττουσιν, ἀλλ' ἑκάστην ἐν ᾧ συνέτυχε, τό
τε ταῖς μετὰ νώνας καὶ καλάνδας ἁπλῶς ἁπάσαις[3]
προστρίψασθαι τὴν δεισιδαιμονίαν ἀπιθανώτατον.

῝Ορα δὴ μή, καθάπερ τῶν μηνῶν τὸν μὲν πρῶτον
ὀλυμπίοις θεοῖς ἱέρωσαν, τὸν δὲ δεύτερον χθονίοις
ἐν ᾧ καὶ καθαρμούς τινας τελοῦσι καὶ τοῖς κατ-
270 οιχομένοις ἐναγίζουσιν, οὕτω καὶ[4] τῶν ἡμερῶν τὰς
μὲν οἷον ἀρχὰς καὶ κυρίας ὥσπερ εἴρηται τρεῖς
οὔσας ἑορτασίμους καὶ ἱερὰς ἔθεντο, τὰς δ' ἐφεξῆς
δαίμοσι καὶ φθιτοῖς ἐπιφημίσαντες ἀποφράδας καὶ
ἀπράκτους ἐνόμισαν. καὶ γὰρ ῝Ελληνες ἐν τῇ
νουμηνίᾳ τοὺς θεοὺς σεβόμενοι, τὴν δευτέραν ἥρωσι
καὶ δαίμοσιν ἀποδεδώκασι καὶ τῶν κρατήρων ὁ
δεύτερος ἥρωσιν ἐπικίρναται καὶ ἡρωίσι. καὶ ὅλως
ἀριθμός τις ὁ χρόνος, ἀριθμοῦ δὲ θεῖον ἡ ἀρχή·
μονὰς γάρ ἐστιν. ἡ δὲ μετ' αὐτὴν δυὰς ἀντίπαλος
B τῇ ἀρχῇ καὶ ἀρτίων πρώτη. τὸ δ' ἄρτιον ἐνδεὲς

---

[1] ἀλογίας] ἀντιλογίας in some mss.
[2] Ἀλάδα the usual spelling: Ἀλλιάδα.
[3] ἁπάσαις] all mss. but one have ἁπάσας.
[4] καὶ omitted in all mss. but E.

---

[a] The traditional date of the battle was July 18, 390 b.c.
[b] Cf. Life of Camillus, chap. xix. 8 (138 d).
[c] As the Kalends, the Nones, and the Ides have the same
names in every month. [d] 269 b, supra.
[e] That is, the spirits of the men and women of the Heroic

42

further, and involve in the same circumspection the day after the Nones and the day after the Kalends?

Or does this contain many irrational assumptions? For it was on a different day that they were defeated in battle,[a] a day which they call Alliensis from the river, and make a dread day of expiation [b]; and although they have many ill-omened days, they do not observe them under the same names [c] in each month, but each in the month in which it occurs; and it is thus quite incredible that the superstition should have attached itself simply to all the days that follow immediately after the Nones or the Kalends.

Consider the following analogy: just as they have dedicated the first month to the gods of Olympus, and the second, in which they perform certain rites of purification and sacrifice to the departed, to the gods of the lower world, so also in regard to the days of the month they have established three as festive and holy days, as I have stated,[d] which are, as it were, fundamental and sovereign days; but the days which follow immediately they have dedicated to the spirits and the dead, and have come to regard them as ill-omened and unsuitable for business. In fact, the Greeks worship the gods on the day of the new moon; the next day they have duly assigned to the heroes and spirits, and the second bowl of wine is mixed in honour of the heroes and heroines.[e] And speaking generally, time is a sort of number; and the beginning of number is divine, for it is the monad. But after it is the dyad, antagonistic to the beginning number, and the first of the even numbers. The even numbers are imperfect, in-

Age who dwelt after death in the Isles of the Blest or in Hades.

(270) καὶ ἀτελὲς καὶ ἀόριστον, ὥσπερ αὖ τὸ περιττὸν
ὥρισται καὶ περαίνει καὶ τέλειόν ἐστι. διὸ καὶ
νῶναι μὲν ἐπιβάλλουσι διὰ πέμπτης καλάνδαις,
νώναις δ' εἰδοὶ δι' ἐνάτης. ὁρίζουσι γὰρ οἱ περιτ-
τοὶ τὰς ἀρχάς· οἱ δὲ μετὰ τὰς ἀρχὰς ἄρτιοι ὄντες
οὐκ ἔχουσι τάξιν οὐδὲ δύναμιν, ὅθεν οὐκ ἄρχονται
πράξεως οὐδ' ἀποδημίας ἐν ταύταις.

Ἦ καὶ τὸ τοῦ Θεμιστοκλέους ἔχει λόγον, ἐρίσαι
ποτὲ τὴν ὑστεραίαν πρὸς τὴν ἑορτήν, ἐκείνης μὲν
ἀσχολίαν καὶ κόπον ἐχούσης πολύν, αὐτὴν δὲ
παρέχουσαν¹ μετὰ σχολῆς καὶ ἡσυχίας ἀπολαῦσαι
τῶν παρεσκευασμένων πρὸς τὴν ἑορτήν· ἀποκρίνα-
C σθαι² δὲ πρὸς ταῦτα τὴν ἑορτήν " ἀληθῆ λέγεις,
ἀλλ' ἐμοῦ μὴ γενομένης οὐδ' ἂν σὺ ἦσθα³ "; ταῦτα
δ' ὁ Θεμιστοκλῆς πρὸς τοὺς αὖθις ἔλεγε στρατηγοὺς
τῶν Ἀθηναίων ὡς οὐκ ἂν οὐδαμοῦ φανέντας, εἰ μὴ
τὴν πόλιν αὐτὸς ἔσωσεν.

Ἐπεὶ τοίνυν πᾶσα μὲν ἀξία σπουδῆς ἀποδημία
καὶ πρᾶξις οἰκονομίας δεῖται καὶ παρασκευῆς,
Ῥωμαῖοι δὲ τὸ παλαιὸν ἐν ταῖς ἑορταῖς οὐδὲν
ᾠκονόμουν οὐδ' ἐφρόντιζον ἀλλ' ἢ περὶ τοὺς θεοὺς
ἠσχολοῦντο καὶ τοῦτ' ἔπραττον, ὥσπερ ἔτι νῦν
προκηρύττουσιν οἱ ἱερεῖς ἐπὶ τὰς θυσίας βαδίζοντες,
εἰκότως εὐθὺς οὐκ ἐξεδήμουν μετὰ τὰς ἑορτὰς οὐδ'
ἔπραττον (ἀπαράσκευοι γὰρ ἦσαν), ἀλλ' ἐκφροντί-

¹ αὐτὴν δὲ παρέχουσαν Bernardakis : αὐτὴ δὲ παρέχουσα.
² ἀποκρίνασθαι Aldine edition : ἀποκρίνεσθαι.
³ ἦσθα 320 F, infra, and Life of Themistocles : ἦς.

─────────

ᵃ Cf. 264 A, supra, also Moralia, 374 A, 387 F, 429 A,
1002 A, 1012 E.
ᵇ Cf. 320 F, infra; Life of Themistocles, xviii. (121 B).
The context of 345 C, infra, makes it very probable that

complete, and indeterminate, just as the odd numbers are determinate, completing, and perfect.[a] Wherefore, in like manner, the Nones succeed the Kalends at an interval of five days and the Ides succeed the Nones at an interval of nine days. For the odd numbers define the beginnings, but the even numbers, since they occur after the beginnings, have no position nor power ; therefore on these days they do not begin any business or travel.

Or has also the saying of Themistocles [b] some foundation in reason ? For once upon a time, said he, the Day-After had an altercation with the Feast-Day on the ground that the Feast-Day had much labour and toil, whereas she herself provided the opportunity of enjoying in leisure and quiet all the things prepared for the festival. To this the Feast-Day replied, " You are quite right ; but if I had not been, you would not be ! " This story Themistocles related to the Athenian generals who succeeded him, to show that they would have been nowhere, if he himself had not saved the city.

Since, therefore, all travel and all business of importance needs provision and preparation, and since in ancient days the Romans, at the time of festivals, made no provision or plan for anything, save only that they were engaged in the service of their gods and busied themselves with this only, just as even to this day the priests cause such a proclamation to be made in advance as they proceed on their way to sacrifice ; so it was only natural that they did not set out on a journey immediately after their festivals, nor did they transact any business, for they were

the essay *De Gloria Atheniensium* began with this favourite story of Plutarch's.

D ζοντες οἴκοι καὶ παρασκευαζόμενοι τὴν ἡμέραν
(270) ἐκείνην διετέλουν.

Ἡ καθάπερ ἔτι νῦν προσευξάμενοι καὶ προσκυνή-
σαντες ἐν τοῖς ἱεροῖς ἐπιμένειν καὶ καθίζειν εἰώθασιν, οὕτως οὐκ εὐθὺς ἐπέβαλλον ταῖς ἱεραῖς
ἡμέραις τὰς ἐνεργούς, ἀλλ' ἐποίουν τι διάλειμμα
καὶ διάστημα, πολλὰ τῶν πραγμάτων δυσχερῆ καὶ
ἀβούλητα φερόντων;

26. " Διὰ τί λευκὰ φοροῦσιν ἐν τοῖς πένθεσιν αἱ
γυναῖκες ἱμάτια καὶ λευκοὺς κεκρυφάλους; "

Πότερον ὡς τοὺς μάγους φασὶν πρὸς τὸν Ἅιδην
καὶ τὸ σκότος ἀντιταττομένους, τῷ δὲ φωτεινῷ καὶ
λαμπρῷ συνεξομοιοῦντας ἑαυτοὺς τοῦτο ποιεῖν;

Ἤ, καθάπερ τὸ σῶμα τοῦ τεθνηκότος ἀμφι-
E εννύουσι λευκοῖς, καὶ τοὺς προσήκοντας ἀξιοῦσι; τὸ
δὲ σῶμα κοσμοῦσιν οὕτως, ἐπεὶ μὴ δύνανται τὴν
ψυχήν· βούλονται δ' ἐκείνην λαμπρὰν καὶ καθαρὰν
προπέμπειν, ὡς ἀφειμένην ἤδη καὶ διηγωνισμένην
μέγαν ἀγῶνα καὶ ποικίλον.

Ἤ τὸ μὲν λιτὸν ἐν τούτοις μάλιστα καὶ τὸ
ἁπλοῦν πρέπει; τῶν δὲ βαπτῶν τὰ μὲν καὶ
πολυτέλειαν ἐμφαίνει τὰ δὲ περιεργίαν· οὐ γὰρ
ἧττον ἔστι πρὸς τὸ μέλαν ἢ τὸ ἁλουργὸν εἰπεῖν,
F " δολερὰ μὲν τὰ εἵματα, δολερὰ δὲ τὰ χρώματα.¹ "
τὸ δ' αὐτόχρουν μέλαν οὐχ ὑπὸ τέχνης ἀλλὰ

¹ χρίματα Hatzidakis and S. A. Naber; cf. Herod. iii. 22
and Moralia, 646 в and 863 е.

---

^a Cf. Life of Numa, xiv. (69 е–70 а) ; Propertius ii. 28. 45-
46 ; see also Lewy in Philologus, lxxxiv. p. 378.

unprepared ; but that day they always spent at home making their plans and preparations.

Or is it even as men now, who have offered their prayers and oblations, are wont to tarry and sit a while in the temples,[a] and so they would not let busy days succeed holy days immediately, but made some pause and breathing-space between, since business brings with it much that is distasteful and undesired ?

26. Why do women in mourning wear white robes and white head-dresses ?

Do they do this, as men say the Magi do, arraying themselves against Hades and the powers of darkness, and making themselves like unto Light and Brightness ?

Or is it that, just as they clothe the body of the dead in white, they think it proper that the relatives should also wear this colour ? They adorn the body thus since they cannot so adorn the soul ; and they wish to send forth the soul bright and pure, since it is now set free after having fought the good fight in all its manifold forms.

Or are plainness and simplicity most becoming on these occasions ? Of the dyed garments, some reflect expense, others over-elaboration ; for we may say no less with reference to black than to purple : " These be cheating garments, these be cheating colours." [b] That which is naturally black is dyed not through art, but by nature ; and when it is

---

[b] Apparently a misquotation of Herodotus, iii. 22. 1 : otherwise misquoted in *Moralia*, 646 B and 863 E. *Cf.* also Clement of Alexandria, *Stromateis*, i. x. 48. 6 (p. 344 Potter).

φύσει βαπτόν ἐστι, καὶ μεμειγμένον τῷ σκιώδει
κεκράτηται.¹ μόνον οὖν τὸ λευκὸν εἰλικρινὲς καὶ
ἀμιγὲς καὶ ἀμίαντόν ἐστι βαφῇ καὶ ἀμίμητον²·
οἰκειότατον οὖν τοῖς θαπτομένοις. καὶ γὰρ ὁ τε-
θνηκὼς ἁπλοῦν τι γέγονε καὶ ἀμιγὲς καὶ καθαρόν,
ἀτεχνῶς οὐδὲν ἀλλ' ἢ φαρμάκου δευσοποιοῦ τοῦ
σώματος ἀπηλλαγμένος. ἐν δ' Ἄργει λευκὰ φοροῦσιν ἐν τοῖς πένθεσιν, ὡς Σωκράτης φησίν,
ὑδατόκλυστα.

27. "Διὰ τί πᾶν τεῖχος ἀβέβηλον καὶ ἱερὸν
271 νομίζουσι, τὰς δὲ πύλας οὐ νομίζουσιν;"

Ἢ καθάπερ ἔγραψε Βάρρων τὸ μὲν τεῖχος ἱερὸν
δεῖ νομίζειν, ὅπως ὑπὲρ αὐτοῦ μάχωνται προθύμως
καὶ ἀποθνήσκωσιν; οὕτω γὰρ δοκεῖ καὶ Ῥωμύλος
ἀποκτεῖναι τὸν ἀδελφὸν ὡς ἄβατον καὶ ἱερὸν τόπον
ἐπιχειροῦντα διαπηδᾶν καὶ ποιεῖν ὑπερβατὸν καὶ
βέβηλον.

Τὰς δὲ πύλας οὐχ οἷόν τ' ἦν ἀφιερῶσαι, δι' ὧν
ἄλλα τε πολλὰ τῶν ἀναγκαίων καὶ τοὺς νεκροὺς
ἐκκομίζουσιν. ὅθεν οἱ πόλιν ἀπ' ἀρχῆς κτίζοντες
ὅσον ἂν μέλλωσι τόπον ἀνοικοδομεῖν ἔπίασιν ἀρό-
τρῳ, βοῦν ἄρρενα καὶ θήλειαν ὑποζεύξαντες· ὅταν
δὲ τὰ τείχη περιορίζωσι, τὰς τῶν πυλῶν χώρας
B διαμετροῦντες τὴν ὕνιν ὑφαιροῦσι, καὶ μεταφέρου-

---

¹ κεκράτηται] κέκραται in some mss.
² ἀμίμητον] ἄμικτον Meziriacus.

ᵃ This apparently means : Naturally black wool may be
dyed purple or any other strong dark colour. It is possible,
however, that Plutarch wrote κέκραται (and so several mss.) :
" it is modified when combined with a dark colour."
ᵇ Cf. Plato, Republic, 729 D-E.

combined with a dark colour, it is overpowered.[a]
Only white,[b] therefore, is pure, unmixed, and un-
contaminated by dye, nor can it be imitated ; wherefore it is most appropriate for the dead at burial.
For he who is dead has become something simple,
unmixed, and pure, once he has been released from
the body, which is indeed to be compared with a
stain made by dyeing. In Argos, as Socrates [c] says,
persons in mourning wear white garments washed
in water.

27. Why do they regard all the city wall as inviolable and sacred, but not the gates ?

Is it, as Varro has written, because the wall must
be considered sacred that men may fight and die
with enthusiasm in its defence ? It was under such
circumstances, it seems, that Romulus killed his
brother because he was attempting to leap across a
place that was inviolable and sacred, and to make it
traversable and profane.

But it was impossible to consecrate the gates, for
through them they carry out many other objection-
able things and also dead bodies.[d] Wherefore the
original founders of a city yoke a bull and a
cow, and mark out with a plough all the land on
which they intend to build [e] ; and when they are
engaged in tracing [f] the circuit of the walls, as they
measure off the space intended for gates, they lift
up the ploughshare and thus carry the plough across,

[c] Müller, *Frag. Hist. Graec.* iv. 498.
[d] *Cf. Moralia,* 518 B.
[e] *Cf.* Varro, *De Lingua Latina,* v. 143, *Res Rusticae,* ii.
1. 9 ; Dionysius of Halicarnassus, *Roman Antiquities,* i. 88 ;
Ovid, *Fasti,* iv. 819 ff.
[f] *Cf. Life of Romulus,* xi. (23 D).

(271) σιν οὕτω τὸ ἄροτρον, ὡς τὴν ἀρουμένην πᾶσαν
ἱερὰν καὶ ἄσυλον ἐσομένην.

28. "Διὰ τί τοὺς παῖδας, ὅταν ὀμνύωσι τὸν
Ἡρακλέα, κωλύουσιν ὑπὸ στέγῃ τοῦτο ποιεῖν καὶ
κελεύουσιν εἰς ὕπαιθρον προϊέναι;"

Πότερον, ὡς ἔνιοι λέγουσιν, οὐκ οἰκουρίᾳ τὸν
Ἡρακλέα χαίρειν ἀλλ' ὑπαίθρῳ βίῳ καὶ θυραυλίαις
νομίζοντες;

"Η μᾶλλον, ὅτι τῶν θεῶν οὐκ ἐπιχώριος οὗτος
ἀλλὰ πόρρωθεν καὶ ξένος; οὐδὲ γὰρ τὸν Διόνυσον
ὀμνύουσιν ὑπὸ στέγῃ,¹ ξένον ὄντα καὶ αὐτόν, εἴπερ
ἐστὶ ἀπὸ Νύσης.²

C   "Η ταῦτα μὲν λέγεται καὶ παίζεται πρὸς τοὺς
παῖδας, ἄλλως δ' ἐπίσχεσίς ἐστι τῆς πρὸς τὸν
ὅρκον εὐχερείας καὶ ταχύτητος τὸ γιγνόμενον, ὡς
Φαβωρῖνος ἔλεγε; τὸ γὰρ ὥσπερ ἐκ παρασκευῆς
μέλλησιν ἐμποιεῖ καὶ βουλεύσασθαι δίδωσι. συμ-
βάλοιτο δ' ἄν τις τῷ Φαβωρίνῳ πρὸς τὸ μὴ κοινὸν
ἀλλ' ἴδιον εἶναι τοῦ θεοῦ τούτου τὸ γιγνόμενον ἐκ
τῶν περὶ Ἡρακλέους λεγομένων. ἱστορεῖται γὰρ
οὕτως³ εὐλαβὴς γεγονέναι πρὸς ὅρκον, ὥσθ' ἅπαξ
ὀμόσαι καὶ μόνῳ Φυλεῖ τῷ Αὐγέου· διὸ καὶ τὴν
Πυθίαν προφέρειν τὰ ὅρκια πάντα⁴ Λακεδαιμονίοις
ὡς ἐμπεδοῦσι λῷον εἴη καὶ ἄμεινον.

D   29. "Διὰ τί τὴν γαμουμένην οὐκ ἐῶσιν αὐτὴν
ὑπερβῆναι τὸν οὐδὸν τῆς οἰκίας, ἀλλ' ὑπεραίρουσιν
οἱ προπέμποντες;"

¹ στέγῃ as above: all mss. except E have στέγην.
² ἀπὸ Νύσης F.C.B.: διόννσος.
³ οὕτως Wyttenbach: οὗτος.
⁴ πάντα F.C.B.: ταῦτα.

50

since they hold that all the land that is ploughed is to be kept sacred and inviolable.

28. WHY do they tell children, whenever they would swear by Hercules, not to do so under a roof, and bid them go out into the open air ? [a]

Is it, as some relate, because they believe that Hercules had no pleasure in staying in the house, but rejoiced in a life in the open air and a bed under the stars ?

Or is it rather because Hercules is not one of the native gods, but a foreigner from afar ? For neither do they swear under a roof by Bacchus, since he also is a foreign god if he is from Nysa.

Or is this but said in jest to the children, and what is done is really a check upon over-readiness and hastiness to swear, as Favorinus stated ? For what is done following, as it were, upon preparation produces delay and allows deliberation. Yet one might urge against Favorinus the fact that this custom is not common, but peculiar to Hercules, as may be seen from the legend about him : for it is recorded that he was so circumspect regarding an oath that he swore but once and for Phyleus, the son of Augeas, alone. Wherefore they say that the prophetic priestess also brought up against the Spartans all the oaths they had sworn, saying that it would be better and much more to be desired if they would keep them ! [b]

29. WHY do they not allow the bride to cross the threshold of her home herself, but those who are escorting her lift her over ? [c]

[a] Cf. Varro, De Lingua Latina, v. 66.
[b] Cf. Moralia, 229 B and the note (Vol. III. p. 372).
[c] Cf. Life of Romulus, xv. (26 D-E).

(271)　Πότερον ὅτι καὶ τὰς πρώτας γυναῖκας ἁρπάσαντες
οὕτως εἰσήνεγκαν, αὐταὶ δ' οὐκ εἰσῆλθον;

῍Η βούλονται δοκεῖν εἰσιέναι βιαζομένας οὐχ
ἑκούσας, ὅπου μέλλουσι διαλύειν τὴν παρθενίαν;

῍Η συμβολόν ἐστι τοῦ μηδ' ἐξιέναι δι' αὐτῆς μηδὲ
καταλιπεῖν τὴν οἰκίαν, εἰ μὴ βιασθείη, καθάπερ καὶ
εἰσῆλθε βιασθεῖσα; καὶ γὰρ παρ' ἡμῖν ἐν Βοιωτίᾳ
καίουσι πρὸ τῆς θύρας τὸν ἄξονα τῆς ἁμάξης, ἐμ-
φαίνοντες δεῖν τὴν νύμφην ἐμμένειν ὡς ἀνῃρημένου
τοῦ ἀπάξοντος.

30.　" Διὰ τί τὴν νύμφην εἰσάγοντες λέγειν κελεύ-
E ουσιν, ' ὅπου σὺ Γάιος,[1] ἐγὼ Γαΐα '; "

Πότερον ὥσπερ ἐπὶ ῥητοῖς εὐθὺς εἴσεισι τῷ
κοινωνεῖν ἁπάντων καὶ συνάρχειν, καὶ τὸ μὲν δη-
λούμενόν ἐστιν " ὅπου σὺ κύριος καὶ οἰκοδεσπότης,
καὶ ἐγὼ κυρία καὶ οἰκοδέσποινα "; τοῖς δ' ὀνόμασι
τούτοις ἄλλως[2] κέχρηνται κοινοῖς οὖσιν, ὥσπερ οἱ
νομικοὶ Γάιον Σήιον καὶ Λούκιον Τίτιον, καὶ οἱ
φιλόσοφοι Δίωνα καὶ Θέωνα παραλαμβάνουσιν.

῍Η διὰ Γαΐαν Καικιλίαν καλὴν καὶ ἀγαθὴν
γυναῖκα, τῶν Ταρκυνίου παίδων ἑνὶ συνοικήσασαν,
ἧς ἐν τῷ τοῦ Σάγκτου ἱερῷ χαλκοῦς ἀνδριὰς
ἕστηκεν; ἔκειτο δὲ πάλαι καὶ σανδάλια καὶ
ἄτρακτος, τὸ μὲν οἰκουρίας αὐτῆς, τὸ δ' ἐνερ-
γείας σύμβολον.

---

[1] Γάιος] all mss. except E have γαὶς.
[2] ἄλλως] all mss. except E have ἄλλοις.

---

[a] " Ubi tu Gaius, ego Gaia."
[b] " John Doe and Richard Roe."
[c] Cf. Moralia, 1061 c.
[d] Probably not the same as Tanaquil, wife of Tarquinius
Priscus ; but cf. Pliny, Natural History, viii. 48 (194).

Is it because they carried off by force also the first Roman brides and bore them in in this manner, and the women did not enter of their own accord ?

Or do they wish it to appear that it is under constraint and not of their own desire that they enter a dwelling where they are about to lose their virginity ?

Or is it a token that the woman may not go forth of her own accord and abandon her home if she be not constrained, just as it was under constraint that she entered it ? So likewise among us in Boeotia they burn the axle of the bridal carriage before the door, signifying that the bride must remain, since her means of departure has been destroyed.

30. Why do they, as they conduct the bride to her home, bid her say, " Where you are Gaius, there am I Gaia " [a] ?

Is her entrance into the house upon fixed terms, as it were, at once to share everything and to control jointly the household, and is the meaning, then, " Wherever you are lord and master, there am I lady and mistress " ? These names are in common use also in other connexions, just as jurists speak of Gaius Seius and Lucius Titius,[b] and philosophers of Dion and Theon.[c]

Or do they use these names because of Gaia Caecilia,[d] consort of one of Tarquin's sons, a fair and virtuous woman, whose statue in bronze stands in the temple of Sanctus ? [e] And both her sandals and her spindle were, in ancient days, dedicated there as tokens of her love of home and of her industry respectively.

[e] We should probably emend to Sancus ; the same mistake is made in the mss. of Propertius, iv. 9. 71-74, where see the excellent note of Barber and Butler.

F 31. "Διὰ τί ὁ πολυθρύλητος ᾄδεται Ταλάσιος
ἐν τοῖς γάμοις;"

Πότερον ἀπὸ τῆς ταλασίας; καὶ γὰρ τὸν
τάλαρον τάλασον[1] ὀνομάζουσι· καὶ τὴν νύμφην
εἰσάγοντες νάκος ὑποστρωννύασιν[2]· αὐτὴ δ' εἰσ-
φέρει μὲν ἡλακάτην καὶ τὴν ἄτρακτον, ἐρίῳ δὲ τὴν
θύραν περιστέφει τοῦ ἀνδρός.

Ἢ τὸ λεγόμενον ὑπὸ τῶν ἱστορικῶν ἀληθές, ὅτι
νεανίας ἦν τις λαμπρὸς ἐν τοῖς πολεμικοῖς καὶ
τἄλλα χρηστὸς ὄνομα Ταλάσιος; ἐπεὶ δ' ἥρπαζον
οἱ Ῥωμαῖοι τὰς τῶν Σαβίνων θυγατέρας ἐλθούσας
272 ἐπὶ θέαν, ἐκομίζετο τῷ Ταλασίῳ παρθένος ἐκπρεπὴς τὴν ὄψιν ὑπὸ δημοτικῶν τινων καὶ πελατῶν[3]
τοῦ Ταλασίου, βοώντων ὑπὲρ ἀσφαλείας καὶ τοῦ
μηδένα πελάζειν μηδ' ἀντιλαμβάνεσθαι τῆς παιδός,
ὡς Ταλασίῳ γυνὴ φέροιτο. τιμῶντες οὖν οἱ λοιποὶ
τὸν Ταλάσιον καὶ συνευχόμενοι καὶ συνευφημοῦντες
εἵποντο καὶ παρέπεμπον· ὅθεν, εὐτυχοῦς γάμου
B γενομένου, καὶ τοῖς ἄλλοις εἰθίσθησαν ἐπιφωνεῖν
τὸν Ταλάσιον, ὥσπερ Ἕλληνες τὸν Ὑμέναιον.

32. "Διὰ τί τοῦ Μαΐου μηνὸς περὶ τὴν πανσέ-
ληνον ἀπὸ τῆς ξυλίνης γεφύρας εἴδωλα ῥιπτοῦντες
ἀνθρώπων εἰς τὸν ποταμὸν Ἀργείους τὰ ῥιπτού-
μενα καλοῦσιν;"

Ἢ τὸ παλαιὸν οἱ περὶ τὸν τόπον οἰκοῦντες

---

[1] τάλασον Xylander : τάλαντον.
[2] ὑποστρωννύασιν] all mss. except E have ὑποστρωννύουσιν.
[3] πελατῶν Wyttenbach : πελαστῶν.

---

[a] The traditional Roman spelling seems to be with -ss-.
[b] Cf. Life of Romulus, xv. (26 c), Life of Pompey, iv.
(620 f) ; Livy, i. 9. 12.

31. Why is the far-famed " Talassio " [a] sung at the marriage ceremony ? [b]

Is it derived from *talasia* (spinning) ? For they call the wool-basket (*talaros*) *talasus*. When they lead in the bride, they spread a fleece beneath her ; she herself brings with her a distaff and her spindle, and wreaths her husband's door with wool.

Or is the statement of the historians true ? They relate that there was a certain young man, brilliant in military achievements and valuable in other ways, whose name was Talasius ; and when the Romans were carrying off the daughters of the Sabines who had come to see the games, a maiden of particularly beautiful appearance was being carried off for him by some plebeian retainers of his. To protect their enterprise and to prevent anyone from approaching and trying to wrest the maiden from them, they shouted continually that she was being brought as a wife for Talasius (*Talasio*). Since, therefore, everyone honoured Talasius, they followed along and provided escort, joining in the good wishes and acclamations. Wherefore since Talasius's marriage was happy, they became accustomed to invoke Talasius in other marriages also, even as the Greeks invoke Hymen.

32. Why is it that in the month of May at the time of the full moon they throw into the river from the Pons Sublicius figures of men, calling the images thrown Argives ? [c]

Is it because in ancient days the barbarians who

---

[c] Cf. 285 A, *infra*, and Ovid, *Fasti*, v. 621 ff. ; Varro, *De Lingua Latina*, v. 45 ; Dionysius of Halicarnassus, *Roman Antiquities*, i. 38. 2-3. Plutarch means the *Argei*, the origin and meaning of which is a mystery (see V. Rose's edition, pp. 98 ff.).

(272) βάρβαροι τοὺς ἁλισκομένους Ἕλληνας οὕτως ἀπώλ-
λυσαν; Ἡρακλῆς δὲ θαυμασθεὶς ὑπ' αὐτῶν ἔπαυσε
μὲν τὴν ξενοκτονίαν, ἐδίδαξε δὲ τὸ ἔθος καὶ τὴν
δεισιδαιμονίαν ἀπομιμουμένους εἴδωλα ῥιπτεῖν, Ἀργείους δὲ τοὺς Ἕλληνας οἱ παλαιοὶ πάντας ὁμαλῶς
προσηγόρευον. εἰ μὴ νὴ Δία τῶν Ἀρκάδων πολεμίους καὶ τοὺς Ἀργείους διὰ τὴν γειτνίασιν ἡγου-
C μένων, οἱ περὶ Εὔανδρον ἐκ τῆς Ἑλλάδος φυγόντες
καὶ κατοικήσαντες αὐτόθι τὴν μνησικακίαν καὶ τὴν
ἔχθραν διεφύλαττον.

33. " Διὰ τί τὸ παλαιὸν οὐκ ἐδείπνουν ἔξω χωρὶς
τῶν υἱῶν ἔτι τὴν παιδικὴν ἡλικίαν ἐχόντων; "
Ἦ τοῦτο μὲν καὶ Λυκοῦργος εἴθισε, τοὺς παῖδας
ἐπεισάγων τοῖς φιδιτίοις, ὅπως ἐθίζωνται μὴ
θηριωδῶς μηδ' ἀτάκτως ἀλλὰ μετ' εὐλαβείας
ταῖς ἡδοναῖς προσφέρεσθαι, τοὺς πρεσβυτέρους οἷον
ἐπισκόπους καὶ θεατὰς ἔχοντες; οὐκ ἔλαττον δὴ
τοῦτο καὶ[1] τοὺς πατέρας αὐτοὺς μᾶλλον αἰδεῖσθαι
καὶ σωφρονεῖν τῶν υἱῶν παρόντων· ὅπου γὰρ ἀν-
αισχυντοῦσι γέροντες, ὥς φησιν ὁ Πλάτων, ἐνταῦθ'
ἀνάγκη καὶ νέους ἀναισχυντοτάτους εἶναι.

34. " Διὰ τί τῶν ἄλλων Ῥωμαίων ἐν τῷ Φε-
D βρουαρίῳ μηνὶ ποιουμένων χοὰς καὶ ἐναγισμοὺς
τοῖς τεθνηκόσι Δέκιμος Βροῦτος, ὡς Κικέρων
ἱστόρηκεν, ἐν τῷ Δεκεμβρίῳ τοῦτ' ἔπραττεν; ἦν

[1] δὴ τοῦτο καὶ] δὲ τούτου καὶ τὸ H. Richards.

lived in these parts used to destroy thus the Greeks
whom they captured ?   But Hercules, who was much
admired by them, put an end to their murder of
strangers and taught them to throw figures into the
river, in imitation of their superstitious custom.
The men of old used to call all Greeks alike Argives ;
unless it be, indeed, since the Arcadians regarded
the Argives also as their enemies because of their
immediate proximity, that, when Evander and his
men [a] fled from Greece and settled here, they continued to preserve their ancient feud and enmity.

33. WHY in ancient days did they never dine out
without their sons, even when these were still but
children ?

Did Lycurgus introduce this custom also, and bring
boys to the common meals that they might become
accustomed to conduct themselves toward their pleasures, not in a brutish or disorderly way, but with
discretion, since they had their elders as supervisors
and spectators, as it were ?   No less important is the
fact that the fathers themselves would also be more
decorous and prudent in the presence of their sons ;
for " where the old are shameless," as Plato[b] remarks,
" there the young also must needs be lost to all sense
of shame."

34. WHY is it that while the other Romans make
libations and offerings to the dead in the month of
February, Decimus Brutus, as Cicero [c] has recorded,
used to do so in the month of December ?   This was

---

[a] Who were Arcadians ; cf. Virgil, Aeneid, viii. 52-151.
[b] Laws, 729 c; also cited or referred to Moralia, 14 B,
71 B, 144 F.
[c] De Legibus, ii. 21. 54.

(272) δ' οὗτος ὁ Λυσιτάνειαν ἐπελθὼν καὶ πρῶτος ἐπ-
έκεινα στρατῷ διαβὰς τὸν τῆς Λήθης ποταμόν.''

Πότερον, ὥσπερ ἡμέρας ληγούσης καὶ μηνὸς
φθίνοντος εἰώθασιν ἐναγίζειν οἱ πολλοί, λόγον ἔχει
καὶ τοῦ ἐνιαυτοῦ καταστρέφοντος ἐν τῷ τελευταίῳ
μηνὶ τιμᾶν τοὺς τεθνηκότας; ἔστι δὲ τῶν μηνῶν
τελευταῖος ὁ Δεκέμβριος.

Ἢ χθονίων μὲν αἱ τιμαὶ θεῶν, τιμᾶν δὲ τοὺς
χθονίους ὡραῖόν ἐστι, τῶν καρπῶν ἁπάντων εἰλη-
E φότων συντέλειαν;

Ἢ ὅτε κινοῦσι τὴν γῆν ἀρχόμενοι σπόρου με-
μνῆσθαι μάλιστα τῶν κάτω προσήκει;

Ἢ Κρόνῳ μὲν οὗτος ὁ μὴν ὑπὸ Ῥωμαίων
καθιέρωται, Κρόνον δὲ τῶν κάτω θεῶν οὐ τῶν
ἄνω νομίζουσιν;

Ἢ μεγίστης αὐτοῖς ἑορτῆς τῶν Κρονίων καθ-
εστώσης καὶ συνουσίας τε πλείστας καὶ ἀπολαύσεις
ἔχειν δοκούσης, ἔδοξε καὶ ταύτης ἀπονέμειν τινὰς
ἀπαρχὰς τοῖς τεθνηκόσιν;

Ἢ τοῦτο, τὸ[1] μόνον Βροῦτον ἐναγίζειν ἐν τῷ μηνὶ
τούτῳ, καθόλου ψεῦδός ἐστι; καὶ γὰρ τῇ Λαρεντίᾳ
ποιοῦσι τὸν ἐναγισμὸν καὶ χοὰς ἐπιφέρουσιν ἐπὶ τὸν
τάφον τοῦ Δεκεμβρίου μηνός.

35. '' Διὰ τί δὲ τὴν Λαρεντίαν, ἑταίραν γεγενη-
F μένην, οὕτω τιμῶσιν;''

Ἄλλην γὰρ εἶναι Λαρεντίαν Ἄκκαν ἱστοροῦσι
τὴν Ῥωμύλου τροφόν, ἣν τῷ Ἀπριλλίῳ μηνὶ

---

[1] τοῦτο, τὸ Bernardakis: τοῦτο.

---

[a] 136 B.C.   Cf. Appian, Spanish Wars (72), 74 ; and
Florus, Epitome, ii. 17. 12.

[b] That is, according to Brutus's reckoning.   For the
common people February continued to be the month of the

the Brutus who invaded Lusitania, and was the first to visit those remote places, and cross the river Lethê with an army.[a]

Since most peoples are accustomed to make offerings to the dead at the close of the day and at the end of the month, is it not reasonable also to honour the dead in the last month [b] at the turn of the year ? And December is the last month.

Or do these honours belong to deities beneath the earth, and is it the proper season to honour these deities when all the crops have attained consummation ?

Or is it most fitting to remember those below when men are stirring the earth at the beginning of seed-time ?

Or is it because this month has been consecrated to Saturn by the Romans, and they regard Saturn as an infernal, not a celestial god ?

Or is it that then their greatest festival, the Saturnalia, is set ; and it is reputed to contain the most numerous social gatherings and enjoyments, and therefore Brutus deemed it proper to bestow upon the dead first-fruits, as it were, of this festival also ?

Or is this statement, that Brutus alone sacrificed to the dead in this month, altogether a falsehood ? For it is in December that they make offerings to Larentia and bring libations to her sepulchre.

35. And why do they thus honour Larentia who was at one time a courtesan ?

They record that there was another Larentia, Acca,[c] the nurse of Romulus, whom they honour in

Parentalia, and February was once the last month (*cf.* 268 b, *supra*).

[c] *Cf.* W. F. Otto, *Wiener Studien*, xxxv. 62 ff.

τιμῶσι. τῇ δ᾽ ἑταίρᾳ Λαρεντίᾳ Φαβόλαν ἐπί-
κλησιν εἶναι λέγουσιν, ἐγνωρίσθη δὲ διὰ τοιαύτην
αἰτίαν. ζάκορός τις Ἡρακλέους, ὡς ἔοικεν, ἀπο-
λαύων σχολῆς ἔθος εἶχεν ἐν πεττοῖς καὶ κύβοις τὰ
πολλὰ διημερεύειν· καί ποτε, τῶν εἰωθότων παίζειν
σὺν αὐτῷ καὶ μετέχειν τῆς τοιαύτης διατριβῆς κατὰ
τύχην μηδενὸς παρόντος, ἀδημονῶν τὸν θεὸν πρου-
καλεῖτο διαβαλέσθαι τοῖς κύβοις πρὸς αὐτὸν ὥσπερ
ἐπὶ ῥητοῖς, νικήσας μὲν εὑρέσθαι τι παρὰ τοῦ θεοῦ
273 χρηστόν, ἂν δὲ λειφθῇ, δεῖπνον αὐτὸς τῷ θεῷ
παρασχεῖν καὶ μείρακα καλὴν συναναπαυσομένην.
ἐκ τούτου δὲ τοὺς κύβους προθέμενος, τὸν μὲν
ὑπὲρ ἑαυτοῦ, τὸν[1] δ᾽ ὑπὲρ τοῦ θεοῦ βαλὼν ἐλείφθη.
ταῖς οὖν προκλήσεσιν ἐμμένων τράπεζάν τε λαμ-
προτέραν παρεσκεύασε τῷ θεῷ, καὶ τὴν Λαρεντίαν
παραλαβὼν ἐμφανῶς ἑταιροῦσαν εἱστίασε καὶ κατ-
έκλινεν ἐν τῷ ἱερῷ καὶ τὰς θύρας ἀπιὼν ἔκλεισε.
λέγεται δὲ νύκτωρ ἐντυχεῖν αὐτῇ τὸν θεὸν οὐκ
ἀνθρωπίνως καὶ κελεῦσαι βαδίζειν ἕωθεν εἰς ἀγοράν,
Β ᾧ δ᾽ ἂν ἐντύχῃ πρώτῳ, προσέχειν μάλιστα καὶ
ποιεῖσθαι φίλον. ἀναστᾶσαν οὖν τὴν Λαρεντίαν
βαδίζειν, καὶ συντυχεῖν τινι τῶν πλουσίων ἀγάμων
δὲ καὶ παρηκμακότων ὄνομα Ταρρουτίῳ[2]· γνωρι-
σθεῖσαν δὲ τούτῳ καὶ ζῶντος ἄρχειν τοῦ οἴκου καὶ
κληρονομῆσαι τελευτήσαντος· ὕστερον δὲ χρόνοις

---

[1] τὸν . . . τὸν] τὴν . . . τὴν in all mss. except E.
[2] Ταρρουτίῳ] Carrutius in Macrobius, *Saturnalia*, i. 10. 14
and 17.

the month of April. But they say that the surname
of the courtesan Larentia was Fabula. She became
famous for the following reason [a] : a certain keeper
of the temple of Hercules enjoyed, it seems, considerable leisure and had the habit of spending the greater
part of the day at draughts and dice ; and one day, as
it chanced, there was present no one of those who were
wont to play with him and share the occupation of
his leisure. So, in his boredom, he challenged the
god to throw dice with him on fixed terms, as it
were : if he should win, he was to obtain some
service from the god ; but if he should lose, he was
to furnish a supper for the god at his own expense
and provide a comely girl to spend the night with
him. Thereupon he brought out the dice, and threw
once for himself and once for the god, and lost.
Abiding, therefore, by the terms of his challenge
he prepared a somewhat sumptuous repast for the
god and fetched Larentia, who openly practised the
profession of courtesan. He feasted her, put her to
bed in the temple, and, when he departed, locked the
doors. The tale is told that the god visited her in
the night, not in mortal wise, and bade her on the
morrow go into the forum, and pay particular attention to the first man she met, and make him her
friend. Larentia arose, therefore, and, going forth,
met one of the wealthy men that were unwed and
past their prime, whose name was Tarrutius. With
this man she became acquainted, and while he lived
she presided over his household, and when he died,
she inherited his estate ; and later, when she herself

    [a] Cf. *Life of Romulus*, chap. v. (19 F ff.) ; Macrobius,
Saturnalia, i. 10. 11-17 ; Augustine, *De Civitate Dei*, vi. 7 ;
Tertullian, *Ad Nationes*, ii. 10.

(273) αὐτὴν τελευτῶσαν τῇ πόλει τὴν οὐσίαν ἀπολιπεῖν· διὸ τὰς τιμὰς ἔχειν ταύτας.

36. " Διὰ τί πύλην μίαν θυρίδα καλοῦσι, τὴν γὰρ ' φενέστραν¹ ' τοῦτο σημαίνει,² καὶ παρ' αὐτὴν ὁ καλούμενος Τύχης θάλαμός ἐστι; "

Πότερον ὅτι Σέρβιος ὁ βασιλεὺς εὐτυχέστατος γενόμενος δόξαν ἔσχε τῇ Τύχῃ συνεῖναι φοιτώσῃ C διὰ θυρίδος πρὸς αὐτόν;

Ἢ τοῦτο μὲν μῦθός ἐστιν, ἐπεὶ δὲ Ταρκυνίου Πρίσκου τοῦ βασιλέως ἀποθανόντος ἡ γυνὴ Τανα- κυλλὶς ἔμφρων οὖσα καὶ βασιλικὴ διὰ θυρίδος προκύψασα τοῖς πολίταις ἐνέτυχε καὶ συνέπεισεν ἀποδεῖξαι βασιλέα τὸν Σέρβιον, ἔσχε ταύτην ὁ τόπος τὴν ἐπωνυμίαν;

37. " Διὰ τί τῶν τοῖς θεοῖς ἀνατιθεμένων μόνα τὰ σκῦλα νενόμισται περιορᾶν ἀφανιζόμενα τῷ χρόνῳ, καὶ μήτε προκινεῖν³ μήτ' ἐπισκευάζειν; "

Πότερον ἵνα τὴν δόξαν οἰόμενοι τοῖς πρώτοις συνεκλιπεῖν ἀεί τι πρόσφατον ὑπόμνημα τῆς ἀρετῆς D ζητῶσι κομίζειν;

Ἢ μᾶλλον ὅτι τοῦ χρόνου τὰ σημεῖα τῆς πρὸς τοὺς πολεμίους διαφορᾶς ἀμαυροῦντος, αὐτοὺς ἀνα- λαμβάνειν καὶ καινοποιεῖν ἐπίφθονόν ἐστι καὶ φιλ- απέχθημον; οὐδὲ γὰρ παρ' Ἕλλησιν οἱ πρῶτοι

¹ φενέστραν as in 322 F and elsewhere : φαινέστραν.
² σημαίνει] an obvious correction for σημαίνειν, the infinitive and the indicative being not infrequently confused in the mss.

62

died, she left her property to the State; and for that
reason she has these honours.

36. WHY do they call one of the gates the Window,
for this is what *fenestra* means; and why is the so-
called Chamber of Fortune beside it? [a]

Is it because King Servius, the luckiest of mortals,
was reputed to have converse with Fortune, who
visited him through a window?

Or is this but a fable, and is the true reason that
when King Tarquinius Priscus died, his wife Tanaquil, a sensible and a queenly woman, put her head
out of a window and, addressing the citizens, persuaded them to appoint Servius king, and thus the
place came to have this name? [b]

37. WHY is it that of all the things dedicated to the
gods it is the custom to allow only spoils of war to
disintegrate with the passage of time, and not to
move them beforehand [c] nor repair them?

Is it in order that men may believe that their
repute deserts them at the same time with the
obliteration of their early memorials, and may ever
seek to bring in some fresh reminder of valour?

Or is it rather that, as time makes dim the
memorials of their dissension with their enemies, it
would be invidious and malicious to restore and
renew them? Nor among the Greeks, either, do

[a] Cf. 322 F, *infra*; Ovid, *Fasti*, vi. 569 ff.
[b] Cf. 323 D, *infra*; Livy, i. 41.
[c] That is, to move them away before they fell to pieces;
for the ancients used to clear out their temples periodically.

---

[3] προκινεῖν F.C.B.; προσκαινοῦν Wyttenbach; προσκατ-
τύειν (?) S. A. Naber: προσκυνεῖν.

(273) λίθινον καὶ χαλκοῦν στήσαντες τρόπαιον εὐδοκι-
μοῦσιν.

38. " Διὰ τί Κόιντος Μέτελλος ἀρχιερεὺς γενόμενος καὶ τἆλλα δοκῶν φρόνιμος εἶναι καὶ πολιτικὸς
ἀνὴρ ἐκώλυεν οἰωνίζεσθαι μετὰ τὸν Σεξτίλιον μῆνα
τὸν νῦν Αὔγουστον προσαγορευόμενον; "

Πότερον ὅτι καθάπερ ἡμέρας ἀκμαζούσης ἢ
ἀρχομένης πράττομεν τὰ τοιαῦτα καὶ μηνὸς ἱσταμένου καὶ αὐξομένου, τὰς δ' ἀποκλίτους ὡς ἀχρη-
E ματίστους φυλαττόμεθα, παραπλησίως τὸν μετὰ
μῆνας ὀκτὼ χρόνον ὥσπερ ἑσπέραν τινὰ τοῦ ἐνιαυτοῦ καὶ δείλην ἀποκλίνοντος ἤδη καὶ φθίνοντος
ἐνόμιζεν¹;

"Η καὶ τοῖς ὄρνισι χρηστέον ἀκμαίοις καὶ τε-
λείοις; εἰσὶ δὲ πρὸ τοῦ θέρους τοιοῦτοι· περὶ δὲ
τὸ φθινόπωρον οἱ μὲν ἀσθενεῖς καὶ νοσώδεις, οἱ δὲ
νεοττοὶ καὶ ἀτελεῖς, οἱ δὲ παντάπασι φροῦδοι διὰ
τὴν ὥραν ἐκτοπίζοντες.

39. " Διὰ τί τοῖς μὴ στρατευομένοις μὲν ἐν
στρατοπέδῳ δ' ἄλλως ἀναστρεφομένοις οὐκ ἐξῆν
ἄνδρα βαλεῖν πολέμιον οὐδὲ τρῶσαι; "

Καὶ τοῦτο Κάτων ὁ πρεσβύτης ἐν ἐπιστολῇ τινι
δεδήλωκε, γράφων πρὸς τὸν υἱὸν καὶ κελεύων, εἰ
F παρεθείη τῆς στρατείας ἀποπληρώσας τὸν χρόνον,

---

¹ ἐνόμιζεν Xylander: νομίζειν.

ᵃ As did the Boeotians after Leuctra: Cicero, De Inventione, ii. 23 (69) ; cf. Diodorus, xiii. 24. 5-6. Of course
this means substituting for the impromptu suit of armour,
set on a stake, a permanent replica ; but memorials of

they that first erected a trophy of stone or of bronze [a] stand in good repute.

38. WHY did Quintus Metellus,[b] when he became *pontifex maximus*, with his reputation for good sense in all other matters as well as in his statesmanship, prevent divination from birds after the month Sextilis, which is now called August?

Is it that, even as we attend to such matters in the middle of the day or at dawn, or in the beginning of the month when the moon is waxing, and avoid the declining days and hours as unsuitable for business, so likewise did Metellus regard the period of time after the first eight months as the evening or late afternoon, so to speak, of the year, since then it is declining and waning?

Or is it because we should observe birds when they are in their prime and in perfect condition? And this they are before the summer-time; but towards autumn some are weak and sickly, others but nestlings and not full-grown, and still others have vanished completely, migrating because of the time of year.

39. WHY were men who were not regularly enlisted, but merely tarrying in the camp, not allowed to throw missiles at the enemy or to wound them?

This fact Cato the Elder [c] has made clear in one of his letters to his son, in which he bids the young man to return home if he has completed his term of service and has been discharged; or, if he should

battles had been popular for many years before this time. *Cf. Moralia*, 401 C-D.

[b] Q. Caecilius Metellus Pius, consul 80 B.C.

[c] *Cf.* Cicero, *De Officiis*, i. 11 (37).

ὑποστρέφειν· ἢ προσμένοντα λαβεῖν παρὰ τοῦ στρατηγοῦ τὸ ἐξεῖναι τρῶσαι καὶ ἀνελεῖν πολέμιον.

Πότερον ὅτι τὴν ἀνάγκην μόνην ἐξουσίαν εἶναι[1]
δεῖ τοῦ ἀνελεῖν ἄνθρωπον, ὁ δ' ἄνευ νόμου καὶ
προστάγματος τοῦτο ποιῶν ἀνδροφόνος ἐστί; διὸ
καὶ Χρυσάνταν ἐπῄνεσεν ὁ Κῦρος, ὅτι μέλλων
ἀναιρεῖν πολέμιον καὶ τὴν κοπίδα διηρμένος, ἀκούσας τὸ ἀνακλητικὸν ἀφῆκε τὸν ἄνδρα καὶ οὐκ
ἔπαισεν ὡς κεκωλυμένος.

Ἢ δεῖ τὸν συνιστάμενον πολεμίοις καὶ μαχό-
274 μενον, ἂν ἀποδειλιάσῃ, μὴ ἀνυπεύθυνον εἶναι μηδ'
ἀθῷον; οὐ γὰρ οὕτω βαλών τινα καὶ τρώσας
ὠφέλησεν, ὡς φυγὼν καὶ ἀναχωρήσας ἔβλαψεν.
ὁ μὲν οὖν ἀφειμένος στρατείας ἀπήλλακται τῶν
στρατιωτικῶν νόμων· ὁ δ' αἰτησάμενος τὸ πράττειν
τὰ τῶν στρατευομένων πάλιν ἑαυτὸν ὑπεύθυνον τῷ
νόμῳ καὶ τῷ στρατηγῷ δέδωκεν.

40. '' Διὰ τί τῷ ἱερεῖ τοῦ Διὸς οὐκ ἔξεστιν ἐν
ὑπαίθρῳ ἀλείφεσθαι; ''

Πότερον ὅτι καὶ παῖδας γυμνοῦσθαι πατρὸς ὁρῶν-
τος καὶ πενθεροῦ γαμβρὸν οὐχ ὅσιον ἦν οὐδὲ καλόν,
B οὐδὲ συνελούοντο τὸ παλαιὸν ἀλλήλοις; πατὴρ δ'
ὁ Ζεὺς καὶ τὸ ἐν ὑπαίθρῳ μάλιστά πως εἶναι δοκεῖ
τοῦ Διὸς ἐνώπιον.

Ἤ, καθάπερ ἐν ναῷ καὶ ἱερῷ γυμνοῦν ἑαυτὸν
ἀθέμιτόν ἐστιν, οὕτω τὸν ὕπαιθρον ἀέρα καὶ τὸν

---

[1] εἶναι] δοῦναι E. Kurtz.

[a] Cf. Xenophon, Cyropaedia, iv. 1. 3 ; and the note on
Moralia, 236 E (Vol. III. p. 420).
[b] Cf. Aulus Gellius, x. 15.

stay over, to obtain permission from his general to
wound or slay an enemy.

Is it because sheer necessity alone constitutes a
warrant to kill a human being, and he who does
so illegally and without the word of command is
a murderer ? For this reason Cyrus also praised
Chrysantas [a] who, when he was about to kill an
enemy, and had his weapon raised to strike, heard
the recall sounded and let the man go without striking him, believing that he was now prevented from
so doing.

Or must he who grapples with the enemy and
fights not be free from accountability nor go unscathed should he play the coward ? For he does
not help so much by hitting or wounding an enemy
as he does harm by fleeing or retreating. He,
therefore, who has been discharged from service is
freed from military regulations ; but he who asks
leave to perform the offices of a soldier renders himself again accountable to the regulations and to his
general.

40. WHY is it not allowed the priest of Jupiter
(*Flamen Dialis*) to anoint himself in the open air ? [b]

Is it because it used not to be proper or decent for
sons to strip in their father's sight, nor a son-in-law
in the presence of his father-in-law, nor in ancient
days did they bathe together ? [c] Now Jupiter is
our father, and whatever is in the open air is in some
way thought to be particularly in his sight.

Or, just as it is against divine ordinance to strip oneself in a shrine or a temple, so also did they scrupulously avoid the open air and the space beneath the

----

[c] *Cf.* Cicero, *De Oratore*, ii. 55 (224), with Wilkins's note.

(274) ὑπουράνιον, ὄντα καὶ θεῶν καὶ δαιμόνων μεστόν,
ἐξευλαβοῦντο; διὸ καὶ τὰ πολλὰ τῶν ἀναγκαίων
ὑπὸ στέγῃ δρῶμεν ἐπικρυπτόμενοι καὶ ἐπικαλυπτό-
μενοι ταῖς οἰκίαις πρὸς τὸ θεῖον.

Ἢ[1] τὰ μὲν μόνῳ τῷ ἱερεῖ, τὰ δὲ πᾶσιν ὑπὸ τοῦ
νόμου προστέτακται διὰ τοῦ ἱερέως; διὸ καὶ παρ'
ἡμῖν τὸ μὲν στεφανηφορεῖν καὶ κομᾶν καὶ μὴ[2]
σιδηροφορεῖν μηδὲ τοῖς Φωκέων ὅροις ἐμβαίνειν
C ἴδια λειτουργήματα τοῦ ἄρχοντός ἐστι· τὸ δ'
ὀπώρας μὴ γεύεσθαι πρὸ ἰσημερίας μετοπωρινῆς
μηδ' ἄμπελον τέμνειν πρὸ ἰσημερίας ἐαρινῆς ὁμοῦ
τι πᾶσι δηλοῦται διὰ τοῦ ἄρχοντος· ἑκατέρου γὰρ
ὁ καιρὸς ἐκεῖνός ἐστι.

Τὸν αὐτὸν οὖν τρόπον, ὡς ἔοικε, καὶ τοῦ παρὰ
Ῥωμαίοις ἱερέως ἴδιόν ἐστι τὸ μήθ' ἵππῳ χρῆσθαι
μήτε πλείονας νύκτας ἀποδημεῖν τριῶν μήτ' ἀπο-
τίθεσθαι τὸν πῖλον, ἀφ' οὗ καὶ " φλᾶμεν " κέκληται.
D πολλὰ δ' ἄλλα δηλοῦται πᾶσι διὰ τοῦ ἱερέως· ὧν ἕν
ἐστι καὶ τὸ ἐν ὑπαίθρῳ μὴ ἀλείφεσθαι. τὸ γὰρ
ξηραλοιφεῖν ὑφεωρῶντο Ῥωμαῖοι σφόδρα, καὶ τοῖς
Ἕλλησιν οἴονται μηδὲν οὕτως αἴτιον δουλείας
γεγονέναι καὶ μαλακίας ὡς τὰ γυμνάσια καὶ τὰς
παλαίστρας πολὺν ἄλυν καὶ σχολὴν ἐντικτούσας[3]
ταῖς πόλεσι καὶ κακοσχολίαν[4] καὶ τὸ παιδεραστεῖν

---

[1] ἢ added by Meziriacus (καὶ in E).
[2] μὴ added by Meziriacus.
[3] ἐντικτούσας] ἐντεκούσας in all mss. except E.
[4] κακοσχολίαν] Wyttenbach suggests ἀδολεσχίαν.

---

[a] Livy, v. 52. 13, says "not even one night." Cf. also
Tacitus, Annals, iii. 58 and 71.
[b] Cf. Life of Numa, chap. vii. (64 c) ; Life of Marcellus,
chap. v. (300 c) ; Varro, De Lingua Latina, v. 84 ; Festus,
68

heavens, since it was full of gods and spirits ? Wherefore also we perform many necessary acts under a roof, hidden and concealed by our houses from the view of Divine powers.

Or are some regulations prescribed for the priest alone, while others are prescribed for all by the law through the priest ? Wherefore also, in my country, to wear a garland, to wear the hair long, not to have any iron on one's person, and not to set foot within the boundaries of Phocis, are the special functions of an archon ; but not to taste fruit before the autumnal equinox nor to prune a vine before the vernal equinox are prohibitions disclosed to practically all alike through the archon ; for those are the proper seasons for each of these acts.

In the same way, then, it is apparently a special obligation of the Roman priest also not to use a horse nor to be absent from the city more than three nights *a* nor to lay aside the cap from which he derives the name of *flamen.b* But many other regulations are revealed to all through the priest, and one of them is the prohibition not to anoint oneself in the open air. For the Romans used to be very suspicious of rubbing down with oil, and even to-day they believe that nothing has been so much to blame for the enslavement and effeminacy of the Greeks as their gymnasia and wrestling - schools, which engender much listless idleness and waste of time in their cities, as well as paederasty and the ruin of the bodies of

s.v. *Flamen Dialis*; Dionysius of Halicarnassus, *Roman Antiquities*, ii. 64. 2. Varro's etymology is " Flamen quasi filamen " ; Plutarch must have pronounced φλᾶμεν " ph(i)-lamen," with " *ph* " a true aspirate as in " u*ph*ill," else there would be no justification for the alternative derivation from *pileus* (*Numa*, vii.).

(274) καὶ τὸ διαφθείρειν τὰ σώματα τῶν νέων ὕπνοις καὶ
περιπάτοις καὶ κινήσεσιν εὐρύθμοις καὶ διαίταις
ἀκριβέσιν, ὑφ᾽ ὧν ἔλαθον ἐκρυέντες τῶν ὅπλων καὶ
ἀγαπήσαντες ἀνθ᾽ ὁπλιτῶν καὶ ἱππέων ἀγαθῶν
εὐτράπελοι καὶ παλαιστρῖται καλοὶ¹ λέγεσθαι. ταῦτα
Ε γοῦν ἔργον ἐστὶν ἀποφυγεῖν εἰς ὕπαιθρον ἀποδυο-
μένους· οἱ δὲ κατ᾽ οἰκίαν ἀλειφόμενοι καὶ θεραπεύοντες ἑαυτοὺς οὐδὲν ἁμαρτάνουσι.

41. '' Διὰ τί τὸ παλαιὸν νόμισμα πῇ μὲν εἶχεν
Ἰανοῦ διπρόσωπον εἰκόνα, πῇ δὲ πλοίου πρύμναν
ἢ πρῷραν ἐγκεχαραγμένην; ''

Πότερον ὡς οἱ πολλοὶ λέγουσιν ἐπὶ τιμῇ τοῦ
Κρόνου πλοίῳ διαπεράσαντος εἰς Ἰταλίαν;

'' Ἢ τοῦτο μὲν ἔστιν ἐπὶ πολλῶν λέγειν, καὶ γὰρ
Ἰανὸς καὶ Εὔανδρος καὶ Αἰνείας ἐκ θαλάττης
προσεκομίσθησαν, ἐκεῖνο δ᾽ ἄν τις μᾶλλον εἰκάσειεν
ὅτι τὰ μὲν καλὰ ταῖς πόλεσίν ἐστι τὰ δ᾽ ἀναγκαῖα·
F καὶ μέγιστον τῶν μὲν καλῶν ἡ εὐνομία, τῶν δ᾽
ἀναγκαίων ἡ εὐπορία· ἐπεὶ τοίνυν εὐκοσμίαν² μὲν
Ἰανὸς κατέστησεν αὐτοῖς ἐξημερώσας τὸν βίον,
ἀφθονίαν δὲ παρέχει τῶν ἀναγκαίων ὁ ποταμὸς
πλόιμος ὢν καὶ τὰ μὲν ἐκ θαλάττης τὰ δ᾽ ἀπὸ τῆς
χώρας κατακομίζων, σύμβολον ἔσχε τὸ νόμισμα
τοῦ μὲν νομοθέτου τὸ δίμορφον ὡς εἴρηται διὰ τὴν
μεταβολήν, τοῦ δὲ ποταμοῦ τὸ πορθμεῖον.

Ἑτέρῳ δ᾽ ἐχρήσαντο νομίσματι βοῦν ἔχοντι καὶ

¹ καλοὶ] all mss. except E have καὶ καλοὶ.
² εὐκοσμίαν] εὐνομίαν in some mss.

the young men with regulated sleeping, walking, rhythmical movements, and strict diet; by these practices they have unconsciously lapsed from the practice of arms, and have become content to be termed nimble athletes and handsome wrestlers rather than excellent men-at-arms and horsemen. It is hard work, at any rate, when men strip in the open air, to escape these consequences; but those who anoint themselves and care for their bodies in their own houses commit no offence.

41. Why did their ancient coinage have stamped on one side a double-faced likeness of Janus, on the other the stern or the prow of a ship? [a]

Is it, as many affirm, in honour of Saturn who crossed over to Italy in a ship?

Or, since this might be said of many, inasmuch as Janus, Evander, and Aeneas all landed in Italy after a voyage by sea, one might rather conjecture thus: some things are excellent for States, others are necessary; and of the excellent things good government is the chief, and of the necessary things facility of provision. Since, therefore, Janus established for them an ordered government by civilizing their life, and since the river, which was navigable and permitted transportation both from the sea and from the land, provided them with an abundance of necessities, the coinage came to have as its symbol the twofold form of the lawgiver, as has been stated,[b] because of the change he wrought, and the vessel as symbol of the river.

They also used another kind of coinage, stamped

[a] *Cf.* Athenaeus, 692 E; Ovid, *Fasti*, i. 229 ff.; Pliny, *Natural History*, xxxiii. 3 (45); Macrobius, *Saturnalia*, i. 7. 21-22. [b] 269 A, *supra*.

πρόβατον καὶ ὗν παράσημον, εὐποροῦντες ἀπὸ τῶν
θρεμμάτων μάλιστα καὶ τὴν περιουσίαν ἀπὸ τούτων ἔχοντες· διὸ καὶ τῶν ὀνομάτων πολλὰ τοῖς
275 παλαιοῖς, Συίλλιοι[1] καὶ Βουβολκοὶ καὶ Πόρκιοι
ἦσαν, ὡς Φενεστέλλας[2] εἴρηκεν.

42. " Διὰ τί τῷ τοῦ Κρόνου ναῷ χρῶνται ταμιείῳ[3] τῶν δημοσίων χρημάτων, ἅμα δὲ καὶ
φυλακτηρίῳ τῶν συμβολαίων; "

Πότερον ὅτι δόξα κατεῖχε καὶ λόγος οὐκ εἶναι
πλεονεξίαν ἐν ἀνθρώποις οὐδ' ἀδικίαν Κρόνου
βασιλεύοντος, ἀλλὰ πίστιν καὶ δικαιοσύνην;

Ἤ ὅτι καρπῶν εὑρετὴς[4] καὶ[5] γεωργίας ἡγεμὼν ὁ
θεός; ἡ γὰρ ἅρπη τοῦτο σημαίνει καὶ οὐχ ὡς
γέγραφεν Ἀντίμαχος Ἡσιόδῳ πειθόμενος

λέχρις[6] δὲ δρεπάνῳ τέμνων ἀπὸ μήδεα πατρὸς
Οὐρανοῦ Ἀκμονίδεω λάσιος Κρόνος ἀντι-
τέτυκτο.

καρπῶν δ' ἀφθονία καὶ διάθεσις γένεσίς ἐστι νο-
B μίσματος· διὸ τὸν αἴτιον καὶ φύλακα ποιοῦνται τῆς
εὐδαιμονίας. μαρτυρεῖ δὲ τούτῳ τὸ τὰς ἀγομένας
δι' ἐννέα ἡμερῶν ἐπ' ἀγορὰν συνόδους, νουνδίνας
δὲ καλουμένας, ἱερὰς τοῦ Κρόνου νομίζεσθαι· πρά-

---

[1] Συίλλιοι Xylander (cf. Life of Publicola, chap. xi.):
Συέλλιοι.

[2] Φενεστέλλας the proper spelling: φαινεστέλλας.

[3] ταμιείῳ, the regular form: ταμείῳ.

[4] εὑρετὴς several mss., as Bücheler had conjectured (cf.
956 A); ἀγέτης Abresch: ἀρετῆς.

[5] καὶ H. Richards: ἤ.   [6] λέχρις Xylander: λέχριε.

---

[a] Is Plutarch thinking of the *suovetaurilia*? Mr E. T.
Newell, President of the American Numismatic Society, has
been kind enough to inform me that no early Roman coinage
bears these symbols.

with the figures of a bull, a ram, and a boar,[a] because their prosperity came mostly from their live stock, and from these they also derived their affluence. This is the reason why many of the names of the ancient families are such as the Suillii, Bubulci, Porcii,[b] as Fenestella [c] has stated.

42. WHY do they use the temple of Saturn as the public treasury and also as a place of storage for records of contracts ? [d]

Is it because the opinion and tradition prevailed that when Saturn was king there was no greed or injustice among men, but good faith and justice ?

Or is it because the god was the discoverer of crops and the pioneer in husbandry ? For this is what his sickle signifies and not as Antimachus,[e] following Hesiod,[f] has written :

Here with sickle in hand was wrought the form of rough
    Cronus
Maiming his sire at his side, who is Uranus, offspring of
    Acmon.

Now abundant harvests and their disposal are what give rise to a monetary system ; therefore they make the god who is the cause of their good fortune its guardian also. Testimony to support this may be found in the fact that the markets held every eight days and called *nundinae* [g] are considered sacred to

---

[b] Cf. *Life of Publicola,* chap. xi. (103 B) ; Varro, quoted by Nonius Marcellus, p. 189. 21 (ed. Müller).

[c] Peter, *Frag. Hist. Rom.* p. 272, *Annales,* Frag. 5.

[d] Cf. *Life of Publicola,* xii. (103 C).

[e] Kinkel, *Epicorum Graec. Frag.* p. 287, Antimachus, Frag. 35.

[f] *Theogony,* 160 ff. ; cf. Apollonius Rhodius, iv. 984-986.

[g] That is, the ninth day, by the Roman inclusive system of reckoning (cf. Macrobius, *Saturnalia,* i. 16. 34).

(275) σεως γὰρ καὶ ὠνῆς περιουσία καρπῶν ἀρχὴν
παρέσχεν.

Ἦ ταῦτα μέν ἐστι παλαιά, πρῶτος δὲ ταμιεῖον
ἀπέδειξε τὸ Κρόνιον, τῶν βασιλέων καταλυθέντων,
Οὐαλέριος Ποπλικόλας πειθόμενος εὐερκῆ καὶ
καταφανῆ καὶ δυσεπιβούλευτον εἶναι τὸν τόπον;

43. " Διὰ τί δ' οἱ πρεσβεύοντες εἰς ῾Ρώμην ὁπο-
θενοῦν ἐπὶ τὸν τοῦ Κρόνου ναὸν βαδίζοντες ἀπο-
C γράφονται πρὸς τοὺς ἐπάρχους τοῦ ταμιείου;"

Πότερον ὡς ξένου τοῦ Κρόνου γενομένου καὶ διὰ
τοῦτο τοῖς ξένοις χαίροντος, ἢ καὶ τοῦτο λύεται
τῇ ἱστορίᾳ; τὸ γὰρ παλαιόν, ὡς ἔοικεν, οἱ ταμίαι
ξένια τοῖς πρεσβεύουσιν ἔπεμπον (ἐκαλεῖτο δὲ
" λαύτια[1] " τὰ πεμπόμενα), καὶ νοσούντων ἐπ-
εμέλοντο καὶ τελευτήσαντας ἔθαπτον ἐκ δημοσίου·
νῦν δ' ὑπὸ πλήθους τῶν ἀφικνουμένων πρέσβεων
ἐκλέλειπται τὸ τῆς δαπάνης, μένει δ' ἔτι τὸ τοῖς
ἐπάρχοις τοῦ ταμιείου προεντυγχάνειν διὰ τῆς
ἀπογραφῆς.

44. " Διὰ τί τῷ ἱερεῖ τοῦ Διὸς οὐκ ἔξεστιν ὀμόσαι;"

Πότερον ὅτι βάσανός τις ἐλευθέρων ὁ ὅρκος ἐστί,
δεῖ δ' ἀβασάνιστον εἶναι καὶ τὸ σῶμα καὶ τὴν
ψυχὴν τοῦ ἱερέως;
D Ἦ ὅτι περὶ μικρῶν ἀπιστεῖσθαι τὸν τὰ θεῖα καὶ
μέγιστα πεπιστευμένον οὐκ εἰκός ἐστιν;
Ἦ ὅτι πᾶς ὅρκος εἰς κατάραν τελευτᾷ τῆς ἐπι-

---

[1] λαύτια Abresch : λαύτεια.

---

[a] Presumably the *quaestores aerarii*.

Saturn, for it was the superabundance of the harvest that initiated buying and selling.

Or is this a matter of ancient history, and was Valerius Publicola the first to make the temple of Saturn the treasury, when the kings had been overthrown, because he believed that the place was well-protected, in plain sight, and hard to attack secretly ?

43. Why do the ambassadors to Rome, from whatever country they come, proceed to the temple of Saturn, and register with the prefects of the treasury ?

Is it because Saturn was a foreigner, and consequently takes pleasure in foreigners, or is the solution of this question also to be found in history ? For it seems that in early days the treasurers [a] used to send gifts to the ambassadors, which were called *lautia*, and they cared for the ambassadors when they were sick, and buried them at public expense if they died ; but now, owing to the great number of embassies that come, this expensive practice has been discontinued ; yet there still remains the preliminary meeting with the prefects of the treasury in the guise of registration.

44. Why may not the priest of Jupiter (*Flamen Dialis*) take an oath ? [b]

Is it because an oath is a kind of test to prove that men are free-born, and neither the body nor the soul of the priest must be subjected to any test ?

Or is it because it is unreasonable to distrust in trivial affairs him who is entrusted with holy matters of the greatest importance ?

Or is it because every oath concludes with a curse

Cf. Livy, xxxi. 50 ; Aulus Gellius, x. 15.

(275) ὁρκίας, κατάρα δὲ δύσφημον καὶ σκυθρωπόν; ὅθεν
οὐδ᾽ ἄλλοις ἐπαρᾶσθαι νομίζεται τοὺς ἱερεῖς. ἐπ-
ῃνέθη γοῦν Ἀθήνησιν ἡ ἱέρεια μὴ θελήσασα κατ-
αράσασθαι τῷ Ἀλκιβιάδη τοῦ δήμου κελεύοντος·
ἔφη γὰρ εὐχῆς οὐ κατάρας ἱέρεια γεγονέναι.

Ἡ κοινὸς ὁ τῆς ἐπιορκίας κίνδυνος, ἂν ἀνὴρ
ἀσεβὴς καὶ ἐπίορκος εὐχῶν κατάρχηται καὶ ἱερῶν
ὑπὲρ τῆς πόλεως;

E   45. '' Διὰ τί τῶν Οὐενεραλίων[1] τῇ ἑορτῇ πολὺν
οἶνον ἐκχέουσιν ἐκ τοῦ ἱεροῦ τῆς Ἀφροδίτης; ''

Πότερον, ὡς οἱ πλεῖστοι λέγουσι, Μεζέντιος[2] ὁ
Τυρρηνῶν στρατηγὸς ἔπεμψε πρὸς Αἰνείαν σπεν-
δόμενος ἐπὶ τῷ λαβεῖν τὸν ἐπέτειον οἶνον; ἀρ-
νησαμένου δ᾽ ἐκείνου, τοῖς Τυρρηνοῖς ὑπέσχετο
κρατήσας μάχη δώσειν τὸν οἶνον· Αἰνείας δὲ τὴν
ὑπόσχεσιν αὐτοῦ πυθόμενος τοῖς θεοῖς τὸν οἶνον
καθιέρωσε, καὶ μετὰ τὸ νικῆσαι συναγαγὼν τὸ
καρπευθὲν ἐξέχεε πρὸ τοῦ ἱεροῦ τῆς Ἀφροδίτης.

Ἡ καὶ τοῦτο σύμβολόν ἐστι τοῦ χρῆναι νήφοντας
ἑορτάζειν ἀλλὰ μὴ μεθύοντας, ὡς τῶν θεῶν μᾶλλον
τοῖς ἐκχέουσι χαιρόντων τὸν πολὺν ἄκρατον ἢ τοῖς
πίνουσι;

F   46. '' Διὰ τί τὸν τῆς Ὅρτας ναὸν ἀνεῳγμένον
εἶχον οἱ παλαιοὶ διὰ παντός; ''

Πότερον, ὡς Ἀντίστιος Λαβεὼν[3] ἱστόρηκε, τοῦ

---

[1] Οὐενεραλίων] Οὐιναλίων Ursinus.
[2] Μεζέντιος Xylander : βυζάντιος.
[3] Ἀντίστιος Λαβεὼν Xylander : Ἀντίστιχος Λάκων.

---

[a] Cf. Life of Alcibiades, xxii. (202 F).
[b] Cf. Ovid, Fasti, iv. 877 ff. ; Dionysius of Halicarnassus,
Roman Antiquities, i. 65 ; Pliny, Natural History, xiv.

on perjury, and a curse is an ill-omened and gloomy thing ? This is the reason why priests may not even invoke curses upon others. At any rate the priestess at Athens who was unwilling to curse Alcibiades at the people's bidding won general approval, for she declared that she had been made a priestess of prayer, not of cursing.[a]

Or is it because the danger of perjury is a public danger if an impious and perjured man leads in prayer and sacrifice on behalf of the State ?

45. WHY on the festival of the Veneralia do they pour out a great quantity of wine from the temple of Venus ? [b]

Is it true, as most authorities affirm, that Mezentius, general of the Etruscans, sent to Aeneas and offered peace on condition of his receiving the year's vintage ? But when Aeneas refused, Mezentius promised his Etruscans that when he had prevailed in battle, he would give them the wine. Aeneas learned of his promise and consecrated the wine to the gods, and after his victory he collected all the vintage and poured it out in front of the temple of Venus.

Or is this also symbolic, indicating that men should be sober and not drunken on festival days, since the gods take more pleasure in those who spill much strong drink than in those who imbibe it ?

46. WHY did the men of old keep the temple of Horta continually open ?

Is it, as Antistius Labeo has stated, that since " to

12 (88), where the authority cited is Varro. Plutarch speaks of the festival of Vinalia (April 23) as Veneralia perhaps because Venus (together with Jupiter) was the protecting deity of the vine.

παρορμᾶν " ὁρτάρι " λεγομένου, τὴν οἷον ἐγκε-
λευομένην πρὸς τὰ καλὰ καὶ παρορμῶσαν θεὸν
Ὅρταν λεγομένην ᾤοντο δεῖν ὡς ἐνεργὸν ἀεὶ
μηδέποτε μέλλειν μηδ' ἀποκεκλεῖσθαι μηδ' ἐλινύειν[1];

Ἢ μᾶλλον ὡς νῦν ὀνομάζουσιν αὐτὴν Ὥραν
μηκυνομένης τῆς προτέρας συλλαβῆς, ἐπιστρεφῆ
276 τινα καὶ πολυωρητικὴν θεόν, ἣν διαφυλακτικὴν
καὶ φροντιστικὴν οὖσαν οὐδέποτε ῥάθυμον οὐδ' ὀλί-
γωρον εἶναι τῶν ἀνθρωπίνων ἐνόμιζον;

Ἢ, καθάπερ ἄλλα πολλά, καὶ τοῦτο τῶν Ἑλ-
ληνικῶν ὀνομάτων ἐστὶ καὶ δηλοῖ θεὸν ἐπισκο-
ποῦσαν καὶ ἐφορῶσαν; ὅθεν ὡς ἀκοιμήτου καὶ
ἀΰπνου διὰ παντὸς ἀνεῳγμένον ἦν τὸ ἱερὸν αὐτῆς.

Εἰ μέντοι τὴν ὥραν ὀρθῶς ὁ Λαβεὼν ἀπὸ τοῦ
παρορμᾶν ὠνομάσθαι δέδειχε,[2] σκόπει μὴ τὸν
" ὡράτωρα[3] " προτρεπτικόν τινα καὶ παρορμη-
τικὸν ὄντα σύμβουλον ἢ δημαγωγὸν οὕτως ὠνομάσθαι φατέον, οὐκ ἀπὸ τῆς ἀρᾶς καὶ εὐχῆς ὡς
ἔνιοι λέγουσι.

B   47. " Διὰ τί τὸ τοῦ Ἡφαίστου ἱερὸν ἔξω πόλεως ὁ Ῥωμύλος ἱδρύσατο; "

Πότερον διὰ τὴν μυθολογουμένην πρὸς Ἄρη
ζηλοτυπίαν τοῦ Ἡφαίστου δι' Ἀφροδίτην υἱὸς
εἶναι δοκῶν Ἄρεος οὐκ ἐποιήσατο σύνοικον οὐδ'
ὁμόπολιν αὐτόν;

Ἢ τοῦτο μὲν ἀβέλτερον, ᾠκοδομήθη δ' ὁ ναὸς
ἐξ ἀρχῆς συνέδριον καὶ βουλευτήριον ἀπόρρητον
αὐτῷ μετὰ Τατίου τοῦ συμβασιλεύσαντος, ὅπως

---

[1] ἐλινύειν Xylander : κλειννύειν.
[2] δέδειχε] δέδεικται in all MSS. except E (δέδεκται Bernardakis).   [3] ὡράτωρα F.C.B. : ὡράτορα.

urge on " is expressed by *hortari*, Horta is the goddess who urges us on, as it were, and incites us to noble actions ; and thus they thought that, since she was ever active, she should never be procrastinating nor shut off by herself nor unemployed ?

Or rather do they call her, as at present, Hora, with the first syllable lengthened, an attentive and very considerate goddess, who, since she was protective and thoughtful, they felt was never indifferent nor neglectful of human affairs ?

Or is this too, like many other Latin words, a Greek word, and does it signify the supervising and guardian goddess ?   Hence her temple was continually open since she neither slumbers nor sleeps.

If, however, Labeo be right in pointing out that Hora is derived from " *parorman* " [a] (to urge on), consider whether we must not declare that *orator* is thus to be derived, since an orator is a counsellor or popular leader who stimulates, as it were, and incites ; and it is not to be derived from " imprecating " or " praying " (*orare*), as some assert.

47. WHY did Romulus build the temple of Vulcan outside the city ?

Was it in consequence of Vulcan's fabled jealousy of Mars because of Venus [b] that Romulus, the reputed son of Mars, did not give Vulcan a share in his home or his city ?

Or is this a foolish explanation, and was the temple originally built as a secret place of assembly and council-chamber for himself and his colleague Tatius,

---

[a] Plutarch here (in *hōra, hŏrman*, (h)*ōrator*), as often, makes havoc of etymology and quantity.

[b] *Cf.* Homer, *Od.* viii. 266-359.

(276) συνιόντες ἐνταῦθα μετὰ τῶν γερόντων ἄνευ τοῦ
παρενοχλεῖσθαι καθ' ἡσυχίαν βουλεύοιντο περὶ τῶν
πραγμάτων;

Ἢ πρὸς ἐμπρησμὸν ἄνωθεν ἐπισφαλῶς τῆς
Ῥώμης ἐχούσης, ἔδοξε τιμᾶν μὲν ἐξοικίσαι δὲ τῆς
πόλεως τὸν θεόν;

C   48. '' Διὰ τί τῇ τῶν Κωνσυαλίων[1] ἑορτῇ καὶ τοὺς
ἵππους καὶ τοὺς ὄνους στεφανοῦσι καὶ σχολάζειν
ἐῶσι; ''

Πότερον ὅτι Ποσειδῶνι μὲν ἄγουσιν Ἱππείῳ τὴν
ἑορτήν, ὁ δ' ὄνος τῷ ἵππῳ συναπολαύει καὶ
συμμετέχει τῆς ἀδείας;

Ἢ ὅτι, ναυτιλίας φανείσης καὶ κομιδῆς κατὰ
θάλατταν, ὑπῆρξέ τις ἀμωσγέπως ῥᾳστώνη καὶ
ἀνάπαυσις τοῖς ὑποζυγίοις;

49. '' Διὰ τί τοὺς παραγγέλλοντας ἀρχὴν[2] ἔθος
ἦν ἐν ἱματίῳ τοῦτο ποιεῖν ἀχίτωνας, ὡς Κάτων
ἱστόρηκε; ''

Πότερον ἵνα μὴ δεκάζωσιν ἀργύριον ἐν τῷ κόλπῳ
κομίζοντες;

D   Ἢ μᾶλλον ὅτι τοὺς ἀξίους ἄρχειν οὐ γένεσιν
οὐδὲ χρήμασιν οὐδὲ δόξαις ἀλλὰ τραύμασι καὶ
ὠτειλαῖς ἔκρινον; ὅπως οὖν ταῦτα καθορῷτο τοῖς
ἐντυγχάνουσιν, ἀχίτωνες ἐπὶ τὰς παραγγελίας[3]
κατῄεσαν;

Ἢ καθάπερ τῷ δεξιοῦσθαι καὶ παρακαλεῖν καὶ
ὑποπίπτειν, οὕτω τῇ γυμνότητι ταπεινοῦντες ἑαυτοὺς ἐδημαγώγουν;

---

[1] Κωνσυαλίων Meziriacus : Κωνσταλίων.
[2] ἀρχὴν Meziriacus : ἄρχειν.
[3] παραγγελίας Wyttenbach : ἐπαγγελίας.

80

that here they might convene with the senators and take counsel concerning public affairs in quiet without being disturbed ?

Or was it that since Rome, from the very beginning, has been in great danger from conflagrations, they decided to show honour to this god, but to place his temple outside of the city ? [a]

48. WHY is it that at the festival of the Consualia they place garlands on both the horses and the asses and allow them to rest ?

Is it because they celebrate this festival in honour of Poseidon, god of horses,[b] and the ass enjoys a share in the horse's exemption ?

Or is it that since navigation and transport by sea have been discovered, pack animals have come to enjoy a certain measure of ease and rest ?

49. WHY was it the custom for those canvassing for office to do so in the toga without the tunic, as Cato has recorded ? [c]

Was it in order that they might not carry money in the folds of their tunic and give bribes ?

Or was it rather because they used to judge candidates worthy of office, not by their family nor their wealth nor their repute, but by their wounds and scars ? Accordingly that these might be visible to those that encountered them, they used to go down to their canvassing without tunics.

Or were they trying to commend themselves to popular favour by thus humiliating themselves by their scanty attire, even as they do by hand-shaking, personal appeals, and fawning behaviour ?

[a] *Cf.* Vitruvius, i. 7. 1.
[b] *Cf. Life of Romulus*, chap. xiv. (25 D).
[c] *Cf. Life of Coriolanus*, chap. xiv. (219 F–220 A).

(276)   50. " Διὰ τί ὁ ἱερεὺς τοῦ Διός, ἀποθανούσης
αὐτῷ τῆς γυναικός, ἀπετίθετο τὴν ἀρχήν, ὡς
'Ατήιος[1] ἱστόρηκε; "

Πότερον ὅτι τοῦ μὴ λαβόντος ὁ λαβὼν εἶτ' ἀποβαλὼν γυναῖκα γαμετὴν ἀτυχέστερος; ὁ μὲν γὰρ
τοῦ γεγαμηκότος οἶκος τέλειος, ὁ δὲ τοῦ γήμαντος
εἶτ' ἀποβαλόντος οὐκ ἀτελὴς μόνον ἀλλὰ καὶ
πεπηρωμένος.

Ε   Ἢ συνιερᾶται μὲν ἡ γυνὴ τῷ ἀνδρί, ὡς καὶ
πολλὰ τῶν ἱερῶν οὐκ ἔστι δρᾶσαι μὴ γαμετῆς
συμπαρούσης, τὸ δὲ γαμεῖν εὐθὺς ἑτέραν ἀπο-
βαλόντα τὴν προτέραν οὔτ' ἴσως δυνατὸν οὔτ'
ἄλλως ἐπιεικές; ὅθεν οὐδ' ἀποπέμψασθαι πρότερον
ἐξῆν, οὐδὲ νῦν, ὡς ἔοικεν, ἔξεστιν, ἀλλ' ἐφ' ἡμῶν
ἐπέτρεψεν ἐντευχθεὶς Δομετιανός. οἱ δ' ἱερεῖς παρ-
εγένοντο τῇ τοῦ γάμου διαλύσει, πολλὰ φρικώδη
καὶ ἀλλόκοτα καὶ σκυθρωπὰ δρῶντες.

Ἧττον δ' ἄν τις τοῦτο θαυμάσειε προσιστορήσας
ὅτι καὶ τῶν τιμητῶν θατέρου τελευτήσαντος ἔδει
Φ   καὶ τὸν ἕτερον[2] πεπαῦσθαι τῆς ἀρχῆς· ἀποθανόντος
δὲ τιμητοῦ Λιβίου Δρούσου Σκαῦρος Αἰμίλιος
συνάρχων οὐκ ἐβούλετο τὴν ἀρχὴν ἀπείπασθαι,
μέχρι οὗ τῶν δημάρχων τινὲς αὐτὸν ἐκέλευον εἰς
τὸ δεσμωτήριον ἀπάγεσθαι.

51. " Διὰ τί τῶν Λαρήτων, οὓς ἰδίως ' πραιστίτεις ' καλοῦσι, τούτοις κύων παρέστηκεν, αὐτοὶ δὲ
κυνῶν διφθέραις ἀμπέχονται; "

Ἢ πραιστίτεις μὲν οἱ προεστῶτές εἰσι, τοὺς δὲ

---

[1] 'Ατήιος Xylander: τήιος.
[2] ἕτερον] all mss. except E have ἑταῖρον.

────────────────

[a] Cf. Aulus Gellius, x. 15.

50. Why did the priest of Jupiter (*Flamen Dialis*) resign his office if his wife died, as Ateius has recorded ?[a]

Is it because the man who has taken a wife and then lost her is more unfortunate than one who has never taken a wife ? For the house of the married man is complete, but the house of him who has married and later lost his wife is not only incomplete, but also crippled.

Or is it because the wife assists her husband in the rites, so that many of them cannot be performed without the wife's presence, and for a man who has lost his wife to marry again immediately is neither possible perhaps nor otherwise seemly ? Wherefore it was formerly illegal for the *flamen* to divorce his wife ; and it is still, as it seems, illegal, but in my day Domitian once permitted it on petition. The priests were present at that ceremony of divorce and performed many horrible, strange, and gloomy rites.[b]

One might be less surprised at this resignation of the *flamen* if one should adduce also the fact that when one of the censors died, the other was obliged to resign his office [c] ; but when the censor Livius Drusus died, his colleague Aemilius Scaurus was unwilling to give up his office until certain tribunes ordered him to be led away to prison.

51. Why is a dog placed beside the Lares that men call by the special name of *praestites*, and why are the Lares themselves clad in dog-skins ? [d]

Is it because " those that stand before " are termed

---

[b] *Cf. Cambridge Ancient History*, vol. vii. p. 422.
[c] *Cf.* Livy, v. 31. 6, 7 ; vi. 27. 4, 5 ; ix. 34.
[d] *Cf.* Ovid, *Fasti*, v. 129 ff.

προεστῶτας οἴκου φυλακτικοὺς εἶναι προσήκει, καὶ
φοβεροὺς μὲν τοῖς ἀλλοτρίοις, ὥσπερ ὁ κύων ἐστίν,
ἠπίους δὲ καὶ πράους τοῖς συνοικοῦσιν;

Ἢ μᾶλλον, ὃ λέγουσιν ἔνιοι Ῥωμαίων, ἀληθές
ἐστι καί, καθάπερ οἱ περὶ Χρύσιππον οἴονται
277 φιλόσοφοι φαῦλα δαιμόνια περινοστεῖν, οἷς οἱ θεοὶ
δημίοις χρῶνται καὶ[1] κολασταῖς ἐπὶ τοὺς ἀνοσίους
καὶ ἀδίκους ἀνθρώπους, οὕτως οἱ Λάρητες ἐρινυώ-
δεις τινές εἰσι καὶ ποίνιμοι δαίμονες, ἐπίσκοποι
βίων καὶ οἴκων; διὸ καὶ κυνῶν δέρμασιν ἀμπέχονται, καὶ κύων πάρεδρός ἐστιν, ὡς δεινοῖς οὖσιν
ἐξιχνεῦσαι καὶ μετελθεῖν τοὺς πονηρούς.

52. '' Διὰ τί τῇ καλουμένῃ Γενείτῃ Μάνῃ κύνα
θύουσι καὶ κατεύχονται μηδένα χρηστὸν ἀποβῆναι
τῶν οἰκογενῶν;''

Ἢ ὅτι δαίμων ἐστὶν ἡ Γενείτα περὶ τὰς γενέσεις
καὶ τὰς λοχείας τῶν φθαρτῶν; ῥύσιν γάρ τινα
σημαίνει τοὔνομα καὶ γένεσιν ἢ ῥέουσαν γένεσιν.
B ὥσπερ οὖν οἱ Ἕλληνες τῇ Ἑκάτῃ, καὶ τῇ Γενείτῃ
κύνα Ῥωμαῖοι θύουσιν ὑπὲρ τῶν οἰκογενῶν. Ἀργείους δὲ Σωκράτης φησὶ τῇ Εἰλιονείᾳ[2] κύνα θύειν
διὰ τὴν ῥᾳστώνην τῆς λοχείας. τὸ δὲ τῆς εὐχῆς
πότερον οὐκ ἐπ᾽ ἀνθρώπων ἐστὶν οἰκογενῶν, μηδένα
χρηστὸν γενέσθαι ἀλλὰ κυνῶν; χαλεποὺς γὰρ εἶναι
δεῖ καὶ φοβεροὺς τοὺς κύνας.

---

[1] καὶ added by Bernardakis.
[2] Εἰλιονείᾳ] Εἰλειθυίᾳ Amyot.

---

[a] Cf. Moralia, 361 ʙ, 419 ᴀ, 1051 c.
[b] Cf. Pliny, Natural History, xxix. 4 (58).

praestites, and, also because it is fitting that those who stand before a house should be its guardians, terrifying to strangers, but gentle and mild to the inmates, even as a dog is ?

Or is the truth rather, as some Romans affirm, that, just as the philosophic school of Chrysippus[a] think that evil spirits stalk about whom the gods use as executioners and avengers upon unholy and unjust men, even so the Lares are spirits of punishment like the Furies and supervisors of men's lives and houses ? Wherefore they are clothed in the skins of dogs and have a dog as their attendant, in the belief that they are skilful in tracking down and following up evil-doers.

52. Why do they sacrifice a bitch to the goddess called Geneta Mana[b] and pray that none of the household shall become " good " ?

Is it because Geneta is a spirit concerned with the generation and birth of beings that perish ? Her name means some such thing as " flux and birth " or " flowing birth." [c] Accordingly, just as the Greeks sacrifice a bitch to Hecatê,[d] even so do the Romans offer the same sacrifice to Geneta on behalf of the members of their household. But Socrates[e] says that the Argives sacrifice a bitch to Eilioneia by reason of the ease with which the bitch brings forth its young. But does the import of the prayer, that none of them shall become "good," refer not to the human members of a household, but to the dogs ? For dogs should be savage and terrifying.

[c] An attempt to derive the name from *genitus* (*-a, -um*) and *manare*.
[d] *Cf.* 280 c, *infra*.
[e] Müller, *Frag. Hist. Graec.* iv. p. 498.

(277) Ἡ διὰ τὸ χρηστοὺς[1] κομψῶς[2] λέγεσθαι τοὺς
τελευτῶντας αἰνιττόμενοι διὰ τῆς εὐχῆς[3] αἰτοῦνται
μηδένα τῶν συνοίκων ἀποθανεῖν; οὐ δεῖ δὲ τοῦτο
θαυμάζειν· καὶ γὰρ Ἀριστοτέλης ἐν ταῖς Ἀρκάδων
C πρὸς Λακεδαιμονίους συνθήκαις γεγράφθαι φησὶ
μηδένα χρηστὸν ποιεῖν βοηθείας χάριν τοῖς λακωνίζουσι τῶν Τεγεατῶν, ὅπερ εἶναι μηδένα ἀπο-
κτιννύναι.

53. "Διὰ τί τοῖς Καπετωλίοις θέας ἄγοντες ἔτι
νῦν κηρύττουσι Σαρδιανοὺς ὠνίους, καὶ γέρων τις
ἐπὶ χλευασμῷ προάγεται παιδικὸν ἐναψάμενος
περιδέραιον, ὃ καλοῦσι βοῦλλαν; "

Ἦ ὅτι Ῥωμύλῳ πολὺν χρόνον ἐπολέμησαν οἱ
λεγόμενοι Οὐήιοι Τυρρηνῶν, καὶ ταύτην τὴν πόλιν
ἐσχάτην εἷλε, καὶ πολλοὺς αἰχμαλώτους ἀπεκήρυξε
μετὰ τοῦ βασιλέως ἐπισκώπτων αὐτοῦ τὴν ἠλιθιό-
D τητα καὶ τὴν ἀβελτερίαν; ἐπεὶ δὲ Λυδοὶ μὲν ἦσαν
οἱ Τυρρηνοὶ ἐξ ἀρχῆς, Λυδῶν δὲ μητρόπολις αἱ[4]
Σάρδεις, οὕτω τοὺς Οὐηίους ἀπεκήρυττον· καὶ
μέχρι νῦν ἐν παιδιᾷ τὸ ἔθος διαφυλάττουσι.

54. "Διὰ τί τὰ κρεοπώλια 'μάκελλα' καὶ
'μακέλλας' καλοῦσι; "

Πότερον ἀπὸ τῶν μαγείρων τοὔνομα διαφθαρέν,
ὥσπερ ἄλλα πολλά, τῇ συνηθείᾳ κεκράτηκε; καὶ
γὰρ τὸ κάππα πρὸς τὸ γάμμα συγγένειαν ἔχει παρ'

---

[1] χρηστοὺς Polus : ἀχρήστους.
[2] κομψῶς Xylander : καὶ κομψούς.
[3] εὐχῆς] ἀρχῆς some mss.
[4] αἱ] omitted in all mss. except E.

---

[a] Frag. 592 (ed. V. Rose); cf. Moralia, 292 B, infra.
[b] Cf. χρηστὲ χαῖρ on Greek tombstones.

Or, because of the fact that the dead are gracefully called " the good," are they in veiled language asking in their prayer that none of their household may die ?   One should not be surprised at this ; Aristotle,[a] in fact, says that there is written in the treaty of the Arcadians with the Spartans : " No one shall be made good [b] for rendering aid to the Spartan party in Tegea " ; that is, no one shall be put to death.

53. WHY do they even now, at the celebration of the Capitoline games, proclaim " Sardians for sale ! ",[c] and why is an old man led forth in derision, wearing around his neck a child's amulet which they call a *bulla* [d] ?

Is it because the Etruscans called Veians fought against Romulus for a long time, and he took this city last of all [e] and sold at auction many captives together with their king, taunting him for his stupidity and folly ?   But since the Etruscans were originally Lydians, and Sardis was the capital city of the Lydians, they offered the Veians for sale under this name ; and even to this day they preserve the custom in sport.

54. WHY do they call the meat-markets *macella* and *macellae* ?

Is this word corrupted from *mageiroi* (cooks) and has it prevailed, as many others have, by force of habit ?   For *c* and *g* have a close relationship in

[c] So apparently Plutarch ; but the Latin *Sardi venales* can mean nothing but " Sardinians for sale."   Plutarch, or his authority, has confused *Sardi* with *Sardiani* (Sardians).

[d] *Cf. Life of Romulus*, xxv. (33 E).

[e] This is quite contrary to the traditional account (*cf.* for example, Livy, vi. 21-23), according to which Veii was not captured until 396 B.C.

(277) αὐτοῖς· ὀψὲ γὰρ ἐχρήσαντο τῷ γάμμα Καρβιλίου[1]
Σπορίου προσεξευρόντος· καὶ τὸ λάμβδα πάλιν τοῖς
ἀπολισθάνουσι τοῦ ρ δι' ἀμβλύτητα τῆς γλώττης
ὑπόκειται τραυλιζόμενον.

E   ῍Η καὶ τοῦτο λυτέον τῇ ἱστορίᾳ; λέγεται γὰρ ἐν
Ῥώμῃ βίαιον ἄνδρα καὶ λῃστρικὸν γενόμενον καὶ
περικόψαντα πολλούς, Μάκελλον τοὔνομα, μόγις
ἁλῶναι καὶ κολασθῆναι· ἐκ δὲ τῶν χρημάτων αὐτοῦ
δημόσιον οἰκοδομηθῆναι κρεοπώλιον ἀπ' ἐκείνου
κτησάμενον τὴν προσηγορίαν.

55. "Διὰ τί ταῖς Ἰανουαρίαις εἰδοῖς περιιέναι
δέδοται τοῖς αὐληταῖς τὴν πόλιν ἐσθῆτας γυναικείας φοροῦντας;"

   ῍Η διὰ τὴν λεγομένην αἰτίαν; μεγάλας γάρ, ὡς
F ἔοικε, τιμὰς ἐκαρποῦντο, τοῦ βασιλέως Νομᾶ δόντος
αὐτοῖς διὰ τὴν πρὸς τὸ θεῖον ὁσιότητα· ταύτας
δ' ὕστερον ἀφαιρεθέντες ὑπὸ τῆς ἀνθυπατικῆς
δεκαδαρχίας ἀπεχώρησαν ἐκ τῆς πόλεως. ἦν οὖν
ἐπιζήτησις αὐτῶν καί τις ἥπτετο δεισιδαιμονία τῶν
ἱερέων ἄναυλα θυόντων. ἐπεὶ δ' οὐκ ἐπείθοντο
μεταπεμπομένοις ἀλλ' ἐν τῷ Τίβουρι[2] διέτριβον,
ἀνὴρ ἀπελεύθερος κρύφα τοῖς ἄρχουσιν ἐπηγγείλατο κατάξειν αὐτούς. καὶ παρασκευάσας θοίνην
ἄφθονον ὡς τεθυκὼς θεοῖς ἐκάλεσε τοὺς αὐλητάς·
καὶ γύναια παρῆν ἅμα τῷ πότῳ καὶ παννυχὶς
συνεκροτεῖτο παιζόντων καὶ χορευόντων. εἶτ'

---

[1] Καρβιλίου Xylander : Καρβειλίου.
[2] τῷ Τίβουρι Petavius : τῇ βούριδι or βούρι.

---

[a] Cf. 278 E, infra.
[b] Cf. Livy, ix. 30 ; Ovid, Fasti, vi. 653 ff. ; Valerius
Maximus, ii. 5. 4 ; see also Classical Weekly, 1921, p. 51.

Latin, and it was only after many years that they made use of *g*, which Spurius Carvilius [a] introduced. And *l*, again, is substituted lispingly for *r* when people make a slip in the pronunciation of *r* because of the indistinctness of their enunciation.

Or must this problem also be solved by history ? For the story goes that there once lived in Rome a violent man, a robber, Macellus by name, who despoiled many people and was with great difficulty caught and punished ; from his wealth the public meat-market was built, and it acquired its name from him.

55. WHY is it that on the Ides of January the flute-players are allowed to walk about the city wearing the raiment of women [b] ?

Is it for the reason commonly alleged ? They used to enjoy, as it seems, great honours, which King Numa had given them by reason of his piety towards the gods. Because they were later deprived of these honours by the *decemviri*, who were invested with consular power,[c] they withdrew from the city. There was, accordingly, inquiry made for them, and a certain superstitious fear seized upon the priests when they sacrificed without flutes. But when the flute-players would not hearken to those sent to summon them to return, but remained in Tibur, a freedman secretly promised the officials to bring them back. On the pretext of having sacrificed to the gods, he prepared a sumptuous banquet and invited the flute-players. Women were present, as well as wine, and a party lasting all the night was being celebrated with merriment and dancing, when

[c] *Consulari potestate.*

ἐξαίφνης ὁ ἄνθρωπος ἐμβαλὼν λόγον ὡς τοῦ
278 πάτρωνος ἐπιόντος αὐτῷ καὶ ταραττόμενος[1] συν-
έπεισε τοὺς αὐλητὰς ἀναβάντας ἐφ᾽ ἁμάξας δέρρεσι
κύκλῳ περικαλυπτομένας εἰς τὸ Τίβουρι κομίζε-
σθαι. τοῦτο δ᾽ ἦν ἀπάτη· περιαγαγὼν γὰρ τὰς
ἁμάξας οὐ συνορῶντας αὐτοὺς διὰ τὸν οἶνον καὶ τὸ
σκότος ἔλαθεν εἰς Ῥώμην καταγαγὼν ἅπαντας
ἕωθεν· ἐτύγχανον δ᾽ οἱ πολλοὶ διὰ τὴν παννυχίδα
καὶ τὸν πότον ἐν ἐσθῆσιν ἀνθιναῖς καὶ γυναικείαις
ὄντες. ὡς οὖν ἐπείσθησαν ὑπὸ τῶν ἀρχόντων καὶ
B διηλλάγησαν, ἐνομίσθη τὴν ἡμέραν ἐκείνην οὕτως
ἀμπεχομένους σοβεῖν διὰ τῆς πόλεως.

56. " Διὰ τί τὸ τῆς Καρμέντης ἱερὸν ἐξ ἀρχῆς
δοκοῦσιν αἱ μητέρες ἱδρύσασθαι καὶ νῦν μάλιστα
σέβονται; "

Λέγεται γάρ τις λόγος, ὡς ἐκωλύθησαν ὑπὸ τῆς
βουλῆς αἱ γυναῖκες ὀχήμασι χρῆσθαι ζευκτοῖς·
συνέθεντο οὖν[2] ἀλλήλαις μὴ κυΐσκεσθαι μηδὲ τίκτειν, ἀμυνόμεναι τοὺς ἄνδρας, ἄχρις οὗ μετέγνωσαν
καὶ συνεχώρησαν αὐταῖς· γενομένων δὲ παίδων
εὐτεκνοῦσαι καὶ πολυτεκνοῦσαι τὸ τῆς Καρμέντης
ἱερὸν ἱδρύσαντο.

Τὴν δὲ Καρμένταν οἱ μὲν[3] Εὐάνδρου μητέρα
C λέγουσιν οὖσαν ἐλθεῖν εἰς Ἰταλίαν ὀνομαζομένην
Θέμιν, ὡς δ᾽ ἔνιοι, Νικοστράτην· ἐμμέτρους δὲ
χρησμοὺς ᾄδουσαν ὑπὸ τῶν Λατίνων Καρμένταν
ὀνομάζεσθαι· τὰ γὰρ ἔπη " κάρμινα " καλοῦσιν.

---

[1] ταραττόμενος] ταραττομένους Helmbold.
[2] οὖν] in E only.
[3] οἱ μὲν Wyttenbach: οἶμαι.

---

[a] Cf. Livy, v. 25. 9, and xxxiv. 1 and 8.

suddenly the freedman interrupted, saying that his patron was coming to see him, and, in his perturbation, he persuaded the flute-players to climb into wagons, which were screened round about with skins, to be conveyed back to Tibur. But this was a trick, for he turned the wagons around, and, without being detected, since the flute-players comprehended nothing because of the wine and the darkness, at dawn he had brought them all to Rome. Now the majority of them happened to be clad in raiment of feminine finery because of the nocturnal drinking-bout ; when, therefore, they had been persuaded and reconciled by the officials, it became their custom on that day to strut through the city clad in this manner.

56. Why are the matrons supposed to have founded the temple of Carmenta originally, and why do they reverence it now above all others ?

There is a certain tale repeated that the women were prevented by the senate from using horse-drawn vehicles [a] ; they therefore made an agreement with one another not to conceive nor to bear children, and they kept their husbands at a distance, until the husbands changed their minds and made the concession to them. When children were born to them, they, as mothers of a fair and numerous progeny, founded the temple of Carmenta.

Some assert that Carmenta was the mother of Evander and that she came to Italy ; that her name was Themis, or, as others say, Nicostratê ; and that because she chanted oracles in verse, she was named Carmenta by the Latins, for they call verses *carmina.*

(278) Οἱ δὲ Μοῖραν ἡγοῦνται τὴν Καρμένταν εἶναι καὶ
διὰ τοῦτο θύειν αὐτῇ τὰς μητέρας. ἔστι δὲ τοῦ
ὀνόματος τὸ ἔτυμον " ἐστερημένη νοῦ " διὰ τὰς
θεοφορήσεις. ὅθεν οὐ τὰ κάρμινα τῇ Καρμέντῃ
τοὔνομα παρέσχεν, ἀλλὰ μᾶλλον ἀπ' ἐκείνης
ἐκλήθη διὰ τὸ τοὺς χρησμοὺς ἐν ἔπεσι καὶ μέτροις
ἐνθουσιῶσαν ᾄδειν.

57. " Διὰ τί τῇ Ῥουμίνῃ θύουσαι γάλα κατα-
σπένδουσι τῶν ἱερῶν, οἶνον δ' οὐ προσφέρουσιν; "

Ἡ ῥοῦμαν Λατῖνοι τὴν θηλὴν καλοῦσι, καὶ
Ῥουμινᾶλιν[1] ὀνομασθῆναι λέγουσιν, παρ' ὅσον ἡ
λύκαινα τῷ Ῥωμύλῳ τὴν θηλὴν παρέσχεν; ὥσπερ
D οὖν ἡμεῖς τὰς τρεφούσας τὰ παιδία γάλακτι θη-
λονὰς[2] ἀπὸ τῆς θηλῆς καλοῦμεν, οὕτως ἡ Ῥουμίνα
θηλώ τις[3] οὖσα καὶ τιθήνη καὶ κουροτρόφος οὐ
προσίεται τὸν ἄκρατον ὡς βλαβερὸν ὄντα τοῖς
νηπίοις.

58. " Διὰ τί τῶν συγκλητικῶν τοὺς μὲν πατέρας
συγγεγραμμένους, τοὺς δ' ἁπλῶς πατέρας προσηγόρευον; "

Ἡ τοὺς μὲν ἐξ ἀρχῆς κατανεμηθέντας ὑπὸ τοῦ
Ῥωμύλου πατέρας ἐκάλουν καὶ πατρικίους, οἷον
εὐπατρίδας ὄντας, πατέρας αὑτῶν ἔχοντας ἀπο-
δεῖξαι· τοὺς δ' ὕστερον ἐπεγγραφέντας ἐκ τῶν
δημοτικῶν συγγεγραμμένους πατέρας ὠνόμασαν;

---

[1] Ῥουμινᾶλιν Bernardakis : ῥουμάναλιν.
[2] θηλονὰς] θηλοὺς Valckenaer.
[3] θηλώ τις Valckenaer : θηλωτὶς (-ης).

But others think that Carmenta is a Fate, and that this is the reason why the matrons sacrifice to her. The true meaning of the name is " deprived of sense," [a] by reason of her divine transports. Wherefore Carmenta was not so named from *carmina*, but rather *carmina* from her, because, in her divine frenzy, she chanted oracles in verse and metre.[b]

57. Why do the women that sacrifice to Rumina pour milk over the offerings, but make no oblation of wine in the ceremony ?

Is it because the Latins call the teat *ruma*, and assert that Ruminalis [c] acquired its name inasmuch as the she-wolf offered its teat to Romulus ? Therefore, as we call wet-nurses *thelonai* from *thele* (teat), even so Rumina is she that gives suck, the nurse and nurturer of children ; she does not, therefore, welcome pure wine, since it is harmful for babes.

58. Why did they use to address some of the senators as Conscript Fathers, others merely as Fathers ? [d]

Is it because they used to call those senators originally assigned to that body by Romulus fathers and patricians, that is to say " well-born," since they could point out their fathers,[e] while they called those who were later enrolled from the commoners conscript fathers ?

[a] That is, *carens mente*.
[b] Cf. *Life of Romulus*, xxi. (31 A) ; Dionysius of Halicarnassus, *Roman Antiquities*, i. 31 ; Strabo, v. 33, p. 230 ; Ovid, *Fasti*, i. 619 ff.
[c] Cf. 320 D, *infra*, and *Life of Romulus*, iv. (19 D); Ovid, *Fasti*, ii. 411 ff.
[d] Cf. *Life of Romulus*, xiii. (25 A).
[e] Cf. Livy, x. 8. 10.

PLUTARCH'S MORALIA

(278)   59. " Διὰ τί κοινὸς ἦν βωμὸς Ἡρακλέους καὶ
Μουσῶν;"

E   Ἢ ὅτι γράμματα τοὺς περὶ Εὔανδρον ἐδίδαξεν
Ἡρακλῆς, ὡς Ἰόβας ἱστόρηκε; καὶ τὸ πρᾶγμα
σεμνὸν ἐνομίζετο, φίλους καὶ συγγενεῖς διδασκόν-
των· ὀψὲ δ' ἤρξαντο μισθοῦ διδάσκειν, καὶ πρῶτος
ἀνέῳξε γραμματοδιδασκαλεῖον Σπόριος Καρβίλιος,
ἀπελεύθερος Καρβιλίου τοῦ πρώτου γαμετὴν ἐκ-
βαλόντος.

60. " Διὰ τί, δυοῖν βωμῶν Ἡρακλέους ὄντων,
οὐ μεταλαμβάνουσι γυναῖκες οὐδὲ γεύονται τῶν ἐπὶ
τοῦ μείζονος θυομένων;"

Πότερον ὅτι τῶν ἱερῶν αἱ περὶ τὴν Καρμένταν
F ὑστέρησαν, ὑστέρησε δὲ καὶ τὸ Πιναρίων γένος·
ὅθεν εἰργόμενοι τῆς θοίνης ἑστιωμένων τῶν ἄλλων
Πινάριοι προσηγορεύθησαν· ἢ διὰ τὰ μυθολογού-
μενα περὶ τοῦ χιτῶνος καὶ τῆς Δηιανείρας;

61. " Διὰ τί τὸν θεὸν ἐκεῖνον, ᾧ μάλιστα τὴν
Ῥώμην σῴζειν προσήκει καὶ φυλάττειν, εἴτ' ἐστὶν
ἄρρην εἴτε θήλεια, καὶ λέγειν ἀπείρηται καὶ ζητεῖν καὶ ὀνομάζειν; ταύτην δὲ τὴν ἀπόρρησιν
ἐξάπτουσι δεισιδαιμονίας, ἱστοροῦντες Οὐαλέριον
Σωρανὸν ἀπολέσθαι κακῶς διὰ τὸ ἐξειπεῖν."

Πότερον, ὡς τῶν Ῥωμαϊκῶν τινες ἱστορήκασιν,

---

[a] Müller, *Frag. Hist. Graec.* iii. p. 470.
[b] *Cf.* 277 D, *supra.*
[c] *Cf.* the note on 267 c, *supra.*
[d] An attempt to derive the word from Greek πεινῶ, " be
hungry ": see further Livy, i. 7 ; Dionysius of Halicarnassus,
Roman Antiquities, i. 40.

94

59. WHY did Hercules and the Muses have an altar in common ?

Is it because Hercules taught Evander's people the use of letters, as Juba[a] has recorded ? And this action was held to be noble on the part of men who taught their friends and relatives. It was a long time before they began to teach for pay, and the first to open an elementary school was Spurius Carvilius,[b] a freedman of the Carvilius[c] who was the first to divorce his wife.

60. WHY, when there are two altars of Hercules, do women receive no share nor taste of the sacrifices offered on the larger altar ?

Is it because the friends of Carmenta came late for the rites, as did also the clan of the Pinarii ? Wherefore, as they were excluded from the banquet while the rest were feasting, they acquired the name *Pinarii* (Starvelings).[d] Or is it because of the fable of Deianeira and the shirt ?[e]

61. WHY is it forbidden to mention or to inquire after or to call by name that deity, whether it be male or female, whose especial province it is to preserve and watch over Rome ?[f] This prohibition they connect with a superstition and relate that Valerius Soranus came to an evil end because he revealed the name.

Is it because, as certain Roman writers have

[e] The shirt anointed with the blood of Nessus which Deianeira supposed to be a love charm. She sent the shirt to Heracles and thereby brought about his death ; hence Heracles may be supposed to hate all women ; see Sophocles, *Trachiniae*, or Ovid, *Heroides*, ix.

[f] *Cf.* Macrobius, *Saturnalia*, iii. 9. 3 ; Pliny, *Natural History*, xxviii. 4 (18).

ἐκκλήσεις εἰσὶ καὶ γοητεῖαι θεῶν, αἷς νομίζοντες
καὶ αὐτοὶ θεούς τινας ἐκκεκλῆσθαι παρὰ τῶν πολε-
279 μίων καὶ μετῳκηκέναι πρὸς αὐτοὺς[1] ἐφοβοῦντο τὸ
αὐτὸ παθεῖν ὑφ᾽ ἑτέρων; ὥσπερ οὖν Τύριοι δεσμοὺς
ἀγάλμασι λέγονται περιβαλεῖν, ἕτεροι δ᾽ αἰτεῖν
ἐγγυητὰς ἐπὶ λουτρὸν ἢ καθαρμόν τινα προπέμποντες, οὕτως ᾤοντο Ῥωμαῖοι τὸ ἄρρητον καὶ τὸ
ἄγνωστον ἀσφαλεστάτην εἶναι θεοῦ καὶ βεβαιο-
τάτην φρουράν.

Ἢ καθάπερ Ὁμήρῳ πεποίηται τὸ

γαῖα δ᾽ ἔτι[2] ξυνὴ πάντων

ὅπως οἱ ἄνθρωποι τοὺς θεοὺς πάντας σέβωνται καὶ
τιμῶσι τὴν γῆν κοινῶς ἔχοντας,[3] οὕτως ἀπεκρύ-
ψαντο τὸν κύριον τῆς σωτηρίας οἱ παλαιοὶ Ῥωμαῖοι, βουλόμενοι μὴ μόνον τοῦτον ἀλλὰ πάντας
ὑπὸ τῶν πολιτῶν τοὺς θεοὺς τιμᾶσθαι;

B   62. " Διὰ τί τῶν λεγομένων Φιτιαλέων,[4] Ἑλληνιστὶ δ᾽ οἷον εἰρηνοποιῶν καὶ[5] σπονδοφόρων, ὁ
καλούμενος ' πάτερ πατρᾶτος ' ἐνομίζετο μέγιστος;
ἔστι δ᾽ οὗτος, ᾧ πατὴρ ζῇ καὶ παῖδες εἰσίν· ἔχει
δὲ καὶ νῦν προνομίαν τινὰ καὶ πίστιν· οἱ γὰρ
στρατηγοὶ τὰ δι᾽ εὐμορφίαν καὶ ὥραν ἐπιμελοῦς
δεόμενα καὶ σώφρονος φυλακῆς σώματα τούτοις
παρακατατίθενται."

---

[1] αὐτοὺς Hatzidakis : αὐτούς.
[2] ἔτι Homer : ἐστὶ.
[3] ἔχοντας Meziriacus : ἔχοντες.
[4] Φιτιαλέων Bernardakis : φιδαλέων (-ίων E).
[5] καὶ added by H. J. Rose.

---

[a] Cf., for example, Dionysius of Halicarnassus, *Roman
Antiquities*, xiii. 3; Livy, v. 21 (the *evocatio* of Juno from
Veii); Macrobius, *Saturnalia*, iii. 9. 7 and 14-16.

recorded, there are certain evocations and enchantments affecting the gods, by which the Romans also believed that certain gods had been called forth[a] from their enemies, and had come to dwell among themselves, and they were afraid of having this same thing done to them by others ? Accordingly, as the Tyrians[b] are said to have put chains upon their images, and certain other peoples are said to demand sureties when they send forth their images for bathing or for some other rite of purification, so the Romans believed that not to mention and not to know the name of a god was the safest and surest way of shielding him.

Or as Homer[c] has written,

> Earth is yet common to all,

so that mankind should reverence and honour all the gods, since they possess the earth in common, even so did the Romans of early times conceal the identity of the god who was the guardian of their safety, since they desired that not only this god, but all the gods should be honoured by the citizens ?

62. WHY, among those called *Fetiales*, or, as we should say in Greek, peace-makers or treaty-bringers, was he who was called *pater patratus* considered the chief ? The *pater patratus*[d] is a man whose father is still alive and who has children ; even now he possesses a certain preferment and confidence, for the praetors entrust to him any wards whose beauty and youth require a careful and discreet guardianship.

[b] *Cf.* Diodorus, xvii. 41. 8 ; Quintus Curtius, iv. 3. 21.
[c] *Il.* xv. 193.
[d] Plutarch here mistakenly explains *patrimus* instead of *patratus* : contrast Livy, i. 24. 6 ; Tacitus, *Hist.* iv. 53.

(279)   Πότερον ὅτι τὸ αἰδεῖσθαι τοὺς παῖδας αὐτοῖς καὶ
τὸ φοβεῖσθαι τοὺς πατέρας πρόσεστιν· ἢ τοὔνομα
τὴν αἰτίαν ὑπαγορεύει; βούλεται γὰρ εἶναι τὸ
" πατρᾶτον " οἱονεὶ συμπεπερασμένον καὶ πεπε-
ρατωμένον, ὡς τελειοτέρου τῶν ἄλλων ὄντος ᾧ
C συμβέβηκε πατέρα κεκτημένῳ πατρὶ γενέσθαι.
    Ἢ δεῖ τὸν ὅρκων καὶ εἰρήνης προϊστάμενον
" ἅμα πρόσω καὶ ὀπίσω "[1] καθ᾽ Ὅμηρον ὁρᾶν; εἴη
δ᾽ ἂν μάλιστα τοιοῦτος, ᾧ παῖς ἔστιν ὑπὲρ οὗ
βουλεύεται, καὶ πατὴρ μεθ᾽ οὗ βουλεύεται.

    63. " Διὰ τί τῷ καλουμένῳ ῾ ῥῆγι σακρώρουμ ᾿
(οὗτος δ᾽ ἐστὶ βασιλεὺς ἱερῶν) ἀπείρηται καὶ ἄρχειν
καὶ δημηγορεῖν; "
    Ἢ τὸ παλαιὸν οἱ βασιλεῖς τὰ πλεῖστα καὶ μέ-
γιστα τῶν ἱερῶν ἔδρων καὶ τὰς θυσίας ἔθυον αὐτοὶ
μετὰ τῶν ἱερέων; ἐπεὶ δ᾽ οὐκ ἐμετρίαζον ἀλλ᾽
D ἦσαν ὑπερήφανοι καὶ βαρεῖς, τῶν μὲν Ἑλλήνων οἱ
πλεῖστοι τὴν ἐξουσίαν αὐτῶν περιελόμενοι μόνον
τὸ θύειν τοῖς θεοῖς ἀπέλιπον, Ῥωμαῖοι δὲ παντάπασι τοὺς βασιλεῖς ἐκβαλόντες ἄλλον ἐπὶ τὰς
θυσίας ἔταξαν, οὔτ᾽ ἄρχειν ἐάσαντες οὔτε δημα-
γωγεῖν, ὅπως μόνον ἐν τοῖς ἱεροῖς βασιλεύεσθαι[2]
δοκῶσι καὶ βασιλείαν διὰ τοὺς θεοὺς ὑπομένειν.
ἔστι γοῦν τις ἐν ἀγορᾷ θυσία πρὸς τῷ λεγομένῳ
Κομιτίῳ[3] πάτριος, ἣν θύσας ὁ βασιλεὺς κατὰ τάχος
ἄπεισι φεύγων ἐξ ἀγορᾶς.

[1] πρόσσω καὶ ὀπίσσω Homer, Il. i. 343, Od. xxiv. 452.
[2] βασιλεύεσθαι Wyttenbach: βουλεύεσθαι.
[3] Κομιτίῳ Bernardakis: Κομητίῳ.

---

[a] Il. i. 343, Od. xxiv. 452 ; cf. Shakespeare, Hamlet,
iv. iv. 37 ; Shelley, Ode to a Skylark (18th stanza).

Is it because there attaches to these men respect for their children and reverence for their fathers? Or does the name suggest the reason? For *patratus* means, as it were, "completed" or "perfected," since he to whose lot it has fallen to become a father while he still has a father is more perfect than other men.

Or should the man who presides over oaths and treaties of peace be, in the words of Homer,[a] one "looking before and after"? Such a man above all others would be he that has a son to plan for and a father to plan with.

63. Why is the so-called *rex sacrorum*, that is to say "king of the sacred rites," forbidden to hold office or to address the people?[b]

Is it because in early times the kings performed the greater part of the most important rites, and themselves offered the sacrifices with the assistance of the priests? But when they did not practise moderation, but were arrogant and oppressive, most of the Greek states took away their authority, and left to them only the offering of sacrifice to the gods; but the Romans expelled their kings altogether, and to offer the sacrifices they appointed another, whom they did not allow to hold office or to address the people, so that in their sacred rites only they might seem to be subject to a king, and to tolerate a kingship only on the gods' account.[c] At any rate, there is a sacrifice traditionally performed in the forum at the place called Comitium, and, when the *rex* has performed this, he flees from the forum as fast as he can.[d]

[b] *Cf.* Livy, ii. 2. 1-2; ix. 34. 12; xl. 42.
[c] *Ibid.* iii. 39. 4.
[d] The *Regifugium*: *cf.* Ovid, *Fasti*, ii. 685 ff.: see the *Cambridge Ancient History*, vol. vii. p. 408.

(279)   64. " Διὰ τί τὴν τράπεζαν οὐκ εἴων ἀναιρεῖσθαι
κενήν, ἀλλὰ πάντως τινὸς ἐπόντος; "

E   Πότερον αἰνιττόμενοι τὸ δεῖν ἀεί τι τοῦ παρόντος
εἰς τὸ μέλλον ὑπολιπεῖν καὶ τῆς αὔριον ἐν τῇ
σήμερον μνημονεύειν, ἢ νομίζοντες ἀστεῖον εἶναι
τὸ συστέλλειν καὶ ἀνέχειν τὴν ὄρεξιν ἔτι παρούσης
τῆς ἀπολαύσεως; ἧττον γὰρ ἐπιθυμοῦσι τῶν ἀπόντων ἐθισθέντες ἀπέχεσθαι τῶν παρόντων.

"Ἢ καὶ πρὸς οἰκέτας φιλάνθρωπον τὸ ἔθος; οὐ
γὰρ οὕτω λαμβάνοντες ὡς μεταλαμβάνοντες ἀγα-
πῶσι, κοινωνεῖν τρόπον τινὰ τραπέζης ἡγούμενοι
τοῖς δεσπόταις.

"Ἢ τῶν ἱερῶν οὐδέποτε δεῖ κενὸν οὐδὲν περιορᾶν,
ἱερὸν δ' ἡ τράπεζα;

65. " Διὰ τί τῇ νύμφῃ τὸ πρῶτον οὐκ ἐντυγχάνει
F μετὰ φωτὸς ὁ ἀνὴρ ἀλλὰ διὰ σκότους; "

Πότερον ὅτι αἰδεῖται πρὶν ἢ συνελθεῖν ἀλλοτρίαν
νομίζων, ἢ καὶ πρὸς ἰδίαν προσιέναι μετ' αἰδοῦς
ἐθιζόμενος;

"Ἢ, καθάπερ ὁ Σόλων ἔγραψε μήλου κυδωνίου
τὴν νύμφην ἐντραγοῦσαν εἰς τὸν θάλαμον βαδίζειν,
ὅπως τὸ πρῶτον ἄσπασμα μὴ δυσχερὲς γένηται
μηδ' ἀχάριστον, οὕτως ὁ[1] Ῥωμαῖος νομοθέτης,
εἰ δή τι προσῆν ἄτοπον τῷ σώματι καὶ δυσχερές,
ἔκρυψεν;

"Ἢ διαβολή τίς ἐστιν ἀφροδισίων παρανόμων τὸ

---

[1] ὁ] in E only.

---

[a] Cf. Moralia, 702 D ff.
[b] Cf. Horace, Satires, ii. 6. 66-67.

64. Why did they not allow the table to be taken away empty, but insisted that something should be upon it ? [a]

Was it that they were symbolizing the necessity of ever allowing some part of the present provision to remain over for the future, and to-day to be mindful of to-morrow, or did they think it polite to repress and restrain the appetite while the means of enjoyment was still at hand ? For persons who have accustomed themselves to refrain from what they have are less likely to crave for what they have not.

Or does the custom also show a kindly feeling towards the servants ? For they are not so well satisfied with taking as with partaking, since they believe that they thus in some manner share the table with their masters.[b]

Or should no sacred thing be suffered to be empty, and the table is a sacred thing ?

65. Why does the husband approach his bride for the first time, not with a light, but in darkness ?

Is it because he has a feeling of modest respect, since he regards her as not his own before his union with her ? Or is he accustoming himself to approach even his own wife with modesty ?

Or, as Solon [c] has given directions that the bride shall nibble a quince before entering the bridal chamber, in order that the first greeting may not be disagreeable nor unpleasant, even so did the Roman legislator, if there was anything abnormal or disagreeable connected with the body, keep it concealed ?

Or is this that is done a manner of casting infamy

[c] Cf. *Moralia*, 138 D ; *Life of Solon*, chap. xx. (89 c).

γιγνόμενον, ὡς καὶ τοῖς νομίμοις¹ αἰσχύνης τινὸς
προσούσης;

66. " Διὰ τί τῶν ἱπποδρόμων εἷς Φλαμίνιος
καλεῖται; "
280 "Ἢ ὅτι, Φλαμινίου τινὸς τῶν παλαιῶν τῇ πόλει
χώραν ἐπιδόντος, ἐχρῶντο ταῖς προσόδοις εἰς τοὺς
ἱππικοὺς ἀγῶνας· ἔτι δὲ περιόντων χρημάτων,
κατεσκεύασαν ὁδόν, ἣν καὶ αὐτὴν Φλαμινίαν προσ-
ηγόρευσαν;

67. " Διὰ τί ' λικτώρεις ' τοὺς ῥαβδούχους ὀνομάζουσι; "
Πότερον ὅτι καὶ συνέδεον τοὺς ἀκολασταίνοντας
οὗτοι καὶ τῷ Ῥωμύλῳ παρηκολούθουν ἱμάντας ἐν
τοῖς κόλποις κομίζοντες; τὸ δὲ δεσμεύειν " ἀλ-
λιγᾶρε " λέγουσιν οἱ πολλοὶ Ῥωμαίων, οἱ δὲ καθ-
αρεύοντες ἐν τῷ διαλέγεσθαι " λιγᾶρε."
"Ἢ νῦν μὲν παρέγκειται τὸ κ, πρότερον δέ
" λιτώρεις " ἐκαλοῦντο, λειτουργοί τινες ὄντες περὶ
B τὸ δημόσιον; ὅτι γὰρ λῆτον ἄχρι νῦν τὸ δημόσιον
ἐν πολλοῖς τῶν Ἑλλήνων νόμων γέγραπται, οὐδένα
ὡς ἔπος εἰπεῖν λέληθε.

68. " Διὰ τί κύνα θύουσιν οἱ Λούπερκοι; Λούπερκοι δ᾽ εἰσὶν οἱ τοῖς Λουπερκαλίοις γυμνοὶ δια-
θέοντες ἐν περιζώμασι καὶ καθικνούμενοι σκύτει
τῶν ἀπαντώντων."

---

¹ νομίμοις Xylander and some mss.: νόμοις.

ᵃ The consul defeated at Trasimene. The circus was
built *circa* 221 B.C.; *cf.* Varro, *De Lingua Latina*, v. 154.
ᵇ The Via Flaminia ran from the Pons Mulvius up the

upon unlawful amours, since even lawful love has a certain opprobrium connected with it ?

66. Why is one of the hippodromes called Flaminian ?

Is it because a certain Flaminius [a] long ago bestowed some land upon the city and they used the revenues for the horse-races ; and, as there was money still remaining, they made a road, and this they also called Flaminian ? [b]

67. Why do they call the rod-bearers " lictors " ? [c]

Is it because these officers used both to bind unruly persons and also to follow in the train of Romulus with straps in their bosoms ? Most Romans use *alligare* for the verb " to bind," but purists, when they converse, say *ligare*. [d]

Or is the *c* but a recent insertion, and were they formerly called *litores*, that is, a class of public servants ? The fact that even to this day the word " public " is expressed by *leitos* in many of the Greek laws has escaped the attention of hardly anyone.

68. Why do the Luperci sacrifice a dog ? [e] The Luperci are men who race through the city on the Lupercalia, lightly clad in loin-cloths, striking those whom they meet with a strip of leather.

Tiber Valley to Narnia in Umbria ; later it was extended over the Apennines to the Port of Ariminum.

[c] *Cf. Life of Romulus*, chap. xxvi. (34 A) ; Aulus Gellius, xii. 3.

[d] *Cf.* Festus, *s.v. lictores* ; Valgius Rufus, frag. 1 (*Gram. Rom. Frag.* i. p. 484).

[e] *Cf.* 290 D, *infra* ; *Life of Romulus*, chap. xxi. (31 B ff.) ; *Life of Numa*, chap. xix. (72 E) ; *Life of Caesar*, chap. lxi. (736 D) ; *Life of Antony*, chap. xii. (921 B-C) ; Varro, *De Lingua Latina*, vi. 13 ; scholium on Theocritus, ii. 12.

(280) Πότερον ὅτι καθαρμός ἐστι τῆς πόλεως τὰ
δρώμενα; καὶ γὰρ¹ τὸν μῆνα " Φεβρουάριον " καλοῦσι καὶ νὴ Δία τὴν ἡμέραν ἐκείνην " φεβράτην,"
καὶ " φεβρᾶρε "² τό τινι³ σκυτῶν εἴδει⁴ καθ-
ικνεῖσθαι, τοῦ ῥήματος τὸ καθαίρειν σημαίνοντος·
τῷ δὲ κυνὶ πάντες⁵ ὡς ἔπος εἰπεῖν Ἕλληνες ἐχρῶντο
C καὶ χρῶνταί γε μέχρι νῦν ἔνιοι σφαγίῳ πρὸς τοὺς
καθαρμούς· καὶ τῇ Ἑκάτῃ σκυλάκια μετὰ τῶν
ἄλλων καθαρσίων ἐκφέρουσι καὶ περιμάττουσι
σκυλακίοις τοὺς ἁγνισμοῦ δεομένους, περισκυλακι-
σμὸν τὸ τοιοῦτον γένος τοῦ καθαρμοῦ καλοῦντες.⁶

Ἢ λύκος μὲν ὁ λοῦπός ἐστι καὶ Λύκαια τὰ
Λουπερκάλια, λύκῳ δὲ κύων πολέμιος καὶ διὰ
τοῦτο θύεται τοῖς Λυκαίοις;

Ἢ ὅτι τοὺς Λουπέρκους ὑλακτοῦσι καὶ παρα-
λυποῦσιν οἱ κύνες ἐν τῇ πόλει διαθέοντας;

Ἢ Πανὶ μὲν ἡ θυσία γίγνεται, Πανὶ δὲ κύων
προσφιλὲς διὰ τὰ αἰπόλια;

69. " Διὰ τί τῷ καλουμένῳ Σεπτομουντίῳ παρεφύλαττον ὀχήμασι ζευκτοῖς μὴ χρῆσθαι, καὶ μέχρι
νῦν οἱ τῶν παλαιῶν μὴ καταφρονοῦντες παρα-
D φυλάττουσι; τὸ δὲ Σεπτομούντιον ἄγουσιν ἐπὶ τῷ
τὸν ἕβδομον λόφον τῇ πόλει προσκατανεμηθῆναι
καὶ τὴν Ῥώμην ἑπτάλοφον γενέσθαι."

---

¹ γὰρ in E only.
² φεβρᾶρε F.C.B. ; φεβρουάρε Pantazides : φεβράριν.
³ Helmbold for τὸ τῶν.   ⁴ εἴδει Capps : ἤθει.
⁵ πάντες] πάντως in all mss. except E.
⁶ καλοῦντες] δηλοῦντες in one ms. at least (E).

ᵃ Cf. 277 B, supra, and 290 D, infra.
ᵇ That the puppies were later sacrificed we may infer from
the practice elsewhere and on other occasions.

Is it because this performance constitutes a rite of purification of the city ? In fact they call this month February, and indeed this very day, *februata* ; and to strike with a kind of leather thong they call *februare*, the word meaning " to purify." Nearly all the Greeks used a dog as the sacrificial victim for ceremonies of purification ; and some, at least, make use of it even to this day. They bring forth for Hecatê [a] puppies along with the other materials for purification, and rub round about with puppies [b] such persons as are in need of cleansing, and this kind of purification they call *periskylakismos* (" puppifrication ").

Or is it that *lupus* means " wolf " and the Lupercalia is the Wolf Festival, and that the dog is hostile to the wolf, and for this reason is sacrificed at the Wolf Festival ?

Or is it that the dogs bark at the Luperci and annoy them as they race about in the city ?

Or is it that the sacrifice is made to Pan, and a dog is something dear to Pan because of his herds of goats ?

69. Why on the festival called Septimontium [c] were they careful to refrain from the use of horse-drawn vehicles ; and why even to this day are those who do not contemn ancient customs still careful about this ? The festival Septimontium they observe in commemoration of the addition to the city of the seventh hill, by which Rome was made a city of seven hills.

[c] On this festival see J. B. Carter, *American Journal of Archaeology* (2nd Series), xii. pp. 172 ff. ; H. Last in the *Cambridge Ancient History*, vol. vii. pp. 355 ff.

105

(280)   Πότερον, ὡς ἔνιοι τῶν Ῥωμαϊκῶν ἐπινοοῦσι,
διὰ τὸ μήπω συνεζεῦχθαι τοῖς μέρεσι παντελῶς
τὴν πόλιν;

"Η τοῦτο μὲν ἄλλως " οὐ πρὸς Διόνυσόν" ἐστιν·
ἔργου δὲ μεγάλου τοῦ πρὸς τὸν συνοικισμὸν ἐκ-
τελεσθέντος, οἰόμενοι τὴν πόλιν ἤδη πεπαῦσθαι
προϊοῦσαν εἰς τὸ πρόσθεν, ἔπαυσαν μὲν αὐτοὺς
ἀνέπαυσαν δὲ τῶν ὑποζυγίων τὰ συμπονήσαντα
καὶ παρέσχον ἀπολαῦσαι τῇ σχολῇ τῆς κοινῆς
ἑορτῆς;

E   "Η πᾶσαν μὲν ἐβούλοντο κοσμεῖν ἀεὶ καὶ τιμᾶν
ἑορτὴν τοὺς πολίτας παρόντας, μάλιστα δὲ τὴν
ἐπὶ τῷ συνοικισμῷ τῆς πόλεως ἀγομένην· ἵν' οὖν
τὴν πόλιν, ἧς ἐστιν ἡ ἑορτή, μὴ ἀπολείπωσιν, οὐκ
ἐφεῖτο χρῆσθαι ζεύγεσιν ἐκείνην τὴν ἡμέραν;

70.   " Διὰ τί τοὺς **κατεγνωσμένους**[1] ἐπὶ κλοπαῖς
ἢ δουλικοῖς τισιν ἄλλοις ἁμαρτήμασι ' φουρκιφέρους '[2] καλοῦσιν; "

"Η καὶ τοῦτο τῆς τῶν παλαιῶν ἐπιμελείας
τεκμήριόν ἐστιν; ὁ γὰρ οἰκότριβος ἰδίου κατα-
γνούς τινα μοχθηρίαν ἐκέλευε διπλοῦν ξύλον, ὃ ταῖς
ἁμάξαις ὑφιστᾶσιν, ἀράμενον διὰ τῆς συνοικίας ἢ
τῆς γειτνιάσεως διεξελθεῖν ὑπὸ πάντων ὁρώμενον,
F ὅπως ἀπιστοῖεν αὐτῷ καὶ φυλάττοιντο πρὸς τὸ
λοιπόν· τὸ δὲ ξύλον ἡμεῖς μὲν στήριγμα,[3] Ῥωμαῖοι

---

[1] κατεγνωσμένους Wyttenbach : ἀπεγνωσμένους.
[2] φουρκιφέρους F.C.B. : φουρκίφερας.
[3] στήριγμα Xylander : στήρητα.

106

Is it, as some of the Roman writers conceive, because the city had not yet been completely joined together in all its parts ?

Or has this " nothing to do with Dionysus " [a] ? But did they imagine, when their great task of consolidation had been accomplished, that the city had now ceased from further extension ; and they rested themselves, and gave respite to the pack-animals, which had helped them in their labours, and afforded the animals an opportunity to enjoy the general festival with no work to do ?

Or did they wish that the presence of the citizens should adorn and honour every festival always, and, above all, that one which was held in commemoration of the consolidation of the city ? Wherefore in order that they might not leave the City, in whose honour the festival was being held, it was not permitted to make use of vehicles on that day.

70. WHY do they call such persons as stand convicted of theft or of any other servile offences *furciferi* ? [b]

Is this also evidence of the carefulness of the men of old ? For anyone who had found guilty of some knavery a slave reared in his own household used to command him to take up the forked stick, which they put under their carts, and to proceed through the community or the neighbourhood, observed of all observers, that they might distrust him and be on their guard against him in the future. This stick we call a prop, and the Romans *furca* (" fork ") ;

[a] " Nothing to do with the case " : *cf. Moralia*, 615 A, and Lucian, *Dionysus*, 5, with Harmon's note (L.C.L. vol. i. p. 55) ; see also *Moralia* 388 E and 612 E.
[b] *Cf. Life of Coriolanus*, chap. xxiv. (225 D).

δὲ " φοῦρκαν " ὀνομάζουσι· διὸ καὶ " φούρκιφερ "
ὁ τοῦτο περιενεγκὼν καλεῖται.

71. " Διὰ τί τῶν κυριττόντων βοῶν ὑπὲρ τοῦ
φυλάττεσθαι τὸν ἐντυγχάνοντα χόρτον τῷ κέρατι
προσδοῦσιν; "
῾Η διὰ κόρον καὶ πλησμονὴν ἐξυβρίζουσι καὶ
βόες καὶ ἵπποι καὶ ὄνοι καὶ ἄνθρωποι; ὥς που
καὶ Σοφοκλῆς πεποίηκε

σὺ δὲ σφαδάζεις πῶλος ὡς εὐφορβίᾳ,
γαστήρ τε γάρ σου καὶ γνάθος πλήρης πέλει.[1]

διὸ καὶ Μᾶρκον Κράσσον οἱ Ῥωμαῖοι χόρτον ἔχειν
ἔφασαν· ἐφυλάττοντο γὰρ αὐτὸν οἱ τοὺς ἄλλους ἐν
281 τῇ πολιτείᾳ σπαράττοντες ὡς ἀμυντικὸν καὶ δυσεπι-
χείρητον. οὐ μὴν ἀλλ᾽ ὕστερον ἐλέχθη πάλιν, ὅτι
Κράσσου Καῖσαρ ἀφῃρήκει τὸν χόρτον· ἀντέστη
γὰρ αὐτῷ πρῶτος ἐν τῇ πολιτείᾳ καὶ κατεφρόνησε.

72. " Διὰ τί τῶν ἐπ᾽ οἰωνοῖς ἱερέων, οὓς Αὔσπι-
κας πρότερον Αὔγουρας δὲ νῦν καλοῦσιν, ᾤοντο
δεῖν ἀεὶ τοὺς λαμπτῆρας ἀνεῳγμένους εἶναι καὶ τὸ
πῶμα μὴ ἐπικεῖσθαι; "
῾Η καθάπερ οἱ Πυθαγορικοὶ μικρὰ μεγάλων
ἐποιοῦντο σύμβολα κωλύοντες " ἐπὶ χοίνικος καθῆσθαι " καὶ " πῦρ μαχαίρᾳ μὴ σκαλεύειν," οὕτως
B οἱ παλαιοὶ πολλοῖς αἰνίγμασιν ἐχρῶντο καὶ μάλιστα
πρὸς τοὺς ἱερεῖς, οἷόν ἐστι καὶ τὸ τοῦ λαμπτῆρος;

---

[1] πέλει added by Pearson (Cobet ἀεί: Ahrens βορᾶς).

[a] Nauck, *Trag. Graec. Frag.* p. 311, Sophocles, Frag.
764; or Pearson, no. 848; *cf.* Aeschylus, *Agamemnon*, 1640-
1641; Menander, *Hero*, 16-17 (p. 291 ed. Allinson in
L.C.L.).

wherefore also he who has borne it about is called *furcifer* (" fork-bearer ").

71. WHY do they tie hay to one horn of vicious bulls to warn anyone who meets them to be on guard ?

Is it because bulls, horses, asses, men, all wax wanton through stuffing and gorging ? So Sophocles [a] has somewhere written,

> You prance, as does a colt, from glut of food,
> For both your belly and your cheeks are full.

Wherefore also the Romans used to say that Marcus Crassus [b] had hay on his horn : for those who heckled the other chief men in the State were on their guard against assailing him, since they knew that he was vindictive and hard to cope with. Later, however, another saying was bandied about, that Caesar had pulled the hay from Crassus ; for Caesar was the first to oppose Crassus in public policy and to treat him with contumely.

72. WHY did they think that the priests that take omens from birds, whom they formerly called *Auspices*, but now *Augures*, should always keep their lanterns open and put no cover on them ?

Were they like the Pythagoreans,[c] who made small matters symbols of great, forbidding men to sit on a peck measure or to poke a fire with a sword ; and even so did the men of old make use of many riddles, especially with reference to priests ; and is the question of the lantern of this sort ? For the

[b] *Cf. Life of Crassus,* chap. vii. (547 c) ; Horace, *Satires,* i. 4. 34 " faenum habet in cornu ; longe fuge ! "
[c] *Cf.* 290 E, *infra,* and the notes on *Moralia,* 12 D-E (Vol. I. p. 58).

(281) ἔοικε γὰρ ὁ λαμπτὴρ τῷ περιέχοντι τὴν ψυχὴν
σώματι. φῶς γάρ ἐστιν ἡ ἐντὸς ψυχὴ καὶ δεῖ τὸ
συνετὸν καὶ φρόνιμον ἀεὶ ἀναπεπταμένον αὐτῆς
εἶναι καὶ δεδορκὸς καὶ μηδέποτε συγκεκλεῖσθαι
μηδ' ἄποπτον μένειν.[1]

Πνευμάτων δ' ὄντων, οὐκ εὐσταθοῦσιν οἱ ὄρνιθες
οὐδὲ βέβαια σημεῖα παρέχουσι διὰ τὴν πλάνην
καὶ τὴν ἀνωμαλίαν. διδάσκουσιν οὖν τῷ ἔθει μὴ
πνευμάτων ὄντων ἀλλὰ νηνεμίας καὶ καταστάσεως
ἐπὶ ταῦτα προϊέναι τοὺς οἰωνοπόλους, ὅτε δύνανται
τοῖς λαμπτῆρσιν ἀνεῳγμένοις χρῆσθαι.

C 73. '' Διὰ τί δ' ἀπείρητο τοῖς ἕλκος ἔχουσιν
ἱερεῦσιν ἐπ' οἰωνῶν καθέζεσθαι[2] ; ''

Πότερον καὶ τοῦτο σύμβολόν ἐστι τοῦ μηδὲν
δακνομένους μηδ' οἷον ἕλκος ἴδιον καὶ πάθος
ἔχοντας ἐν τῇ ψυχῇ τὰ θεῖα χρηματίζειν, ἀλλ'
ἀλύπους καὶ ἀκεραίους καὶ ἀπερισπάστους ὄντας;

Ἢ κατὰ λόγον ἐστίν, εἰ μήθ' ἱερείῳ χρήσαιτ' ἄν
τις ἕλκος ἔχοντι πρὸς θυσίαν μήτ' ὄρνισι πρὸς
οἰωνισμόν, ἔτι μᾶλλον ἐφ' ἑαυτῶν φυλάττεσθαι τὰ
τοιαῦτα, καὶ καθαροὺς γενομένους καὶ ἀσινεῖς καὶ
ὁλοκλήρους ἐπὶ τὰ παρὰ τῶν θεῶν σημαινόμενα
βαδίζειν; τὸ γὰρ ἕλκος ἔοικε πήρωσίς[3] τις εἶναι
D καὶ μιασμὸς τοῦ σώματος.

74. '' Διὰ τί μικρᾶς Τύχης ἱερὸν ἱδρύσατο Σερούιος Τούλλιος ὁ βασιλεὺς ἣν ' βρέβεμ ' καλοῦσι;''

Πότερον ὅτι μικρὸς ὢν ἐν ἀρχῇ καὶ ταπεινὰ

---

[1] ἄποπτον μένειν F.C.B. : ἀποπνεόμενον.
[2] καθέζεσθαι Wyttenbach : καθίζεσθαι.
[3] πήρωσίς Meziriacus : πώρωσίς.

---

[a] Cf. Moralia, 1130 B.

lantern is like the body which encompasses the soul ;
the soul within is a light [a] and the part of it that
comprehends and thinks should be ever open and
clear-sighted, and should never be closed nor remain
unseen.

Now when the winds are blowing the birds are unsteady, and do not afford reliable signs because of
their wandering and irregular movements. Therefore by this custom they instruct the augurs not to
go forth to obtain these signs when the wind is
blowing, but only in calm and still weather when
they can use their lanterns open.

73. WHY was it forbidden to priests that had any
sore upon their bodies to sit and watch for birds of
omen ?

Is this also a symbolic indication that those who
deal with matters divine should be in no way suffer-
ing from any smart, and should not, as it were, have
any sore or affection in their souls, but should be un-
troubled, unscathed, and undistracted ?

Or is it only logical, if no one would use for sacrifice a victim afflicted with a sore, or use such birds
for augury, that they should be still more on their
guard against such things in their own case, and be
pure, unhurt, and sound when they advance to in-
terpret signs from the gods ? [b] For a sore seems to
be a sort of mutilation or pollution of the body.

74. WHY did King Servius Tullius build a shrine of
Little Fortune, which they call *Brevis* ? [c]

Is it because although, at the first, he was a man of
little importance and of humble activities and the

[b] *Cf. Moralia*, 383 B ; Leviticus, xxii. 17-21.
[c] Hartman's theory that Plutarch is rendering *Occasio*
= *Fortuna Brevis*) is very doubtful.

(281) πράττων καὶ γεγονὼς ἐκ μητρὸς αἰχμαλώτου διὰ
τὴν τύχην ἐβασίλευσε τῆς Ῥώμης· ἢ αὕτη μὲν ἡ
μεταβολὴ μέγεθος ἐμφαίνει τύχης μᾶλλον ἢ μικρότητα, πάντων δὲ μάλιστα Σερούιος ἔοικε τὴν τῆς
τύχης ἐκθειάσας δύναμιν ἐπιφημίσαι πράξεσιν
E ἁπάσαις; οὐ γὰρ μόνον Τύχης εὐέλπιδος καὶ
ἀποτροπαίου καὶ μειλιχίας καὶ πρωτογενείας καὶ
ἄρρενος ἱερὰ κατεσκεύασεν, ἀλλ' ἔστιν ἰδίας Τύχης
ἱερόν, ἕτερον δ' ἐπιστρεφομένης, ἄλλο¹ παρθένου·
καὶ τί ἄν τις ἐπεξίοι τὰς ἄλλας ἐπωνυμίας, ὅπου
Τύχης ἰξευτρίας² ἱερόν ἐστιν, ἣν βισκᾶταν³ ὀνομάζουσιν, ὡς πόρρωθεν ἡμῶν ἁλισκομένων ὑπ' αὐτῆς
καὶ προσισχομένων τοῖς πράγμασιν;

Ὅρα δὴ μὴ καταμαθὼν τὸ παρὰ μικρὸν ἀεὶ τῆς
τύχης μέγα δυνάμενον, καὶ ὅτι τῷ γενέσθαι τι
μικρὸν ἢ μὴ γενέσθαι τι πολλάκις ὑπῆρξεν ἐνίοις
τυχεῖν ἢ διαμαρτεῖν τῶν μεγίστων, μικρᾶς Τύχης
ἱερὸν ἱδρύσατο, προσέχειν διδάσκων τοῖς πράγμασι
καὶ μὴ καταφρονεῖν διὰ μικρότητα τῶν ἐντυγ-
χανόντων.

75. " Διὰ τί λύχνον οὐκ ἐσβέννυσαν, ἀλλ' αὐτὸν
ὑφ' ἑαυτοῦ περιεώρων μαραινόμενον; "

Πότερον ὡς συγγενὲς καὶ ἀδελφικὸν σεβόμενοι
τοῦ ἀσβέστου καὶ ἀθανάτου πυρός, ἢ καὶ τοῦτο
σύμβολόν ἐστι τοῦ μὴ δεῖν τὸ ἔμψυχον, ἂν μὴ

¹ ἄλλο Dübner: ἄλλο δ' εὐέλπιδος ἄλλο, apparently repeated
from above.
² ἰξευτρίας Stephanus (cf. 322 F): ἰξευτηρίας.
³ βισκᾶταν] βισκατρίκεμ Meziriacus.

ᵃ Cf. 273 B, supra.
ᵇ Cf. 322 F, infra: the Latin equivalents here are perhaps

son of a captive woman, yet, owing to Fortune, he became king of Rome ? Or does this very change reveal the greatness rather than the littleness of Fortune, and does Servius beyond all other men seem to have deified the power of Fortune,[a] and to have set her formally over all manner of actions ? For he not only built shrines [b] of Fortune the Giver of Good Hope, the Averter of Evil, the Gentle, the First-Born,[c] and the Male ; but there is also a shrine of Private Fortune, another of Attentive Fortune, and still another of Fortune the Virgin. Yet why need anyone review her other appellations, when there is a shrine of the Fowler's Fortune, or *Viscata*, as they call her, signifying that we are caught by Fortune from afar and held fast by circumstances ?

Consider, however, whether it be not that Servius observed the mighty potency of Fortune's ever slight mutation, and that by the occurrence or non-occurrence of some slight thing, it has often fallen to the lot of some to succeed or to fail in the greatest enterprises, and it was for this reason that he built the shrine of Little Fortune, teaching men to give great heed to events, and not to despise anything that they encountered by reason of its triviality.

75. Why did they not extinguish a lamp, but suffered it to go out of itself ? [d]

Did they reverence it as akin and closely related to the inextinguishable and undying fire, or is this also a symbolic indication that we should not destroy

Felix (?), *Averrunca, Obsequens, Primigenia, Virilis, Privata, Respiciens, Virgo, Viscata.*
  [c] Cf. 289 B, *infra.*
  [d] Cf. *Moralia*, 702 D ff.

113

βλάπτῃ, διαφθείρειν μηδ᾽ ἀναιρεῖν, ὡς ζῴῳ¹ τοῦ
πυρὸς ἐοικότος; καὶ γὰρ τροφῆς δεῖται καὶ αὐτο-
κίνητόν ἐστιν καὶ σβεννύμενον φωνὴν ἀφίησιν
ὥσπερ φονευόμενον.

Ἡ διδάσκει τὸ ἔθος ἡμᾶς ὅτι δεῖ μήτε πῦρ
μήθ᾽ ὕδωρ μήτ᾽ ἄλλο τι τῶν ἀναγκαίων αὐτοὺς
ἄδην ἔχοντας διαφθείρειν, ἀλλ᾽ ἐᾶν χρῆσθαι τοὺς
δεομένους καὶ ἀπολείπειν ἑτέροις, ὅταν αὐτοὶ
μηκέτι χρείαν ἔχωμεν;

282 76. '' Διὰ τί τὰς ἐν τοῖς ὑποδήμασι σεληνίδας
οἱ διαφέρειν δοκοῦντες εὐγενείᾳ φοροῦσιν; ''

Πότερον, ὡς Κάστωρ φησί, σύμβολόν ἐστι
τοῦτο τῆς λεγομένης οἰκήσεως ἐπὶ τῆς σελήνης² καὶ
ὅτι μετὰ τὴν τελευτὴν αὖθις αἱ ψυχαὶ τὴν σελήνην
ὑπὸ πόδας ἕξουσιν, ἢ τοῖς παλαιοτάτοις τοῦθ᾽
ὑπῆρχεν ἐξαίρετον; οὗτοι δ᾽ ἦσαν Ἀρκάδες τῶν
ἀπ᾽³ Εὐάνδρου Προσελήνων λεγομένων.

Ἢ, καθάπερ ἄλλα πολλά, καὶ τοῦτο τοὺς ἐπαιρο-
μένους καὶ μέγα φρονοῦντας ὑπομιμνήσκει⁴ τῆς
ἐπ᾽ ἀμφότερον τῶν ἀνθρωπίνων μεταβολῆς παρά-
δειγμα ποιουμένους τὴν σελήνην, ὡς

B ἐξ ἀδήλου πρῶτον ἔρχεται νέα
πρόσωπα καλλύνουσα καὶ πληρουμένη,
χὥταν περ αὑτῆς εὐπρεπεστάτη⁵ φανῇ,
πάλιν διαρρεῖ κἀπὶ⁶ μηδὲν ἔρχεται;

---

¹ ζῴῳ Dübner : ζώου.   ² τῆς σελήνης E : ταῖς σελήναις.
³ ἀπ᾽] ἐπ᾽ Xylander and Kronenberg.
⁴ ὑπομιμνήσκει a patent correction : ὑπομιμνήσκειν.
⁵ εὐπρεπεστάτη, Moralia, 517 D : εὐγενεστάτη (εὐγανεστάτη?
Pohlenz).
⁶ κἀπὶ] κεὶς τὸ in the Life of Demetrius, chap. xlv.

ᵃ Cf. Isidore, Origines, xix. 34 ; Juvenal, vii. 192.

nor do away with any living thing, if it does us no harm, since fire is like a living thing ? For it needs sustenance, it moves of itself, and when it is extinguished it gives out a sound as if it were being slain.

Or does this custom teach us that we should not destroy fire, water, or any other necessity when we have enough and to spare, but should allow those who have need of these things to use them, and should leave them for others when we ourselves no longer have any use for them ?

76. Why do they that are reputed to be of distinguished lineage wear crescents on their shoes ? [a]

Is this, as Castor says,[b] an emblem of the fabled residence in the moon, and an indication that after death their souls will again have the moon beneath their feet [c] ; or was this the special privilege of the most ancient families ? These were Arcadians of Evander's following, the so-called Pre-Lunar [d] people.

Or does this also, like many another custom, remind the exalted and proud of the mutability, for better or worse, in the affairs of men, and that they should take the moon as an illustration [e] :

> When out of darkness first she comes anew
> Her face she shows increasing fair and full ;
> And when she reaches once her brightest sheen,
> Again she wastes away and comes to naught ?

[b] Jacoby, *Frag. der griech. Hist.* 250, Frag. 16.
[c] *Cf. Moralia*, 943 a ff.
[d] *Cf.* Aristotle, Frag. 591 (ed. V. Rose); Apollonius Rhodius, iv. 264 ; scholium on Aristophanes, *Clouds*, 398.
[e] Nauck, *Trag. Graec. Frag.* p. 315, Sophocles, Frag. 787 ; or Pearson, no. 871 : the full quotation may be found in *Life of Demetrius*, xlv. (911 c). *Cf.* the variants there and in *Moralia*, 517 D.

(282) Ἡ πειθαρχίας ἦν μάθημα βασιλευομένους[1] μὴ
δυσχεραίνειν, ἀλλ' ὥσπερ ἡ σελήνη προσέχειν
ἐθέλει τῷ κρείττονι καὶ δευτερεύειν

ἀεὶ παπταίνουσα πρὸς αὐγὰς ἠελίοιο

κατὰ τὸν Παρμενίδην, οὕτω τὴν δευτέραν τάξιν
ἀγαπᾶν χρωμένους τῷ ἡγεμόνι καὶ τῆς ἀπ' ἐκείνου
δυνάμεως καὶ τιμῆς ἀπολαύοντας;

77. " Διὰ τί τὸν μὲν ἐνιαυτὸν τοῦ Διὸς νομίζουσι, τοὺς δὲ μῆνας τῆς Ἥρας; "

C   "Ἡ ὅτι τῶν μὲν ἀοράτων θεῶν καὶ νοητῶν βασι-
λεύουσι Ζεὺς καὶ Ἥρα, τῶν δ' ὁρατῶν ἥλιος καὶ
σελήνη; ποιεῖ δ' ὁ μὲν ἥλιος τὸν ἐνιαυτόν, ἡ δὲ
σελήνη τοὺς μῆνας. δεῖ δὲ μὴ νομίζειν ἁπλῶς
εἰκόνας ἐκείνων τούτους, ἀλλ' αὐτὸν ἐν ὕλῃ Δία
τὸν ἥλιον, καὶ αὐτὴν τὴν Ἥραν ἐν ὕλῃ τὴν σελήνην.
διὸ καὶ Ἰουνῶνεμ[2] ἐπονομάζουσι τὴν Ἥραν, τὸ
νέον ἢ τὸ νεώτερον ἐμφαίνοντος τοῦ ὀνόματος ἀπὸ
τῆς σελήνης· καὶ Λουκῖναν Ἥραν καλοῦσιν οἷον
φωτεινὴν[3] ἢ φωτίζουσαν· καὶ νομίζουσιν ἐν ταῖς
λοχείαις καὶ ὠδῖσι βοηθεῖν, ὥσπερ καὶ τὴν σελήνην,

διὰ κυάνεον[4] πόλον ἄστρων
D   διά τ' ὠκυτόκοιο σελάνας·

εὐτοκεῖν γὰρ ἐν ταῖς πανσελήνοις μάλιστα δοκοῦσιν.

---

[1] βασιλευομένους] βουλευομένων in some mss.

[2] Ἰουνῶνεμ an early correction (in the Vossianus according to Wyttenbach): ἴουνον.

[3] φωτεινὴν] φαεινὴν in most mss.

[4] κυάνεον] λαμπρὸν as quoted by Macrobius.

---

[a] Diels, *Frag. der Vorsokratiker*, i. p. 162, Parmenides,
no. B 15.

[b] Timotheus, Frag. 28 (ed. Wilamowitz-Möllendorff);

Or was it a lesson in obedience to authority,
teaching them not to be disaffected under the government of kings, but to be even as the moon, who is
willing to give heed to her superior and to be a second
to him,

> Ever gazing in awe at the rays of the bright-gleaming
> Sun-god,

as Parmenides [a] puts it; and were they thus to be
content with their second place, living under their
ruler, and enjoying the power and honour derived
from him?

77. Why do they believe that the year belongs to
Jupiter, but the months to Juno?

Is it because Jupiter and Juno rule the invisible,
conceptual deities, but the sun and moon the visible
deities? Now the sun makes the year and the moon
the months; but one must not believe that the sun
and moon are merely images of Jupiter and Juno, but
that the sun is really Jupiter himself in his material
form and in the same way the moon is Juno. This
is the reason why the Romans apply the name Juno
to our Hera, for the name means "young" or "junior,"
so named from the moon. And they also call her
Lucina, that is "brilliant" or "light-giving"; and they
believe that she aids women in the pangs of child-
birth, even as the moon [b]:

> On through the dark-blue vault of the stars,
> Through the moon that brings birth quickly;

for women are thought to have easiest travail at the
time of the full moon.

Edmonds, *Lyra Graeca*, iii. p. 331; better Diels, *Anthologia
Lyrica Graeca*, ii. p. 152. *Cf. Moralia*, 659 A; Macrobius,
Saturnalia, vii. 16. 28; see also Roscher, *Lexikon der gr.
und röm. Mythologie*, vol. i. coll. 571-572.

(282)   78. " Διὰ τί τῶν οἰωνῶν ὁ καλούμενος ἀριστερὸς αἴσιος; "

Πότερον οὐκ ἔστι τοῦτ' ἀληθές, ἀλλὰ παρακρούεται πολλοὺς ἡ διάλεκτος[1]; τὸ γὰρ ἀριστερὸν " σίνιστρον " ὀνομάζουσι, τὸ δ' ἐφεῖναι[2] " σίνερε " καὶ " σίνε " λέγουσιν, ὅταν ἐφεῖναι[2] παρακαλῶσι. τὸν οὖν ἐφιέντα τὴν πρᾶξιν οἰωνὸν σινιστέριον ὄντα σίνιστρον οὐκ ὀρθῶς ὑπολαμβάνουσιν οἱ πολλοὶ καὶ ὀνομάζουσιν.

Ἤ, καθάπερ Διονύσιός φησιν, Ἀσκανίῳ τῷ Αἰνείου παραταττομένῳ πρὸς Μεζέντιον ἀστραπῆς
E ἐν ἀριστερᾷ νικηφόρου γενομένης οἰωνισαμένοις[3] καὶ πρὸς τὸ λοιπὸν οὕτω παραφυλάττουσιν; ἤ, ὡς ἄλλοι τινές, Αἰνείᾳ τούτου συμπεσόντος; καὶ γὰρ Θηβαῖοι τῷ ἀριστερῷ κέρατι τρεψάμενοι τοὺς πολεμίους καὶ κρατήσαντες ἐν Λεύκτροις, διετέλεσαν ἐν πάσαις ταῖς μάχαις τῷ ἀριστερῷ τὴν ἡγεμονίαν ἀποδιδόντες.

Ἤ μᾶλλον, ὡς Ἰόβας φησί, τοῖς πρὸς τὰς ἀνατολὰς ἀποβλέπουσιν ἐν ἀριστερᾷ γίγνεται τὸ βόρειον, ὃ δὴ τοῦ κόσμου δεξιὸν ἔνιοι τίθενται καὶ καθυπέρτερον;

Ὅρα δὲ μὴ φύσει τοῖς εὐωνύμοις ἀσθενεστέροις οὖσιν οἱ προϊστάμενοι[4] τῶν οἰωνῶν οἷον ἀναρρων
F νύουσι καὶ ὑπερείδουσι τὸ ἐλλιπὲς τῆς δυνάμεως ἐπανισοῦντες.

---

[1] διάλεκτος] διαλεκτικός in practically all mss.
[2] ἐφεῖναι Xylander: ἀφεῖναι.
[3] οἰωνισαμένοις F.C.B.; οἰωνισαμένῳ Rose: οἰωνισάμενοι.
[4] προϊστάμενοι Abresch, supported by one ms.: παριστάμενοι.

118

78. WHY of birds is the one called " left-hand " a bird of good omen ?

Is this not really true, but is it the peculiarity of the language which throws many off the track ? For their word for " left " is *sinistrum* ; " to permit " is *sinere* ; and they say *sine* when they urge giving permission. Accordingly the bird which permits the augural action to be taken, that is, the *avis sinisteria*, the vulgar are not correct in assuming to be *sinistra* and in calling it so.

Or is it, as Dionysius [a] says, that when Ascanius, son of Aeneas, was drawing up his army against Mezentius, and his men were taking the auspices, a flash of lightning, which portended victory, appeared on the left, and from that time on they observe this practice in divination ? Or is it true, as certain other authorities affirm, that this happened to Aeneas ? As a matter of fact, the Thebans, when they had routed and overpowered their enemies on the left wing at Leuctra,[b] continued thereafter to assign to the left the chief command in all battles.

Or [c] is it rather, as Juba [d] declares, that as anyone looks eastward, the north is on the left, and some make out the north to be the right, or upper, side of the universe ?

But consider whether it be not that the left is by nature the weaker side, and they that preside over auguries try to strengthen and prop its deficient powers by this method of equalization.

[a] Dionysius of Halicarnassus, *Roman Antiquities*, ii. 5. 5 ; Virgil, *Aeneid*, ix. 630, and Conington's note on Virgil, *Georgics*, iv. 7.
[b] *Cf. Life of Pelopidas*, xxiii. (289 D-E).
[c] *Cf. Moralia*, 363 E, 888 B.
[d] Müller, *Frag. Hist. Graec.* iii. p. 471.

Ἦ τὰ ἐπίγεια καὶ θνητὰ τοῖς οὐρανίοις καὶ
θείοις ἀντικεῖσθαι νομίζοντες ᾤοντο τὰ πρὸς ἡμᾶς
ἀριστερὰ τοὺς θεοὺς ἀπὸ τῶν δεξιῶν προπέμπειν;

79. '' Διὰ τί τοῦ θριαμβεύσαντος εἶτ᾽ ἀποθανόντος καὶ καέντος ἐξῆν ὀστέον λαβόντας εἰς τὴν
πόλιν εἰσφέρειν καὶ κατατίθεσθαι, ὡς Πύρρων ὁ
Λιπαραῖος ἱστόρηκεν;''

Ἦ τιμῆς ἕνεκα τοῦ τεθνηκότος; καὶ γὰρ ἄλλοις
ἀριστεῦσι καὶ στρατηγοῖς ἔδωκαν οὐκ αὐτοὺς
μόνον ἀλλὰ καὶ τοὺς ἀπ᾽ αὐτῶν ἐνθάπτεσθαι
τῇ ἀγορᾷ, καθάπερ Οὐαλερίῳ καὶ Φαβρικίῳ· καί
283 φασι τούτων ἀπογόνοις ἀποθανοῦσι καὶ κομισθεῖσιν
εἰς ἀγορὰν ὑφίεσθαι δᾷδα καιομένην, εἶτ᾽ εὐθὺς
αἴρεσθαι, χρωμένων ἀνεπιφθόνως τῇ τιμῇ καὶ τὸ
ἐξεῖναι μόνον ἐκβεβαιουμένων.

80. '' Διὰ τί τοὺς θριαμβεύσαντας ἑστιῶντες ἐν
δημοσίῳ παρῃτοῦντο τοὺς ὑπάτους, καὶ πέμποντες
παρεκάλουν μὴ ἐλθεῖν ἐπὶ τὸ δεῖπνον;''

Ἦ καὶ τόπον ἔδει τῷ θριαμβεύσαντι κλισίας τὸν[1]
ἐντιμότατον ἀποδίδοσθαι καὶ προπομπὴν μετὰ τὸ
δεῖπνον; ταῦτα δ᾽ οὐκ ἔξεστιν ἑτέρῳ γίγνεσθαι τῶν
ὑπάτων παρόντων, ἀλλ᾽ ἐκείνοις.

81. '' Διὰ τί περιπόρφυρον ὁ δήμαρχος οὐ φορεῖ,
B τῶν ἄλλων ἀρχόντων φορούντων;''

Ἦ τὸ παράπαν οὐδ᾽ ἐστὶν ἄρχων; οὐδὲ γὰρ
ῥαβδούχους ἔχουσι οὐδ᾽ ἐπὶ δίφρου καθήμενοι

---

[1] κλισίας τὸν Cobet: καὶ σίαστον.

ᵃ Müller, *Frag. Hist. Graec.* iv. p. 479.
ᵇ Cf. *Life of Publicola*, chap. xxiii. (109 D).
ᶜ Cf. Valerius Maximus, ii. 8. 6.
ᵈ The *toga praetexta*.

Or was it that they believed earthly and mortal matters to be antithetical to things heavenly and divine, and so thought that whatever was on the left for us the gods were sending forth from the right ?

79. WHY was it permitted to take up a bone of a man who had enjoyed a triumph, and had later died and been cremated, and carry it into the city and deposit it there, as Pyrrhon *a* of Lipara has recorded ?

Was it to show honour to the dead ? In fact, to other men of achievement, as well as to generals, they granted, not only for themselves, but also for their descendants, the right to be buried in the Forum, as they did to Valerius *b* and to Fabricius ; and they relate that when descendants of these men die and have been conveyed to the Forum, a lighted torch is placed beneath the body and then immediately withdrawn ; thus they enjoy the honour without exciting envy, and merely confirm their prerogative.

80. WHY was it that when they gave a public banquet for men who had celebrated a triumph, they formally invited the consuls and then sent word to them requesting them not to come to the dinner ? *c*

Was it because it was imperative that the place of honour at table and an escort home after dinner should be assigned to the man who had triumphed ? But these honours can be given to no one else when the consuls are present, but only to them.

81. WHY does not the tribune wear a garment with the purple border,*d* although the other magistrates wear it ?

Is it because he is not a magistrate at all ? For tribunes have no lictors, nor do they transact business

121

(283) χρηματίζουσιν, οὐδ' ἔτους ἀρχῇ καθάπερ οἱ
λοιποὶ πάντες ἄρχοντες εἰσίασιν,[1] οὐδὲ παύονται
δικτάτωρος αἱρεθέντος ἀλλὰ πᾶσαν ἀρχὴν ἐκείνου
μετατιθέντος εἰς ἑαυτὸν αὐτοὶ μόνοι διαμένουσιν,
ὥσπερ οὐκ ὄντες ἄρχοντες ἀλλ' ἑτέραν τινὰ τάξιν
ἔχοντες. ὡς δὲ τῶν ῥητόρων ἔνιοι τὴν παραγραφὴν
οὐ βούλονται δίκην εἶναι, τοὐναντίον τῇ δίκῃ
δρῶσαν· ἡ μὲν γὰρ εἰσάγει καὶ ποιεῖ κρίσιν, ἡ δ'
ἀναιρεῖ καὶ λύει· τὸν αὐτὸν τρόπον οἴονται τὴν
δημαρχίαν κώλυσιν ἀρχῆς μᾶλλον εἶναι καὶ πρὸς
C ἀρχὴν ἀντίταξιν ἢ ἀρχήν. τὸ γὰρ ἐνστῆναι πρὸς
δύναμιν ἄρχοντος καὶ τὴν ἄγαν ἐξουσίαν ἀφελεῖν
ἐξουσία καὶ δυναμίς ἐστιν αὐτῆς.

"Η ταῦτα μὲν ἄν τις εἴποι καὶ τὰ τοιαῦτα χρώμενος εὑρησιλογίᾳ· τῆς δὲ δημαρχίας τὴν γένεσιν
ἐκ τοῦ δήμου λαμβανούσης τὸ δημοτικὸν ἰσχυρόν
ἐστι, καὶ μέγα τὸ μὴ μεῖζον φρονεῖν τῶν λοιπῶν
ἀλλ' ὁμοιοῦσθαι καὶ σχήματι καὶ στολῇ καὶ διαίτῃ
τοῖς ἐπιτυγχάνουσι τῶν πολιτῶν. ὁ γὰρ ὄγκος
ὑπάτῳ προσήκει καὶ στρατηγῷ, τὸν δὲ δήμαρχον,
ὡς Γάιος Κουρίων ἔλεγε, καταπατεῖσθαι δεῖ, καὶ
D μὴ σεμνὸν εἶναι τῇ ὄψει μηδὲ δυσπρόσοδον μηδὲ
τοῖς πολλοῖς χαλεπόν, ἀλλ' ὑπὲρ τῶν ἄλλων ἄοκνον[2]
τοῖς δὲ πολλοῖς εὐμεταχείριστον. ὅθεν οὐδ' οἰκίας
αὐτοῦ κλείεσθαι νενόμισται θύραν, ἀλλὰ καὶ νύκτωρ
ἀνέῳγε καὶ μεθ' ἡμέραν ὥσπερ λιμὴν καὶ καταφυγὴ
τοῖς δεομένοις. ὅσῳ δὲ μᾶλλον ἐκταπεινοῦται τῷ

---

[1] εἰσίασιν Meziriacus: εἰσιν.
[2] ἄοκνον added by F.C.B. to fill a lacuna.

[a] They entered upon their office December 10th : Dionysius of Halicarnassus, *Roman Antiquities*, vi. 89. 2 ; Livy,
xxxix. 52.

seated on the curule chair, nor do they enter their office at the beginning of the year *a* as all the other magistrates do, nor do they cease from their functions when a dictator is chosen ; but although he transfers every other office to himself, the tribunes alone remain, as not being officials but as holding some other position. Even as some advocates will not have it that a demurrer is a suit, but hold that its effect is the opposite of that of a suit ; for a suit brings a case into court and obtains a judgement, while a demurrer takes it out of court and quashes it; in the same way they believe that the tribuneship is a check on officialdom and a position to offer opposition to magistracy rather than a magistracy. For its authority and power consist in blocking the power of a magistrate and in the abrogation of excessive authority.

Or one might expound these matters and others like them, if one were to indulge in the faculty of invention ; but since the tribunate derives its origin from the people, the popular element in it is strong ; and of much importance is the fact that the tribune does not pride himself above the rest of the people, but conforms in appearance, dress, and manner of life to ordinary citizens. Pomp and circumstance become the consul and the praetor ; but the tribune, as Gaius Curio used to say, must allow himself to be trodden upon ; he must not be proud of mien, nor difficult of access nor harsh to the multitude, but indefatigable on behalf of others and easy for the multitude to deal with. Wherefore it is the custom that not even the door of his house shall be closed, but it remains open both night and day as a haven of refuge for such as need it. The more humble he is

(283) σχήματι,[1] τοσούτῳ μᾶλλον αὔξεται τῇ δυνάμει.
κοινὸν γὰρ αὐτὸν ἀξιοῦσι τῇ χρείᾳ καὶ πᾶσιν
ἐφικτὸν ὥσπερ βωμὸν εἶναι, τῇ δὲ τιμῇ ποιοῦσιν
ἱερὸν καὶ ἅγιον καὶ ἄσυλον· ὅπου κἂν βαδίζων ἐν
δημοσίῳ πάθῃ τι,[2] νόμος ἐστὶ καθαίρεσθαι καὶ
ἀγνίζεσθαι τὸ σῶμα καθάπερ μεμιασμένον.

E   82. " Διὰ τί τῶν στρατηγῶν αἱ ῥάβδοι συνδεδε-
μέναι προσηρτημένων τῶν πελέκεων φέρονται; "
     Πότερον ὅτι σύμβολόν ἐστι τοῦ μὴ δεῖν πρόχειρον
εἶναι καὶ λελυμένην τὴν ὀργὴν τοῦ ἄρχοντος, ἢ
διατριβὴν καὶ μέλλησιν ἐμποιοῦν τῇ ὀργῇ τὸ λύειν
ἀτρέμα τὰς ῥάβδους πολλάκις ἐποίησε μεταγνῶναι
περὶ τῆς κολάσεως; ἐπεὶ δὲ τῆς κακίας τὸ μὲν
ἰάσιμόν ἐστι τὸ δ' ἀνήκεστον, αἱ μὲν ῥάβδοι νου-
F θετοῦσι τὸ μεταθέσθαι δυνάμενον, οἱ[3] δὲ πελέκεις
ἀποκόπτουσι τὸ ἀνουθέτητον.

     83. " Διὰ τί τοὺς καλουμένους Βλετονησίους
βαρβάρους ὄντας ἄνθρωπον τεθυκέναι θεοῖς πυθό-
μενοι, μετεπέμψαντο τοὺς ἄρχοντας αὐτῶν ὡς
κολάσοντες, ἐπεὶ δὲ νόμῳ τινὶ τοῦτ' ἐφαίνοντο
πεποιηκότες, ἐκείνους μὲν ἀπέλυσαν, ἐκώλυσαν δὲ
πρὸς τὸ λοιπόν; αὐτοὶ δ' οὐ πολλοῖς ἔτεσιν ἔμπροσθεν δύο μὲν ἄνδρας δύο δὲ γυναῖκας ἐν τῇ βοῶν
ἀγορᾷ λεγομένῃ, τοὺς μὲν Ἕλληνας, τοὺς δὲ Γαλάτας, ζῶντας κατώρυξαν· φαίνεται γὰρ ἄτοπον

---

[1] σχήματι Wyttenbach: σώματι.
[2] πάθῃ τι suggested by Bernardakis: πᾶσι.
[3] οἱ Bernardakis: αἱ.

in outward appearance, the more is he increased in power. They think it meet that he shall be available for the common need and be accessible to all, even as an altar ; and by the honour paid to him they make his person holy, sacred, and inviolable.[a] Wherefore if anything happen to him when he walks abroad in public, it is even customary for him to cleanse and purify his body as if it had been polluted.

82. Why are the rods of the praetors carried in bundles with axes attached ?

Is it because this is a symbolic indication that the temper of the official should not be too quick or unrestrained ? Or does the deliberate unfastening of the rods, which creates delay and postponement of his fit of temper, oftentimes cause him to change his mind about the punishment ? Now since some bad-ness is curable, but other badness is past remedy, the rods correct that which may be amended and the axes cut off the incorrigible.

83. When the Romans learned that the people called Bletonesii,[b] a barbarian tribe, had sacrificed a man to the gods, why did they send for the tribal rulers with intent to punish them, but, when it was made plain that they had done thus in accordance with a certain custom, why did the Romans set them at liberty, but forbid the practice for the future ? Yet they them-selves, not many years before, had buried alive two men and two women, two of them Greeks, two Gauls, in the place called the Forum Boarium. It certainly

---

[a] Cf. Livy, iii. 55. 6-7 ; Dionysius of Halicarnassus, Roman Antiquities, vi. 89. 2-3.

[b] Of Bletisa in Spain, according to Cichorius, Römische Studien (Berlin, 1922).

ταῦτα μὲν ποιεῖν αὐτούς, ἐπιτιμᾶν δὲ βαρβάροις ὡς οὐχ ὅσια ποιοῦσι.''

284 Πότερον τὸ μὲν θεοῖς θύειν ἀνθρώπους ἀνόσιον ἡγοῦντο, τὸ δὲ δαίμοσιν ἀναγκαῖον· ἢ τοὺς μὲν ἔθει καὶ νόμῳ τοῦτο πράττοντας ἁμαρτάνειν ἐνόμιζον, αὐτοὶ δὲ προσταχθέντες ἐκ τῶν Σιβυλλείων ἔπραξαν; λέγεται γὰρ Ἐλβίαν τινὰ παρθένον ὀχουμένην ἐφ' ἵππου βληθῆναι κεραυνῷ, καὶ γυμνὸν μὲν εὑρεθῆναι κείμενον τὸν ἵππον, γυμνὴν δ' αὐτὴν ὡς ἐπίτηδες ἀνηγμένου τοῦ χιτῶνος ἀπὸ τῶν ἀπορρήτων, ὑποδημάτων δὲ καὶ δακτυλίων καὶ κεκρυφάλου διερριμμένων χωρὶς ἄλλων ἀλλαχόθι, τοῦ δὲ στόματος ἔξω προβεβληκότος τὴν B γλῶσσαν. ἀποφηναμένων δὲ τῶν μάντεων δεινὴν μὲν αἰσχύνην ταῖς ἱεραῖς παρθένοις εἶναι καὶ γενήσεσθαι περιβόητον, ἅψεσθαι δέ τινα καὶ ἱππέων ὕβριν, ἐμήνυσε βάρβαρος[1] τινὸς ἱππικοῦ θεράπων τρεῖς παρθένους τῶν ἑστιάδων, Αἰμιλίαν καὶ Λικινίαν καὶ Μαρκίαν,[2] ὑπὸ ταὐτὸ διεφθαρμένας καὶ συνούσας πολὺν χρόνον ἀνδράσιν, ὧν εἷς ἦν Βετούτιος Βάρρος[3] τοῦ μηνυτοῦ δεσπότης. ἐκεῖναι μὲν οὖν ἐκολάσθησαν ἐξελεγχθεῖσαι, τῆς δὲ πράξεως δεινῆς φανείσης, ἔδοξεν ἀνερέσθαι[4] τὰ Σιβύλλεια τοὺς ἱερεῖς. εὑρεθῆναι δέ φασι χρησμοὺς ταῦτά τε C προδηλοῦντας ὡς ἐπὶ κακῷ γενησόμενα, καὶ προστάττοντας ἀλλοκότοις τισὶ δαίμοσι καὶ ξένοις ἀποτροπῆς ἕνεκα τοῦ ἐπιόντος προέσθαι δύο μὲν

---

[1] βάρβαρος Madvig: βαρβάρου.
[2] Μαρκίαν Wyttenbach: μαρτίαν.
[3] Βετούτιος Βάρρος Wyttenbach: βουτέτιος βάρβαρος (βετούτιος in some mss.).
[4] ἀνερέσθαι Xylander: ἀναιρεῖσθαι.

seems strange that they themselves should do this, and yet rebuke barbarians on the ground that they were acting with impiety.

Did they think it impious to sacrifice men to the gods, but necessary to sacrifice them to the spirits ? Or did they believe that men who did this by tradition and custom were sinning, whereas they themselves did it by command of the Sibylline books ? For the tale is told that a certain maiden, Helvia, was struck by lightning while she was riding on horseback, and her horse was found lying stripped of its trappings ; and she herself was naked, for her tunic had been pulled far up as if purposely ; and her shoes, her rings, and her head-dress were scattered apart here and there, and her open mouth allowed the tongue to protrude. The soothsayers declared that it was a terrible disgrace for the Vestal Virgins, that it would be bruited far and wide, and that some wanton outrage would be found touching the knights also. Thereupon a barbarian slave of a certain knight gave information against three Vestal Virgins, Aemilia, Licinia, and Marcia, that they had all been corrupted at about the same time, and that they had long entertained lovers, one of whom was Vetutius Barrus,[a] the informer's master. The Vestals, accordingly, were convicted and punished ; but, since the deed was plainly atrocious, it was resolved that the priests should consult the Sibylline books. They say that oracles were found foretelling that these events would come to pass for the bane of the Romans, and enjoining on them that, to avert the impending disaster, they should offer as a sacrifice to certain

---

[a] *Cf.* Cicero, *Brutus*, 46 (169) ; Horace, *Satires*, i. 6. 30, if the emendation is right.

(284) Ἕλληνας, δύο δὲ Γαλάτας ζῶντας αὐτόθι κατ-
ορυγέντας.

84. '' Διὰ τί τὴν τῆς ἡμέρας ἀρχὴν ἐκ μέσης
νυκτὸς λαμβάνουσι; ''

Πότερον ὅτι ἡ πολιτεία στρατιωτικὴν ἐν ἀρχῇ
σύνταξιν εἶχε, τὰ δὲ πολλὰ νύκτωρ ἐν ταῖς στρατείαις προλαμβάνεται τῶν χρησίμων; ἢ πράξεως
μὲν ἀρχὴν ἐποιοῦντο τὴν ἀνατολήν, παρασκευῆς δὲ
τὴν νύκτα; δεῖ γὰρ παρασκευασαμένους πράττειν,
ἀλλὰ μὴ παρασκευάζεσθαι πράττοντας, ὡς Μύσων
πρὸς Χίλωνα τὸν σοφὸν εἰπεῖν λέγεται ἐν χειμῶνι
θρίνακα τεκταινόμενος.

D Ἢ καθάπερ ἡ μεσημβρία πέρας ἐστὶ τοῖς πολλοῖς
τοῦ τὰ δημόσια καὶ σπουδαῖα πράττειν, οὕτως
ἀρχὴν ἔδοξε ποιεῖσθαι τὸ μεσονύκτιον; τεκμήριον
δὲ τούτου[1] μέγα τὸ μὴ ποιεῖσθαι Ῥωμαῖον ἄρχοντα
συνθήκας μηδ' ὁμολογίας μετὰ μέσον ἡμέρας.

Ἢ δύσει μὲν καὶ ἀνατολῇ λαμβάνειν ἀρχὴν
ἡμέρας καὶ τελευτὴν οὐ[2] δυνατόν ἐστιν; ὡς μὲν
γὰρ οἱ πολλοὶ τῇ αἰσθήσει διορίζουσιν ἡμέρας μὲν
ἀρχὴν τὴν πρώτην ἀνάσχεσιν τοῦ ἡλίου, νυκτὸς δὲ
τὴν[3] τελευταίαν ἀπόκρυψιν λαμβάνοντες, οὐχ ἕξομεν
E ἰσημερίαν, ἀλλ' ἣν μάλιστα τῇ ἡμέρα νύκτα παρ-
ισοῦσθαι δοκοῦμεν, αὕτη τῆς ἡμέρας ἐλάττων

_____

[1] τούτου Wyttenbach : τοῦτο.
[2] οὐ] Petavius's conjecture, found in A only.
[3] τὴν added by Bernardakis.

strange and alien spirits two Greeks and two Gauls, buried alive on the spot.[a]

84. WHY do they reckon the beginning of the day from midnight ? [b]

Is it because the Roman State was based originally on a military organization and most of the matters that are of use on campaigns are taken up beforehand at night ? Or did they make sunrise the beginning of activity, and night the beginning of preparation ? For men should be prepared when they act, and not be making their preparations during the action, as Myson,[c] who was fashioning a grain-fork in winter-time, is reported to have remarked to Chilon the Wise.

Or, just as noon is for most people the end of their transaction of public or serious business, even so did it seem good to make midnight the beginning ? A weighty testimony to this is the fact that a Roman official does not make treaties or agreements after midday.

Or is it impossible to reckon the beginning and end of the day by sunset and sunrise ? For if we follow the method by which most people formulate their definitions, by their perceptions, reckoning the first peep of the sun above the horizon as the beginning of day, and the cutting off of its last rays as the beginning of night, we shall have no equinox ; but that night which we think is most nearly equal to the day will plainly be less than that day by the diameter of

---

[a] Cf. Life of Marcellus, chap. iii. (299 D) ; Livy, xxii. 57.

[b] Cf. Pliny, Natural History, ii. 77 (188) ; Aulus Gellius, iii. 2 ; Macrobius, Saturnalia, i. 3.

[c] Similar foresight regarding a plough instead of a fork is reported by Diogenes Laertius, i. 106.

φανεῖται τῷ τοῦ ἡλίου μεγέθει. ὃ δ' αὖ πάλιν οἱ
μαθηματικοὶ ταύτην ἰώμενοι τὴν ἀτοπίαν τίθενται,
τὸ τοῦ ἡλίου κέντρον, ὅταν ἅψηται τοῦ ὁρίζοντος,
ἡμέρας διορισμὸν εἶναι καὶ νυκτός, ἀναίρεσίς ἐστι
τῆς ἐναργείας. συμβήσεται γάρ, ἔτι πολλοῦ φωτὸς
ὑπὲρ¹ γῆν ὄντος καὶ τοῦ ἡλίου καταλάμποντος
ἡμᾶς, μηδέπω ἡμέραν ὁμολογεῖν ἀλλ' ἔτι νύκτα
εἶναι. ἐπεὶ τοίνυν ἐν ταῖς ἀνατολαῖς καὶ δύσεσι
τοῦ ἡλίου δύσληπτός ἐστιν ἡ ἀρχὴ διὰ τὰς εἰρη-
μένας ἀλογίας, ἀπολείπεται τὸ μεσουρανοῦν ἢ τὸ
ἀντιμεσουρανοῦν αὐτοῦ λαμβάνειν ἀρχήν. βέλτιον
F δὲ τὸ δεύτερον· φέρεται γὰρ ἐκ μεσημβρίας ἐπὶ τὰς
δύσεις ἀφ' ἡμῶν, ἐκ δὲ μεσονυκτίου πρὸς ἡμᾶς
ἐπὶ τὰς ἀνατολάς.

85. " Διὰ τί τὰς γυναῖκας οὔτ' ἀλεῖν εἴων οὔτ'
ὀψοποιεῖν τὸ παλαιόν;"

Ἦ τὰς συνθήκας διαμνημονεύοντες, ἃς ἐποιήσαντο πρὸς τοὺς Σαβίνους; ἐπεὶ γὰρ ἥρπασαν τὰς
θυγατέρας αὐτῶν εἶτα πολεμήσαντες διηλλάγησαν,
ἐν ταῖς ἄλλαις ὁμολογίαις καὶ τοῦτ' ἐγράφη, μήτ'
ἀλεῖν ἀνδρὶ Ῥωμαίῳ γυναῖκα μήτε μαγειρεύειν.

86. " Διὰ τί τοῦ Μαΐου μηνὸς οὐκ ἄγονται
γυναῖκας;"

Πότερον ὅτι μέσος ἐστὶ τοῦ Ἀπριλλίου καὶ τοῦ
285 Ἰουνίου μηνός, ὧν τὸν μὲν Ἀφροδίτης τὸν δ'
Ἥρας, γαμηλίων θεῶν, ἱερὸν νομίζοντες προ-
λαμβάνουσι μικρὸν ἢ περιμένουσιν;

---

¹ ὑπὲρ Xylander: ὑπό.

ᵃ Long before Plutarch's day the Greeks had calculated
the angle subtended by the sun with an accuracy that stood
the test of centuries, and was not modified until comparatively

the sun.[a] But then again the remedy which the mathematicians apply to this anomaly, decreeing that the instant when the centre of the sun touches the horizon is the boundary between day and night, is a negation of plain fact; for the result will be that when there is still much light over the earth and the sun is shining upon us, we cannot admit that it is day, but must say that it is already night. Since, therefore, the beginning of day and night is difficult to determine at the time of the risings and settings of the sun because of the irrationalities which I have mentioned, there is left the zenith or the nadir of the sun to reckon as the beginning. The second is better; for from noon on the sun's course is away from us to its setting, but from midnight on its course is towards us to its rising.

85. Why in the early days did they not allow their wives to grind grain or to cook?[b]

Was it in memory of the treaty which they made with the Sabines? For when they had carried off the Sabines' daughters, and later, after warring with the Sabines, had made peace, it was specified among the other articles of agreement that no Sabine woman should grind grain for a Roman or cook for him.

86. Why do men not marry during the month of May?[c]

Is it because this month comes between April and June, of which they regard April as sacred to Venus and June as sacred to Juno, both of them divinities of marriage; and so they put the wedding a little earlier or wait until later?

recent times. *Cf.* Archimedes, *Arenarius*, i. 10 (J. L. Heiberg's ed. ii. p. 248).
  [b] *Cf. Life of Romulus*, chap. xv. (26 D), xix. (30 A).
  [c] *Cf.* Ovid, *Fasti*, v. 489.

(285) Ἢ ὅτι τῷ μηνὶ τούτῳ τὸν μέγιστον ποιοῦνται τῶν καθαρμῶν, νῦν μὲν εἴδωλα ῥιπτοῦντες ἀπὸ τῆς γεφύρας εἰς τὸν ποταμὸν πάλαι δ' ἀνθρώπους; διὸ καὶ τὴν Φλαμινίκαν,[1] ἱερὰν τῆς Ἥρας εἶναι δοκοῦσαν, νενόμισται σκυθρωπάζειν, μήτε λουομένην τηνικαῦτα μήτε κοσμουμένην.

Ἢ ὅτι πολλοὶ Λατίνων ἐν τῷ μηνὶ τούτῳ τοῖς
B κατοιχομένοις ἐναγίζουσι; καὶ διὰ τοῦτ' ἴσως Ἑρμῆν ἐν αὐτῷ σέβονται καὶ Μαίας ἐπώνυμός ἐστιν.

Ἤ, καθάπερ ἔνιοι λέγουσιν, ὁ μὲν Μάιος ἀπὸ τῆς πρεσβυτέρας, ὁ δ' Ἰούνιος ἀπὸ τῆς νεωτέρας ἡλικίας ὠνόμασται; γάμῳ δὲ ἁρμοδιώτερον τὸ νέον, ὡς καὶ Εὐριπίδης φησίν·

> ἀλλ' ᾖ[2] τὸ γῆρας τὴν Κύπριν χαίρειν ἐᾷ,
> ἥ τ' Ἀφροδίτη τοῖς γέρουσιν ἄχθεται.

οὐ γαμοῦσιν οὖν ἐν τῷ Μαΐῳ, περιμένοντες τὸν Ἰούνιον, ὃς εὐθύς ἐστι μετὰ τὸν Μάιον.

87. "Διὰ τί τῶν γαμουμένων αἰχμῇ δορατίου τὴν κόμην διακρίνουσιν;"

Ἆρα σύμβολόν ἐστι τοῦτο τοῦ βίᾳ καὶ μετὰ
C πολέμου γαμηθῆναι τὰς πρώτας, ἢ μανθάνουσιν ἀνδράσι συνοικοῦσαι μαχίμοις καὶ πολεμικοῖς ἄθρυπτον καὶ ἄθηλυν καὶ ἀφελῆ προσίεσθαι καλλωπισμόν; ὥσπερ ὁ Λυκοῦργος ἀπὸ πρίονος καὶ

---

[1] Φλαμινίκαν Xylander : φλαμινίβαν.
[2] ᾖ Kvičala and F.C.B. : ἤ.

[a] Cf. 272 B, supra.
[b] The mother of Mercury.
[c] From the Aeolus of Euripides ; Nauck, Trag. Graec. Frag. p. 369, Euripides, no. 23 : cf. Moralia, 786 A, 1094 F.

Or is it because in this month they hold their most important ceremony of purification, in which they now throw images from the bridge into the river,[a] but in days of old they used to throw human beings? Wherefore it is the custom that the Flaminica, reputed to be consecrate to Juno, shall wear a stern face, and refrain from bathing and wearing ornaments at this time.

Or is it because many of the Latins make offerings to the departed in this month? And it is for this reason, perhaps, that they worship Mercury in this month and that the month derives its name from Maia.[b]

Or is May, as some relate, named after the older (*maior*) and June after the younger generation (*iunior*)? For youth is better fitted for marriage, as Euripides[c] also says:

> Old age bids Love to take her leave for aye
> And Aphroditê wearies of the old.

They do not, therefore, marry in May, but wait for June which comes next after May.

87. Why do they part the hair of brides with the point of a spear?[d]

Does this symbolize the marriage of the first Roman wives[e] by violence with attendant war, or do the wives thus learn, now that they are mated to brave and warlike men, to welcome an unaffected, unfeminine, and simple mode of beautification? Even as Lycurgus,[f] by giving orders to make the

---

[a] Cf. *Life of Romulus*, chap. xv. (26 E).

[e] The Sabine women.

[f] Cf. *Moralia*, 189 E, 227 c, 997 c; and the *Life of Lycurgus*, chap. xiii. (47 c); cf. also *Comment. on Hesiod*, 42 (Bernardakis, vol. vii. p. 72).

(285) πελέκεως κελεύσας τὰ θυρώματα ταῖς οἰκίαις
ποιεῖν καὶ τὰς ὀροφάς, ἄλλῳ δὲ μὴ χρῆσθαι τὸ
παράπαν ἐργαλείῳ, πᾶσαν ἐξέβαλε περιεργίαν καὶ
πολυτέλειαν.

Ἢ τὴν διάστασιν αἰνίττεται τὸ γιγνόμενον, ὡς
μόνῳ σιδήρῳ τοῦ γάμου διακριθησομένου;

Ἢ τὰ μὲν πλεῖστα τῶν γαμικῶν εἰς τὴν Ἥραν
ἀνῆπτο[1]; Ἥρας δ᾽ ἱερὸν τὸ δόρυ νενόμισται, καὶ
τῶν ἀγαλμάτων αὐτῆς δόρατι στηρίζεται τὰ
πλεῖστα καὶ Κυρῖτις ἡ θεὸς ἐπωνόμασται, τὸ γὰρ
D δόρυ " κύριν[2] " ἐκάλουν οἱ παλαιοί· διὸ καί φασι
Κυρῖνον ὀνομασθῆναι τὸν Ἐννάλιον.

88. " Διὰ τί τὸ τελούμενον εἰς θέας Λοῦκαρ
καλοῦσιν; "

Ἢ ὅτι πολλὰ ἔστιν ἄλση[3] περὶ τὴν πόλιν ἀν-
ειμένα θεοῖς, ἃ καλοῦσι " λούκους," καὶ τὴν ἀπὸ
τούτων πρόσοδον εἰς τὰς θέας ἀνήλισκον;

89. " Διὰ τί τὰ Κυρινάλια μωρῶν ἑορτὴν ὀνομάζουσιν; "

Ἢ ὅτι τὴν ἡμέραν ταύτην ἀποδεδώκεσαν, ὡς
Ἰόβας φησί, τοῖς τὰς αὑτῶν φρατρίας ἀγνοοῦσιν;
ἢ τοῖς μὴ θύσασιν, ὥσπερ οἱ λοιποί, κατὰ φυλὰς
ἐν τοῖς Φουρνικαλίοις δι᾽ ἀσχολίαν ἢ ἀποδημίαν ἢ
ἄγνοιαν ἐδόθη τῇ ἡμέρᾳ ταύτῃ τὴν ἑορτὴν ἐκείνην
ἀπολαβεῖν;

---

[1] ἀνῆπτο E : ἀνῆπτον.
[2] κύριν Aldine ed. and Xylander : κοῦριν.
[3] ἄλση Xylander : ἄλλα.

---

[a] See Roscher, *Lexikon der gr. und röm. Mythologie*, ii. coll.
588-592.
[b] *Cf. Life of Romulus*, chap. xxix. (36 в) ; Dionysius of

134

doors and roofs of houses with the saw and the axe only, and to use absolutely no other tool, banished all over-refinement and extravagance.

Or does this procedure hint at the manner of their separation, that with steel alone can their marriage be dissolved ?

Or is it that most of the marriage customs were connected with Juno ?[a] Now the spear is commonly held to be sacred to Juno, and most of her statues represent her leaning on a spear, and the goddess herself is surnamed *Quiritis* ; for the men of old used to call the spear *curis* ; wherefore they further relate that Enyalius is called Quirinus by the Romans.[b]

88. WHY do they call the money expended upon public spectacles *Lucar* ?

Is it because round about the city there are, consecrated to gods, many groves which they call *luci*, and they used to spend the revenue from these on the public spectacles ?

89. WHY do they call the Quirinalia the Feast of Fools ?[c]

Is it because, as Juba[d] states, they apportioned that day to men who did not know their own kith and kin ?[e] Or was it granted to those who, because of some business, or absence from Rome, or ignorance, had not sacrificed with the rest of their tribe on the Fornacalia, that, on this day, they might take their due enjoyment of that festival ?

Halicarnassus, *Roman Antiquities*, ii. 48 ; Ovid, *Fasti*, ii. 475 ff.

[c] Cf. Ovid, *Fasti*, ii. 513 ff.
[d] Müller, *Frag. Hist. Graec.* iii. p. 470.
[e] *Curiae.*

E 90. " Διὰ τί τῷ Ἡρακλεῖ γιγνομένης θυσίας
(285) ἄλλον οὐδένα θεῶν ὀνομάζουσιν οὐδὲ φαίνεται κύων
ἐντὸς τῶν περιβόλων, ὡς Βάρρων ἱστόρηκεν;"

"Ἡ θεὸν μὲν ἄλλον οὐκ ὀνομάζουσι διὰ τὸ τοῦτον
ἡμίθεον νομίζειν; ὡς δέ φασιν ἔνιοι, καὶ μετὰ
τῶν ἀνθρώπων ὄντος ἔτι βωμὸν ἱδρύσασθαι τὸν
Εὔανδρον αὐτοῦ καὶ θυσίαν προσαγαγεῖν. κυνὶ δὲ
πάντων μάλιστα τῶν ζῴων ἐπολέμησε· καὶ γὰρ
F οὗτος[1] αὐτῷ ἀεὶ πολλὰ πράγματα παρέσχ᾽ ὡς[2]
ὁ Κέρβερος· καὶ ἐπὶ πᾶσι, τοῦ Λικυμνίου παιδὸς
Οἰωνοῦ διὰ κύνα φονευθέντος ὑπὸ τῶν Ἱππο-
κοωντιδῶν, ἀναγκασθεὶς μάχην συνάψαι τῶν τ᾽
ἄλλων φίλων πολλοὺς ἀπέβαλε καὶ τὸν ἀδελφὸν
Ἰφικλέα.

91. " Διὰ τί τοῖς πατρικίοις οὐκ ἐξῆν περὶ τὸ
Καπετώλιον κατοικεῖν;"

Πότερον ὅτι Μᾶρκος Μάλλιος[3] αὐτόθι κατοικῶν
ἐπεχείρησε τυραννίδι, δι᾽[4] ὃν ἀπώμοτόν φασιν εἶναι
τῷ οἴκῳ μηδενὶ Μαλλίων[5] ὄνομα Μάρκου γενέσθαι.
"Ἡ παλαιὸς ἦν φόβος οὗτος; Ποπλικόλαν γοῦν
ἄνδρα δημοτικώτατον οὐκ ἐπαύσαντο διαβάλλοντες
μὲν οἱ δυνατοὶ δεδιότες δ᾽ οἱ πολλοί, μέχρι οὗ τὴν
οἰκίαν αὐτὸς κατέσκαψεν ἐπικεῖσθαι τῇ ἀγορᾷ
δοκοῦσαν.

---

[1] οὗτος] ὁ Ὄρθος Wehl.

[2] ὡς Naber: καὶ.

[3] Μάλλιος Bernardakis, as elsewhere: μάλιος.

[4] δι᾽ added by Meziriacus.

[5] Μαλλίων Bernardakis, as elsewhere: μαλίῳ.

---

[a] Cf. Pliny, Natural History, x. 29 (79).

[b] Dionysius of Halicarnassus, Roman Antiquities, i. 40.
2 ; Livy, i. 7. 12.

90. Why is it that, when the sacrifice to Hercules takes place, they mention by name no other god, and why is a dog never seen within his enclosure,[a] as Varro has recorded ?

Do they make mention of no other god because they regard Hercules as a demigod ? But, as some [b] relate, even while he was still on earth, Evander erected an altar to him and brought him sacrifice. And of all animals he contended most with a dog, for it is a fact that this beast always gave him much trouble, Cerberus, for instance. And, to crown all, when Oeonus, Licymnius's son, had been murdered by the sons of Hippocoön [c] because of a dog, Hercules was compelled to engage in battle with them, and lost many of his friends and his brother Iphicles.

91. Why was it not permitted the patricians to dwell about the Capitoline ?

Was it because Marcus Manlius,[d] while he was dwelling there, tried to make himself king ? They say that because of him the house of Manlius was bound by an oath that none of them should ever bear the name of Marcus.

Or does this fear date from early times ? At any rate, although Publicola [e] was a most democratic man, the nobles did not cease traducing him nor the commoners fearing him, until he himself razed his house, the situation of which was thought to be a threat to the Forum.

---

[c] *Cf.* Apollodorus, ii. 7. 3 with Frazer's note (L.C.L. vol. i. p. 251).

[d] *Cf. Life of Camillus*, chap. xxxvi. (148 D); Livy, vi. 20. 13-14.

[e] *Cf. Life of Publicola*, chap. x. (102 C-D).

92. " Διὰ τί τῷ σώσαντι πολίτην ἐν πολέμῳ
286 δρύινον διδόασι στέφανον; "

Πότερον ὅτι πανταχοῦ καὶ ῥαδίως ἔστιν εὐ-
πορῆσαι δρυὸς ἐπὶ στρατείας;

Ἢ ὅτι Διὸς καὶ Ἥρας ἱερὸς ὁ στέφανός ἐστιν,
οὓς πολιούχους νομίζουσιν;

Ἢ παλαιὸν ἀπ᾽ Ἀρκάδων τὸ ἔθος, οἷς ἔστι τις
συγγένεια πρὸς τὴν δρῦν; πρῶτοι γὰρ ἀνθρώπων
γεγονέναι δοκοῦσιν ἐκ γῆς, ὥσπερ ἡ δρῦς τῶν
φυτῶν.

93. " Διὰ τί γυπὶ χρῶνται μάλιστα πρὸς τοὺς
οἰωνισμούς; "

Πότερον ὅτι καὶ Ῥωμύλῳ δώδεκα γῦπες ἐφάνη-
σαν ἐπὶ τῇ κτίσει τῆς Ῥώμης; ἢ ὅτι τῶν ὀρνίθων
ἥκιστα συνεχὴς καὶ συνήθης οὗτος; οὐδὲ γὰρ
νεοττιᾷ γυπὸς ἐντυχεῖν ῥαδίως ἔστιν, ἀλλὰ πόρρω-
B θέν ποθεν ἐξαπίνης καταίρουσι· διὸ καὶ σημειώδης
ἡ ὄψις αὐτῶν ἐστιν.

Ἢ καὶ τοῦτο παρ᾽ Ἡρακλέους ἔμαθον; εἰ λέγει
ἀληθῶς Ἡρόδωρος, ὅτι πάντων μάλιστα γυπὶν ἐπὶ
πράξεως ἀρχῇ φανεῖσιν ἔχαιρεν Ἡρακλῆς, ἡγούμενος δικαιότατον εἶναι τὸν γῦπα τῶν σαρκοφάγων
ἁπάντων· πρῶτον μὲν γὰρ οὐδενὸς ἅπτεται ζῶντος
οὐδ᾽ ἀποκτίννυσιν ἔμψυχον οὐδὲν ὡς ἀετοὶ καὶ
ἱέρακες καὶ τὰ νυκτίνομα· χρῆται δὲ τοῖς ἄλλως[1]
ἀποθανοῦσιν. ἔπειτα καὶ τούτων τὰ ὁμόφυλα

---

[1] ἄλλως Wyttenbach : ἄλλοις.

[a] Cf. *Life of Coriolanus*, chap. iii. (214 E-F); Pliny,
Natural History, xvi. 4 (11-14); Polybius, vi. 39. 6; Aulus
Gellius, v. 6.

[b] Müller, *Frag. Hist. Graec.* ii. p. 31: cf. *Life of*

92. Why do they give a chaplet of oak leaves to the man who has saved the life of a citizen in time of war ? [a]

Is it because it is easy to find an abundance of oak leaves everywhere on a campaign ?

Or is it because the chaplet is sacred to Jupiter and Juno, whom they regard as guardians of the city ?

Or is the custom an ancient inheritance from the Arcadians, who have a certain kinship with the oak ? For they are thought to have been the first men sprung from the earth, even as the oak was the first plant.

93. Why do they make most use of vultures in augury ?

Is it because twelve vultures appeared to Romulus at the time of the founding of Rome ? Or is it because this is the least frequent and familiar of birds ? For it is not easy to find a vulture's nest, but these birds suddenly swoop down from afar ; wherefore the sight of them is portentous.

Or did they learn this also from Hercules ? If Herodorus [b] tells the truth, Hercules delighted in the appearance of vultures beyond that of all other birds at the beginning of any undertaking, since he believed that the vulture was the most righteous of all flesh-eating creatures ; for, in the first place, it touches no living thing, nor does it kill any animate creature, as do eagles and hawks and the birds that fly by night ; but it lives upon that which has been killed in some other way. Then again, even of these

---

Romulus, ix. (23 a-b) ; Pliny, *Natural History*, x. 6 (19) ; Aelian, *De Natura Animalium*, ii. 46.

(286) παρίησι· πετεινοῦ γὰρ οὐδεὶς ἑώρακε γῦπα γενόμενον, ὡς ἀετοὶ καὶ ἱέρακες μάλιστα τὰ συγγενῆ
C διώκουσι καὶ κόπτουσι.   καίτοι κατ' Αἰσχύλον

ὄρνιθος ὄρνις πῶς ἂν ἁγνεύοι φαγών;

ἀνθρώποις δ' ὡς ἔπος εἰπεῖν ἀβλαβέστατός ἐστιν,
οὔτε καρπὸν ἀφανίζων οὔτε φυτὸν οὔτε ζῷον ἥμερον
κακουργῶν.   εἰ δ', ὡς Αἰγύπτιοι μυθολογοῦσι, θῆλυ
πᾶν τὸ γένος ἐστὶ καὶ κυΐσκονται δεχόμεναι κατα-
πνέοντα τὸν ἀπηλιώτην ὥσπερ τὰ δένδρα τὸν ζέφυ-
ρον, καὶ παντάπασιν ἁπλανῆ τὰ σημεῖα καὶ βέβαια
γίγνεσθαι πιθανόν ἐστιν ἀπ' αὐτῶν.   ἐν δὲ τοῖς
ἄλλοις αἱ περὶ τὰς ὀχείας σοβήσεις ἔτι δ' ἁρπαγαὶ
καὶ φυγαὶ καὶ διώξεις πολὺ τὸ θορυβῶδες καὶ
ἀκατάστατον ἔχουσι.

94. "Διὰ τί τοῦ Ἀσκληπιοῦ τὸ ἱερὸν ἔξω τῆς
πόλεώς ἐστι;"

D   Πότερον ὅτι τὰς ἔξω διατριβὰς ὑγιεινοτέρας
ἐνόμιζον εἶναι τῶν ἐν ἄστει; καὶ γὰρ Ἕλληνες ἐν
τόποις καὶ καθαροῖς καὶ ὑψηλοῖς ἐπιεικῶς ἱδρυμένα
τὰ Ἀσκληπιεῖα ἔχουσιν.

Ἢ ὅτι τὸν θεὸν ἐξ Ἐπιδαύρου μετάπεμπτον
ἥκειν νομίζουσιν, Ἐπιδαυρίοις δ' οὐ κατὰ πόλιν
ἀλλὰ πόρρω τὸ Ἀσκληπιεῖον ἔστιν;

Ἢ ὅτι τοῦ δράκοντος ἐκ τῆς τριήρους κατὰ τὴν
νῆσον ἀποβάντος καὶ ἀφανισθέντος αὐτὸν ᾤοντο
τὴν ἵδρυσιν ὑφηγεῖσθαι τὸν θεόν;

---

[a] Suppliants, 226.
[b] Cf. Pliny, Natural History, xxix. 1 (16) ; 4 (72) ; Livy,
x. 47, Epitome, xi.
[c] The Insula Tiberina.

it leaves its own kind untouched ; for no one has ever seen a vulture feeding on a bird, as eagles and hawks do, pursuing and striking their own kind particularly. And yet, as Aeschylus [a] says,

> How can a bird that feeds on birds be pure ?

And we may say that it is the most harmless of birds to men, since it neither destroys any fruit or plant nor injures any domesticated animal. But if, as the Egyptians fable, the whole species is female, and they conceive by receiving the breath of the East Wind, even as the trees do by receiving the West Wind, then it is credible that the signs from them are altogether unwavering and certain. But in the case of the other birds, their excitements in the mating season, as well as their abductions, retreats, and pursuits, have much that is disturbing and unsteady.

94. Why is the shrine of Aesculapius [b] outside the city ?

Is it because they considered it more healthful to spend their time outside the city than within its walls ? In fact the Greeks, as might be expected, have their shrines of Asclepius situated in places which are both clean and high.

Or is it because they believe that the god came at their summons from Epidaurus, and the Epidaurians have their shrine of Asclepius not in the city, but at some distance ?

Or is it because the serpent came out from the trireme into the island,[c] and there disappeared, and thus they thought that the god himself was indicating to them the site for building ?

141

(286)   95. '' Διὰ τί νενόμισται τοὺς ἁγνεύοντας ὀσπρίων
ἀπέχεσθαι; ''

Πότερον, ὡς οἱ Πυθαγορικοί, τοὺς μὲν κυάμους
ἀφωσιοῦντο διὰ τὰς λεγομένας αἰτίας, τὸν δὲ
E λάθυρον καὶ τὸν ἐρέβινθον ὡς παρωνύμους τοῦ
ἐρέβους καὶ τῆς λήθης;

῍Η ὅτι πρὸς τὰ περίδειπνα καὶ τὰς προκλήσεις
τῶν νεκρῶν μάλιστα χρῶνται τοῖς ὀσπρίοις;

῍Η μᾶλλον ὅτι δεῖ πρὸς τὰς ἁγνείας καὶ ἁγιστείας
καθαρὰ καὶ λιτὰ τὰ σώματα ἔχειν· ἔστι δὲ τὰ
ὄσπρια πνευματώδη καὶ περίττευμα ποιεῖ πολλῆς
καθάρσεως δεόμενον.

῍Η ὅτι καὶ πρὸς συνουσίαν παρορμᾷ διὰ τὸ
φυσῶδες καὶ πνευματικόν;

96. '' Διὰ τί τῶν παναγῶν παρθένων τὰς δια-
F φθαρείσας ἄλλως οὐ κολάζουσιν, ἀλλὰ ζώσας
κατορύττουσι; ''

Πότερον ὅτι καίουσι τοὺς ἀποθανόντας, θάπτειν
δὲ πυρὶ τὴν τὸ πῦρ τὸ θεῖον ὁσίως μὴ φυλάξασαν
οὐκ ἦν δίκαιον;

῍Η σῶμα ταῖς μεγίσταις καθωσιωμένον ἁγι-
στείαις ἀναιρεῖν καὶ προσφέρειν ἱερᾷ γυναικὶ χεῖρας
οὐ θεμιτὸν ἐνόμιζον; αὐτὴν οὖν ἀποθανεῖν μη-
χανώμενοι δι' αὐτῆς, κατεβίβαζον ὑπὸ γῆν εἰς
οἴκημα πεποιημένον, ὅπου καὶ λύχνος ἔκειτο καιό-

---

[a] Cf. Pliny, Natural History, xviii. 12 (118-119); Aulus
Gellius, x. 15. 12.

[b] Cf., for example, Juvenal, xv. 9 '' porrum et caepe nefas
violare et frangere morsu ''; Horace, Satires, ii. 6. 63;
Epistles, i. 12. 21.

[c] The numerous reasons suggested may be found in
Pauly-Wissowa, Real-Encyclopädie, vol. iii. coll. 619-620.

[d] Plutarch elsewhere uses a similar expression (παρθένος

95. WHY is it the customary rule that those who are practising holy living must abstain from legumes ? [a]

Did they, like the followers of Pythagoras,[b] religiously abstain from beans for the reasons which are commonly offered,[c] and from vetch and chickpea, because their names (*lathyros* and *erebinthos*) suggest Lethê and Erebus ?

Or is it because they make particular use of legumes for funeral feasts and invocations of the dead ?

Or is it rather because one must keep the body clean and light for purposes of holy living and lustration ? Now legumes are a flatulent food and produce surplus matter that requires much purgation.

Or is it because the windy and flatulent quality of the food stimulates desire ?

96. WHY do they inflict no other punishment on those of the Holy Maidens [d] who have been seduced, but bury them alive ? [e]

Is it because they cremate their dead, and to use fire in the burial of a woman who had not guarded the holy fire in purity was not right ?

Or did they believe it to be against divine ordinance to annihilate a body that had been consecrated by the greatest of lustral ceremonies, or to lay hands upon a holy woman ? Accordingly they devised that she should die of herself ; they conducted her underground into a chamber built there, in which had been placed a lighted lamp, a loaf of bread,

ἱέρεια) for the vestal virgins, *e.g.* in his *Life of Publicola*, chap. viii. (101 B) or *Moralia*, 89 E.

[e] Cf. *Life of Numa*, chap. x. (67 A-C) ; Ovid, *Fasti*, vi. 457-460 ; Dionysius of Halicarnassus, *Roman Antiquities*, ii. 67. 4, viii. 89. 5 ; Pliny, *Epistles*, iv. 11. 6.

μενος καὶ ἄρτος καὶ γάλακτός τι καὶ ὕδατος· εἶτα
287 γῇ τὸ οἴκημα κατέκρυπτον ἄνωθεν. καὶ οὐδὲ τοῦτον τὸν τρόπον ἀφοσιωσάμενοι τὴν δεισιδαιμονίαν
ἐκπεφεύγασιν, ἀλλὰ μέχρι νῦν ἐναγίζουσιν οἱ ἱερεῖς
ἐκεῖ βαδίζοντες ἐπὶ τὸν τόπον.

97. " Διὰ τί ταῖς Δεκεμβρίαις εἰδοῖς ἱππο-
δρομίας γενομένης ὁ νικήσας δεξιόσειρος[1] Ἄρει
θύεται, καὶ τὴν μὲν οὐρὰν ἀποκόψας τις ἐπὶ τὴν
Ῥηγίαν[2] καλουμένην κομίζει καὶ τὸν βωμὸν αἱμάτ-
τει, περὶ δὲ τῆς κεφαλῆς οἱ μὲν ἀπὸ τῆς ἱερᾶς
ὁδοῦ λεγομένης οἱ δ' ἀπὸ τῆς Συβούρης[3] κατα-
βάντες διαμάχονται; "

Πότερον, ὡς ἔνιοι λέγουσιν, ἵππῳ τὴν Τροίαν
ἡλωκέναι νομίζοντες ἵππον κολάζουσιν, ἅτε δὴ καὶ
γεγονότες

B   Τρώων ἀγλαὰ τέκνα μεμιγμένα παισὶ Λατίνων·

Ἢ ὅτι θυμοειδὲς καὶ πολεμικὸν καὶ ἀρήιον ὁ
ἵππος ἐστὶ τὰ δὲ προσφιλῆ μάλιστα καὶ πρόσφορα
θύουσι τοῖς θεοῖς, ὁ δὲ νικήσας θύεται διὰ τὸ νίκης
καὶ κράτους[4] οἰκεῖον εἶναι τὸν θεόν;

Ἢ μᾶλλον ὅτι τοῦ θεοῦ στάσιμον τὸ ἔργον ἐστὶ
καὶ νικῶσιν οἱ μένοντες ἐν τάξει τοὺς μὴ μένοντας
ἀλλὰ φεύγοντας, καὶ κολάζεται τὸ τάχος ὡς δειλίας
ἐφόδιον, καὶ μανθάνουσι συμβολικῶς ὅτι σωτήριον
οὐκ ἔστι τοῖς φεύγουσι;

---

[1] δεξιόσειρος Abresch : δεξιὸς ἱερὸς.
[2] Ῥηγίαν Life of Numa, chap. xiv. : ῥήγειναν.
[3] Συβούρης as elsewhere : σιβούρης.
[4] κράτους Meziriacus and E : κράτος.

144

and some milk and water. Thereafter they covered over the top of the chamber with earth. And yet not even by this manner of avoiding the guilt have they escaped their superstitious fear, but even to this day the priests proceed to this place and make offerings to the dead.

97. Why is it that after the chariot-race on the Ides of December [a] the right-hand trace-horse of the winning team is sacrificed to Mars, and then some-one cuts off its tail, and carries it to the place called Regia and sprinkles its blood on the altar, while some come down from the street called the Via Sacra, and some from the Subura, and fight for its head ?

Is it, as some [b] say, that they believe Troy to have been taken by means of a horse ; and therefore they punish it, since, forsooth, they are

Noble scions of Trojans commingled with children of Latins.[c]

Or is it because the horse is a spirited, warlike, and martial beast, and they sacrifice to the gods creatures that are particularly pleasing and appropriate for them ; and the winner is sacrificed because Mars is the specific divinity of victory and prowess ?

Or is it rather because the work of the god demands standing firm, and men that hold their ground defeat those that do not hold it, but flee ? And is swiftness punished as being the coward's resource, and do they learn symbolically that there is no safety for those who flee ?

[a] Presumably an error of Plutarch's : he means the tenth month, October : cf. Festus, s.v. October equus, p. 178. 5.
[b] Such as the historian Timaeus : cf. Polybius xii. 4b.
[c] A verse made in imitation of Homer, Il. xviii. 337 (or xxiii. 23), blended with a part of x. 424.

(287)   98. " Διὰ τί οἱ τιμηταὶ τὴν ἀρχὴν παραλαβόντες
οὐδὲν ἄλλο πράττουσι πρότερον[1] ἢ τὴν τροφὴν ἀπο-
C μισθοῦσι τῶν ἱερῶν χηνῶν καὶ τὴν γάνωσιν τοῦ
ἀγάλματος; "

Πότερον ἀπὸ τῶν εὐτελεστάτων ἀρχόμενοι καὶ
μὴ πολλῆς δεομένων δαπάνης μηδὲ πραγματείας;

Ἡ παλαιά τις αὕτη χάρις ἀπομνημονεύεται τοῖς
ζῴοις ἀπὸ τῶν Κελτικῶν, ὅτι τοὺς βαρβάρους
ὑπερβαίνοντας ἤδη τὸ περιτείχισμα τοῦ Καπε-
τωλίου νύκτωρ οἱ χῆνες ᾔσθοντο τῶν κυνῶν καθ-
ευδόντων καὶ βοῇ τοὺς φύλακας ἐπήγειραν;

Ἡ φύλακες ὄντες οἱ τιμηταὶ τῶν μεγίστων, καὶ
προσῆκον[2] ἐπισκοπεῖν καὶ πολυπραγμονεῖν αὐτοῖς
ἱερὰ καὶ δημόσια καὶ βίους καὶ ἤθη καὶ διαίτας, τὸ
φυλακτικώτατον ζῷον εὐθὺς ἐν λόγῳ τίθενται, καὶ
ἅμα τῇ τούτων ἐπιμελείᾳ προτρέπονται τοὺς πολί-
D τας μὴ ἀμελεῖν μηδὲ ῥᾳθυμεῖν τῶν ἱερῶν;

Ἡ δὲ γάνωσις τοῦ ἀγάλματος ἀναγκαία· ταχὺ
γὰρ ἐξανθεῖ τὸ μίλτινον, ᾧ τὰ παλαιὰ τῶν ἀγαλμάτων ἔχρωζον.

99. " Διὰ τί τῶν ἄλλων ἱερέων τὸν καταδικα-
σθέντα καὶ φυγόντα παύοντες ἕτερον αἱροῦνται,
τοῦ δ' αὔγουρος, ἕως ζῇ, κἂν ἐπὶ τοῖς μεγίστοις
ἀδικήμασι καταγνῶσιν, οὐκ ἀφαιροῦνται τὴν ἱερω-

[1] πρότερον Madvig: πρῶτον.
[2] προσῆκον] προσηκόντων in all mss. but one (προσήκοντος
Meziriacus).

---

[a] Cf. Pliny, Natural History, x. 22 (51).
[b] The statue of Jupiter Capitolinus: Pliny, Natural
History, xxxiii. 7 (112).

98. Why do the censors, when they take office, do nothing else before they contract for the food of the sacred geese [a] and the polishing of the statue ? [b]

Is it that they begin with the most trivial things, matters that require little expense or trouble ?

Or is this a commemoration of an old debt of gratitude owed to these creatures for their services in the Gallic wars ? [c] For when in the night the barbarians were already climbing over the rampart of the Capitol, the geese perceived the invaders, although the dogs were asleep, and waked the guards by their clamour.

Or is it because the censors are guardians of the most important matters, and, since it is their duty to oversee and to busy themselves with sacred and State affairs and with the lives, morals, and conduct of the people, they immediately take into account the most vigilant of creatures, and at the same time by their care of the geese they urge the citizens not to be careless or indifferent about sacred matters ?

But the polishing [d] of the statue is absolutely necessary ; for the red pigment, with which they used to tint ancient statues, rapidly loses its freshness.

99. Why is it that, if any one of the other priests is condemned and exiled, they depose him and elect another, but the augur, as long as he lives, even if they find him guilty of the worst offences, they do not

[c] Cf. 325 c-d, infra ; Life of Camillus, xxvii. (142 d ff.) ; Livy, v. 47 ; Dionysius of Halicarnassus, Roman Antiquities, xiii. 7-8 ; Diodorus, xiv. 116.

[d] The high polish of the Roman statues is very noticeable in contrast with the duller surface of Greek statues. This is one of the factors in the controversy over the genuineness of the Hermes of Praxiteles at Olympia.

(287) σύνην; ' αὔγουρας ' δὲ τοὺς ἐπὶ τῶν οἰωνῶν καλοῦσι."

Πότερον, ὡς ἔνιοι λέγουσι, βούλονται μηδένα τὰ τῶν ἱερῶν ἀπόρρητα γιγνώσκειν, ὃς οὐκ ἔστιν ἱερεύς;

῍Η κατειλημμένον ὅρκοις τὸν αὔγουρα μηδενὶ φράσειν τὰ τῶν ἱερῶν ἀπολῦσαι τῶν ὅρκων οὐ

E θέλουσιν ἰδιώτην γενόμενον;

῍Η τιμῆς οὐκ ἔστιν οὐδ' ἀρχῆς ἀλλ' ἐπιστήμης ὄνομα καὶ τέχνης ὁ αὔγουρ; ὅμοιον οὖν τῷ τὸν μουσικὸν ἀποψηφίσασθαι μουσικὸν μὴ εἶναι καὶ τὸν ἰατρὸν ἰατρὸν τὸ κωλύειν μάντιν εἶναι τὸν μάντιν, ἀφελέσθαι μὴ δυναμένους τὴν δύναμιν αὐτοῦ, κἂν ἀφέλωνται τὴν προσηγορίαν. ἄλλον δ' οὐ καθιστᾶσιν εἰκότως τὸν ἐξ ἀρχῆς ἀριθμὸν τῶν αὐγούρων φυλάττοντες.

100. '' Διὰ τί ταῖς Αὐγούσταις εἰδοῖς, Σεξτιλίαις δὲ πρότερον λεγομέναις, ἑορτάζουσιν αἵ τε δοῦλαι

F καὶ οἱ δοῦλοι πάντες, αἱ δὲ γυναῖκες μάλιστα ῥύπτεσθαι τὰς κεφαλὰς καὶ καθαίρειν[1] ἐπιτηδεύουσιν; ''

῍Η διὰ τὸ[2] Σερούιον τὸν βασιλέα κατὰ ταύτην τὴν ἡμέραν ἐξ αἰχμαλώτου γενέσθαι θεραπαινίδος ἄδειαν ἔργων ἔχουσιν οἱ θεράποντες, τὸ δὲ πλύνειν τὰς κεφαλὰς ἀρξάμενον ἀπὸ τῶν θεραπαινίδων διὰ τὴν ἑορτὴν ἄχρι τῶν ἐλευθέρων προῆλθεν;

101. '' Διὰ τί κοσμοῦσι τοὺς παῖδας τοῖς περιδεραίοις, ἃ βούλλας καλοῦσι; ''

Πότερον ἐπὶ τιμῇ τῶν ἡρπασμένων γυναικῶν,

---

[1] καθαίρειν] καθαίρεσθαι in one ms. (E).
[2] τὸ Bernardakis and one ms.: τὸν.

deprive of his priesthood ? [a] They call " augurs " the men who are in charge of the omens.

Is it, as some say, because they wish no one who is not a priest to know the secrets of the holy rites ?

Or, because the augur is bound by oaths to reveal the sacred matters to no one, are they unwilling to release him from his oath as would be the case if he had been reduced to private status ?

Or is " augur " a name denoting, not a rank or office, but knowledge and skill ? Then to prevent a soothsayer from being a soothsayer would be like voting that a musician shall not be a musician, nor a physician a physician ; for they cannot deprive him of his ability, even if they take away his title. They naturally appoint no successor since they keep the original number of augurs.

100. WHY is it that on the Ides of August, formerly called Sextilis, all the slaves, female and male, keep holiday, and the Roman women make a particular practice of washing and cleansing their heads ?

Do the servants have release from work because on this day King Servius was born from a captive maid-servant ? [b] And did the washing of their heads begin with the slave-women, because of their holiday, and extend itself to free-born women ?

101. WHY do they adorn their children's necks with amulets which they call *bullae* ? [c]

Was it, like many another thing, in honour of their

---

[a] *Cf.* Pliny, *Letters*, iv. 8. 1.
[b] *Cf.* 323 B-C, *infra.*
[c] *Cf. Life of Romulus*, xx. (30 c) ; Pliny, *Natural History*, xxxiii. 1 (10) ; Macrobius, *Saturnalia*, i. 6. 7-17.

ὥσπερ ἄλλα πολλά, καὶ τοῦτ᾽ ἐψηφίσαντο τοῖς ἐξ
αὐτῶν γεννωμένοις ὑπάρχειν;

"Η τὴν Ταρκυνίου τιμῶντες ἀνδραγαθίαν; λέγεται γὰρ ἔτι παῖς ὢν ἐν τῇ μάχῃ τῇ πρὸς Λατίνους
238 ἅμα καὶ Τυρρηνοὺς ἐμβαλεῖν εἰς τοὺς πολεμίους,
ἀπορρυεὶς δὲ τοῦ ἵππου καὶ τοὺς ἐπιφερομένους
ἰταμῶς ὑποστὰς ἐπιρρῶσαι τοὺς ῾Ρωμαίους· γενομένης δὲ λαμπρᾶς τροπῆς τῶν πολεμίων καὶ μυρίων
ἑξακισχιλίων ἀναιρεθέντων, τοῦτο λαβεῖν ἀριστεῖον
παρὰ τοῦ πατρὸς καὶ βασιλέως.

"Η τοῖς παλαιοῖς οἰκετῶν μὲν ἐρᾶν ὥραν ἐχόντων
οὐκ ἦν ἄδοξον οὐδ᾽ αἰσχρόν, ὡς ἔτι νῦν αἱ κωμῳ-
δίαι μαρτυροῦσιν, ἐλευθέρων δὲ παίδων ἰσχυρῶς
ἀπείχοντο,[1] καὶ ὅπως μηδὲ γυμνοῖς ἐντυχόντες
B ἀμφιγνοήσειαν, ἐφόρουν οἱ παῖδες τὸ παράσημον;

"Η καὶ πρὸς εὐταξίαν ἐστὶ φυλακτήριον τοῦτο,
καὶ τρόπον τινὰ τοῦ ἀκολάστου χαλινός, αἰσχυ-
νομένων ἀνδροῦσθαι πρὶν ἢ τὸ παιδικὸν ἀποθέσθαι
παράσημον;

"Ο μὲν γὰρ οἱ περὶ Βάρρωνα λέγουσιν οὐ πιθανόν
ἐστι, τῆς βουλῆς[2] ὑπὸ Αἰολέων βόλλας προσ-
αγορευομένης, τοῦτο σύμβολον εὐβουλίας περιτίθε-
σθαι τοὺς παῖδας.

'Αλλ᾽ ὅρα μὴ καὶ τοῦτο διὰ τὴν σελήνην φοροῦσι.
τὸ γὰρ φαινόμενον σχῆμα τῆς σελήνης, ὅταν ᾖ
διχόμηνος, οὐ σφαιροειδὲς ἀλλὰ φακοειδές ἐστι καὶ

---

[1] ἰσχυρῶς ἀπείχοντο] παντελῶς ἀπέσχοντο in one ms. (E), and
παντελῶς may well be right.
[2] βουλῆς Xylander and Meziriacus: βούλλης.

150

wives, who had been made theirs by force, that they voted this also as a traditional ornament for the children born from them ?

Or is it to honour the manly courage of Tarquin ? For the tale is told that, while he was still but a boy, in the battle against the combined Latin and Etruscan forces he charged straight into the enemy ; and although he was thrown from his horse, he boldly withstood those that hurled themselves upon him, and thus gave renewed strength to the Romans. A brilliant rout of the enemy followed, sixteen thousand were killed, and he received this amulet as a prize of valour from his father the king.

Or did the Romans of early times account it not disreputable nor disgraceful to love male slaves in the flower of youth, as even now their comedies [a] testify, but they strictly refrained from boys of free birth ; and that they might not be in any uncertainty, even when they encountered them unclad, did the boys wear this badge ?

Or is this a safeguard to insure orderly conduct, a sort of bridle on incontinence, that they may be ashamed to pose as men before they have put off the badge of childhood ?

What Varro and his school say is not credible : that since *boulê* (counsel) is called *bolla* by the Aeolians, the boys put on this ornament as a symbol of good counsel.

But consider whether they may not wear it because of the moon. For the visible shape of the moon at the first quarter is not like a sphere, but like a lentil-

---

[a] The so-called *togatae*, of which no complete specimen has survived ; the *palliatae* of Plautus and Terence, being based on the Greek New Comedy, would prove nothing.

(288) δισκοειδές, ὡς δ' Ἐμπεδοκλῆς οἴεται, καὶ τὸ ὑποκείμενον.

102. " Διὰ τί τῶν παίδων τοῖς μὲν ἄρρεσιν ἐνα-
C ταίοις, τοῖς δὲ θήλεσιν ὀγδοαίοις τὰ ὀνόματα τίθενται; "

"Ἢ τὸ μὲν προτέροις τοῖς θήλεσιν αἰτίαν ἔχει τὴν φύσιν; καὶ γὰρ αὔξεται τὸ θῆλυ καὶ ἀκμάζει καὶ τελειοῦται πρότερον τοῦ ἄρρενος. τῶν δ' ἡμε-ρῶν τὰς μετὰ τὴν ἑβδόμην λαμβάνουσιν· ἡ γὰρ ἑβδόμη σφαλερὰ τοῖς νεογνοῖς πρός τε τἆλλα καὶ τὸν ὀμφαλόν· ἑβδομαῖος γὰρ ἀπολύεται τοῖς πλείστοις· ἕως δ'[1] ἀπολυθῇ, φυτῷ μᾶλλον ἢ ζῴῳ προσέοικε τὸ νήπιον.

D "Ἢ καθάπερ οἱ Πυθαγορικοὶ τοῦ ἀριθμοῦ τὸν μὲν ἄρτιον θῆλυν ἄρρενα δὲ τὸν περιττὸν ἐνόμιζον; γόνιμος γάρ ἐστι καὶ κρατεῖ τοῦ ἀρτίου συν-τιθέμενος. καὶ διαιρουμένων εἰς τὰς μονάδας ὁ μὲν ἄρτιος καθάπερ τὸ θῆλυ χώραν μεταξὺ κενὴν ἐνδίδωσι, τοῦ δὲ περιττοῦ μόριον ἀεί τι πλῆρες ὑπολείπεται· διὸ τὸν μὲν ἄρρενι τὸν δὲ θήλει πρόσφορον νομίζουσιν.

"Ἢ ὅτι τῶν ἀριθμῶν ἁπάντων τὰ μὲν ἐννέα πρῶ-τός ἐστι τετράγωνος ἀπὸ περιττοῦ καὶ τελείου τῆς τριάδος, τὰ δ' ὀκτὼ πρῶτος κύβος ἀπὸ ἀρτίου τῆς δυάδος· δεῖ δὲ τὸν μὲν ἄνδρα[2] τετράγωνον εἶναι καὶ περιττὸν καὶ τέλειον, τὴν δὲ γυναῖκα καθάπερ
E τὸν κύβον ἑδραῖον καὶ οἰκουρὸν καὶ δυσμετακίνητον.

---

[1] δ'] δ' ἂν Bernardakis, but not necessarily required.
[2] ἄνδρα added by Polus and found in one ms.

---

[a] Cf. Moralia, 891 c ; Diogenes Laertius, viii. 77 ; Diels, Frag. der Vorsokratiker, i. p. 210, A 60.

seed or a quoit ; and, as Empedocles [a] thinks, so also is the matter of which the moon is composed.

102. Why do they name boys when they are nine days old, but girls when they are eight days old ?

Does the precedence of the girls have Nature as its cause ? It is a fact that the female grows up, and attains maturity and perfection before the male. As for the days, they take those that follow the seventh ; for the seventh is dangerous for newly-born children in various ways and in the matter of the umbilical cord ; for in most cases this comes away on the seventh day ; but until it comes off, the child is more like a plant than an animal.[b]

Or did they, like the adherents of Pythagoras, regard the even number as female and the odd number as male ?[c] For the odd number is generative, and, when it is added to the even number, it prevails over it. And also, when they are divided into units, the even number, like the female, yields a vacant space between, while of the odd number an integral part always remains. Wherefore they think that the odd is suitable for the male, and the even for the female.

Or is it that of all numbers nine [d] is the first square from the odd and perfect triad, while eight is the first cube from the even dyad ? Now a man should be four-square,[e] eminent, and perfect ; but a woman, like a cube, should be stable, domestic, and difficult to remove from her place. And this should be added,

[b] Cf. Aulus Gellius, xvi. 16. 2-3.
[c] Cf. 264 A, supra.
[d] Cf. Moralia, 744 A-B.
[e] Cf. Bergk, Poet. Lyr. Graec., Simonides, Frag. 5 (or Edmonds, Lyra Graeca, in L.C.L. ii. p. 284).

(288) τοῦτο δὲ προσληπτέον ὅτι τὰ μὲν ὀκτὼ κύβος ἐστὶν
ἀπὸ δυάδος, τὰ δ᾽ ἐννέα τετράγωνος ἀπὸ τριάδος·
χρῶνται δὲ δυσὶ μὲν ὀνόμασιν αἱ θήλειαι τρισὶ δ᾽ οἱ
ἄρρενες.

103. " Διὰ τί τοὺς ἀπάτορας ' σπορίους ' υἱοὺς
καλοῦσιν; "

Οὐ γάρ, ὡς Ἕλληνες νομίζουσι καὶ λέγουσιν
οἱ ῥήτορες ἐν ταῖς δίκαις, συμφορητοῦ τινος καὶ
κοινοῦ σπέρματος γεγόνασιν, ἀλλ᾽ ἔστιν ὁ Σπόριος
τῶν πρώτων ὀνομάτων, ὡς ὁ Σέξτος καὶ ὁ Δέκιμος
καὶ ὁ Γάιος. τὰ δὲ πρῶτα τῶν ὀνομάτων οὐχ
ὁλογραφοῦσιν ἀλλ᾽ ἢ δι᾽ ἑνὸς γράμματος, ὡς τὸν
Τίτον καὶ τὸν Λούκιον καὶ τὸν Μᾶρκον, ἢ διὰ
δυοῖν, ὡς τὸν Τιβέριον καὶ τὸν Γναῖον, ἢ διὰ
τριῶν, ὡς τὸν Σέξτον καὶ τὸν Σερούιον. ἔστιν οὖν
καὶ ὁ Σπόριος τῶν διὰ δυοῖν γραφομένων, τοῦ σ
F καὶ τοῦ π. γράφουσι δὲ διὰ τούτων καὶ τοὺς
ἀπάτορας " σίνε πάτρε[1] " οἷον ἄνευ πατρός, τῷ μὲν
σ τὸ " σίνε " τῷ δὲ π τὸ " πάτρε "[1] σημαίνοντες.
τοῦτ᾽ οὖν τὴν πλάνην ἐποίησε, τὸ διὰ τῶν αὐτῶν
γραμμάτων τὸ " σίνε πάτρε "[1] καὶ τὸν Σπόριον
γράφεσθαι.

Λεκτέον δὲ καὶ τὸν ἕτερον λόγον, ἔστι δ᾽ ἀτοπώ-
τερος· τοὺς γὰρ Σαβίνους φασὶ τὸ τῆς γυναικὸς
αἰδοῖον ὀνομάζειν σπόριον, εἶθ᾽ οἷον ἐφυβρίζοντας
οὕτω προσαγορεύειν τὸν ἐκ γυναικὸς ἀγάμου καὶ
ἀνεγγύου γεγενημένον.

104. " Διὰ τί τὸν Διόνυσον ' Λίβερουμ Πάτρεμ '
καλοῦσι; "

---

[1] πάτρε an obvious correction : πάτρις.

154

that eight is the cube of two and nine the square of three ; women have two names, men have three.

103. Why do they call children of unknown fathers *spurii* ? [a]

Now the reason is not, as the Greeks believe and lawyers in court are wont to assert, that these children are begotten of some promiscuous and common seed ; but Spurius is a first name like Sextus and Decimus and Gaius. They do not write first names in full, but by one letter, as Titus (T.) and Lucius (L.) and Marcus (M.) ; or by two, as Tiberius (Ti.) and Gnaeus (Cn.) ; or by three, as Sextus (Sex.) and Servius (Ser.). Spurius, then, is one of those written by two letters : Sp. And by these two letters they also denote children of unknown fathers, *sine patre,*[b] that is " without a father " ; by the *s* they indicate *sine* and by the *p patre.* This, then, caused the error, the writing of the same abbreviation for *sine patre* and for Spurius.

I must state the other explanation also, but it is somewhat absurd : They assert that the Sabines use the word *spurius* for the *pudenda muliebria*, and it later came about that they called the child born of an unmarried, unespoused woman by this name, as if in mockery.

104. Why do they call Bacchus *Liber Pater* (" Free Father ") ? [c]

[a] *Cf.* Gaius, *Institutiones*, i. 64 ; Valerius Maximus, *De Praenominibus*, 6 (p. 590 of Kempf's ed.).
[b] The MSS. have *sine patris* ; did Plutarch, or some Greek copyist, confuse the Latin genitive and ablative, since they are one in Greek ?
[c] *Cf.* Petronius, *Satyricon*, 41, and Housman's commentary in *Classical Review*, xxxii. p. 164.

Πότερον ὡς ἐλευθερίας πατέρα τοῖς πιοῦσι γιγ-
289 νόμενον; γίγνονται γὰρ οἱ πολλοὶ θρασεῖς καὶ
παρρησίας ὑποπιμπλῶνται περὶ τὰς μέθας· ἢ ὅτι
τὴν λοιβὴν παρέσχεν; ἤ, ὡς Ἀλέξανδρός φησιν,
ἀπὸ τοῦ περὶ¹ Ἐλευθερὰς τῆς Βοιωτίας Ἐλευθερέως Διονύσου προσαγορευομένου;

105. " Διὰ τίνα αἰτίαν ἐν ταῖς δημοσίαις ἑορταῖς
ἔθος οὐκ ἔστι γαμεῖσθαι παρθένους, αἱ δὲ χῆραι
γαμοῦνται; "

Πότερον, ὡς ὁ Βάρρων εἴρηκεν, ὅτι λυπούμεναι
μὲν αἱ παρθένοι γαμοῦνται, χαίρουσαι² δ' αἱ γυναῖκες, ἑορτῇ δὲ δεῖ³ μηδὲν λυπουμένους ποιεῖν
μηδὲ πρὸς ἀνάγκην;

Ἢ μᾶλλον ὅτι ταῖς μὲν παρθένοις καλὸν μὴ
B ὀλίγων ταῖς δὲ χῆραις αἰσχρὸν πολλῶν παρόντων⁴
γαμεῖσθαι; ζηλωτὸς γὰρ ὁ πρῶτος γάμος ὁ δὲ
δεύτερος ἀπευκταῖος· αἰσχύνονται γάρ, ἂν ζώντων
τῶν προτέρων ἑτέρους λαμβάνωσιν, ὀδύρονται δέ,
ἂν ἀποθανόντων. ὅθεν ἡσυχίᾳ χαίρουσι μᾶλλον ἢ
θορύβοις καὶ προπομπαῖς. αἱ δ' ἑορταὶ περισπῶσι
τοὺς πολλούς, ὥστε τοῖς τοιούτοις μὴ σχολάζειν.

Ἢ ὅτι καὶ τὰς Σαβίνων θυγατέρας ἁρπάσαντες
ἐν ἑορτῇ παρθένους οὔσας εἰς πόλεμον κατέστησαν,
ἐξοιωνίσαντο τὸ γαμεῖν παρθένους ἐν ἱεραῖς
ἡμέραις;

---

¹ περὶ] παρ' in one ms. (E).
² χαίρουσαι E : χαίρουσι.
³ δὲ δεῖ Wyttenbach : δὲ.
⁴ παρόντων Meziriacus : ὄντων.

Is it because he is the father of freedom to drinkers?
For most people become bold and are abounding in
frank speech when they are in their cups.[a] Or is
it because he has provided the means for libations?
Or is it derived, as Alexander [b] asserts, from Dionysus
Eleuthereus,[c] so named from Eleutherae in Boeotia?

105. FOR what reason is it not the custom for
maidens to marry on public holidays, but widows do
marry at this time? [d]

Is it, as Varro has remarked, that maidens are
grieved over marrying, but older women are glad,
and on a holiday one should do nothing in grief or
by constraint?

Or is it rather because it is seemly that not a few
should be present when maidens marry, but disgraceful that many should be present when widows
marry? Now the first marriage is enviable; but
the second is to be deprecated, for women are
ashamed if they take a second husband while the
first husband is still living, and they feel sad if they
do so when he is dead. Wherefore they rejoice
in a quiet wedding rather than in noise and processions. Holidays distract most people, so that they
have no leisure for such matters.

Or, because they seized the maiden daughters of
the Sabines at a holiday festival, and thereby became involved in war, did they come to regard it as
ill-omened to marry maidens on holy days?

[a] Cf. Moralia, 716 B.
[b] Müller, Frag. Hist. Graec. iii. p. 244; Alexander
Polyhistor.
[c] Cf. the inscription on the chair of the priest of Dionysus
in the theatre at Athens, Ἱερέως Διονύσου Ἐλευθερέως.
[d] Cf. Macrobius, Saturnalia, i. 15. 21.

(289)   106. " Διὰ τί Ῥωμαῖοι Τύχην σέβονται Πριμι-
γένειαν, ἣν ἄν τις εἴποι πρωτογένειαν;"

C   Ἀρ᾽ ὅτι Σερουίῳ κατὰ τύχην, ὥς φασιν, ἐκ
θεραπαινίδος γενομένῳ βασιλεῦσαι τῆς Ῥώμης
ἐπιφανῶς ὑπῆρξεν; οὕτω γὰρ οἱ πολλοὶ Ῥωμαίων
ὑπειλήφασιν.

Ἦ μᾶλλον ὅτι τῆς Ῥώμης ἡ τύχη παρέσχε τὴν
ἀρχὴν καὶ τὴν γένεσιν;

Ἦ φυσικώτερον ἔχει λόγον τὸ πρᾶγμα καὶ
φιλοσοφώτερον, ὡς τὴν τύχην πάντων οὖσαν ἀρχὴν
καὶ τὴν φύσιν ἐκ τοῦ κατὰ τύχην συνισταμένην,
ὅταν τισὶν ὡς ἔτυχεν ἀποκειμένοις[1] τάξις ἐγ-
γένηται;

107. " Διὰ τί τοὺς περὶ τὸν Διόνυσον τεχνίτας
' ἱστρίωνας ' Ῥωμαῖοι καλοῦσιν;"

Ἦ δι᾽ ἣν αἰτίαν Κλούβιος Ῥοῦφος ἱστόρηκε;
D φησὶ γὰρ ἐν τοῖς πάνυ παλαιοῖς χρόνοις Γαΐου τε
Σουλπικίου καὶ Λικινίου Στόλωνος ὑπατευόντων,
λοιμώδη νόσον ἐν Ῥώμῃ γενομένην πάντας ὁμαλῶς
διαφθεῖραι τοὺς ἐπὶ σκηνὴν προερχομένους· δεη-
θεῖσιν οὖν αὐτοῖς ἐκ Τυρρηνίας ἐλθεῖν πολλοὺς καὶ
ἀγαθοὺς τεχνίτας, ὧν τὸν πρωτεύοντα δόξῃ καὶ
χρόνον[2] πλεῖστον ἐνευημεροῦντα τοῖς θεάτροις Ἴ-
στρον ὀνομάζεσθαι· καὶ διὰ τοῦτο πάντας " ἱστρίωνας " ἀπ᾽ ἐκείνου προσαγορεύεσθαι.

---

[1] ἀποκειμένοις] ὑποκειμένοις E. Kurtz.
[2] χρόνον Dübner: χρόνῳ.

158

106. Why do the Romans reverence Fortuna Primigenia,[a] or " First-born," as one might translate it ?

Is it because by Fortune, as they say, it befell Servius, born of a maidservant, to become a famous king of Rome ? This is the assumption which the majority of Romans make.

Or is it rather because Fortune supplied the origin and birth of Rome ?[b]

Or does the matter have an explanation more natural and philosophic, which assumes that Fortune is the origin of everything, and Nature acquires its solid frame by the operation of Fortune, whenever order is created in any store of matter gathered together at haphazard.

107. Why do the Romans call the Dionysiac artists [c] *histriones* [d] ?

Is it for the reason that Cluvius Rufus [e] has recorded ? For he states that in very ancient times, in the consulship of Gaius Sulpicius and Licinius Stolo,[f] a pestilential disease arose in Rome and destroyed to a man all persons appearing on the stage. Accordingly, at the request of the Romans, there came many excellent artists from Etruria, of whom the first in repute and the one who for the longest time enjoyed success in their theatres, was named Hister ; and therefore all actors are named *histriones* from him.

[a] Cf. 281 E, *supra*, 322 F, *infra* ; Cicero, *De Legibus*, ii. 11 ; Livy, xxxiv. 53.
[b] Cf. 320 B ff., *infra*.   [c] Cf. *Moralia*, 87 F.
[d] Cf. Livy, vii. 2 ; closely followed by Valerius Maximus, ii. 4. 4.
[e] Peter, *Frag. Hist. Rom.* p. 314, Cluvius, Frag. 4.
[f] In 361 B.C.

(289)   108. '' Διὰ τί δὲ τὰς ἐγγὺς γένους οὐ γαμοῦσι; ''

Πότερον αὔξειν τοῖς γάμοις βουλόμενοι τὰς οἰκειότητας καὶ συγγενεῖς πολλοὺς ἐπικτᾶσθαι, E διδόντες ἑτέροις καὶ λαμβάνοντες παρ' ἑτέρων γυναῖκας;

'Ἢ φοβούμενοι τὰς ἐν τοῖς γάμοις τῶν συγγενῶν διαφορὰς ὡς τὰ φύσει δίκαια προσαπολλυούσας;

'Ἢ πολλῶν βοηθῶν τὰς γυναῖκας ὁρῶντες δι' ἀσθένειαν δεομένας, οὐκ ἐβούλοντο τὰς ἐγγὺς γένους συνοικίζειν, ὅπως, ἂν οἱ ἄνδρες ἀδικῶσιν αὐτάς, οἱ συγγενεῖς βοηθῶσιν;

109. '' Διὰ τί τῷ ἱερεῖ τοῦ Διός, ὃν Φλάμινα Διᾶλιν καλοῦσιν, οὐκ ἐξῆν ἀλεύρου θιγεῖν, οὐδὲ ζύμης; ''

'Ἢ τὸ μὲν ἄλευρον ἀτελὴς τροφὴ καὶ ἄπεπτός ἐστιν; οὔτε γὰρ ὃ ἦν μεμένηκεν ὁ πυρὸς οὔθ' ὃ δεῖ γενέσθαι γέγονεν ὁ ἄρτος, ἀλλὰ καὶ τὴν σπέρματος F δύναμιν ἀπολώλεκεν ἅμα καὶ τὴν σιτίου χρείαν οὐκ ἔσχηκε. διὸ καὶ '' μυλήφατον '' ὁ ποιητὴς '' ἄλφιτον '' ἐκ μεταφορᾶς ὠνόμασεν[1] ὥσπερ φονευόμενον ἐν τῷ ἀλέτῳ καὶ φθειρόμενον.

'Ἡ δὲ ζύμη καὶ γέγονεν ἐκ φθορᾶς αὐτὴ καὶ φθείρει τὸ φύραμα μειγνυμένη· γίγνεται γὰρ ἄτονον καὶ ἀδρανὲς καὶ ὅλως ἔοικε σῆψις ἡ ζύμωσις εἶναι· πλεονάσασα γοῦν ἀποξύνει παντάπασι καὶ φθείρει τὸ ἄλευρον.

---

[1] ὠνόμασεν] ὠνόμακεν in all mss. except E.

---

^a Cf. Aulus Gellius, x. 15. 19.
^b Homer, Od. ii. 355 : '' mill-slaughtered.''
^c Cf. Moralia, 659 B.

108. WHY do they not marry women who are closely akin to them ?

Do they wish to enlarge their relationships by marriage and to acquire many additional kinsmen by bestowing wives upon others and receiving wives from others ?

Or do they fear the disagreements which arise in marriages of near kin, on the ground that these tend to destroy natural rights ?

Or, since they observed that women by reason of their weakness need many protectors, were they not willing to take as partners in their household women closely akin to them, so that if their husbands wronged them, their kinsmen might bring them succour ?

109. WHY was it not permitted for the priest of Jupiter, whom they call the *Flamen Dialis*, to touch either flour or yeast ? [a]

Is it because flour is an incomplete and crude food ? For neither has it remained what it was, wheat, nor has it become what it must become, bread ; but it has both lost the germinative power of the seed and at the same time it has not attained to the usefulness of food. Wherefore also the Poet by a metaphor applied to barley-meal the epithet *mylephatos*,[b] as if it were being killed or destroyed in the grinding.

Yeast is itself also the product of corruption, and produces corruption in the dough with which it is mixed ; for the dough becomes flabby and inert, and altogether the process of leavening seems to be one of putrefaction [c] ; at any rate if it goes too far, it completely sours and spoils the flour.

110. "Διὰ τί καὶ σαρκὸς ὠμῆς ἀπείρηται τῷ ἱερεῖ ψαύειν;"

Πότερον ὠμοφαγίας πάνυ πόρρωθεν ἀποτρέπει τὸ ἔθος, ἢ δι' ἣν τὸ ἄλευρον αἰτίαν ἀφοσιοῦνται καὶ τὸ 290 κρέας; οὔτε γάρ ἐστι ζῷον οὔτ' ὄψον ἤδη γέγονεν. ἡ γὰρ ἕψησις καὶ ὄπτησις ἀλλοίωσις οὖσα καὶ μετακόσμησις ἐξίστησι τὴν μορφήν, τὸ δὲ πρόσφατον καὶ ὠμὸν οὐδὲ τὴν ὄψιν ἔχει καθαρὰν καὶ ἀμίαντον, ἀλλ' εἰδεχθῆ καὶ ἑλκώδη.

111. "Διὰ τί δὲ κυνὸς καὶ αἰγὸς ἐκέλευον ἀπέχεσθαι τὸν ἱερέα, μήθ' ἁπτόμενον μήτ' ὀνομάζοντα;"

Πότερον τῆς μὲν αἰγὸς βδελυττόμενοι τὸ ἀκόλαστον καὶ δυσῶδες, ἢ φοβούμενοι τὸ νοσηματικόν; δοκεῖ γὰρ ἐπιληψίᾳ καταλαμβάνεσθαι μάλιστα τῶν ζῴων καὶ προσαναχρώννυσθαι τοῖς φαγοῦσιν ἢ θιγοῦσιν ὑπὸ τοῦ πάθους ἐχομένης.[1] αἰτίαν δὲ B λέγουσι τὴν στενότητα τῶν πνευματικῶν πόρων πολλάκις ἐπιλαμβανομένων,[2] τεκμαιρόμενοι τῇ λεπτότητι τῆς φωνῆς. καὶ γὰρ ἀνθρώπων ὅσοις ἐπιληπτίζουσι συμβαίνει φθέγγεσθαι, μηκασμῷ παραπλησίαν φωνὴν ἀφιᾶσι.

Τῷ δὲ κυνὶ τοῦ μὲν ἀκολάστου καὶ δυσώδους ἧττον ἴσως μέτεστι· καίτοι φασὶν ἔνιοι μήτε τῆς Ἀθηναίων ἀκροπόλεως ἐπιβαίνειν κύνα μήτε τῆς Δηλίων νήσου διὰ τὴν ἐμφανῆ μεῖξιν, ὥσπερ βοῶν καὶ συῶν καὶ ἵππων ἐν θαλάμοις ἀλλ'

---

[1] ἐχομένης] ἐχομένοις in most mss.
[2] ἐπιλαμβανομένων F.C.B.: ἐπιλαμβανομένην.

110. Why is this priest also forbidden to touch raw flesh?

Is this custom intended to deter people completely from eating raw meat, or do they scrupulously repudiate flesh for the same reason as flour? For neither is it a living creature nor has it yet become a cooked food. Now boiling or roasting, being a sort of alteration and mutation, eliminates the previous form; but fresh raw meat does not have a clean and unsullied appearance, but one that is repulsive, like a fresh wound.

111. Why did they bid the priest avoid the dog and the goat, neither touching them nor naming them?

Did they loathe the goat's lasciviousness and foul odour, or did they fear its susceptibility to disease? For it is thought to be subject to epilepsy beyond all other animals, and to infect persons who eat it [a] or touch it when it is possessed of the disease. The reason, they say, is the narrowness of the air passages, which are often suddenly contracted; this they deduce from the thinness of its voice. So also in the case of men, if they chance to speak during an epileptic fit, the sound they make is very like a bleat.

The dog has, perhaps, less of lasciviousness and foul odour. Some, however, assert that a dog may not enter either the Athenian acropolis [b] or the island of Delos [c] because of its open mating, as if cattle and swine and horses mated within the walls of a chamber

[a] Contrast Pliny, *Natural History*, xxviii. 16 (226), who says that goat's meat was given for epilepsy.

[b] *Cf. Comparison of Demetrius and Antony*, chap. iv. (95-97 B); Dionysius of Halicarnassus, *De Dinarcho*, 3.

[c] *Cf.* Strabo, x. 5. 5, p. 684 (Meineke).

(290) οὐκ ἐμφανῶς καὶ ἀνέδην ὀχευόντων. τὴν γὰρ
ἀληθινὴν αἰτίαν ἀγνοοῦσιν ὅτι μάχιμον ὄντα τὸν
C κύνα τῶν ἀσύλων καὶ ἁγίων ἐξείργουσιν ἱερῶν,
ἀσφαλῆ καταφυγὴν τοῖς ἱκέταις διδόντες. εἰκὸς
μὲν οὖν ἐστι καὶ τὸν ἱερέα τοῦ Διὸς ὥσπερ ἔμψυχον
καὶ ἱερὸν ἄγαλμα[1] καταφύξιμον ἀνεῖσθαι τοῖς δεομένοις καὶ ἱκετεύουσι, μηδενὸς ἀπείργοντος μηδ'
ἐκφοβοῦντος. διὸ κλινίδιον μὲν ἦν αὐτοῦ κείμενον
ἐν τῷ θυρῶνι τῆς οἰκίας· ὁ δὲ προσπεσὼν τοῖς
γόνασι τὴν ἡμέραν ἐκείνην ἄδειαν εἶχε πληγῶν καὶ
κολάσεως· εἰ δὲ δεσμώτης φθαίη[2] προσελθών,
ἐλύετο· τοὺς δὲ δεσμοὺς ἐκτὸς οὐ κατὰ θύρας
ἀλλ' ὑπὲρ τοῦ στέγους ἀπερρίπτουν. οὐδὲν οὖν
ὄφελος ἦν οὕτως αὐτὸν ἥμερον παρέχειν καὶ φιλάνθρωπον, εἰ κύων προειστήκει δεδιττόμενος καὶ
ἀπερύκων τοὺς προσφυγεῖν δεομένους.

D Οὐ μὴν οὐδὲ καθαρεύειν ᾤοντο παντάπασιν οἱ
παλαιοὶ τὸ ζῷον· καὶ γὰρ Ὀλυμπίων μὲν[3] οὐδενὶ
θεῶν καθιέρωται, χθονίᾳ δὲ δεῖπνον Ἑκάτῃ πεμπό-
μενος εἰς τριόδους ἀποτροπαίων καὶ καθαρσίων
ἐπέχει μοῖραν. ἐν δὲ Λακεδαίμονι τῷ φονικωτάτῳ
θεῶν Ἐνυαλίῳ σκύλακας ἐντέμνουσι· Βοιωτοῖς δὲ
δημοσίᾳ καθαρμός ἐστι κυνὸς διχοτομηθέντος τῶν
μερῶν διεξελθεῖν· αὐτοὶ δὲ Ῥωμαῖοι τοῖς Λυκαίοις,
ἃ Λουπερκάλια καλοῦσιν, ἐν τῷ καθαρσίῳ μηνὶ
κύνα θύουσιν. ὅθεν οὐκ ἀπὸ τρόπου τοῖς
τὸν ὑπέρτατον καὶ καθαρώτατον εἰληφόσι[4] θερα-

---

[1] ἄγαλμα Dübner : καὶ ἄγαλμα or ἄγαλμα καί.
[2] φθαίη] ἔφθη in one ms. (E).
[3] καὶ γὰρ Ὀλυμπίων μὲν Wyttenbach : (καὶ) ὀλυμπίων μὲν
γάρ.
[4] εἰληφόσι] εἰληχόσι H. Richards and Kronenberg.

and not openly and without restraint! For these persons are ignorant of the true reason: because the dog is a belligerent creature they exclude it from inviolable and holy shrines, thereby offering a safe place of refuge for suppliants. Accordingly it is likely that the priest of Jupiter also, since he is, as it were, the animate embodiment and sacred image of the god, should be left free as a refuge for petitioners and suppliants, with no one to hinder them or to frighten them away. For this reason his couch was placed in the vestibule of his house, and anyone who fell at his knees had immunity from beating or chastisement all that day; and if any prisoner succeeded in reaching the priest, he was set free, and his chains they threw outside, not by the doors, but over the roof. So it would have been of no avail for him to render himself so gentle and humane, if a dog had stood before him frightening and keeping away those who had need of a place of refuge.

Nor, in fact, did the men of old think that this animal was wholly pure, for it was never sacrificed to any of the Olympian gods; and when it is sent to the cross-roads as a supper for the earth-goddess Hecatê,[a] it has its due portion among sacrifices that avert and expiate evil. In Sparta they immolate puppies to the bloodiest of the gods, Enyalius; and in Boeotia the ceremony of public purification is to pass between the parts of a dog which has been cut in twain. The Romans themselves, in the month of purification,[b] at the Wolf Festival, which they call the Lupercalia, sacrifice a dog. Hence it is not out of keeping that those who have attained to the office of serving the

---

[a] Cf. 277 B, 280 C, supra; Life of Romulus, xxi. (31 E).

[b] February; cf. 280 B, supra.

πεύειν θεὸν ἀπειρῆσθαι κύνα ποιεῖσθαι συνήθη καὶ σύνοικον.

E   112. " Διὰ τίνα δ' αἰτίαν οὐδὲ κιττοῦ θιγεῖν ἐφεῖτο[1] τῷ ἱερεῖ τοῦ Διός, οὐδ' ὁδὸν διελθεῖν ἀναδενδράδος ἄνωθεν διατεταμένης; "

"Ἡ τοῦτο μὲν ὅμοιόν ἐστι τῷ " μὴ ἐσθίειν ἐπὶ δίφρου,[2] " " μηδ' ἐπὶ χοίνικος καθῆσθαι," " μηδὲ σάρον ὑπερβαίνειν," οὐ ταῦτα τῶν Πυθαγορικῶν δεδιότων καὶ φυλαττομένων ἀλλ' ἕτερα τούτοις ἀπαγορευόντων; καὶ γὰρ τὸ ὑπ' ἄμπελον ὑποπορεύεσθαι τὴν ἀναφορὰν ἐπὶ τὸν οἶνον εἶχεν, ὡς οὐ θεμιτὸν τῷ ἱερεῖ μεθύσκεσθαι. τῶν γὰρ μεθυσκομένων ὑπὲρ κεφαλῆς ὁ οἶνός ἐστι καὶ πιέζονται
F καὶ ταπεινοῦνται, δέον ὑπερτέρους εἶναι καὶ κρατεῖν ἀεὶ τῆς ἡδονῆς ταύτης ἀλλὰ μὴ κρατεῖσθαι.

Τὸν δὲ κιττὸν πότερον ὡς ἄκαρπον καὶ ἄχρηστον ἀνθρώποις, ἀδρανῆ δὲ καὶ δι' ἀσθένειαν ἑτέρων ὀχούντων δεόμενον, σκιᾷ δὲ καὶ χλωρότητος ὄψει γοητεύοντα τοὺς πολλούς, οὐκ ᾤοντο δεῖν ἀσύμβολον ἐν ταῖς οἰκίαις μάτην ἐντρέφεσθαι καὶ περιπλέκεσθαι, βλαβερὸν ὄντα τοῖς προσδεχομένοις
291 φυτοῖς; ἢ ὡς[3] τῆς γῆς ἐχόμενον; διὸ τῶν μὲν Ὀλυμπίων ἱερῶν εἴργεται, καὶ οὔτ' ἐν Ἥρας Ἀθήνησιν οὔτε Θήβησιν ἐν Ἀφροδίτης ἴδοι τις ἂν κιττόν· Ἀγριωνίοις[4] δὲ καὶ Νυκτελίοις, ὧν τὰ πολλὰ διὰ σκότους δρᾶται, πάρεστιν.

---

[1] ἐφεῖτο as in 291 B, infra : ἐφίετο.
[2] ἐπὶ δίφρου as in 354 E : ἀπὸ δίφρου.
[3] ἢ ὡς added by Titchener and Pohlenz.
[4] Ἀγριωνίοις Meziriacus and Wyttenbach : ἄγριον ἴοις.

---

[a] Cf. Aulus Gellius, x. 15. 12.

highest and purest god should be forbidden to make
a dog their familiar companion and housemate.

112. For what reason was it forbidden the priest of
Jupiter to touch ivy or to pass along a road overhung
by a vine growing on a tree ? [a]

Is this second question like the precepts : " Do not
eat seated on a stool," " Do not sit on a peck measure,"
" Do not step over a broom " ?   For the followers of
Pythagoras [b] did not really fear these things nor
guard against them, but forbade other things through
these.   Likewise the walking under a vine had reference to wine, signifying that it is not right for the
priest to get drunk ; for wine is over the heads of
drunken men, and they are oppressed and humbled
thereby, when they should be above it and always
master this pleasure, not be mastered by it.

Did they regard the ivy as an unfruitful plant,
useless to man, and feeble, and because of its weakness needing other plants to support it, but by its
shade and the sight of its green fascinating to most
people ?   And did they therefore think that it should
not be uselessly grown in their homes nor be allowed
to twine about in a futile way, contributing nothing,
since it is injurious to the plants forming its support ?
Or is it because it cleaves to the ground ? [c] Wherefore
it is excluded from the ritual of the Olympian gods, nor
can any ivy be seen in the temple of Hera at Athens,
or in the temple of Aphroditê at Thebes ; but it has
its place in the Agrionia [d] and the Nyctelia, [e] the rites
of which are for the most part performed at night.

[b] Cf. 281 A, supra ; Moralia, 727 c.
[c] It clings to the earth, unless it finds support, and is
therefore unacceptable to the higher gods.
[d] Cf. 299 F, infra.   [e] Cf. Moralia, 364 F.

(291) Ἦ καὶ τοῦτο συμβολικὴ θιάσων καὶ βακχευ-
μάτων ἀπαγόρευσις ἦν; αἱ γὰρ ἔνοχοι τοῖς
βακχικοῖς πάθεσι γυναῖκες εὐθὺς ἐπὶ τὸν κιττὸν
φέρονται, καὶ σπαράττουσι δραττόμεναι ταῖς χερσὶ
καὶ διεσθίουσαι τοῖς στόμασιν· ὥστε μὴ παντελῶς
ἀπιθάνους εἶναι τοὺς λέγοντας ὅτι καὶ πνεῦμα
B μανίας ἔχων ἐγερτικὸν καὶ παρακινητικὸν ἐξίστησι
καὶ ταράττει,[1] καὶ ὅλως ἄοινον ἐπάγει μέθην καὶ
χαρὰν[2] τοῖς ἐπισφαλῶς πρὸς ἐνθουσιασμὸν ἔχουσι.

113. " Διὰ τί τοῖς ἱερεῦσι τούτοις ἀρχὴν οὐκ
ἐφεῖτο λαβεῖν οὐδὲ μετελθεῖν, ἀλλὰ ῥαβδούχῳ τε
χρῶνται καὶ δίφρον ἡγεμονικὸν ἐπὶ τιμῇ καὶ παρα-
μυθίᾳ τοῦ μὴ ἄρχειν ἔχουσι; "

Πότερον, ὡς ἐνιαχοῦ τῆς Ἑλλάδος ἀντίρροπον
ἦν τὸ τῆς ἱερωσύνης ἀξίωμα πρὸς τὸ τῆς βασιλείας,
καὶ μὴ τοὺς[3] τυχόντας ἱερεῖς ἀπεδείκνυσαν;

Ἦ μᾶλλον ὅτι τῶν μὲν ἱερέων ὡρισμένας πράξεις
ἐχόντων τῶν δ᾽ ἀρχόντων[4] ἀτάκτους καὶ ἀορίστους
C οὐκ ἦν δυνατὸν εἰς ἓν ἅμα τῶν καιρῶν συμπεσόντων ἑκατέρῳ παρεῖναι τὸν αὐτόν, ἀλλ᾽ ἔδει θάτερα
πολλάκις ἀμφοτέρων ἐπειγόντων ἀπολείποντα νῦν
μὲν ἀσεβεῖν[5] τοὺς θεούς, νῦν δὲ βλάπτειν τοὺς
πολίτας;

Ἦ[6] ταῖς ἀνθρωπίναις ἐνορῶντες ἀρχαῖς οὐκ ἐλάτ-
τονα τῆς ἐξουσίας τὴν ἀνάγκην προσοῦσαν, καὶ τὸν
ἄρχοντα δήμου, καθάπερ Ἱπποκράτης ἔφη τὸν

---

[1] ταράττει Wyttenbach (*cf.* 136 c): σπαράττει.
[2] χαρὰν Wyttenbach (κάρον Meziriacus): χάριν.
[3] τοὺς added by F.C.B.
[4] τῶν δ᾽ ἀρχόντων seems to be required by the context.
Meziriacus wrote τῶν δ᾽ ἀρχῶν and one ms. has τῶν δὲ
δημοσίων.
[5] ἀσεβεῖν Xylander: εὐσεβεῖν.   [6] ἦ] οἱ all mss. but one.

Or was this also a symbolic prohibition of Bacchic revels and orgies? For women possessed by Bacchic frenzies rush straightway for ivy and tear it to pieces, clutching it in their hands and biting it with their teeth; so that not altogether without plausibility are they who assert that ivy, possessing as it does an exciting and distracting breath of madness, deranges persons and agitates them, and in general brings on a wineless drunkenness and joyousness in those that are precariously disposed towards spiritual exaltation.[a]

113. WHY were these priests not allowed to hold office nor to solicit it, yet they have the service of a lictor and the right to a curule chair as an honour and a consolation for holding no office?[b]

Is this similar to the conditions in some parts of Greece where the priesthood had a dignity commensurate with that of the kingship, and they appointed as priests no ordinary men?

Or was it rather that since priests have definite duties, whereas officials have duties which are irregular and undefined, if the occasions for these duties happened to coincide, it was impossible for the same man to be present at both, but oftentimes, when both duties were pressing, he had to neglect one of them and at one time commit impiety against the gods, and at another do hurt to his fellow-citizens?

Or did they observe that there is implicit in the government of men no less constraint than authority, and that the ruler of the people, as Hippocrates[c] said

---

[a] Plutarch's fullest treatment of the properties of ivy will be found in *Moralia*, 648 B–649 F.

[b] *Cf.* Aulus Gellius, x. 15. 4.

[c] In the *De Flatibus*: vol. vi. p. 213 (ed. Chartier); vol. i. p. 569 (Kühn); *cf.* Lucian, *Bis Accusatus*, 1.

(291) ἰατρόν, δεινὰ μὲν ὁρῶντα δεινῶν[1] δ' ἁπτόμενον, ἐπ'
ἀλλοτρίοις δὲ κακοῖς ἰδίας λύπας καρπούμενον, οὐχ
ὅσιον ἡγοῦντο θύειν θεοῖς καὶ ἱερῶν κατάρχεσθαι
γενόμενον ἐν καταδίκαις καὶ θανατώσεσι πολιτῶν,
πολλάκις δὲ καὶ συγγενῶν καὶ οἰκείων, οἷα καὶ
Βρούτῳ συνέτυχε;

[1] δεινῶν] ἀηδῶν in both Hippocrates and Lucian, cited in
note c on page 169.

of the physician, must see dreadful things and touch dreadful things and reap painful emotions of his own from the ills of other men ? Did they, then, think it impious for a man to offer sacrifice to the gods, and to take the lead in the sacred rites, if he was concerned in pronouncing judgements and sentences of death upon citizens, and often upon kinsmen and members of his household, such as fell to the lot of Brutus ? [a]

[a] The first consul, who condemned his own sons to death ; cf. Livy, ii. 5 ; *Life of Publicola*, chap. vi. (99 E-F).

THE GREEK QUESTIONS
(QUAESTIONES GRAECAE)

INTRODUCTION

In the *Greek Questions*, as in the *Roman Questions*, Plutarch endeavours to give the reason or explanation of fifty-nine matters concerned with Greek life. The vast majority of them are customs or names and, as the explanations are usually historical, they often go back to very early times. A full commentary may be found in W. R. Halliday, *The Greek Questions of Plutarch* (Oxford, 1928), an excellent work, embodying also much of the modern speculation in regard to primitive religion.

The sources for the information contained in this essay seem to be somewhat varied, but there is little doubt that Aristotle's account of the numerous *Greek Constitutions* was Plutarch's principal source. The matter is treated at length by Halliday.

J. J. Hartman (*Mnemosyne*, xli. p. 216, or *De Plutarcho scriptore et philosopho*, p. 139) is the only modern scholar who has doubted the authenticity of the attribution to Plutarch of this work [a]; the author was not primarily interested in ethical matters, according to Hartman, and hence cannot be Plutarch. J. B. Titchener [b] has promised a discussion of this

---

[a] " Sed praeterea totus liber mera est doctrinae ostentatio, . . . Chaeronensi mentium medico prorsus indigna."

[b] See *The MS. Tradition of Plutarch's Aetia Graeca and Aetia Romana* (Urbana, Illinois, 1924), p. 9.

matter, but stylistic considerations alone seem to make it uncertain whether the work is correctly attributed to Plutarch.

A few of the topics treated in the *Greek Questions* appear also in other works of Plutarch, but the number naturally is not large.

The MS. tradition is good; the few difficulties found are generally with single words.

The work is No. 166 in Lamprias's list of Plutarch's works, where the title is given as Αἰτίαι Ἑλλήνων.

ΑΙΤΙΑ ΕΛΛΗΝΙΚΑ

1. " Τίνες οἱ ἐν Ἐπιδαύρῳ κονίποδες καὶ ἄρτυ-
Ε νοι; "

Οἱ μὲν τὸ πολίτευμα ἔχοντες[1] ὀγδοήκοντα καὶ
ἑκατὸν ἄνδρες ἦσαν· ἐκ δὲ τούτων ᾑροῦντο βου-
λευτάς, οὓς " ἀρτύνους " ἐκάλουν. τοῦ δὲ δήμου
τὸ πλεῖστον ἐν ἀγρῷ διέτριβεν· ἐκαλοῦντο δὲ
" κονίποδες, " ὡς συμβαλεῖν ἔστιν ἀπὸ τῶν ποδῶν
γνωριζόμενοι κεκονιμένων, ὁπότε κατέλθοιεν εἰς
τὴν πόλιν.

2. " Τίς ἡ παρὰ Κυμαίοις ὀνοβάτις; "

F Τῶν γυναικῶν τὴν ἐπὶ μοιχείᾳ ληφθεῖσαν ἀγα-
γόντες εἰς ἀγορὰν ἐπὶ λίθου τινὸς ἐμφανῆ πᾶσι
καθίστασαν· εἶθ᾿ οὕτως ἀνεβίβαζον ἐπ᾿ ὄνον, καὶ
τὴν πόλιν κύκλῳ περιαχθεῖσαν ἔδει πάλιν ἐπὶ τὸν
αὐτὸν λίθον καταστῆναι καὶ τὸ λοιπὸν ἄτιμον
διατελεῖν, " ὀνοβάτιν " προσαγορευομένην. τὸν δὲ
λίθον ἀπὸ τούτου οὐ καθαρὸν νομίζοντες ἀφωσιοῦντο.

Ἦν δὲ καὶ φυλάκτου τις ἀρχὴ παρ᾿ αὐτοῖς· ὁ δὲ
ταύτην ἔχων τὸν μὲν ἄλλον χρόνον ἐτήρει τὸ

---

[1] ἔχοντες Wyttenbach to fill a lacuna; Bernardakis prefers
διέποντες, and E. Capps διοικοῦντες.

---

[a] This was the serf-class liberated by the tyrants : *cf.*
Cambridge Ancient History, vol. iii. p. 554.

THE GREEK QUESTIONS

1. Who were the " dusty-feet " and the " directors " in Epidaurus ?

There were one hundred and eighty men who directed the State. From these they used to elect councillors whom they called " directors." But the majority of the populace spent their life in the country. They were called " dusty-feet " [a] since, as one may conjecture, they were recognized by their dust-covered feet whenever they came down to the city.

2. Who was the " woman that rode on a donkey " at Cumae ?

Any woman taken in adultery they used to bring into the market-place and set her on a certain stone in plain sight of everyone. In like manner they then proceeded to mount her upon a donkey, and when she had been led about the circuit of the entire city, she was required again to take her stand upon the same stone, and for the rest of her life to continue in disgrace, bearing the name " donkey-rider." After this ceremony they believed that the stone was unclean and they used ritually to purify it.

The citizens of Cumae had also a certain office called the Guards. The man who held this office used to watch the prison most of the time, but he

δεσμωτήριον, εἰς δὲ τὴν βουλὴν ἐν τῷ νυκτερινῷ
292 συλλόγῳ παριὼν ἐξῆγε τοὺς βασιλεῖς τῆς χειρὸς
καὶ κατεῖχε, μέχρι περὶ αὐτῶν ἡ βουλὴ διαγνοίη,
πότερον ἀδικοῦσιν ἢ οὔ, κρύβδην φέρουσα τὴν
ψῆφον.

3. " Τίς παρὰ Σολίοις[1] ἡ ὑπεκκαύστρια; "
Τὴν τῆς Ἀθηνᾶς ἱέρειαν οὕτω καλοῦσιν, ὅτι
ποιεῖταί τινας θυσίας καὶ ἱερουργίας ἀποτροπαίους.

4. " Τίνες ἐν Κνίδῳ οἱ ἀμνήμονες καὶ τίς ὁ
ἀφεστήρ; "
Ἑξήκοντα προκρίτοις ἀνδράσιν[2] ἐκ τῶν ἀρίστων
οἷον ἐπισκόποις ἐχρῶντο διὰ βίου καὶ προβούλοις
τῶν μεγίστων· ἐκαλοῦντο δ' " ἀμνήμονες," ὡς ἂν
B τις εἰκάσειε, διὰ τὸ ἀνυπεύθυνον, εἰ μὴ νὴ Δία
πολυμνήμονές τινες ὄντες. ὁ δὲ τὰς γνώμας
ἐρωτῶν " ἀφεστήρ."

5. " Τίνες οἱ παρ' Ἀρκάσι καὶ Λακεδαιμονίοις
χρηστοί; "
Λακεδαιμόνιοι Τεγεάταις διαλλαγέντες ἐποιήσαντο συνθήκας καὶ στήλην ἐπ' Ἀλφειῷ κοινὴν
ἀνέστησαν, ἐν ᾗ μετὰ τῶν ἄλλων γέγραπται
" Μεσσηνίους ἐκβαλεῖν ἐκ τῆς χώρας, καὶ μὴ
ἐξεῖναι ' χρηστοὺς ' ποιεῖν." ἐξηγούμενος οὖν ὁ
Ἀριστοτέλης τοῦτό φησι δύνασθαι τὸ μὴ ἀπο-

---

[1] Σολίοις Wyttenbach : Σόλοις.
[2] προκρίτοις ἀνδράσιν Meziriacus : προκρίτους ἄνδρας.

---

[a] W. R. Halliday, in *Harvard Studies in Classical
Philology*, xxxvi. 165-177, suggests that "cohen" (= priest)
may be contained in this word.
[b] Grote thus connected *aphestēr* with the Spartan *apo-*

178

came to the nocturnal assemblies of the council and
led out the kings by the hand and kept them out,
until by secret ballot the council had decided on
their case, whether they had done wrong or no.

3. WHO is She that Kindles the Fire (*hypekkaus-
tria*) [a] among the people of Soli ?

This is the name which they give to the priestess of
Athena because she performs certain sacrifices and
ceremonies to avert evil.

4. WHO were the Forgetful Ones (*Amnemones*) at
Cnidus, and who was the Dismisser [b] (*Aphester*) ?

They were wont to employ sixty men chosen from
the nobles, and appointed for life, as overseers and
preliminary advisers in matters of the greatest importance. They were called the Forgetful Ones, one
might conjecture, because they could not be held to
account for their actions ; unless, indeed, it was because they were men who remembered many things.[c]
He who asked them their opinions was the Dismisser.

5. WHO are the " good " among the Arcadians and
the Spartans ?

When the Spartans had come to terms with the
Tegeans, they made a treaty and set up in common
a pillar by the Alpheius. On this, among other
matters, was inscribed : " The Messenians must be
expelled from the country ; it shall not be lawful to
make men good." [d] Aristotle,[e] then, in explaining
this, states that it means that no one shall be put

---

statēr of *Life of Lycurgus*, chap. vi. (43 c) ; but the matter
is very doubtful ; *cf.* van Herwerden, *Lex. Supp. Graec.*

[c] On the *lucus a non lucendo* principle, as Halliday well
suggests ; or else ἀμ-μνήμονες, as van Herwerden supposes.

[d] *Cf.* χρηστὲ χαῖρε on Greek tombstones.

[e] Frag. 592 (V. Rose) ; *cf.* 277 B-C, *supra.*

(292) κτιννύναι βοηθείας χάριν τοῖς λακωνίζουσι τῶν
Τεγεατῶν.

6. '' Τίς ὁ παρ' 'Οπουντίοις κριθολόγος; ''
Οἱ πλεῖστοι τῶν Ἑλλήνων πρὸς τὰς πάνυ
C παλαιὰς θυσίας ἐχρῶντο ταῖς κριθαῖς, ἀπαρχομένων
τῶν πολιτῶν. τὸν μὲν οὖν ἐπὶ τῶν θυσιῶν ἄρχοντα
καὶ ταύτας κομιζόμενον τὰς ἀπαρχὰς '' κριθο-
λόγον '' ὠνόμαζον. δύο δ' ἦσαν ἱερεῖς παρ' αὐτοῖς,
ὁ μὲν περὶ τὰ θεῖα τεταγμένος, ὁ δὲ περὶ τὰ δαιμόνια.

7. '' Τίνες αἱ πλωιάδες νεφέλαι; ''
Τὰς ὑπόμβρους μάλιστα καὶ περιφερομένας
ἐκάλουν '' πλωιάδας,'' ὡς Θεόφραστος ἐν τετάρτῃ
περὶ μεταρσίων εἴρηκε κατὰ λέξιν, '' ἐπεὶ καὶ αἱ
πλωιάδες αὗται νεφέλαι καὶ αἱ συνεστῶσαι,
D ἀκίνητοι δὲ καὶ τοῖς χρώμασιν ἔκλευκοι, δηλοῦσι
διαφοράν τινα τῆς ὕλης, ὡς οὔτ' ἐξυδατουμένης
οὔτ' ἐκπνευματουμένης.''

8. '' Τίς ὁ παρὰ Βοιωτοῖς πλατιοικέτας¹; ''
Τοὺς οἰκίᾳ γειτνιῶντας ἢ χωρίοις ὁμοροῦντας
αἰολίζοντες οὕτω καλοῦσιν ὡς τὸ πλησίον² ἔχοντας.
παραθήσομαι δὲ λέξιν μίαν ἐκ τοῦ θεσμοφυλακίου
νόμου, πλειόνων οὐσῶν. . . .ᵃ

9. '' Τίς ὁ παρὰ Δελφοῖς ὁσιωτὴρ καὶ διὰ τί
βύσιον ἕνα τῶν μηνῶν καλοῦσιν; ''

---

¹ πλατιοικέτας Bechtel : πλατυχαίτας.
² πλησίον Wyttenbach : πλεῖστον.

ᵃ The copyist seems to have omitted the quotation.

to death because of assistance given to the Spartan
party in Tegea.

6. WHO is "he that selects barley" (*krithologos*)
among the Opuntians ?

For sacrifices of very ancient origin most of the
Greeks used to employ barley, which the citizens
offered as first-fruits of the harvest. Accordingly
they called the officer who presided at the sacrifices
and brought these first-fruits the Barley-selector.
They had two priests : one appointed for sacrifices to
the gods, the other for sacrifices to the spirits.

7. WHAT were the "floating clouds" ?

They used to call clouds "floating" which particularly threatened rain and were in constant motion, as
Theophrastus has stated in the fourth book of his
Meteorology. The passage reads thus : "Since also
these floating clouds and these compact clouds, which
are immovable and very white in colour, exhibit a
certain difference of substance which is filled neither
with water nor with wind."

8. WHO is the "near-dweller" (*platioiketas*) among
the Boeotians ?

This is the name they give in the Aeolian dialect
to persons who dwell in the next house or occupy
adjoining property. signifying that they hold land
near at hand. I shall add one phrase from the Edict
of the Guardians of the Law, although there are
several more . . .[a]

9. WHO is the Consecrator (*hosiōtēr*) among the
Delphians and why do they call one of the months
"Bysios" ?

" 'Οσιωτῆρα " μὲν καλοῦσι τὸ θυόμενον ἱερεῖον,
ὅταν " ὅσιος " ἀποδειχθῇ. πέντε δ' εἰσὶν ὅσιοι
διὰ βίου, καὶ τὰ πολλὰ μετὰ τῶν προφητῶν δρῶσιν
οὗτοι καὶ συνιερουργοῦσιν, ἅτε[1] γεγονέναι δοκοῦντες
ἀπὸ Δευκαλίωνος.

E   Ὁ δὲ " βύσιος " μήν, ὡς μὲν οἱ πολλοὶ νομίζουσι, φύσιός ἐστιν· ἔαρος γὰρ ἄρχει καὶ τὰ πολλὰ
φύεται τηνικαῦτα καὶ διαβλαστάνει. τὸ δ' ἀληθὲς
οὐκ ἔχει οὕτως· οὐ γὰρ ἀντὶ τοῦ φ τῷ β χρῶνται
Δελφοί, καθάπερ Μακεδόνες " Βίλιππον[2] " καὶ
" βαλακρὸν " καὶ " Βερονίκην " λέγοντες, ἀλλ'
ἀντὶ τοῦ π· καὶ γὰρ τὸ πατεῖν " βατεῖν " καὶ τὸ
πικρὸν " βικρὸν " ἐπιεικῶς καλοῦσιν. ἔστιν οὖν
πύσιος ὁ " βύσιος," ἐν ᾧ πυστιῶνται καὶ πυνθά-
νονται τοῦ θεοῦ· τοῦτο[3] γὰρ ἔννομον[4] καὶ πάτριον.
ἐν τῷ μηνὶ γὰρ τούτῳ χρηστήριον ἐγίγνετο καὶ
ἑβδόμην ταύτην νομίζουσι τοῦ θεοῦ γενέθλιον,
F καὶ πολύφθοον[5] ὀνομάζουσιν οὐ διὰ τὸ πέττεσθαι
φθόϊς, ἀλλὰ πολυπευθῆ καὶ πολυμάντευτον οὖσαν.
ὀψὲ γὰρ ἀνείθησαν αἱ κατὰ μῆνα μαντεῖαι τοῖς
δεομένοις, πρότερον δ' ἅπαξ ἐθεμίστευεν ἡ Πυθία
τοῦ ἐνιαυτοῦ κατὰ ταύτην τὴν ἡμέραν, ὡς Καλλι-
293 σθένης καὶ Ἀναξανδρίδης ἱστορήκασι.

10. " Τί τὸ φυξίμηλον; "
    Τῶν μικρῶν ἐστι καὶ χαμαιζήλων φυτῶν, ὧν

---

[1] ἅτε Xylander: ᾇ, or οἱ or ὡς.
[2] Βίλιππον Basel ed. of 1542: βίλιππον γὰρ.
[3] τοῦτο Bernardakis: τὸ.   [4] ἔννομον Weniger: ἐννοεῖν.
[5] πολύφθοον Aldine edition: πολύφθονον.

---

[a] Cf. Moralia, 365 A, 437 A.
[b] Ibid. 717 D ; for the connexion of the number seven with
the birth of Apollo see Callimachus, Hymn iv. 251 ff.

They call the victim that is sacrificed Consecrator whenever an Holy One [a] is appointed. There are five Holy Ones, who hold office for life; they do a great many things with the co-operation of the oracle-interpreters and with them take part in the holy rites, since they are thought to have descended from Deucalion.

The month " Bysios," as many think, is the month of growth (*physios*); for it begins the spring and during it many plants spring up and come into bloom. But this is not the truth of the matter, for Delphians do not use *b* in place of *ph* (as Macedonians do who say " Bilip " and " balacros " and " Beronicê "), but in place of *p*; thus they naturally say " broceed " for " proceed " and " bainful " for " painful." Accordingly " Bysios " is " pysios," the month of oracular inquiry, in which men ask questions and obtain responses from the god; for this is the legitimate and traditional procedure. In this month, then, oracles used to be given and the seventh day of this month they consider the birthday of the god.[b] They call this day the day of Many Utterances (*Polyphthoös*) not because they then bake cakes (*phthoïs*),[c] but because it is a day when many inquire of the god and receive many oracles. For only recently have monthly oracles been given out to inquirers; formerly the prophetic priestess was wont to give responses but once a year on this day, as Callisthenes [d] and Anaxandrides have recorded.

10. WHAT is the " sheep-escaper " ?
It is one of the small plants that grow close to the

[c] *Cf.* Athenaeus, 647 D, 502 B.
[d] *Cf.* Jacoby, *Frag. der griech. Hist.* 124 F 49.

(293) ἐπιόντα τοὺς βλαστοὺς τὰ βοσκήματα κολούει καὶ
ἀδικεῖ καὶ λυμαίνεται τὴν αὔξησιν· ὅταν οὖν
ἀναραμόντα μέγεθος λάβῃ καὶ διαφύγῃ τὸ βλά-
πτεσθαι ὑπὸ τῶν ἐπινεμομένων,[1] " φυξίμηλα "
καλεῖται. τὸ δὲ μαρτύριον Αἰσχύλος.

11. " Τίνες οἱ ἀποσφενδόνητοι; "

Κέρκυραν τὴν νῆσον Ἐρετριεῖς κατῴκουν· Χαρι-
κράτους δὲ πλεύσαντος ἐκ Κορίνθου μετὰ δυνάμεως
καὶ τῷ πολέμῳ κρατοῦντος, ἐμβάντες εἰς τὰς ναῦς
B οἱ Ἐρετριεῖς ἀπέπλευσαν οἴκαδε. προαισθόμενοι
δ' οἱ πολῖται, τῆς χώρας εἶργον αὐτοὺς καὶ ἀποβαίνειν ἐκώλυον σφενδονῶντες. μὴ δυνάμενοι δὲ
μήτε πεῖσαι μήτε βιάσασθαι πολλοὺς καὶ ἀπαρ-
αιτήτους ὄντας, ἐπὶ Θρᾴκης ἔπλευσαν καὶ κατα-
σχόντες χωρίον, ἐν ᾧ πρότερον οἰκῆσαι Μέθωνα
τὸν Ὀρφέως πρόγονον ἱστοροῦσι, τὴν μὲν πόλιν
ὠνόμασαν Μεθώνην, ὑπὸ δὲ τῶν προσοίκων " ἀποσφενδόνητοι " προσωνομάσθησαν.

12. " Τίς ἡ παρὰ Δελφοῖς Χάριλλα[2]; "

Τρεῖς ἄγουσι Δελφοὶ ἐννεαετηρίδας κατὰ τὸ ἑξῆς,
C ὧν τὴν μὲν Σεπτήριον καλοῦσι, τὴν δ' Ἡρωΐδα,
τὴν δὲ Χάριλλαν.[2]

Τὸ μὲν οὖν Σεπτήριον ἔοικε μίμημα τῆς πρὸς
τὸν Πύθωνα τοῦ θεοῦ μάχης εἶναι καὶ τῆς μετὰ
τὴν μάχην ἐπὶ τὰ Τέμπη φυγῆς καὶ ἐκδιώξεως.

[1] ἐπινεμομένων Wyttenbach and E: ἐπιγενομένων.
[2] Χάριλλα . . . Χαρίλλαν Hatzidakis: Χάριλα . . . Χαρίλαν.

[a] Nauck, *Trag. Graec. Frag.* p. 123, Aeschylus, Frag. 447.

ground, whose shoots the grazing animals attack, cutting off the tops and injuring them and so spoiling the growth. But when these plants grow up and gain some size and escape injury from the flocks which graze upon them, then they are called " sheep-escapers." The evidence for this is Aeschylus.[a]

11. Who are the " Men repulsed by slings " ?

Men from Eretria used to inhabit the island of Corcyra. But Charicrates sailed thither from Corinth with an army and defeated them in war ; so the Eretrians embarked in their ships and sailed back home. Their fellow-citizens, however, having learned of the matter before their arrival, barred their return to the country and prevented them from disembarking by showering upon them missiles from slings. Since the exiles were unable either to persuade or to overcome their fellow-citizens, who were numerous and inexorable, they sailed to Thrace and occupied a territory in which, according to tradition, Methon, the ancestor of Orpheus, had formerly lived. So the Eretrians named their city Methonê, but they were also named by their neighbours the " Men repulsed by slings."

12. Who was " Charilla " among the Delphians ?

The Delphians celebrate three festivals one after the other which occur every eight [b] years, the first of which they call Septerion, the second Heroïs, and the third Charilla.

Now the Septerion seems to be a representation of Apollo's fight with the Python and the flight to Tempê and pursuit that followed the battle.[b] Some indeed

[b] Cf. Moralia, 421 c.

185

(293) οἱ μὲν γὰρ φυγεῖν ἐπὶ τῷ φόνῳ φασὶ χρῄζοντα
καθαρσίων, οἱ δὲ τῷ Πύθωνι τετρωμένῳ καὶ φεύ-
γοντι κατὰ τὴν ὁδόν, ἣν νῦν ἱερὰν καλοῦμεν,
ἐπακολουθεῖν καὶ μικρὸν ἀπολειφθῆναι τῆς τελευτῆς·
κατέλαβε γὰρ αὐτὸν ἐκ τοῦ τραύματος ἄρτι τεθνηκότα καὶ κεκηδευμένον ὑπὸ τοῦ παιδός, ᾧ ὄνομα
ἦν Αἴξ, ὡς λέγουσι. τὸ μὲν οὖν Σεπτήριον τούτων
ἢ τοιούτων τινῶν ἀπομίμησίς ἐστιν ἑτέρων.

Τῆς δ' Ἡρωίδος τὰ πλεῖστα μυστικὸν ἔχει λόγον,
D ὃν ἴσασιν αἱ Θυιάδες, ἐκ δὲ τῶν δρωμένων φανερῶς
Σεμέλης ἄν τις ἀναγωγὴν εἰκάσειε.

Περὶ δὲ τῆς Χαρίλλης[1] τοιαῦτά τινα μυθολογοῦσι.
λιμὸς ἐξ αὐχμοῦ τοὺς Δελφοὺς κατέσχε, καὶ πρὸς
τὰς θύρας τοῦ βασιλέως ἐλθόντες μετὰ τέκνων καὶ
γυναικῶν ἱκέτευον. ὁ δὲ τῶν ἀλφίτων καὶ τῶν
χεδρόπων μετεδίδου τοῖς γνωριμωτέροις αὐτῶν· οὐ
γὰρ ἦν ἱκανὰ πᾶσιν. ἐλθούσης δὲ παιδὸς ἔτι
μικρᾶς ὀρφανῆς γονέων καὶ προσλιπαρούσης, ἐρ-
ράπισεν αὐτὴν ὑποδήματι καὶ τῷ προσώπῳ τὸ
ὑπόδημα προσέρριψεν· ἡ δέ, πενιχρά τις οὖσα καὶ
ἔρημος οὐκ ἀγεννὴς δὲ[2] τὸ ἦθος, ἐκποδὼν γενομένη
E καὶ λύσασα τὴν ζώνην ἀνήρτησεν ἑαυτήν. ἐπι-
τείνοντος δὲ τοῦ λιμοῦ καὶ νοσημάτων προσ-
γενομένων, ἀνεῖλεν ἡ Πυθία τῷ βασιλεῖ Χάριλλαν[1]
ἱλάσκεσθαι παρθένον αὐτοθάνατον. μόλις οὖν ἀνευ-
ρόντες ὅτι τοὔνομα τοῦτ' ἦν τῇ ῥαπισθείσῃ παιδί,
μεμειγμένην τινὰ καθαρμῷ θυσίαν ἀπετέλεσαν, ἣν

[1] Χαρίλλης . . . Χάριλλαν Hatzidakis: Χαρίλας . . . Χάριλαν.
[2] δὲ Hutten: τε or τις.

---

[a] Cf. Moralia, 418 A-B ; Aelian, Varia Historia, iii. 1, for
this festival.
[b] Cf. Moralia, 249 E-F.

affirm that Apollo fled because he desired purification as a consequence of the slaughter he had done, others that he was following the wounded Python as he fled along the road which we now call the Sacred Way, and was only a little late for the monster's death ; for he overtook him when he had just died from the effects of the wound and had been buried by his son, whose name, as they say, was Aix. The Septerion, then, is a representation of these matters or certain matters of a similar nature.[a]

The greater part of the Heroïs has a secret import which the Thyiads [b] know ; but from the portions of the rites that are performed in public one might conjecture that it represents the evocation of Semelê.

The story of Charilla which they relate is somewhat as follows : A famine following a drought oppressed the Delphians, and they came to the palace of their king with their wives and children and made supplication. The king gave portions of barley and legumes to the more notable citizens, for there was not enough for all. But when an orphaned girl, who was still but a small child, approached him and importuned him, he struck her with his sandal and cast the sandal in her face. But, although the girl was poverty-stricken and without protectors, she was not ignoble in character ; and when she had withdrawn, she took off her girdle and hanged herself. As the famine increased and diseases also were added thereto, the prophetic priestess gave an oracle to the king that he must appease Charilla, the maiden who had slain herself. Accordingly, when they had discovered with some difficulty that this was the name of the child who had been struck, they performed a certain sacrificial rite combined with purification,

ἐπιτελοῦσιν ἔτι καὶ νῦν δι᾽ ἐννέα ἐτῶν. προκάθηται
μὲν γὰρ ὁ βασιλεὺς τῶν ἀλφίτων καὶ τῶν χεδρόπων
ἐπιδιδοὺς πᾶσι καὶ ξένοις καὶ πολίταις, κομίζεται
δὲ τῆς Χαρίλλης[1] παιδικὸν εἴδωλον· ὅταν οὖν πάντες
F λάβωσιν, ὁ μὲν βασιλεὺς ῥαπίζει τῷ ὑποδήματι τὸ
εἴδωλον, ἡ δὲ τῶν Θυιάδων ἀρχηγὸς ἀραμένη
κομίζει πρός τινα τόπον φαραγγώδη, κἀκεῖ σχοινίον
περιάψαντες τῷ τραχήλῳ τοῦ εἰδώλου κατορύτ-
τουσιν, ὅπου τὴν Χάριλλαν[1] ἀπαγξαμένην ἔθαψαν.

13. '' Τί τὸ πτωχικὸν κρέας παρ᾽ Αἰνιᾶσι; ''
Πλείονες γεγόνασιν Αἰνιάνων μεταναστάσεις.
πρῶτον μὲν γὰρ οἰκοῦντες περὶ τὸ Δώτιον πεδίον
ἐξέπεσον ὑπὸ Λαπιθῶν εἰς Αἴθικας. ἐκεῖθεν τῆς
Μολοττίας τὴν περὶ τὸν Αὔαν[2] χώραν κατέσχον,
ὅθεν ὠνομάσθησαν Παραυαῖοι.[3] μετὰ ταῦτα Κίρρα
294 κατέσχον· ἐν δὲ Κίρρᾳ[4] καταλεύσαντες[5] Οἴνοκλον
τὸν βασιλέα, τοῦ θεοῦ προστάξαντος, εἰς τὴν περὶ
τὸν Ἴναχον χώραν κατέβησαν οἰκουμένην ὑπ᾽
Ἰναχιέων καὶ Ἀχαιῶν. γενομένου δὲ χρησμοῦ
τοῖς μὲν ἂν μεταδῶσι τῆς χώρας ἀποβαλεῖν ἅπασαν,
τοῖς δ᾽ ἂν λάβωσι παρ᾽ ἑκόντων καθέξειν, Τέμων,
ἀνὴρ ἐλλόγιμος τῶν Αἰνιάνων, ἀναλαβὼν ῥάκια
καὶ πήραν ὡς[6] προσαίτης ὢν ἀφίκετο πρὸς τοὺς
Ἰναχιεῖς· ὕβρει δὲ καὶ πρὸς γέλωτα τοῦ βασιλέως
B βῶλον ἐπιδόντος αὐτῷ, δεξάμενος εἰς τὴν πήραν

---

[1] Χαρίλλης . . . Χάριλλαν Hatzidakis: Χαρίλας . . . Χάριλαν.
[2] Αὔαν seems required by the ending of the adjective below
rather than Αὔον (Xylander from Stephanus Byzantius):
Ἀραούαν.
[3] Παραυαῖοι Xylander (as in Thuc. ii. 80, and elsewhere):
Παραοῦαι. [4] Κίρρᾳ Hatzidakis and Kontos: Κίρρῃ.
[5] καταλεύσαντες Xylander: καταπλεύσαντες.
[6] ὡς Wyttenbach: καί.

which even now they continue to perform every eight years. For the king sits in state and gives a portion of barley-meal and legumes to everyone, alien and citizen alike, and a doll-like image of Charilla is brought thither. When, accordingly, all have received a portion, the king strikes the image with his sandal. The leader of the Thyiads picks up the image and bears it to a certain place which is full of chasms ; there they tie a rope round the neck of the image and bury it in the place where they buried Charilla after she had hanged herself.

13. WHAT is the "beggar's meat" among the Aenianians ?

There have been several migrations of the Aenianians. For first, when they inhabited the region about the Dotian plain, they were expelled by the Lapiths to Aethicia.[a] From there they proceeded to take possession of the region of Molossia about the river Auas, from which they received the name Parauaei. After this they took possession of Cirrha. There, when they had stoned to death Oenoclus,[a] their king, at the command of the god, they descended to the country about the Inachus, which was inhabited by Inachians and Achaeans. Since an oracle had declared that if the Inachians gave away any part of their country, they should lose it all, and that if the Aenianians received any part of the land from willing givers, they should gain possession of it, Temon, a notable man among the Aenianians, donned rags and wallet and came to the Inachians in the guise of a beggar. In scorn and mockery their king gave him a clod of earth, which Temon accepted,

[a] *Cf.* 297 B-C, *infra.*

189

(294) ἐνέβαλε καὶ καταφανὴς[1] ἦν ἠγαπηκὼς τὸ δῶρον
ἀπεχώρησε γὰρ εὐθὺς οὐδὲν προσαιτήσας. οἱ
δὲ πρεσβύτεροι θαυμάσαντες ἀνεμιμνήσκοντο τοῦ
χρησμοῦ, καὶ τῷ βασιλεῖ προσιόντες ἔλεγον μὴ
καταφρονῆσαι μηδὲ προέσθαι τὸν ἄνθρωπον. αἰσθόμενος οὖν ὁ Τέμων τὴν διάνοιαν αὐτῶν ὥρμησε
φεύγειν, καὶ διέφυγεν εὐξάμενος τῷ Ἀπόλλωνι
καθ' ἑκατόμβης.

Ἐκ δὲ τούτου μονομαχοῦσιν οἱ βασιλεῖς, καὶ
τὸν τῶν Ἰναχιέων Ὕπεροχον ὁ τῶν Αἰνιάνων
Φήμιος ὁρῶν μετὰ κυνὸς αὐτῷ προσφερόμενον οὐκ
C ἔφη δίκαια ποιεῖν, δεύτερον ἐπάγοντα μαχόμενον·
ἀπελαύνοντος δὲ τοῦ Ὑπερόχου τὸν κύνα καὶ
μεταστρεφομένου, λίθῳ βαλὼν ὁ Φήμιος αὐτὸν
ἀναιρεῖ. κτησάμενοι δὲ τὴν χώραν, τοὺς Ἰναχιεῖς
μετὰ τῶν Ἀχαιῶν ἐκβαλόντες, τὸν μὲν λίθον
ἐκεῖνον ὡς ἱερὸν σέβονται καὶ θύουσιν αὐτῷ καὶ
τοῦ ἱερείου τῷ δημῷ περικαλύπτουσιν. ὅταν δὲ
τῷ Ἀπόλλωνι τὴν ἑκατόμβην ἀποδιδῷσι, τῷ Διὶ
βοῦν καθιερεύσαντες, μερίδα τοῖς Τέμωνος ἀπογόνοις ἐξαίρετον νέμουσι, καὶ " πτωχικὸν κρέας "
ἐπονομάζουσι.

14. " Τίνες οἱ παρ' Ἰθακησίοις Κολιάδαι καὶ τίς
ὁ φάγιλος; "

Τῷ Ὀδυσσεῖ μετὰ τὴν μνηστηροφονίαν οἱ ἐπι-
τήδειοι τῶν τεθνηκότων ἐπανέστησαν, μεταπεμ-
φθεὶς δ' ὑπ' ἀμφοτέρων διαιτητὴς Νεοπτόλεμος
D ἐδικαίωσε τὸν μὲν Ὀδυσσέα μεταναστῆναι καὶ
φεύγειν ἐκ τῆς Κεφαλληνίας καὶ Ζακύνθου καὶ

---

[1] καταφανὴς F.C.B.; ἐμφανὴς Meziriacus; οὐκ ἀφανὴς
H. Richards (all amounting to the same thing): ἀφανὴς.

placed within his wallet, and was evidently satisfied with the gift ; for he straightway withdrew
without asking for anything more. The Inachian
elders were astonished, but, recalling the oracle,
they went to the king and told him not to make light
of the fellow nor to let him get away. Temon, then,
perceiving their intent, hastened his flight and made
his escape after vowing a hecatomb to Apollo.

After this affair the two kings engaged in single
combat, and Phemius, king of the Aenianians, ob-
serving the Inachian king, Hyperochus, advancing
to meet him accompanied by a dog, said that Hyperochus was acting unfairly in bringing on a second
combatant. But while Hyperochus was driving
off the dog and had his back turned, Phemius hit
him with a stone and killed him. The Aenianians
gained possession of the country, driving out the
Inachians together with the Achaeans, and they
revere that stone as sacred, and sacrifice to it and
cover it round about with the fat of the sacrificial
victim ; and whenever they pay the hecatomb to
Apollo, they sacrifice a bull to Zeus ; and they set
aside a select portion of the flesh for the descendants
of Temon, and this they call the " beggar's meat."

14. Who are the " Coliadae " among the inhabitants of Ithaca and what is the *phagilos* ?

After the slaughter of the suitors the relatives
of the dead men rose up against Odysseus; but
Neoptolemus was sent for by both parties to act as
arbiter.[a] He adjudged that Odysseus should depart
from the country and be exiled for homicide from
Cephallenia, Zacynthus, and Ithaca ; and that the

---

[a] *Cf.* Apollodorus, *Epitome*, vii. 40.

(294) Ἰθάκης ἐφ' αἵματι, τοὺς δὲ τῶν μνηστήρων ἑταίρους καὶ οἰκείους ἀποφέρειν ποινὴν Ὀδυσσεῖ τῶν εἰς τὸν οἶκον ἀδικημάτων καθ' ἕκαστον ἐνιαυτόν. αὐτὸς μὲν οὖν εἰς Ἰταλίαν¹ μετέστη· τὴν δὲ ποινὴν τῷ υἱεῖ καθιερώσας ἀποφέρειν ἐκέλευσε τοὺς Ἰθακησίους. ἦν δ' ἄλφιτα οἶνος κηρία ἔλαιον ἄλες ἱερεῖα πρεσβύτερα '' φαγίλων ''· '' φάγιλον '' δέ φησιν Ἀριστοτέλης τὸν ἀμνὸν εἶναι. τοὺς δὲ περὶ Εὔμαιον ἐλευθερώσας ὁ Τηλέμαχος κατέμειξεν εἰς τοὺς πολίτας, καὶ τὸ γένος ἐστὶ Κολιαδῶν² ἀπ' Εὐμαίου καὶ Βουκολιδῶν³ ἀπὸ Φιλοιτίου.

15. '' Τίς ἡ ξυλίνη κύων παρὰ Λοκροῖς; ''

E   Φυσκίου τοῦ Ἀμφικτύονος υἱὸς ἦν Λοκρός· ἐκ δὲ τούτου καὶ Καβύης Ὀποῦς.⁴ πρὸς ὃν ὁ πατὴρ διενεχθεὶς καὶ συχνοὺς τῶν πολιτῶν ἀναλαβὼν περὶ ἀποικίας ἐμαντεύετο. τοῦ δὲ θεοῦ φήσαντος κτίζειν πόλιν ὅπουπερ ἂν τύχῃ δηχθεὶς ὑπὸ κυνὸς ξυλίνης, ὑπερβαίνων εἰς τὴν ἑτέραν θάλατταν ἐπάτησε κυνόσβατον. ἐνοχληθεὶς δὲ τῇ πληγῇ διέτριψεν ἡμέρας αὐτόθι πλείονας, ἐν αἷς καταμαθὼν τὸ χωρίον ἔκτισε πόλεις Φύσκον⁵ καὶ
F Οἰάνθειαν,⁶ καὶ τὰς ἄλλας, ὅσας οἱ κληθέντες Ὀζόλαι Λοκροὶ κατῴκησαν.

Ὀζόλας δὲ Λοκροὺς οἱ μὲν διὰ τὸν Νέσσον, οἱ δὲ διὰ⁷ τὸν Πύθωνα δράκοντα κληθῆναι λέγουσιν,

¹ Ἰταλίαν] Αἰτωλίαν Hartman.
² Κολιαδῶν Xylander and one ms.: κολιδῶν.
³ Βουκολιδῶν V. Rose (cf. Eustathius on Il. xv. 338, p. 1018): βουκολιῶν.
⁴ Ὀποῦς V. Rose (cf. Eustathius on Il. ii. 531, p. 277): λοκρός.
⁵ Φύσκον F.C.B.: Φυσκεῖς is the gentile name. Cf. S.G.D.I. 1529 a 15.   ⁶ Οἰάνθειαν F.C.B.: Ὑάνθειαν.
⁷ δὲ διὰ Bernardakis: δὲ.

companions and the relatives of the suitors should recompense Odysseus each year for the injuries which they had done to his estate. Odysseus accordingly departed to Italy ; but the recompense he formally transferred to his son, and ordered the inhabitants of Ithaca to pay it to him. The recompense consisted of barley, wine, honeycombs, olive-oil, salt, and beasts for sacrifice that were older than *phagiloi* ; according to Aristotle's[a] statement, a lamb is a *phagilos*. Now Telemachus bestowed freedom upon Eumaeus and his associates, and incorporated them among the citizens ; and the clan of the Coliadae is descended from Eumaeus, and that of the Bucolidae from Philoetius.[b]

15. WHAT is "the wooden dog" among the Locrians?
Locrus was the son of Physcius, the son of Amphictyon. The son of Locrus and Cabyê was Opus. His father quarrelled with Opus and taking many of the citizens with him he went to seek an oracle concerning a colony. The god told him to found a city where he should chance to be bitten by a wooden dog, and, as he was crossing to the other sea, he trod upon a dog-brier.[c] Greatly troubled by the wound, he spent several days there, during which he explored the country and founded the cities Physcus and Oeantheia and the other cities which the so-called Ozolian Locrians inhabited.

Some say that the Locrians are called Ozolian because of Nessus ; others say that it is because of the serpent Python, since their bodies were washed up

[a] Frag. 507 (ed. V. Rose).
[b] Eumaeus was the swineherd and Philoetius the cowherd of Odysseus.
[c] *Cf.* Athenaeus, 70 C-D.

ἐκβρασθέντας ὑπὸ τῆς θαλάττης καὶ σαπέντας ἐν
τῇ τῶν Λοκρῶν χώρᾳ. τινὲς δὲ κώδια καὶ τραγέας
τοὺς ἀνθρώπους φοροῦντας καὶ τὰ πλεῖστα συνόντας
αἰπολίοις γενέσθαι δυσώδεις. ἔνιοι δὲ τοὐναντίον
πολυάνθεμον τὴν χώραν οὖσαν ὑπ᾽ εὐωδίας τοὔνομα λαβεῖν· ὧν ἐστι καὶ Ἀρχύτας ὁ Ἀμφισσεύς·
γέγραφε γὰρ οὕτω·

295 τὰν¹ βοτρυοστέφανον μυρίπνουν Μάκυναν ἐ-
ραννάν.¹

16. " Τί τὸ καλούμενον ὑπὸ Μεγαρέων ἀφάβρωμα; "

Νῖσος, ἀφ᾽ οὗ προσηγορεύθη Νίσαια, βασιλεύων
ἐκ Βοιωτίας ἔγημεν Ἀβρώτην,² Ὀγχήστου θυγατέρα, Μεγαρέως δ᾽ ἀδελφήν, γυναῖκα καὶ τῷ φρονεῖν
ὡς ἔοικε περιττὴν καὶ σώφρονα διαφερόντως.
ἀποθανούσης δ᾽ αὐτῆς, οἵ τε Μεγαρεῖς ἐπένθησαν
ἑκουσίως καὶ ὁ Νῖσος ἀιδίαν τινὰ μνήμην καὶ δόξαν
αὐτῆς καταστῆναι³ βουλόμενος ἐκέλευε⁴ τὰς ἀστὰς⁵
B φορεῖν ἣν ἐκείνη στολὴν ἐφόρει, καὶ τὴν στολὴν
" ἀφάβρωμα " δι᾽ ἐκείνην ὠνόμασε. δοκεῖ δὲ
τῇ δόξῃ τῆς γυναικὸς καὶ ὁ θεὸς βοηθῆσαι· πολλάκις γὰρ τὰς ἐσθῆτας ἀλλάξαι βουλομένας τὰς
Μεγαρίδας χρησμῷ διεκώλυσε.

17. " Τίς ὁ δορίξενος⁶; "
Τὸ παλαιὸν ἡ Μεγαρὶς ᾠκεῖτο κατὰ κώμας, εἰς
πέντε μέρη νενεμημένων τῶν πολιτῶν. ἐκαλοῦντο

¹ τὰν and ἐραννάν are necessary for τὴν and ἐραννήν of the
mss. if the words are Doric.
² Ἀβρώτην Crönert: Ἀβρώτην.
³ καταστῆναι] καταστῆσαι H. Richards and some mss.
⁴ ἐκέλευε] ἐκέλευσε Bernardakis.

194

by the sea and rotted away in the country of the Locrians. But some say that these men wear fleeces and goatskins and for the most part spend their time with herds of goats, and thus became evil-smelling.[a] But some, on the contrary, assert that, since the country has many flowers, it acquired its name from sweet odour. Among these is also Archytas [b] of Amphissa, for he has written thus :

> Lovely Macyna, wreathed with clusters of grapes and fragrant with perfume.

16. WHAT is it that the Megarians call *aphabroma*?

When Nisus, from whom Nisaea acquired its name, was king, he took a wife from Boeotia, Habrotê, daughter of Onchestus, the sister of Megareus, a woman who, as it appears, was both exceptionally intelligent and remarkably discreet. When she died, the Megarians mourned her with one accord, and Nisus, wishing that her memory and her repute should be established everlastingly, ordered the women of the city to wear the garment that she used to wear ; and because of her he called the garment *apha-broma*. Even the god seems to have furthered the repute of this woman, for often, when the Megarian women wished to make a change in their raiment, he prevented them by an oracle.

17. WHAT is the " spear-friend " ?

In days of old the Megarid used to be settled in village communities with the citizens divided into five groups. They were called Heraeïs, Piraeïs,

---

[a] *Cf.* Pausanias, x. 38.
[b] Powell, *Collectanea Alexandrina*, p. 23.

---

[5] τὰς ἀστὰς Bryan : τὰ ὀστᾶ (Μεγαρίδας in two MSS. can be defended).   [6] δορίξενος] δορύξενος in nearly all MSS.

(295) δ' Ἡραεῖς καὶ Πιραεῖς καὶ Μεγαρεῖς καὶ Κυνοσου-
ρεῖς καὶ Τριποδίσκιοι.¹ τῶν δὲ Κορινθίων πόλεμον
αὐτοῖς ἐξεργασαμένων πρὸς ἀλλήλους (ἀεὶ γὰρ
ἐπεβούλευον ὑφ' αὑτοῖς ποιήσασθαι τὴν Μεγαρικήν),
C ὅμως δι' ἐπιείκειαν ἡμέρως ἐπολέμουν καὶ συγ-
γενικῶς. τοὺς μὲν γὰρ γεωργοῦντας οὐδεὶς ἠδίκει
τὸ παράπαν, τοὺς δ' ἁλισκομένους λύτρον τι τεταγ-
μένον ἔδει καταβαλεῖν, καὶ τοῦτ' ἐλάμβανον ἀφέντες,
πρότερον δ' οὐκ εἰσέπραττον, ἀλλ' ὁ λαβὼν αἰχμάλωτον ἀπῆγεν οἴκαδε, καὶ μεταδοὺς ἁλῶν καὶ
τραπέζης ἀπέπεμπεν οἴκαδε. ὁ μὲν οὖν τὰ λύτρα
κομίσας ἐπῃνεῖτο καὶ φίλος ἀεὶ διετέλει τοῦ
λαβόντος ἐκ δοριαλώτου '' δορίξενος² '' προσ-
αγορευόμενος· ὁ δ' ἀποστερήσας οὐ μόνον παρὰ
τοῖς πολεμίοις ἀλλὰ καὶ παρὰ τοῖς πολίταις ὡς
ἄδικος καὶ ἄπιστος ἠδόξει.

18. '' Τίς ἡ παλιντοκία; ''

Μεγαρεῖς Θεαγένη τὸν τύραννον ἐκβαλόντες,
D ὀλίγον χρόνον ἐσωφρόνησαν κατὰ τὴν πολιτείαν·
εἶτα πολλὴν κατὰ Πλάτωνα καὶ ἄκρατον αὐτοῖς
ἐλευθερίαν τῶν δημαγωγῶν οἰνοχοούντων, δια-
φθαρέντες παντάπασι τά τ' ἄλλα τοῖς πλουσίοις
ἀσελγῶς προσεφέροντο, καὶ παριόντες εἰς τὰς
οἰκίας αὐτῶν οἱ πένητες ἠξίουν ἑστιᾶσθαι καὶ
δειπνεῖν πολυτελῶς· εἰ δὲ μὴ τυγχάνοιεν, πρὸς βίαν
καὶ μεθ' ὕβρεως ἐχρῶντο πᾶσι. τέλος δὲ δόγμα
θέμενοι, τοὺς τόκους ἀνεπράττοντο παρὰ τῶν

---

¹ Τριποδίσκιοι van Herwerden: τριποδισκαῖοι or τριπο-
δισκοῦνοι.   ² δορίξενος] δορύξενος in nearly all mss.

ᵃ Cf. 304 ε, infra.   ᵇ Cf. Thucydides, i. 126.
ᶜ Cf. Plato, Republic, 562 D.

Megareis, Cynosureis, and Tripodiscioi. Although the Corinthians brought about a civil war among them, for the Corinthians were ever plotting to get Megara under their control, none the less, because of their fair-mindedness, they conducted their wars in a civilized and a kinsmanly way. For no one did any harm at all to the men working in the fields, and when anyone was captured, he but needed to pay a certain specified ransom ; this his captors received after they had set him free, and did not collect it earlier ; but he who took a prisoner conducted the man to his house and, after sharing with him salt and food, sent him home. He, accordingly, who brought his ransom, was highly regarded and continued thenceforward to be a friend of his captor ; and, as a consequence of his capture by the spear, he was now called " spear-friend." But anyone who failed to pay the ransom was held in disrepute as dishonest and faithless, not only among his enemies, but also among his fellow-citizens.

18. What is " return-interest " ? [a]

When the Megarians had expelled Theagenes,[b] their despot, for a short time they were sober and sensible in their government. But later when the popular leaders poured a full and heady draught of freedom for them, as Plato [c] says, they were completely corrupted and, among their shocking acts of misconduct toward the wealthy, the poor would enter their homes and insist upon being entertained and banqueted sumptuously. But if they did not receive what they demanded, they would treat all the household with violence and insult. Finally they enacted a decree whereby they received back again the

(295) δανειστῶν οὓς δεδωκότες ἐτύγχανον, " παλιντοκίαν " τὸ γιγνόμενον προσαγορεύσαντες.

19. " Τίς ἡ Ἀνθηδών, περὶ ἧς ἡ Πυθιὰς εἶπε

E ' πῖν' οἶνον τρυγίαν, ἐπεὶ οὐκ Ἀνθηδόνα ναίεις '

(ἡ γὰρ ἐν Βοιωτοῖς οὐκ ἔστι πολύοινος); "

Τὴν Καλαύρειαν¹ Εἰρήνην τὸ παλαιὸν ὠνόμαζον
ἀπὸ γυναικὸς Εἰρήνης, ἣν ἐκ Ποσειδῶνος καὶ
Μελανθείας τῆς Ἀλφειοῦ γενέσθαι μυθολογοῦσιν.
ὕστερον δὲ τῶν περὶ Ἄνθον² καὶ Ὑπέραν³ αὐτόθι
κατοικούντων, Ἀνθηδονίαν καὶ Ὑπέρειαν ἐκάλουν
τὴν νῆσον. εἶχε δ' ὁ χρησμὸς οὕτως, ὡς Ἀριστοτέλης φησί,

πῖν' οἶνον τρυγίαν, ἐπεὶ οὐκ Ἀνθηδόνα ναίεις
οὐδ' ἱερὰν Ὑπέραν, ὅθι γ' ἄτρυγον⁴ οἶνον ἔπινες.

F ταῦτα μὲν ὁ Ἀριστοτέλης. ὁ δὲ Μνασιγείτων
φησὶν Ὑπέρας³ ἀδελφὸν ὄντα τὸν Ἄνθον ἔτι
νήπιον ἀπολέσθαι, καὶ τὴν Ὑπέραν³ κατὰ ζήτησιν
αὐτοῦ πλανωμένην εἰς Φερὰς πρὸς Ἄκαστον⁵
ἐλθεῖν, ὅπου κατὰ τύχην ὁ Ἄνθος ἐδούλευεν οἰνο-
χοεῖν τεταγμένος. ὡς οὖν εἰστιῶντο, τὸν παῖδα
προσφέροντα τῇ ἀδελφῇ τὸ ποτήριον ἐπιγνῶναι
καὶ εἰπεῖν πρὸς αὐτὴν ἡσυχῇ

πῖν' οἶνον τρυγίαν, ἐπεὶ οὐκ Ἀνθηδόνα ναίεις.

¹ Καλαύρειαν the approved form, Bernardakis: Καλαυριὰν.
² Ἄνθον as below: Ἄνθην. (The genders are confused in the
MSS. Ἄνθος is presumably masc. and Ὑπέρα fem. but cf.
Athenaeus, 31 c.)
³ Ὑπέρα, etc., F.C.B.: Ὑπέρη, etc.
⁴ γ' ἄτρυγου Wechel: ὅτι κἂν τρύγα.
⁵ Ἄκαστον Bryan: ἄκαστον ἢ ἄδραστον.

interest which they chanced to have paid to their creditors, calling the measure " return-interest."

19. WHICH is the Anthedon to which the utterance of the prophetic priestess refers :

> Drink wine turbid with lees, since thou dwellest not in Anthedon,

for Anthedon in Boeotia is not rich in wine ?

In days of old they used to call Calaureia by the name of Eirenê, from the woman Eirenê who, as legend has it, was born of Poseidon and Melantheia, the daughter of the Alpheius. But later, when the companions of Anthus and Hypera settled there, they called the island Anthedonia and Hypereia. According to Aristotle [a] the oracle ran as follows :

> Drink wine turbid with lees, since thou dwellest not in Anthedon,
> No, nor in Hypera holy ; for wine without lees thou didst drink there.

This, then, is Aristotle's version. But Mnasigeiton says that Anthus, the brother of Hypera, disappeared from home while he was still a child, and that Hypera, while she was wandering about in search of him, came to Pherae to the house of Acastus, where it chanced that Anthus was the slave appointed to be cupbearer. While they were feasting the boy recognized his sister, as he was bearing her cup to her, and said to her softly

> Drink wine turbid with lees, since thou dwellest not in Anthedon.

[a] Frag. 597 (ed. V. Rose) ; *cf.* Frag. 596 and Athenaeus, 31 B-C.

20. " Τίς ὁ λεγόμενος ἐν Πριήνῃ παρὰ δρυῒ σκότος; "

296 Σάμιοι καὶ Πριηνεῖς πολεμοῦντες ἀλλήλοις, τὰ μὲν ἄλλα μετρίως ἐβλάπτοντο καὶ ἔβλαπτον, μάχης δὲ μεγάλης γενομένης, χιλίους Σαμίων οἱ Πριηνεῖς ἀπέκτειναν· ἑβδόμῳ δ' ὕστερον ἔτει Μιλησίοις συμβαλόντες παρὰ τὴν καλουμένην δρῦν τοὺς ἀρίστους ὁμοῦ τι καὶ πρώτους ἀπέβαλον τῶν πολιτῶν· ὅτε καὶ Βίας ὁ σοφὸς εἰς Σάμον ἐκ Πριήνης πρεσβεύσας εὐδοκίμησε. ταῖς δὲ Πριηνέων γυναιξὶν ὡμοῦ[1] τοῦ πάθους τούτου καὶ τῆς συμφορᾶς ἐλεεινῆς γενομένης, ἀρὰ κατέστη καὶ ὅρκος περὶ τῶν μεγίστων B " ὁ παρὰ δρυῒ σκότος " διὰ τὸ παῖδας αὐτῶν καὶ πατέρας καὶ ἄνδρας ἐκεῖ φονευθῆναι.

21. " Τίνες οἱ παρὰ Κρησὶ λεγόμενοι κατακαῦται; "

Τυρρηνούς φασι τὰς Ἀθηναίων θυγατέρας καὶ γυναῖκας ἐκ Βραύρωνος ἁρπάσαντας, ὁπηνίκα Λῆμνον καὶ Ἴμβρον κατῴκουν, εἶτ' ἐκπεσόντας, εἰς τὴν Λακωνικὴν ἀφικέσθαι καὶ γενέσθαι ἐπιμειξίαν αὐτοῖς μέχρι παίδων γενέσεως πρὸς τὰς ἐγχωρίους γυναῖκας· ἐκ δ' ὑποψίας καὶ διαβολῆς πάλιν ἀναγκασθέντας[2] ἐκλιπεῖν τὴν Λακωνικήν, μετὰ παίδων καὶ γυναικῶν εἰς Κρήτην κατᾶραι, C Πόλλιν ἡγεμόνα καὶ Δελφὸν[3] ἔχοντας. ἐκεῖ δὲ

---

[1] ὡμοῦ Madvig : ὁμοῦ.
[2] ἀναγκασθέντας Wyttenbach : ἀναγκασθέντες.
[3] Πόλλιν ἡγεμόνα καὶ Δελφὸν Wyttenbach, as attested elsewhere, cf. 247 D : πόλιν ἡγεμόνα τὸν ἀδελφόν.

---

[a] Cf. Aristotle, Frag. 576 (ed. V. Rose).

20. WHAT is it that is called in Prienê "the darkness by the Oak " ?

When the Samians and the Prienians were at war with each other, on the other occasions they suffered injuries and inflicted injuries to a moderate degree only ; but when a great battle took place, the people of Prienê slew one thousand Samians. Six years later they engaged the Milesians at a place called the Oak, and lost practically all the best and the foremost of their citizens. At this time also the sage Bias was sent on an embassy from Prienê to Samos and won high repute. For the women of Prienê this was a cruel experience and a pitiable calamity, and it became established as a curse and an oath in the most important matters to swear by "the darkness by the Oak," because of the fact that there their sons, their fathers, and their husbands had been slaughtered.[a]

21. WHO are they that are called "burners" among the Cretans ?

They relate that the Tyrrhenians who, at the time when they inhabited Lemnos and Imbros, carried off the daughters and wives of the Athenians from Brauron, later, when they had been expelled from there, came to Sparta and consorted with the women of the country even to the begetting of children. But again, as the result of suspicions and false accusations, they were forced to leave the Spartan country. With their children and wives they effected a landing in Crete with Pollis and Delphus as their leaders.[b] There, while they were fighting

[b] Cf. Moralia, 247 A-F, and the note there (Vol. III. p. 496).

(296) πολεμοῦντας τοῖς κατέχουσι τὴν Κρήτην, πολλοὺς
περιορᾶν τῶν ἐν ταῖς μάχαις ἀποθνησκόντων
ἀτάφους, τὸ μὲν πρῶτον ἀσχόλους διὰ τὸν πόλεμον
ὄντας καὶ τὸν κίνδυνον, ὕστερον δὲ φεύγοντας
ἅπτεσθαι νεκρῶν ἐφθαρμένων ὑπὸ χρόνου καὶ
διερρυηκότων. τὸν οὖν Πόλλιν ἐξευρόντα τιμάς
τινας καὶ προνομίας καὶ ἀτελείας ἀποδοῦναι τὰς
μὲν τοῖς ἱερεῦσι τῶν θεῶν, τὰς δὲ τοῖς ταφεῦσι τῶν
τετελευτηκότων, ἐπιφημίσαντα καὶ ταύτας δαίμοσι
χθονίοις, ὅπως ἀναφαίρετοι διαμένοιεν· ὀνομασθῆναι
δὲ τοὺς μὲν ἱερεῖς, τοὺς δὲ " κατακαύτας."

Εἶτα[1] κλήρῳ διαλαχεῖν πρὸς τὸν Δελφὸν[2] καὶ
D πολιτεύεσθαι μὲν αὐτοὺς καθ' αὐτούς, ἔχειν δὲ μετὰ
τῶν ἄλλων φιλανθρώπων καὶ ἄδειαν ἀδικημάτων,
οἷς οἱ ἄλλοι Κρῆτες εἰώθασι χρῆσθαι πρὸς ἀλλήλους
ἄγοντες λαθραίως καὶ ἀποφέροντες· ἐκείνους γὰρ
οὐδὲν ἀδικεῖν οὐδὲ κλέπτειν οὐδὲν οὐδ' ἀφαιρεῖσθαι.

22. " Τίς ὁ παίδων τάφος παρὰ Χαλκιδεῦσι; "
Κόθος καὶ Αἶκλος[3] οἱ Ξούθου παῖδες εἰς Εὔβοιαν
ἧκον οἰκήσοντες, Αἰολέων τότε τὰ πλεῖστα τῆς
νήσου κατεχόντων. ἦν δὲ τῷ Κόθῳ λόγιον εὖ
πράξειν καὶ περιέσεσθαι τῶν πολεμίων, ἐὰν
πρίηται τὴν χώραν. ἀποβὰς οὖν μετ' ὀλίγων[4]
ἐνέτυχε παίζουσι παιδαρίοις παρὰ τὴν θάλατταν·
E συμπαίζων οὖν αὐτοῖς καὶ φιλοφρονούμενος ἔδειξε

---

[1] The sentence εἶτα . . . Δελφόν follows διαμένοιεν in the mss.
Transposed by Halliday.

[2] Δελφὸν Wyttenbach, as attested elsewhere, cf. 247 D:
ἀδελφόν.

[3] Αἶκλος Xylander: ἄρκλος.

[4] ὀλίγων Meziriacus: ὀλίγον.

the possessors of the island, they suffered many of the men who had been slain in the battles to lie unburied, because at first they had no leisure to bury them because of the war and the danger, and later because they shrank from touching corpses that had been decomposed and putrefied by the lapse of time. Accordingly Pollis devised certain honours, privileges, and immunities, and some of these he bestowed on the priests of the gods, others upon them that buried the dead. These honours he put in the keeping of the spirits of the underworld in order that they might continue for ever irrevocable. The one class received the name of priests, and the other that of " burners."

Then Pollis made a division by lot with Delphus, and they governed separate and independent states ; and, along with other humane provisions which they enjoyed, they had freedom from the injuries which the other Cretans are wont to inflict upon one another through stealthy plundering and pillaging. For to the Tyrrhenian communities they do no injury, nor do they steal anything from them or dispossess them of anything.

22. WHAT is the " Children's Tomb " among the Chalcidians ?

Cothus and Aeclus, the sons of Xuthus, came to Euboea to dwell at a time when the Aeolians possessed the greater part of the island. It had been prophesied to Cothus that he should have great success and get the better of his enemies if he bought the land. When he had landed on the island with a few men, he encountered little children playing by the sea. So he joined in their play, and in a kindly spirit showed them many playthings

παίγνια πολλὰ τῶν ξενικῶν. ὡς δ᾽ ἑώρα τοὺς
παῖδας ἐπιθυμοῦντας λαβεῖν, οὐκ ἔφησεν αὐτοῖς
δώσειν ἄλλως, εἰ μὴ τῆς γῆς λάβοι παρ᾽ αὐτῶν·
οἱ δὲ παῖδες οὕτως ἀναιρούμενοι χαμᾶθεν[1] ἐδίδο-
σαν καὶ τὰ παίγνια λαβόντες ἀπηλλάγησαν. οἱ
δ᾽ Αἰολεῖς αἰσθόμενοι τὸ γεγονός, καὶ τῶν πολεμίων αὐτοῖς ἐπιπλεόντων, ὑπ᾽ ὀργῆς καὶ λύπης δι-
εχρήσαντο τοὺς παῖδας. ἐτάφησαν δὲ παρὰ τὴν
ὁδὸν ᾗ βαδίζουσιν ἐκ πόλεως ἐπὶ τὸν Εὔριπον,
καὶ ὁ τόπος " τάφος παίδων " καλεῖται.

23. " Τίς ὁ μιξαρχαγέτας[2] ἐν Ἄργει καὶ τίνες
F οἱ ἐλάσιοι; "

" Μιξαρχαγέταν[2] " τὸν Κάστορα καλοῦσι καὶ
νομίζουσι παρ᾽ αὐτοῖς τεθάφθαι· τὸν δὲ Πολυ-
δεύκην ὡς ἕνα τῶν Ὀλυμπίων σέβονται. τοὺς δὲ
τὰς ἐπιληψίας ἀποτρέπειν δοκοῦντας " ἐλασίους "
μὲν ὀνομάζουσι, δοκοῦσι δὲ τῶν Ἀλεξίδας τῆς
Ἀμφιαράου θυγατρὸς ἀπογόνων εἶναι.

24. " Τί τὸ παρ᾽ Ἀργείοις λεγόμενον ἔγκνισμα; "
Τοῖς ἀποβαλοῦσί τινα συγγενῶν ἢ συνήθων ἔθος
ἐστὶ μετὰ τὸ πένθος εὐθὺς τῷ Ἀπόλλωνι θύειν,
ἡμέραις δ᾽ ὕστερον τριάκοντα τῷ Ἑρμῇ. νομίζουσι γάρ, ὥσπερ τὰ σώματα τῶν ἀποθανόντων
δέχεσθαι τὴν γῆν, οὕτω τὰς ψυχὰς τὸν Ἑρμῆν·
297 τοῦ δ᾽ Ἀπόλλωνος τῷ ἀμφιπόλῳ κριθὰς διδόντες
λαμβάνουσι κρέας τοῦ ἱερείου, καὶ τὸ πῦρ

---

[1] χαμᾶθεν Pierson : χαμαῖθεν.
[2] μιξαρχαγέτας (-ν) Xylander : μιξαρχαγεύτας (-ν).

---

[a] Cf. Müller, *Frag. Hist. Graec.* iv. p. 498.

from foreign lands. But when he saw that the children were desirous of having them for their own, he refused to give them unless he too should receive some earth from the children. So they picked up some from the ground and gave it to Cothus, and then, taking the playthings, departed. But the Aeolians discovered what had happened, and, when their enemies sailed against them, they made away with the children under stress of anger and grief. The children were buried beside the road which leads from the city to the Euripus, and the place is called the Children's Tomb.

23. Who is the "Associate-founder" (*mixarchagetas*) at Argos, and who are the " Averters " (*elasioi*) ?

They call Castor the Associate-founder, and think that he is buried in Argive territory, but Polydeuces they reverence as one of the Olympians. Persons who have the reputed ability to turn away attacks of epilepsy they call Averters, and these are thought to be of the descendants of Alexida, the daughter of Amphiaraüs.

24. What is that which is called an *enknisma* (a roast) among the Argives ? [a]

It is the custom for those who have lost a relative or an intimate friend to sacrifice to Apollo [b] immediately after the mourning, and again thirty days later to Hermes. For they believe that, just as the earth receives the bodies of the dead, even so Hermes receives their souls. They give barley to the priest of Apollo and receive some meat of the sacrificial

---

[b] For " Apollo " Halliday suggests with some plausibility "Pluto " ; but Apollo, as the god who cleanses from pollution (καθάρσιος), is almost a commonplace in Greek literature.

(297) ἀποσβέσαντες ὡς μεμιασμένον παρ' ἑτέρων δ' ἐν-
αυσάμενοι, τοῦτο τὸ κρέας ὀπτῶσιν " ἔγκνισμα "
προσαγορεύοντες.

25. " Τίς ἀλάστωρ ἀλιτήριος παλαμναῖος; "

Οὐ γὰρ πειστέον τοῖς λέγουσιν " ἀλιτηρίους "
κεκλῆσθαι τοὺς ἐπιτηροῦντας ἐν τῷ λιμῷ τὸν
ἀλοῦντα καὶ διαρπάζοντας· ἀλλ' " ἀλάστωρ " μὲν
κέκληται ὁ ἄληστα καὶ πολὺν χρόνον μνημονευ-
θησόμενα δεδρακώς, " ἀλιτήριος " δ' ὃν ἀλεύασθαι
καὶ φυλάξασθαι διὰ μοχθηρίαν καλῶς εἶχε. ταῦτα,
φησὶν ὁ Σωκράτης,[c] ἐν διφθέραις χαλκαῖς γεγρά-
φασι.

B 26. " Τίνος ἔχεται διανοίας τὸ τοὺς ἀπάγοντας
εἰς Κασσιοπαίαν τὸν βοῦν ἐξ Αἰνίδος[1] τὰς παρθένους προπεμπούσας ἐπᾴδειν ἄχρι τῶν ὅρων

μήποτε νοστήσαιτε φίλην ἐς πατρίδα γαῖαν; "

Αἰνιᾶνες ὑπὸ Λαπιθῶν ἐξαναστάντες τὸ πρῶτον
ᾤκησαν περὶ τὴν Αἰθικίαν,[2] εἶτα περὶ τὴν Μολοτ-
τίδα καὶ Κασσιοπαίαν· οὐδὲν δὲ χρηστὸν ἀπὸ τῆς
χώρας ἔχοντες, ἀλλὰ καὶ χαλεποῖς χρώμενοι προσ-
C οίκοις εἰς τὸ Κιρραῖον πεδίον ἧκον, Οἰνόκλου[3] τοῦ
βασιλέως ἄγοντος αὐτούς. ἐκεῖ δὲ μεγάλων αὐχμῶν γενομένων, κατὰ χρησμὸν ὡς λέγεται τὸν

---

[1] Αἰνίδος F.C.B., cf. Αἰνίδι S.G.D.I. 1431 (for Αἰνίᾳ?);
Αἰνίας Bernardakis; Αἰνιάνων Wyttenbach: Αἴνου.
[2] Αἰθικίαν F.C.B., cf. 293 F: Αἰθακίαν.
[3] Οἰνόκλου . . . Οἰνόκλον] Ὀνόκλου . . . Ὄνοκλον, most mss.
Cf. 294 A.

---

[a] Cf. Moralia, 523 A-B.   [b] Ibid. 418 B.
[c] Socrates of Argos; cf. Müller, Frag. Hist. Graec. v.
p. 498.

victim ; and when they have put out their fire, since they believe it to be polluted, and have relighted it from the hearth of others, they proceed to roast this flesh which they call *enknisma*.

25. WHAT is an *alastor*, an *aliterios*, a *palamnaeos*?

We certainly must not believe those who say that persons who, during a famine, set a watch upon the miller and plunder him are called *aliterioi*.[a] But he who has done unforgettable (*alesta*) things,[b] things that will be remembered for a long time, is called *alastor* ; and he whom it were well to avoid (*aleuasthai*) and to guard against because of his wickedness is called *aliterios*. These things, according to the statement of Socrates,[c] they have written on tablets of bronze.

26. WHAT is the intent of the custom by which the maidens who serve as an escort for the men who lead the bull from Aenis to Cassiopaea chant until they reach the boundary,

Never may ye return to the well-loved soil of your homeland?[d]

When the Aenianians had been driven out of their country by the Lapiths,[e] they dwelt first of all about Aethicia, and later about Molossia and Cassiopaea. But, since they had no benefit from the country, and, in addition, had to deal with ungentle peoples on their borders, they came to the Cirrhaean plain under the leadership of Oenoclus, their king. But great droughts befell them there, and, as it is related, in accordance with an oracle they stoned

[a] Adapted from Homer, *Od.* xviii. 148 (=xix. 298).
[e] *cf.* 293 F–294 C, *supra.*

(297) Οἴνοκλον[1] καταλεύσαντες καὶ πάλιν πλανηθέντες,
εἰς ταύτην ἀφίκοντο τὴν χώραν, ἣν νῦν ἔχουσιν,
ἀγαθὴν καὶ πάμφορον οὖσαν. ὅθεν εἰκότως εὔχονται τοῖς θεοῖς εἰς τὴν παλαιὰν πατρίδα μὴ
ἐπανελθεῖν, ἀλλ' αὐτοῦ καταμένειν εὐδαιμονοῦντας.

27. " Τί δήποτε παρὰ Ῥοδίοις εἰς τὸ τοῦ Ὀκρι-
δίωνος ἡρῷον οὐκ εἰσέρχεται κῆρυξ; "

Ἢ ὅτι Ὄχιμος τὴν θυγατέρα Κυδίππην ἐν-
εγγύησεν Ὀκριδίωνι; Κέρκαφος δ' ἀδελφὸς ὢν
Ὀχίμου τῆς δὲ παιδὸς ἐρῶν, ἔπεισε τὸν κήρυκα
D (διὰ κηρύκων γὰρ ἔθος ἦν τὸ μετέρχεσθαι τὰς
νύμφας), ὅταν παραλάβῃ τὴν Κυδίππην, πρὸς ἑαυτὸν ἀγαγεῖν. τούτου δὲ πραχθέντος, ὁ μὲν Κέρκαφος ἔχων τὴν κόρην ἔφυγεν, ὕστερον δὲ τοῦ
Ὀχίμου γηράσαντος ἐπανῆλθε. τοῖς δὲ Ῥοδίοις
ἔθος[2] κατέστη κήρυκα μὴ προσιέναι τῷ τοῦ Ὀκρι-
δίωνος ἡρῴῳ διὰ τὴν γενομένην ἀδικίαν.

28. " Τί δήποτε παρὰ Τενεδίοις εἰς τὸ τοῦ
Τένου ἱερὸν οὐκ ἔξεστιν αὐλητὴν εἰσελθεῖν οὐδ'
Ἀχιλλέως ἐν τῷ ἱερῷ μνησθῆναι; "

Ἢ ὅτι τῆς μητρυιᾶς τὸν Τένην διαβαλούσης ὡς
βουλόμενον αὐτῇ συγγενέσθαι Μόλπος[3] ὁ αὐλητὴς
E τὰ ψευδῆ κατεμαρτύρησεν αὐτοῦ, διὰ τοῦτο τῷ
Τένῃ συνέπεσε φεύγειν εἰς Τένεδον μετὰ τῆς
ἀδελφῆς; Ἀχιλλεῖ δὲ λέγεται τὴν μητέρα Θέτιν
ἰσχυρῶς ἀπαγορεῦσαι[4] μὴ ἀνελεῖν τὸν Τένην ὡς

---

[1] Οἴνοκλον] Ὄνοκλον most mss.   Cf. 294 A.
[2] ἔθος is omitted in some mss.
[3] Μόλπος] Εὔμολπος Apollodorus, Epitome, iii. 24.
[4] ἀπαγορεῦσαι] ἀγορεῦσαι in all mss. but one.

Oenoclus.[a] Then they wandered on and came to this country which they now possess, a goodly country, productive of all manner of crops ; wherefore it is with good reason that they pray to the gods that they may not return again to their ancient fatherland, but may remain here in prosperity.

27. Why is it that among the Rhodians a herald does not enter the shrine of the hero Ocridion ?

Is it because Ochimus affianced his daughter Cydippê to Ocridion ? But Cercaphus, who was the brother of Ochimus, was in love with the maiden and persuaded the herald (for it used to be the custom to use heralds to fetch the brides), when he should receive Cydippê, to bring her to him. When this had been accomplished, Cercaphus fled with the maiden ; but later, when Ochimus had grown old, Cercaphus returned to his home again. But the custom became established among the Rhodians that a herald should not approach the shrine of Ocridion because of the wrong that had been done.

28. Why is it that among the inhabitants of Tenedos a flute-player may not enter the shrine of Tenes, nor may anyone mention Achilles' name within the shrine ?

Is it that, when Tenes' stepmother [b] falsely accused him of wishing to lie with her, Molpus the flute-player bore false witness against him, and because of this it came about that Tenes had to flee to Tenedos with his sister ? But as for Achilles, it is said that his mother Thetis straitly forbade him to kill Tenes, since

---

[a] Cf. 293 F–294 A, supra.
[b] Cf. Apollodorus, Epitome, iii. 23-26, with Frazer's notes (L.C.L. vol. ii. pp. 193 ff.).

τιμώμενον ὑπ' Ἀπόλλωνος, καὶ παρεγγυῆσαι ἑνὶ
τῶν οἰκετῶν, ὅπως προσέχῃ καὶ ἀναμιμνῇσκῃ, μὴ
λάθοι κτείνας ὁ Ἀχιλλεὺς τὸν Τένην. ἐπεὶ δὲ
τὴν Τένεδον κατατρέχων ἐδίωκε τὴν ἀδελφὴν τοῦ
F Τένου καλὴν οὖσαν ἀπαντήσας θ' ὁ Τένης ἠμύνετο
πρὸ τῆς ἀδελφῆς, καὶ ἡ μὲν ἐξέφυγεν ὁ δὲ Τένης
ἀνῃρέθη· ὁ δ' Ἀχιλλεὺς πεσόντα γνωρίσας[1] τὸν
μὲν οἰκέτην ἀπέκτεινεν ὅτι παρὼν οὐκ ἀνέμνησε,
τὸν δὲ Τένην ἔθαψεν οὗ νῦν τὸ ἱερόν ἐστι, καὶ οὔτ'
αὐλητὴς εἴσεισιν οὔτ' Ἀχιλλεὺς ὀνομάζεται.

29. " Τίς ὁ παρ' Ἐπιδαμνίοις πωλήτης; "
Ἐπιδάμνιοι γειτνιῶντες Ἰλλυριοῖς ᾐσθάνοντο
τοὺς ἐπιμειγνυμένους αὐτοῖς πολίτας γιγνομένους
πονηροὺς καὶ φοβούμενοι νεωτερισμὸν ᾑροῦντο πρὸς
τὰ τοιαῦτα συμβόλαια καὶ τὰς ἀμείψεις καθ'
ἕκαστον ἐνιαυτὸν ἕνα τῶν δεδοκιμασμένων παρ'
αὐτοῖς, ὃς ἐπιφοιτῶν τοῖς βαρβάροις παρεῖχεν
298 ἀγορὰν καὶ διάθεσιν πᾶσι τοῖς πολίταις " πωλήτης "
προσαγορευόμενος.

30. " Τίς ἡ περὶ Θρᾴκην Ἀραίνου[2] ἀκτή; "
Ἄνδριοι καὶ Χαλκιδεῖς πλεύσαντες εἰς Θρᾴκην
οἰκήσεως ἕνεκα Σάνην μὲν πόλιν ἐκ προδοσίας
κοινῇ παρέλαβον, τὴν δ' Ἄκανθον ἐκλελοιπέναι
τοὺς βαρβάρους πυνθανόμενοι, δύο κατασκόπους
ἔπεμψαν. ὡς δὲ τῇ πόλει προσιόντες παντάπασι
πεφευγότας ᾐσθάνοντο τοὺς πολεμίους, ὁ μὲν
Χαλκιδικὸς προεξέδραμεν ὡς καταληψόμενος τοῖς
Χαλκιδεῦσι τὴν πόλιν, ὁ δ' Ἄνδριος οὐ συνεξανύτων

---

[1] γνωρίσας] ἐγνώρισε in one ms. (E).
[2] Ἀραίνου] Ἀραίου ? Bernardakis; ἀραοῦ, ἀράνου most mss.

Tenes was honoured by Apollo; and she commissioned one of the servants to be on guard, and to remind Achilles lest he should unwittingly slay Tenes. But when Achilles was overrunning Tenedos and was pursuing Tenes' sister, who was a beautiful maiden, Tenes met him and defended his sister; and she escaped, though Tenes was slain. When he had fallen, Achilles recognized him, and slew the servant because he had, although present, not reminded him; and he buried Tenes where his shrine now stands and neither does a flute-player enter it nor is Achilles mentioned there by name.

29. Who is the "Seller" among the Epidamnians?
The Epidamnians were neighbours of the Illyrians and perceived that such of their citizens as associated with the Illyrians were becoming corrupted; and, since they feared a revolution, they used to select one of the most reputable of their fellow-citizens each year to conduct such commercial dealings and barters. This man visited the barbarians and provided them with a market and an opportunity for all the citizens to display what they had to sell: thus he was called the "Seller."

30. What is the "Beach of Araenus" in Thrace?
When the Andrians and Chalcidians sailed to Thrace to settle there, they jointly seized the city of Sanê, which was betrayed to them; but when they learned that the barbarians had abandoned Acanthus, they sent out two scouts. When these were approaching the city, they perceived that the enemy had all fled; so the Chalcidian ran forward to take possession of the city for Chalcis, but the Andrian, since he could not cover the distance so rapidly as

(298) ἠκόντισε τὸ δόρυ, καὶ ταῖς πύλαις ἐμπαρέντος
B μέγα βοήσας[1] Ἀνδρίων ἔφη παισὶν αἰχμῇ προ-
κατειλῆφθαι τὴν πόλιν. ἐκ τούτου διαφορᾶς γενομένης, ἄνευ πολέμου συνέβησαν Ἐρυθραίοις καὶ
Σαμίοις καὶ Παρίοις χρήσασθαι περὶ πάντων δικασταῖς. ἐπεὶ δ' οἱ μὲν Ἐρυθραῖοι καὶ οἱ Σάμιοι τὴν
ψῆφον Ἀνδρίοις ἤνεγκαν, οἱ δὲ Πάριοι Χαλκι-
δεῦσιν, ἀρὰς ἔθεντο περὶ τὸν τόπον τοῦτον οἱ
Ἄνδριοι κατ' αὐτῶν μήτε δοῦναι γυναῖκα Παρίοις
μήτε λαβεῖν παρ' αὐτῶν· καὶ διὰ τοῦτο προσ-
ηγόρευσαν " ἀκτὴν Ἀραίνου,[2] " πρότερον ὀνομαζομένην Δράκοντος.

31. " Διὰ τί τοῖς Θεσμοφορίοις αἱ τῶν Ἐρε-
τριέων γυναῖκες οὐ πρὸς πῦρ ἀλλὰ πρὸς ἥλιον
ὀπτῶσι τὰ κρέα, καὶ Καλλιγένειαν οὐ καλοῦσιν; "
C " Ἢ ὅτι ταῖς αἰχμαλώτοις, ἃς ἦγεν ἐκ Τροίας
Ἀγαμέμνων, ἐνταῦθα συνέβη Θεσμοφόρια θύειν,
πλοῦ δὲ φανέντος ἐξαίφνης ἀνήχθησαν ἀτελῆ τὴν
θυσίαν καταλιποῦσαι;

32. " Τίνες οἱ ἀεὶναῦται παρὰ Μιλησίοις; "
Τῶν περὶ Θόαντα καὶ Δαμασήνορα τυράννων
καταλυθέντων, ἑταιρεῖαι δύο τὴν πόλιν κατέσχον,
ὧν ἡ μὲν ἐκαλεῖτο Πλουτὶς ἡ δὲ Χειρομάχα.[3]
κρατήσαντες οὖν οἱ δυνατοὶ καὶ τὰ πράγματα

---

[1] μέγα βοήσας Patzig : μετὰ βοῆς or βολῆς.
[2] Ἀραίνου] Ἀραίου ? Bernardakis ; ἀραοῦ, ἀράνου most mss.
[3] Χειρομάχα] Χειρομάχη?

[a] Plutarch, or his source, imagined that this meant " Beach
of Vowing."
[b] The name of the third and last day of this festival at
Athens ; probably also a cult title applied to some goddess,
perhaps to Demeter.   [c] " Capital and Labour."

his rival, hurled his spear, and when it was firmly
implanted in the city gates, he called out in a loud
voice that by his spear the city had been taken into
prior possession for the children of the Andrians. As
a result of this a dispute arose, and, without going
to war, they agreed to make use of Erythraeans,
Samians, and Parians as arbitrators concerning the
whole matter. But when the Erythraeans and the
Samians gave their vote in favour of the Andrians,
and the Parians in favour of the Chalcidians, the
Andrians, in the neighbourhood of this place, made
a solemn vow against the Parians that they would
never give a woman in marriage to the Parians nor
take one from them. And for this reason they called
the place the Beach of Araenus,[a] although it had
formerly been named the Serpent's Beach.

31. WHY is it that at the Thesmophoria the Eretrian
women cook their meat, not by fire, but by the
rays of the sun; and why do they not call upon
Calligeneia?[b]

Is it because it happened that the captive women
whom Agamemnon was bringing home from Troy
were celebrating the Thesmophoria at this place,
but when conditions for sailing suddenly appeared
favourable, they put out to sea leaving behind them
the sacrifice uncompleted?

32. WHO are the Perpetual Sailors among the
Milesians?

When the despots associated with Thoas and
Damasenor had been overthrown, two political parties
came into control of the city, one of which was called
Plutis, the other Cheiromacha.[c] When, accordingly,
the men of influence gained the upper hand and

213

(298) περιστήσαντες εἰς τὴν ἑταιρείαν, ἐβουλεύοντο περὶ
τῶν μεγίστων ἐμβαίνοντες εἰς τὰ πλοῖα καὶ πόρρω
D τῆς γῆς ἐπανάγοντες· κυρώσαντες δὲ τὴν γνώμην
κατέπλεον, καὶ διὰ τοῦτ' " ἀειναῦται " προσηγορεύθησαν.

33. " Τί δήποτε Χαλκιδεῖς τὸν περὶ τὸ Πυρ-
σόφιον τόπον ' ἀκμαίων λέσχην ' καλοῦσι; "

Τὸν Ναύπλιόν φασιν ὑπὸ τῶν Ἀχαιῶν διωκό-
μενον Χαλκιδεῖς ἱκετεῦσαι, καὶ τὰ μὲν περὶ τῆς
αἰτίας ἀπολογεῖσθαι, τὰ δ' αὐτὸν ἀντεγκαλεῖν τοῖς
Ἀχαιοῖς. ἐκδιδόναι μὲν αὐτὸν οἱ Χαλκιδεῖς οὐκ
ἐμέλλησαν· δεδιότες δὲ μὴ δόλῳ φονευθῇ, φυ-
λακὴν ἔδοσαν αὐτῷ τοὺς ἀκμάζοντας νεανίσκους
καὶ κατέστησαν εἰς τὸν τόπον τοῦτον, ὅπου συνῆσαν
ἀλλήλοις ἅμα καὶ τὸν Ναύπλιον παρεφύλαττον.

E 34. " Τίς ὁ βοῦν εὐεργέτῃ θύσας; " [a]

Πλοῖον ὥρμει περὶ τὴν Ἰθακησίαν ληστρικόν,
ἐν ᾧ πρεσβύτης ἐτύγχανε μετὰ κεραμίων ἐχόντων
πίτταν. τούτῳ[1] οὖν κατὰ τύχην προσέσχε πορ-
θμεὺς Ἰθακήσιος ὀνόματι Πυρρίας, καὶ τὸν πρεσ-
βύτην ἐρρύσατο μηδενὸς δεόμενος, ἀλλὰ πεισθεὶς
ὑπ' αὐτοῦ καὶ οἰκτίρας· προσέλαβε δὲ καὶ τῶν
κεραμίων, τοῦ πρεσβύτου κελεύσαντος. ἀπαλ-
λαγέντων δὲ τῶν ληστῶν καὶ γενομένης ἀδείας, ὁ
πρεσβύτης τοῖς κεραμίοις τὸν Πυρρίαν προσαγαγὼν

---

[1] τούτῳ] ταύτῃ in most mss.

[a] Possibly " sacrificed an ox to his benefactor "; but an
animal sacrifice to a living man seems incredible.

214

brought matters into the control of their party, they used to deliberate about matters of the greatest importance by embarking in their ships and putting out to a considerable distance from the land. But when they had come to a final decision, they sailed back ; and because of this they acquired the appellation of Perpetual Sailors.

33. Why do the Chalcidians call the neighbourhood of the Beacon " the Young Men's Club " ?

They relate that Nauplius, when he was being pursued by the Achaeans, came as a suppliant to the Chalcidians ; and on the one hand he defended himself in regard to the indictment brought against him, and on the other hand brought a counter-charge against the Achaeans. The Chalcidians had no intention of surrendering him ; but, since they were afraid that he might be slain by treachery, they gave him a guard of young men in the prime of their youth and stationed them in this place, where they lived together and at the same time served as a guard for Nauplius.

34. Who was the man that slew an ox for *a* his benefactor ?

Anchored off the island of Ithaca was a pirate vessel in which there chanced to be an old man with earthenware jars containing pitch. By chance a ferryman of Ithaca, by name Pyrrhias, put off to the ship and rescued the old man without asking for any reward, but because he had been persuaded by the old man and pitied him. He did, however, accept some of the jars, for the old man bade him do so. But when the pirates had departed and there was nothing to fear, the old man led Pyrrhias to the jars,

215

F χρυσίον ἐδείκνυεν ἐν αὐτοῖς πολὺ καὶ ἀργύριον τῇ
πίττῃ καταμεμειγμένον. ἐξαίφνης οὖν ὁ Πυρρίας
πλούσιος γενόμενος τά τ' ἄλλ' εὖ περιεῖπε τὸν
γέροντα καὶ βοῦν ἔθυσεν αὐτῷ. ὃ καὶ παροιμια-
ζόμενοι λέγουσιν " οὐδεὶς[1] εὐεργέτῃ βοῦν ἔθυσεν
ἀλλ' ἢ Πυρρίας."

35. " Τί δήποτε ταῖς κόραις τῶν Βοττιαίων
ἔθος ἦν λέγειν χορευούσαις ' ἴωμεν εἰς 'Αθήνας '; "
Κρῆτάς φασιν εὐξαμένους ἀνθρώπων ἀπαρχὴν
εἰς Δελφοὺς ἀποστεῖλαι, τοὺς δὲ πεμφθέντας, ὡς
299 ἑώρων οὐδεμίαν οὖσαν εὐπορίαν, αὐτόθεν εἰς
ἀποικίαν ὁρμῆσαι· καὶ πρῶτον μὲν ἐν 'Ιαπυγίᾳ
κατοικῆσαι,[2] ἔπειτα τῆς Θρᾴκης τοῦτον τὸν τόπον
κατασχεῖν, ἀναμεμειγμένων αὐτοῖς 'Αθηναίων.
ἔοικε γὰρ μὴ διαφθείρειν ὁ Μίνως οὓς ἔπεμπον
'Αθηναῖοι κατὰ τὸν δασμὸν ᾐθέους, ἀλλὰ κατέχειν
παρ' ἑαυτῷ λατρεύοντας. ἐξ ἐκείνων οὖν τινες
γεγονότες καὶ νομιζόμενοι Κρῆτες εἰς Δελφοὺς
συναπεστάλησαν. ὅθεν αἱ θυγατέρες τῶν Βοττιαίων ἀπομνημονεύουσαι τοῦ γένους ᾖδον ἐν ταῖς
ἑορταῖς " ἴωμεν εἰς 'Αθήνας."

36. " Διὰ τί τὸν Διόνυσον αἱ τῶν 'Ηλείων
γυναῖκες ὑμνοῦσαι παρακαλοῦσι βοέῳ ποδὶ παρα-
B γίγνεσθαι πρὸς αὐτάς; ἔχει δ' οὕτως ὁ ὕμνος.

---

[1] οὐδεὶς] οὐδὲ εἷς Meziriacus.
[2] κατοικῆσαι] κατοικεῖν all mss. but one (E), but cf., for
example, 297 B.

---

[a] Plutarch (Life of Theseus, chap. xvi. p. 6 E ff.) states
that his source for this is Aristotle's Constitution of the
Bottiaeans (Frag. 485 (ed. V. Rose)); cf. Edmonds, Lyra
Graeca (in L.C.L. iii. 540).
[b] For Dionysus as a bull cf. e.g. Athenaeus 35 E, 38 E.

216

and in them showed him much gold and silver mixed with the pitch. So Pyrrhias, suddenly becoming rich, treated the old man well in various ways, and also slew an ox for him. Wherefore men make use of this as a proverbial expression : " No one but Pyrrhias has slain an ox for his benefactor."

35. WHY was it the custom for the Bottiaean maidens to chant as they danced, " Let us go to Athens [a] " ?

They relate that the Cretans in accordance with a vow sent a consecrated offering of men to Delphi ; but the men who had been sent, when they saw that there was no abundance there, set out from Delphi to found a colony. They settled first in Iapygia, but later occupied this region of Thrace. There were some Athenians included among them ; for it appears that Minos did not destroy the young persons whom the Athenians sent him for tribute, but kept them by him as servants. Accordingly, some who were descended from these Athenians and had come to be considered Cretans were included in this company sent to Delphi. Wherefore the daughters of the Bottiaeans, in remembrance of their lineage, were wont to sing in their festivals, " Let us go to Athens."

36. WHY is it that the women of the Eleans, when they sing hymns to Dionysus, call upon him to come to them " with the foot of a bull " [b] ? The hymn [c] runs as follows :

[c] The text is uncertain ; Hartman has attempted a reconstruction in *Mnemosyne*, xli. 217 ; *cf.* also the other references in E. Diehl, *Anthologia Lyrica Graeca*, ii. p. 206. *Cf.* also *Moralia*, 364 F ; Pausanias, vi. 26. 1 ; Bergk, *Poet. Lyr. Graec.* iii. p. 656, or Edmonds, *Lyra Graeca* (L.C.L. iii. 510).

(299)

ἐλθεῖν, ἥρω Διόνυσε,
Ἀλεῖον[1] ἐς ναὸν
ἁγνὸν σὺν Χαρίτεσσιν
ἐς ναὸν
τῷ βοέῳ ποδὶ θύων.'

εἶτα δὶς ἐπᾴδουσιν ' ἄξιε[2] ταῦρε.' ''

Πότερον ὅτι καὶ βουγενῆ προσαγορεύουσι καὶ
ταῦρον[3] ἔνιοι τὸν θεὸν ἢ τῷ μεγάλῳ ποδὶ '' βοέῳ ''
λέγουσιν, ὡς '' βοῶπιν '' ὁ ποιητὴς τὴν μεγαλ-
όφθαλμον καὶ '' βουγάιον '' τὸν μεγάλαυχον;

Ἢ μᾶλλον, ὅτι τοῦ βοὸς ὁ πούς ἀβλαβής ἐστι
τὸ δὲ κερασφόρον[4] ἐπιβλαβές, οὕτω τὸν θεὸν παρακαλοῦσι πρᾶον ἐλθεῖν καὶ ἄλυπον;

Ἢ ὅτι καὶ ἀρότου[5] καὶ σπόρου πολλοὶ τὸν θεὸν
ἀρχηγὸν γεγονέναι νομίζουσι;

C   37. '' Διὰ τί Ταναγραίοις πρὸ τῆς πόλεως ἔστιν
Ἀχίλλειον, τόπος οὕτω προσαγορευόμενος; ἔχ-
θρα γὰρ αὐτῷ μᾶλλον ἢ φιλία λέγεται γεγονέναι
πρὸς τὴν πόλιν, ἁρπάσαντι μὲν τὴν μητέρα τοῦ
Ποιμάνδρου Στρατονίκην, ἀποκτείναντι δ' υἱὸν
Ἐφίππου[6] Ἀκέστορα.''

Ποίμανδρος τοίνυν ὁ Ἐφίππου πατήρ, ἔτι τῆς
Ταναγρικῆς κατὰ κώμας οἰκουμένης, ἐν τῷ καλουμένῳ Στέφοντι πολιορκούμενος ὑπὸ τῶν Ἀχαιῶν
διὰ τὸ μὴ βούλεσθαι συστρατεύειν, ἐξέλιπε τὸ
χωρίον ἐκεῖνο νύκτωρ καὶ τὴν Ποιμανδρίαν ἐτείχισε.

---

[1] Ἀλεῖον Cobet ; Ἀλείων Bergk : ἄλιον.
[2] ἐπᾴδουσι, Νάξιε Cobet.
[3] ταῦρον] κερασφόρον Kronenberg.
[4] κερασφόρον] κέρας Kronenberg.
[5] ἀρότου Wyttenbach : ἀρότρου.
[6] Ἐφίππου] Wyttenbach would omit.

> Come, O hero Dionysus,
> To thy Elean holy
> Temple, with the Graces,
> To thy temple
> With thy bull's foot hasting.

Then they chant twice the refrain : " O worthy bull."

Is it because some address the god as " kine-born " or as " bull " ? Or by " ox-foot " do they mean " with thy mighty foot," even as the Poet used " ox-eyed " [a] to signify " large-eyed," and " bully " [b] for " loud-mouthed " ?

Or is it rather because the foot of the bull is harmless, but the part that bears horns is harmful, and thus they call upon the god to come in a gentle and painless manner ?

Or is it because many believe that the god was the pioneer in both ploughing and sowing ?

37. WHY do the people of Tanagra have before their city an Achilleum, that is, a place bearing this name ? For it is related that Achilles actually had more enmity than friendship for the city, since he carried off Stratonicê, the mother of Poemander, and slew Acestor, the son of Ephippus.[c]

While the territory of Tanagra was still inhabited in village communities, Poemander, the father of Ephippus, had been besieged by the Achaeans in the place called Stephon, because of his unwillingness to join their expedition.[d] But he abandoned that stronghold by night and fortified Poemandria.[e]

---

[a] Homer, *Il.* i. 551 and often.
[b] βουγάιος, *Il.* xiii. 824 : *Od.* xviii. 79.
[c] A grandson of Poemander.
[d] Against Troy.　　　　[e] *Cf.* Pausanias, ix. 20. 1.

(299) παρὼν δὲ Πολύκριθος ὁ ἀρχιτέκτων διαφαυλίζων τὰ
D ἔργα καὶ καταγελῶν ὑπερήλατο τὴν τάφρον. ὀργισθεὶς ὁ Ποίμανδρος ὥρμησε λίθον ἐμβαλεῖν αὐτῷ
μέγαν, ὃς ἦν αὐτόθι κεκρυμμένος ἐκ παλαιοῦ, Νυκτελίοις ἱεροῖς ἀποκείμενος[1]· τοῦτον ἀνασπάσας ὑπ'
ἀγνοίας ὁ Ποίμανδρος ἔβαλε, καὶ τοῦ μὲν Πολυ-
κρίθου διήμαρτε, Λεύκιππον δὲ τὸν υἱὸν ἀπέκτεινεν.
ἔδει μὲν οὖν κατὰ τὸν νόμον ἐκ τῆς Βοιωτίας μετα-
στῆναι, ἐφέστιον καὶ ἱκέτην ξένον[2] γενόμενον· οὐκ
ἦν δὲ ῥᾴδιον, ἐμβεβληκότων εἰς τὴν Ταναγρικὴν
τῶν Ἀχαιῶν. ἔπεμψεν οὖν Ἔφιππον τὸν υἱὸν
Ἀχιλλέως δεησόμενον. ὁ δὲ καὶ τοῦτον εἰσάγει
πείσας καὶ Τληπόλεμον τὸν Ἡρακλέους καὶ Πηνέ-
λεων τὸν Ἱππάλκμου, συγγενεῖς ἅπαντας αὐτῶν[3]
E ὄντας. ὑφ' ὧν ὁ Ποίμανδρος εἰς Χαλκίδα συν-
εκπεμφθεὶς καὶ καθαρθεὶς παρ' Ἐλεφήνορι τὸν
φόνον, ἐτίμησε τοὺς ἄνδρας καὶ τεμένη πᾶσιν
ἐξεῖλεν, ὧν τὸ Ἀχιλλέως καὶ τοὔνομα διατετήρηκεν.

38. "Τίνες οἱ παρὰ Βοιωτοῖς Ψολόεις καὶ τίνες
αἱ Ὀλεῖαι[4];"
Τὰς Μινύου θυγατέρας φασὶ Λευκίππην καὶ
Ἀρσινόην καὶ Ἀλκαθόην μανείσας ἀνθρωπίνων
ἐπιθυμῆσαι κρεῶν καὶ διαλαχεῖν περὶ τῶν τέκνων·
Λευκίππης λαχούσης παρασχεῖν Ἵππασον τὸν υἱὸν
διασπάσασθαι· κληθῆναι τοὺς μὲν ἄνδρας αὐτῶν
F δυσειματοῦντας ὑπὸ λύπης καὶ πένθους "Ψολόεις,"

---

[1] ἀποκείμενος Wyttenbach: ἐπικείμενος.
[2] ξένον] ξένου E. Kurtz.
[3] αὐτῶν E. Kurtz: αὐτῶν or αὐτῷ (E).
[4] αἱ Ὀλεῖαι Meziriacus: αἰολεῖαι or αἰολῖαι.

[a] These rites resembled those of the rending and resurrection of Osiris; cf. Moralia 367 F.

Polycrithus the master-builder, however, who was present, spoke slightingly of the fortifications and, in derision, leaped over the moat. Poemander was enraged and hastened to throw at him a great stone which had been hidden there from ancient days, set aside for use in the ritual of the Nyctelia.[a] This stone Poemander snatched up in his ignorance, and hurled. He missed Polycrithus, but slew his son Leucippus. According to the law, therefore, he had to depart from Boeotia and become a suppliant at a stranger's hearth. But this was not easy, since the Achaeans had invaded the territory of Tanagra. Accordingly he sent his son Ephippus to appeal to Achilles. Ephippus, by his persuasive words, brought to his father Achilles, as well as Tlepolemus, the son of Heracles, and Peneleös, the son of Hippalcmas, all of them interrelated. Poemander was escorted by them to Chalcis, and there at the house of Elephenor he was purified of the murder. Therefore he honoured these heroes and set apart sacred precincts for them all, and of these the precinct of Achilles has still kept its name.

38. Who are the "Psoloeis" and who the "Oleiae" among the Boeotians?

They relate that the daughters of Minyas, Leucippê and Arsinoê and Alcathoê, becoming insane, conceived a craving for human flesh, and drew lots for their children.[b] The lot fell upon Leucippê to contribute her son Hippasus to be torn to pieces, and their husbands, who put on ill-favoured garments for very grief and sorrow, were called "Grimy" (Psoloeis);

[b] Cf. Aelian, Varia Historia, iii. 42; Antonius Liberalis, Metamorphoses, x. Ovid's account (Met. iv. 1 ff.; 389 ff.) is rather different and omits the murder of Hippasus.

αὐτὰς δὲ " Ὀλείας " οἷον ὀλοάς.[1]   καὶ μέχρι νῦν
Ὀρχομένιοι τὰς ἀπὸ τοῦ γένους οὕτω καλοῦσι.
καὶ γίγνεται παρ' ἐνιαυτὸν ἐν τοῖς Ἀγριωνίοις
φυγὴ καὶ δίωξις αὐτῶν ὑπὸ τοῦ ἱερέως τοῦ Διονύσου
ξίφος ἔχοντος.   ἔξεστι δὲ τὴν καταληφθεῖσαν
ἀνελεῖν, καὶ ἀνεῖλεν ἐφ' ἡμῶν Ζωΐλος ὁ ἱερεύς.
ἀπέβη δ' εἰς οὐδὲν χρηστὸν αὐτοῖς, ἀλλ' ὅ τε
Ζωΐλος ἔκ του[2] τυχόντος ἑλκυδρίου[3] νοσήσας καὶ
300 διασαπεὶς πολὺν χρόνον ἐτελεύτησαν, οἵ τ' Ὀρχομένιοι δημοσίαις βλάβαις καὶ καταδίκαις περι-
πεσόντες ἐκ τοῦ γένους τὴν ἱερωσύνην μετέστησαν,
ἐκ πάντων αἱρούμενοι τὸν ἄριστον.

39. " Διὰ τί τοὺς εἰς τὸ Λύκαιον εἰσελθόντας
ἑκουσίως καταλεύουσιν οἱ Ἀρκάδες· ἂν δ' ὑπ'
ἀγνοίας, εἰς Ἐλευθερὰς ἀποστέλλουσι; "

Πότερον ὡς ἐλευθερουμένων αὐτῶν διὰ τὴν
ἀπόλυσιν ἔσχεν ὁ λόγος πίστιν, καὶ τοιοῦτόν ἐστι
τὸ " εἰς Ἐλευθεράς," οἷον τὸ " εἰς Ἀμελοῦς
B χώραν " καὶ τὸ " ἥξεις εἰς Ἀρέσαντος ἕδος " ;

Ἢ κατὰ τὸν μῦθον ἐπεὶ μόνοι τῶν Λυκάονος[4]
παίδων Ἐλευθὴρ καὶ Λέβαδος[5] οὐ μετέσχον τοῦ
περὶ τὸν Δία μιάσματος ἀλλ' εἰς Βοιωτίαν ἔφυγον,
καὶ Λεβαδεῦσιν ἔστιν ἰσοπολιτεία πρὸς Ἀρκάδας,

---

[1] αὐτὰς . . . ὀλοάς Meziriacus : τὰς αἰολείας (καὶ οἰωνολόας
in E) οἰωνολόας.   [2] ἔκ του F.C.B. : ἐκ τοῦ.
[3] ἑλκυδρίου (the better attested form) Hatzidakis : ἑλκειδίου
or ἑλκυδίου.   [4] Λυκάονος the usual form : Λυκάωνος.
[5] Λέβαδος the better spelling : Λεβεάδος.

---

[a] Cf. Moralia, 717 A ; 291 A supra.
[b] The serving of human flesh.   Cf. Ovid, Metamorphoses,

but the Minyads themselves were called "Oleiae," that is to say, 'Murderesses.' And even to-day the people of Orchomenus give this name to the women descended from this family ; and every year, at the festival of Agrionia,[a] there takes place a flight and pursuit of them by the priest of Dionysus with sword in hand. Any one of them that he catches he may kill, and in my time the priest Zoïlus killed one of them. But this resulted in no benefit for the people of Orchomenus ; but Zoïlus fell sick from some slight sore and, when the wound had festered for a long time, he died. The people of Orchomenus also found themselves involved in some suits for damages and adverse judgements ; wherefore they transferred the priesthood from Zoïlus's family and chose the best man from all the citizens to fill the office.

39. WHY do the Arcadians stone persons who voluntarily enter the Lycaeon ; but if such persons enter through ignorance, they send them away to Eleutherae ?

Is it because they were released and set free that this story gained credence, and is the expression " to Free Town " (*Eleutherae*) of the same sort as " to the land of Sans Souci " and " you will come to the Seat of Satisfaction " ?

Or is it in accordance with the legend, since Eleuther and Lebadus were the only sons of Lycaon that had no share in the abomination prepared for Zeus,[b] but instead they fled to Boeotia, and there is community of citizenship between the people of Lebadeia and the Arcadians, and do they accordingly

i. 163 ff. and Frazer's note on Apollodorus, *Bibliotheca* iii. 8. 1 (L.C.L. vol. i. pp. 390 ff.).

(300) εἰς Ἐλευθερὰς οὖν ἀποπέμπουσι τοὺς ἐν τῷ ἀβάτῳ
τοῦ Διὸς ἀκουσίως γενομένους;

Ἢ ὡς Ἀρχίτιμος ἐν τοῖς Ἀρκαδικοῖς ἐμβάντας
τινὰς κατ᾽ ἄγνοιάν φησιν ὑπ᾽ Ἀρκάδων παρα-
δοθῆναι Φλιασίοις, ὑπὸ δὲ Φλιασίων Μεγαρεῦσιν,
ἐκ δὲ Μεγαρέων εἰς Θήβας κομιζομένους περὶ τὰς
Ἐλευθερὰς ὕδατι καὶ βρονταῖς καὶ διοσημίαις
ἄλλαις κατασχεθῆναι; ἀφ᾽ οὗ δὴ καὶ τὸν τόπον
Ἐλευθερὰς ἔνιοί φασι προσαγορεύεσθαι.

C   Τὸ μέντοι σκιὰν μὴ πίπτειν ἀπὸ τοῦ ἐμβάντος
εἰς τὸ Λύκαιον λέγεται μὲν οὐκ ἀληθῶς, ἔσχηκε[1]
δὲ πίστιν ἰσχυράν. πότερον τοῦ ἀέρος εἰς νέφη
τρεπομένου καὶ σκυθρωπάζοντος ἐπὶ τοῖς εἰσιοῦσιν;
ἢ ὅτι θανατοῦται μὲν ὁ ἐμβάς, τῶν δ᾽ ἀποθανόντων
οἱ Πυθαγορικοὶ λέγουσι τὰς ψυχὰς μὴ ποιεῖν
σκιὰν μηδὲ σκαρδαμύττειν; ἢ σκιὰν μὲν ὁ ἥλιος
ποιεῖ, τὸν δ᾽ ἥλιον ἀφαιρεῖται τοῦ ἐμβάντος ὁ νόμος;

Καὶ τοῦτ᾽ αἰνιττόμενοι λέγουσι· καὶ γὰρ ἔλαφος
ὁ ἐμβὰς καλεῖται. διὸ καὶ Κανθαρίωνα τὸν Ἀρκάδα
πρὸς Ἠλείους αὐτομολήσαντα πολεμοῦντας Ἀρκάσι
καὶ διαβάντα μετὰ λείας τὸ ἄβατον, καταλυθέντος
D δὲ τοῦ πολέμου καὶ[2] φυγόντα εἰς Σπάρτην, ἐξέδοσαν
οἱ Λακεδαιμόνιοι τοῖς Ἀρκάσι, τοῦ θεοῦ κελεύσαντος ἀποδιδόναι τὸν ἔλαφον.

---

[1] ἔσχηκε Wyttenbach : ἐσχηκέναι.
[2] καὶ] Hutten would omit.

send away to Eleutherae those who involuntarily enter the inviolate sanctuary of Zeus ?

Or is it as Architimus [a] relates in his *Arcadian History*, that certain men who entered through ignorance were handed over by the Arcadians to the Phliasians, and by the Phliasians to the Megarians, and, as they were being conducted from Megara to Thebes, they were stopped near Eleutherae [b] by rain and thunder and other signs from heaven ? Whence, in fact, some assert that the place acquired the name of Eleutherae.

The tale, however, that no shadow is cast by a person who enters the Lycaeon is not true, although it has acquired widespread credence.[c] Is it because the air turns to clouds, and lowers darkly upon those who enter ? Or is it because he that enters is condemned to death, and the followers of Pythagoras declare that the spirits of the dead cast no shadow,[d] neither do they blink ? Or is it because it is the sun which causes shadow, but the law deprives him that enters of the sunlight ?

This too they relate allegorically : he that enters is called a " deer." Wherefore, when Cantharion the Arcadian deserted to the Eleans while they were at war with the Arcadians, and with his booty crossed the inviolate sanctuary, even though he fled to Sparta after peace had been made, the Spartans surrendered him to the Arcadians, since the god ordered them to give back " the deer."

[a] Müller, *Frag. Hist. Graec.* vol. iv. p. 317.
[b] A town in Attica not far from the borders of Boeotia.
[c] *Cf.* Pausanias, viii. 38. 6 ; Polybius, xvi. 12. 7, whose source is Theopompus.
[d] *Cf. Moralia*, 564 D. See also Dante, *Purgatorio*, iii. 25-30, 94-97.

40. " Τίς Εὔνοστος ἥρως ἐν Τανάγρᾳ καὶ διὰ τίνα
αἰτίαν τὸ ἄλσος αὐτοῦ γυναιξὶν ἀνέμβατόν ἐστιν; "
Ἐλιέως τοῦ Κηφισοῦ καὶ Σκιάδος Εὔνοστος ἦν
υἱός, ᾧ φασιν ὑπὸ νύμφης Εὐνόστας ἐκτραφέντι
τοῦτο γενέσθαι τοὔνομα. καλὸς δ᾽ ὢν καὶ δίκαιος
οὐχ ἧττον ἦν σώφρων καὶ αὐστηρός· ἐρασθῆναι δ᾽
αὐτοῦ λέγουσιν Ὄχναν, μίαν τῶν Κολωνοῦ θυγα-
E τέρων, ἀνεψιὰν οὖσαν. ἐπεὶ δὲ πειρῶσαν ὁ Εὔνοστος ἀπετρέψατο καὶ λοιδορήσας ἀπῆλθεν εἰς τοὺς
ἀδελφοὺς κατηγορήσων, ἔφθασεν ἡ παρθένος τοῦτο
πράξασα κατ᾽ ἐκείνου καὶ παρώξυνε τοὺς ἀδελφοὺς
Ἔχεμον[1] καὶ Λέοντα καὶ Βουκόλον ἀποκτεῖναι τὸν
Εὔνοστον, ὡς πρὸς βίαν αὐτῇ συγγεγενημένον.
ἐκεῖνοι μὲν οὖν ἐνεδρεύσαντες ἀπέκτειναν τὸν
F νεανίσκον. ὁ δ᾽ Ἐλιεὺς ἐκείνους ἔδησεν· ἡ δ᾽
Ὄχνη μεταμελομένη καὶ γέμουσα ταραχῆς, ἅμα
μὲν αὐτὴν ἀπαλλάξαι θέλουσα τῆς διὰ τὸν ἔρωτα
λύπης, ἅμα δ᾽ οἰκτίρουσα τοὺς ἀδελφοὺς ἐξήγγειλε
πρὸς τὸν Ἐλιέα πᾶσαν τὴν ἀλήθειαν, ἐκεῖνος δὲ
Κολωνῷ. Κολωνοῦ δὲ δικάσαντος, οἱ μὲν ἀδελφοὶ
τῆς Ὄχνης ἔφυγον, αὐτὴ δὲ κατεκρήμνισεν ἑαυτήν,
ὡς Μυρτὶς ἡ Ἀνθηδονία ποιήτρια μελῶν ἱστόρηκε.

Τοῦ δ᾽ Εὐνόστου τὸ ἡρῷον καὶ τὸ ἄλσος οὕτως
ἀνέμβατον ἐτηρεῖτο[2] καὶ ἀπροσπέλαστον γυναιξίν,
ὥστε πολλάκις σεισμῶν ἢ αὐχμῶν ἢ διοσημιῶν
ἄλλων γενομένων ἀναζητεῖν καὶ πολυπραγμονεῖν
ἐπιμελῶς τοὺς Ταναγραίους, μὴ λέληθε γυνὴ τῷ
301 τόπῳ πλησιάσασα, καὶ λέγειν ἐνίους, ὧν ὁ Κλείδαμος ἦν, ἀνὴρ ἐπιφανής, ἀπηντηκέναι αὐτοῖς τὸν
Εὔνοστον ἐπὶ θάλατταν βαδίζοντα λουσόμενον, ὡς

---

[1] Ἔχεμον] ὄχεμον some mss.
[2] ἐτηρεῖτο Wyttenbach : ἐτήρει.

40. Who was the hero Eunostus in Tanagra, and why may no women enter his grove?

Eunostus was the son of Elieus, who was the son of Cephisus, and Scias. They relate that he acquired his name because he was brought up by the nymph Eunosta. Handsome and righteous as he was, he was no less virtuous and ascetic. They say that Ochnê, his cousin, one of the daughters of Colonus, became enamoured of him; but when Eunostus repulsed her advances and, after upbraiding her, departed to accuse her to her brothers, the maiden forestalled him by doing this very thing against him. She incited her brothers, Echemus, Leon, and Bucolus, to kill Eunostus, saying that he had consorted with her by force. They, accordingly, lay in ambush for the young man and slew him. Then Elieus put them in bonds; but Ochnê repented, and was filled with trepidation and, wishing to free herself from the torments caused by her love, and also feeling pity for her brothers, reported the whole truth to Elieus, and he to Colonus. And when Colonus had given judgement, Ochnê's brothers were banished, and she threw herself from a precipice, as Myrtis,[a] the lyric poetess of Anthedon, has related.

But the shrine and the grove of Eunostus were so strictly guarded against entry and approach by women that, often, when earthquakes or droughts or other signs from heaven occurred, the people of Tanagra were wont to search diligently and to be greatly concerned lest any woman might have approached the place undetected; and some relate, among them Cleidamus, a man of prominence, that Eunostus met them on his way to the sea to bathe

---

[a] *Cf.* Edmonds, *Lyra Graeca*, iii. p. 3.

(301) γυναικὸς ἐμβεβηκυίας εἰς τὸ τέμενος. ἀναφέρει δὲ
καὶ Διοκλῆς ἐν τῷ περὶ ἡρῴων συντάγματι δόγμα
Ταναγραίων, περὶ ὧν ὁ Κλείδαμος ἀπήγγειλεν.

41. '' Πόθεν ἐν τῇ Βοιωτίᾳ περὶ τὸν Ἐλεῶνα
ποταμὸς Σκάμανδρος ὠνομάσθη; ''

Δήιμαχος ὁ Ἐλεῶνος υἱός, ἑταῖρος ὢν Ἡρακλέους, μετέσχε τῆς ἐπὶ Τροίαν στρατείας· τοῦ δὲ
πολέμου μῆκος ὡς ἔοικε λαμβάνοντος, ἐρασθεῖσαν
αὐτοῦ Γλαυκίαν τὴν Σκαμάνδρου θυγατέρα προσ-
δεξάμενος ἔγκυον ἐποίησεν, εἶτ' αὐτὸς μὲν ἔπεσε
B μαχόμενος τοῖς Τρωσίν· ἡ δὲ Γλαυκία φοβουμένη
κατάφωρος γενέσθαι κατέφυγε καὶ τῷ Ἡρακλεῖ[1]
κατεῖπεν αὐτῆς τὸν ἔρωτα καὶ τὴν γενομένην
πρὸς τὸν Δήιμαχον ὁμιλίαν. ὁ δ' ἅμα μὲν οἴκτῳ
τῆς γυναικὸς ἅμα δὲ χαίρων τῷ ὑπολείπεσθαι
γένος ἀνδρὸς ἀγαθοῦ καὶ συνήθους, ἀνέλαβε τὴν
Γλαυκίαν εἰς τὰς ναῦς, καὶ τεκοῦσαν υἱὸν ἀγαγὼν
ἐν τῇ Βοιωτίᾳ ἀπέδωκε τῷ Ἐλεῶνι καὶ τὸ παιδίον
καὶ αὐτήν. ὠνομάσθη δ' ὁ παῖς Σκάμανδρος καὶ
τῆς χώρας ἐβασίλευσε. καὶ τὸν μὲν Ἴναχον
ποταμὸν ἀφ' αὑτοῦ[2] Σκάμανδρον, τὸ δὲ πλησίον
ῥεῦμα Γλαυκίαν ἀπὸ τῆς μητρὸς ὠνόμασεν· Ἀκι-
δοῦσαν δὲ τὴν κρήνην ἀπὸ τῆς ἑαυτοῦ γυναικός, ἐξ
C ἧς ἔσχε τρεῖς θυγατέρας, ἃς τιμῶσιν ἄχρι νῦν
'' παρθένους '' προσαγορεύοντες.

42. '' Ἀπὸ τίνος ἐρρήθη[3] τὸ παροιμιῶδες Αὖτα
κυρία; ''

Δείνων[4] ὁ Ταραντῖνος στρατηγῶν, ἀνὴρ δ' ὢν

---

[1] τῷ Ἡρακλεῖ stands before κατέφυγε in the mss.; transferred here by Helmbold.
[2] ἀφ' αὑτοῦ Helmbold : ἀπ' αὐτοῦ.
[3] ἐρρήθη Bernardakis : ἐρρέθη or ἐρέθη.

because a woman had set foot within the sacred precinct. And Diocles [a] also, in his treatise upon the *Shrines of Heroes*, quotes a decree of the people of Tanagra concerning the matters which Cleidamus reported.

41. FROM what cause was a river in Boeotia in the vicinity of Eleon called Scamander ?

Deïmachus, the son of Eleon and a companion of Heracles, took part in the expedition against Troy. But since, as it appears, the war was dragging on, he welcomed to his quarters Glaucia, the daughter of Scamander, who had fallen in love with him, and got her with child ; then he himself fell in fighting against the Trojans. But Glaucia, fearing detection, fled for refuge, and told Heracles of her love and of her association with Deïmachus. And he, both through pity for the woman, and for joy that the stock of a brave man who was his close friend should thus survive, took Glaucia on board his fleet ; and when she gave birth to a son, he brought both the child and the mother, and delivered them to Eleon in Boeotia. The child was named Scamander, and he became the king of the country ; and he named the Inachus river Scamander after himself, and the stream near by he called Glaucia from his mother. The spring Acidusa he named after his wife ; and from her he had three daughters whom even to this day they honour under the name of the " Maidens."

42. WHENCE arose the proverbial saying, " This is valid " ?

When Deinon of Tarentum, a brave soldier, was

[a] Müller, *Frag. Hist. Graec.* iii. p. 78.

[4] Δείνων Crönert : Δίνων.

(301) ἀγαθὸς ἐν τοῖς πολεμικοῖς, ἀποχειροτονησάντων
αὐτοῦ τινα γνώμην τῶν πολιτῶν, ὡς ὁ κῆρυξ
ἀνεῖπε τὴν νικῶσαν, αὐτὸς ἀνατείνας τὴν δεξιάν,
" ἅδε," εἶπε, " κρείσσων "· οὕτω γὰρ ὁ Θεόφραστος
ἱστόρηκε. προσιστόρηκε δὲ καὶ ὁ Ἀπολλόδωρος
Ταραντίνων[1] τοῦ κήρυκος, " αὗται πλείους,"
εἰπόντος, " ἀλλ' αὗται," φάναι, " βελτίους," καὶ
ἐπικυρῶσαι τὴν τῶν ἐλαττόνων χειροτονίαν.

D 43. " Πόθεν ἡ τῶν Ἰθακησίων πόλις Ἀλαλ-
κομεναὶ προσηγορεύθη; "

Διὰ τὸ τὴν Ἀντίκλειαν ὑπὸ Σισύφου βιασθεῖσαν
ἐν τῇ παρθενίᾳ τὸν Ὀδυσσέα συλλαβεῖν· ὑπὸ
πλειόνων δ' ἐστὶν εἰρημένον. Ἴστρος δ' ὁ Ἀλε-
ξανδρεὺς ἐν ὑπομνήμασι προσιστόρηκεν, ὅτι τῷ
Λαέρτῃ δοθεῖσα πρὸς γάμον καὶ ἀναγομένη, περὶ
τὸ Ἀλαλκομένιον[2] ἐν τῇ Βοιωτίᾳ τὸν Ὀδυσσέα
τέκοι, καὶ διὰ τοῦτ' ἐκεῖνος ὥσπερ μητροπόλεως[3]
ἀναφέρων τοὔνομα τὴν ἐν Ἰθάκῃ πόλιν οὕτω φησὶ
προσαγορεύεσθαι.[4]

44. " Τίνες ἐν Αἰγίνῃ οἱ μονοφάγοι; "

E Τῶν ἐπὶ τὴν Τροίαν στρατευσάντων Αἰγινητῶν
πολλοὶ μὲν ἐν ταῖς μάχαις ἀπώλοντο, πλείονες δὲ
κατὰ πλοῦν ὑπὸ[5] τοῦ χειμῶνος. ὀλίγους οὖν τοὺς
περιλειπομένους οἱ προσήκοντες ὑποδεξάμενοι,
τοὺς δ' ἄλλους πολίτας ὁρῶντες ἐν πένθεσι καὶ
λύπαις ὄντας, οὔτε χαίρειν ᾤοντο δεῖν φανερῶς

---

[1] Ταραντίνων F.C.B.: ἐν Ῥυτίνῳ.
[2] Ἀλαλκομένιον the spelling elsewhere: ἀλαλκομένειον.
[3] μητροπόλεως Stephanus: μεσοπόλεως.
[4] φησὶ προσαγορεύεσθαι] προσαγορεύσειε Hutten.
[5] ὑπὸ Wyttenbach: ἀπό.

general, his fellow-citizens voted to reject a certain proposal of his. When the herald reported the prevailing majority, he held up his right hand and said, " But this is stronger." This is Theophrastus's [a] version of the story ; but Apollodorus has a supplementary version, that when the herald of the Tarentines proclaimed, " These are in the majority," Deinon said, " But these are better ! " and validated the vote of the minority.

43. FOR what reason was the city of the Ithacans called Alalcomenae ?

Because Anticleia, while yet a virgin, was violated by Sisyphus and conceived Odysseus. This is related by several authorities [b] ; but Ister [c] of Alexandria in his *Commentaries* has in addition recorded that when Anticlea had been given in marriage to Laërtes and was being conducted to his home, she gave birth to Odysseus near the Alalcomenium in Boeotia. And for this reason, as though referring the name to that of a mother-city, he states that the city in Ithaca acquired its name.

44. WHO were the " solitary eaters " in Aegina ?

Of the Aeginetans who were engaged in the war against Troy many perished in the battles there, but even more were destroyed by the storm on the returnvoyage. So there were but few who survived, and when their relatives had welcomed them home, and observed that the other citizens were in mourning and sorrow, they deemed it proper neither to rejoice

[a] Frag. 133 (ed. Wimmer).
[b] *Cf.* Sophocles, *Philoctetes*, 417, with Jebb's note ; Frag. 567 (ed. Pearson), with the note.
[c] Müller, *Frag. Hist. Graec.* i. p. 426.

οὔτε θύειν τοῖς θεοῖς, ἀλλὰ κρύφα καὶ κατ᾽ οἰκίαν
ἕκαστοι τοὺς σεσωσμένους ἀνελάμβανον ἑστιάσεσι
καὶ φιλοφροσύναις, αὐτοὶ διακονούμενοι πατράσι
καὶ συγγενέσι καὶ ἀδελφοῖς καὶ οἰκείοις, ἀλλοτρίου
μηδενὸς παρεισιόντος. ταῦτ᾽ οὖν ἀπομιμούμενοι
F τῷ Ποσειδῶνι θυσίαν ἄγουσι τοὺς καλουμένους
" θιάσους," ἐν ᾗ καθ᾽ αὑτοὺς ἐφ᾽ ἡμέρας ἑκκαίδεκα
μετὰ σιωπῆς ἑστιῶνται, δοῦλος δ᾽ οὐ πάρεστιν·
εἶτα ποιήσαντες ᾿Αφροδίσια διαλύουσι τὴν ἑορτήν·
ἐκ δὲ τούτου " μονοφάγοι " καλοῦνται.

45. " Διὰ τί τοῦ Λαβρανδέως[1] Διὸς ἐν Καρίᾳ
τὸ ἄγαλμα πέλεκυν ἠρμένον οὐχὶ δὲ σκῆπτρον ἢ
κεραυνὸν πεποίηται; "
"Οτι ῾Ηρακλῆς ῾Ιππολύτην ἀποκτείνας καὶ μετὰ
τῶν ἄλλων ὅπλων αὐτῆς λαβὼν τὸν πέλεκυν ᾿Ομ-
φάλῃ δῶρον ἔδωκεν.[2] οἱ δὲ μετ᾽ ᾿Ομφάλην Λυδῶν
βασιλεῖς ἐφόρουν αὐτὸν ὥς τι τῶν ἄλλων ἱερῶν ἐκ
302 διαδοχῆς παραλαμβάνοντες, ἄχρι Κανδαύλης ἀπ-
αξιώσας ἑνὶ τῶν ἑταίρων φορεῖν ἔδωκεν. ἐπεὶ δὲ
Γύγης ἀποστὰς ἐπολέμει πρὸς αὐτόν, ἦλθεν
῎Αρσηλις ἐκ Μυλασέων[3] ἐπίκουρος τῷ Γύγῃ μετὰ
δυνάμεως, καὶ τόν τε Κανδαύλην καὶ τὸν ἑταῖρον
αὐτοῦ διέφθειρε,[4] καὶ τὸν πέλεκυν εἰς Καρίαν
ἐκόμισε μετὰ τῶν ἄλλων λαφύρων. καὶ Διὸς
ἄγαλμα κατασκευάσας τὸν πέλεκυν ἐνεχείρισε, καὶ

---

[1] Λαβρανδέως Wyttenbach (from Herodotus, v. 119): λα-
βραδέως.
[2] ἔδωκε F.C.B.: δέδωκεν.
[3] Μυλασέων Xylander: μυλέων.
[4] διέφθειρε Helmbold: διαφθείρει.

nor to sacrifice to the gods openly ; but secretly and separately in their own houses they received with feasting and good cheer those who had reached home in safety. They themselves waited upon their fathers and kinsmen, their brothers and relatives, and no one outside the family was allowed to enter. It is, then, in imitation of this that they hold a sacrifice to Poseidon, which is called *thiasoi,*[a] in which they feast by themselves in silence for sixteen days, and no slave is present. Then, when they have celebrated the Aphrodisia, they terminate the festival. For this reason they are called " solitary eaters."

45. WHY is it that the statue of the Labrandean Zeus in Caria is fashioned holding an axe, but not a sceptre or a thunderbolt ?

Because when Heracles had slain Hippolytê, together with her other arms he took her axe and gave it as a present to Omphalê. The Lydian kings who succeeded Omphalê used to carry it as a part of the sacred regalia, handing it down one to the other until it came to Candaules. He deemed it of little worth and gave it to one of his Companions [b] to carry. But when Gyges [c] revolted and was at war with Candaules, Arselis came from Mylasa with an army as an ally for Gyges and slew both Candaules and his Companion and brought the axe to Caria together with the other spoils. He therefore constructed a statue of Zeus and placed the axe in its hand, and

[a] Club-dinner.
[b] Technically a Hellenistic court office, but Plutarch seems to assume such a relation in early Lydian history.
[c] The many ancient variants of the Gyges legend are collected and discussed by K. F. Smith, *American Jour. Phil.*, 1902, pp. 261 ff., 362 ff. ; 1920, pp. 1 ff.

(302) Λαβρανδέα[1] τὸν θεὸν προσηγόρευσε· Λυδοὶ γάρ
" λάβρυν " τὸν πέλεκυν ὀνομάζουσι.

46. " Διὰ τί Τραλλιανοὶ καθαρτῆρα καλοῦσι τὸν
B ὄροβον καὶ χρῶνται μάλιστα πρὸς τὰς ἀφοσιώσεις
καὶ τοὺς καθαρμούς; "

Ἢ ὅτι Λέλεγες καὶ Μινύαι τὸ παλαιὸν ἐξελά-
σαντες αὐτοὺς τὴν πόλιν καὶ τὴν χώραν κατέσχον,[2]
ὕστερον δ' οἱ Τραλλιανοὶ κατελθόντες καὶ κρατήσαντες, ὅσοι τῶν Λελέγων οὐ διεφθάρησαν οὐδ'
ἔφυγον ἀλλὰ δι' ἀμηχανίαν βίου καὶ ἀσθένειαν
ὑπελείφθησαν αὐτόθι, τούτων οὐδένα λόγον ἔχοντες
οὔτε ζώντων οὔτ' ἀπολλυμένων νόμον ἔθεντο τὸν
κτείναντα Μινύην ἢ Λελέγην[3] Τραλλιανῶν καθαρὸν
εἶναι, μέδιμνον ὀρόβων ἀπομετρήσαντα τοῖς οἰκείοις
τοῦ φονευθέντος;

47. " Διὰ τί παρὰ τοῖς Ἠλείοις παροιμιῶδές
C ἐστι τὸ ' δεινότερα Σαμβίκου παθεῖν '; "

Λέγεταί τινα Σάμβικον Ἠλεῖον ἔχοντα πολλοὺς
ὑφ' ἑαυτῷ συνεργοὺς πολλὰ περικόψαι τῶν ἐν
Ὀλυμπίᾳ χαλκῶν ἀναθημάτων καὶ ἀποδόσθαι,
τέλος δὲ συλῆσαι τὸ τῆς ἐπισκόπου Ἀρτέμιδος
ἱερόν· τοῦτο δ' ἐστὶ μὲν ἐν Ἤλιδι, καλεῖται δ'
Ἀρισταρχεῖον. εὐθὺς οὖν μετὰ ταύτην τὴν ἱεροσυλίαν ἁλόντα βασανίζεσθαι δι' ἐνιαυτοῦ περὶ
ἑκάστου τῶν κεκοινωνηκότων ἀνακρινόμενον, καὶ
οὕτως ἀποθανεῖν καὶ τὴν παροιμίαν ἐπὶ τοῖς
ἐκείνου πάθεσι γενέσθαι.

---

[1] Λαβρανδέα Wyttenbach (from Herodotus, v. 119): λα-
βραδέα.
[2] κατέσχον F.C.B.: κατεῖχον.
[3] Λελέγην] λέλεγα some mss.

called the god Labrandeus ; for the Lydians call the axe *labrys*.[a]

46. WHY is it that the people of Tralles call vetch " purifier " and make particular use of it for expiations and purifications ?

Is it because the Leleges and Minyae in days of old drove them out and took possession of their city and their land, and because later the Trallians returned and prevailed, and as many of the Leleges as had not been slain nor had fled away, but had been left behind there because of their destitution and weakness—of these they took no account either of their life or of their death, and they established a law that any Trallian who killed a Minyan or a Lelegian should be free from pollution when he had measured out a bushel of vetch to the relatives of the murdered man ?

47. WHY is there a proverb among the Eleans " to suffer more terribly than Sambicus " ?

The story is told that a certain Sambicus, an Elean, at the head of a numerous group of confederates, cut many pieces from the bronze votive statues in Olympia and sold them, and finally he despoiled the shrine of Artemis the Guardian. This is in Elis and is called the Aristarcheum. Immediately, then, after this sacrilege, he was caught and tortured for a year, being interrogated about each of his confederates in turn ; and in this manner he died and the proverb arose from his sufferings.

[a] One is reminded of the many representations of the double axe on Cretan monuments.

235

(302)   48. '' Διὰ τί ἐν Λακεδαίμονι παρὰ τὸ τῶν Λευκιππίδων ἱερὸν ἵδρυται τοῦ Ὀδυσσέως ἡρῷον;''
       Ἐργῖνος,¹ εἷς τῶν Διομήδους ἀπογόνων, ὑπὸ
D Τημένου πεισθεὶς ἐξέκλεψε τὸ παλλάδιον ἐξ
Ἄργους, συνειδότος Λεάγρου καὶ συνεκκλέπτοντος·
ἦν δ' οὗτος εἷς τῶν Τημένου συνήθων. ὕστερον δὲ
τῷ Τημένῳ γενόμενος δι' ὀργῆς ὁ Λέαγρος εἰς
Λακεδαίμονα μετέστη τὸ παλλάδιον κομίζων. οἱ
δὲ βασιλεῖς δεξάμενοι προθύμως ἱδρύσαντο πλησίον τοῦ τῶν Λευκιππίδων ἱεροῦ, καὶ πέμψαντες
εἰς Δελφοὺς διεμαντεύοντο περὶ σωτηρίας αὐτοῦ
καὶ φυλακῆς. ἀνελόντος δὲ τοῦ θεοῦ ἕνα τῶν ὑφ-
ελομένων τὸ παλλάδιον φύλακα ποιεῖσθαι, κατεσκεύασαν αὐτόθι τοῦ Ὀδυσσέως τὸ ἡρῷον, ἄλλως
τε καὶ προσήκειν τῇ πόλει τὸν ἥρωα διὰ τὸν τῆς
Πηνελόπης γάμον ὑπολαβόντες.

E   49. '' Διὰ τί ταῖς Χαλκηδονίαις ἔθος ἐστίν, ὅταν
ἀνδράσιν ἀλλοτρίοις ἐντύχωσι, μάλιστα δ' ἄρχουσι,
τὴν ἑτέραν περικαλύπτεσθαι παρειάν;''
       Πόλεμος ἦν αὐτοῖς πρὸς Βιθυνοὺς ἐκ πάσης
παροξυνομένοις προφάσεως· Ζειποίτου δὲ βασιλεύ-
σαντος τούτων,² πανστρατιᾷ, καὶ Θρακῶν ἐπικουρίας
προσγενομένης, ἐπυρπόλουν καὶ κατέτρεχον τὴν
χώραν. ἐπιθεμένου δὲ τοῦ Ζειποίτου περὶ τὸ
καλούμενον Φάλιον αὐτοῖς, κακῶς ἀγωνισάμενοι
διὰ θράσος καὶ ἀταξίαν ὑπὲρ ὀκτακισχιλίους ἀπ-
F έβαλον στρατιώτας· καὶ παντελῶς μὲν οὐκ ἀν-
ῃρέθησαν τότε, Ζειποίτου Βυζαντίοις χαρισαμένου
τὰς διαλύσεις· πολλῆς δὲ τὴν πόλιν ἐρημίας ἀνδρῶν

---

¹ Ἐργῖνος Bernardakis: ἐργίαιος.
² τούτων Helmbold: αὐτῶν.

48. WHY at Sparta is a shrine of Odysseus built near the shrine of the daughters of Leucippus ?

Erginus, one of the descendants of Diomedes, was persuaded by Temenus to steal the Palladium from Argos ; this he did with the knowledge and help of Leagrus, who was one of Temenus's friends. But later Leagrus became incensed at Temenus and removed to Sparta, taking the Palladium with him. The Spartan kings received it eagerly, and gave it a place near the shrine of the daughters of Leucippus, and they sent to Delphi to obtain an oracle concerning its safety and preservation. When the god gave oracle that one of those who had purloined the Palladium should be made its guardian, the Spartans constructed there the shrine of Odysseus, especially since, because of his marriage with Penelopê,[a] they reckoned that this hero had close relations with their city.

49. WHY is it the custom for the women of Chalcedon, whenever they encounter strange men, and especially officials, to veil one cheek ?

The Chalcedonians were involved in a war against the Bithynians, to which they were provoked by all kinds of reasons. When Zeipoetes became king of Bithynia, the Chalcedonians, in full force and with the addition of Thracian allies, devastated the country with fire and sword. When Zeipoetes attacked them near the so-called Phalion, they fought badly through rashness and lack of discipline, and lost over eight thousand soldiers. It was only because Zeipoetes granted an armistice to please the Byzantines that they were not completely annihilated at that time. Since, then, there was a great scarcity of men

---

[a] The daughter of the Spartan Icarius.

κατεχούσης, αἱ μὲν πλεῖσται γυναῖκες ὑπ' ἀνάγκης
ἀπελευθέροις καὶ μετοίκοις συνῴκησαν· αἱ δ'
ἀνανδρίαν ἀντὶ τοιούτων ἑλόμεναι γάμων, αὐταί[1]
δι' αὑτῶν ἔπραττον ὅτου δεηθεῖεν παρὰ δικασταῖς
καὶ ἄρχουσιν, ἀπάγουσαι θάτερον μέρος τοῦ
303 προσώπου τῆς καλύπτρας. αἱ δὲ γεγαμημέναι δι'
αἰσχύνην ἀναμιμούμεναι ταύτας ὡς ἑαυτῶν βελ-
τίονας εἰς ἔθος ὅμοιον κατέστησαν.

50. '' Διὰ τί πρὸς τὸ τοῦ Ἀγήνορος τέμενος τὰς
οἶς προσελαύνοντες οἱ Ἀργεῖοι βιβάζουσιν; ''

Ἢ ὅτι κάλλιστα προβάτων ὁ Ἀγήνωρ ἐπ-
εμελήθη καὶ πλεῖστα ποίμνια τῶν βασιλέων ἐ-
κτήσατο;

51. '' Διὰ τί Βαλλαχράδας ἑαυτοὺς Ἀργείων
παῖδες ἐν ἑορτῇ τινι παίζοντες ἀποκαλοῦσιν; ''

Ἢ ὅτι τοὺς πρώτους ὑπ' Ἰνάχου καταχθέντας
ἐκ τῶν ἄκρων[2] εἰς τὰ πεδία ἀχράσι διατραφῆναι
λέγουσιν; ἀχράδας δὲ πρῶτον ἐν Πελοποννήσῳ
Β φανῆναι τοῖς Ἕλλησιν, ἔτι τῆς χώρας ἐκείνης
Ἀπίας προσαγορευομένης· ὅθεν ἄπιοι αἱ[3] ἀχράδες
ἐπωνομάσθησαν.[4]

52. '' Τίς ἡ αἰτία, δι' ἣν Ἠλεῖοι τὰς ὀνοθόρους[5]
ἵππους ἐκτὸς ὅρων ἀπάγοντες βιβάζουσιν; ''

Ἢ ὅτι πάντων τῶν βασιλέων φιλιππότατος ὢν
ὁ Οἰνόμαος καὶ μάλιστα τὸ ζῷον ἀγαπήσας τοῦτ'

---

[1] αὐταί Dübner: αὗται.
[2] ἄκρων Madvig; ὁρῶν Wyttenbach: ἀγρῶν.
[3] αἱ Bernardakis: omitted in most mss, two having οἱ.
[4] ἐπωνομάσθησαν] μετωνομάσθησαν in nearly all mss.
[5] ὀνοθόρους F.C.B.: ἐνόδας. (It seems almost certain that
the first three letters of ἐνόδας must have been ὀνο-.)

throughout the city, most of the women were forced to consort with freedmen and resident aliens. But those women who preferred to have no husband at all rather than a marriage of this sort, themselves conducted whatever business they needed to transact with the judges or the officials, drawing aside one part of the veil that covered their faces. And the married women, for very shame, followed the example of these, who, they felt, were better than themselves, and also changed to a similar custom.

50. WHY is it that the Argives drive their sheep to the precinct of Agenor when they wish to mate them ?

Is it because Agenor took most excellent care of his sheep and acquired more flocks than any other king ?

51. WHY is it that Argive children in a certain festival call themselves, in jest, " Pear-throwers " ?

Is it because the first men that were led down by Inachus from the mountains to the plain lived, as they say, on wild pears ? They also say that wild pears were first discovered by the Greeks in the Peloponnesus at a time when that country was still called Apia,[a] wherefore wild pears were named *apioi.*

52. WHAT is the reason why the Eleans lead their mares outside the boundaries of their country to mate them with asses ? [b]

Is it because of all kings Oenomaüs was the most fond of horses, and, since he particularly loved

[a] *Cf.* Pausanias, ii. 5. 7; Aelian, *Varia Historia*, iii. 39.

[b] *Cf.* Herodotus, iv. 30; Pausanias, v. 5. 2; 9. 2; mules were not bred in Elis because of a curse, and this, seemingly, should be the meaning here; but the corruption in the text of one word, which should have designated asses, has made the mules somewhat dubious.

(303) ἐπηράσατο πολλὰ καὶ δεινὰ κατὰ τῶν ἵππους[1]
ὀχευόντων ἐν Ἤλιδι, καὶ φοβούμενοι τὴν κατάραν
ἐκείνην ἀφοσιοῦνται;

53. '' Διὰ τί παρὰ Κνωσσίοις ἔθος ἦν ἁρπάζειν
τοῖς δανειζομένοις τὸ ἀργύριον; ''
Ἤ ὅπως ἀποστεροῦντες ἔνοχοι τοῖς βιαίοις ὦσι
καὶ μᾶλλον κολάζωνται;

C 54. '' Τίς ἡ αἰτία, δι' ἣν ἐν Σάμῳ τὴν Δεξι-
κρέοντος Ἀφροδίτην καλοῦσι; ''
Πότερον ὅτι τὰς γυναῖκας αὐτῶν ὑπὸ τρυφῆς καὶ
ὕβρεως ἀκόλαστα ποιούσας Δεξικρέων ἀνὴρ ἀγύρ-
της καθαρμῷ χρησάμενος ἀπήλλαξεν;
Ἤ ὅτι ναύκληρος ὢν ὁ Δεξικρέων ἔπλευσεν εἰς
Κύπρον ἐπ' ἐμπορίᾳ, καὶ μέλλοντα γεμίζειν τὴν
ναῦν[2] ἡ Ἀφροδίτη ἐκέλευσεν[3] ὕδωρ ἐμβαλόμενον καὶ
μηδὲν ἄλλο πλεῖν τὴν ταχίστην; πεισθεὶς δὲ καὶ
πολὺ ὕδωρ ἐνθέμενος ἐξέπλευσεν, εἶτα νηνεμίας
καὶ γαλήνης ἐν τῷ πελάγει κατασχούσης, διψῶσι
τοῖς ἄλλοις ἐμπόροις καὶ ναυκλήροις ὕδωρ πιπρά-
σκων ἀργύριον πολὺ συνήθροισεν. ἐκ δὲ τούτου
D κατασκευάσας τὴν θεὸν ἀφ' ἑαυτοῦ προσηγόρευσεν.
εἰ δὴ τοῦτ' ἀληθές ἐστι, φαίνεται οὐχ ἕνα πλουτίσαι,
πολλοὺς δὲ σῶσαι δι' ἑνὸς ἡ θεὸς θελήσασα.

55. '' Διὰ τί τοῖς Σαμίοις, ὅταν τῷ Ἑρμῇ τῷ
χαριδότῃ θύωσι, κλέπτειν ἐφεῖται τῷ βουλομένῳ
καὶ λωποδυτεῖν; ''

---

[1] ἵππους Wyttenbach : ἵππων or ἵππον.
[2] τὴν ναῦν added by Wyttenbach.
[3] ἡ Ἀφροδίτη ἐκέλευσεν Wyttenbach from E : τὴν ἀφροδίτην
κελεύειν.

this animal, he laid many terrible curses upon any that should thus mate horses in Elis ; and it is in fear of that curse that they endeavour to keep clear of it ?

53. Why was it the custom among the Cnossians for those who borrowed money to snatch it ?

Was it that if they defaulted they might be liable to the charge of violence, and so be punished the more ?

54. What is the reason why in Samos they invoke the Aphroditê of Dexicreon ?

Is it because a sorcerer Dexicreon, making use of a rite of purification, freed the women of Samos from the unbridled licentiousness in which they indulged because of their great luxury and wantonness?

Or is it because Dexicreon was a shipmaster and sailed to Cyprus on a trading voyage, and, when he was about to freight his ship, Aphroditê bade him put into it water and nothing else, and set sail as quickly as possible ? He obeyed and, putting much water aboard the ship, sailed away ; after a time the wind died down and the ship was becalmed in the open sea. To the other merchants and shipmasters, who were athirst, he sold the water and amassed much money. Wherefore he fashioned an image of the goddess and called it by his own name. If this is really true, it appears that the goddess wished not to make one man rich, but to save the lives of many through one man.

55. Why is it that whenever the Samians are engaged in sacrificing to Hermes the Giver of Joy they allow whoever so desires to steal from them and filch their clothes ?

241

(303) Ὅτι κατὰ χρησμὸν ἐκ τῆς νήσου μεταστάντες
εἰς Μυκάλην ἀπὸ λῃστείας δέκα ἔτη διεγένοντο·
καὶ μετὰ ταῦτα πλεύσαντες αὖθις εἰς τὴν νῆσον,
ἐκράτησαν τῶν πολεμίων.[1]

56. " Ἀπὸ τίνος Πάναιμα τόπος ἐν τῇ Σαμίων
νήσῳ καλεῖται; "

E   Ἢ ὅτι φεύγουσαι Διόνυσον[2] αἱ Ἀμαζόνες ἐκ τῆς
Ἐφεσίων χώρας εἰς Σάμον διέπλευσαν· ὁ δὲ
ποιησάμενος πλοῖα καὶ διαβὰς μάχην συνῆψε καὶ
πολλὰς αὐτῶν ἀπέκτεινε περὶ τὸν τόπον τοῦτον,
ὃν διὰ τὸ πλῆθος τοῦ ῥυέντος αἵματος οἱ θεώμενοι
Πάναιμα θαυμάζοντες ἐκάλουν; τῶν δ' ἐλεφάντων[3] ἀποθανεῖν τινες λέγονται περὶ τὸ Φλοιὸν καὶ
τὰ ὀστᾶ δείκνυται αὐτῶν· τινὲς δὲ λέγουσι καὶ τὸ
Φλοιὸν ὑπ'[4] ἐκείνων ῥαγῆναι φθεγγομένων μέγα τι
καὶ διάτορον.

57. " Ἀπὸ ποίας αἰτίας ὁ ἀνδρῶν ἐν Σάμῳ
πεδήτης καλεῖται; "

Τῶν γεωμόρων ἐχόντων τὴν πολιτείαν μετὰ τὴν
Δημοτέλους σφαγὴν καὶ τὴν κατάλυσιν τῆς ἐκείνου
F   μοναρχίας, οἱ Μεγαρεῖς Περινθίοις ἐπεστράτευσαν
ἀποίκοις οὖσι Σαμίων πέδας κομίζοντες, ὡς λέγεται,
ἐπὶ τοὺς αἰχμαλώτους. ταῦτα δ' οἱ γεωμόροι
πυνθανόμενοι βοήθειαν ἔπεμπον κατὰ τάχος, στρατηγοὺς μὲν ἀποδείξαντες ἐννέα, ναῦς δὲ πληρώ-

---

[1] πολεμίων Helmbold : πολεμίων οἱ σάμιοι.
[2] Διόνυσον Wyttenbach : διονύσιον.
[3] ἐλεφάντων Wilamowitz-Möllendorff (cf. Hermes, xxxiii.
528); φθειράντων F.C.B. : φάντων.
[4] ὑπ' Halliday and one ms. : ἐπ'.

---

[a] Cf. Pausanias, vii. 2. 7.   [b] " Allblood."

Because in obedience to an oracle they changed their abode from Samos to Mycalê and supported themselves by piracy there for ten years ; and after this they sailed again to Samos and overcame their enemies.

56. FROM what does the place Panhaema on the island of Samos derive its name ?

Is it because the Amazons sailed from the country of the Ephesians [a] across to Samos when they were endeavouring to escape from Dionysus? But he built boats and crossed over and, joining battle, slew many of them near this place, which the spectators in amazement called Panhaema [b] because of the vast quantity of blood shed there. And of the elephants [c] some are said to have been slain near Phloeum, and their bones are pointed out there ; but some relate that Phloeum also was cleft by them as they uttered a loud and piercing cry.

57. FOR what reason is the great hall in Samos called the Hall of Fetters ?

After the murder of Demoteles and the dissolution of his monarchic government the Land-owners [d] controlled the State, and at this time the Megarians made an expedition against the Perinthians, who were colonists of the Samians ; as it is related, they brought with them fetters for their captives. When the Land-owners learned of this, they dispatched aid to the Perinthians with all speed, appointing nine

[c] Wilamowitz and Halliday emend to ἐλεφάντων. This has, at first view, some plausibility, but completely lacks corroborative evidence. Nonnus, *Dionysiaca*, xxvi. 326 ff. is not by any means parallel.

[d] Thucydides, viii. 21, recounts the later struggles of the Land-owners and the People.

σαντες τριάκοντα. τούτων ἐκπλέουσαι δύο πρὸ
304 τοῦ λιμένος ὑπὸ κεραυνοῦ διεφθάρησαν· οἱ δὲ
στρατηγοὶ ταῖς ἄλλαις πλεύσαντες ἐνίκων τοὺς
Μεγαρέας καὶ ζῶντας αὐτῶν ἔλαβον ἑξακοσίους.
ἐπαρθέντες δὲ τῇ νίκῃ διενοοῦντο καταλύειν τὴν
οἴκοι γεωμόρων ὀλιγαρχίαν. ἀφορμὴν δὲ παρέσχον
οἱ προεστῶτες τῆς πολιτείας, γράψαντες αὐτοῖς
ὅπως τοὺς αἰχμαλώτους τῶν Μεγαρέων κομίσωσι
ταῖς αὐτῶν ἐκείνων πέδαις δεδεμένους. λαβόντες
οὖν τὰ γράμματα ταῦτα καὶ δείξαντες κρύφα τισὶ[1]
B τῶν Μεγαρέων ἔπεισαν αὐτοὺς συστῆναι μεθ'
αὐτῶν καὶ τὴν πόλιν ἐλευθερῶσαι· βουλευομένοις
δὲ κοινῇ περὶ τῆς πράξεως ἔδοξε τῶν πεδῶν τοὺς
κρίκους διακροτῆσαι, καὶ περιθέντας οὕτω τοῖς
σκέλεσι τῶν Μεγαρέων ἀναλαβεῖν πρὸς τὰς ζώνας
ἱμᾶσιν, ὅπως μὴ περιρρέωσι μηδ' ἐκβαίνωσι τῶν
σκελῶν[2] ἐν τῷ βαδίζειν χαλαρῶν γενομένων. οὕτω
δὲ τοὺς ἄνδρας ἐνσκευάσαντες καὶ ξίφος ἑκάστῳ
δόντες, ἐπεὶ κατέπλευσαν εἰς Σάμον καὶ ἀπέβησαν,
ἦγον αὐτοὺς δι' ἀγορᾶς εἰς τὸ βουλευτήριον, ὁμοῦ
τι πάντων τῶν γεωμόρων συγκαθεζομένων. εἶτα
σημείου δοθέντος, οἱ Μεγαρεῖς προσπεσόντες
ἔκτεινον τοὺς ἄνδρας. οὕτω δὲ τῆς πόλεως ἐλευ-
C θερωθείσης, τούς τε βουλομένους τῶν Μεγαρέων
πολίτας ἐποιήσαντο καὶ κατασκευάσαντες οἶκον
εὐμεγέθη τὰς πέδας ἀνέθηκαν, καὶ ἀπὸ τούτου
" πεδήτης " ὁ οἶκος ὠνομάσθη.

58. " Διὰ τί παρὰ Κῴοις ὁ τοῦ Ἡρακλέους
ἱερεὺς ἐν Ἀντιμαχείᾳ γυναικείαν ἐνδεδυμένος

[1] τισὶ Wyttenbach: τοῖς.   [2] τῶν σκελῶν Helmbold: αὐτῶν.
244

generals and manning thirty ships. Two of these
ships, as they were sailing out, were destroyed by a
thunderbolt in front of the harbour; but the generals
kept on with the others, defeated the Megarians, and
took six hundred of them alive. Elated by their
victory, they conceived the project of overthrowing
the oligarchy of the Land-owners at home. Now
the officials in charge of the government had provided
an occasion for undertaking this, by writing to the
generals to bring back the captive Megarians bound
in their own fetters. The generals, accordingly,
took the letter, and secretly showed it to certain
of the Megarians and persuaded them to join with
themselves and free the city. When they took
counsel together concerning the deed, they decided
to knock loose the rings that fastened the fetters, and
in this condition to put them on the legs of the
Megarians, holding them up with thongs to their
girdles, so that the fetters might not slip down
and fall off when their legs became relaxed in
walking. Having thus equipped the men and given
a sword to each, they sailed back to Samos and disembarked, and there they led the Megarians through
the market-place to the council-chamber, where practically all the Land-owners were sitting together.
Then, at a given signal, the Megarians fell upon
them and slew them. When the city had thus been
freed, they made citizens of those Megarians who
so desired; and they constructed a great building
and dedicated the fetters there; and from this the
building was called the Hall of Fetters.

58. WHY is it that among the Coans the priest of
Heracles at Antimacheia dons a woman's garb, and

(3)4) ἐσθῆτα καὶ τὴν κεφαλὴν ἀναδούμενος μίτρᾳ κατ-
άρχεται τῆς θυσίας·''

Ἡρακλῆς ταῖς ἐξ ναυσὶν ἀπὸ Τροίας ἀναχθεὶς
ἐχειμάσθη, καὶ τῶν ἄλλων[1] διαφθαρεισῶν μιᾷ μόνῃ
πρὸς τὴν Κῶν ὑπὸ τοῦ πνεύματος ἐλαυνόμενος
ἐξέπεσε κατὰ τὸν Λακητῆρα καλούμενον, οὐδὲν
D ἄλλο περισώσας ἢ τὰ ὅπλα καὶ τοὺς ἄνδρας.
ἐντυχὼν δὲ προβάτοις ᾔτει κριὸν ἕνα παρὰ τοῦ
νέμοντος· ὁ δ' ἄνθρωπος ἐκαλεῖτο μὲν Ἀνταγόρας,
ἀκμάζων δὲ τῇ ῥώμῃ τοῦ σώματος ἐκέλευσεν αὐτῷ[2]
διαπαλαῖσαι τὸν Ἡρακλέα, κἂν καταβάλῃ, τὸν
κριὸν φέρεσθαι. καὶ συμπεσόντος αὐτῷ τοῦ Ἡρακλέους ἐς χεῖρας, οἱ Μέροπες τῷ Ἀνταγόρᾳ παρα-
βοηθοῦντες, οἱ δ' Ἕλληνες τῷ Ἡρακλεῖ, μάχην
καρτερὰν συνῆψαν, ἐν ᾗ λέγεται τῷ πλήθει κατα-
πονούμενος ὁ Ἡρακλῆς καταφυγεῖν πρὸς γυναῖκα
Θρᾷτταν καὶ διαλαθεῖν ἐσθῆτι γυναικείᾳ κατα-
E κρύψας ἑαυτόν. ἐπεὶ δὲ τῶν Μερόπων αὖθις
κρατήσας καὶ καθαρθεὶς ἐγάμει τὴν Χαλκιόπην,[3]
ἀνέλαβε στολὴν ἀνθινήν. διὸ θύει μὲν ὁ ἱερεὺς
ὅπου τὴν μάχην συνέβη γενέσθαι, τὰς δὲ νύμφας
οἱ γαμοῦντες δεξιοῦνται γυναικείαν στολὴν περι-
θέμενοι.

59. '' Πόθεν ἐν Μεγάροις γένος ἁμαξοκυλιστῶν;''
Ἐπὶ τῆς ἀκολάστου δημοκρατίας, ἣ καὶ τὴν
παλιντοκίαν ἐποίησε καὶ τὴν ἱεροσυλίαν, ἐπορεύετο
θεωρία Πελοποννησίων εἰς Δελφοὺς διὰ τῆς Με-

---

[1] ἄλλων E. Capps: νεῶν.
[2] αὐτῷ Dübner: αὐτῷ.
[3] Χαλκιόπην Wyttenbach, from Apollodorus, *Bibliotheca*,
ii. 7. 8: Ἀλκιόπου.

fastens upon his head a woman's head-dress before he begins the sacrifice ?

Heracles, putting out with his six ships from Troy, encountered a storm ; and when his other ships had been destroyed, with the only one remaining he was driven by the gale to Cos. He was cast ashore upon the Laceter, as the place is called, with nothing salvaged save his arms and his men. Now he happened upon some sheep and asked for one ram from the shepherd. This man, whose name was Antagoras, was in the prime of bodily strength, and bade Heracles wrestle with him ; if Heracles could throw him, he might carry off the ram. And when Heracles grappled with him, the Meropes came to the aid of Antagoras, and the Greeks to help Heracles, and they were soon engaged in a mighty battle. In the struggle it is said that Heracles, being exhausted by the multitude of his adversaries, fled to the house of a Thracian woman ; there, disguising himself in feminine garb, he managed to escape detection. But later, when he had overcome the Meropes in another encounter, and had been purified, he married Chalciopê and assumed a gay-coloured raiment. Wherefore the priest sacrifices on the spot where it came about that the battle was fought, and bridegrooms wear feminine raiment when they welcome their brides.

59. WHENCE came the clan of " Wagon-rollers " among the Megarians ?

In the time of the unbridled democracy which brought about both the return-interest[a] and the temple sacrilege, a sacred mission of Peloponnesians passed through the Megarid, on its way to Delphi and

---

[a] *Cf.* 295 C-D, *supra.*

F γαρικῆς καὶ κατηυλίσθησαν[1] ἐν Αἰγείροις παρὰ τὴν
(304) λίμνην μετὰ παίδων καὶ γυναικῶν ὡς ἔτυχεν ἐν
ταῖς ἁμάξαις. τῶν δὲ Μεγαρέων οἱ θρασύτατοι
μεθυσθέντες, ὕβρει καὶ ὠμότητι τὰς ἁμάξας
ἀνακυλίσαντες εἰς τὴν λίμνην ἐνεώσαντο, ὥστε
πολλοὺς ἀποπνιγῆναι τῶν θεωρῶν. οἱ μὲν οὖν
Μεγαρεῖς δι' ἀταξίαν τῆς πολιτείας ἠμέλησαν τοῦ
ἀδικήματος, οἱ δ' Ἀμφικτύονες, ἱερᾶς τῆς θεωρίας
οὔσης, ἐπιστραφέντες τοὺς μὲν φυγῇ τοὺς δὲ
θανάτῳ τῶν ἐναγῶν ἐζημίωσαν. οἱ δ' ἀπὸ τοῦ
γένους " ἁμαξοκυλισταί " προσηγορεύθησαν.

---

[1] κατηυλίσθησαν Wyttenbach : κατεκυλίσθησαν.

had encamped, as chance dictated, in their wagons, with their wives and children, in Aegeiri beside the lake. But the boldest spirits among the Megarians, inflamed with wine, in their insolence and savagery rolled back the wagons and pushed them into the lake, so that many members of the mission were drowned. Now because of the unsettled state of their government the Megarians took no notice of the crime; but the Amphictyonic Assembly, since the mission was sacred, took cognizance of the matter and punished some of the guilty men with banishment and others with death. The descendants of these men were called " Wagon-rollers."

GREEK AND ROMAN
PARALLEL STORIES
(PARALLELA GRAECA ET ROMANA)

INTRODUCTION

THE *Greek and Roman Parallel Stories* (sometimes called
the *Parallela Minora*) are a puzzle. The use of some
strange and barbarous forms, the substitution of " the
aforesaid " [a] for the usual pronoun of reference (though
this is, to be sure, a prominent characteristic of the
work of Polybius), and above all the atrocious style in
which the work is written make it impossible that
this could reasonably be regarded as the work of
Plutarch,[b] though some scholars, fortunately unknown to Hartman, have actually regarded this work
as one of the sins of Plutarch's otherwise stainless
youth.

Yet a work of this name is included in Lamprias's
list, No. 128 under the title Διηγήσεις Παράλληλοι
Ἑλληνικαὶ καὶ Ῥωμαϊκαί and several of these tales
are quoted in full [c] in almost the exact words of our
MS. text by Joannes Stobaeus. But the excessive
ineptitude of the language quite excludes the pos-
sibility that the work before us can be Plutarch's, if
indeed he ever wrote a book of this sort.

S. Luria, in *Rheinisches Museum*, lxxviii. (1929) p. 94,

---

[a] On προειρημένος see W. Schmid, *Der Atticismus*, iii. pp.
147 ff.

[b] Contrariwise see Parthenius, translated by S. Gaselee, in
the L.C.L. p. 289 note.

[c] Only the first, however, is assigned to Plutarch.

253

has suggested that the *Parallela* and the *De Fluviis*[a] are parodies after the manner of Lucian's *True History*; and both Hercher and Hartman have expressed the opinion that both works are by the same anonymous author, chiefly because it is difficult to imagine that *two* such fools as the author of each discloses himself to be could ever have lived! The confusion that the author (ingeniously ?) introduces, the forced simplicity of his glaring misnomers, his many references to authorities that Hercher[b] has attempted to show never existed,[c] all have been thought to suggest that the *Parallela* is a parody of the comparisons in the *Lives*; but J. Schlereth, in his excellent dissertation *De Plutarchi quae feruntur Parallela Minora* (Freiburg, 1931), has with great learning and acumen attempted to disprove this thesis.[d] His work may be consulted by anyone who may be curious about the sources, the language, or the purpose of the *Parallela Minora*.

Wilhelm Schmid (*Philologische Wochenschrift* 1932, coll. 625-634) has reviewed Schlereth's work with great care. Both Schmid and Nachstädt hold that the citations from otherwise unknown authors are

[a] Bernardakis's ed. vol. vii. pp. 282-328.

[b] *Plutarchi libellus de fluviis* (Leipzig, 1851). Schlereth, however, has severely criticized Hercher's conclusions. On the sources of *De Fluviis* see Atenstädt, *Hermes*, lvii. pp. 219 ff.

[c] Yet Müller receives them all as Fragmenta Historicorum Graecorum. It has not been thought worth while to include in the notes the references to Müller, since no additional information is to be found there. All the references, however, will be found in the recent Teubner edition.

[d] It must be noted that many of the points which Plutarch has selected for comparison in the *Lives*, that is, in the so-called Συγκρίσεις, are very tenuous, not to say inept. They would lend themselves readily to parody. On the Σύγκρισις see further F. Focke, *Hermes*, lviii. pp. 327 ff.

genuine, not falsifications of the compiler. Nachstädt, accordingly in the Teubner edition of 1934, gives all the references, and also adds, for convenient comparison, the most important passages from Stobaeus, Lydus, and a *gnomologicum Parisinum*, published by Sternbach in 1893, which seem to have the same original as the text of the present work.

ΣΥΝΑΓΩΓΗ ΙΣΤΟΡΙΩΝ
ΠΑΡΑΛΛΗΛΩΝ
ΕΛΛΗΝΙΚΩΝ ΚΑΙ ΡΩΜΑΙΚΩΝ

305   Τὰς ἀρχαίας ἱστορίας διὰ τὰ παράδοξα τῆς πράξεως οἱ πλεῖστοι νομίζουσι πλάσματα καὶ μύθους
B τυγχάνειν· εὑρὼν δ' ἐγὼ καὶ ἐν τοῖς νῦν χρόνοις
γεγονότα ὅμοια, τὰ ἐν τοῖς Ῥωμαϊκοῖς καιροῖς
συμβεβηκότα ἐξελεξάμην, καὶ ἑκάστῳ πράγματι
ἀρχαίῳ νεωτέραν ὁμοίαν διήγησιν ὑπέταξα, ἀνα-
γράψας καὶ τοὺς ἱστορήσαντας ἄνδρας.

1. ΔΑΤΙΣ ὁ Περσῶν σατράπης μετὰ τριάκοντα
μυριάδων εἰς Μαραθῶνα παραγενόμενος, πεδίον τῆς
Ἀττικῆς, καὶ στρατοπεδευσάμενος πόλεμον τοῖς
ἐγχωρίοις κατήγγειλεν· Ἀθηναῖοι δὲ τοῦ βαρ-
βαρικοῦ πλήθους καταφρονήσαντες ἐνακισχιλίους
ἔπεμψαν, στρατηγοὺς ποιήσαντες Κυνέγειρον Πολύ-
C ζηλον Καλλίμαχον Μιλτιάδην. συμβληθείσης δὲ
τῆς παρατάξεως, Πολύζηλος μὲν ὑπεράνθρωπον[1]
φαντασίαν θεασάμενος τὴν ὅρασιν ἀπέβαλε καὶ
τυφλὸς ἐγένετο[2]· Καλλίμαχος δὲ πολλοῖς περιπεπαρ-
μένος δόρασι καὶ νεκρὸς ἐστάθη· Κυνέγειρος δὲ Περσικὴν ἀναγομένην ναῦν κατασχὼν[3] ἐχειροκοπήθη.

---

[1] ὑπεράνθρωπον Bernardakis: ὑπὲρ ἄνθρωπον.
[2] καὶ τυφλὸς ἐγένετο] καὶ τυφλὸς ὢν ἀνεῖλε τεσσαράκοντα ὀκτὼ
Stobaeus.   [3] κατασχὼν] κατέχων Stobaeus.

256

GREEK AND ROMAN PARALLEL STORIES

THE greater part of mankind think that tales of ancient events are inventions and myths because of the incredible elements which they contain. But since I have discovered that similar events have happened in this modern era, I have singled out crises of Roman history ; and, to parallel each ancient happening, I have subjoined a more modern instance. I have also recorded my authorities.

1. DATIS, the Persian satrap, came to Marathon, a plain of Attica, with an army of three hundred thousand, encamped there, and declared war on the inhabitants of the country. The Athenians, however, contemning the barbarian host, sent out nine thousand men, and appointed as generals Cynegeirus, Polyzelus, Callimachus, and Miltiades. When this force had engaged the enemy, Polyzelus, having seen a supernatural vision, lost his sight, and became blind. Callimachus was pierced with so many spears that, dead though he was, he stood upright [a] ; and Cynegeirus, seizing hold of a Persian ship that was putting out to sea, had his hand chopped off.[b]

[a] Contrast Lucan, iv. 787 " compressum turba stetit omne cadaver"; Ammianus Marcellinus, xviii. 8. 12.
[b] *Cf.* Herodotus, vi. 114 ; Stobaeus, *Florilegium*, vii. 63 (iii. p. 328 Hense).

(305) ΑΣΔΡΟΥΒΑΣ βασιλεὺς Σικελίαν καταλαβόμενος
πόλεμον 'Ρωμαίοις κατήγγειλε· Μέτελλος δὲ ὑπὸ
τῆς συγκλήτου στρατηγὸς χειροτονηθεὶς ἐγκρατὴς
ἐγένετο τῆς νίκης ταύτης, ἐν ᾗ Λεύκιος Γλαύκων
εὐγενὴς ἀνήρ, τὴν 'Ασδρούβα κατέχων ναῦν, ἀμφοτέρας ἀπέβαλε τὰς χεῖρας· καθάπερ ἱστορεῖ
D 'Αριστείδης Μιλήσιος ἐν πρώτῃ Σικελικῶν, παρ'
οὗ τὴν ὑπόθεσιν ἔμαθε Διονύσιος ὁ Σικελιώτης.

2. ΞΕΡΞΗΣ μετὰ πεντακοσίων μυριάδων 'Αρτε-
μισίῳ προσορμίσας πόλεμον τοῖς ἐγχωρίοις κατ-
ήγγειλεν· 'Αθηναῖοι δὲ συγκεχυμένοι κατάσκοπον
ἔπεμψαν 'Αγησίλαον, τὸν Θεμιστοκλέους ἀδελφόν,
καίπερ Νεοκλέους τοῦ πατρὸς αὐτοῦ κατ' ὄναρ
ἑωρακότος ἀμφοτέρας ἀποβεβληκότα τὰς χεῖρας.
παραγενόμενος δὲ εἰς τοὺς βαρβάρους[1] ἐν σχήματι
Περσικῷ Μαρδόνιον ἕνα τῶν σωματοφυλάκων
ἀνεῖλεν ὑπολαμβάνων Ξέρξην εἶναι.[2] συλληφθεὶς
E δὲ πρὸς τῶν πέριξ[3] δέσμιος ἤχθη πρὸς τὸν βασιλέα.
βουθυτεῖν δὲ τοῦ προειρημένου μέλλοντος ἐπὶ τῷ
τοῦ ἡλίου βωμῷ, τὴν δεξιὰν ἐπέθηκε χεῖρα, καὶ
ἀστενάκτως[4] ὑπομείνας τὴν ἀνάγκην τῶν βασάνων
ἠλευθερώθη τῶν δεσμῶν εἰπών, " πάντες ἐσμὲν[5]
τοιοῦτοι 'Αθηναῖοι· εἰ δ' ἀπιστεῖς, καὶ τὴν ἀριστε-
ρὰν ἐπιθήσω." φοβηθεὶς δὲ ὁ Ξέρξης φρουρεῖσθαι
αὐτὸν προσέταξε· καθάπερ ἱστορεῖ 'Αγαθαρχίδης
Σάμιος ἐν δευτέρᾳ τῶν Περσικῶν.

ΠΟΡΣΙΝΑΣ Τούσκων βασιλεὺς πέραν ποταμοῦ
Θύμβρεως στρατεύσας ἐπολέμησε 'Ρωμαίοις, καὶ
F τὴν ἀπὸ σιτίων φερομένην εὐθηνίαν 'Ρωμαίοις

[1] εἰς τοὺς β.] εἰς πλῆθος τῶν βαρβάρων Stobaeus.
[2] εἶναι] ὑπάρχειν Stobaeus.

HASDRUBAL the king seized Sicily and declared war on the Romans. Metellus was elected general by the Senate and was victor in the battle in which Lucius Glauco, a patrician, seizing hold of Hasdrubal's ship, lost both his hands. This Aristeides the Milesian relates in the first book of his *Sicilian History* ; from him Dionysius Siculus learned the facts.

2. XERXES with five million men anchored near Artemisium and declared war on the inhabitants. The Athenians were in confusion and sent Agesilaüs, the brother of Themistocles, as a spy, although his father Neocles had seen in a dream his son deprived of both his hands. Agesilaüs, arriving among the barbarians in Persian garb, slew Mardonius, one of the king's bodyguards, supposing him to be Xerxes. He was arrested by the bystanders and led in bonds to the king. The aforesaid king was about to offer sacrifice at the altar of the Sun, and Agesilaüs placed his right hand upon the altar ; and when he had endured the cruel torture without a groan, he was freed from his bonds, whereupon he declared, " All we Athenians are men of this sort ; if you do not believe me, I will place my left hand also on the altar." Xerxes was frightened and gave command that he be kept under guard.[a] This Agatharchides the Samian relates in the second book of his *Persian History*.

PORSENNA, king of the Etruscans, made a foray on the other side of the river Tiber and warred against the Romans ; he intercepted their abundant supply

---

[a] Stobaeus, *Florilegium*, vii. 64 (iii. p. 330 Hense).

---

[3] πρὸς τῶν πέριξ] ὑπὸ τῶν δορυφόρων Stobaeus.
[4] ἀστενάκτως] ἀστένακτος some MSS. and Stobaeus.
[5] πάντες ἐσμὲν Bernardakis from Stobaeus : πάντες μὲν.

μέσην λαβὼν λιμῷ τοὺς προειρημένους ἔτρυχε.
τῆς δὲ συγκλήτου συγκεχυμένης, Μούκιος τῶν
ἐπισήμων ἀνὴρ λαβὼν τετρακοσίους ἀπὸ τῶν ὑπάτων ὁμήλικας ἐν ἰδιωτικῷ σχήματι τὸν ποταμὸν
διῆλθεν. ἰδὼν δὲ τὸν σωματοφύλακα τοῦ τυράννου
τὰ ἐπιτήδεια διαδιδόντα τοῖς στρατηγοῖς, ὑπολαβὼν
αὐτὸν τὸν Πορσίναν εἶναι ἀνεῖλεν. ἀχθεὶς δ' ἐπὶ
τὸν βασιλέα τοῖς ἐμπύροις ἐπέθηκε τὴν δεξιὰν
306 χεῖρα καὶ στέξας τὰς ἀλγηδόνας εὐψύχως ἐμειδία-
σεν εἰπών, " βάρβαρε, λέλυμαι, κἂν μὴ θέλῃς· καὶ
ἴσθι ἡμᾶς κατὰ σοῦ τετρακοσίους ὄντας ἐν τῷ
στρατοπέδῳ, οἵ σε ἀνελεῖν ζητοῦμεν." ὁ δὲ φοβηθεὶς σπονδὰς πρὸς Ῥωμαίους ἐποιήσατο· καθάπερ
ἱστορεῖ Ἀριστείδης ὁ Μιλήσιος ἐν τρίτῃ ἱστοριῶν.

3. ΑΡΓΕΙΩΝ καὶ Λακεδαιμονίων ὑπὲρ Θυρεάτιδος
χώρας πολεμούντων, οἱ Ἀμφικτύονες ἔκριναν πο-
λεμῆσαι τριακοσίους ἑκατέρων[1] καὶ τῶν νικησάντων
εἶναι τὴν χώραν. Λακεδαιμόνιοι μὲν οὖν Ὀθρυά-
δην ἐποίησαν στρατηγὸν Ἀργεῖοι δὲ Θέρσανδρον.
πολεμούντων δὲ δύο ἐκ τῶν Ἀργείων περιελεί-
B φθησαν, Ἀγήνωρ[2] καὶ Χρόμιος[3] οἵτινες εἰς τὴν πόλιν
ἤγγειλαν τὴν νίκην. ἐρημίας[4] δ' ὑπαρχούσης ὁ
Ὀθρυάδης ἐπιζήσας καὶ ἡμικλάστοις δόρασιν ἐπ-
ερειδόμενος τὰς τῶν νεκρῶν ἁρπάζων[5] ἀσπίδας περιείλετο· καὶ τρόπαιον στήσας ἐκ τοῦ ἰδίου

[1] τριακοσίους (= τ') ἑκατέρων E. Kurtz, as in Herodotus and
Stobaeus: ἑκατέρους.

[2] Ἀγήνωρ] Ἀλκήνωρ Herod. i. 82; Stobaeus, Flor. vii. 67.

[3] Χρόμιος] the mss. of some authors give χρομίος.

[4] ἐρημίας E. Kurtz, S. A. Naber, H. Richards: ἠρεμίας,
which, however, can be defended.

of grain and oppressed the aforesaid with famine.[a]
The senate was in confusion; but Mucius one of
the nobles, with the consuls' authorization, took four
hundred men of his own age in civilian dress, and
crossed the river. He observed one of the tyrant's
bodyguards distributing provisions to the officers and,
supposing him to be Porsenna, killed him. When he
was led to the king, he put forth his right hand into
the sacrificial fire; and dissembling his torments
with a stout heart, he said with a smile, "Ruffian, I
am free, whether you will or no. Know that there
are against you even now in your camp four hundred
of us that seek to slay you." Porsenna was
frightened, and made a truce with the Romans.[b]
This Aristeides the Milesian relates in the third book
of his *Histories*.

3. When Argives and Spartans were contending for
the Thyreatis, the Amphictyonic Assembly decreed
that three hundred of each should fight, and the
country should belong to the victors. The Spartans
accordingly made Othryades their general, and the
Argives made Thersander theirs. In the battle two
of the Argives survived, Agenor and Chromius, who
brought to their city the report of their victory. But
when the battlefield was deserted, Othryades revived
and, supporting himself on spear-shafts broken in
two, despoiled and stripped the corpses of their
shields; and when he had erected a trophy, he wrote

---

[a] This passage is repeated in 307 D, *infra*.
[b] *Cf.* Livy, ii. 12.

---

[5] ἁρπάζων] σκυλεύσας Herodotus and Stobaeus; ἁπάντων
some mss. The verbal variants in Stobaeus are too numerous to be recorded here. He has almost another version.

(306) αἵματος ἐπέγραψε " Διὶ τροπαιούχῳ." καὶ τῶν
δύο¹ στάσιν ἐχόντων, οἱ Ἀμφικτύονες αὐτόπται
γενόμενοι Λακεδαιμονίους προκρίνουσι· καθάπερ
Χρύσερμος ἐν τρίτῳ Πελοποννησιακῶν.

ΡΩΜΑΙΟΙ πρὸς Σαμνίτας πόλεμον ἔχοντες στρατηγὸν ἐχειροτόνησαν Ποστούμιον Ἀλβῖνον.² οὗτος
κατὰ τὰς καλουμένας φορκούλας Καυδίνας³ (ἔστι δὲ
C τόπος στενώτατος) ἐνεδρευθεὶς τρεῖς ἀπέβαλε λε-
γεῶνας καὶ αὐτὸς καιρίως τρωθεὶς ἔπεσε. βαθείας
δὲ νυκτὸς ὀλίγον ἐπιζήσας περιείλετο τῶν ἀνῃρη-
μένων πολεμίων τὰς ἀσπίδας, καὶ εἰς τὸ αἷμα τὴν
χεῖρα βαπτίσας ἔστησε τρόπαιον ἐπιγράψας " Ῥωμαῖοι κατὰ Σαμνιτῶν Διὶ τροπαιούχῳ." Μάξιμος⁴
δὲ ὁ ἐπικληθεὶς Λαίμαργος, στρατηγὸς πεμφθεὶς
καὶ παραγενόμενος ἐπὶ τὸν τόπον, ἰδὼν τὸ τρόπαιον
τὸν οἰωνὸν ἀσμένως ἐδέξατο· καὶ συμβαλὼν ἐνίκησε
καὶ αἰχμάλωτον λαβὼν τὸν βασιλέα εἰς Ῥώμην
ἔπεμψεν· ὡς Ἀριστείδης ὁ Μιλήσιος ἐν τρίτῃ
Ἰταλικῶν.

4. ΠΕΡΣΩΝ μετὰ πεντακοσίων μυριάδων ἐπὶ τὴν
Ἑλλάδα ἐρχομένων,⁵ Λεωνίδας ἅμα τριακοσίοις
D ἐπέμφθη εἰς Θερμοπύλας ὑπὸ Λακεδαιμονίων.
εὐωχουμένοις⁶ δ' ἐκεῖ ἐπέκειτο τὸ τῶν βαρβάρων
πλῆθος· καὶ ὁ Λεωνίδας εἶπεν ἰδὼν τοὺς βαρβάρους,

¹ δήμων Pohlenz.
² Ποστούμιον Ἀλβῖνον Guarinus and Xylander ; Μισούνιον
Ἀμβλιρηνόν.
³ φορκούλας Καυδίνας Holsten : φορκοῦντας κλαυδίνας.
⁴ μάξιμος one ms. : Μάιος or Μάϊμος.
⁵ ἐρχομένων] φερομένων Stobaeus, Flor. vii. 64. Stobaeus
has other minor variants besides those recorded below.
⁶ εὐωχουμένοις Dübner from Stobaeus : εὐωχουμένων or
εὐωχούμενον.

with his own blood upon it : ' To Zeus, Guardian of Trophies.' And when the two peoples still disputed over the victory, the Amphictyonic Assembly, after a personal inspection of the battlefield, decided in favour of the Spartans.[a] Thus Chrysermus in the third book of his *Peloponnesian History*.

THE ROMANS in a war with the Samnites elected Postumius Albinus general.[b] He was ambushed at a place called the Caudine Forks (it is a very narrow pass) and lost three legions, and himself fell mortally wounded. But in the dead of night he revived for a little and despoiled the enemy's corpses of their shields. With these he set up a trophy and, dipping his hand in his blood, wrote upon it : " The Romans from the Samnites to Jupiter Feretrius." But Maximus, surnamed the Glutton,[c] was dispatched as general and when he had come to the place and had seen the trophy, he gladly accepted the omen. He attacked the enemy and conquered, and taking their king prisoner, sent him to Rome. Thus Aristeides the Milesian in the third book of his *Italian Histories*.

4. WHEN THE PERSIANS were marching with five million men against Greece, Leonidas was sent by the Spartans to Thermopylae with three hundred men. While they were eating and drinking there, the barbarian host attacked them ; and when Leonidas saw

[a] *Cf.* Herodotus, i. 82 ; Stobaeus, *Florilegium*, vii. 68 (iii. p. 333, Hense) ; Valerius Maximus, iii. 2. ext. 4. Stobaeus quotes the story on the authority of Theseus, and, while his account has quite the same context, there is a great difference in wording.

[b] He was consul 321 B.C. according to Livy, ix. 1. ff., but his death after his defeat was not so dramatic as is here depicted.

[c] Gurges ; *cf.* Macrobius, *Saturnalia*, iii. 13. 6.

(306) '' οὕτως ἀριστᾶτε ὡς ἐν ''Αιδου δειπνήσοντες.''
καὶ ὁρμήσας κατὰ τῶν βαρβάρων καὶ πολλοῖς περι-
παρεὶς δόρασιν ἀνέβη ἐπὶ τὸν Ξέρξην[1] καὶ τὸ
διάδημα ἀφείλετο.[2] οὗ ἀποθανόντος ὁ βάρβαρος
τέμνει[3] τὴν καρδίαν[4] καὶ εὗρε δασεῖαν· ὡς 'Αριστείδης ἐν πρώτῃ Περσικῶν.

ΡΩΜΑΙΟΙ πρὸς Ποινοὺς πόλεμον ἔχοντες ἔπεμψαν τριακοσίους καὶ στρατηγὸν Φάβιον Μάξιμον.
Ε συμβαλὼν δ' ἀπέβαλε πάντας, αὐτὸς δὲ καιρίως
τρωθεὶς μεθ' ὁρμῆς ἐπὶ τὸν 'Αννίβαν ἠνέχθη, καὶ
καθελὼν τὸ διάδημα συναπέθανεν αὐτῷ, καθάπερ
ἱστορεῖ 'Αριστείδης ὁ Μιλήσιος.

5. κατα Κελαινὰς[5] πόλιν τῆς Φρυγίας χάσμα
μεθ' ὕδατος γενόμενον πολλὰς οἰκίας αὐτάνδρους
εἰς τὸν βυθὸν εἵλκυσε.[6] Μίδας δὲ ὁ βασιλεὺς
χρησμὸν ἔλαβεν, ἐὰν τὸ τιμιώτατον ἐμβάλῃ, συν-
ελεύσεσθαι· ὁ δὲ χρυσὸν καὶ ἄργυρον ἐμβαλὼν
F οὐδὲν ἐβοήθησεν. ''Αγχουρος δὲ υἱὸς τοῦ Μίδα
λογισάμενος μηδὲν εἶναι τιμιώτερον ἐν βίῳ ψυχῆς
ἀνθρωπίνης, δοὺς περιπλοκὰς τῷ γεννήσαντι καὶ[7]
τῇ γυναικὶ Τιμοθέᾳ, ἔφιππος εἰς τὸν τόπον τοῦ
χάσματος ἠνέχθη. συνελθούσης δὲ τῆς γῆς χρύσεον βωμὸν ἐποίησεν 'Ιδαίου Διὸς ἁψάμενος τῇ

---

[1] ἀνέβη . . . Ξέρξην] μεθ' ὁρμῆς ἐπὶ Ξέρξην ἠνέχθη Stobaeus.
[2] τὸ διάδημα ἀφείλετο] περιελόμενος αὐτοῦ τὸ διάδημα πρὸ τῶν
τραυμάτων κατέσχε καὶ αἱμορραγήσας ἐξέπνευσεν Stobaeus.
[3] τέμνει] ἐκτέμνει van Herwerden.
[4] τέμνει τὴν καρδία] ἀνατεμὼν δὲ ὁ βασιλεὺς τοῦ προειρημένου
τὸ στῆθος εὗρεν αὐτοῦ τὴν καρδίαν τριχῶν γέμουσαν Stobaeus.
[5] Κελαινὰς Stobaeus, vii. 66 : κελαινόν.
[6] εἵλκυσε] καθείλκυσε Stobaeus.
[7] καὶ] καὶ ἀποταξάμενος Stobaeus.

the barbarians, he said, "Eat your lunch now as if you were to dine in the other world." [a]   And when he rushed against the barbarians, and was pierced by many a spear, he made his way up to Xerxes and snatched off his crown.   When he was dead the barbarian king cut out his heart and found it covered with hair.[b]   So Aristeides in the first [c] book of his *Persian History*.

WHEN THE ROMANS were at war with the Carthaginians, they dispatched three hundred men and Fabius Maximus as their general.   He attacked the enemy and lost all his men, but he himself, although mortally wounded, with a mad rush reached Hannibal and knocked down his crown, and so died with him. This Aristeides the Milesian relates.

5. AT the city of Celaenae in Phrygia the earth yawned open, together with a heavy rain, and dragged down many homesteads with their inhabitants into the depths.   Midas the king received an oracle that if he should throw his most precious possession into the abyss, it would close.   He cast in gold and silver, but this availed nothing.   But Anchurus, the son of Midas, reasoning that there is nothing in life more precious than a human life, embraced his father and his wife Timothea, and rode on his horse into the abyss.   When the earth had closed, Midas made an altar of Idaean Zeus golden

---

[a] *Cf. Moralia*, 225 D, and the note there (Vol. III. p. 350).

[b] *Cf.* Stobaeus, *Florilegium*, vii. 65 (iii. 330 Hense); Lydus, *De Mensibus* 167 (p. 179 Wünsch).

[c] Stobaeus says, " in the third."

χειρί.[1] οὗτος ὁ βωμὸς περὶ ἐκεῖνον τὸν καιρόν, ἐν
ᾧ τὸ χάσμα συνέβη γενέσθαι, λίθινος[2] γίγνεται·
τῆς δὲ ὡρισμένης προθεσμίας παρελθούσης, χρύ-
σεος ὁρᾶται· ὡς Καλλισθένης ἐν δευτέρῳ Μεταμορφώσεων.

ΔΙΑ μέσης τῆς ἀγορᾶς ῥέων ὁ Τίβερις διὰ μῆνιν
Ταρπηίου[3] Διὸς μέγιστον ἀπέρρηξε χάσμα[4] καὶ πολλὰς οἰκίας ἐβύθισε· χρησμὸς δ' ἐδόθη λήξεσθαι, ἐὰν
τὸ τίμιον ἐμβάλωσι. τῶν δὲ χρυσὸν καὶ ἄργυρον
307 ἐμβαλλόντων, Κούρτιος τῶν ἐπισήμων νέος τὸν
χρησμὸν νοήσας καὶ λογισάμενος τὴν ψυχὴν τιμιω-
τέραν, ἔφιππον ἑαυτὸν ἔρριψεν εἰς τὸ χάσμα καὶ
τοὺς οἰκείους ἐξέσωσε τῶν κακῶν· ὡς Ἀριστείδης
ἐν τετταρακοστῷ Ἰταλικῶν.

6. ΤΩΝ ἅμα Πολυνείκει εὐωχουμένων λοχαγῶν
ἀετὸς καταπτὰς τὸ Ἀμφιάρεω ἐβάστασε δόρυ εἰς
ὕψος καὶ εἴασε· τὸ δὲ παγὲν ἐν γῇ δάφνη ἐγένετο.
τῇ δ' ὑστεραίᾳ πολεμούντων κατ' ἐκεῖνο κατεπόθη
ὁ Ἀμφιάρεως ἅμα[5] τῷ ἅρματι, ἔνθα νῦν πόλις
Ἅρμα καλεῖται· ὡς Τρισίμαχος ἐν τρίτῳ Κτίσεων.
Β ΡΩΜΑΙΩΝ πρὸς Πύρρον Ἠπειρώτην πολεμούντων
Αἰμίλιος Παῦλος χρησμὸν ἔλαβε νικῆσαι, βωμὸν

---

[1] χρύσεον βωμόν . . . τῇ χειρί] Μίδας βωμὸν ἱδρύσατο Διὸς
Ἰδαίου, ὃν χρύσεον ἐποίησε ταῖς χερσὶν ἀψάμενος Stobaeus, who
has a clearer and fuller text.

[2] λίθινος Stobaeus: λίθος.

[3] Ταρπηίου S. A. Naber: ταρσίου.

[4] χάσμα Aldine edition, Stegmann, and S. A. Naber: χῶμα.

[5] ἅμα added by H. Richards.

---

[a] The " golden touch " of Midas.

by a touch of his hand.[a] This altar becomes stone at that time of the year when this yawning of the earth occurred ; but when this limit of time has passed, it is seen to be golden.[b] So Callisthenes in the second book of his *Metamorphoses*.

BECAUSE of the wrath of Jupiter Tarpeius[c] the Tiber coursed through the middle of the Forum, broke open a very large abyss and engulfed many houses. An oracle was given that this would end if they threw in their precious possession. As they were casting in gold and silver, Curtius, a youth of noble family, apprehended the meaning of the oracle, and, reasoning that human life is more precious, he hurled himself on horseback into the abyss, and saved his people from their miseries.[d] So Aristeides in the fortieth book of his *Italian History*.

6. WHEN the captains that accompanied Polyneices were feasting, an eagle swooped down and carried the spear of Amphiaraüs up to a height and then let it drop. The spear became fixed in the earth and was changed into a laurel. The next day, when the captains were fighting, at that very spot Amphiaraüs was swallowed up with his chariot, where now is the city that is called Harma.[e] So Trisimachus in the third book of his *Founding of Cities*.

WHEN THE ROMANS were fighting against Pyrrhus of Epeirus, Aemilius Paulus received an oracle that he should be victorious if he would build an altar where

[b] *Cf.* Stobaeus, vii. 66 (iii. 331 Hense).
[c] That is, Capitolinus (*e.g.* Ovid, *Fasti*, vi. 34).
[d] *Cf.* Livy, vii. 6 ; or Dionysius of Halicarnassus, *Roman Antiquities*, xiv. 11. The story is often referred to.
[e] " City of the Chariot " ; *cf.* Pausanias, ix. 19. 4, and the scholium on Clement of Alexandria, *Protrepticus*, ii. 11. 1.

(307) ἐὰν ποιήσῃ, ἔνθα ἂν ἴδῃ χάσματι κρυπτόμενον ἄνδρα τῶν ἐπισήμων μετὰ ἅρματος. μετὰ τρεῖς ἡμέρας Οὐαλέριος Κονᾶτος κατ' ὄναρ ἰδὼν ἀναλαβεῖν
ἱερέως κόσμον (καὶ γὰρ ἦν μαντικῆς ἔμπειρος),
στρατηγήσας καὶ πολλοὺς φονεύσας ὑπὸ γῆς κατεπόθη. ὁ Αἰμίλιος δὲ βωμὸν ἱδρύσας ἐνίκησε καὶ
ἑκατὸν ἑξήκοντα πυργοφόρους ἐλέφαντας εἰς Ῥώμην κατέπεμψεν. ὁ δὲ βωμὸς μαντεύεται κατ'
ἐκεῖνον τὸν καιρόν, καθ' ὃν ἐνικήθη Πύρρος· ὡς
ἱστορεῖ Κριτόλαος[1] ἐν τρίτῃ Ἠπειρωτικῶν.

7. ΠΥΡΑΙΧΜΗΣ βασιλεὺς Εὐβοέων ἐπολέμει Βοιω-
C τοῖς. ὃν Ἡρακλῆς ἔτι νέος ὢν ἐνίκησε· πώλοις δὲ
προσδήσας καὶ εἰς δύο μέρη διελὼν τὸν Πυραίχμην,
ἄταφον ἔρριψεν. ὁ δὲ τόπος προσαγορεύεται " πῶλοι Πυραίχμου," κεῖται δὲ παρὰ ποταμὸν Ἡρά-
κλειον, χρεμετισμὸν δ' ἀναδίδωσι πινόντων ἵππων·
ὡς ἐν τρίτῳ περὶ Ποταμῶν.

ΤΟΥΛΛΟΣ Ὁστίλιος βασιλεὺς Ῥωμαίων ἐπολέμησεν
Ἀλβανοῖς, βασιλέως ὄντος Μετίου Φουφετίου,[2] καὶ
τὴν μάχην πολλάκις ὑπερέθετο. οἱ δ' ὡς ἡττημένου[3] εἰς εὐωχίαν ἐτράπησαν· οἰνωμένοις δ'
ἐπέθετο, καὶ τὸν βασιλέα δύο πώλοις συζεύξας δι-
εσπάραξεν· ὡς Ἀλέξαρχος ἐν τετάρτῃ Ἰταλικῶν.

D 8. ΦΙΛΙΠΠΟΣ Μεθώνην καὶ Ὄλυνθον βουλόμενος πορθῆσαι[4] καὶ βιαζόμενος ἐπὶ τῷ Σανδάνῳ

---

[1] Κριτόλαος Helmbold, as in 308 A, infra: κριτόλας.
[2] Μετίου Φουφετίου] φουφεντίου in some MSS. and in Dionysius
consistently Μεττίου Φουφεττίου.
[3] ἡττημένου F.C.B.: ἡττωμένου. ὡς added by Dübner.
[4] πορθῆσαι] λεηλατεῖν Stobaeus.

---

[a] " Quis significetur, quaerere non est operae pretium "

he should see a man of the nobles with his chariot swallowed up in an abyss. Three days later Valerius Conatus in a dream saw a vision which commanded him to don his priestly raiment (he was, in fact, an expert augur). When he had led forth his men and slain many of the enemy, he was swallowed up by the earth. Aemilius built an altar, gained a victory, and sent back an hundred and sixty turreted elephants to Rome. The altar delivers oracles at that time of year when Pyrrhus was vanquished. This Critolaüs relates in the third book of his *Epeirote History*.

7. PYRAECHMES, king of the Euboeans, was at war with the Boeotians. Heracles, while still a youth, vanquished him. He tied Pyraechmes to colts, tore his body into two parts, and cast it forth unburied. The place is called " Colts of Pyraechmes." It is situated beside the river Heracleius, and it gives forth a sound of neighing when horses drink of it. So in the third book of *Concerning Rivers*.[a]

TULLUS Hostilius, King of the Romans, waged war with the Albans, whose king was Metius Fufetius. And Tullus repeatedly postponed battle. But the Albans, assuming his defeat, betook themselves to feasting and drinking. When they were overcome by wine, Tullus attacked them, and, tying their king to two colts, tore him apart.[b] So Alexarchus in the fourth book of his *Italian History*.

8. PHILIP wished to plunder Methonê and Olynthus and, while he was attempting to force a crossing at

(Wyttenbach); at any rate not the author of the *De Fluviis* in Bernardakis, vol. vii.

[b] *Cf.* Livy, i. 28, *ad fin.* or Dionysius of Halicarnassus, *Roman Antiquities*, iii. 30, *ad fin.*

(307) ποταμῷ διαβῆναι πέραν,[1] ὑπό τινος τῶν Ὀλυνθίων
Ἀστέρος ὀνόματι ἐτοξεύθη τὸν ὀφθαλμόν εἰπόντος,

Ἀστὴρ Φιλίππῳ θανάσιμον πέμπει βέλος·

ὁ δ᾽ ὀπίσω διανηξάμενος πρὸς τοὺς οἰκείους σῴζε-
ται ἀπολέσας[2] τὸν ὀφθαλμόν· ὡς Καλλισθένης ἐν
τρίτῳ Μακεδονικῶν.

ΠΟΡΣΙΝΑΣ Τούσκων βασιλεὺς πέραν Θύμβρεως[3]
ποταμοῦ στρατεύσας ἐπολέμησε Ῥωμαίοις, καὶ τὴν
ἀπὸ σιτίων φερομένην εὐθηνίαν μέσην λαβὼν λιμῷ
τοὺς προειρημένους ἔτρυχεν. Ὁράτιος δὲ Κόκλης
E στρατηγὸς χειροτονηθεὶς τὴν ξυλίνην κατελάβετο
γέφυραν καὶ τὸ πλῆθος τῶν βαρβάρων διαβῆναι
βουλόμενον ἐπεῖχε. πλεονεκτούμενος δὲ ὑπὸ τῶν
πολεμίων προσέταξε τοῖς ὑποτεταγμένοις κόπτειν
τὴν γέφυραν, καὶ τὸ πλῆθος τῶν βαρβάρων διαβῆναι
βουλόμενον ἐκώλυσε. βέλει δὲ τὸν ὀφθαλμὸν
πληγεὶς ῥίψας ἑαυτὸν εἰς τὸν ποταμόν, διενήξατο εἰς
τοὺς οἰκείους· ὡς Θεότιμος ἐν δευτέρῳ Ἰταλικῶν.

9. Ο ΠΕΡΙ τοῦ Ἰκαρίου μῦθος, ᾧ Διόνυσος
ἐπεξενώθη· Ἐρατοσθένης ἐν τῇ Ἠριγόνῃ.

ΚΡΟΝΟΣ ἐπιξενωθεὶς γεωργῷ, ᾧ ἦν θυγάτηρ καλὴ
Ἐντωρία, ταύτην[4] ἐβιάσατο[5] καὶ ἐτέκνωσεν υἱοὺς
F Ἰανὸν Ὕμνον Φαῦστον Φήλικα. διδάξας οὖν τὸν
τρόπον τῆς τοῦ οἴνου πόσεως καὶ τῆς ἀμπέλου

---

[1] πέραν] εἰς τὸ πέραν Stobaeus.

[2] ἀπολέσας] ἀποβαλὼν Stobaeus. Stobaeus has some other
variants and a slightly amplified, but no better, text.

[3] Θύμβρεως seems to be the preferred form of the genitive:
θύμβριος.

[4] ταύτην Dübner: ἦν.   [5] ἐβιάσατο] ἐβιάζετο most mss.

---

[a] Cf. Diodorus, xvi. 34. 5 ; Stobaeus, Florilegium, vii. 67
(iii. p. 332 Hense).

the Sandanus river, his eye was pierced by an arrow
from the bow of a certain Olynthian named Aster,
who uttered these words :

> Aster to Philip sends this deadly shaft.

But Philip swam back to his friends and was saved,
although he lost his eye.[a] So Callisthenes in the
third book of his *Macedonian History*.

PORSENNA, king of the Etruscans, made a foray on
the other side of the river Tiber and warred against the
Romans, and, by intercepting their abundant supply
of grain, he oppressed the aforesaid with famine.[b]
But Horatius Cocles, who was elected general, took
possession of the Wooden Bridge and checked the
barbarian horde that sought to cross. But as he was
being worsted by the enemy, he ordered his sub-
ordinates to cut down the bridge, and so thwarted the
barbarian horde that sought to cross. When his
eye was struck by an arrow, he threw himself into the
river and swam across to his friends. So Theotimus
in the second book of his *Italian History*.[c]

9. THE STORY of Icarius who entertained Dionysus :
Eratosthenes in his *Erigonê*.[d]

SATURN, when once he was entertained by a farmer[e]
who had a fair daughter named Entoria, seduced her
and begat Janus, Hymnus, Faustus, and Felix. He
then taught Icarius the use of wine and viniculture,

---

[b] Repeated from 305 E-F, *supra*.
[c] And Macaulay in *Horatius at the Bridge*.
[d] *Cf.* Powell, *Collectanea Alexandrina*, pp. 64 ff., for the
fragments of the *Erigonê*. Powell is no doubt right in
ignoring this passage, of which Wyttenbach remarks
" Noster tenebrio omnia turbavit."
[e] Presumably Icarius.

ἠξίωσε καὶ τοῖς γείτοσι μεταδοῦναι. ποιήσαντες δ'
αὐτὸ καὶ πιόντες παρὰ τὸ σύνηθες εἰς ὕπνον κατ-
ηνέχθησαν βαρύτερον τοῦ δέοντος· οἱ δὲ πεφαρμα-
κῶσθαι δόξαντες, λίθοις βάλλοντες τὸν Ἰκάριον
ἀπέκτειναν· οἱ δὲ θυγατρίδαι¹ ἀθυμήσαντες βρόχῳ
308 τὸν βίον κατέστρεψαν. λοιμοῦ δὲ κατασχόντος
Ῥωμαίους, ἔχρησεν ὁ Πύθιος λωφήσειν, ἐὰν ἐξ-
ιλάσωνται τοῦ Κρόνου τὴν μῆνιν καὶ τοὺς δαίμονας
τῶν ἀνόμως ἀπολομένων. Λουτάτιος δὲ Κάτλος,
ἀνὴρ τῶν ἐπισήμων, κατεσκεύασε τῷ θεῷ τέμενος
τὸ κείμενον σύνεγγυς τοῦ Ταρπηίου ὄρους, καὶ
τὸν ἄνω βωμὸν ἱδρύσατο τετραπρόσωπον ἢ διὰ
τοὺς θυγατρίδας¹ ἢ ὅτι τετραμερὴς ὁ ἐνιαυτός ἐστι,
καὶ μῆνα κατέδειξεν Ἰανουάριον. ὁ δὲ Κρόνος
πάντας κατηστέρισεν. καὶ οἱ μὲν καλοῦνται προ-
τρυγητῆρες, ὁ δ' Ἰανὸς προανατέλλων· δείκνυται
δ' ὁ ἀστὴρ πρὸ τῶν ποδῶν τῆς παρθένου· ὡς Κριτόλαος ἐν τετάρτῃ Φαινομένων.

B   10. ΠΕΡΣΩΝ τὴν Ἑλλάδα λεηλατούντων Παυ-
σανίας ὁ τῶν Λακεδαιμονίων στρατηγὸς πεντακόσια χρυσοῦ τάλαντα παρὰ Ξέρξου λαβὼν ἔμελλε
προδιδόναι τὴν Σπάρτην. φωραθέντος δὲ τούτου,
Ἀγησίλαος² ὁ πατὴρ μέχρι τοῦ ναοῦ τῆς Χαλ-
κιοίκου συνεδίωξεν Ἀθηνᾶς, καὶ τὰς θύρας τοῦ
τεμένους πλίνθῳ φράξας³ λιμῷ ἀπέκτεινεν· ἡ

¹ θυγατρίδαι and θυγατρίδας would presumably be θυγατριδοῖ
and θυγατριδοῦς in better Greek.
² Ἀγησίλαος] Ἡγησίλαος some mss. and Stobaeus; Κλεόμ-
βροτος in margin of one ms. of Stobaeus.
272

and told him that he should share his knowledge with his neighbours also. When the neighbours did so and drank more than is customary, they fell into an unusually deep sleep. Imagining that they had been poisoned, they pelted Icarius with stones and killed him ; and his grandchildren in despair ended their lives by hanging themselves. When a plague had gained a wide hold among the Romans, Apollo gave an oracle that it would cease if they should appease the wrath of Saturn and the spirits of those who had perished unlawfully. Lutatius Catulus, one of the nobles, built for the god the precinct which lies near the Tarpeian Rock. He made the upper altar with four faces, either because of Icarius's grandchildren or because the year has four parts ; and he designated a month January. Saturn placed them all among the stars. The others are called Harbingers of the Vintage,[a] but Janus rises before them. His star is to be seen just in front of the feet of Virgo. So Critolaüs in the fourth book of his *Phaenomena*.

10. WHEN THE PERSIANS were plundering Greece, Pausanias, the Spartan general, accepted five hundred talents of gold from Xerxes and intended to betray Sparta. But when he was detected, Agesilaüs,[b] his father, helped to pursue him to the temple of Athena of the Brazen House ; the father walled up the doors of the shrine with bricks and killed his son by starva-

[a] *Cf.* Aratus, *Phaenomena*, 138, who mentions only one star of this name, the Vindemiator, which ushers in the autumn.

[b] A mistake for Cleombrotus.

---

[3] πλίνθῳ φράξας] πλίνθοις ἐμφράξας Stobaeus, *Flor.* xxxix. 31.

(308) δὲ μήτηρ καὶ ἄταφον ἔρριψεν· ὡς Χρύσερμος
ἐν δευτέρῳ Ἱστορικῶν.[1]

ΡΩΜΑΙΟΙ πρὸς Λατίνους πολεμοῦντες ἐχειροτόνησαν στρατηγὸν Πόπλιον Δέκιον· νεανίσκος δέ τις
C τῶν ἐπισήμων πένης τοὔνομα Κάσσιος Βροῦτος ἐπὶ
ῥητῷ μισθῷ νυκτὸς τὰς πύλας ἀνοῖξαι ἐβουλήθη.
φωραθεὶς δὲ εἰς ναὸν ἔφυγεν Ἀθηνᾶς Αὐξιλιαρίας.[2]
Κάσσιος δὲ Σίγνιφερ ὁ πατὴρ αὐτοῦ κατέκλεισε καὶ
λιμῷ διέφθειρε καὶ ἄταφον ἔρριψεν· ὡς Κλειτώνυμος ἐν Ἰταλικῶν.[3]

11. ΔΑΡΕΙΟΣ ὁ Πέρσης ἐπὶ Γρανικῷ πολεμήσας
Ἀλεξάνδρῳ καὶ ἑπτὰ σατράπας ἀποβαλὼν καὶ ἅρ-
ματα δρεπανηφόρα δύο καὶ πεντακόσια, συμβαλεῖν
ἔμελλε τῇ ἑξῆς. Ἀριοβαρζάνης δὲ ὁ υἱὸς συμπαθῶς διακείμενος πρὸς Ἀλέξανδρον ὑπισχνεῖτο
τὸν πατέρα προδώσειν. ἀγανακτήσας δὲ ὁ πατὴρ
ἐτραχηλοκόπησεν· ὡς Ἀρητάδης Κνίδιος ἐν τρίτῳ
Μακεδονικῶν.

D ΒΡΟΥΤΟΣ ὑπὸ πάντων ὕπατος χειροτονηθεὶς ἐφυ-
γάδευσε τὸν Ὑπερήφανον Ταρκύνιον τυραννικῶς
ἀναστρεφόμενον. ὁ δ' ἐλθὼν εἰς Τούσκους ἐπολέμει Ῥωμαίοις. οἱ δὲ υἱοὶ[4] τὸν πατέρα προδοῦναι
ἠβουλήθησαν. ἐμφανέντας δ' ἐτραχηλοκόπησεν[5]·
ὡς Ἀριστείδης Μιλήσιος ἐν τοῖς Ἰταλικοῖς.

12. ΕΠΑΜΕΙΝΩΝΔΑΣ ὁ τῶν Θηβαίων στρατηγὸς

---

[1] Ἱστορικῶν] Περσικῶν Stobaeus. Stobaeus has a slightly
fuller text, but derived from the same source, as the mistake
of Agesilaüs (for Cleombrotus) shows.
[2] Αὐξιλιαρίας Budaeus: αὐξιληρίας.
[3] ἐν Ἰταλικῶν] ἐν ι' Ἰταλικῶν?   [4] υἱοὶ Turnebus: τοῦσκοι.
[5] ἐμφανέντας δ' ἐτραχηλοκόπησεν F.C.B., cf. 312 D: ἐμ-
πεσόντων δὲ τραχηλοκοπῆσαι.

tion.[a] His mother also cast his body forth unburied.[b] So Chrysermus in the second book of his *Histories*.

THE ROMANS in their war with the inhabitants of Latium elected Publius Decius general. A certain poor, but noble, youth named Cassius Brutus wished to open the gates at night for a stated sum of money. He was detected and fled to the temple of Minerva Auxiliaria. Cassius Signifer, his father, shut him in, killed him by starvation, and cast him forth unburied. So Cleitonymus in his *Italian History*.

11. WHEN DARIUS the Persian had fought with Alexander at the Granicus, and had lost seven satraps and five hundred and two scythe-bearing chariots, he intended to attack again on the next day. But Ariobarzanes, his son, who was kindly disposed toward Alexander, promised to betray his father. But the father fell into a rage and cut off his head. So Aretades of Cnidus in the third book of his *Macedonian History*.

BRUTUS, unanimously elected consul, drove into exile Tarquin the Proud, who was comporting himself despotically. Tarquin went to the Etruscans and began to wage war against the Romans. But Tarquin's sons wished to betray their father. But they were detected, and Tarquin cut off their heads. So Aristeides the Milesian in his *Italian History*.

12. EPAMEINONDAS, the Theban general, when he

[a] *Cf.* Thucydides, i. 134 : what Ps.-Plut. tells us here of Pausanias's father is related of his mother Theano in Diodorus, xi. 45. 6; Polyaenus, *Stratagemata*, viii. 51; Cornelius Nepos, *Life of Pausanias*, 5.

[b] Stobaeus, *Florilegium*, xxxix. 31 (iii. p. 728 Hense).

ἔχων πρὸς Λακεδαιμονίους πόλεμον καὶ ἀρχαιρε-
σιῶν ἀγομένων ἧκεν ἐς πατρίδα, παραγγείλας
τῷ παιδὶ Στησιμβρότῳ μὴ συμβάλλειν.[1] Λακεδαιμόνιοι μαθόντες τὴν ἀπουσίαν ἐβλασφήμουν τὸν
νεανίαν ὡς ἄνανδρον· ὁ δ' ἀγανακτήσας καὶ ἐπι-
E λαθόμενος τοῦ πατρὸς συνέβαλε καὶ ἐνίκησεν· ὁ δὲ
πατὴρ βαρέως ἐνέγκας στεφανώσας ἐτραχηλοκόπησεν, ὡς Κτησιφῶν ἱστορεῖ ἐν τρίτῳ Βοιωτιακῶν.

ΡΩΜΑΙΟΙ πρὸς Σαμνίτας πόλεμον ἔχοντες ἐχειροτόνησαν Μάλλιον τὸν Ἐπιτάκτην ἐπικληθέντα.
οὗτος διὰ χειροτονίαν ὑπατικὴν εἰς Ῥώμην πορευόμενος τῷ υἱῷ προσέταξε μὴ συμβαλεῖν. οἱ δὲ
Σαμνῖται μαθόντες βλασφημίαις ἐξουδένιζον τὸν
νεανίαν· ὁ δὲ ταραχθεὶς ἐνίκησεν· Μάλλιος δ'
αὐτὸν ἐτραχηλοκόπησεν· καθάπερ ἱστορεῖ Ἀριστείδης Μιλήσιος.

F 13. ΗΡΑΚΛΗΣ τοῦ Ἰόλης γάμου ἀποτυχὼν τὴν
Οἰχαλίαν ἐπόρθησεν. ἡ δ' Ἰόλη ἀπὸ τοῦ τείχους
ἔρριψεν ἑαυτήν. συνέβη δέ, κολπωθείσης ὑπὸ ἀνέ-
μου τῆς ἐσθῆτος, μηδὲν παθεῖν· καθάπερ ἱστορεῖ
Νικίας Μαλλώτης.[2]

ΡΩΜΑΙΟΙ πολεμοῦντες πρὸς Τούσκους[3] ἐχειροτόνησαν Βαλέριον Τορκουᾶτον. οὗτος θεασάμενος
τοῦ βασιλέως τὴν θυγατέρα τοὔνομα Κλουσίαν
ᾐτεῖτο παρὰ τοῦ Τούσκου τὴν θυγατέρα, μὴ τυχὼν
δ' ἐπόρθει τὴν πόλιν. ἡ δὲ Κλουσία ἀπὸ τῶν
309 πύργων ἔρριψεν ἑαυτήν· προνοίᾳ δ' Ἀφροδίτης
κολπωθείσης τῆς ἐσθῆτος, διεσώθη ἐπὶ τὴν γῆν·

---

[1] συμβάλλειν] συμβαλεῖν Hatzidakis.
[2] Μαλλώτης Hercher : μαλεώτης.
[3] Τούσκους F.C.B. : τροῦσκον.

was waging war against the Spartans, returned home at the season of the elections, giving orders to his son Stesimbrotus not to engage the enemy. But the Spartans learned of Epameinondas's absence and taunted the youth with lack of manliness. He became indignant and, forgetting his father's command, engaged the enemy and conquered. But his father being deeply offended, crowned the youth[a] and cut off his head. This Ctesiphon relates in the third book of his *Boeotian History*.

WHEN THE ROMANS were engaged in war against the Samnites, they appointed Manlius, called Imperiosus, general. As he was journeying to Rome for the consular elections, he ordered his son not to engage the enemy. But the Samnites learned of this and insultingly called the youth a nobody. He was provoked and defeated them, but Manlius cut off his head. This Aristeides the Milesian relates.

13. HERACLES failed in his suit for Iolê's hand and sacked Oechalia. Iolê threw herself down from the wall; but it came about, since her garment was billowed out by the wind, that she suffered no harm. This Nicias of Mallus relates.

WHEN THE ROMANS were warring against the Etruscans, they elected Valerius Torquatus general. When he beheld the king's daughter, whose name was Clusia, he asked the Etruscan for his daughter; but when he failed to obtain her, he attempted to sack the city. Clusia threw herself down from the battlements; but by the foresight of Venus her garment billowed out, and she came safely to the ground. The

---

[a] Thus recognizing him as victorious.

(309) ἦν ὁ στρατηγὸς διέφθειρε, καὶ τούτων[1] πάντων
ἕνεκα ἐξωρίσθη κοινῷ δόγματι ὑπὸ Ῥωμαίων εἰς
Κόρσικαν νῆσον πρὸ τῆς Ἰταλίας· ὡς Θεόφιλος ἐν
τρίτῳ Ἰταλικῶν.

14. ΠΟΙΝΩΝ καὶ Σικελιωτῶν τὴν κατὰ Ῥωμαίων
B συμμαχίαν ἑτοιμαζόντων, Μέτελλος στρατηγὸς
μόνῃ τῇ Ἑστίᾳ οὐκ ἔθυσεν· ἡ δὲ πνεῦμα ἀντ-
έπνευσε ταῖς ναυσί. Γάιος δὲ Ἰούλιος μάντις εἶπε
λωφῆσαι, ἐὰν προθύσῃ τὴν θυγατέρα. ὁ δ᾽
ἀναγκασθεὶς Μετέλλαν[2] τὴν θυγατέρα προσῆγεν· ἡ
δὲ Ἑστία ἐλεήσασα δάμαλιν ὑπέβαλε καὶ αὐτὴν
ἐκόμισεν εἰς Λανούιον,[3] καὶ ἱέρειαν τοῦ σεβομένου
παρ᾽ αὐτοῖς δράκοντος ἀπέδειξεν· ὡς Πυθοκλῆς ἐν
τρίτῃ Ἰταλικῶν.

ΕΝ ΑΤΛΙΔΙ τῆς Βοιωτίας τὰ περὶ Ἰφιγένειαν
ὁμοίως ἱστορεῖ Μένυλλος[4] ἐν πρώτῳ Βοιωτιακῶν.

15. ΒΡΕΝΝΟΣ Γαλατῶν βασιλεὺς λεηλατῶν τὴν
Ἀσίαν ἐπὶ Ἔφεσον ἦλθε, καὶ ἠράσθη παρθένου
Δημονίκης·[5] ἡ δὲ συνελθεῖν ὑπέσχετο, ἐὰν τὰ ψέλλια
καὶ τὸν κόσμον τῶν γυναικῶν[6] δῷ αὐτῇ, καὶ τὴν
C Ἔφεσον προδοῦναι· ὁ δ᾽ ἠξίωσε τοὺς στρατιώτας
ἐμβαλεῖν εἰς τὸν κόλπον ὃν εἶχον χρυσὸν[7] τῆς
φιλαργύρου. ποιησάντων δὲ ὑπὸ τῆς δαψιλείας

---

[1] διέφθειρε, καὶ τούτων F.C.B. (καὶ τούτων Hutten): ἔφθειρε καὶ διὰ τούτων.
[2] Μετέλλαν Xylander: μεταλίαν or μεταλλίαν.
[3] Λανούιον Xylander and Bücheler: λαμούσιον.
[4] Μένυλλος Müller, F.H.G. iv. p. 452: μέρυλλος.

general violated her, and for all these reasons was
banished by public decree of the Romans to Corsica,
an island off Italy. So Theophilus in the third book
of his *Italian History*.

14. WHEN THE CARTHAGINIANS and Siceliots were
negotiating an alliance against the Romans, Vesta
was the only divinity to whom Metellus, the general,
did not sacrifice. She, accordingly, sent a contrary
wind against his ships. Gaius Julius, the augur, said
that it would abate if Metellus should sacrifice his
daughter. Forced by necessity, he brought forward
his daughter Metella. But Vesta took pity, substituted a heifer, transported the maiden to Lanuvium,[a]
and appointed her priestess of the serpent that is
worshipped by the people there. So Pythocles in the
third book of his *Italian History*.

THE LIKE FATE of Iphigeneia at Aulis in Boeotia
Menyllus relates in the first book of his *Boeotian
History*.

15. BRENNUS, king of the Gauls, when he was
ravaging Asia, came to Ephesus and fell in love with
a maiden Demonicê. She promised to satisfy his
desires and also to betray Ephesus, if he would give
her the Gauls' bracelets and feminine ornaments. But
Brennus required his soldiers to throw into the lap
of the avaricious woman the gold which they were
wearing. This they did, and she was buried alive by

[a] *Cf.* Propertius, iv. 8. 3.

---

[5] Δημονίκης Stobaeus, x. 71: δημοτικῆς.
[6] τὸν κόσμον τῶν γυναικῶν] καὶ τοὺς ὅρμους Stobaeus.
[7] ὃν εἶχον χρυσὸν] τὸν χρυσὸν ὅσον εἶχον κόσμου χάριν (*ut infra*)
Stobaeus.

(309) τοῦ χρυσοῦ ζῶσα κατεχώσθη· καθάπερ ἱστορεῖ
Κλειτοφῶν ἐν πρώτῳ Γαλατικῶν.[1]

ΤΑΡΠΗΙΑ[2] τῶν εὐσχημόνων παρθένων τοῦ Καπι-
τωλίου φύλαξ, Ῥωμαίων πρὸς Σαβίνους[3] πολεμούντων, ὑπέσχετο τῷ Τατίῳ δώσειν εἴσοδον εἰς
τὸ Ταρπήιον ὄρος, ἐὰν μισθὸν λάβῃ τοὺς ὅρμους,
οὓς ἐφόρουν κόσμου χάριν. Σαβῖνοι δὲ νοήσαντες
ζῶσαν κατέχωσαν· ὡς Ἀριστείδης Μιλήσιος ἐν
Ἰταλικοῖς.

16. ΤΕΓΕΑΤΑΙΣ καὶ Φενάταις χρονίου πολέμου
D γενομένου, ἔδοξε[4] τριδύμους ἀδελφοὺς πέμψαι τοὺς
μαχησομένους περὶ τῆς νίκης. καὶ Τεγεᾶται μὲν
οὖν τοὺς Ῥηξιμάχου παῖδας, Φενεᾶται δὲ τοὺς
Δημοστράτου προεβάλλοντο.[5] συμβληθείσης δὲ τῆς
μάχης, ἐφονεύθησαν τῶν Ῥηξιμάχου δύο· ὁ δὲ
τρίτος τοὔνομα Κριτόλαος στρατηγήματι περι-
εγένετο τῶν δύο· προσποιητὴν γὰρ φυγὴν σκηψά-
μενος καθ' ἕνα τῶν διωκόντων ἀνεῖλε. καὶ ἐλθόν-
τος οἱ μὲν ἄλλοι συνεχάρησαν, μόνη δ' οὐκ ἐχάρη[7]
ἡ ἀδελφὴ Δημοδίκη· πεφονεύκει γὰρ αὐτῆς τὸν
κατηγγυημένον ἄνδρα Δημόδικον. ἀναξιοπαθήσας
δὲ ὁ Κριτόλαος ἀνεῖλεν αὐτήν. φόνου δ' ἀγόμενος

---

[1] ἐν πρώτῳ Γαλατικῶν] ἐκ τοῦ εʹ Ἰταλικῶν Stobaeus. Stobaeus
has also other unimportant variants and amplifications.
[2] Ταρπηΐα Turnebus : ταρσία, ταρτησιά, or ταρμισία.
[3] Σαβίνους Schott : Ἀλβανούς.
[4] ἔδοξε] συνεφώνησε Stobaeus, *Flor.* xxxix. 32.
[5] προεβάλλοντο] ἔπεμψαν Stobaeus.

the abundance of gold.[a]   This Cleitophon relates in the first book of his *Gallic History*.

TARPEIA, one of the maidens of honourable estate, was the guardian of the Capitol when the Romans were warring against the Sabines. She promised Tatius that she would give him entry to the Tarpeian Rock if she received as pay the necklaces [b] which the Sabines wore for adornment. The Sabines understood the import and buried her alive. So Aristeides the Milesian in his *Italian History*.

16. WHEN a war between the Tegeans and the Pheneans had continued for a long time, it was agreed to send triplet brothers to determine the victory by their fighting. The Tegeans accordingly chose to represent them the sons of Rheximachus, and the Pheneans the sons of Demostratus. When battle was joined, two of Rheximachus's sons were slain. But the third, Critolaüs by name, by a stratagem succeeded in surviving his two brothers. For he devised the ruse of simulated flight, and so killed one after another of his pursuers. And when he came home all the rest rejoiced with him ; but his sister Demodicê alone did not rejoice, for he had slain her betrothed, Demodicus. Critolaüs, smarting under such undeserved treatment, killed her. He was prosecuted for murder by his

---

[a] *Cf.* Stobaeus, *Florilegium*, x. 70 (iii. p. 426 Hense).

[b] The usual specification was " what they bore on their left arms " (*cf. Life of Romulus*, xvii. (27 F–28 D); Livy, i. 11), but, to judge from Stobaeus's version of the preceding paragraph, its source probably contained " necklaces," and so a strict parallelism requires " necklace " here!

---

[6] τῶν δύο] τῶν ἀντιπάλων Stobaeus.

[7] μόνη δ᾽ οὐκ ἐχάρη] οὐ συνεχάρη μόνη τῷ προειρημένῳ Stobaeus.

E ὑπὸ τῆς μητρὸς ἀπελύθη τοῦ ἐγκλήματος[1]· ὡς
Δημάρατος ἐν δευτέρῳ Ἀρκαδικῶν.

ΡΩΜΑΙΟΙ καὶ Ἀλβανοὶ πολεμοῦντες τριδύμους
προμάχους εἵλοντο, καὶ Ἀλβανοὶ μὲν Κουριατίους,[2]
Ῥωμαῖοι δὲ Ὡρατίους. συμβληθείσης δὲ τῆς
μάχης, οἱ Κουριάτιοι[2] δύο τῶν ἐναντίων ἀνεῖλον·
ὁ δὲ περίλοιπος φυγῇ προσποιητῇ συμμάχῳ
χρώμενος ἐφόνευσε καθ᾿ ἕνα τῶν ἐπιδιωκόντων.
χαρέντων δὲ πάντων, μόνη ἡ ἀδελφὴ οὐ συνεχάρη
Ὡρατία τὸν κατηγγυημένον ἄνδρα Κουριάτιον[2]
ἀνῃρηκότι· ὁ δ᾿ ἐφόνευσε τὴν ἀδελφήν· ὡς φησιν
F Ἀριστείδης ὁ Μιλήσιος ἐν Ἰταλικοῖς.

17. ΕΝ ΙΛΙΩΙ τοῦ ναοῦ τῆς Ἀθηνᾶς ἐμπρησθέντος,
προσδραμὼν Ἶλος τὸ διοπετὲς ἥρπασε παλλάδιον
καὶ ἐτυφλώθη· οὐ γὰρ ἐξῆν[3] ὑπ᾿ ἀνδρὸς βλέπεσθαι·
ὕστερον δ᾿ ἐξιλασάμενος ἀνέβλεψεν· ὡς Δέρκυλλος
ἐν πρώτῳ Κτίσεων.

ΑΝΤΥΛΟΣ[4] ἀνὴρ τῶν ἐπισήμων πορευόμενος εἰς τὸ
προάστειον ὑπὸ κοράκων ἐπεσχέθη παιόντων ταῖς
πτέρυξι. φοβηθεὶς δὲ τὸν οἰωνὸν εἰς Ῥώμην
310 ὑπέστρεψεν. ἰδὼν δὲ τὸ τέμενος τῆς Ἑστίας καιό-
μενον καὶ τὸ παλλάδιον ἁρπάσας ἐτυφλώθη· ὕστερον
δ᾿ ἀνέβλεψεν ἐξιλασάμενος· ὡς Ἀριστείδης Μιλήσιος ἐν Ἰταλικοῖς.

---

[1] τοῦ ἐγκλήματος some mss. and Stobaeus: τῶν ἐγκλημάτων.
Some other slight amplifications and variations may be
found in the text of Stobaeus, but the two versions are often
in exact agreement.

[2] Κουριατίους, etc., an obvious correction, Guarinus:
κορατίους or κουρατίους.

[3] ἐξῆν Wyttenbach: ἐξόν.

[4] Ἀντύλος] Μέτελλος Basel ed. of 1542, and Guarinus.

mother, but was acquitted of the charge.[a] So
Demaratus in the second book of his *Arcadian History*.

WHEN THE ROMANS and the Albans were at war, they
chose triplets as their champions, the Albans the
Curiatii, the Romans the Horatii. When the battle
was joined, the Curiatii killed two of their opponents ;
but the survivor made use of simulated flight to help
him, and killed one after another of his pursuers.
Amid the universal rejoicing his sister Horatia alone
did not rejoice with him ; for he had slain her
betrothed, Curiatius. So Horatius killed his sister.[b]
This Aristeides the Milesian narrates in his *Italian
History*.

17. WHEN the shrine of Athena in Ilium was in
flames, Ilus rushed up and seized the Palladium, a
statue which had fallen from heaven, and was
blinded : for the Palladium might not be looked upon
by man. But later, when he had placated the
goddess, he regained his sight. So Dercyllus in the
first book of his *Foundations of Cities*.

WHEN ANTYLUS,[c] one of the noblemen, was on
his way to the outskirts of the city, he was checked
by crows which struck at him with their wings.
Frightened by the omen, he returned to Rome. He
saw that the shrine of Vesta was on fire, seized the
Palladium, and was blinded. But later he regained
his sight when he had placated the goddess. So
Aristeides the Milesian in his *Italian History*.

---

[a] *Cf.* Stobaeus, *Florilegium*, xxxix. 32 (iii. p. 729 Hense).
[b] *Cf.* Livy, i. 24-26.
[c] Some would write " Metellus " and make it refer to
Caecilius Metellus, the Pontifex Maximus; *cf.* Seneca
Rhetor, *Controversiae*, iv. 2 ; Pliny, *Natural History*, vii. 43
(141); *cf.* also Livy, *Periocha*, xix. and Ovid, *Fasti*, vi. 437 ff.

PLUTARCH'S MORALIA

(310) 18. ΘΡΑΙΚΕΣ 'Αθηναίοις πολεμοῦντες χρησμὸν
ἔλαβον, ὡς, ἐὰν Κόδρου φείσωνται, νικῆσαι· ὁ δὲ
δρέπανον λαβὼν ἧκεν εἰς τοὺς ἐναντίους ἐν εὐτελοῦς
σχήματι, καὶ ἕνα φονεύσας ὑπὸ θατέρου ἀνῃρέθη·
οὕτω τ' ἐνίκησαν οἱ 'Αθηναῖοι· ὡς Σωκράτης[1] ἐν
δευτέρῳ Θρακικῶν.

ΠΟΠΛΙΟΣ Δέκιος 'Ρωμαῖος πρὸς 'Αλβανοὺς πολεμῶν ὄναρ εἶδεν, ἐὰν ἀποθάνῃ, ῥώμην προσ-
B ποιήσειν 'Ρωμαίοις. ἐλθὼν εἰς μέσους καὶ πολλοὺς
φονεύσας ἀνῃρέθη. ὁμοίως δὲ καὶ ὁ υἱὸς αὐτοῦ
Δέκιος ἐν τῷ πρὸς Γάλλους πολέμῳ τοὺς 'Ρω-
μαίους διέσωσεν· ὡς 'Αριστείδης Μιλήσιος.

19. ΚΤΑΝΙΠΠΟΣ γένει Συρακούσιος μόνῳ Διονύσῳ
οὐκ ἔθυεν· ὁ δὲ θεὸς ὀργισθεὶς μέθην ἐνέσκηψε,
καὶ ἐν τόπῳ σκοτεινῷ τὴν θυγατέρα ἐβιάσατο
Κυάνην· ἡ δὲ τὸν δακτύλιον περιελομένη ἔδωκε τῇ
τροφῷ ἐσόμενον ἀναγνώρισμα. λοιμωξάντων δὲ
καὶ τοῦ Πυθίου εἰπόντος μὲν δεῖν τὸν ἀσεβῆ τροπαίοις θεοῖς σφαγιάσαι, τῶν δ' ἄλλων ἀγνοούντων
C τὸν χρησμόν, γνοῦσα ἡ Κυάνη καὶ ἐπιλαβομένη τῶν
τριχῶν εἷλκε, καὶ αὐτὴ κατασφάξασα τὸν πατέρα
ἑαυτὴν ἐπέσφαξε· καθάπερ Δοσίθεος ἐν τῷ τρίτῳ
Σικελικῶν.

ΤΩΝ Διονυσίων ἐν τῇ 'Ρώμῃ ἀγομένων 'Αρούντιος[2] ἐκ γενετῆς ὑδροπότης ἐξουδένιζε τὴν τοῦ θεοῦ
δύναμιν· ὁ δὲ μέθην ἐνέβαλε, καὶ ἐβιάσατο τὴν

---

[1] Σωκράτης] Σώστρατος Stobaeus, vii. 67. Stobaeus's version
differs greatly in its language, and is about twice as long.
[2] 'Αρούντιος Oswald: ἀρνούτιος or ἀρνούσιος.

---

[a] Cf. Stobaeus, Florilegium, vii. 67 (iii. p. 332 Hense).
[b] Cf. Livy, viii. 9; x. 28; also Moralia, 499 B.

18. WHEN THE THRACIANS were at war with the Athenians, they received an oracle that they would be victorious if they should spare Codrus; but Codrus took a scythe and, in the guise of a poor man, went to meet the enemy. He slew one and was killed by the second, and thus the Athenians gained the victory.[a] So Socrates in the second book of his *Thracian History*.

WHEN PUBLIUS Decius, a Roman, was warring against the Albans, he saw in a dream that, if he should die, his death would bring strength to the Romans. He went into the thick of the battle, slew many, and was himself slain. In like manner did his son Decius also save the Romans in the war against the Gauls.[b] So Aristeides the Milesian.

19. To DIONYSUS alone did Cyanippus, a Syracusan, omit to sacrifice. The god was angry and cast upon him a fit of drunkenness, in which he violated his daughter Cyanê in a dark place. She took off his ring and gave it to her nurse to be a mark of recognition. When the Syracusans were oppressed by a plague, and the Pythian god pronounced that they should sacrifice the impious man to the Averting Deities, the rest had no understanding of the oracle; but Cyanê knew, and seized her father by the hair and dragged him forth; and when she had herself cut her father's throat, she killed herself upon his body in the same manner. So Dositheüs in the third book of his *Sicilian History*.

WHEN THE BACCHANALIAN revels were being celebrated at Rome, Aruntius, who had been from birth a water-drinker, set at naught the power of the god. But Dionysus cast a fit of drunkenness upon him, and

(310) θυγατέρα Μεδουλλῖναν. ἡ δὲ ἐκ δακτυλίου γνοῦσα
τὸ γένος καὶ πρεσβύτερα τῆς ἡλικίας φρονήσασα,
μεθύσασα τὸν πατέρα καὶ στεφανώσασα ἤγαγεν ἐπὶ
τὸν βωμὸν τῆς Ἀστραπῆς καὶ δακρύσασα ἀνεῖλε
τὸν ἐπίβουλον τῆς παρθενίας· ὡς Ἀριστείδης ἐν
τρίτῃ Ἰταλικῶν.

D   20. ΕΡΕΧΘΕΥΣ πρὸς Εὔμολπον πολεμῶν ἔμαθε
νικῆσαι, ἐὰν τὴν θυγατέρα προθύσῃ, καὶ συγ-
κοινωνήσας τῇ γυναικὶ Πραξιθέᾳ προέθυσε τὴν
παῖδα. μέμνηται Εὐριπίδης ἐν Ἐρεχθεῖ.[1]

MAPIOΣ[2] πρὸς Κίμβρους πόλεμον ἔχων καὶ ἡττώ-
μενος ὄναρ εἶδεν ὅτι νικήσει, ἐὰν τὴν θυγατέρα
προθύσῃ· ἦν δ᾽ αὐτῷ Καλπουρνία· προκρίνας δὲ
τῆς φύσεως τοὺς πολίτας ἔδρασε καὶ ἐνίκησε. καὶ
ἔτι καὶ νῦν βωμοὶ εἰσὶ δύο ἐν Γερμανίᾳ, οἳ κατ᾽
ἐκεῖνον τὸν καιρὸν ἦχον σαλπίγγων ἀποπέμπουσιν·
E ὡς Δωρόθεος ἐν τετάρτῳ Ἰταλικῶν.

21. ΚΥΑΝΙΠΠΟΣ τῷ γένει Θετταλὸς ἐπὶ θήραν
συνεχῶς ἐξῄει· ἡ δὲ νεόνυμφος αὐτοῦ ὑπολαβοῦσα
διὰ τὸ πολλάκις ἐν ὕλαις μένειν συνήθειαν ἔχειν
μεθ᾽ ἑτέρας, κατ᾽ ἴχνος ἠκολούθησε τῷ Κυανίππῳ·
καὶ ἔν τινι κατακρυβεῖσα συνδένδρῳ, τὸ μέλλον

---

[1] Ἐρεχθεῖ] Δημαράτου ἐν τρίτῳ Τραγῳδουμένων Stobaeus,
Flor. xxxix. 33. Stobaeus has an expanded version, but
obviously drawn from the same source.
[2] Μάριος (from Clement of Alexandria) Xylander: μάνιος.

---

[a] Fulgora; cf. Moralia, 499 B–C. The garlands marked
him as a victim for sacrifice.
[b] Cf. 313 B and the note.

he violated his daughter Medullina. But she recognized from a ring his relationship and devised a plan wiser than her years ; making her father drunk, and crowning him with garlands, she led him to the altar of Divine Lightning,[a] and there, dissolved in tears, she slew the man who had plotted against her virginity. So Aristeides in the third book of his *Italian History*.

20. WHEN ERECHTHEUS was at war with Eumolpus,[b] he learned that he would conquer if he sacrificed his daughter before the battle, and, communicating this to his wife Praxithea, he sacrificed his daughter.[c] Euripides [d] records this in the *Erechtheus*.

WHEN MARIUS was fighting the Cimbri and was being worsted, he saw in a dream that he would conquer if he sacrificed his daughter before the battle ; for he had a daughter Calpurnia. Since he placed his fellow-citizens before the ties of nature, he did the deed and won the victory. And even to this day there are two altars in Germany which at that time of year send forth the sound of trumpets. So Dorotheüs in the fourth book of his *Italian History*.[e]

21. CYANIPPUS, a Thessalian by birth, used continually to go forth to hunt, but his wife, whom he had but lately wed, suspected him of intimacy with another woman, because of his habit of frequently passing the night in the forest, and she followed on the track of Cyanippus. Hiding herself in a thicket,

[c] *Cf.* Stobaeus, *Florilegium*, xxxix. 33 (iii. p. 730 Hense) ; Clement of Alexandria, *Protrepticus*, iii. 42 ; Eusebius, *Praepar. Evang* iv. 16. 12.
[d] *Cf.* Nauck, *Trag. Graec. Frag.* pp. 464 ff.
[e] *Cf.* Eusebius, *l.c.* and Lydus, *De Mensibus*, 147 (p. 165 Wünsch).

ἀπεκαραδόκει. τῶν δὲ κλάδων σεισθέντων οἱ κύνες[1] θηρίον εἶναι δόξαντες ὥρμησαν καὶ τὴν φίλανδρον ἀλόγου δίκην ζῴου διεσπάραξαν. ὁ δὲ Κυάνιππος τῆς[2] ἀνελπίστου πράξεως αὐτόπτης γενόμενος ἑαυτὸν ἀπέσφαξεν[3]· ὡς Παρθένιος[4] ὁ ποιητής.

F   ΕΝ Συβάρει πόλει τῆς Ἰταλίας νέος περίβλεπτος τὸ κάλλος Αἰμίλιος φιλοκύνηγος ἦν· ἡ δὲ νεόνυμφος δόξασα ἑτέρᾳ συνεῖναι εἰσήει εἰς τὴν νάπην. τῶν δὲ δένδρων σεισθέντων, οἱ κύνες ἐπιδραμόντες διέσπασαν· ὁ δὲ ἐπέσφαξεν ἑαυτόν· ὡς Κλειτώνυμος ἐν δευτέρῳ Συβαριτικῶν.

22. ΣΜΥΡΝΑ Κινύρου θυγάτηρ διὰ μῆνιν Ἀφροδίτης ἠράσθη τοῦ γεννήσαντος, καὶ τῇ τροφῷ τὴν

311   ἀνάγκην τοῦ ἔρωτος ἐδήλωσεν· ἡ δὲ δόλῳ ὑπῆγε[5] τὸν δεσπότην· ἔφη γὰρ γείτονα παρθένον ἐρᾶν αὐτοῦ καὶ αἰσχύνεσθαι ἐν φανερῷ προσιέναι. ὁ δὲ συνήει. ποτὲ δὲ θελήσας τὴν ἐρῶσαν μαθεῖν φῶς ᾔτησεν, ἰδὼν δὲ ξιφήρης τὴν ἀσελγεστάτην ἐδίωκεν. ἡ δὲ κατὰ πρόνοιαν Ἀφροδίτης εἰς ὁμώνυμον δένδρον μετεμορφώθη· καθὰ Θεόδωρος ἐν ταῖς Μεταμορφώσεσιν.

ΟΥΑΛΕΡΙΑ Τουσκλαναρία κατὰ μῆνιν Ἀφροδίτης

---

[1] τῶν δὲ κλάδων . . . κύνες] τῶν δὲ πέριξ κλάδων αἰφνιδίως σεισθέντων οἱ στιβευταὶ κύνες is a fair sample of Stobaeus's version, Flor. lxiv. 33.

[2] τῆς added from Stobaeus.

[3] ἀπέσφαξεν] ἐπικατέσφαξεν Stobaeus; διεχρήσατο Parthenius.

[4] Παρθένιος] Σωστράτου ἐν β΄ Κυνηγετικῶν Stobaeus.

[5] ὑπῆγε] ἐνήδρευσεν Stobaeus, Flor. lxiv. 34. Stobaeus has quite a different version; only a few words and the last complete sentence (κατὰ πρόνοιαν . . . μετεμορφώθη) are the same.

she awaited events. But some branches were shaken
by her movements, and the dogs, thinking that she
was a wild animal, rushed upon her and tore to pieces
the loving wife like a brute beast. Cyanippus was a
witness of this unexpected event and slew himself.[a]
So the poet Parthenius.[b]

IN SYBARIS, a city of Italy, a young man Aemilius,
greatly admired for his beauty, was very fond of
hunting. But his wife, whom he had but lately wed,
thought that he was consorting with another woman
and entered the dell. The trees were shaken by her
movements and the dogs rushed upon her and tore
her to pieces ; and her husband slew himself. So
Cleitonymus in the second book of his *History of
Sybaris.*

22. THROUGH the wrath of Aphroditê, Smyrna, the
daughter of Cinyras, fell in love with her father, and
revealed to her nurse the all-compelling force of her
love. The nurse led on her master by a trick ; for she
declared that a neighbouring maiden was in love with
him and was too modest to approach him openly ; and
Cinyras consorted with her. But on one occasion,
wishing to learn the identity of his mistress, he called
for a light ; but when he saw her, sword in hand he
pursued this most wanton woman. But by the foresight of Aphroditê she was changed into the tree
that bears her name.[c] So Theodorus in his *Metamorphoses.*

THROUGH the wrath of Venus, Valeria Tusculanaria

---

[a] *Cf.* Stobaeus, *Florilegium*, lxiv. 33 (iv. p. 471 Hense).
[b] *Love Romances*, x., with Gaselee's note (in L.C.L. p. 289).
[c] Stobaeus, *Florilegium*, lxiv. 34 (iv. p. 472 Hense):
cf. Ovid, *Metamorphoses*, x. 298 ff.; Apollodorus, iii. 14. 3,
with Frazer's note (L.C.L. vol. ii. p. 84).

(311) ἐρασθεῖσα Οὐαλερίου τοῦ πατρὸς τῇ τροφῷ ἀν-
εκοίνωσεν· ἡ δὲ τὸν δεσπότην δόλῳ ὑπῆλθεν,
εἰποῦσα ὡς αἰδεῖται κατ' ὄψιν μίσγεσθαι, τῶν τε
B γειτόνων εἶναί τινα[1] παρθένον. καὶ οἰνωθεὶς ὁ
πατὴρ ᾔτει φῶς, ἡ δὲ τροφὸς φθάσασα διήγειρεν,
ἥτις ἐπὶ τὰς ἀγροικίας ᾔει[2] ἐγκύμων τυγχάνουσα·
ποτὲ δὲ κατὰ κρημνῶν ἐνεχθείσης, τὸ βρέφος ἔζη·
κατιοῦσα δ' ἐγκύμων κατέστη καὶ εἰς τὸν ὡρισμένον χρόνον ἐγέννησεν Αἰγίπανα, κατὰ τὴν Ῥωμαίων φωνὴν Σιλουᾶνον. ὁ δὲ Οὐαλέριος ἀθυμήσας
κατὰ τῶν αὐτῶν ἔρριψε[3] κρημνῶν· ὡς Ἀριστείδης
Μιλήσιος ἐν τρίτῳ Ἰταλικῶν.

23. ΜΕΤΑ τὴν Ἰλίου πόρθησιν ἐξεβράσθη Διο-
μήδης εἰς Λιβύην, ἔνθα Λύκος ἦν βασιλεὺς ἔθος
ἔχων τοὺς ξένους Ἄρει τῷ πατρὶ θύειν. Καλλιρρόη
C δὲ ἡ θυγάτηρ ἐρασθεῖσα Διομήδους τὸν πατέρα
προέδωκε, καὶ τὸν Διομήδην ἔσωσε λύσασα τῶν
δεσμῶν· ὁ δὲ ἀμελήσας τῆς εὐεργέτιδος ἀπέπλευσεν·
ἡ δὲ βρόχῳ ἐτελεύτησεν· ὡς Ἰόβας ἐν τρίτῃ
Λιβυκῶν.

ΚΑΛΠΟΥΡΝΙΟΣ Κράσσος ἀνὴρ τῶν ἐπισήμων,
Ῥηγούλῳ συστρατευόμενος, ἐπέμφθη εἰς Μασ-
σύλους[4] πορθήσων φρούριόν τι δυσάλωτον τοὔνομα
Γαραίτιον. αἰχμάλωτος δὲ ληφθεὶς ἔμελλε θύεσθαι
τῷ Κρόνῳ. Βισαλτία δέ, τοῦ βασιλέως θυγάτηρ,
D ἐρασθεῖσα προέδωκε τὸν πατέρα καὶ νικηφόρον

---

[1] τινα F.C.B.: τὴν (in E only).

[2] τὰς ἀγροικίας ᾔει Helmbold: ταῖς ἀγροικίαις ἦν. But the
version is much condensed. If we had a version in Stobaeus,
probably much would be clearer.

[3] ἔρριψε] ἑαυτὸν ἔρριψε?

fell in love with her father Valerius, and imparted her secret to her nurse. The nurse deceived her master by a trick, saying that there was someone who was too modest to consort with him openly, but that she was a maiden of the neighbourhood. The father, sodden with wine, kept calling for a light ; but the nurse was quick enough to wake the daughter, who went to the country, since she was with child. Once on a time she threw herself down from a cliff, but the child still lived. Returning home, she found her pregnancy inescapable, and in due time gave birth to Aegipan, called in the Roman tongue Silvanus. But Valerius, in a fit of despair, hurled himself down from the same cliff. So Aristeides the Milesian in the third book of his *Italian History*.

23. AFTER the sack of Troy Diomedes was cast up on the Libyan coast where Lycus was king, whose custom it was to sacrifice strangers to his father Ares. But Callirrhoê, the king's daughter, fell in love with Diomedes and betrayed her father : loosing Diomedes from his bonds, she saved him. But he, without regard for his benefactor, sailed away, and she ended her life with a halter. So Juba in the third book of his *Libyan History*.

CALPURNIUS CRASSUS, one of the noblemen who had campaigned with Regulus, was dispatched against the Massylians to sack a certain stronghold by name Garaetium, a place difficult to capture. He was taken captive and was destined to be sacrificed to Saturn ; but Bisaltia, daughter of the king, fell in love with him, betrayed her father, and gave her lover the

---

⁴ Μασσύλους Xylander : μεσεύσουλους or μεσόλους.

(311) ἐκεῖνον ἐποίησεν. ἀναστρέψαντος δ' αὐτοῦ, ἡ κόρη κατέσφαξεν ἑαυτήν· ὡς Ἡσιάναξ[1] ἐν τρίτῳ Λιβυκῶν.

24. ΠΡΙΑΜΟΣ Πολύδωρον ἐξέθετο εἰς Θρᾴκην μετὰ χρυσίου πρὸς Πολυμήστορα τὸν γαμβρόν, ὡς ἐγγὺς[2] ἦν τοῦ πορθεῖσθαι ἡ πόλις. ὁ δὲ[3] μετὰ τὴν ἅλωσιν ἀπέκτεινε τὸν παῖδα, ὡς ἂν κερδήσῃ τὸν χρυσόν. Ἑκάβη δ' ἐπὶ τοὺς τόπους παραγενομένη καὶ σοφισαμένη ὡς χρυσὸν δώσουσα ἅμα ταῖς αἰχμαλωτίσι ταῖς χερσὶν[4] ἐξετύφλωσεν· ὡς Εὐριπίδης ὁ τραγῳδοποιός.

ΑΝΝΙΒΑ Καμπανοὺς λεηλατοῦντος, Λούκιος Θύμβρις τὸν υἱὸν Ῥούστιον μετὰ χρημάτων ἔθετο πρὸς E Οὐαλέριον Γέστιον ὄντα γαμβρόν. ὁ δὲ νενίκηκεν. ἀκούσας δὲ ὁ Καμπανὸς φιλαργυρίᾳ παρέβη τὰ δίκαια τῆς φύσεως, τὸν παῖδα φονεύσας. ὁ δὲ Θύμβρις διὰ τῆς ἀγροικίας πορευόμενος καὶ τῷ σώματι τοῦ παιδὸς ἐντυχὼν ἔπεμψεν ἐπὶ τὸν γαμβρὸν ὡς δείξων θησαυρούς· ἐλθόντα δ' ἐτύφλωσε καὶ ἐσταύρωσεν. ὡς Ἀριστείδης ἐν τρίτῳ Ἰταλικῶν.

25. ΦΩΚΟΥ ὄντος ἐκ Ψαμάθης Αἰακῷ καὶ στεργομένου, Τελαμὼν ἦγεν ἐπὶ θήραν· καὶ συὸς ἐπιφανέντος κατὰ τοῦ μισουμένου ἐπαφῆκε τὸ δόρυ καὶ ἐφόνευσεν. ὁ δὲ πατὴρ ἐφυγάδευσεν· ὡς Δωρόθεος ἐν πρώτῳ Μεταμορφώσεων.

F ΓΑΙΟΣ Μάξιμος ἔχων υἱοὺς Σιμίλιον καὶ Ῥῆσον·

---

[1] Ἡσιάναξ] Ἡγησιάναξ C. Müller.
[2] ὡς ἐγγὺς Stegmann : ὡς δ' ἐγγὺς.
[3] ὁ δὲ (δὲ Stegmann) added by Uhde.
[4] χερσὶν] κερκίσιν Musgrave from Euripides, *Hecuba*, 1153.

[a] In the *Hecuba*.

victory. But when he returned home, the maiden slew herself. So Hesianax in the third book of his *Libyan History*.

24. PRIAM sent away Polydorus with gold to Thrace to his son-in-law Polymestor, because the city was on the point of being sacked. But, after its capture, Polymestor killed the child that he might gain the gold. Hecuba, however, came to the country and, tricking him with the promise of gold, put out his eyes with her own hands, assisted by the captive women. So Euripides[a] the tragedian.

WHEN HANNIBAL was ravaging Campania, Lucius Tiberis placed his son Rustius together with his possessions in the hands of Valerius Gestius, who was his son-in-law ; but Hannibal was victorious. When the Campanian heard this, through his love of money he violated the rights of nature and slew the child. But when Tiberis was journeying through the country-side and came upon the body of his son, he sent to his son-in-law, pretending that he would show him treasures ; but when he came, Tiberis put out his eyes and nailed him to a cross. So Aristeides in the third book of his *Italian History*.

25. TELAMON led out to hunt Phocus, the beloved son of Aeacus by his wife Psamathê. When a boar appeared, Telamon threw his spear at his hated brother and killed him. But his father drove him into exile.[b] So Dorotheüs in the first book of his *Metamorphoses*.

GAIUS Maximus had two sons, Similius and Rhesus,

[b] *Cf.* Frazer on Apollodorus, iii. 12. 6 (L.C.L. vol. ii. p. 57).

293

τοῦτον ἐγέννησεν ἐξ Ἀμερίας νόθον[1]· ὁ Ῥῆσος
οὗτος ἐν κυνηγεσίῳ ἀπέκτεινε τὸν ἀδελφὸν καὶ
ὑποστρέψας τὸ σύμπτωμα τύχης εἶπεν οὐ κρίσεως
γεγονέναι. ὁ δὲ γνοὺς τἀληθὲς ἐφυγάδευσεν· ὡς
Ἀριστοκλῆς ἐν τρίτῳ Ἰταλικῶν.

312   26. ΑΡΗΣ Ἀλθαίᾳ συνῆλθε καὶ Μελέαγρον ποιή-
σας * * *[2] ὡς Εὐριπίδης ἐν Μελεάγρῳ.

ΣΕΠΤΙΜΙΟΣ Μάρκελλος γήμας Σιλουίαν τὰ πολλὰ
κυνηγίῳ προσέκειτο· τὴν δὲ νεόνυμφον ἐν σχήματι
ποιμένος Ἄρης βιασάμενος ἐγκύμονα ἐποίησε,
καὶ ὡμολόγησεν ὅστις ἦν καὶ δόρυ ἔδωκε, τὴν
γένεσιν τοῦ μέλλοντος τίκτεσθαι φάσκων ἐν αὐτῷ[3]
ἀποκεῖσθαι. ἀπέτεκεν οὖν Σεπτιμίῳ[4] Τουσκῖνον.
Μάμερκος δὲ ὑπὲρ εὐκαρπίας θύων θεοῖς μόνης
ἠμέλησε Δήμητρος. ἡ δὲ κάπρον ἔπεμψε. συν-
αθροίσας δὲ πολλοὺς ἐκεῖνος[5] κυνηγέτας ἀνεῖλε,
Β καὶ τὴν κεφαλὴν καὶ τὸ δέρος τῇ κατηγγυημένῃ
γυναικὶ κατεχώρησε. Σκυμβράτης δὲ καὶ Μουθίας
οἱ μητράδελφοι περιείλοντο τῆς κόρης. ἀγανακτήσας δ' ἀνεῖλε τοὺς συγγενεῖς· ἡ δὲ μήτηρ τὸ δόρυ
κατέκαυσεν· ὡς Μένυλλος ἐν τρίτῳ Ἰταλικῶν.

27. ΤΕΛΑΜΩΝ ὁ Αἰακοῦ καὶ Ἐνδηΐδος ἐλθὼν εἰς
Εὔβοιαν[6] διέφθειρε τὴν Ἀλκοθόου Ἐρίβοιαν[7] καὶ
* * *[8] νυκτὸς ἔφυγεν. ὁ δὲ πατὴρ αἰσθόμενος καὶ

---

[1] νόθον· van Herwerden: Κόνων.
[2] A lacuna of about twenty-five letters in E.
[3] ἐν αὐτῷ] ἑαυτῷ in nearly all mss.
[4] ἀπέτεκεν οὖν Σεπτιμίῳ van Herwerden: ἀπέκτεινε γοῦν
Σεπτίμιος.   [5] ἐκεῖνος] Τουσκῖνος van Herwerden.
[6] Εὔβοιαν] Μέγαρα (Meziriacus) is in accord with tradition.
[7] διέφθειρε τὴν Ἀλκοθόου Ἐρίβοιαν added by Meziriacus.
[8] A lacuna of about seventy-five letters in E.

of whom this Rhesus, whom he begat from Ameria out of wedlock, killed his brother during a hunt; and when he returned home, he declared that the mischance was accidental, not deliberate. But his father recognized the truth and banished him. So Aristocles in the third book of his *Italian History*.

26. ARES consorted with Althaea and begat Meleager. . . .[a] So Euripides in his *Meleager*.[b]

SEPTIMIUS MARCELLUS, who was wedded to Silvia, was much given to hunting. Mars, in the guise of a shepherd, violated the young bride, and got her with child. He acknowledged his identity and gave her a spear-shaft, declaring that with it the life of her child that was to be born was inseparably united. She duly bore for Septimius a son Tuscinus. Now the only divinity that Mamercus neglected when he was sacrificing to the gods for a bountiful harvest was Ceres, and she sent a wild boar. But Tuscinus assembled many huntsmen, slew it, and presented the head and the hide to his affianced bride ; but Scymbrates and Muthias, his mother's brothers, took them away from the maiden. Tuscinus was enraged and slew his kinsmen, but his mother burned the spear-shaft. So Menyllus in the third book of his *Italian History*.

27. TELAMON, the son of Aeacus and Endeïs, came to Euboea, ⟨violated the daughter of Alcothoüs, Eriboea⟩[c] and escaped by night. But when her

---

[a] There is obviously something omitted here.
[b] *Cf.* Nauck, *Trag. Graec. Frag.* pp. 525 ff. ; Frazer on Apollodorus, i. 8. 2 (L.C.L. vol. i. p. 64).
[c] Conjecturally restored ; there is a lacuna in the MSS. ; *cf.* Frazer on Apollodorus, iii. 12. 7 (L.C.L. vol. ii. p. 60).

(312) τῶν πολιτῶν τινα ὑποπτεύσας ἔδωκε τὴν κόρην
καταποντωθῆναί τινι τῶν δορυφόρων. ὁ δ' ἐλεήσας
ἀπημπόλησε· προσσχούσης δὲ τῆς νεὼς Σαλαμῖνι
Τελαμὼν ὠνήσατο· ἡ δ' ἔτεκεν Αἴαντα· ὡς Ἀρητάδης Κνίδιος ἐν δευτέρῳ Νησιωτικῶν.

C ΛΟΥΚΙΟΣ Τρώσκιος θυγατέρα εἶχε Φλωρεντίαν
ἀπὸ τῆς Πατρίδος· ταύτην ἔφθειρε Καλπούρνιος
Ῥωμαῖος. ὁ δὲ παρέδωκε τὴν κόρην κατα-
ποντίσαι· ἐλεηθεῖσα δὲ ὑπὸ τοῦ δορυφόρου πι-
πράσκεται· καὶ[1] κατὰ τύχην τῆς νεὼς προσσχούσης
εἰς Ἰταλίαν, Καλπούρνιος ὠνήσατο καὶ ἐποιήσατο
ἐξ αὐτῆς Κόντρουσκον.

28. ΑΙΟΛΟΣ τῶν κατὰ Τυρρηνίαν βασιλεὺς ἔσχεν
ἐξ Ἀμφιθέας θυγατέρας ἓξ καὶ ἴσους ἄρρενας·
Μακαρεὺς δὲ ὁ νεώτατος[2] ἔρωτι ἔφθειρε μίαν, ἡ
δὲ παιδίον ἐκύησεν. ἐμφανεῖσα[3] δὲ καὶ ξίφους
D πεμφθέντος ὑπὸ τοῦ πατρὸς ἄνομον[4] κρίνασα
ἑαυτὴν διεχρήσατο· ὁμοίως δὲ καὶ ὁ Μακαρεύς·
ὡς Σώστρατος ἐν δευτέρᾳ Τυρρηνικῶν.

ΠΑΠΙΡΙΟΣ Τόλουκερ[5] γήμας Ἰουλίαν Πούλχραν[6]
ἔσχεν ἓξ θυγατέρας καὶ ἴσους[7] ἄρρενας. τούτων ὁ πρεσβύτατος Παπίριος Ῥωμάνος τῆς
ἀδελφῆς ἐρασθεὶς Κανουλίας ἔγκυον ἐποίησε.
μαθὼν δὲ ὁ πατὴρ τῇ θυγατρὶ ξίφος ἔπεμψεν· ἡ

---

[1] καὶ in E only.
[2] νεώτατος] πρεσβύτατος Stobaeus, *Flor.* lxiv. 35.
[3] ἐμφανεῖσα F.C.B. (*cf.* Stobaeus, Αἴολος δὲ περὶ τούτων
μαθὼν τῇ θυγατρὶ ξίφος ἔπεμψεν): ἐμπεσοῦσα.
[4] ἄνομον] ὁ νόμον Müller; ὡς νόμον δεξαμένη τὸν σίδηρον
Stobaeus.

father discovered the matter and suspected someone of the citizens, he gave the girl to one of his guardsmen to be cast into the sea. But the guardsman took pity on her, and sold her into slavery. When the ship on which she was put in at Salamis, Telamon bought her, and she bore Ajax. So Aretades the Cnidian in the second book of his *History of the Islands*.

LUCIUS TROSCIUS had by Patris a daughter Florentia. Calpurnius, a Roman, violated her, and Lucius delivered over the maiden to be thrown into the sea. But she was pitied by the guardsman and sold into slavery; and by chance her ship put in at Italy, Calpurnius bought her, and had from her Contruscus.

28. AEOLUS, king of the Etruscans, begat from Amphithea six daughters and the like number of sons. Macareus, the youngest, for love violated one of his sisters and she became pregnant. Her plight was discovered and her father sent her a sword; she judged herself a law-breaker and made away with herself. Macareus also did likewise.[a] So Sostratus in the second book of his *Etruscan History*.

PAPIRIUS TOLUCER married Julia Pulchra and begat six daughters and the like number of sons. The eldest, Papirius Romanus, fell in love with his sister Canulia and got her with child. Their father learned of it and sent his daughter a sword. She killed

---

[a] *Cf.* Stobaeus, *Florilegium*, lxiv. 35 (iv. p. 472 Hense); Ovid, *Heroïdes*, xi.

---

5 Τόλουκερ] Οὐόλουκερ Amyot.
6 Πούλχραν Aldine ed. : ἀπόλχραν.
7 ἴσους] τοὺς ἴσους in most MSS.

δὲ ἑαυτὴν ἀνεῖλε· τὸ αὐτὸ δὲ καὶ ὁ Ῥωμᾶνος
ἔπραξεν· ὡς Χρύσιππος ἐν τῷ πρώτῳ Ἰταλικῶν.

29. ΑΡΙΣΤΩΝΥΜΟΣ[1] Ἐφέσιος υἱὸς Δημοστράτου
ἐμίσει γυναῖκας, ὄνῳ δ᾽ ἐμίσγετο· ἡ δὲ κατὰ χρόνον
ἔτεκε κόρην εὐειδεστάτην Ὀνόσκελιν[2] τοὔνομα· ὡς
Ἀριστοκλῆς[3] ἐν δευτέρᾳ Παραδόξων.

Ε   ΦΟΥΛΟΤΙΟΣ Στέλλος μισῶν γυναῖκας ἵππῳ συν-
εμίσγετο· ἡ δὲ κατὰ χρόνον ἔτεκε κόρην εὔμορφον
καὶ ὠνόμασαν[4] Ἔποναν· ἔστι δὲ θεὸς πρόνοιαν ποιου-
μένη ἵππων· ὡς Ἀγησίλαος ἐν τρίτῳ Ἰταλικῶν.

30. ΣΑΡΔΙΑΝΟΙ πρὸς Σμυρναίους πόλεμον ἔχοντες
περὶ τὰ τείχη ἐστρατοπεδεύσαντο, καὶ διὰ πρέσβεων
ἔπεμψαν μὴ πρότερον ἀναχωρῆσαι, ἐὰν μὴ τὰς
γυναῖκας συνελθεῖν αὐτοῖς συγχωρήσωσι. τῶν δὲ
Σμυρναίων διὰ τὴν ἀνάγκην μελλόντων πάσχειν

F κακῶς, θεραπαινὶς ἦν μία τῶν εὐσχημόνων, ἣ προσ-
δραμοῦσα ἔφη τῷ δεσπότῃ Φιλάρχῳ, " δεῖ τὰς
θεραπαίνας κοσμήσαντας ἀντ᾽ ἐλευθέρων πέμπειν."
ὃ δὴ καὶ ἔδρασαν. οἱ δὲ κοπωθέντες ὑπὸ τῶν
θεραπαινῶν ἑάλωσαν. ὅθεν καὶ νῦν παρὰ Σμυρ-
313 ναίοις ἑορτὴ λέγεται Ἐλευθέρια,[5] ἐν ᾗ αἱ δοῦλαι
τὸν κόσμον τῶν ἐλευθέρων φοροῦσιν· ὡς Δοσίθεος
ἐν τρίτῳ Λυδιακῶν.

---

[1] Ἀριστώνυμος Xylander and some mss.: ἀρίστων
ἀριστώνυμος (probably dittography).
[2] Ὀνόσκελιν] Ὀνοσκελίαν Stobaeus, *Flor.* lxiv. 37; Ὀνο-
σκελίδα Meineke.
[3] Ἀριστοκλῆς from Stobaeus : ἀριστοτέλης.
[4] ὠνόμασαν F.C.B.: ὠνόμασεν.
[5] Ἐλευθέρια Wyttenbach: ἐλευθερία.

herself; Romanus also did the same. So Chrysippus in the first book of his *Italian History*.

29. ARISTONYMUS of Ephesus, the son of Demostratus, hated women and used to consort with an ass; and in due time the ass gave birth to a very beautiful maiden, Onoscelis[a] by name. So Aristocles in the second book of his *Strange Events*.

FULVIUS STELLUS hated women and used to consort with a mare and in due time the mare gave birth to a beautiful girl and they named her Epona. She is the goddess that is concerned with the protection of horses. So Agesilaüs in the third book of his *Italian History*.

30. THE PEOPLE OF SARDIS, when they were engaged in war against the people of Smyrna, encamped round about the walls, and sent word through ambassadors that they would never retire unless the people of Smyrna would agree to let their wives consort with them. The Smyrnaeans, because of the compelling necessity, were in a fair way to suffer grievously; but there was a certain maid-servant to one of the better class who ran up to her master Philarchus and said, "You must dress up the maid-servants and send them in place of free-born women." And this, in fact, they did. The men of Sardis were quite exhausted by the serving-maids, and so were taken captive; whence even now the people of Smyrna have a festival called Eleutheria in which the maid-servants wear the adornments of free women. So Dositheüs in the third book of his *Lydian History*.

[a] "The girl with ass's legs": *cf.* the scholium on Aristophanes, *Ecclesiazusae*, 1048; Stobaeus, *Florilegium*, lxiv. 37 (iv. p. 473 Hense).

(313) ΑΤΕΠΟΜΑΡΟΣ Γάλλων βασιλεὺς 'Ρωμαίοις πολεμῶν
ἔφη μὴ πρότερον ἀναχωρῆσαι, ἐὰν μὴ τὰς γυναῖκας εἰς συνουσίαν ἐκδῶσι. τῶν δὲ διὰ συμβουλὴν
θεραπαινίδων[1] πεμψάντων τὰς δούλας κοπωθέντες
οἱ βάρβαροι τῇ ἀλήκτῳ συνουσίᾳ ὑπνώθησαν. ἡ δὲ
'Ρητᾶνα (αὕτη γὰρ ἦν τοῦτο συμβουλεύσασα)
ἀγρίας ἐπιλαβομένη συκῆς ἀναβαίνει εἰς τὸ τεῖχος
καὶ μηνύει τοῖς ὑπάτοις· οἱ δ' ἐπελθόντες ἐνίκησαν.
ἀφ' οὗ καὶ ἑορτὴ θεραπαινῶν καλεῖται· ὡς 'Αριστ-
B εἴδης Μιλήσιος ἐν πρώτῃ 'Ιταλικῶν.

31. ΑΘΗΝΑΙΩΝ πόλεμον ἐχόντων πρὸς Εὔμολπον
καὶ τῆς εὐθηνίας μὴ ἐπαρκούσης Πύρανδρος ταμίας
τῶν δημοσίων ὑπέσπασε[2] τὸ μέτρον φειδωλῶς
χρώμενος· οἱ δ' ἐγχώριοι ὡς προδότην ὑπο-
πτεύσαντες λιθόλευστον ἐποίησαν· ὡς Καλλισθένης
ἐν τρίτῳ Θρᾳκικῶν.

ΡΩΜΑΙΩΝ πρὸς Γάλλους πολεμούντων καὶ τῆς
εὐθηνίας μὴ ἀρκούσης Κίννας τοῦ δήμου τὸ σιτόμετρον ὑπέσπασε· 'Ρωμαῖοι δὲ ὡς ἀντιποιούμενον
αὐτὸν τῆς βασιλείας λιθόλευστον ἐποίησαν· ὡς
'Αριστείδης ἐν τρίτῳ 'Ιταλικῶν.

32. ΕΝ τῷ Πελοποννησιακῷ πολέμῳ Πεισί-
C στρατος 'Ορχομένιος τοὺς μὲν εὐγενεῖς ἐμίσει,
τοὺς δ' εὐτελεῖς ἐφίλει. ἐβουλεύσαντο δὲ οἱ ἐν τῇ
βουλῇ φονεῦσαι, καὶ διακόψαντες αὐτὸν εἰς τοὺς
κόλπους ἔβαλον, καὶ τὴν γῆν ἔξυσαν. ὁ δὲ δημότης

---

[1] θεραπαινίδων] E has θεραπαινίδος, as Pantazides had
conjectured.
[2] ὑπέσπασε Helmbold : ὑπεσπάσατο.

[a] Cf. Life of Romulus, xxix. (36 E-F); Life of Camillus,
xxxiii. (145 F ff.); Macrobius, Saturnalia, i. 11. 35-39.

WHEN ATEPOMARUS, king of the Gauls, was at war with the Romans, he said he would never retire unless the Romans should surrender their wives for intercourse. But the Romans, on the advice of their maid-servants, sent slave-women; and the barbarians, exhausted by unremitting intercourse, fell asleep. But Rhetana (for she had been the author of this advice), by taking hold of a wild fig-tree, climbed upon the wall and informed the consuls; and the Romans attacked and conquered. From this the Servants' Festival takes its name.[a] So Aristeides the Milesian in the first book of his *Italian History*.

31. WHEN THE ATHENIANS were engaged in a war against Eumolpus,[b] and their supply of food was insufficient, Pyrander, the treasurer of the public funds, secretly reduced the unit of measure and distributed food very sparingly. But his countrymen suspected that he was a traitor and stoned him to death. So Callisthenes in the third book of his *Thracian History*.

WHEN THE ROMANS were waging war against the Gauls, and their supply of food was insufficient, Cinna secretly reduced the distribution of grain to the people. But the Romans stoned him to death on the suspicion that he had designs on the kingship. So Aristeides in the third book of his *Italian History*.

32. DURING the Peloponnesian War Peisistratus of Orchomenus hated the aristocracy and strongly favoured the poorer citizens. The members of the Council plotted to kill him; they cut him up into bits, thrust these into the folds of their garments, and scraped the earth clean. But the crowd of commoners

---

[b] *Cf.* 310 D, *supra*; Frazer on Apollodorus, iii. 15. 4 (L.C.L. vol. ii. p. 110).

(313) ὄχλος ὑπόνοιαν λαβὼν ἔδραμεν εἰς τὴν βουλήν. ὁ
δὲ νεώτερος υἱὸς τοῦ βασιλέως Τλησίμαχος εἰδὼς
τὴν συνωμοσίαν ἀπὸ τῆς ἐκκλησίας ἀπέσπασε τὸν
ὄχλον, εἰπὼν ἑωρακέναι τὸν πατέρα μεθ' ὁρμῆς
εἰς τὸ Πισαῖον ὄρος φέρεσθαι, μείζονα μορφὴν
ἀνθρώπου κεκτημένον. καὶ οὕτως ἠπατήθη ὁ
ὄχλος· ὡς Θεόφιλος ἐν δευτέρῳ Πελοποννησιακῶν.

ΔΙΑ τοὺς ἀστυγείτονας πολέμους ἡ σύγκλητος
D τῶν Ῥωμαίων τοῦ δήμου τὸ σιτόμετρον ᾖρε·
Ῥωμύλος δὲ ὁ βασιλεὺς βαρέως ἐνεγκὼν τῷ δήμῳ
ἀπέδωκε· πολλοὺς δὲ τῶν μειζόνων ἐκόλαζεν. οἱ
δὲ φονεύσαντες αὐτὸν ἐν τῇ συγκλήτῳ βουλῇ καὶ
διακόψαντες[1] εἰς τοὺς κόλπους ἔβαλον. Ῥωμαῖοι
δὲ μετὰ πυρὸς εἰς τὴν σύγκλητον ἔδραμον. Ἰούλιος[2]
δὲ Πρόκλος[3] τῶν ἐπισήμων ἀνὴρ εἶπε τὸν Ῥωμύλον
ἐν ὄρει ἑωρακέναι μείζονα παντὸς ἀνθρώπου θεόν
τε γεγενῆσθαι.[4] Ῥωμαῖοι δὲ πιστεύσαντες ἀν-
εχώρησαν· ὡς Ἀριστόβουλος ἐν τρίτῳ Ἰταλικῶν.

33. ΠΕΛΟΨ Ταντάλου καὶ Εὐρυανάσσης γήμας
Ἱπποδάμειαν ἔσχεν Ἀτρέα καὶ Θυέστην, ἐκ δὲ
E Δαναΐδος νύμφης Χρύσιππον, ὃν πλέον τῶν γνησίων
ἔστερξε. Λάιος δὲ ὁ Θηβαῖος ἐπιθυμήσας ἥρπασεν
αὐτόν. καὶ συλληφθεὶς ὑπὸ Θυέστου καὶ Ἀτρέως
ἐλέους ἔτυχε παρὰ Πέλοπος διὰ τὸν ἔρωτα. Ἱππο-
δάμεια δ' ἀνέπειθεν Ἀτρέα καὶ Θυέστην ἀναιρεῖν

---

[1] διακόψαντες Bernardakis (as above): κόψαντες.
[2] Ἰούλιος in the other accounts (Meziriacus); Αἴλιος
Wyttenbach: αἴτιος.
[3] πρόκλος Guarinus: Πρᾶος.
[4] θεόν τε γεγενῆσθαι Helmbold: θεὸν γεγενῆσθαι.

---

[a] Cf. *Life of Romulus*, chap. xxviii. (35 A ff.); *Life of*

caught a suspicion of this deed and hurried to the Council. Tlesimachus, however, the younger son of the king, was privy to the plot and drew the crowd away from the assembly by declaring that he had seen his father, endowed with more than mortal stature, being swiftly borne toward mount Pisa ; and thus the crowd was deceived. So Theophilus in the second book of his *Peloponnesian History*.

BECAUSE of the wars with neighbouring States the Roman Senate had done away with the distribution of grain to the people ; but Romulus the king could not brook this, restored the dole to the people, and punished many of the more prominent men. They slew him in the Senate, cut him into bits, and thrust these into the folds of their garments ; but the Roman people ran with fire to the Senate-house. Julius Proculus, however, one of the prominent men, declared that on a mountain he had seen Romulus with greater stature than any mortal's and that he had become a god. The Romans believed him and withdrew.[a] So Aristobulus in the third book of his *Italian History*.

33. PELOPS, the son of Tantalus and Euryanassa, married Hippodameia and begat Atreus and Thyestes ; but by the nymph Danaïs he had Chrysippus, whom he loved more than his legitimate sons. But Laïus the Theban conceived a desire for him and carried him off ; and, although he was arrested by Thyestes and Atreus, he obtained mercy from Pelops because of his love. But Hippodameia tried to persuade Atreus and Thyestes to do away with Chrysippus,

Numa, chap. ii. (60 c ff.) ; Dionysius of Halicarnassus, *Roman Antiquities*, ii. 63 ; Livy, i. 16 ; Cicero, *De Republica*, i. 10. 20.

αὐτόν, εἰδυῖα ἔσεσθαι ἔφεδρον βασιλείας. τῶν δ'
ἀρνησαμένων, αὐτὴ τῷ μύσει τὰς χεῖρας ἔχρισε.
νυκτὸς γὰρ βαθείας κοιμωμένου Λαΐου, τὸ ξίφος
ἑλκύσασα καὶ τρώσασα τὸν Χρύσιππον ἐγκατα-
πήγνυσι τὸ ξίφος. ὑπονοηθεὶς δὲ ὁ Λάιος διὰ τὸ
ξίφος ῥύεται ὑπὸ ἡμιθνῆτος τοῦ Χρυσίππου τὴν
ἀλήθειαν ὁμολογήσαντος· ὁ δὲ θάψας τὴν Ἱπποδάμειαν ἐξώρισεν· ὡς Δοσίθεος ἐν Πελοπίδαις.

F   ΗΒΙΟΣ Τολίειξ γήμας Νουκερίαν ἔσχε δύο παῖδας
ἐκ ταύτης. ἔσχε δὲ καὶ ἐξ ἀπελευθέρας κάλλει
περίβλεπτον Φίρμον, ὃν τῶν γνησίων μᾶλλον
ἔστεργε. ἡ δὲ Νουκερία πρὸς τὸν πρόγονον μισο-
πονήρως διακειμένη τοὺς παῖδας ἀνέπειθεν αὐτὸν
ἀναιρεῖν.[1] τῶν δ' εὐσεβῶς ἀνανευσάντων, αὐτὴ τὸν
314 φόνον ἐνείργησε, καὶ[2] νυκτὸς τοῦ σωματοφύλακος
τὸ ξίφος ἑλκύσασα καιρίως ἔτρωσε τὸν κοιμώμενον,
ἐγκαταλιποῦσα τὸ ξίφος. τοῦ δὲ σωματοφύλακος
ὑποπτευθέντος, ὁ παῖς τὴν ἀλήθειαν λέγει. ὁ δὲ
τοῦτον θάψας τὴν γυναῖκα ἐφυγάδευσεν· ὡς
Δοσίθεος ἐν τρίτῳ Ἰταλικῶν.

34. ΘΗΣΕΥΣ ταῖς ἀληθείαις παῖς Ποσειδῶνος,
ἔχων δ' ἐξ Ἱππολύτης Ἀμαζόνος Ἱππόλυτον,
ἐπέγημε μητρυιὰν Φαίδραν τὴν Μίνωος, ἥτις τοῦ
προγόνου εἰς ἐπιθυμίαν ἐμπεσοῦσα τὴν τροφὸν
ἔπεμψεν· ὁ δὲ καταλείψας Ἀθήνας καὶ εἰς Τροιζῆνα
παραγενόμενος κυνηγεσίαις προσανέκειτο. τῆς δὲ
B προαιρέσεως ἡ ἀσελγὴς ἀποτυχοῦσα ψευδεῖς κατὰ

───────────
[1] αὐτὸν ἀναιρεῖν Stephanus, *ut supra*: φονεύειν.
[2] καὶ added by Hutten.

───────────
[a] *Cf.* Pausanias, vi. 20. 7 ; Apollodorus, iii. 5. 5 ; Athe-

since she knew that he would be a contestant for the kingship ; but when they refused, she stained her hands with the pollution.   For at dead of night, when Laïus was asleep, she drew his sword, wounded Chrysippus, and fixed the sword in his body.   Laïus was suspected because of the sword, but was saved by Chrysippus who, though half-dead, acknowledged the truth.   Pelops buried Chrysippus and banished Hippodameia.[a]   So Dositheüs in his *Descendants of Pelops*.

EBIUS TOLIEIX married Nuceria and had from her two sons ; and he had also, from a freedwoman, Firmus, conspicuous for his beauty, whom he loved more than his legitimate sons.   Nuceria was disposed to hate her stepson and tried to persuade her sons to kill him ; but when they righteously refused, she herself effected the murder.   By night she drew the sword of Firmus's body-guard and mortally wounded the boy as he slept, leaving the sword behind in his body.   The guard was suspected, but the boy told the truth.   Ebius buried his son and banished his wife.   So Dositheüs in the third book of his *Italian History*.

34. THESEUS, who was actually the son of Poseidon, begat a son Hippolytus from Hippolytê the Amazon and took a second wife, Phaedra, the daughter of Minos, who thus became a stepmother.   Phaedra fell in love with her stepson, and sent her nurse to him ; but he left Athens and, coming to Troezen, devoted himself to hunting.   But when the wanton woman failed to obtain her cherished desire, she

naeus, 602 F ;   scholium on Euripides, *Phoenissae*, 1760 ; Aelian, *Varia Historia*, xiii. 5.

(314) τοῦ σώφρονος ἐπιστολὰς ἐχάραξε καὶ βρόχῳ τὸ ζῆν
ἀνήρτησε.[1] Θησεὺς δὲ πιστεύσας ᾐτήσατο παρὰ
Ποσειδῶνος ἀπολέσθαι τὸν Ἱππόλυτον, ἐκ τῶν
τριῶν εὐχῶν ἃς εἶχε παρ' αὐτοῦ. ὁ δὲ παρ'
αἰγιαλὸν ἐπὶ ἅρματος τυχόντι ταῦρον ἔπεμψε καὶ
ἐπτόησε τοὺς ἵππους, οἳ συνέτριψαν τὸν Ἱππόλυτον.

κομμινιος Σοῦπερ Λαυρεντῖνος ἔχων υἱὸν ἐξ
Ἐγερίας νύμφης Κομμίνιον ἐπήγαγε μητρυιὰν
Γιδίκαν· ἥτις ἐρασθεῖσα τοῦ προγόνου καὶ ἀποτυχοῦσα βρόχῳ κατέστρεψε τὸν βίον, ἐπιστολὰς
καταλείψασα ψευδεῖς. ὁ δὲ Κομμίνιος ἀναγνοὺς
C τὰ ἐγκλήματα καὶ τῷ ζήλῳ πιστεύσας ἐπεκαλέσατο
τὸν Ποσειδῶνα. ὁ δὲ τῷ παιδὶ ἐπὶ ἅρματος
ὀχουμένῳ ταῦρον ἔδειξε, καὶ οἱ ἵπποι τὸν νέον
σύραντες ἀπώλεσαν· ὡς Δοσίθεος ἐν τρίτῳ
Ἰταλικῶν.

35. ΛΟΙΜΟΥ κατασχόντος Λακεδαίμονα, ἔχρησεν
ὁ θεὸς παύσασθαι, ἐὰν παρθένον εὐγενῆ κατὰ ἔτος
θύωσιν.[2] Ἑλένης δέ ποτε κληρωθείσης καὶ προ-
αχθείσης κεκοσμημένης, ἀετὸς καταπτὰς ἥρπασε
τὸ ξίφος καὶ ἐς τὰ βουκόλια κομίσας ἐπὶ δάμαλιν
καθῆκεν[3]· ὅθεν ἀπέσχοντο τῆς παρθενοκτονίας· ὡς
Ἀριστόδημος ἐν Τρίτῃ Μυθικῇ Συναγωγῇ.

D ΛΟΙΜΟΥ κατασχόντος Φαλερίους[4] καὶ φθορᾶς

---

[1] τὸ ζῆν ἀνήρτησε] τὸν βίον περιέγραψε Stobaeus, lxiv. 38.
Stobaeus's slightly amplified version agrees very exactly until
the last sentence, which is utterly different both in language
and construction.

[2] θύωσιν E: θύσωσιν.   [3] καθῆκεν S. A. Naber: κατέθηκεν.
[4] Φαλερίους Amyot: χαλερίους.

---

[a] Cf. Stobaeus, Florilegium, lxiv. 38 (iv. 474 Hense),
and Euripides, Hippolytus.

indited a false letter against the chaste youth and ended her life with a halter. Theseus believed the letter and asked from Poseidon the destruction of Hippolytus as fulfilment of one of the three wishes which he had as a concession from Poseidon. The god sent a bull to confront Hippolytus as he was driving along the shore in his chariot and terrified the horses, which crushed Hippolytus.[a]

COMMINIUS SUPER of Laurentum begat a son Comminius from the nymph Egeria and took a second wife Gidica, who thus became a stepmother. She fell in love with her stepson and, failing to obtain her desire, put an end to her life with a halter, leaving behind her a lying letter. Comminius read the accusations, believed the invidious charge, and called upon Neptune, who placed a bull in the youth's path as he was riding in a chariot ; and the young man's horses ran away with him and killed him. So Dositheüs in the third book of his *Italian History*.

35. WHEN A PLAGUE had overspread Sparta, the god gave an oracle that it would cease if they sacrificed a noble maiden each year. Once when Helen had been chosen by lot and had been led forward adorned for the sacrifice, an eagle swooped down, snatched up the sword, carried it to the herds of cattle, and let it fall on a heifer ; wherefore the Spartans refrained from the slaying of maidens.[b] So Aristodemus in his Third Collection of Fables.

WHEN A PLAGUE had gained a wide hold on the city of Falerii, and many perished of it, an oracle

[b] *Cf.* Lydus, *De Mensibus*, 147 (p. 165 Wünsch) ; Tzetzes, *Scholia on Lycophron*, ii. 63 and 92 ed. Scheer. For human victims at Sparta *cf.* Porphyry, *De Abstinentia*, ii. 55.

(314) γενομένης, χρησμὸς ἐδόθη λωφῆσαι τὸ δεινόν, ἐὰν παρθένον τῇ "Ηρᾳ θύωσιν κατ᾽ ἐνιαυτόν. ἀεὶ δὲ τῆς δεισιδαιμονίας μενούσης κατὰ κλῆρον λαχομένῃ[1] Οὐαλερία Λουπέρκα[2] σπασαμένη τὸ ξίφος, * * *[3] ἀετὸς καταπτὰς ἥρπασε καὶ ἐπὶ τῶν ἐμπύρων ἔθηκε ῥάβδον μικρὰν ἔχουσαν σφῦραν, τὸ δὲ ξίφος ἐπέβαλε δαμάλει τινὶ παρὰ τὸν ναὸν βοσκομένῃ. νοήσασα δὲ ἡ παρθένος καὶ τὴν βοῦν θύσασα καὶ τὴν σφῦραν ἄρασα, κατ᾽ οἰκίαν περιῆλθε, καὶ τοὺς ἀσθενοῦντας ἠρέμα πλήττουσα διήγειρεν, ἐρρῶσθαι ἑνὶ ἑκάστῳ λέγουσα. ὅθεν καὶ νῦν τὸ μυστήριον τελεῖται· ὡς Ἀριστείδης ἐν ἐννεακαι-
E δεκάτῳ Ἰταλικῶν.

36. ΦΥΛΟΝΟΜΗ Νυκτίμου καὶ Ἀρκαδίας θυγάτηρ ἐκυνήγει σὺν τῇ Ἀρτέμιδι· Ἄρης δ᾽ ἐν σχήματι ποιμένος ἔγκυον ἐποίησεν. ἡ δὲ τεκοῦσα διδύμους παῖδας καὶ φοβουμένη τὸν πατέρα ἔρριψεν εἰς τὸν Ἐρύμανθον. οἱ δὲ κατὰ πρόνοιαν ἀκινδύνως περιφερόμενοι προσηνέχθησαν ἐν κοίλῃ δρυΐ· λύκαινα δ᾽ ἐμφωλεύουσα τοὺς μὲν ἰδίους σκύμνους εἰς τὸν ῥοῦν ἔρριψε, τοῖς δὲ βρέφεσι θηλὴν παρέσχε. Γύλιφος[4] δὲ ποιμὴν αὐτόπτης γενόμενος καὶ ἀναλαβὼν τοὺς παῖδας ὡς ἰδίους ἔθρεψε, τὸν μὲν καλέσας Λύκαστον τὸν δὲ Παρράσιον, τοὺς δια-
F δεξαμένους τὴν βασιλείαν τῶν Ἀρκάδων· ὡς Ζώπυρος Βυζάντιος ἐν τῷ τρίτῳ Ἱστορικῶν.

ΑΜΟΥΛΙΟΣ πρὸς Νομίτορα τὸν ἀδελφὸν τυραννικῶς διακείμενος, τὸν μὲν υἱὸν Αἴνιτον ἐπὶ κυνηγίᾳ

[1] λαχομένη F.C.B.: καλουμένη.
[2] Λουπέρκα Guarinus: τουπέρκα.
[3] There is probably a lacuna here; E alone adds ἤγετο εἰς θυσίαν. [4] Γύλιφος Crönert: τύλιφος.

was given that the terror would abate if they sacrificed a maiden to Juno each year. This superstitious practice persisted and once, as a maiden chosen by lot, Valeria Luperca, had drawn the sword, an eagle swooped down, snatched it up, and placed a wand tipped with a small hammer upon the sacrificial offerings ; but the sword the eagle cast down upon a certain heifer which was grazing near the shrine. The maiden understood the import : she sacrificed the heifer, took up the hammer, and went about from house to house, tapping the sick lightly with her hammer and rousing them, bidding each of them to be well again ; whence even to this day this mystic rite is performed. So Aristeides in the nineteenth book of his *Italian History*.

36. PHYLONOMÊ, the daughter of Nyctimus and Arcadia, was wont to hunt with Artemis ; but Ares, in the guise of a shepherd, got her with child. She gave birth to twin children and, fearing her father, cast them into the Erymanthus ; but by some divine providence they were borne round and round without peril, and found haven in the trunk of a hollow oak-tree. A wolf, whose den was in the tree, cast her own cubs into the stream and suckled the children. A shepherd, Gyliphus, was witness of this event and, taking up the children, reared them as his own, and named them Lycastus and Parrhasius, the same that later succeeded to the throne of Arcadia.[a] So Zopyrus of Byzantium in the third book of his *Histories*.

AMULIUS, being despotically disposed toward his brother Numitor, killed his brother's son Aenitus

[a] *Cf.* Lydus, *De Mensibus*, 150 (p. 168 Wünsch).

ἀνεῖλε, τὴν δὲ θυγατέρα Σιλουίαν ἢ Ἰλίαν[1] τῆς
Ἥρας ἱέρειαν ἐποιήσατο. ταύτην Ἄρης ἐγκύμονα
ποιεῖ· ἡ δ' ἔτεκε διδύμους, ὡμολόγησέ τε τῷ
τυράννῳ τὴν ἀλήθειαν. ὁ δὲ φοβηθεὶς ἀμφοτέρους
κατεπόντισε, βαλὼν παρὰ τὰς ὄχθας τοῦ Θύμβρεως.
315 οἱ δὲ προσηνέχθησαν ἐν τόπῳ, ἔνθα λύκαινα ἦν
φωλεύουσα νεοτόκος· καὶ τοὺς μὲν σκύμνους
ἔρριψε, τὰ δὲ βρέφη ἔτρεφε. Φαῦστος[2] δὲ ποιμὴν
αὐτόπτης γενόμενος τοὺς παῖδας ἀνέθρεψε, καὶ τὸν
μὲν Ῥῶμον τὸν δὲ Ῥωμύλον προσηγόρευσε, τοὺς
κτίστας Ῥώμης· ὡς Ἀριστείδης Μιλήσιος ἐν τοῖς
Ἰταλικοῖς.

37. ΜΕΤΑ τὴν Ἰλίου ἅλωσιν Ἀγαμέμνων μετὰ
Κασάνδρας ἀνῃρέθη. Ὀρέστης δὲ παρὰ Στροφίῳ
ἀνατραφεὶς τοὺς φονεῖς τοῦ πατρὸς ἐτιμωρήσατο·
ὡς Πύρανδρος ἐν τετάρτῳ Πελοποννησιακῶν.

ΦΑΒΙΟΣ ΦΑΒΡΙΚΙΑΝΟΣ τοῦ μεγάλου συγγενὴς
Φαβίου, πορθήσας Τούξιον μητρόπολιν Σαννιτῶν,
B τὴν παρ' αὐτοῖς τιμωμένην νικηφόρον Ἀφροδίτην
ἔπεμψεν εἰς Ῥώμην. τούτου γυνὴ Φαβία[3] μοι-
χευθεῖσα ὑπό τινος εὐπρεποῦς νεανίου τοὔνομα
Πετρωνίου Οὐαλεντίνου, τὸν ἄνδρα ἐδολοφόνησε.
Φαβία δὲ θυγάτηρ[4] τὸν ἀδελφὸν ἔτι νήπιον Φαβρι-
κιανὸν τῶν κινδύνων ἐρρύσατο καὶ ἔπεμψε κρύφα
τραφησόμενον. ἀκμάσας δὲ ὁ νεανίας τήν τε
μητέρα καὶ τὸν μοιχὸν ἀπέκτεινε, καὶ ἀπελύθη ὑπὸ
τῆς συγκλήτου· ὡς ἱστορεῖ Δοσίθεος ἐν τρίτῳ
Ἰταλικῶν.

---

[1] ἢ Ἰλίαν Bryan : ἐν ἰουλίᾳ.
[2] Φαῦστος] Φαυστύλος Bryan.
[3] Φαβία] a few inferior MSS. have πετρωνία here and omit
Πετρωνίου below.

in hunting, and his daughter Silvia, or Ilia, he made a
priestess of Juno. But Mars got Silvia with child.
She gave birth to twins and acknowledged the truth
to the despot ; he became frightened and threw both
the children into the water by the banks of the Tiber.
But they found a haven at a place where was the den
of a wolf which had recently whelped. She abandoned
her cubs and suckled the children. A shepherd
Faustus was witness of this event and reared the
children ; he named them Remus and Romulus, who
became the founders of Rome.[a] So Aristeides the
Milesian in his *Italian History*.

37. AFTER the capture of Troy Agamemnon together with Cassandra was slain. But Orestes was
reared in the house of Strophius, and took vengeance
on the murderers of his father. So Pyrander in the
fourth book of his *Peloponnesian History*.

FABIUS FABRICIANUS, a kinsman of Fabius Maximus,
sacked Tuxium,[b] the chief city of the Samnites, and
sent to Rome the statue of Venus Victrix, which was
held in honour among the Samnites. His wife Fabia,
debauched by a certain handsome youth whose name
was Petronius Valentinus, slew her husband by
treachery. But a daughter Fabia rescued from
danger her brother Fabricianus, who was still a young
child, and sent him away secretly to be reared elsewhere. When he reached manhood he slew his
mother and her lover, and was absolved from guilt by
the senate. This Dositheüs relates in the third book
of his *Italian History*.

---

[a] Contrast 320 D, *infra*.
[b] Bovianum ?

---

[4] θυγάτηρ added by Helmbold.

(315)   38. ΒΟΥΣΙΡΙΣ, παῖς Ποσειδῶνος καὶ Ἀνίππης τῆς Νείλου, τοὺς παριόντας ὑπούλῳ φιλοξενίᾳ κατέθυε. μετῆλθε δ' αὐτὸν ἡ τῶν τετελευτηκότων C νέμεσις· Ἡρακλῆς γὰρ ἐπιτεθεὶς τῷ ῥοπάλῳ διεχρήσατο· ὡς Ἀγάθων Σάμιος.

ΗΡΑΚΛΗΣ τὰς Γηρυόνου βοῦς ἐλαύνων δι' Ἰταλίας ἐπεξενώθη Φαύνῳ βασιλεῖ, ὃς ἦν Ἑρμοῦ παῖς καὶ τοὺς ξένους τῷ γεννήσαντι ἔθυεν· ἐπιχειρήσας δὲ τῷ Ἡρακλεῖ ἀνῃρέθη· ὡς Δέρκυλλος ἐν τρίτῳ Ἰταλικῶν.

39. ΦΑΛΑΡΙΣ Ἀκραγαντίνων τύραννος ἀποτόμως[1] τοὺς παριόντας ξένους ἐστρέβλου καὶ ἐκόλαζε. Πέριλλος δὲ τῇ τέχνῃ χαλκουργὸς δάμαλιν κατασκευάσας χαλκῆν ἔδωκε τῷ βασιλεῖ, ὡς ἂν τοὺς ξένους κατακαίῃ ζῶντας ἐν αὐτῇ· ὁ δὲ μόνον τότε γενόμενος δίκαιος αὐτὸν ἐνέβαλεν. ἐδόκει δὲ D μυκηθμὸν ἀναδιδόναι ἡ δάμαλις· ὡς ἐν δευτέρῳ Αἰτίων.

ΕΝ ΑΙΓΕΣΤΗΙ πόλει τῆς Σικελίας ἐγένετό τις ὠμὸς τύραννος Αἰμίλιος Κενσωρῖνος. οὗτος τοὺς καινότερα βασανιστήρια κατασκευάσαντας ἐδωροδόκει. εἷς δέ τις Ἀρούντιος Πατέρκουλος δημιουργήσας ἵππον χαλκοῦν τῷ προειρημένῳ δῶρον ἔδωκεν, ἵν' ἐμβάλλῃ[2] ἀστούς.[3] ὁ δὲ τότε πρῶτον

---

[1] ἀποτόμως] ἀπότομος some mss. (ἀπότομος καὶ ἀπαθὴς ὑπάρχων, Stobaeus, *Flor.* xlix. 49). The text of Stobaeus, slightly amplified, plainly comes from the same original.
[2] ἵν' ἐμβάλλῃ van Herwerden (confirmed by ἐνέβαλε in another ms. version): ἵνα βάλλῃ.
[3] ἀστούς van Herwerden: αὐτούς.

[a] Cf. *Life of Theseus*, xi. (5 B); Frazer's note on Apollodorus, ii. 5. 11 (L.C.L. vol. i. pp. 224-225). "Quis . . . inlaudati nescit Busiridis aras?" (Virgil, *Georgics*, iii. 4-5).

38. Busiris, the son of Poseidon and Anippê, daughter of the Nile, with treacherous hospitality was wont to sacrifice such persons as passed his way. But there came upon him vengeance for those that had perished by his hand. For Heracles attacked him with his club and slew him.[a] So Agathon of Samos.

When Hercules was driving through Italy the cattle of Geryon, he was entertained by king Faunus, the son of Mercury, who was wont to sacrifice his guests to the god that was his father. But when he attacked Hercules, he was slain. So Dercyllus in the third book of his *Italian History*.

39. Phalaris, the tyrant of Agrigentum, used to inflict most cruel torture and torment upon the strangers that passed his way. Perillus, a bronze-founder by trade, made a bronze heifer and gave it to the king that he might burn the strangers in it alive. But Phalaris on this one occasion proved himself a just man and threw into it the artisan; the heifer seemed to give forth a sound of bellowing.[b] So in the second book of *Causes*.[c]

In Segesta, a city of Sicily, there lived a certain cruel despot, Aemilius Censorinus, who used to reward with gifts those who invented more novel forms of torture; and a certain Arruntius Paterculus constructed a horse of bronze and gave it as a gift to the aforesaid that he might cast the citizens therein. But on this occasion, for the first

---

[b] *Cf.* Stobaeus, *Florilegium*, xlix. 49 (iv. p. 318 Hense).

[c] Probably, as Bentley conjectured, the *Aetia* of Callimachus (*cf.* Mair's edition, L.C.L. p. 203). Schneider's objections Schlereth has shown to be irrelevant.

(315) νομίμως ἀναστραφεὶς τὸν χαρισάμενον πρότερον
ἔβαλεν ὡς ἄν, ἣν ἐπενόησε βάσανον ἄλλοις, αὐτὸς
πάθῃ πρῶτος. τοῦτον συλλαβὼν ἀπὸ τοῦ Ταρπηίου[1]
ὄρους ἔρριψε. καὶ δοκοῦσιν οἱ ἀποτόμως βασιλεύ-
σαντες ἀπ᾿ ἐκείνου Αἰμίλιοι προσαγορεύεσθαι· ὡς
E Ἀριστείδης ἐν τετάρτῳ Ἰταλικῶν.

40. ΕΥΗΝΟΣ Ἄρεος καὶ Στερόπης τὴν Οἰνομάου
γήμας Ἀλκίππην ἐγέννησε θυγατέρα Μάρπησσαν,
ἣν παρθένον ἐφρούρει. καὶ[2] Ἴδας ὁ Ἀφαρέως[3]
ἁρπάσας ἐκ χοροῦ ἔφυγεν. ὁ δὲ πατὴρ διώξας καὶ
μὴ συλλαβὼν εἰς τὸν Λυκόρμαν ἔρριψεν ἑαυτὸν
ποταμὸν καὶ ἀθάνατος ἐγένετο· ὡς Δοσίθεος ἐν
πρώτῳ Αἰτωλικῶν.[4]

ΑΝΝΙΟΣ δὲ Τούσκων βασιλεὺς ἔχων θυγατέρα
εὔμορφον τοὔνομα Σαλίαν,[5] παρθένον ἐτήρει. Κάθητος δ᾿ ἐκ τῶν ἐπισήμων ἰδὼν τὴν παρθένον παί-
ζουσαν ἠράσθη, καὶ μὴ στέγων τὸν ἔρωτα ἥρπασε
F καὶ ἦγεν εἰς Ῥώμην. ὁ δὲ πατὴρ ἐπιδιώξας καὶ
μὴ συλλαβὼν ἥλατο εἰς τὸν Παρεούσιον ποταμόν, ὃς Ἀνίων μετωνομάσθη· τῇ δὲ Σαλίᾳ συγ-
γενόμενος Κάθητος ἐποιήσατο Λατῖνον καὶ Σάλιον,
ἀφ᾿ ὧν οἱ εὐγενέστατοι κατῆγον τὸ γένος· ὡς
Ἀριστείδης Μιλήσιος καὶ Ἀλέξανδρος ὁ Πολυΐστωρ
ἐν τρίτῳ Ἰταλικῶν.

41. ΗΓΗΣΙΣΤΡΑΤΟΣ ἀνὴρ Ἐφέσιος ἐμφύλιον φόνον

---

[1] Ταρπηίου the usual form : ταρπίου.
[2] καὶ before Ἴδας follows Ἀφαρέως in the mss.
[3] Ἀφαρέως Xylander from Apollodorus and De Fluviis : ἀφάρητος.
[4] Αἰτωλικῶν Petavius and some mss. : Ἰταλικῶν.
[5] σαλίαν E : σιλίαν or στιλίαν.

---

[a] Cf. Pseudo-Plutarch, De Fluviis, viii. 1 (Bernardakis,
314

time, the despot behaved in a just manner and thrust first the giver of the gift into the horse, so that he himself should be the first to experience the torment which he had devised for others. Then he seized the man and hurled him from the Tarpeian Rock. It is believed that those who rule with great cruelty are called Aemilii from this Aemilius. So Aristeides in the fourth book of his *Italian History*.

40. EVENUS, the son of Ares and Steropê, married Alcippê, the daughter of Oenomaüs, and begat a daughter Marpessa,[a] whom he endeavoured to keep a virgin. Idas, the son of Aphareus, seized her from a band of dancers and fled. Her father gave chase; but, since he could not capture them, he hurled himself into the Lycormas[b] river and became immortal. So Dositheüs in the first book of his *Aetolian History*.

ANNIUS, king of the Etruscans, had a beautiful daughter named Salia, whom he endeavoured to keep a virgin. But Cathetus, one of the nobles, saw the maiden at play and fell in love with her; nor could he control his passion, but seized her and set out with her for Rome. Her father gave chase, but since he could not capture them, he leaped into the river Pareüsium, and from him its name was changed to Anio. And Cathetus consorted with Salia and begat Latinus and Salius, from whom the most noble patricians traced their descent. So Aristeides the Milesian, and also Alexander Polyhistor in the third book of his *Italian History*.

41. HEGESISTRATUS, an Ephesian, having murdered

vol. vii. p. 296); Frazer's note on Apollodorus, i. 7. 8 (L.C.L. vol. i. p. 62).
[b] An earlier name for the river Evenus in Aetolia.

δράσας ἔφυγεν εἰς Δελφοὺς καὶ ἠρώτα τὸν θεὸν
ποῦ οἰκήσειεν. ὁ δ' Ἀπόλλων ἀνεῖλεν[1] ἔνθα ἂν
ἴδῃ χορεύοντας ἀγροίκους θαλλοῖς ἐλαίας ἐστεφανω-
316 μένους. γενόμενος δὲ κατά τινα[2] τόπον τῆς Ἀσίας
καὶ θεασάμενος φύλλοις ἐλαίας ἐστεφανωμένους
γεωργοὺς καὶ χορεύοντας, ἔκτισεν αὐτοῦ πόλιν καὶ
ἐκάλεσεν Ἐλαιοῦντα· ὡς Πυθοκλῆς ὁ Σάμιος ἐν
τρίτῳ Γεωργικῶν.

ΤΗΛΕΓΟΝΟΣ Ὀδυσσέως καὶ Κίρκης ἐπ' ἀναζήτησιν
τοῦ πατρὸς πεμφθεὶς ἔμαθε πόλιν κτίσαι, ἔνθα
ἂν ἴδῃ γεωργοὺς ἐστεφανωμένους καὶ χορεύοντας.
γενόμενος δὲ κατά τινα τόπον τῆς Ἰταλίας καὶ
θεασάμενος ἀγροίκους πρινίνοις κλάδοις ἐστεφανωμένους καὶ ὀρχήσει προσευκαιροῦντας, ἔκτισε
πόλιν, ἀπὸ τοῦ συγκυρήματος Πρίνιστον ὀνομάσας,
ἣν Ῥωμαῖοι παραγώγως Πραίνεστον καλοῦσιν· ὡς
B ἱστορεῖ Ἀριστοκλῆς ἐν τρίτῳ Ἰταλικῶν.

---

[1] ἀνεῖλεν Bernardakis : ἀνεῖπεν.
[2] κατά τινα van Herwerden : κατὰ τὸν.

one of his kinsmen, fled to Delphi, and inquired of the
god where he should make his home. And Apollo
answered: "Where you shall see rustics dancing,
garlanded with olive-branches." When he had come
to a certain place in Asia and had observed farmers
garlanded with olive-leaves and dancing, there he
founded a city and called it Elaeüs.[a] So Pythocles
the Samian in the third book of his *Treatise on
Husbandry*.

When Telegonus, the son of Odysseus and Circê,
was sent to search for his father, he was instructed
to found a city where he should see farmers garlanded
and dancing. When he had come to a certain place in
Italy, and had observed rustics garlanded with twigs
of oak (*prininoi*) and diverting themselves with dancing, he founded a city, and from the coincidence
named it Prinistum, which the Romans, by a slight
change, call Praenestê. So Aristocles relates in the
third book of his *Italian History*.

---

[a] "City of Olives."

ON THE FORTUNE OF THE
ROMANS
(DE FORTUNA ROMANORUM)

INTRODUCTION

PLUTARCH's essay on the *Fortune of the Romans*, like the following essays, is very plainly an epideictic oration. Where and when it was delivered, or whether it was ever delivered at all, we have no means of ascertaining. Hartman feels very sure that it was delivered to a Roman audience in the early days of Plutarch's sojourn at Rome, and was intended to commend the speaker to other Romans besides his personal friends there.

The thesis that Fortune was responsible for the great Roman empire would hardly be pleasing to Romans, but Plutarch is careful to point out that the high character of many individual Romans also contributed to the Roman success. In fact the essay might well bear the double title of *Fortune or Virtues*,[a] as does the essay on Alexander. Plutarch was thoroughly familiar with the interpretations of Roman history then fashionable, and in this essay he gives a colourful sketch of as much as will serve his purpose. Much that is here may also be found elsewhere in Plutarch's writings.

The essay comes to a somewhat abrupt conclusion, and many have thought it unfinished; the same is true of the essays immediately following. One may

---

[a] This name it actually does bear in seven (out of a total of about twenty-six) MSS.

wonder whether a time limit was set for these orations, as in the courts at Athens where the time allowed was measured by the water-clock or clepsydra. We may note, however, that these orations are of quite unequal length.

The text is fairly good, and the majority of the MS. mistakes have been corrected by the various editors and commentators. The essay is No. 175 in Lamprias's list of Plutarch's works.

ΠΕΡΙ ΤΗΣ ΡΩΜΑΙΩΝ ΤΥΧΗΣ

C 1. Αἱ πολλοὺς πολλάκις ἠγωνισμέναι καὶ μεγάλους ἀγῶνας Ἀρετὴ καὶ Τύχη πρὸς ἀλλήλας
μέγιστον ἀγωνίζονται τὸν παρόντα, περὶ τῆς
Ῥωμαίων ἡγεμονίας διαδικαζόμεναι ποτέρας γέγονεν ἔργον καὶ ποτέρα τὴν τηλικαύτην δύναμιν
γεγέννηκεν. οὐ γὰρ μικρὸν ἔσται τῇ περιγενομένῃ
τοῦτο μαρτύριον, μᾶλλον δ᾽ ἀπολόγημα πρὸς
κατηγορίαν. κατηγορεῖται δ᾽ Ἀρετὴ μὲν ὡς καλὸν
μὲν¹ ἀνωφελὲς δέ, Τύχη δ᾽ ὡς ἀβέβαιον μὲν ἀγαθὸν
δέ· καὶ τὴν μὲν ἄκαρπα πονεῖν λέγουσι, τὴν δ᾽
ἄπιστα δωρεῖσθαι. τίς οὖν οὐχὶ λέξει, τῇ ἑτέρᾳ
τῆς Ῥώμης προστεθείσης, ἢ λυσιτελέστατον
D Ἀρετήν, εἰ τηλικαῦτα τοὺς ἀγαθοὺς δέδρακεν
ἀγαθά, ἢ βεβαιότατον εὐτυχίαν, χρόνον ἤδη τοσοῦτον ἃ δέδωκε τηροῦσαν;

Ἴων μὲν οὖν ὁ ποιητὴς ἐν τοῖς δίχα μέτρου καὶ
καταλογάδην αὐτῷ γεγραμμένοις φησὶν ἀνομοιό-
τατον πρᾶγμα τῇ σοφίᾳ τὴν τύχην οὖσαν ὁμοιο-
τάτων πραγμάτων γίγνεσθαι δημιουργόν· αὔξουσιν
ἀμφότεραι, προσκοσμοῦσιν ἄνδρας, εἰς δόξαν
ἀνάγουσιν, εἰς δύναμιν, εἰς ἡγεμονίαν. τί δεῖ
τὰ πολλὰ μηκύνειν ἐξαριθμούμενον; αὐτὴν τὴν
τὰ πάντα γεννῶσαν ἡμῖν καὶ φέρουσαν φύσιν οἱ

¹ καλὸν μὲν Reiske and a few mss.: καλόν.

ON THE FORTUNE OF THE ROMANS

1. Virtue and Fortune, who have often engaged in many great contests, are now engaging each other in the present contest, which is the greatest of all ; for in this they are striving for a decision regarding the hegemony of Rome, to determine whose work it is and which of them created such a mighty power. For to her who is victorious this will be no slight testimonial, but rather a defence against accusation. For Virtue is accused of being a fair thing, but unprofitable ; Fortune of being a thing inconstant, but good. Virtue's labours, they say, are fruitless, Fortune's gifts untrustworthy. Who, then, will not declare, when Rome shall have been added to the achievements of one of the contestants, either that Virtue is a most profitable thing if she has done such good to good men, or that Good Fortune is a thing most steadfast if she has already preserved for so long a time that which she has bestowed ?

The poet Ion [a] in his prose works observes that Fortune is a thing very dissimilar to Wisdom, and yet she becomes the creator of things very similar : they both bring increase and added honours to men, they lead them on to high repute, to power, to dominion. What need to be tedious by enumerating the many examples ? Even Nature herself, who creates and

[a] Cf. Moralia, 717 B.

323

μὲν τύχην εἶναι νομίζουσιν, οἱ δὲ σοφίαν. διὸ
E καλόν τι τῇ Ῥώμῃ καὶ ζηλωτὸν ὁ ἐνεστὼς λόγος
ἀξίωμα περιτίθησιν, εἰ διαπορῦμεν ὑπὲρ[1] αὐτῆς,
ὡς ὑπὲρ γῆς καὶ θαλάττης καὶ οὐρανοῦ καὶ ἄστρων,
πότερον κατὰ τύχην συνέστηκεν ἢ κατὰ πρόνοιαν.
   2. Ἐγὼ δέ, ὅτι μέν, εἰ καὶ πάνυ πρὸς ἀλλήλας
ἀεὶ πολεμοῦσι καὶ διαφέρονται Τύχη καὶ Ἀρετή,
πρός γε τηλικαύτην σύμπηξιν ἀρχῆς καὶ δυνάμεως
εἰκός ἐστιν αὐτὰς σπεισαμένας συνελθεῖν καὶ
συνελθούσας ἐπιτελειῶσαι καὶ συναπεργάσασθαι
τῶν ἀνθρωπίνων ἔργων τὸ κάλλιστον, ὀρθῶς ὑπο-
νοεῖν οἴομαι. καὶ νομίζω, καθάπερ Πλάτων φησὶν
ἐκ πυρὸς καὶ γῆς ὡς ἀναγκαίων τε καὶ πρώτων
γεγονέναι τὸν σύμπαντα κόσμον, ἵν' ὁρατός[2] τε
F γένηται καὶ ἁπτός, γῆς μὲν τὸ ἐμβριθὲς καὶ στάσιμον αὐτῷ συμβαλομένης, πυρὸς δὲ χρῶμα καὶ
μορφὴν καὶ κίνησιν· αἱ δ' ἐν μέσῳ φύσεις, ὕδωρ
καὶ ἀήρ, μαλάξασαι καὶ σβέσασαι τὴν ἑκατέρου
τῶν ἄκρων ἀνομοιότητα συνήγαγον καὶ ἀνεμείξαντο
τὴν ὕλην δι' αὑτῶν· οὕτως ἄρα καὶ ὁ τὴν Ῥώμην
ὑποβαλόμενος χρόνος μετὰ θεοῦ τύχην καὶ ἀρετὴν
317 ἐκέρασε καὶ συνέζευξεν, ἵν' ἑκατέρας λαβὼν τὸ
οἰκεῖον ἀπεργάσηται πᾶσιν ἀνθρώποις ἑστίαν ἱερὰν
ὡς ἀληθῶς καὶ ἀνησιδώραν[3] καὶ " πεῖσμα " μόνι-
μον καὶ στοιχεῖον ἀΐδιον, ὑποφερομένοις τοῖς
πράγμασιν " ἀγκυρηβόλιον σάλου καὶ πλάνης,"
ὡς φησι Δημόκριτος. ὡς γὰρ οἱ φυσικοὶ τὸν

---

[1] ὑπὲρ] περὶ some early editions. and many mss.
[2] ὁρατός Plato : προσόρατός.
[3] ἀνησιδώραν Iunius and a few mss.: ὀνησιδώραν.

---

[a] That is, Wisdom.

produces all things for us, some think to be Fortune, others Wisdom. Wherefore our present discourse does, in a measure, bestow a fair and enviable dignity upon Rome, if we raise the question over her, even as we do over earth and sea, heaven and stars, whether she has come to her present state by Fortune or by Forethought.[a]

2. I believe myself to be right in suspecting that, even if Fortune and Virtue are engaged in a direct and continual strife and discord with each other, yet, at least for such a welding together of dominion and power, it is likely that they suspended hostilities and joined forces ; and by joining forces they co-operated in completing this most beautiful of human works. Even as Plato [b] asserts that the entire universe arose from fire and earth as the first and necessary elements, that it might become visible and tangible, earth contributing to it weight and stability, and fire contributing colour, form, and movement ; but the medial elements, water and air, by softening and quenching the dissimilarity of both extremes, united them and brought about the composite nature of Matter through them ; in this way, then, in my opinion, did Time lay the foundation for the Roman State and, with the help of God, so combine and join together Fortune and Virtue that, by taking the peculiar qualities of each, he might construct for all mankind a Hearth, in truth both holy and beneficent, a steadfast cable, a principle abiding for ever, "an anchorage from the swell and drift," as Democritus [c] says, amid the shifting conditions of human affairs. For even as

[b] *Timaeus*, 28 B, 31 B–32 B.
[c] Diels, *Frag. der Vorsokratiker*, ii. 88, Frag. B 148 : *cf. Moralia*, 495 E.

(317) κόσμον λέγουσιν οὐκ εἶναι πάλαι¹ κόσμον οὐδ'
ἐθέλειν τὰ σώματα συνελθόντα καὶ συμμιγέντα
κοινὸν ἐκ πάντων εἶδος τῇ φύσει παρασχεῖν, ἀλλὰ
τῶν μὲν ἔτι μικρῶν καὶ σποράδην φερομένων καὶ
διολισθανόντων καὶ ὑποφευγόντων τὰς ἐναπολήψεις²
καὶ περιπλοκάς, τῶν δ' ἁδροτέρων καὶ συνεστηκό-
B των ἤδη δεινοὺς ἀγῶνας πρὸς ἄλληλα καὶ διαταρα-
χὰς λαμβανόντων, κλύδωνα καὶ βρασμὸν εἶναι καὶ
φθόρου καὶ πλάνης καὶ ναυαγίων μεστὰ πάντα,
πρίν γε τὴν γῆν μέγεθος λαβοῦσαν ἐκ τῶν συνιστα-
μένων καὶ φερομένων ἱδρυθῆναί πως αὐτὴν καὶ τοῖς
ἄλλοις ἵδρυσιν ἐν αὐτῇ καὶ περὶ αὐτὴν παρασχεῖν,
οὕτω τῶν μεγίστων ἐν ἀνθρώποις δυνάμεων καὶ
ἡγεμονιῶν κατὰ τύχας ἐλαυνομένων καὶ συμφερο-
μένων ὑπὸ τοῦ μηδένα κρατεῖν βούλεσθαι δὲ πάντας,
ἀμήχανος ἦν ἡ³ φορὰ⁴ καὶ πλάνη καὶ μεταβολὴ πᾶσα
πάντων, μέχρι οὗ τῆς Ῥώμης ἰσχὺν καὶ αὔξησιν
C λαβούσης καὶ ἀναδησαμένης τοῦτο μὲν ἔθνη καὶ
δήμους ἐν αὐτῇ, τοῦτο δ' ἀλλοφύλους καὶ δια-
ποντίους βασιλέων ἡγεμονίας, ἕδραν ἔσχε τὰ μέγιστα καὶ ἀσφάλειαν, εἰς κόσμον εἰρήνης καὶ ἕνα
κύκλον τῆς ἡγεμονίας ἀπταίστου⁵ περιφερομένης,
πάσης μὲν ἀρετῆς ἐγγενομένης τοῖς ταῦτα μηχα-
νησαμένοις, πολλῆς δὲ καὶ τύχης συνελθούσης,
ὡς ἐνέσται τοῦ λόγου προϊόντος ἐνδείξασθαι.

---

¹ πάλαι added by F.C.B.
² ἐναπολήψεις] ὑπολήψεις nearly all mss.
³ ἦν ἡ Madvig: ἡ.
⁴ φορὰ early editors: φθορά.
⁵ ἀπταίστου F.C.B.: ἄπταιστον.

the physicists [a] assert that the world was in ancient days not a world nor were the atoms willing to coalesce and mix together and bestow a universal form upon Nature, but, since the atoms, which were yet small and were being borne hither and thither, kept eluding and escaping incorporation and entanglement, and the larger, close-compacted atoms were already engaging in terrific struggles and confusion among themselves, there was pitching and tossing, and all things were full of destruction and drift and wreckage until such time as the earth, by acquiring magnitude from the union of the wandering atoms, somehow came to be permanently abiding herself, and provided a permanent abode in herself and round about herself for the other elements ; even so, while the mightiest powers and dominions among men were being driven about as Fortune willed, and were continuing to collide one with another because no one held the supreme power, but all wished to hold it, the continuous movement, drift, and change of all peoples remained without remedy, until such time as Rome acquired strength and growth, and had attached to herself not only the nations and peoples within her own borders, but also royal dominions of foreign peoples beyond the seas, and thus the affairs of this vast empire gained stability and security, since the supreme government, which never knew reverse, was brought within an orderly and single cycle of peace ; for though Virtue in every form was inborn in those who contrived these things, yet great Good Fortune was also joined therewith, as it will be possible to demonstrate as the discourse proceeds.

[a] *Cf. Moralia*, 878 c-f ; *De Anima*, i. 1 (Bernardakis, vol. vii. p. 1).

(317) 3. Νυνὶ δέ μοι δοκῶ τοῦ προβλήματος ὥσπερ
ἀπὸ σκοπιᾶς[1] καθορᾶν ἐπὶ τὴν σύγκρισιν καὶ τὸν
ἀγῶνα τήν τε Τύχην καὶ τὴν Ἀρετὴν βαδιζούσας.
ἀλλὰ τῆς μὲν Ἀρετῆς πρᾶόν τε τὸ βάδισμα καὶ
τὸ βλέμμα καθεστηκός, παρέχει[2] δέ τι καὶ τῷ
D προσώπῳ πρὸς τὴν ἅμιλλαν ἐρύθημα τῆς φιλοτιμίας. καὶ πολὺ μὲν ὑστερεῖ σπευδούσης τῆς Τύχης,
ἄγουσι δ' αὐτὴν καὶ δορυφοροῦσι κατὰ πλῆθος

ἄνδρες ἀρηίφατοι βεβροτωμένα τεύχε' ἔχοντες,

ἐναντίων τραυμάτων ἀνάπλεῳ, αἷμα συμμεμιγ-
μένον ἱδρῶτι σταλάζοντες, ἡμικλάστοις ἐπιβεβη-
κότες λαφύροις. βούλεσθε δὲ πυθώμεθα, τίνες ποτ'
εἰσὶν οὗτοι; Φαβρίκιοί φασιν εἶναι καὶ Κάμιλλοι
καὶ Δέκιοι[3] καὶ Κικιννᾶτοι καὶ Μάξιμοι Φάβιοι καὶ
Κλαύδιοι Μάρκελλοι καὶ Σκιπίωνες. ὁρῶ δὲ καὶ
Γάιον Μάριον ὀργιζόμενον τῇ Τύχῃ, καὶ Μούκιος
ἐκεῖ Σκαιόλας[4] τὴν φλεγομένην χεῖρα δείκνυσι βοῶν
E '' μὴ καὶ ταύτην τῇ Τύχῃ χαρίζῃ; '' καὶ Μάρκος
Ὡράτιος[5] ἀριστεὺς παραποτάμιος Τυρρηνικοῖς
βέλεσι βαρυνόμενος καὶ σκάζοντα μηρὸν παρέχων,
ἐκ βαθείας ὑποφθέγγεται δίνης, '' οὐκοῦν κἀγὼ
κατὰ τύχην πεπήρωμαι; '' τοιοῦτος ὁ τῆς Ἀρετῆς
χορὸς πρόσεισιν ἐπὶ τὴν σύγκρισιν,

βριθὺς ὁπλιτοπάλας δάιος ἀντιπάλοις.

---

[1] σκοπιᾶς] σκοπῆς many mss.
[2] παρέχει] ἐπανθεῖ Cobet; ἐπιτρέχει Stegmann.
[3] Δέκιοι F.C.B.: λούκιοι.
[4] Σκαιόλας Xylander: κέστλας.
[5] Μάρκος Ὡράτιος Basel ed. of 1542: πάκιος καὶ μάρκος.

---

[a] This scene is perhaps imitated from Xenophon, *Memora-*

3. And now, methinks, from my lofty look-out, as it were, from whence I survey the matter in hand, I can descry Fortune and Virtue advancing to be judged and tried one against the other.[a] The gait of Virtue is unhurried, her gaze unwavering ; yet the flush of ambition lends to her countenance some intimation regarding the contest. She follows far behind Fortune, who makes great haste, and in a throng conducting her and guarding her person are

> Heroes slain in the conflict, wearing their blood-stained armour,[b]

men befouled with wounds in front, dripping blood with sweat commingled, trampling upon battered spoils. Is it your desire that we inquire what men are these ? They declare themselves to be the Fabricii, the Camilli, the Decii, the Cincinnati, the Fabii Maximi, the Claudii Marcelli, and the Scipios. I see also Gaius Marius showing anger at Fortune, and yonder Mucius Scaevola is exhibiting his burning hand and crying, " Do you graciously attribute this also to Fortune ? " And Marcus Horatius, the hero of the battle by the Tiber, weighed down by Etruscan shafts and showing his limping limb, cries aloud from the deep whirl of the waters, " Then am I also maimed by Fortune's will ? " Of such character is Virtue's choir that advances to the lists,

> Sturdy contender in arms, baleful to all that oppose.[c]

bilia, ii. 1. 21-34 : Prodicus's Heracles and the contest of the goddesses, Virtue and Vice.

[b] Homer, *Od.* xi. 41.

[c] Bergk, *Poet. Lyr. Graec.* ii. p. 242, or Edmonds, *Elegy and Iambus*, i. p. 420 ; *cf. Moralia*, 334 D, *infra*, 640 A ; *Compar. of Demosthenes and Cicero*, ii. (887 B) ; *cf.* 337 D, *infra*.

329

4. Τῆς δὲ Τύχης ὀξὺ μὲν τὸ κίνημα καὶ θρασὺ
τὸ φρόνημα καὶ μεγάλαυχος[1] ἡ ἐλπίς, φθάνουσα δὲ
τὴν Ἀρετὴν ἐγγύς ἐστιν, οὐ πτεροῖς ἐλαφρίζουσα
κούφοις ἑαυτὴν οὐδ᾽ ἀκρώνυχον ὑπὲρ σφαίρας τινὸς
ἴχνος καθεῖσα[2] περισφαλὴς καὶ ἀμφίβολος πρόσεισιν, εἶτ᾽ ἄπεισιν ἀιδής[3]· ἀλλ᾽ ὥσπερ οἱ Σπαρτιᾶται
F τὴν Ἀφροδίτην λέγουσι διαβαίνουσαν τὸν Εὐρώταν
τὰ μὲν ἔσοπτρα καὶ τοὺς χλίδωνας καὶ τὸν κεστὸν
ἀποθέσθαι, δόρυ δὲ καὶ ἀσπίδα λαβεῖν κοσμουμένην
τῷ Λυκούργῳ· οὕτως ἡ Τύχη καταλιποῦσα Πέρσας
καὶ Ἀσσυρίους Μακεδονίαν μὲν ἐλαφρὰ διέπτη καὶ
ἀπεσείσατο ταχέως Ἀλέξανδρον, καὶ δι᾽ Αἰγύπτου
καὶ Συρίας περιφέρουσα βασιλείας διώδευσε, καὶ
318 Καρχηδονίους στρεφομένη πολλάκις ἐβάστασε· τῷ
δὲ Παλατίῳ προσερχομένη καὶ διαβαίνουσα τὸν
Θύμβριν ὡς ἔοικεν ἔθηκε τὰς πτέρυγας, ἐξέβη τῶν
πεδίλων, ἀπέλιπε τὴν ἄπιστον καὶ παλίμβολον
σφαῖραν. οὕτως εἰσῆλθεν εἰς Ῥώμην ὡς μενοῦσα
καὶ τοιαύτη πάρεστιν ὡς[4] ἐπὶ τὴν δίκην.

οὐ μὲν γὰρ ἀπειθής,[5]

κατὰ Πίνδαρον,

οὐδὲ δίδυμον στρέφουσα πηδάλιον,

ἀλλὰ μᾶλλον

Εὐνομίας καὶ Πειθοῦς ἀδελφὰ
καὶ Προμαθείας[6] θυγάτηρ,

---

[1] μεγάλαυχος F.C.B.: μεγάλαυχον.
[2] καθεῖσα] καταθεῖσα Abresch; τιθεῖσα Cobet.
[3] ἀιδής F.C.B. (Xylander ἀειδής): ἀηδής.
[4] ὡς not in some mss.
[5] μὲν γὰρ ἀπειθής Reiske and one ms. (B): μεγαπένθης and
the like.

330

4. But swift is the pace of Fortune, bold is her spirit, and most vaunting her hopes ; she outstrips Virtue and is close at hand. She does not raise herself in the air on light pinions, nor advance "poised on tip-toe above a globe," in a precarious and hesitant posture, and then depart from sight. But even as the Spartans say that Aphroditê, as she crossed the Eurotas, put aside her mirrors and ornaments and her magic girdle, and took a spear and shield, adorning herself to please Lycurgus, even so Fortune, when she had deserted the Persians and Assyrians, had flitted lightly over Macedonia, and had quickly shaken off Alexander, made her way through Egypt and Syria, conveying kingships here and there ; and turning about, she would often exalt the Carthaginians. But when she was approaching the Palatine and crossing the Tiber, it appears that she took off her wings, stepped out of her sandals, and abandoned her untrustworthy and unstable globe.[a] Thus did she enter Rome, as with intent to abide, and in such guise is she present to-day, as though ready to meet her trial.

> For stubborn is she not,

as Pindar [b] says,

> Nor is the rudder double that she plies ;

but rather is she

> The sister of Good Order and Persuasion, and
> The daughter of Foresight,

[a] This is the Fortuna of Horace, *Carmina*, i. 35 ; *cf.* Dio Chrysostom, *Oration*, lxiii. (p. 591 c-d) ; Galen, *Protrepticus*, 2.

[b] Pindar, Frags. 39-41 (ed. Christ), or Bergk, *Poet. Lyr. Graec.* i. p. 382.

---

[c] ἀδελφὰ καὶ Προμαθείας Schneidewin : ἀδελφὴ καὶ προμηθείας.

(318) ὡς γενεαλογεῖ Ἀλκμάν. τὸ δ' ὑμνούμενον ἐκεῖνο
τοῦ πλούτου κέρας ἔχει διὰ χειρός, οὐκ ὀπώρας ἀεὶ
θαλλούσης μεστόν, ἀλλ' ὅσα φέρει πᾶσα γῆ πᾶσα
B δὲ θάλαττα καὶ ποταμοὶ καὶ μέταλλα καὶ λιμένες,
ἄφθονα καὶ ῥύδην ἐπιχεαμένη. λαμπροὶ δὲ καὶ
διαπρεπεῖς ἄνδρες οὐκ ὀλίγοι μετ' αὐτῆς ὁρῶν-
ται, Πομπίλιος Νομᾶς ἐκ Σαβίνων καὶ Πρίσκος
ἐκ Ταρκυνίων, οὓς ἐπήλυδας βασιλεῖς καὶ ξένους
ἐνιδρύσατο τοῖς Ῥωμύλου θρόνοις· καὶ Παῦλος
Αἰμίλιος ἀπὸ Περσέως καὶ Μακεδόνων ἄτρωτον
στρατὸν ἄγων καὶ νίκην ἄδακρυν θριαμβεύων μεγαλύνει τὴν Τύχην· μεγαλύνει δὲ καὶ Καικίλιος Μέτελλος ὁ Μακεδονικὸς γέρων, ὑπὸ τεττάρων παίδων
ὑπατικῶν ἐκκομιζόμενος, Κοΐντου Βαλεαρικοῦ[1] καὶ
C Λευκίου Διαδημάτα καὶ Μάρκου Μετέλλου καὶ
Γαΐου Καπραρίου, καὶ δυοῖν γαμβρῶν ὑπατικῶν
καὶ θυγατριδῶν κοσμουμένων ἐπιφανέσιν ἀριστείαις
καὶ πολιτείαις. Αἰμίλιος δὲ Σκαῦρος ἐκ ταπεινοῦ
βίου καὶ ταπεινοτέρου γένους καινὸς ἄνθρωπος ἀρθεὶς ὑπ' αὐτῆς προγράφεται τοῦ μεγάλου συνεδρίου.
Κορνήλιον δὲ Σύλλαν ἐκ τῶν Νικοπόλεως τῆς ἑταίρας ἀναλαβοῦσα καὶ βαστάσασα κόλπων ὑψηλό-
τερον τῶν Κιμβρικῶν Μαρίου θριάμβων καὶ τῶν
ἑπτὰ ὑπατειῶν ἐπιτίθησι μοναρχίαις καὶ δικτατω-
ρίαις. ἄντικρυς οὗτος τῇ Τύχῃ μετὰ τῶν πράξεων

---

[1] Βαλεαρικοῦ Basel ed. of 1542 : βαναρίκου.

[a] Bergk, *Poet. Lyr. Graec.* iii. p. 58, Alcman, no. 62 ; or
Edmonds, *Lyra Graeca*, i. p. 90.
[b] An exaggeration ; 100 were killed : *cf. Life of Aemilius
Paulus*, chap. xxi. (266 ᴇ) ; Livy, xliv. 42.
[c] *Cf.* Cicero, *De Finibus*, v. 27 (82) ; *Tusculan Disp.* i.

as Alcman[a] describes her lineage. And she holds
that celebrated Horn of Plenty in her hand, filled not
with fruits of everlasting bloom, but as many as are
the products of the whole earth and of all the seas,
rivers, mines, and harbours, these does she pour forth
in unstinted abundance. Not a few splendid and
distinguished men are seen in her company : Numa
Pompilius from the Sabine country and Priscus from
Tarquinii, whom as adventitious and foreign kings she
set upon the throne of Romulus ; and Aemilius
Paulus, leading back his army without a wound[b]
from Perseus and the Macedonians, triumphing for a
tearless victory, magnifies Fortune. There magnifies
her also the aged Caecilius Metellus Macedonicus,[c]
borne to his grave by four sons of consular rank,
Quintus Baliaricus, Lucius Diadematus,[d] Marcus
Metellus, Gaius Caprarius, and by two sons-in-law of
consular rank, and by grandsons made distinguished
by illustrious deeds and offices. Aemilius Scaurus, a
novus homo,[e] was raised by her from a humble station
and a humbler family to be enrolled as the first man
of the Senate.[f] Cornelius Sulla she took up and
elevated from the embraces of his mistress, Nicopolis,[g]
and designated him for a monarchy and dictatorship
which ranked far above the Cimbrian triumphs and
the seven consulships of Marius. Sulla used openly
to declare himself, together with his exploits, to be

35 (85) ; Velleius Paterculus, i. 11. 7 ; Valerius Maximus,
vii. 1. 1 ; Pliny, *Natural History*, vii. 13. 59 ; 44. 142.

   [d] That is, Vittatus.

   [e] Not literally true ; he was of the gens Aemilia (*cf.*
Cicero, *Pro Murena*, 7 (16)); but his father was engaged in
the charcoal trade, and he had to fight his way as though he
had been a *novus homo.*　　　　　　　　[f] *Princeps senatus.*

   [g] *Life of Sulla*, chap. ii. (452 B-C).

(318) ἑαυτὸν εἰσεποίει, βοῶν κατὰ τὸν Οἰδίποδα τὸν
Σοφοκλέους

D   ἐγὼ δ' ἐμαυτὸν παῖδα τῆς Τύχης νέμω.

καὶ Ῥωμαϊστὶ μὲν Φήλιξ ὠνομάζετο, τοῖς δ'
Ἕλλησιν οὕτως ἔγραφε " Λούκιος Κορνήλιος Σύλ-
λας Ἐπαφρόδιτος.'' καὶ τὰ παρ' ἡμῖν ἐν Χαιρωνείᾳ τρόπαια καὶ τὰ¹ τῶν Μιθριδατικῶν οὕτως
ἐπιγέγραπται, καὶ εἰκότως²· " πλεῖστον γὰρ Ἀφροδίτης '' οὐ " νύξ,'' κατὰ Μένανδρον, ἀλλὰ τύχη
μετέσχηκεν.

5. Ἆρ' οὖν³ ταύτην τις ἀρχὴν ποιησάμενος οἰ-
κείαν ἂν ὑπὲρ τῆς Τύχης ἐπάγοιτο μάρτυρας αὖ
τοὺς⁴ Ῥωμαίους, ὡς τῇ Τύχῃ πλέον ἢ τῇ Ἀρετῇ
νέμοντας; Ἀρετῆς μέν γε παρ' αὐτοῖς ὀψὲ καὶ
μετὰ πολλοὺς χρόνους ἱερὸν ἱδρύσατο Σκιπίων ὁ
E Νομαντῖνος, εἶτα Μάρκελλος⁵ τὸ Οὐιρτοῦτίς τε καὶ
Ὀνώρις προσαγορευόμενον, καὶ τὸ τῆς Μέντις
καλουμένης (Γνώμης ἂν νομίζοιτο) Σκαῦρος Αἰμίλιος, περὶ τὰ Κιμβρικὰ τοῖς χρόνοις γεγονώς· ἤδη
τότε λόγων καὶ σοφισμάτων⁶ καὶ στωμυλίας παρεισρυείσης εἰς τὴν πόλιν ἤρχοντο σεμνύνειν τὰ

¹ καὶ τὰ] κατὰ Reiske and E.
² καὶ εἰκότως] εἰκότως Cobet.
³ οὖν] οὐκ ἂν (οὖν) ? Bernardakis; ἂν added here by F.C.B.;
ἐπάγοιτ' ἂν one ms. (B).
⁴ αὖ τοὺς F.C.B.: αὐτούς.
⁵ Μάρκελλος] most mss. have μάριος.
⁶ σοφισμάτων Reiske from 322 D, infra: σοφιστῶν or σοφι-
στικῶν (B).

ᵃ Oedipus Tyrannus, 1080.
ᵇ Life of Sulla, chap. xxxiv. (473 D-E); Appian, Civil

the adopted child of Fortune, loudly asserting in the words of Sophocles' Oedipus,[a]

> And Fortune's son I hold myself to be.

In the Latin tongue he was called Felix,[b] but for the Greeks he wrote his name thus : Lucius Cornelius Sulla Epaphroditus.[c] And the trophies at my home in Chaeroneia and those of the Mithridatic Wars are thus inscribed, quite appropriately ; for not "Night," as Menander [d] has it, but Fortune has the " greater share in Aphroditê."

5. Might one, then, after proffering this as a suitable introduction, bring on the Romans once more as witnesses in behalf of Fortune, on the ground that they assigned more to Fortune than to Virtue ? At least, it was only recently and after many years that Scipio Numantinus built a shrine of Virtue in Rome ; later Marcellus [e] built what is called the Temple of Virtue and Honour[f]; and Aemilius Scaurus,[g] who lived in the time of the Cimbrian Wars, built the shrine of *Mens* (Mind) so-called, which might be considered a Temple of Reason. For at this time rhetoric, sophistry, and argumentation had already found their way into the City ; and people were beginning to

---

Wars, i. 97; Diodorus, xxxviii. 15; *Corpus Inscriptionum Graecarum*, vii. nos. 264, 372, 413 (=Dittenberger, *Sylloge*³, 747, 752).   [c] That is, *Venustus*.

[d] Koch, *Com. Att. Frag.* iii. 209, Menander, no. 739, or Menander, ed. Allinson (in L.C.L.), p. 528 : *cf. Moralia*, 654 D ; scholia on Theocritus, ii. 10.

[e] *Life of Marcellus*, chap. xxviii. (314 c); Livy, xxvii. 25, xxix. 11 ; Valerius Maximus, i. 1. 8 ; Cicero, *Verrine Orations*, iv. 54 (121) ; *De Natura Deorum*, ii. 23 (61).

[f] The following passage is repeated in the MSS. with some changes *infra*, 322 C-E, where see the note.

[g] Cicero, *De Natura Deorum*, ii. 23 (61).

τοιαῦτα. σοφίας δὲ μέχρι καὶ νῦν ἱερὸν οὐκ ἔστιν
οὐδὲ σωφροσύνης ἢ μεγαλοψυχίας ἢ καρτερίας ἢ
ἐγκρατείας· ἀλλὰ τά γε τῆς Τύχης ἱερὰ λαμπρὰ καὶ
παλαιά, καὶ ὁμοῦ τι τοῖς πρώτοις καταμεμειγμένα
τῆς πόλεως θεμελίοις γέγονε. πρῶτος μὲν γὰρ
ἱδρύσατο Τύχης ἱερὸν Μάρκιος[1] Ἄγκος, ὁ Νομᾶ[2]
F θυγατριδοῦς καὶ τέταρτος ἀπὸ Ῥωμύλου βασιλεὺς
γενόμενος· καὶ τάχα που τῇ τύχῃ τὴν ἀνδρείαν[3]
παρωνόμασεν,[4] ᾗ πλεῖστον εἰς τὸ νικᾶν τύχης μέτ-
εστι. τὸ δὲ τῆς γυναικείας Τύχης κατεσκευά-
σαντο πρὸ Καμίλλου[5] ὅτε Μάρκιον Κοριολανὸν
ἐπάγοντα τῇ πόλει Οὐολούσκους ἀπετρέψαντο[6] διὰ
τῶν γυναικῶν. πρεσβευσάμεναι γὰρ αὗται πρὸς
τὸν ἄνδρα μετὰ τῆς μητρὸς αὐτοῦ καὶ τῆς γυναικός, ἐξελιπάρησαν καὶ κατειργάσαντο φείσασθαι
τῆς πόλεως καὶ τὴν στρατιὰν τῶν βαρβάρων ἀπ-
319 αγαγεῖν. τότε[7] λέγεται τὸ ἄγαλμα τῆς Τύχης ἅμα
τῷ καθιερωθῆναι φωνὴν ἀφεῖναι καὶ εἰπεῖν, "ὁσίῳ[8]
με πόλεως νόμῳ, γυναῖκες ἀσταί, καθιδρύσασθε."

Καὶ μὴν καὶ Φούριος Κάμιλλος, ὅτε τὸ Κελτικὸν
ἔσβεσε πῦρ, καὶ τὴν Ῥώμην ἀντίρροπον χρυσῷ
κεκλιμένην ἀπὸ τοῦ ζυγοῦ καὶ τῆς πλάστιγγος

---

[1] Μάρκιος Basel ed. of 1542 : Μαρκὸς.
[2] ὁ Νομᾶ early eds. and some mss.: ὄνομα.
[3] τῇ τύχῃ τὴν ἀνδρείαν] τὴν τύχην τῇ ἀνδρείᾳ in nearly all mss.
[4] παρωνόμασεν] παρωνόμασαν Meziriacus, but see 322 D,
infra.
[5] πρὸ Καμίλλου Wyttenbach would omit as in 322 E, infra.
[6] ἀπετρέψαντο] ἀπέστρεψαν 322 E, infra; ἀπετρίψαντο Reiske;
ἀπεστρέψαντο Bruhn and some mss.   [7] τότε] ὅτε E. Kurtz.
[8] ὁσίῳ Dionysius Hal. viii. 56; cf. also Life of Coriolanus,
chap. xxxvii.: ὁσίως.

---

[a] Cf. 281 E, supra.

magnify such pursuits. But even to this day they have no shrine of Wisdom or Prudence or Magnanimity or Constancy or Moderation. But of Fortune there are splendid and ancient shrines,[a] all but coeval with the first foundations of the City. For the first to build a temple of Fortune was Ancus Marcius, the grandson of Numa[b] and king fourth in line from Romulus. He, perchance, it was who added the title of *Fortis* to *Fortuna*[c] ; for in Fortune Manly Fortitude shares most largely in the winning of victory. They erected a temple of *Fortuna Muliebris*[d] before the time of Camillus, when, through the offices of their women, they had turned back Marcius Coriolanus, who was leading the Volsci against the City. For a delegation of women, together with his mother and his wife, went to the hero and besought him and gained their request that he spare the City and lead away the foreign army. It is said that at this time, when the statue of Fortune was consecrated, it spoke and said, " Women of the city, you have dedicated me by the holy law of Rome."

And it is a fact that Furius Camillus likewise, when he had quenched the Gallic conflagration and had removed Rome from the balance and scales when her price was being weighed in gold,[e] founded no shrine

---

[b] Cf. *Life of Numa*, chap. xxi. (74 B).

[c] Contrast *Life of Coriolanus*, chap. i. (214 B). W. W. Goodwin's suggestion, that Plutarch misunderstood *Fors Fortuna* in an oblique case (*e.g. Fortis Fortunae*), is not unlikely ; see *e.g.* Tacitus, *Annals*, ii. 41, where the mistake would be easy for a foreigner.

[d] The Women's Fortune : *cf. Life of Coriolanus*, chap. xxxvii. (231 F ff.); Livy, ii. 40. 12 ; Dionysius of Halicarnassus, *Roman Antiquities*, viii. 56. 2 ; Valerius Maximus, i. 8. 4 ; 5. 2.

[e] Cf. *Life of Camillus*, chap. xxix. (143 E).

(319) καθεῖλεν, οὔτ᾽ εὐβουλίας οὔτ᾽ ἀνδρείας, ἀλλὰ Φήμης
ἱδρύσατο καὶ Κληδόνος ἱερὸν¹ παρὰ τὴν Καινὴν
ὁδόν, ὅπου φασὶ πρὸ τοῦ πολέμου Μάρκῳ Καιδικίῳ²
βαδίζοντι νύκτωρ φωνὴν γενέσθαι κελεύουσαν
ὀλίγῳ χρόνῳ Γαλατικὸν πόλεμον προσδέχεσθαι.

Τὴν δὲ πρὸς τῷ ποταμῷ Τύχην " φόρτιν³ "
B καλοῦσιν (ὅπερ ἐστὶν ἰσχυρὰν ἢ ἀριστευτικὴν ἢ
ἀνδρείαν), ὡς τὸ νικητικὸν ἁπάντων κράτος ἔχουσαν. καὶ τόν γε ναὸν⁴ αὐτῆς ἐν τοῖς ὑπὸ Καίσαρος
τῷ δήμῳ καταλειφθεῖσι κήποις ᾠκοδόμησαν, ἡγούμενοι κἀκεῖνον εὐτυχίᾳ γενέσθαι μέγιστον, ὡς
αὐτὸς ἐμαρτύρησε.

6. Περὶ δὲ Γαΐου Καίσαρος ᾐδέσθην ἂν εἰπεῖν,
ὡς ὑπ᾽ εὐτυχίας ἤρθη μέγιστος, εἰ μὴ τοῦτ᾽ αὐτὸς
ἐμαρτύρησεν. ἐπεὶ γὰρ ἀπὸ Βρεντεσίου Πομπήιον
διώκων ἀνήχθη πρὸ μιᾶς ἡμέρας νωνῶν Ἰανουα-
ρίων, χειμῶνος ἐν τροπαῖς ὄντος, τὸ μὲν πέλαγος
ἀσφαλῶς διεπέρασε, τῆς Τύχης τὸν καιρὸν ὑπερ-
θεμένης· εὑρὼν δὲ τὸν Πομπήιον ἄθρουν καὶ πολὺν
C μὲν ἐν γῇ πολὺν δ᾽ ἐν θαλάττῃ μετὰ πασῶν ἅμα
τῶν δυνάμεων καθεζόμενον αὐτὸς ὀλιγοστὸς ὤν, τῆς
μετ᾽ Ἀντωνίου καὶ Σαβίνου στρατιᾶς αὐτῷ βραδυ-
νούσης, ἐτόλμησεν εἰς ἀκάτιον μικρὸν ἐμβὰς καὶ
λαθὼν τόν τε ναύκληρον καὶ τὸν κυβερνήτην ὥς
τινος θεράπων ἀναχθῆναι. σκληρᾶς δὲ πρὸς τὸ

---

¹ ἱερὸν F.C.B. (from νεὼν in the *Life of Camillus*, chap. xxx.)⁵
ἕδος or ἕδη Reiske: ἐκεῖ.
² Καιδικίῳ as elsewhere Xylander: καὶ δεκίῳ.
³ φόρτιν Reiske: ἦν φόρτικαν.
⁴ τόν γε ναὸν Stephanus: τὸ γενναῖον.

ᵃ Perhaps an attempted translation of Aius Locutius; *cf.*
Livy, v. 32. 6 ; 50. 5 ; *Life of Camillus*, chap. xxx.

of Good Counsel or of Valour, but a shrine of Report and Rumour [a] by New Street, where, as they assert, before the war there came to Marcus Caedicius, as he was walking by night, a voice which told him to expect in a short time a Gallic war.

The Fortune whose temple is by the river they call *Fortis*,[b] that is, strong or valiant or manly, as having the power to conquer everything. And her temple they have built in the Gardens bequeathed by Caesar to the People,[c] since they believed that he also reached his most exalted position through good fortune, as he himself has testified.

6. Yet I should hesitate to say of Gaius Caesar that he was raised to his most exalted position by good fortune, if he had not himself testified to this. For when on the fourth day of January he put out from Brundisium in pursuit of Pompey,[d] though it was the time of the winter solstice, yet he crossed the sea in safety ; for Fortune postponed the season. But when he found that Pompey had a compact and numerous army on land and a large fleet on the sea, and was well entrenched with all his forces, while he himself had a force many times smaller, and since his army with Antony and Sabinus was slow in coming, he had the courage to go on board a small boat and put out to sea in the guise of a servant, unrecognized by the captain and the pilot.[e] But there was a violent

---

xxx. (144 c-d) ; Aulus Gellius, xvi. 17 ; Cicero, *De Divinatione*, i. 45 (101) ; ii. 32 (69).

[b] See note *c* on p. 337.

[c] *Cf.* Suetonius, *Divus Julius*, 83 ; Dio Cassius, xliv. 35. 3.

[d] *Cf.* Lucan, *Pharsalia*, v. 406 ff.

[e] *Cf. Moralia*, 206 c-d, and note *b* in L.C.L. Vol. III. p. 226.

(319) ῥεῦμα τοῦ ποταμοῦ γενομένης ἀντιμεταβάσεως καὶ
κλύδωνος ἰσχυροῦ,[1] μεταβαλλόμενον ὁρῶν τὸν κυβερνήτην ἀφεῖλεν ἀπὸ τῆς κεφαλῆς τὸ ἱμάτιον, καὶ
ἀναδείξας ἑαυτόν, " ἴθι," ἔφη, " γενναῖε, τόλμα καὶ
D δέδιθι μηδέν, ἀλλ' ἐπιδίδου τῇ Τύχῃ τὰ ἱστία
καὶ δέχου τὸ πνεῦμα, πιστεύων ὅτι Καίσαρα φέρεις
καὶ τὴν Καίσαρος Τύχην." οὕτως ἐπέπειστο τὴν
Τύχην αὐτῷ συμπλεῖν, συναποδημεῖν, συστρατεύε-
σθαι, συστρατηγεῖν, ἧς ἔργον ἦν γαλήνην μὲν
ἐπιτάξαι θαλάττῃ, θέρος δὲ χειμῶνι, τάχος δὲ τοῖς
βραδυτάτοις, ἀλκὴν δὲ τοῖς ἀθυμοτάτοις, τὸ δὲ τούτων ἀπιστότερον, φυγὴν Πομπηίῳ καὶ Πτολεμαίῳ
ξενοκτονίαν, ἵνα καὶ Πομπήιος πέσῃ καὶ Καῖσαρ
μὴ μιανθῇ.

7. Τί δέ; ὁ τούτου μὲν υἱός, πρῶτος δ' ἀναγο-
ρευθεὶς Σεβαστὸς ἄρξας δὲ τέτταρα καὶ πεντήκοντα
E ἔτη, οὐκ αὐτὸς ἐκπέμπων τὸν θυγατριδοῦν ἐπὶ
στρατείαν εὔξατο τοῖς θεοῖς ἀνδρείαν μὲν αὐτῷ δοῦναι τὴν Σκιπίωνος, εὔνοιαν δὲ τὴν Πομπηίου, Τύχην
δὲ τὴν αὑτοῦ; καθάπερ ἔργῳ μεγάλῳ δημιουργὸν ἐπιγράψας ἑαυτῷ τὴν Τύχην, ἥτις αὐτὸν ἐπι-
θεῖσα Κικέρωνι καὶ Λεπίδῳ καὶ Πάνσᾳ[2] καὶ Ἱρτίῳ
καὶ Μάρκῳ Ἀντωνίῳ,[3] ταῖς ἐκείνων ἀριστείαις καὶ
χερσὶ καὶ νίκαις καὶ στόλοις καὶ πολέμοις[4] καὶ
στρατοπέδοις γενόμενον πρῶτον εἰς ὕψος ἄρασα
καὶ καταβαλοῦσα τούτους, δι' ὧν ἀνέβη, μόνον

---

[1] σκληρᾶς . . . ἰσχυροῦ] several attempts have been made
to emend these two lines, but a comparison with other
accounts will show that the text is sound.

[2] Πάνσᾳ the usual form elsewhere: πάσσα.

[3] Μάρκῳ Ἀντωνίῳ Basel ed. of 1542: ἀντωνίῳ καὶ μάρκῳ.

[4] καὶ πολέμοις] not in most mss.

commotion where heavy surge from without encountered the current of the river, and Caesar, seeing
the pilot changing his course, removed the cloak
from his head and, revealing himself, said, " Go on,
good sir, be brave and fear nothing ! But entrust
your sails to Fortune^a and receive her breeze,
confident because you bear Caesar and Caesar's
Fortune." Thus firmly was he convinced that
Fortune accompanied him on his voyages, his travels,
his campaigns, his commands ; Fortune's task it was
to enjoin calm upon the sea, summer weather upon the
winter-time,^b speed upon the slowest of men, courage
upon the most dispirited, and (more unbelievable
than these) to enjoin flight upon Pompey, and upon
Ptolemy the murder of his guest, that Pompey should
fall and Caesar should escape the stain of his blood.

7. What then ? Caesar's son, who was the first to
be styled Augustus, and who ruled for fifty-four years,
when he was sending forth his grandson to war, did
he not pray to the gods to bestow upon the young
man the courage of Scipio, the popularity of Pompey,
and his own Fortune,^c thus recording Fortune as the
creator of himself, quite as though he were inscribing
the artist's name on a great monument ?^d For it
was Fortune that imposed him upon Cicero, Lepidus,
Pansa, Hirtius, and Mark Antony, and by their
displays of valour, their deeds, victories, fleets, wars,
armies, raised him on high to be the first of Roman
citizens ; and she cast down these men, through
whom he had mounted, and left him to rule alone.

^a Cf. the metaphor of Tacitus, Historiae, i. 52 " panderet
modo sinum et venienti Fortunae occurreret."
^b As above, 319 B : " Fortune postponed the season."
^c Cf. Moralia, 207 E.
^d Cf. Classical Review, xxv. 15.

κατέλιπεν. ἐκείνῳ γὰρ ἐπολιτεύετο Κικέρων καὶ
Λέπιδος ἐστρατήγει καὶ Πάνσας[1] ἐνίκα καὶ Ἵρτιος
F ἔπιπτε καὶ Ἀντώνιος ὕβριζεν. ἐγὼ γὰρ καὶ Κλεο-
πάτραν τῆς τύχης[2] Καίσαρος τίθημι, περὶ ἣν ὡς
ἕρμα κατέδυ καὶ συνετρίβη τηλικοῦτος αὐτοκράτωρ,
ἵν' ᾖ μόνος Καῖσαρ. λέγεται δὲ πολλῆς οἰκειό-
τητος αὐτοῖς καὶ συνηθείας ὑπαρχούσης πολλάκις
σχολαζόντων εἰς παιδιὰν σφαίρας ἢ κύβων ἢ νὴ
Δία θρεμμάτων ἀμίλλης, οἷον ὀρτύγων, ἀλεκτρυό-
νων, ἀεὶ νικώμενον Ἀντώνιον ἀπαλλάττεσθαι· καὶ
τινα τῶν περὶ αὐτὸν ἐπὶ μαντείᾳ[3] σεμνυνόμενον
320 πολλάκις παρρησιάζεσθαι καὶ νουθετεῖν, " ὦ ἄν-
θρωπε, τί σοι πρᾶγμα πρὸς τοῦτον ἔστι τὸν νεανίσκον; φεῦγ' αὐτόν· ἐνδοξότερος εἶ, πρεσβύτερος εἶ,
ἄρχεις πλειόνων, ἐνήθληκας πολέμοις, ἐμπειρίᾳ
διαφέρεις· ἀλλ' ὁ σὸς δαίμων τὸν τούτου φοβεῖται·
καὶ ἡ τύχη σου καθ' ἑαυτήν ἐστι μεγάλη κολακεύει
δὲ τὴν τούτου· ἐὰν μὴ μακρὰν ᾖς,[4] οἰχήσεται μετα-
βᾶσα πρὸς αὐτόν."

8. Ἀλλὰ γὰρ αἱ μὲν ἀπὸ τῶν μαρτύρων πίστεις
τοσαῦται τῇ Τύχῃ πάρεισι. δεῖ δὲ καὶ τὰς ἀπὸ
τῶν πραγμάτων αὐτῶν εἰσάγειν, ἀρχὴν τοῦ λόγου
τὴν ἀρχὴν τῆς πόλεως λαβόντας. εὐθὺς οὖν τίς οὐκ
ἂν εἴποι πρὸς τὴν Ῥωμύλου γένεσιν καὶ σωτηρίαν
B καὶ τροφὴν καὶ αὔξησιν τὴν μὲν Τύχην ὑποβολὰς[5]
κατατεθεῖσθαι τὴν δ' Ἀρετὴν[6] ἐξῳκοδομηκέναι;

---

[1] Πάνσας the usual form elsewhere : πάσσας.
[2] τῆς τύχης H. Richards : τῇ τύχῃ or τὴν τύχην.
[3] μαντείᾳ] μαντείαις in most mss.
[4] ᾖς] ἴῃς Hartman.
[5] ὑποβολὰς Meziriacus : ὑπερβολάς.
[6] τὴν μὲν Τύχην . . . τὴν δ' Ἀρετὴν Meziriacus and Reiske :
ἀρετῆς μὲν . . . τὴν δὲ τύχην.

It was, in fact, for him that Cicero governed the State, that Lepidus commanded armies, that Pansa conquered, that Hirtius fell, that Antony played the wanton. For I reckon even Cleopatra as a part of Caesar's Fortune, on whom, as on a reef, even so great a commander as Antony was wrecked and crushed that Caesar might rule alone. The tale[a] is told of Caesar and Antony that, when there was much familiarity and intimacy between them, they often devoted their leisure to a game of ball or dice or even to fights of pet birds, such as quails or cocks ; and Antony always retired from the field defeated. It is further related[a] that one of his friends, who prided himself on his knowledge of divination, was often wont to speak freely to him and admonish him, " Sir, what business have you with this youth ? Avoid him ! Your repute is greater, you are older, you govern more men, you have fought in wars, you excel in experience ; but your Guardian Spirit fears this man's Spirit. Your Fortune is mighty by herself, but abases herself before his. Unless you keep far away from him, your Fortune will depart and go over to him ! "

8. But enough ! For such important testimonies from her witnesses has Fortune to support her. But we must also introduce the testimony of the very events of history, taking as the beginning of our account the beginning of Rome. To begin with, who would not at once declare touching the birth, the preservation, the nurture, the development of Romulus, that Fortune laid the foundations, and that Virtue finished the building ? In the first place,

[a] *Cf. Life of Antony*, xxxiii. (930 D-E).

(320) πρῶτον μὲν οὖν τὸ περὶ τὴν γένεσιν καὶ τὴν
τέκνωσιν αὐτῶν τῶν ἐνιδρυσαμένων¹ καὶ κτισάντων
τὴν πόλιν εὐτυχίας ἔοικε θαυμαστῆς γενέσθαι.
θεῷ γὰρ ἡ τεκοῦσα μειχθῆναι λέγεται, καὶ καθάπερ
τὸν Ἡρακλέα σπαρῆναί φασιν ἐν μακρᾷ νυκτί, τῆς
ἡμέρας ἐπισχεθείσης παρὰ φύσιν καὶ τοῦ ἡλίου
βραδύναντος, οὕτω περὶ τὴν Ῥωμύλου σπορὰν καὶ
καταβολὴν τὸν ἥλιον ἐκλιπεῖν ἱστοροῦσι, ποιησά-
μενον ἀτρεκῆ σύνοδον πρὸς σελήνην, ᾧπερ² ὁ Ἄρης
C θεὸς ὢν τῇ Σιλβίᾳ θνητῇ συνῆλθε. ταὐτὸ δὲ
συντυχεῖν τῷ Ῥωμύλῳ καὶ περὶ τὴν μετάστασιν
αὐτὴν τοῦ βίου· λέγουσι γὰρ ἐκλείποντος τοῦ ἡλίου
ἠφανίσθαι νώναις καπρατίναις, ἣν ἄχρι νῦν ἡμέραν
ἐπιφανῶς ἑορτάζουσιν.

Ἔπειτα γεννηθέντας αὐτούς, τοῦ τυράννου τάττον-
τος³ ἀνελεῖν, παρέλαβε κατὰ τύχην οὐ βάρβαρος οὐδ'
ἄγριος ὑπηρέτης, ἐλεήμων δέ τις καὶ φιλάνθρωπος,
ὥστε μὴ κτεῖναι· ἀλλὰ τοῦ ποταμοῦ τις ἦν ὄχθη
χλοερῷ λειμῶνι προσκλύζουσα καὶ περισκιαζομένη
χθαμαλοῖς δένδρεσιν· ἐνταῦθα κατέθηκε τὰ βρέφη
πλησίον ἐρινεοῦ τινος, ὃν ῥουμινάλιν ὠνόμαζον.
D εἶτα λύκαινα μὲν νεοτόκος σπαργῶσα καὶ πλημ-
μυροῦσα τοὺς μαστοὺς γάλακτι, τῶν σκύμνων

¹ ἐνιδρυσαμένων] ἱδρυσαμένων Emperius.
² ᾧπερ F.C.B. (ἔωσπερ Pohlenz): ὥσπερ.
³ τάττοντος F.C.B. (as there is some word of ordering in
most of the other accounts); ζητοῦντος Reiske; ἀξιοῦντος
S. A. Naber: αἰτοῦντος.

ᵃ Cf. *Life of Romulus*, chaps. iii.-iv. (19 c-f) ; and 268 f,
278 c, *supra*.
ᵇ Cf. *Life of Romulus*, chap. xxvii. (34 e) ; *Life of
Camillus*, xxxiii. (146 d).

then, it appears that the circumstances surrounding the origin and the birth of the very founders and builders of Rome were of a marvellous good fortune.[a] For their mother is said to have consorted with a god ; and even as they relate that Heracles was conceived during a long night (for the day was retarded in contrariety to nature, and the sun delayed), so regarding the generation and conception of Romulus they record that the sun was eclipsed and came into exact conjunction with the moon at the time when Mars, a god, consorted with the mortal Silvia.[b] And this same thing, they say, happened to Romulus also at the very time of his translation from this life ; for they relate that he disappeared during an eclipse of the sun on the Capratine Nones,[c] on which day, even to the present time, they hold high festival.

Later, when the children were born and the despot gave orders to do away with them, by the decree of Fortune no barbarous or savage servant but a compassionate and humane man received them, with the result that he did not kill them ; but there was a margin of the river, bordering upon a green meadow,[d] shaded round about with lowly shrubs ; and here the servant deposited the infants near a certain wild fig-tree, to which people later gave the name Ruminalis.[e] Then a she-wolf, that had newly whelped, with her dugs distended and overflowing with milk because her young had perished, being

---

[c] July 7th; cf. Life of Romulus, chap. xxix. (36 c) ; Life of Numa, chap. ii. (60 c) ; Müller, Frag. Hist. Graec. iv. 552-553 ; Varro, De Lingua Latina, vi. 18.

[d] Perhaps Plutarch is attempting to give a version of super ripas Tiberis effusus lenibus stagnis . . . in proxima alluvie of Livy, i. 4.

[e] Cf. 278 c, supra.

(320) ἀπολωλότων, αὐτὴ[1] χρῄζουσα κουφισμοῦ, περιέστειξε[2] τὰ βρέφη καὶ θηλὴν ἐπέσχεν, ὥσπερ ὠδῖνα
δευτέραν ἀποτιθεμένη τὴν τοῦ γάλακτος. ἱερὸς δ᾽
ὄρνις Ἄρεος, ὃν δρυοκολάπτην καλοῦσιν, ἐπιφοιτῶν
καὶ προσκαθίζων ἀκρώνυχος, ἐν μέρει τῶν νηπίων
ἑκατέρου στόμα τῇ χηλῇ διοίγων, ἐνετίθει ψώ-
μισμα, τῆς αὑτοῦ τροφῆς ἀπομερίζων. τὸν μὲν οὖν
ἐρινεὸν ῥουμινᾶλιν ὠνόμασαν ἀπὸ τῆς θηλῆς, ἣν ἡ
λύκαινα παρ᾽ αὐτῷ[3] ὀκλάσασα τοῖς βρέφεσι παρέσχε.
μέχρι δὲ πολλοῦ διεφύλαττον οἱ περὶ τὸν τόπον
Ε ἐκεῖνον κατοικοῦντες μηδὲν ἐκτιθέναι τῶν γεννω-
μένων, ἀλλ᾽ ἀναιρεῖσθαι πάντα καὶ τρέφειν, τὸ
Ῥωμύλου πάθος καὶ τὴν ὁμοιότητα τιμῶντες.

Καὶ μὴν τό τε λαθεῖν αὐτοὺς τρεφομένους καὶ
παιδευομένους ἐν Γαβίοις ἀγνοηθῆναί τε[4] Σιλβίας
ὄντας υἱοὺς καὶ θυγατριδοῦς Νομίτορος τοῦ βασιλέως παντάπασι Τύχης κλέμμα καὶ σόφισμα
φαίνεται γεγενημένον, ὅπως μὴ ἀπόλωνται πρὸ
τῶν ἔργων διὰ τὸ γένος, ἀλλ᾽ ἐν αὐτοῖς φανῶσι
τοῖς κατορθώμασι, γνωρίσματα[5] τῆς εὐγενείας τὴν
ἀρετὴν παρέχοντες.

Ἐνταῦθά μοι μεγάλου καὶ φρονίμου στρατηγοῦ
λόγος ἔπεισι Θεμιστοκλέους ῥηθεὶς πρός τινας τῶν
F ὕστερον εὐημερούντων Ἀθήνησι στρατηγῶν καὶ
προτιμᾶσθαι τοῦ Θεμιστοκλέους ἀξιούντων. ἔφη

---

[1] αὐτὴ] αὐτῇ Wyttenbach.
[2] περιέστειξε Bernardakis: περιέπτηξε or περιέπτυξε in
most mss.   [3] αὐτῷ Helmbold: αὐτόν.
[4] τε added by Wyttenbach.
[5] γνωρίσματα] γνώρισμα in the Aldine ed., but the plural is
not unusual in this meaning.

herself in great need of relief, circled around [a] the infants and then gave them suck, thus ridding herself of the pain caused by the milk as if it had been a second birth-pang. And a bird sacred to Mars, which they call the woodpecker, visited them and, perching near on tiptoe, would, with its claw, open the mouth of each child in turn and place therein a morsel, sharing with them a portion of its own food. Wherefore they named this wild fig-tree Ruminalis, from the teat (*ruma*) which the wolf offered to the children as she crouched beside the tree. And for a long time the people who dwelt near this place preserved the custom of never exposing any of the new-born infants, but they acknowledged and reared them all, in honour of Romulus's experience and the similarity of the childrens' case with his.

And, in truth, the fact that they were not discovered while they were being reared and educated in Gabii, and that it was unknown that they were the sons of Silvia and the grandchildren of king Numitor surely appears to have been a furtive and shrewd device of Fortune, so that they might not, because of their lineage, be put to death before performing their tasks, but that they might in their very successes be discovered, by bringing to notice their noble qualities as tokens by which to recognize their high birth.

At this point there occurs to me the remark of a great and prudent general, Themistocles,[b] which was made to certain of the generals who came into favour at Athens after him and felt that they deserved to be rated above him. He said that the Day-After con-

---

[a] *Cf. cursum flexisse* of Livy, i. 4.
[b] *Cf.* 270 B, *supra*, and the note.

γὰρ τὴν ὑστεραίαν ἐρίσαι πρὸς τὴν ἑορτὴν λέ-
γουσαν ὡς ἐκείνη μέν ἐστι κοπώδης καὶ ἄσχολος,
ἐν αὐτῇ δὲ τῶν παρεσκευασμένων ἀπολαύουσι μεθ'
ἡσυχίας. τὴν οὖν ἑορτὴν εἰπεῖν, '' ἀληθῆ λέγεις,
ἀλλ' ἐμοῦ μὴ γενομένης, ποῦ ἂν σὺ ἦσθα;'' '' κἀ-
μοῦ τοίνυν,'' ἔφη, '' μὴ γενομένου περὶ τὰ Μηδικά,
τίς ἂν ὑμῶν ἦν νῦν ὄνησις;'' τοῦτό μοι δοκεῖ πρὸς
τὴν Ῥωμύλου Ἀρετὴν ἡ Τύχη λέγειν, '' λαμπρὰ
μέν τὰ σὰ ἔργα καὶ μεγάλα καὶ θεῖον ὡς ἀληθῶς
321 ἐξέφηνας αἷμα καὶ γένος οὖσαν σεαυτήν· ἀλλ' ὁρᾷς
πόσον ὑστερεῖς μου; εἰ γὰρ ἐγὼ τότε μὴ παρ-
ηκολούθησα χρηστὴ καὶ φιλάνθρωπος, ἀλλ' ἀπέλιπον
καὶ προηκάμην τὰ νήπια, σὺ πῶς ἂν ἐγένου καὶ
πόθεν ἐξέλαμψας; εἰ τότε μὴ θῆλυ θηρίον ἐπῆλθε
φλεγμαῖνον ὑπὸ πλήθους καὶ φορᾶς γάλακτος καὶ
τραφησομένου δεόμενον μᾶλλον ἢ θρέψοντος, ἀλλ'
ἀνήμερόν τι τελέως καὶ λιμῶττον, οὐκ ἂν ἔτι νῦν
τὰ καλὰ ταῦτα βασίλεια καὶ ναοὶ καὶ θέατρα καὶ
περίπατοι καὶ ἀγοραὶ[1] καὶ ἀρχεῖα βοτηρικαὶ[2] καλύβαι
καὶ σταθμοὶ νομέων ἦσαν Ἀλβανὸν ἢ Τυρρηνὸν ἢ
Λατῖνον ἄνδρα δεσπότην προσκυνούντων;'' ἀρχὴ
B μὲν δὴ μέγιστον ἐν παντί, μάλιστα δ' ἐν ἱδρύσει καὶ
κτίσει πόλεως· ταύτην δ' ἡ Τύχη παρέσχε σώσασα
καὶ φυλάξασα τὸν κτίστην· ἡ μὲν γὰρ Ἀρετὴ μέγαν
ἐποίησε Ῥωμύλον, ἡ Τύχη δ' ἄχρι τοῦ γενέσθαι
μέγαν ἐτήρησε.

9. Καὶ μὴν τήν γε Νομᾶ βασιλείαν πολυχρονιω-

---

[1] ἀγοραὶ Xylander and some mss.: ἀγορά.
[2] βοτηρικαὶ Bernardakis: βοτῆραι (βοτῆρες) καὶ.

---

[a] Cf. the Pythagorean ἀρχὴ μέν τοι ἥμισυ παντός (Iam-
blichus, *Life of Pythagoras*, 162).

tended with the Feast-Day, saying that the Feast-Day was full of wearying tasks and labours, but on the Day-After men enjoyed in quiet all things that had been made ready. Then the Feast-Day said, " What you say is true ; but if I had not been, where would you be ? " " And so," said Themistocles, " if I had not been at the time of the Persian Wars, what benefit would now come from you ? " And this, methinks, is what Fortune says to the Virtue of Romulus : " Brilliant and mighty are your deeds, and in very truth you have proved yourself to be divine in blood and birth. But do you observe how far you fall behind me ? For if, at the time of his birth, I had not accompanied him in a helpful and humane guise, but had deserted and abandoned the infants, how could you have come into being and whence had you derived such lustre ? If on that occasion there had not come to them a female beast swollen with the abundance and the burden of her milk, and in need of some creature to be fed rather than of something to yield her sustenance, but if instead there had come some utterly savage and ravening creature, would not even now these fair palaces and temples, theatres, promenades, fora, and public buildings be herdsmen's huts and folds of shepherds who paid homage to some man of Alba or Etruria or Latium as their lord ? " The beginning, as every one knows, is of supreme importance in everything,[a] and particularly in the founding and building of a city ; and this Fortune provided, since she had preserved and protected the founder. For Virtue made Romulus great, but Fortune watched over him until be became great.

9. And in truth, it is generally agreed that a

(321) τάτην γενομένην ὁμολογουμένως εὐτυχία διεκυβέρ-
νησε θαυμαστή. τὸ μὲν γὰρ Ἐγερίαν τινά, νυμφῶν
μίαν δρυάδων, δαίμονα σοφὴν ἔρωτι τἀνδρὸς ἐν
συνουσίᾳ γενομένην, παραπαιδαγωγεῖν καὶ συ-
σχηματίζειν τὴν πολιτείαν ἴσως μυθωδέστερόν ἐστι.
C καὶ γὰρ ἄλλοι λεχθέντες ἅψασθαι γάμων θείων καὶ
θεοῖς ἐράσμιοι γενέσθαι, Πηλεῖς καὶ Ἀγχίσαι καὶ
Ὠρίωνες καὶ Ἡμαθίωνες, οὐ πάντως ἀγαπητῶς
οὐδ' ἀλύπως διεβίωσαν. ἀλλὰ Νομᾶς ἔοικε τὴν
ἀγαθὴν Τύχην ἔχειν ὡς ἀληθῶς σύνοικον καὶ σύν-
εδρον καὶ συνάρχουσαν, ἤ, καθάπερ ἐν κλύδωνι
θολερῷ καὶ τεταραγμένῳ πελάγει, τῇ τῶν προσοίκων καὶ γειτόνων ἔχθρᾳ καὶ χαλεπότητι τὴν πόλιν
φερομένην καὶ φλεγμαίνουσαν ὑπὸ μυρίων πόνων
καὶ διχοστασιῶν παραλαβοῦσα τοὺς μὲν ἀντιτεταγμένους θυμοὺς καὶ φθόνους ὥσπερ πνεύματα
D κατέσβεσεν· οἷα δέ φασι τὰς ἀλκυόνων λοχείας
παραδεξαμένην τὴν θάλατταν ἐν χειμῶνι σῴζειν καὶ
συνεκτιθηνεῖσθαι, τοιαύτην ἀναχεαμένη καὶ περι-
στήσασα γαλήνην πραγμάτων ἀπόλεμον[1] καὶ ἄνοσον
καὶ ἀκίνδυνον καὶ ἄφοβον, νεοσταθεῖ δήμῳ καὶ
κραδαινομένῳ παρέσχε ῥιζῶσαι καὶ καταστῆσαι τὴν
πόλιν αὐξανομένην ἐν ἡσυχίᾳ βεβαίως καὶ ἀνεμπο-
δίστως. ὥσπερ γὰρ ὁλκὰς ἢ τριήρης ναυπηγεῖται
μὲν ὑπὸ πληγῶν καὶ βίας πολλῆς, σφύραις καὶ
ἥλοις ἀρασσομένη καὶ γομφώμασι καὶ πρίοσι καὶ
πελέκεσι, γενομένην δὲ στῆναι δεῖ καὶ παγῆναι

─────────────────────

[1] ἀπόλεμον Reiske and some mss. : καὶ ἀπόλεμον.

─────────────────────

[a] *Cf. Life of Numa*, chap. iv. (61 f ff.) ; Livy, i. 19. 5,

marvellous good Fortune guided the reign of Numa
which endured for so many years.[a] For the tale that a
certain Egeria, a dryad and a wise divinity, consorted
in love with the man, and helped him in instituting
and shaping the government of his State,[b] is perhaps
somewhat fabulous. For other mortals who are said
to have attained divine marriages and to have been
beloved of goddesses, men like Peleus and Anchises,
Orion and Emathion, by no means lived through their
lives in a satisfactory, or even painless, manner. On
the contrary, it appears likely that Numa had Good
Fortune as his true wife, counsellor, and colleague ;
and she took the city in charge when it was being
carried hither and yon amid the enmity and fierceness
of bordering tribes and neighbours, as in the midst of
turbulent billows of a troubled sea and was inflamed
by countless struggles and dissensions; and she calmed
those opposing passions and jealousies as though they
had been but gusts of wind. Even as they relate
that the sea, when it has received the brood of
halcyons in the stormy season, keeps them safe and
assists in their nurture, even such a calm in the affairs
of Rome, free from war or pestilence or danger or
terror, Fortune caused to overspread and surround
the city, and thus afforded the opportunity to a newly
settled and sorely shaken people to take root and to
establish their city on a firm foundation where it might
grow in quiet, securely and unhindered. It is as with a
merchantman or a trireme, which is constructed by
blows and with great violence, and is buffeted by
hammers and nails, bolts and saws and axes, and, when
it is completed, it must remain at rest and grow firm for

21. 3 ; Ovid, *Metamorphoses*, xv. 487 ; *Fasti*, iii. 261 ff. ;
Dionysius of Halicarnassus, *Roman Antiquities*, ii. 60. 5.
  [b] *Cf. Life of Numa*, chap. iv. (62 A).

σύμμετρον χρόνον, ἕως οἵ τε δεσμοὶ κάτοχοι γέ-
E νωνται καὶ συνήθειαν οἱ γόμφοι λάβωσιν· ἐὰν δὲ
ὑγροῖς ἔτι καὶ περιολισθάνουσι τοῖς ἁρμοῖς κατα-
σπασθῇ, πάντα χαλάσει διατιναχθέντα καὶ δέξεται
τὴν θάλατταν· οὕτω τὴν Ῥώμην ὁ μὲν πρῶτος
ἄρχων καὶ δημιουργὸς ἐξ ἀγρίων καὶ βοτήρων
ὥσπερ ἐκ δρυόχων κραταιῶν συνιστάμενος, οὐκ
ὀλίγους πόνους ἔσχεν οὐδὲ μικροῖς ἀντήρεισε πολέμοις καὶ κινδύνοις, ἐξ ἀνάγκης ἀμυνόμενος τοὺς
ἀνθισταμένους πρὸς τὴν γένεσιν καὶ ἵδρυσιν αὐτῆς.

Ὁ δὲ δεύτερος παραλαβὼν χρόνον ἔσχε[1] πῆξαι
καὶ βεβαιῶσαι τὴν αὔξησιν τῇ εὐτυχίᾳ, ἐπι-
λαβόμενος πολλῆς μὲν εἰρήνης πολλῆς δ᾽ ἡσυχίας.
F εἰ δὲ τότε Πορσίνας τις ἐπέβρισε Τυρρηνικὸν χάρακα
καὶ στρατόπεδον παραστήσας τείχεσιν ὑγροῖς ἔτι
καὶ κραδαινομένοις ἤ τις ἐκ Μαρσῶν ἀποστὰς ἀρειμάνιος δυνάστης ἢ Λευκανὸς ὑπὸ φθόνου καὶ φιλονεικίας, ἀνὴρ δύσερις καὶ πολεμοποιός, οἷος ὕστερον
Μουτίλος[2] ἢ Σίλων ὁ θρασὺς ἢ τὸ ἔσχατον Σύλλα
πάλαισμα Τελεσῖνος,[3] ὡς ἀφ᾽ ἑνὸς συνθήματος ὅλην
ἐξοπλίζων τὴν Ἰταλίαν, τὸν φιλόσοφον Νομᾶν
περιεσάλπιζε θύοντα καὶ προσευχόμενον, οὐκ ἂν
ἀντέσχον αἱ πρῶται τῆς πόλεως ἀρχαὶ πρὸς σάλον
322 καὶ κλύδωνα τοσοῦτον οὐδ᾽ εἰς εὐανδρίαν καὶ
πλῆθος ἐπέδωκαν· νῦν δ᾽ ἔοικε[4] τῆς πρὸς τοὺς

---

[1] ἔσχε] ἔπεσχε in nearly all mss. ἀπέσχε might be read.
[2] Μουτίλος Xylander: μουίλος.
[3] Τελεσῖνος, ὡς Basel ed. of 1542: ἢ τελεσῖνος ὅς.
[4] δ᾽ ἔοικε] δέ, ὡς ἔοικε in some mss. (δέ πως Reiske).

---

^a Is this a reminiscence of Plato, *Timaeus*, 81 в ; or of
Polybius, i. 38. 5 ?

a suitable period of time until its bonds hold tight and its fastenings have acquired affinity ; but if it be launched while its joinings are still damp and slippery, these will all be loosened when they are racked by the waves, and will admit the sea. Even so the first ruler and artificer of Rome, in organizing the city from rustics and shepherds, as though building up from a stout keel,[a] took upon himself no few labours, nor of slight moment were the wars and dangers that he withstood in warding off, of necessity, those who opposed the creation and foundation of Rome.

But he who was the second to take over the State gained time by good fortune to consolidate and make assured the enlargement of Rome ; for much peace did he secure for her and much quiet. But if at that time a Porsenna had pressed hard upon the city and had erected an Etruscan stockade and a camp beside the new walls which were still moist and unstable, or if from the Marsi had come some rebellious chief filled with warlike frenzy, or some Lucanian, incited by envy and love of strife, a man contentious and warlike, as later was Mutilus or the bold Silo [b] or Sulla's last antagonist, Telesinus,[c] arming all Italy at one preconcerted signal, as it were—if one of these had sounded his trumpets round about Numa, the lover of wisdom, while he was sacrificing and praying, the early beginnings of the City would not have been able to hold out against such a mighty surge and billow, nor would they ever have increased to such a goodly and numerous people. But as it is, it seems likely that the peace of Numa's reign was a provision to equip

---

[b] Cf. Life of Marius, chap. xxxiii. (424 D).

[c] Life of Sulla, chap. xxix. (470 D) ; Compar. of Lysander and Sulla, iv. (477 F).

(322) ὕστερον πολέμους παρασκευῆς ἐφόδιον Ῥωμαίοις
ἢ τότ' εἰρήνη γενέσθαι, καὶ καθάπερ ἀθλητὴς ὁ
δῆμος ἐκ τῶν κατὰ Ῥωμύλον ἀγώνων ἐν ἡσυχίᾳ
χρόνον ἐτῶν τριῶν καὶ τετταράκοντα σωμασκήσας
τὴν δύναμιν ἀξιόμαχον καταστῆσαι τοῖς ὕστερον
ἀντιταττομένοις. οὐδὲ γὰρ λιμὸν οὐδὲ λοιμὸν οὐδ'
ἀφορίαν γῆς οὐδ' ἀωρίαν τινὸς θέρους ἢ χειμῶνος
ἐν τῷ τότε χρόνῳ παραλυπῆσαι τὴν Ῥώμην λέγουσιν, ὡς οὐκ ἀνθρωπίνης εὐβουλίας ἀλλὰ θείας
Τύχης ἐπιτροπευούσης τῶν καιρῶν ἐκείνων. ἐ-
κλείσθη δ' οὖν τότε καὶ τὸ τοῦ Ἰανοῦ δίπυλον, ὃ
B πολέμου πύλην[1] καλοῦσιν· ἀνέῳγε μὲν γὰρ ὅταν ᾖ
πόλεμος, κλείεται δ' εἰρήνης γενομένης. Νομᾶ δ'
ἀποθανόντος ἀνεῴχθη τοῦ πρὸς Ἀλβανοὺς πολέμου
συρραγέντος. εἶτα μυρίων ἄλλων συνεχῶς ὑπο-
λαμβανόντων πάλιν δι' ἐτῶν ὀγδοήκοντα καὶ
τετρακοσίων ἐκλείσθη μετὰ τὸν πρὸς Καρχηδονίους πόλεμον εἰρήνης γενομένης Γαΐου Ἀτιλίου
καὶ Τίτου Μαλλίου[2] ὑπάτων. μετὰ δὲ τοῦτον τὸν
ἐνιαυτὸν αὖθις ἀνεῴχθη καὶ διέμειναν οἱ πόλεμοι
ἄχρι τῆς ἐν Ἀκτίῳ νίκης Καίσαρος· τότε δ' ἤργησε
τὰ Ῥωμαίων ὅπλα χρόνον οὐ πολύν· αἱ γὰρ ἀπὸ
C Καντάβρων ταραχαὶ καὶ Γαλατίας συρραγεῖσαι Γερ-
μανοῖς συνετάραξαν τὴν εἰρήνην. ἀλλὰ ταῦτα μὲν
εὐτυχίας τῆς Νομᾶ προσιστόρηται μαρτύρια.

10. Τὴν δὲ Τύχην καὶ οἱ μετ' ἐκεῖνον ἐθαύμασαν
βασιλεῖς ὡς πρωτόπολιν καὶ τιθηνὸν καὶ '' φερέ-

---

[1] πύλην Xylander: τύχην.
[2] Μαλλίου added by Xylander from *Life of Numa*, chap. xx.

them for their subsequent wars, and that the people, like an athlete, having, during a period of forty-three years following the contests of Romulus's time, trained themselves in quiet and made their strength staunch enough to cope in battle with those who later arrayed themselves against them. For they relate that no famine nor pestilence nor failure of crops nor any unseasonable occurrence in either summer or winter vexed Rome during that time, as if it were not wise human counsel, but divine Fortune that was Rome's guardian during those crucial days. Therefore at that time the double door of Janus's [a] temple was shut, which the Romans call the Portal of War; for it is open when there is war, but closed when peace has been made. But after Numa died it was opened, since the war with the Albans had broken out. Then countless other wars followed in continuous succession until again, after four hundred and eighty years, it was closed in the peace following the Punic War, when Gaius Atilius and Titus Manlius were consuls.[b] After this year it was again opened and the wars continued until Caesar's victory at Actium.[c] Then the arms of Rome were idle for a time, but not for long; for the tumults caused by the Cantabri and Gaul, breaking forth at the same time with the Germans, disturbed the peace. These facts are added to the record as proofs of Numa's good fortune.

10. And even the kings who succeeded Numa honoured Fortune as the head and foster-parent of

[a] Cf. Life of Numa, chap. xx. (73 A); Livy, i. 19. 2-7; Pliny, Natural History, xxxiv. 7. 33; Suetonius, Augustus, 22.

[b] In 235 B.C. after the First Punic War; references may be found in Pauly-Wissowa, Real-Encycl. xiv. 1207.

[c] In 31 B.C.

(322) πολιν '' τῆς Ῥώμης ἀληθῶς κατὰ Πίνδαρον.[1]
Σέρβιος δὲ Τύλλιος, ἀνὴρ τῶν βασιλέων μάλιστα
καὶ τὴν δύναμιν αὐξήσας τοῦ δήμου καὶ τὸ
πολίτευμα κοσμήσας καὶ τάξιν μὲν ἐπιθεὶς ταῖς
ψηφοφορίαις, τάξιν δὲ ταῖς στρατείαις, τιμητὴς δὲ
πρῶτος καὶ βίων ἐπίσκοπος καὶ σωφροσύνης γενόμενος καὶ δοκῶν ἀνδρειότατος εἶναι καὶ φρονι-
μώτατος, αὐτὸς ἑαυτὸν εἰς τὴν Τύχην ἀνῆπτε καὶ
ἀνεδεῖτο τὴν ἡγεμονίαν ἐξ ἐκείνης, ὥστε καὶ συνεῖναι δοκεῖν αὐτῷ τὴν Τύχην διά τινος θυρίδος

---

[1] After κατὰ Πίνδαρον the mss. have the following passage,
which seems to be repeated from 318 D-F, *supra*. Its excision
was first suggested by Wyttenbach, although others had
earlier noted the repetition: ἔξεστι δ' οὕτω θεωρεῖν. ἱερόν
ἐστιν Ἀρετῆς ἐν Ῥώμῃ τιμώμενον, ὃ Οὐιρτοῦτις αὐτοὶ καλοῦσιν,
ἀλλ' ὀψὲ καὶ μετὰ πολλοὺς χρόνους ἱδρυθὲν ὑπὸ Μαρκέλλου τοῦ
Συρακούσας ἑλόντος. ἔστι δὲ καὶ Γνώμης, ᾗ νὴ Δία Εὐβουλίας
νεώς, ἣν Μέντεμ καλοῦσιν, ἀλλὰ καὶ τοῦτο Σκαῦρος Αἰμίλιος περὶ
D τὰ Κιμβρικὰ τοῖς χρόνοις γεγονὼς καθιέρωσεν, ἤδη τότε λόγων καὶ
σοφισμάτων καὶ στωμυλίας Ἑλληνικῆς εἰς τὴν πόλιν παρεισρυείσης.
σοφίας δὲ ἔτι καὶ νῦν ἱερὸν οὐκ ἔχουσιν οὐδὲ σωφροσύνης οὐδὲ
καρτερίας οὐδὲ μεγαλοψυχίας· ἀλλὰ τά γε τῆς Τύχης ἱερὰ πάμπολλα
καὶ παλαιὰ καὶ λαμπρὰ τιμαῖς πᾶσιν, ὡς ἔπος εἰπεῖν, ἐνίδρυται καὶ
καταμέμεικται τοῖς ἐπιφανεστάτοις μέρεσι καὶ τόποις τῆς πόλεως.
καὶ τὸ μὲν τῆς ἀνδρείας Τύχης ἱερὸν ὑπὸ [ἀπὸ mss.] Μαρκίου
Ἄγκου τοῦ τετάρτου βασιλέως ἱδρυθὲν καὶ ὀνομασθὲν οὕτως, ὅτι
πλεῖστον ἀνδρείας ἡ τύχη [ἢ τύχης mss.] εἰς τὸ νικᾶν μετέσχηκε·
τὸ δὲ τῆς γυναικείας αὖθις ὑπὸ [ἀπὸ mss.] τῶν γυναικῶν αἳ
E Μάρκιον Κοριολᾶνον ἀπέστρεψαν ἐπάγοντα τῇ Ῥώμῃ πολεμίους
καθοσιωθὲν οὐδεὶς ἀγνοεῖ.

---

[a] Cf. Pausanias, iv. 30. 6.

[b] It is possible that in the mss. the next section, which
interrupts the historical sequence, is a copyist's error, being
perhaps copied from an earlier page of the archetype (*sc.*
318 D-F, *supra*) with some slight additions, changes, and
omissions by later copyists. Another theory, however, is

Rome and, as Pindar *a* has it, truly the " Prop of the State." *b*   And Servius Tullius, the man who of all the kings most increased the power of his people, and introduced a well-regulated government and imposed order upon both the holding of elections and military procedure, and became the first censor and overseer of the lives and decorum of the citizens, and held the highest repute for courage and wisdom, of his own initiative attached himself to Fortune and bound his sovereignty fast to her, with the result that it was even thought that Fortune consorted with him, descending into his chamber through a certain

possible: the section before us appeared in Plutarch's first sketch of the essay, and was later modified and completed in chap. v. (*supra*); Plutarch did not himself publish the essay, but after his death the first editor neglected to cancel the present passage (Bruhn and Stegmann.)   A translation follows :

" One may consider the matter thus : there is in Rome an honoured shrine of Virtue which they themselves call the shrine of *Virtus* ; but it was built late and after a considerable lapse of time by Marcellus, who captured Syracuse. There is also a shrine of Reason, or verily of Good Counsel, which they call *Mens* (Mind) ; but this also was dedicated by Aemilius Scaurus, who lived in the era of the Cimbrian Wars, at which time rhetoric and sophistry and Greek argumentation had already found their way into the City. But even now they have no temple of Wisdom or Prudence or Constancy or Magnanimity.   But of Fortune there are very many ancient and splendid temples built with every honour, one might say, and interspersed throughout the most conspicuous districts and localities of the City.   The shrine of the Men's Fortune was built by Ancus Marcius, the fourth king, and so named because Fortune has the largest share with Manly Fortitude for winning the victory. And again, that the shrine of the Women's Fortune was dedicated by the women who turned back Marcius Coriolanus when he was leading enemies against Rome, there is no one who does not know."

PLUTARCH'S MORALIA

καταβαίνουσαν εἰς τὸ δωμάτιον, ἣν¹ νῦν Φενέστελλαν²
F πύλην καλοῦσιν. ἱδρύσατο δ᾽ οὖν Τύχης ἱερὸν ἐν
μὲν Καπετωλίῳ τὸ τῆς Πριμιγενείας λεγομένης,
ὃ πρωτογόνου τις ἂν ἑρμηνεύσειε· καὶ τὸ τῆς
Ὀψεκουέντις, ἣν οἱ μὲν πειθήνιον οἱ δὲ μειλίχιον
εἶναι νομίζουσι. μᾶλλον δὲ τὰς Ῥωμαϊκὰς ἐάσας
ὀνομασίας Ἑλληνιστὶ τὰς δυνάμεις τῶν ἱδρυμάτων
πειράσομαι καταριθμήσασθαι. καὶ γὰρ ἰδίας Τύχης
ἱερόν ἐστιν ἐν Παλατίῳ, καὶ τὸ τῆς ἰξευτρίας, εἰ
καὶ γελοῖον, ἀλλ᾽ ἔχον ἐκ μεταφορᾶς ἀναθεώρησιν,
οἷον ἑλκούσης τὰ πόρρω καὶ κρατούσης συμπροσ-
ισχόμενα. παρὰ δὲ τὴν Μουσκῶσαν³ καλουμένην
323 κρήνην ἔτι παρθένου Τύχης ἱερόν ἐστι καὶ⁴ ἐν
Αἰσκυλίαις⁵ ἐπιστρεφομένης· ἐν δὲ τῷ μακρῷ
στενωπῷ Τύχης βωμὸς εὐέλπιδος⁶· ἔστι δὲ καὶ παρὰ
τὸν τῆς Ἀφροδίτης ἐπιταλαρίου⁷ βωμὸν ἄρρενος
Τύχης ἕδος. ἄλλαι τε μυρίαι Τύχης τιμαὶ καὶ
ἐπικλήσεις, ὧν τὰς πλείστας Σερούιος κατέστησεν,
εἰδὼς ὅτι " μεγάλη ῥοπή, μᾶλλον δ᾽ ὅλον⁸ ἡ Τύχη
παρὰ πάντ᾽ ἐστὶ τὰ τῶν ἀνθρώπων πράγματα,"
καὶ μάλιστά γ᾽ αὐτοῦ⁹ δι᾽ εὐτυχίαν ἐξ αἰχμαλώτου
καὶ πολεμίου γένους εἰς βασιλείαν προαχθέντος.
τοῦ γὰρ Κορνικλάνων ἄστεος ἁλόντος ὑπὸ Ῥω-

---

¹ ἣν F.C.B. (seems to be demanded by 273 B): ὅ.
² Φενέστελλαν Hatzidakis : φαινεστέλλαν.
³ Μουσκῶσαν Basel ed. of 1542 : μουσικῶσαν.
⁴ καὶ added by Hutten.
⁵ Αἰσκυλίαις Meziriacus : ἀβησκύμαις.
⁶ εὐέλπιδος Xylander : εὐέλπιδος ἢ ὡς ἐλπίδος.
⁷ ἐπιταλαρίου] ἐπιταλασίου Bernardakis.
⁸ δ᾽ ὅλον] δὲ τὸ ὅλον in Demosthenes mss.
⁹ αὐτοῦ F.C.B. : αὑτοῦ.

window which they now call the Porta Fenestella.[a]
He, accordingly, built on the Capitoline a temple of
Fortune which is now called the Temple of Fortuna
Primigenia [b] (which one might translate as " First-
Born ") and the Temple of Fortuna Obsequens,[c]
which some think means " obedient " and others
" gracious." However, I prefer to abandon the Latin
nomenclature, and shall endeavour to enumerate
in Greek the different functions of the shrines of
Fortune. There is, in fact, a shrine of Private Fortune
on the Palatine, and the shrine of the Fowler's
Fortune which, even though it be a ridiculous name,
yet gives reason for reflexion on metaphorical
grounds, as if she attracted far-away objects and held
them fast when they come into contact with her.
Beside the Mossy Spring, as it is called, there is even
yet a temple of Virgin Fortune ; and on the Esquiline
a shrine of Regardful [d] Fortune. In the Angiportus
Longus there is an altar of Fortune of Good Hope ;
and there is also beside the altar of Venus of the
Basket a shrine of the Men's Fortune. And there
are countless other honours and appellations of
Fortune, the greater part of which Servius instituted ;
for he knew that " Fortune is of great moment, or
rather, she is everything in human affairs," [e] and particularly since he himself, through good fortune, had
been promoted from the family of a captive enemy
to the kingship. For, when the town of Corniculum

[a] Cf. 273 B, supra.
[b] Cf. 281 E and 289 B-C, supra ; Cicero, De Legibus,
ii. 11. 28 ; Livy, xxix. 36. 8, xxxiv. 53. 5.
[c] With this and the following passage 281 D-F, supra,
should be carefully compared.
[d] Is this meant to be a translation of Redux ?
[e] A literal quotation from Demosthenes, Olynthiac ii. 22.

(323) μαίων, Ὀκρησία[1] παρθένος αἰχμάλωτος, ἧς οὐδὲ
B τὴν ὄψιν οὐδὲ τὸν τρόπον ἠμαύρωσεν ἡ Τύχη,
δοθεῖσα Τανακυλλίδι[2] τῇ Ταρκυνίου γυναικὶ τοῦ
βασιλέως ἐδούλευσε· καὶ πελάτης τις εἶχεν αὐτήν,
οὓς κλιέντης Ῥωμαῖοι καλοῦσιν· ἐκ τούτων ἐγε-
γόνει Σερούιος. οἱ δ' οὔ φασιν, ἀλλὰ παρθένον τὴν
Ὀκρησίαν[1] ἀπάργματα καὶ λοιβὴν ἑκάστοτε λαμβά-
νουσαν ἀπὸ τῆς βασιλικῆς τραπέζης ἐπὶ τὴν ἑστίαν
κομίζειν· καί ποτε τυχεῖν μὲν αὐτήν, ὥσπερ εἰώθει,
τῷ πυρὶ τὰς ἀπαρχὰς ἐπιβάλλουσαν, αἰφνίδιον δὲ
τῆς φλογὸς μαρανθείσης μόριον ἀνδρὸς ἀνατεῖναι
γόνιμον ἐκ τῆς ἑστίας, καὶ τοῦτο τὴν κόρην τῇ
C Τανακυλλίδι[2] φράσαι μόνῃ περίφοβον γενομένην.
τὴν δὲ συνετὴν οὖσαν καὶ φρενήρη κοσμῆσαί τε
τὴν κόρην ὅσα νύμφαις πρέπει καὶ συγκαθεῖρξαι τῷ
φάσματι, θεῖον ἡγουμένην. οἱ μὲν ἥρωος οἰκουροῦ
λέγουσιν, οἱ δ' Ἡφαίστου τὸν ἔρωτα τοῦτον γενέσθαι. τίκτεται γοῦν[3] Σερούιος, καὶ βρέφους ὄντος
ἡ κεφαλὴ σέλας ἀστραπῇ παραπλήσιον ἀπήστραψεν.
οἱ δὲ περὶ Ἀντίαν οὐχ οὕτω λέγουσιν, ἀλλὰ τυχεῖν
μὲν τῷ Σερουίῳ τὴν γυναῖκα Γεγανίαν[4] θνήσκου-
σαν, αὐτὸν δὲ τῆς μητρὸς παρούσης εἰς ὕπνον ἐκ
δυσθυμίας καὶ λύπης ἀποκλιθῆναι· καὶ καθεύδοντος
αὐτοῦ ταῖς γυναιξὶν ὀφθῆναι τὸ πρόσωπον αὐτοῦ
D πυρὶ περιλαμπόμενον· ὅπερ ἦν μαρτύριον αὐτῷ τῆς
ἐκ πυρὸς γενέσεως, σημεῖον δὲ χρηστὸν ἐπὶ τὴν
ἀπροσδόκητον ἡγεμονίαν, ἧς ἔτυχε μετὰ τὴν Ταρ-

---

[1] Ὀκρησία] Ὀκρισία in Dionysius Hal.
[2] Τανακυλλίδι Basel ed. of 1542, and here and elsewhere sometimes in mss.: ταρκυλλίδι.
[3] γοῦν E. Capps: δ' οὖν.
[4] Γεγανίαν Basel ed. of 1542: γετανίαν.

was taken by the Romans, a captive maiden Ocrisia,[a] whose fortune could not obscure either her beauty or her character, was given to be a slave to Tanaquil, the wife of king Tarquin ; and a certain dependent, one of those whom the Romans call *clientes*, had her to wife ; from these parents Servius was born. Others deny this, but assert that Ocrisia was a maiden who took the first-fruits and the libations on all occasions from the royal table and brought them to the hearth ; and once on a time when she chanced, as usual, to be casting the offerings upon the fire, suddenly, as the flames died down, the member of a man rose up out of the hearth ; and this the girl, greatly frightened, told to Tanaquil only. Now Tanaquil was an intelligent and understanding woman, and she decked the maiden in garments such as become a bride, and shut her up in the room with the apparition, for she judged it to be of a divine nature. Some declare that this love was manifested by the Lar of the house, others that it was by Vulcan. At any rate, it resulted in the birth of Servius, and, while he was still a child, his head shone with a radiance very like the gleam of lightning. But Antias[b] and his school say not so, but relate that when Servius's wife Gegania lay dying, in the presence of his mother he fell into a sleep from dejection and grief ; and as he slept, his face was seen by the women to be surrounded by the gleam of fire. This was a token of his birth from fire and an excellent sign pointing to his unexpected accession to the kingship, which he gained after the death of Tarquin, by

[a] *Cf.* Dionysius of Halicarnassus, *Roman Antiquities*, iv. 1 ; Ovid, *Fasti*, vi. 627 ff. ; Livy, i. 39 ; Pliny, *Natural History*, xxxvi. 27. 204.

[b] Peter, *Frag. Hist. Rom.* p. 154, Valerius Antias, Frag. 12.

(323) κυνίου τελευτὴν Τανακυλλίδος σπουδασάσης. ἐπεὶ
πάντων γε τῶν βασιλέων πρὸς μοναρχίαν οὗτος
ἀφυέστατος δοκεῖ γενέσθαι καὶ ἀπροθυμότατος, ὅς
γε τὴν βασιλείαν ἀποθέσθαι διανοηθεὶς ἐκωλύθη·
τελευτῶσα γάρ, ὡς ἔοικεν, ἐξώρκωσε τοῦτον ἐμ-
μεῖναι τῇ ἀρχῇ καὶ προθέσθαι[1] τὴν πάτριον Ῥωμαίων πολιτείαν.[2] οὕτως ἡ Σερουίου βασιλεία
παντάπασι τῆς Τύχης, ἣν ἔλαβέ τε μὴ προσδοκήσας
καὶ μὴ βουλόμενος διεφύλαξεν.

E   11. Ἀλλ' ἵνα μὴ δοκῶμεν ὥσπερ εἰς τόπον
ἀμαυρὸν τὸν παλαιὸν χρόνον ἐκ τῶν λαμπρῶν καὶ
ἐναργῶν τεκμηρίων φεύγειν καὶ ὑποχωρεῖν, φέρε τοὺς
βασιλεῖς ἐάσαντες ἐπὶ τὰς γνωριμωτάτας πράξεις
καὶ τοὺς ἐπιφανεστάτους πολέμους τὸν λόγον μετα-
γάγωμεν, ἐν[3] οἷς πολλὴν τόλμαν καὶ ἀνδρείαν εἶναι[3]

αἰδῶ τε συνεργὸν ἀρετᾶς δοριμάχου,

ὥς φησι Τιμόθεος, τίς οὐκ ἂν ὁμολογήσειεν; ἡ δ'
εὔροια τῶν πραγμάτων καὶ τὸ ῥόθιον τῆς εἰς
τοσαύτην δύναμιν καὶ αὔξησιν ὁρμῆς, οὐ χερσὶν
ἀνθρώπων οὐδ' ὁρμαῖς προχωροῦσαν[4] ἡγεμονίαν,
θείᾳ δὲ πομπῇ καὶ πνεύματι Τύχης ἐπιταχυνο-
F μένην,[5] ἐπιδείκνυται τοῖς ὀρθῶς λογιζομένοις. τρόπαια τροπαίοις ἐπανίσταται καὶ θρίαμβοι θριάμβοις
ἀπαντῶσι, καὶ τὸ πρῶτον αἷμα τῶν ὅπλων ἔτι
θερμὸν ἀποκλύζεται τῷ δευτέρῳ καταλαμβανό-

---

[1] προθέσθαι F.C.B.; μὴ προέσθαι Xylander: προσέσθαι.
[2] πολιτείαν early edd.: πομπείαν, πομπήν.
[3] ἐν and εἶναι added by F.C.B.
[4] προχωροῦσαν Reiske, confirmed by some mss.: προσ-
χωροῦσαν.
[5] ἐπιταχυνομένην Reiske and one late ms.: ἐπιταχυνομένης.

[a] Cf. 273 c, supra.

the zealous assistance of Tanaquil.[a]   Inasmuch as he
of all kings is thought to have been naturally the
least suited to monarchy and the least desirous of it,
he who was minded to resign the kingship,[b] but was
prevented from doing so ; for it appears that Tanaquil
on her death-bed made him swear that he would
remain in power and would ever set before him
the ancestral Roman form of government.   Thus to
Fortune wholly belongs the kingship of Servius, which
he received contrary to his expectations and retained
against his will.

11. That we may not, however, appear to be
retreating and withdrawing from illuminating and
perspicuous testimonials into the dim past, as into a
place of darkness, let us now leave the kings and
transfer our discourse to the most notable deeds
and the most celebrated wars.   And in these wars,
who would not acknowledge that much daring and
courage was needed and also, as Timotheüs[c] has it,

> Shame, the helpmate of warring Valour ?

Yet the smooth flow of events and the impelling
swiftness of Rome's progress to so high a pinnacle of
power and expansion demonstrates to all who reason
aright that the progress of Rome's sovereignty was
not brought about by the handiwork and urging of
human beings, but was speeded on its way by divine
escort and the fair wind of Fortune.   Trophy upon
trophy arises, triumph meets triumph, and the first
blood, while still warm on their arms, is overtaken
and washed away by a second flood.   They count

[b] *Cf.* Livy, i. 48. 9 ; Dionysius of Halicarnassus, *Roman
Antiquities*, iv. 40. 3.
  [c] From the *Persians*: Frag. 14, ed. Wilamowitz; *cf.
Moralia*, 32 D, and Edmonds, *Lyra Graeca*, iii. p. 307.

μενον. τὰς δὲ νίκας ἀριθμοῦσιν οὐ νεκρῶν πλήθει
καὶ λαφύρων, ἀλλὰ βασιλείαις αἰχμαλώτοις καὶ
δεδουλωμένοις ἔθνεσι καὶ νήσοις καὶ ἠπείροις προσ-
οριζομέναις¹ τῷ μεγέθει τῆς ἡγεμονίας. μιᾷ μάχῃ
Φίλιππος ἀπέβαλε Μακεδονίαν,² μιᾷ πληγῇ παρ-
εχώρησεν Ἀντίοχος Ἀσίας, ἅπαξ Καρχηδόνιοι σφα-
324 λέντες ἀπώλεσαν Λιβύην. εἷς ἀνὴρ μιᾶς ὁρμῇ στρατιᾶς Ἀρμενίαν προσεκτήσατο, Πόντον, Εὔξεινον,
Συρίαν, Ἀραβίαν, Ἀλβανούς, Ἴβηρας, τὰ μέχρι
Καυκάσου καὶ Ὑρκανῶν· καὶ τρὶς αὐτὸν ὁ περιρρέων
τὴν οἰκουμένην Ὠκεανὸς εἶδε νικῶντα. Νομάδας
μὲν ἐν Λιβύῃ μέχρι τῶν μεσημβρινῶν ἀνέκοψεν³
ἠιόνων,⁴ Ἰβηρίαν δὲ Σερτωρίῳ συννοσήσασαν ἄχρι
τῆς Ἀτλαντικῆς κατεστρέψατο θαλάττης· τοὺς δ᾽
Ἀλβανῶν βασιλεῖς διωκομένους περὶ⁵ τὸ Κάσπιον
πέλαγος ἔστησε. ταῦτα πάντα κατώρθωσε δημοσίᾳ
τύχῃ χρώμενος, εἶθ᾽ ὑπὸ τῆς ἰδίας ἀνετράπη μοίρας.

B   Ὁ δὲ Ῥωμαίων μέγας δαίμων οὐκ ἐφήμερος
πνεύσας οὐδὲ καιρὸν ἀκμάσας βραχὺν ὡς ὁ Μακεδόνων,⁶ οὐδὲ χερσαῖος μόνον ὡς ὁ Λακώνων οὐδ᾽
ἐνάλιος ὡς ὁ Ἀθηναίων, οὐδ᾽ ὀψὲ κινηθεὶς ὡς ὁ
Περσῶν, οὐδὲ ταχὺ παυσάμενος ὡς ὁ Καρχη-
δονίων⁷· ἀλλ᾽ ἄνωθεν ἐκ πρώτων γενέσεων τῇ πόλει
συνηβήσας καὶ συναυξηθεὶς καὶ συμπολιτευσάμενος,

---

¹ προσοριζομέναις Emperius : προσορμιζομέναις.
² Φίλιππος . . . Μακεδονίαν Basel ed. of 1542 : φίλιππον
. . . μακεδονία.   ³ ἀνέκοψεν Reiske : ἀπέκοψεν.
⁴ ἠιόνων] θινῶν Kronenberg.   ⁵ περὶ Reiske : ἐπὶ.
⁶ Μακεδόνων Bernardakis : μακεδών.
⁷ Καρχηδονίων Bernardakis ; Φωκέων S. A. Naber : Κολο-
φωνίων.

their victories, not by the multitude of corpses and spoils, but by captive kingdoms, by nations enslaved, by islands and continents added to their mighty realm. In one battle Philip lost Macedonia, with one stroke Antiochus was forced to withdraw from Asia, by one defeat the Carthaginians lost Africa. One man [a] in the swift onset of one campaign added to the Roman dominion Armenia, Pontus, the Euxine, Syria, Arabia, the Albanians, the Iberians, and all the territory to the Caucasus and the Hyrcanians ; thrice did the Ocean which encircles the inhabited world see him victorious, for in Africa he drove back the Numidians [b] to the strands of the southern sea ; even as far as the Atlantic Ocean, he subdued Iberia,[c] which had joined in the distemper of Sertorius ; the kings of the Albanians were pursued until he brought them to a halt near the Caspian Sea.[d] All these successes he won through enjoying the Fortune of the Roman commonwealth ; then he was overthrown by his own fate.

But the great Guardian Spirit of Rome sent a favouring breeze, not for one day, nor at its height for a brief time only, like the Macedonian, nor but a land breeze, like the Spartan, nor but a sea breeze, like the Athenian, nor late to rise, like the Persian, nor quick to cease, like the Carthaginian [e] ; but this Spirit, from its first creation, grew in maturity, in might, and

---

[a] *Cf. Life of Pompey*, chap. xlv. (642 E); Housman on Manilius iv. 52.

[b] *Cf. Life of Pompey*, chap. xii. (624 F).

[c] *Ibid.* chaps. xviii.-xxi. (627 D–629 C).

[d] *Ibid.* chap. xxxv. (637 F).

[e] "Carthaginian" is an emendation, the MSS. having "Colophonians" (*cf.* Thucydides, iii. 37). Almost any reasonable guess might serve as well.

(324) καὶ παραμείνας βέβαιος ἐν γῇ καὶ θαλάττῃ καὶ
πολέμοις καὶ εἰρήνῃ καὶ πρὸς βαρβάρους καὶ πρὸς
Ἕλληνας. οὗτος Ἀννίβαν τὸν Καρχηδόνιον, φθόνῳ
καὶ ταῖς πολιτικαῖς δυσμενείαις[1] μηδενὸς οἴκοθεν
C ἐπιρρέοντος, ὥσπερ χείμαρρον ἐξέχεε καὶ κατ-
ανήλωσε περὶ τὴν Ἰταλίαν. οὗτος τὸ Κίμβρων
καὶ τὸ Τευτόνων στράτευμα μεγάλοις διαστήμασι
τόπων καὶ χρόνων ἐχώρισε καὶ διέσπασεν, ἵν᾽
ἀρκέσῃ Μάριος ἑκατέροις ἀνὰ μέρος μαχόμενος,
καὶ μὴ συμπεσοῦσαι τριάκοντα μυριάδες ἀνδρῶν
ἀηττήτων καὶ ἀμάχων ὅπλων ὁμοῦ κατακλύσωσι
τὴν Ἰταλίαν. διὰ τοῦτον[2] Ἀντίοχος μὲν ἠσχολεῖτο
πολεμουμένου Φιλίππου, Φίλιππος δὲ κινδυνεύοντος
Ἀντιόχου προηττημένος ἔπιπτε· Μιθριδάτην δέ,
τοῦ Μαρσικοῦ πολέμου τὴν Ῥώμην ἐπιφλέγοντος,
οἱ Σαρματικοὶ καὶ Βασταρνικοὶ πόλεμοι κατεῖχον·
D Τιγράνην δὲ Μιθριδάτου λαμπροῦ μὲν ὄντος ὑπόνοια
καὶ φθόνος ἐχώριζεν, ἡττωμένῳ δ᾽ ἀνέμειξεν
ἑαυτὸν συναπολέσθαι.

12. Τί δ᾽ οὐχὶ καὶ περὶ τὰς μεγίστας συμφορὰς
ὤρθου τὴν πόλιν ἡ Τύχη; Κελτῶν μὲν περὶ τὸ
Καπετώλιον στρατοπεδευόντων καὶ πολιορκούντων
τὴν ἀκρόπολιν,

    νοῦσον ἀνὰ στρατὸν ὦρσε κακήν, ὀλέκοντο δὲ
        λαοί·

τὴν δὲ νυκτερινὴν ἔφοδον αὐτῶν, λεληθότων πάντας

---

[1] δυσμενείαις] ἔχθραις or χρείαις in other mss.
[2] τοῦτον Reiske and Wyttenbach, and confirmed by a few
mss.: τοῦτο.

---

[a] Cf. Life of Marius, chap. xv. (414 в).
[b] Cf. Life of Flamininus, chap. ix. (374 в); it is interesting to find a critical modern historian interpreting these events

in polity together with the City, and remained constant to it on land and on sea, in war and in peace, against foreigners, against Greeks. This it was that dissipated and exhausted in the confines of Italy, like a mountain torrent, Hannibal the Carthaginian, since no fresh aid flowed to him from home because of jealousy and political enmities. This it was that separated and kept apart by great intervals of space and time the armies of the Cimbri and of the Teutons, that Marius[a] might avail to fight each of them in turn, and that three hundred thousand men of irresistible and invincible arms might not simultaneously invade and overwhelm Italy. Through the agency of this Spirit Antiochus was fully occupied while war was being waged against Philip,[b] and Philip had been vanquished and was falling when Antiochus was making his venture ; the Sarmatian and Bastarnian wars restrained Mithridates[c] during the time when the Marsian war was blazing up against Rome ; suspicion and jealousy kept Tigranes[d] from Mithridates while Mithridates was brilliantly successful, but he joined himself to Mithridates only to perish with him in defeat.

12. And why not admit that Fortune also retrieved the city in times of the greatest disaster ? When the Gauls were encamped round about the Capitol and were besieging the citadel,

> Baneful the plague that she brought on the host, and the people were dying.[e]

And as for the Gauls' nocturnal assault, though they

in almost the same words as Plutarch : see M. Holleaux in the *Cambridge Ancient History*, vol. viii. p. 225.

[c] *Cf.* Appian, *Mithridatica*, 15, 69.

[d] *Cf. Life of Lucullus*, chap. xxii. (505 F–506 A).

[e] Homer, *Il.* i. 10.

(324) ἀνθρώπους, ἡ Τύχη καὶ ταὐτόματον ἔκπυστον
ἐποίησε γενέσθαι.

Περὶ ἧς κἂν βραχεῖ πλείω διελθεῖν ἴσως οὐκ
ἄκαιρόν ἐστι. μετὰ τὴν ἐπ᾽ Ἀλλίᾳ[1] ποταμῷ Ῥωμαίων μεγάλην ἧτταν οἱ μὲν εἰς Ῥώμην κατ-
E άραντες ἀπὸ[2] τῆς φυγῆς καὶ ταραχῆς συνανα-
πλήσαντες τὸν δῆμον ἐξεπτόησαν καὶ διεσκέδασαν,
ὀλίγων εἰς τὸ Καπετώλιον ἀνασκευασαμένων καὶ
διακαρτερούντων. οἱ δ᾽ εὐθὺς ἀπὸ τῆς τροπῆς εἰς
Βηίους συναθροισθέντες ᾑροῦντο δικτάτωρα Φού-
ριον Κάμιλλον, ὃν εὐτυχῶν μὲν καὶ ὑψαυχενῶν ὁ
δῆμος ἀπεσείσατο καὶ κατέβαλε, δίκῃ περιπεσόντα
δημοσίων κλοπῶν· πτήξας δὲ καὶ ταπεινωθεὶς
ἀνεκαλεῖτο μετὰ τὴν ἧτταν, ἐγχειρίζων καὶ παρα-
διδοὺς ἀνυπεύθυνον ἡγεμονίαν. ἵν᾽ οὖν μὴ καιρῷ
δοκῇ νόμῳ δὲ λαμβάνειν[3] ὁ ἀνήρ, μηδ᾽, ὡς ἀπ-
F εγνωκὼς τὴν πόλιν, ὅπλοις ἀρχαιρεσιάζῃ τὰ[4] τοῦ
στρατοῦ σποράδος καὶ πλάνητος, ἔδει τοὺς ἐν
Καπετωλίῳ βουλευτὰς ἐπιψηφίσασθαι τὴν τῶν
στρατιωτῶν γνώμην μαθόντας. ἦν οὖν Γάιος
Πόντιος ἀνὴρ ἀγαθός, καὶ τῶν δεδογμένων αὐτάγγελος ὑποστὰς ἔσεσθαι τοῖς ἐν Καπετωλίῳ μέγαν
ἀνεδέξατο κίνδυνον· ἡ γὰρ ὁδὸς ἦν διὰ τῶν πολεμίων κύκλῳ φυλακαῖς καὶ χάρακι τὴν ἄκραν περι-

---

[1] ἐπ᾽ Ἀλλίᾳ (Ἀλλίᾳ) Basel ed. of 1542: ἐν παλλίᾳ.
[2] ἀπὸ Reiske: ὑπὸ.   [3] λαμβάνειν] λαγχάνειν Patzig.
[4] ἀρχαιρεσιάζῃ τὰ] ἀρχαιρεσιάζηται Madvig.

---

[a] Cf. Life of Camillus, chap. xviii. (137 E); Livy, v.
35-38.
[b] Cf. ibid. chap. xx. (138 F); Livy, v. 39-40.
[c] Cf. Life of Camillus, chap. xii. (134 F).

were noticed by none, yet Fortune and Chance brought about the discovery.

Concerning this assault of the Gauls it will perhaps not be unseasonable to give some additional details, however briefly. After the great defeat of the Romans at the river Allia,[a] some in their flight found a haven in Rome and filled the people with consternation and terror, and caused them to scatter far and wide, although a few went to the Capitol and prepared to stand a siege.[b] Others, immediately after their defeat, gathered together at Veii and appointed as dictator Furius Camillus, whom the people in their prosperity and lofty pride had rejected and deposed because he had become involved in a suit concerning the appropriation of public property.[c] But now, cowed and humbled after their defeat, they were for recalling him, and offered to hand over to him the supreme command, accountable to no one. Accordingly, that he might not be thought to be obtaining office because of the crisis, but in accordance with the law, and that he should not, as if he had given up all hope for the city, be elected by soldiery in a canvass of the remnants of the army, now scattered and wandering, it was necessary that the senators on the Capitoline should vote upon the matter after they had been informed of the decision of the soldiers. Now there was a certain Gaius Pontius,[d] a brave man, who, by volunteering personally to report these resolutions to the Senate on the Capitol, took upon himself great danger. For the way led through the midst of the enemy, who encompassed the citadel with sentries and

---

[d] *Ibid.* chaps. xxv.-xxvii. (141 D–143 A); Livy v. 46. 47; Dionysius of Halicarnassus, *Roman Antiquities*, xiii. 7.

ἐχόντων. ὡς οὖν ἐπὶ τὸν ποταμὸν ἦλθε νύκτωρ,
325 φελλοὺς πλατεῖς ὑποστερνισάμενος καὶ τὸ σῶμα τῇ
κουφότητι τοῦ ὀχήματος παραθέμενος ἀφῆκε τῷ
ῥόῳ· τυχὼν δὲ πράου καὶ σχολαίως ὑποφέροντος
ἥψατο τῆς ἀντιπέρας ὄχθης ἀσφαλῶς, καὶ ἀποβὰς
ἐχώρει πρὸς τὸ τῶν φώτων διάκενον, τῷ τε[1] σκότει
καὶ τῇ σιωπῇ τὴν ἐρημίαν τεκμαιρόμενος· ἐμφὺς δὲ
τῷ κρημνῷ, καὶ ταῖς δεχομέναις τὴν ἐπίβασιν καὶ
παρεχούσαις ἀντίληψιν ἐγκλίσεσι καὶ περιαγωγαῖς
καὶ τραχύτησι τῆς πέτρας παραδοὺς ἑαυτὸν καὶ
ἐπερεισάμενος ἐξίκετο πρὸς τὸ ἄνω πέτρας[2] καὶ
ἀναληφθεὶς ὑπὸ τῶν προφυλάκων ἐδήλωσε τοῖς ἔσω
B τὰ δεδογμένα· καὶ λαβὼν τὸ ψήφισμα πάλιν ᾤχετο
πρὸς τὸν Κάμιλλον.

Ἡμέρας δὲ τῶν βαρβάρων τις ἄλλως τὸν τόπον
περιιὼν ὡς εἶδε τοῦτο μὲν ἴχνη ποδῶν ἀκρώνυχα
καὶ περιολισθήσεις, τοῦτο δ' ἀποτριβὰς καὶ περι-
κλάσεις τῆς ἐπιβλαστανούσης τοῖς γεώδεσι πόας
ὁλκούς τε σώματος πλαγίους καὶ ἀπερείσεις,[3]
ἔφραζε τοῖς ἄλλοις. οἱ δὲ δείκνυσθαι τὴν ὁδὸν
αὐτοῖς[4] ὑπὸ τῶν πολεμίων νομίζοντες ἐπεχείρουν
ἁμιλλᾶσθαι, καὶ τῆς νυκτὸς τὸ ἐρημότατον δια-
φυλάξαντες ἀνέβησαν λαθόντες οὐ μόνον τοὺς φύλακας, ἀλλὰ καὶ τοὺς συνεργοὺς καὶ[5] προκοίτους
τῆς φρουρᾶς κύνας ὕπνῳ κρατηθέντας.

C Οὐ μὴν ἠπόρησεν ἡ τῆς Ῥώμης Τύχη φωνῆς
κακὸν τοσοῦτο μηνῦσαι καὶ φράσαι δυναμένης.
χῆνες ἱεροὶ περὶ τὸν νεὼν τῆς Ἥρας ἐτρέφοντο

---

[1] τε Reiske, confirmed by mss.: τε γάρ.

[2] ἄνω πέτρας F.C.B.; τὰ ἄνω τῆς πέτρας Emperius; ἀντί-
φραγμα (from the Life of Camillus, chaps. xx. and xxv.)
Kronenberg: ἀντιπέρας.   [3] ἀπερείσεις] ἐπερείσεις Reiske.

[4] αὐτοῖς Nachstädt: αὐτοῖς.   [5] καὶ Pohlenz: καὶ τοὺς.

palisades. When, accordingly, he had come by night to the river, he bound broad strips of cork beneath his breast and, entrusting his body to the buoyancy of this support, committed himself to the stream. Encountering a gentle current which bore him slowly down stream, he reached the opposite bank in safety, and, climbing out of the river, advanced toward the section void of lights, inferring from the darkness and quiet that no one was there. Clinging to the precipitous cliff and entrusting himself to the support of sloping and circuitous ways and jagged surfaces of the rock which would allow a foothold or afford a clutch for his hand, he reached the top of the rock ; he was received by the sentries, and made known to those within the decision of the army, and having obtained the decree of the Senate, he returned again to Camillus.

The next day one of the barbarians was wandering idly about this place, when he saw in one spot prints of feet and marks of slipping, and in another the bruising and tearing off of the grass, which grew on the earth of the cliff, and marks of the zigzag dragging and pulling up of a body ; and this he told to the others. They, thinking that the way was pointed out to them by their enemies, attempted to rival them ; and waiting till the very dead of night, they made the ascent, unnoticed not only by the sentinels, but also by the dogs which shared guard duty and formed the outpost, but then were overcome by sleep.

Rome's Fortune, however, did not lack a voice capable of revealing and declaring such a great mischance. Sacred geese [a] were kept near the temple of Juno for

***

[a] *Cf.* 287 c, *supra.*

(325) θεραπεύοντες τὴν θεόν. φύσει μὲν οὖν τὸ ζῷον
εὐθορύβητόν ἐστι καὶ ψοφοδεές· τότε δέ, συντόνου
περὶ τοὺς ἔνδον οὔσης ἀπορίας ἀμελουμένων αὐτῶν,
λεπτὸς ἦν καὶ λιμώδης ὁ ὕπνος, ὥστ' εὐθὺς ᾔσθοντο
τῶν πολεμίων ὑπερφανέντων τῆς στεφάνης καὶ
καταβοῶντες ἰταμῶς προσεφέροντο, καὶ τῇ τῶν
ὅπλων ὄψει μᾶλλον ἐκταραττόμενοι κλαγγῆς δια-
τόρου καὶ τραχείας ἐνεπεπλήκεσαν τὸν τόπον· ὑφ'
D ἧς ἀναστάντες οἱ Ῥωμαῖοι καὶ συμφρονήσαντες τὸ
γενόμενον ἐώσαντο καὶ κατεκρήμνισαν τοὺς πολεμίους. πομπεύει δὲ μέχρι νῦν ἐπὶ μνήμῃ τῶν τότε
συμπτωμάτων[1] κύων μὲν ἀνεσταυρωμένος, χὴν δὲ
μάλα σεμνῶς ἐπὶ στρωμνῆς πολυτελοῦς καὶ φορείου
καθήμενος.

Ἡ δ' ὄψις ἐπιδείκνυται Τύχης ἰσχὺν καὶ πρὸς
ἅπαν εὐπορίαν ἐκ τῶν παραλόγων, ὅταν τι πραγ-
ματεύηται καὶ στρατηγῇ, νοῦν μὲν ἀλόγοις καὶ
ἄφροσιν, ἀλκὴν δὲ καὶ θράσος δειλοῖς ἐντιθείσης. τίς
γὰρ οὐκ ἂν ὡς ἀληθῶς ἐκπλαγείη καὶ θαυμάσειεν
ἐπιμαθὴς[2] γενόμενος καὶ λογισμῷ τινι τὴν τότε
κατήφειαν καὶ τὴν νῦν[3] ὑπάρχουσαν εὐδαιμονίαν
E τῆς πόλεως περιλαβὼν καὶ ἀποβλέψας ναῶν[4] λαμ-
πρότητα καὶ πλοῦτον ἀναθημάτων καὶ τεχνῶν
ἁμίλλας καὶ φιλοτιμίας πόλεων καὶ στεφάνους
βασιλέων, καὶ ὅσα γῆ φέρει καὶ θάλαττα καὶ νῆσοι

---

[1] συμπτωμάτων Xylander and a few mss.; συμπτωμάτων τῇ
τύχῃ Reiske: συμπτωμάτων ἡ τύχη.
[2] ἐπιμαθὴς F.C.B.: θεατὴς E. Kurtz: ἐμπαθὴς.
[3] νῦν added by Reiske and confirmed by two mss.
[4] ναῶν Kronenberg and Stegmann: ἄνω.

the service of the goddess. Now by nature this bird is easily disturbed and frightened by noise ; and at this time, since they were neglected, because dire want oppressed the garrison, their sleep was light, and was made uncomfortable by hunger, with the result that they were at once aware of the enemy as they showed themselves above the edge of the cliff. The geese hissed at them and rushed at them impetuously, and, at the sight of arms, became even more excited, and filled the place with piercing and discordant clamour. By this the Romans were aroused, and, when they comprehended what had happened, they forced back their enemies and hurled them over the precipice. And even to this day, in memory of these events, there are borne in solemn procession a dog impaled on a stake,[a] but a goose perched in state upon a costly coverlet in a litter.

This spectacle exhibits the might of Fortune and the ease with which, whenever she busies herself and takes command, she provides from unexpected sources against all emergencies by implanting intelligence in the unreasoning and senseless, and prowess and daring in the craven. For who would not, truly, be struck with astonishment and amazement when he has come to learn and has embraced in his consideration the former dejection of the city and her present prosperity, and has looked upon the splendour of her temples, the richness of her votive offerings, the rivalry of her arts and crafts, the ambitious efforts of subject cities, the crowns of dependent kings, and all things which the earth contributes and the sea and islands, continents,

---

[a] *Cf.* Pliny, *Natural History*, xxix. 4 (57) ; Aelian, *De Natura Animalium*, xii. 33 ; Lydus, *De Mensibus*, iv. 114 ; Bücheler, *Umbrica*, p. 128.

καὶ ἤπειροι καὶ ποταμοὶ καὶ δένδρα καὶ ζῷα καὶ
πεδία καὶ ὄρη καὶ μέταλλα, πάντων ἀπαρχὰς
ἐριζούσας εἰς κάλλος ὄψει καὶ χάριτι κοσμούσῃ τὸν
τόπον, ὡς ταῦτα παρὰ μικρὸν ἦλθε μὴ γενέσθαι
μηδ' εἶναι; πυρὶ δὲ καὶ σκότει φοβερῷ καὶ ὄρφνῃ
καὶ ξίφεσι βαρβάροις καὶ μιαιφόνοις θυμοῖς κρατου-
μένων πάντων, εὐτελῆ καὶ ἄλογα καὶ ἄτολμα θρέμ-
F ματα σωτηρίας ἀρχὴν παρέσχε, καὶ τοὺς μεγάλους
ἐκείνους ἀριστεῖς καὶ ἡγεμόνας Μαλλίους καὶ
Σερουιλίους[1] καὶ Ποστουμίους καὶ Παπιρίους, τῶν
αὖθις οἴκων γενάρχας, παρ' οὐδὲν ἥκοντας ἀπολέσθαι, χῆνες ἀνέστησαν ὑπὲρ τοῦ πατρίου θεοῦ[2] καὶ
τῆς πατρίδος ἀμύνεσθαι. εἰ δέ, ὥσπερ Πολύβιος
ἐν τῇ δευτέρᾳ βίβλῳ περὶ τῶν τότε τὴν Ῥωμαίων
πόλιν καταλαβόντων ἱστόρηκε Κελτῶν, ἀληθές
ἐστιν, ὅτι προσπεσούσης αὐτοῖς ἀγγελίας φθείρεσθαι
τὰ οἴκοι ὑπὸ τῶν προσοίκων βαρβάρων ἐμβεβληκότων εἰς τὴν χώραν καὶ κρατούντων ἀνεχώρησαν
326 εἰρήνην θέμενοι πρὸς τὸν Κάμιλλον, οὐδ' ἀμφι-
σβήτησις ἔστι πρὸς τὴν Τύχην ὡς οὐχὶ τῆς
σωτηρίας αἰτία κατέστη περισπάσασα τοὺς πολεμίους, μᾶλλον δ' ἀποσπάσασα τῆς Ῥώμης ἀπροσδοκήτως.

13. Ἀλλὰ τί δεῖ περὶ ταῦτα διατρίβειν, ἃ σαφὲς
οὐδὲν οὐδ' ὡρισμένον ἔχει τῷ καὶ τὰ πράγματα[3]
συγχυθῆναι τῶν Ῥωμαίων καὶ διαφθαρῆναι[4] τοὺς
ἐπ[5] αὐτῶν ὑπομνηματισμούς, ὡς Λίβιος ἱστόρηκε;

---

[1] Σερουιλίους Wyttenbach : Σερουίους.
[2] τοῦ πατρίου θεοῦ] τῶν πατρίων θεῶν Reiske.
[3] πράγματα] γράμματα Reiske.
[4] συγχυθῆναι . . . διαφθαρῆναι transposed by Abresch
διαφθαρῆναι . . . συγχυθῆναι.

374

rivers, trees, living creatures, plains, mountains, mines, the first-fruits of everything, vying for beauty in the aspect and grace that adorns this place ? And then comes the thought : how near did all this come to not being created and to not existing at all ! When all things else were overcome by fire and frightful darkness and gloom, by foreign swords and murderous rage, it was poor, irrational, and timorous creatures that contributed the beginning of deliverance ; and those great heroes and commanders, the Manlii, the Servilii, the Postumii, the Papirii, the founders of future illustrious houses, whom naught separated from death, geese aroused to make defence for the god of their fathers and for their fatherland. But if it be true, as Polybius [a] has recorded in his second book, concerning the Gauls who had at this time seized Rome, that, when news suddenly came to them that their domains at home were in danger of being lost to them at the hands of neighbouring barbarians who had invaded their land and were masters of it, they concluded a treaty of peace with Camillus and withdrew—if this be true, then there can be no contention with Fortune that she was not the cause of Rome's preservation, by distracting the enemy, or rather, by abstracting them from Rome quite unexpectedly.

13. But what need is there to dwell on these matters, which offer nothing certain or definite because of the confusion of the events of Roman history and the destruction of contemporary chronicles, as Livy [b] has recorded ? Certainly the

[a] ii. 18. 3. [b] Livy, vi. 1. 2.

---

[5] ἐπ' F.C.B. : ὑπ' (τοὺς ὑπάτων ? = *Fasti Consulares*, Helmbold).

(326) τὰ γὰρ ὕστερον μᾶλλον ὄντα δῆλα καὶ καταφανῆ
δεικνύει τὴν τῆς Τύχης εὐμένειαν, ᾗ ἔγωγε¹ τίθεμαι
καὶ τὴν Ἀλεξάνδρου τελευτήν, ἀνδρὸς εὐτυχήμασι
μεγάλοις καὶ κατορθώμασι λαμπροῖς ὑπὸ θάρσους
B ἀμάχου καὶ φρονήματος ὥσπερ ἄστρου φερομένου
καὶ διᾴττοντος ἐπὶ δυσμὰς ἐξ ἀνατολῶν καὶ βάλ-
λοντος ἤδη τὰς τῶν ὅπλων αὐγὰς εἰς τὴν Ἰταλίαν,
ὡς πρόφασις μὲν ἦν αὐτῷ τῆς στρατείας ὁ Μολοτ-
τὸς Ἀλέξανδρος ὑπὸ Βρεττίων καὶ Λευκανῶν περὶ
Πανδοσίαν κατακεκομμένος· ὁ δ' ἀγών αὐτὸν ὡς
ἀληθῶς ἐπὶ πάντας ἀνθρώπους δόξης ἔρως καὶ
ἡγεμονίας ζῆλον ἔσχε καὶ ἄμιλλαν ὑπερβαλέσθαι τὰ
Διονύσου καὶ Ἡρακλέους πέρατα τῆς στρατη-
λασίας. τῆς δ' Ἰταλίας ἐπυνθάνετο τὴν ἐν Ῥώμῃ
δύναμιν καὶ ἀλκὴν ὥσπερ στόμωμα προτεταγμένην·
C ὄνομα γὰρ καὶ δόξα τούτων ἐπιφανεστάτη δι-
επέμπετο πρὸς αὐτὸν ὥσπερ ἀθλητῶν μυρίοις ἐγ-
γεγυμνασμένων πολέμοις.

        οὐ γὰρ ἀναιμωτί γε διακρινθήμεναι οἴω,

συμπεσόντων ὅπλοις ἀνικήτοις φρονημάτων ἀδου-
λώτων. πλῆθος μὲν γὰρ ἦσαν οὗτοι τρισκαίδεκα
μυριάδων οὐκ ἐλάττους, πολεμικοὶ δὲ καὶ ἀνδρώδεις
ἅπαντες,

                        ἐπιστάμενοι μὲν ἀφ' ἵππων
ἀνδράσι μάρνασθαι καὶ ὅτι χρὴ πεζὸν ἐόντα.

---

¹ ᾗ ἔγωγε Wyttenbach: ἐγὼ δέ.

ᵃ In 330 B.C.; he was the uncle of Alexander the Great.
Cf. Livy, viii. 17. 24.
ᵇ Cf. 332 A infra; Lucian, True History, i. 7.
ᶜ Adapted from Homer, Od. xviii. 149.
ᵈ Cf. Livy, ix. 19. 2, who says 250,000.

376

later events, plainer and clearer as they are, exhibit Fortune's benignity ; and to Fortune I ascribe also the death of Alexander, a man who by great good luck and brilliant successes, the result of his invincible daring and lofty aspirations, was sweeping swiftly through the world like a shooting star from East to West, and was already allowing the lustre of his arms to gleam upon Italy, since the destruction of Alexander the Molossian[a] near Pandosia at the hands of the Bruttians and Lucanians served him as pretext for the campaign. But truly that love of glory which led him against all mankind embraced both an emulous desire for sovereignty and a wish to rival and to pass beyond the limits of Dionysus's and Heracles'[b] expeditions. He learned that Rome's power and courage was arrayed for the protection of Italy like a firm-set battle-line ; for some account of their illustrious name and fame was often transmitted to him, as of athletes thoroughly practised in countless wars.

> Not without spilling of blood could this matter, I deem, have been settled,[c]

had the great aspirations of these two unconquered peoples with their invincible arms clashed with each other. For in numbers at this time the Romans were no fewer than an hundred and thirty thousand men[d] ; and every one of them was warlike and intrepid,[e]

> Knowing on horseback
> How to do battle with men, and even, if need be, dismounted.[f]

---

[a] *Cf.* Livy, ix. 16. 19 ff., for a comparison of Alexander and the Romans.　　　　　[f] Homer, *Od.* ix. 49-50.

ON THE FORTUNE OR THE VIRTUE OF ALEXANDER

(DE ALEXANDRI MAGNI FORTUNA AUT VIRTUTE)

I AND II

INTRODUCTION

AGAIN we have epideictic orations similar to the preceding and the following essays, and the conclusion again is abrupt, as if the speaker had been obliged to stop after a certain period of time had elapsed. Note, however, the very considerable difference in length between the first and the second part of the present work.

We know nothing of the circumstances under which these orations were delivered, but it is quite possible that they were spoken at Rome to show the Romans what an educated Greek could do in the treatment of a controversial subject.

The first oration deals mainly with the manner in which Fortune used Alexander; but much is also said of the manner in which he met the buffetings of Fortune and rose superior to them. In the second oration Fortune is by no means neglected, but rather more is said of Alexander's Virtue; thus it is not surprising to find in Lamprias's list of Plutarch's works two entries: the first, No. 176, *Alexander's Fortune* (Περὶ τῆς 'Αλεξάνδρου τύχης) and the second, No. 186, *Alexander's Virtue* (Περὶ τῆς 'Αλεξάνδρου ἀρετῆς).

Much that is included here is found also in Plutarch's *Life of Alexander*, in Arrian's *Anabasis*, and in other writers cited in the notes.

ON THE FORTUNE OF ALEXANDER

The genuineness of the tradition which ascribes these works to Plutarch (for the attribution had been attacked by A. Schäfer and by L. Weber) has been brilliantly vindicated by W. Nachstädt in his dissertation, *De Plutarchi Declamationibus quae sunt De Alexandri Fortuna (Berliner Beiträge für klassischen Philologie*, ii.), Karl Vogt, Berlin, 1895. This excellent work also contains a discussion of many of the problems which confront the editor of these essays and has been of great service.

ΠΕΡΙ
D ΤΗΣ ΑΛΕΞΑΝΔΡΟΥ ΤΥΧΗΣ Η ΑΡΕΤΗΣ

ΛΟΓΟΣ Α

1. Οὗτος ὁ τῆς Τύχης λόγος ἐστίν, ἴδιον καὶ μόνης αὐτῆς[1] ἔργον ἀποφαινομένης Ἀλέξανδρον. δεῖ δ᾽ ἀντειπεῖν ὑπὲρ φιλοσοφίας, μᾶλλον δ᾽ ὑπὲρ Ἀλεξάνδρου δυσχεραίνοντος καὶ ἀγανακτοῦντος, εἰ προῖκα δόξει καὶ παρὰ τῆς Τύχης λαβεῖν τὴν ἡγεμονίαν, ἣν ὤνιον αἵματος πολλοῦ καὶ τραυμάτων ἐπαλλήλων κτώμενος

E   πολλὰς μὲν ἀΰπνους νύκτας ἴαυεν,
    ἤματα δ᾽ αἱματόεντα διέπρησσεν πολεμίζων

πρὸς ἀμάχους δυνάμεις καὶ ἄπειρα φῦλα καὶ ποταμοὺς ἀπεράτους καὶ πέτρας ἀτοξεύτους, εὐβουλίᾳ καὶ καρτερίᾳ καὶ ἀνδρείᾳ καὶ σωφροσύνῃ παραπεμπόμενος.

2. Οἶμαι δ᾽ ἂν αὐτὸν εἰπεῖν πρὸς τὴν Τύχην τοῖς κατορθώμασιν αὐτὴν ἐπιγράφουσαν, " μή μου διάβαλλε τὴν ἀρετὴν μηδ᾽ ἀφαιροῦ περισπῶσα τὴν δόξαν. Δαρεῖος ἦν σὸν ἔργον, ὃν ἐκ δούλου καὶ

---

[1] αὑτῆς Abresch: αὐτῆς.

ON THE FORTUNE OR THE VIRTUE OF ALEXANDER

I

1. THIS is Fortune's discourse, who declares that Alexander is her own characteristic handiwork, and hers alone. But some rejoinder must be made on behalf of philosophy, or rather on Alexander's behalf, who would be vexed and indignant if he should be thought to have received as a pure gift, even at the hands of Fortune, the supremacy which he won at the price of much blood and of wounds that followed one after another ; and

> Many a night did he spend without sleeping,
> Many a blood-stained day did he pass amid combats unceasing,[a]

against irresistible forces and innumerable tribes, against impassable rivers and mountain fastnesses whose summit no arrow could reach, furthered by wise counsels, steadfast purpose, manly courage, and a prudent heart.

2. I think that if Fortune should try to inscribe her name on his successes, he would say to her, " Slander not my virtues, nor take away my fair fame by detraction. Darius was your handiwork : he who was

---

[a] Adapted from Homer, *Il.* ix. 325-326.

ἀστάνδου βασιλέως κύριον Περσῶν ἐποίησας· καὶ
F Σαρδανάπαλλος, ᾧ τὸ διάδημα τῆς βασιλείας πορφύραν ξαίνοντι περιέθηκας. ἐγὼ δ᾽ εἰς Σοῦσα
νικῶν δι᾽ Ἀρβήλων ἀναβέβηκα, καὶ Κιλικία μοι
πλατεῖαν ἀνέῳξεν Αἴγυπτον, Κιλικίαν δὲ Γράνι-
κος, ὃν Μιθριδάτῃ καὶ Σπιθριδάτῃ νεκροῖς ἐπιβὰς
διεπέρασα. κόσμει σεαυτὴν καὶ σεμνύνου βασιλεῦσιν ἀτρώτοις καὶ ἀναιμάκτοις· ἐκεῖνοι γὰρ
327 εὐτυχεῖς ἦσαν, Ὦχοι καὶ Ἀρταξέρξαι, οὓς εὐθὺς
ἐκ γενετῆς τῷ Κύρου θρόνῳ ἐνίδρυσας. τοὐμὸν δὲ
σῶμα πολλὰ σύμβολα φέρει Τύχης ἀνταγωνιζο-
μένης οὐ συμμαχούσης. πρῶτον ἐν Ἰλλυριοῖς λίθῳ
τὴν κεφαλήν, ὑπέρῳ δὲ τὸν τράχηλον ἠλοήθην·
ἔπειτα περὶ Γράνικον τὴν κεφαλὴν βαρβαρικῇ
μαχαίρᾳ διεκόπην, ἐν δ᾽ Ἰσσῷ ξίφει τὸν μηρόν·
πρὸς δὲ Γάζῃ τὸ μὲν σφυρὸν ἐτοξεύθην, τὸν δ᾽
ὦμον ἐκπεσὼν ἐξ ἕδρας βαρὺς περιεδίνησα[1]· πρὸς
δὲ Μαρακανδάνοις[2] τοξεύματι[3] τὸ τῆς κνήμης ὀστέον
διεσχίσθην· τὰ λοιπὰ δ᾽ Ἰνδῶν πληγαὶ καὶ βίαι

[1] ἐκπεσὼν . . . περιεδίνησα corrupt.
[2] Μαρακανδάνοις Reiske: μαρακάνδαν τοῖς or μαρακαδάρτοις.
[3] τοξεύματι Kronenberg: τοξεύμασι.

---

[a] Cf. 340 c, infra ; Life of Alexander, chap. xviii. (674 D).
Aelian, Varia Historia, xii. 43, says that he was a slave ; and
Strabo, xv. 3. 24, Diodorus, xvii. 5, say that he was not of
the royal family.
[b] Cf. 336 c, infra.   [c] 331 B.C.
[d] The battle of Issus, 333 B.C.   [e] 334 B.C.
[f] Artaxerxes III. (358–338 B.C.).
[g] This wound is elsewhere unknown to history. For
the wounds of Alexander see the excellent tables of Nachstädt,
op. cit. pp. 38–44.

a slave and courier of the king,[a] him did you make the mighty lord of Persia ; and Sardanapalus, upon whose head you placed the royal diadem, though he spent his days in carding purple wool.[b] But I, through my victory at Arbela,[c] went up to Susa, and Cilicia[d] opened the way for me into the broad land of Egypt ; but to Cilicia I came by way of the Granicus,[e] which I crossed, using as a bridge the dead bodies of Mithridates and Spithridates. Adorn yourself, proud Fortune, and vaunt your dominion over kings that never felt a wound nor shed a drop of blood. For they have been Fortune's favourites, men such as Ochus[f] was and Artaxerxes, whom at the very hour of their birth you placed upon the throne of Cyrus. But my body bears many a token of an opposing Fortune and no ally of mine. First, among the Illyrians,[g] my head was wounded by a stone and my neck by a cudgel. Then at the Granicus[h] my head was cut open by an enemy's dagger, at Issus[i] my thigh was pierced by the sword. Next at Gaza[j] my ankle was wounded by an arrow, my shoulder was dislocated, and I whirled heavily round and round. Then at Maracanda[k] the bone of my leg was split open by an arrow. There awaited me towards the last also the buffetings I received among the Indians and the

[h] Cf. 341 A–c, infra; Life of Alexander, chap. xvi. (673 A); Arrian, Anabasis, i. 15. 7 ; Diodorus, xvii. 20.

[i] By Darius, according to Chares (341 c, infra; Life of Alexander, chap. xx. (675 F)) ; but this is unknown to Arrian, Diodorus, Curtius, and Justin.

[j] The text is probably corrupt; in Curtius, iv. 6, we hear of two wounds, and they are quite different ones. One wound is reported in 341 B, infra; Life of Alexander, chap. xxv. (679 B); Arrian, Anabasis, ii. 27. 2.

[k] Cf. 341 B, infra; Arrian, Anabasis, iii. 30. 11 ; Curtius, vii. 6.

Β λιμῶν[1]· ἐν 'Ασπασίοις[2] ἐτοξεύθην τὸν ὦμον, ἐν δὲ
(327) Γανδρίδαις τὸ σκέλος· ἐν Μαλλοῖς βέλει μὲν ἀπὸ
τόξου τὸ στέρνον ἐνερεισθέντι καὶ καταδύσαντι τὸν
σίδηρον, ὑπέρον δὲ πληγῇ παρὰ τὸν τράχηλον, ὅτε
προστεθεῖσαι τοῖς τείχεσιν αἱ κλίμακες ἐκλάσθησαν·
ἐμὲ δ' ἡ Τύχη μόνον συνεῖρξεν οὐδὲ λαμπροῖς ἀντ-
αγωνισταῖς, ἀλλὰ βαρβάροις ἀσήμοις χαριζομένη
τηλικοῦτον ἔργον· εἰ δὲ μὴ Πτολεμαῖος ὑπερέσχε
τὴν πέλτην, Λιμναῖος δὲ πρὸ ἐμοῦ μυρίοις ἀπαντήσας βέλεσιν ἔπεσεν, ἤρειψαν δὲ θυμῷ καὶ βίᾳ
Μακεδόνες τὸ τεῖχος, ἔδει τάφον 'Αλεξάνδρου τὴν
βάρβαρον ἐκείνην καὶ ἀνώνυμον κώμην γενέσθαι."

C 3. Καὶ μὴν τὰ μὲν αὐτῆς τῆς στρατείας, χειμῶ-
νες, αὐχμοί, βάθη ποταμῶν, ἄορνα ὕψη, θηρίων
ὑπερφυεῖς ὄψεις, ἄγριοι δίαιται, μεταβολαὶ δυναστῶν, παλιμπροδοσίαι[3]· τὰ δὲ πρὸ τῆς στρατείας, ἔτι[4]
τοῖς Φιλιππικοῖς πολέμοις ἐπέσπαιρεν ἡ 'Ελλάς,
ἀπεσείοντο δ' αἱ Θῆβαι τῶν ὅπλων τὴν Χαιρωνικὴν
κόνιν ἐκ τοῦ πτώματος ἀνιστάμεναι, καὶ συνῆπτον
αἱ 'Αθῆναι τὰς χεῖρας ὀρέγουσαι· πᾶσα δ' ὕπουλος
ἦν[5] Μακεδονία πρὸς 'Αμύνταν ἀποβλέπουσα καὶ

---

[1] λιμῶν F.C.B., cf. Life of Alexander, chap. lxvi.; θηρίων
van Herwerden; θυμουμένων H. Richards: θυμῶν.
[2] 'Ασπασίοις (as elsewhere) K. Schmidt: ἄπασιν οἷς.
[3] παλιμπροδοσίαι Bryan: πάλιν προδοσίαι.
[4] ἔτι Reiske: ἐπί.
[5] ἦν Bernardakis: ἡ.

---

[a] Cf. Life of Alexander, chap. lxvi. (702 A-B); Arrian,
Anabasis, vi. 24-25.
[b] Cf. Ibid., iv. 23. 3; Curtius, viii. 3.
[c] Nothing is known of this wound.
[d] Cf. 341 c, 343 E ff., infra; Life of Alexander, chap.
lxiii. (700 B ff.); Arrian, Anabasis, vi. 9, 10; Diodorus, xvii.
98; Curtius, ix. 4, 5; Strabo, xv. 1. 33.

violence of famines.[a]   Among the Aspasians [b] my
shoulder was wounded by an arrow, and among the
Gandridae [c] my leg.   Among the Mallians,[d] the shaft
of an arrow sank deep into my breast and buried
its steel ; and I was struck in the neck by a cudgel,
when the scaling-ladders which we had moved up to
the walls were battered down ; and Fortune cooped
me up alone, favouring ignoble barbarians and not
illustrious adversaries with such an exploit.   But
if Ptolemy [e] had not held his shield above me, and
Limnaeus [f] taking his stand before me had not fallen, a
target for ten thousand shafts, and if my Macedonians
had not overthrown the wall with spirit and main
force, then that nameless village in a foreign land
must needs have become the tomb of Alexander."

3. Moreover, there were the trials of the campaign
itself : storms, droughts, deep rivers, the heights of
the Birdless Rock,[g] the monstrous shapes of savage
beasts, an uncivilized manner of life, the constant succession of petty kings and their repeated treachery.
Then there were also the difficulties before his expedition : [h] Greece was still gasping over Philip's
wars ; Thebes, staggering to her feet after her fall,
was shaking the dust of Chaeroneia from her arms,
and Athens was stretching forth a helping hand to
join with Thebes.   All Macedonia was festering with
revolt and looking toward Amyntas and the children

---

[e] Peucestas in *Life of Alexander*, and in Arrian, *Anabasis*.
   [f] Leonnatus according to Arrian (*Anabasis*, vi. 10. 2).
   [g] *Cf. Moralia*, 181 c ; Arrian, *Anabasis*, iv. 28 ; Diodorus,
xvii. 85.   Sir Aurel Stein has identified Aornos with the
plateau of Pir-s'ar (*On Alexander's Track to the Indus*,
Macmillan, 1929).
   [h] *Cf. Life of Alexander*, chap. xi. (670 B).

(327) τοὺς Ἀερόπου παῖδας· ἀνερρήγνυντο δ' Ἰλλυριοί,
καὶ τὰ Σκυθῶν ἐπηωρεῖτο τοῖς προσοίκοις νεωτερί-
ζουσι¹· τὸ δὲ Περσικὸν χρυσίον διὰ τῶν ἑκασταχοῦ
D δημαγωγῶν ῥέον ἐκίνει τὴν Πελοπόννησον· κενοὶ
δ' οἱ Φιλίππου θησαυροὶ χρημάτων, καὶ προσῆν ἔτι
δάνειον, ὡς Ὀνησίκριτος ἱστορεῖ, διακοσίων ταλάντων. ἐν τοσαύτῃ πενίᾳ καὶ πράγμασι ταραχὰς
ἔχουσι μειράκιον ἄρτι τὴν παιδικὴν παραλλάττον
ἡλικίαν ἐθάρρησεν ἐλπίσαι Βαβυλῶνα καὶ Σοῦσα,
μᾶλλον δὲ τὴν πάντων ἀνθρώπων ἀρχὴν εἰς νοῦν
ἐμβαλέσθαι, τοῖς τρισμυρίοις οἷς ἔσχε² πεζοῖς καὶ
τετρακισχιλίοις ἱππεῦσι πιστεύσας· τοσοῦτοι γὰρ
ἦσαν, ὡς Ἀριστόβουλός φησιν· ὡς δὲ Πτολεμαῖος
E ὁ βασιλεύς, τρισμύριοι πεζοὶ πεντακισχίλιοι δ'
ἱππεῖς· ὡς δ' Ἀναξιμένης, τετρακισμύριοι πεζοὶ
καὶ τρισχίλιοι, πεντακισχίλιοι δὲ καὶ πεντακόσιοι
ἱππεῖς. τὸ δὲ λαμπρὸν αὐτῷ καὶ μέγα παρασκευα-
σθὲν ὑπὸ τῆς Τύχης ἐφόδιον ἑβδομήκοντα τάλαντ'
ἦν, ὥς φησιν Ἀριστόβουλος· ὡς δὲ Δοῦρις, τριάκοντα μόνον ἡμερῶν ἐπισιτισμός.

4. Ἄβουλος οὖν καὶ προπετὴς Ἀλέξανδρος ἐξ
εὐτελῶν οὕτως ἐπὶ τηλικαύτην δύναμιν ὁρμώ-
μενος; οὐ μὲν οὖν. τίς γὰρ ἀπὸ μειζόνων ἢ
καλλιόνων ἀφορμῶν ἀνήγετο, μεγαλοψυχίας, συνέσεως, σωφροσύνης, ἀνδραγαθίας, αἷς³ αὐτὸν

---

¹ νεωτερίζουσι Reiske, confirmed by a few mss.: νεωτεροῦσι.
² οἷς ἔσχε F.C.B.: οἴεσθαι.
³ αἷς F.C.B. and Stegmann: οἷς.

---

^a Very little is known of this faction. *Cf.* Diodorus, xiv.
37 and 89. Amyntas later joined Darius and met his death
soon after the battle of Issus.
^b £40,000 or $200,000.

388

of Aëropus[a]; the Illyrians were again rebelling, and trouble with the Scythians was impending for their Macedonian neighbours, who were in the throes of political change; Persian gold flowed freely through the hands of the popular leaders everywhere, and helped to rouse the Peloponnesus; Philip's treasuries were bare of money, and in addition there was owing a loan of two hundred talents[b] (as Onesicritus records). In such poverty[c] and in circumstances fraught with such uncertainty, a stripling, scarcely older than a boy, had the daring to hope for Babylon and Susa; nay more, to conceive the project of dominion over all the world, relying only on the thirty thousand foot and four thousand cavalry which were his; for, according to Aristobulus, that was the full extent of their number. But King Ptolemy puts them at thirty thousand foot and five thousand horse, Anaximenes at forty-three thousand foot, fifty-five hundred horse. And the great and glorious war-chest which Fortune had ready for him was only seventy talents,[d] as Aristobulus[e] says, though Duris[f] says it was provision for only thirty days.

4. Was, then, Alexander ill-advised and precipitate in setting forth with such humble resources to acquire so vast an empire? By no means. For who has ever put forth with greater or fairer equipment than he: greatness of soul, keen intelligence, self-restraint, and manly courage, with which Philosophy

---

[c] For the varying accounts of the wealth and forces of Alexander cf. 342 D, infra; Life of Alexander, chap. xv. (672 A); Arrian, Anabasis, i. 11. 3; and Alexander's own account, according to Arrian, Anabasis, vii. 9. 6 ff.

[d] £14,000 or $70,000.

[e] Cf. 342 D, infra.

[f] Cf. Müller, Frag. Hist. Graec. ii. p. 472.

ἐφωδίαζε φιλοσοφία πρὸς τὴν στρατείαν; ναί,[1]
πλείονας παρ' Ἀριστοτέλους τοῦ καθηγητοῦ ἢ
F παρὰ Φιλίππου τοῦ πατρὸς ἀφορμὰς ἔχων διέβαινεν ἐπὶ Πέρσας. ἀλλὰ τοῖς μὲν γράφουσιν, ὡς
Ἀλέξανδρος ἔφη ποτὲ τὴν Ἰλιάδα καὶ τὴν Ὀδύσσειαν ἀκολουθεῖν αὐτῷ τῆς στρατείας ἐφόδιον,
πιστεύομεν, Ὅμηρον σεμνύνοντες· ἂν δέ τις φῇ τὴν
Ἰλιάδα καὶ τὴν Ὀδύσσειαν παραμύθιον πόνου καὶ
328 διατριβὴν ἕπεσθαι σχολῆς[2] γλυκείας, ἐφόδιον δ'
ἀληθῶς γεγονέναι τὸν ἐκ φιλοσοφίας λόγον καὶ τοὺς
περὶ ἀφοβίας καὶ ἀνδρείας ἔτι δὲ σωφροσύνης καὶ
μεγαλοψυχίας ὑπομνηματισμούς, καταφρονοῦμεν;
ὅτι δηλαδὴ περὶ συλλογισμῶν οὐδὲν οὐδὲ περὶ
ἀξιωμάτων ἔγραψεν,[3] οὐδ' ἐν Λυκείῳ περίπατον
συνέσχεν οὐδ' ἐν Ἀκαδημείᾳ θέσεις εἶπεν· τούτοις
γὰρ ὁρίζουσι φιλοσοφίαν οἱ λόγον αὐτὴν οὐκ ἔργον
νομίζοντες. καίτοι γ' οὐδὲ Πυθαγόρας ἔγραψεν
οὐδ' οὐδὲ Σωκράτης οὐδ' Ἀρκεσίλαος οὐδὲ Καρ-
νεάδης, οἱ δοκιμώτατοι τῶν φιλοσόφων· καὶ οὐκ
ἠσχολοῦντο περὶ πολέμους ἐκεῖνοι τηλικούτους,
B οὐδὲ βασιλεῖς βαρβάρους ἡμεροῦντες οὐδὲ πόλεις
Ἑλληνίδας ἐπικτίζοντες[4] ἀγρίοις ἔθνεσιν οὐδ' ἄθεσμα
καὶ ἀνήκοα φῦλα νόμους διδάσκοντες καὶ εἰρήνην
ἐπῆεσαν, ἀλλὰ καὶ σχολάζοντες τὸ γράφειν παρ-
ίεσαν τοῖς σοφισταῖς. πόθεν οὖν ἐπιστεύθησαν
ἐκεῖνοι φιλοσοφεῖν; ἀφ' ὧν εἶπον ἢ ἀφ' ὧν ἐβίωσαν

---

[1] ναί E. Capps : καὶ.
[2] διατριβὴν σχολῆς Reiske : διατριβῆς καὶ σχολῆς.
[3] ἔγραψεν Bernardakis, to harmonize with the other aorists :
ἔγραφεν.   [4] ἐπικτίζοντες] ἐγκτίζοντες Bernardakis.

[a] Cf. Life of Alexander, chaps. viii. (p. 668 D) and xxvi.
(679 C-D) ; Pliny, Natural History, vii. 29. 108.

herself provided him for his campaign ? Yes, the equipment that he had from Aristotle his teacher when he crossed over into Asia was more than what he had from his father Philip. But although we believe those who record that Alexander once said that the *Iliad* [a] and the *Odyssey* accompanied him as equipment for his campaigns, since we hold Homer in reverence, yet are we to contemn anyone who asserts that the works of Homer accompanied him as a consolation after toil and as a pastime for sweet hours of leisure, but that his true equipment was philosophic teaching, and treatises on Fearlessness and Courage, and Self-restraint also, and Greatness of Soul ? For of course it is obvious that Alexander wrote nothing on the subject of either syllogisms or axioms, nor did he have the opportunity of sharing the walks in the Lyceum, [b] or of discussing propositions in the Academy. For it is by these criteria that those define philosophy who regard it as a theoretical rather than a practical pursuit. And yet even Pythagoras wrote nothing at all, nor did Socrates, nor Arcesilaüs, nor Carneades, who were all most notable among philosophers. Nor were these philosophers continuously occupied with such tremendous wars, nor with spreading civilization among foreign princes, nor in establishing Grecian cities among savage nations, nor did they go on and on, instructing lawless and ignorant tribes in the principles of law and peace ; but, even though they had leisure, they relinquished the writing of philosophy to sophists. Whence, then, comes our belief that they were true philosophers ? Surely from what they said, or from the

[b] That is, of occupying himself with Peripatetic (Aristotelian) philosophy.

(328) ἢ ἀφ᾽ ὧν ἐδίδαξαν. ἀπὸ τούτων κρινέσθω καὶ
᾽Αλέξανδρος· ὀφθήσεται γὰρ οἷς εἶπεν οἷς ἔπραξεν
οἷς ἐπαίδευσε φιλόσοφος.

5. Καὶ πρῶτον τὸ παραδοξότατον, εἰ βούλει,
σκόπει, τοὺς ᾽Αλεξάνδρου μαθητὰς τοῖς Πλάτωνος,
τοῖς Σωκράτους ἀντιπαραβάλλων. εὐφυεῖς οὗτοι
καὶ ὁμογλώσσους ἐπαίδευον, εἰ μηδὲν ἄλλο, φωνῆς
C Ἑλληνίδος συνιέντας· καὶ πολλοὺς οὐκ ἔπεισαν·
ἀλλὰ Κριτίαι καὶ ᾽Αλκιβιάδαι καὶ Κλειτοφῶντες,
ὥσπερ χαλινὸν τὸν λόγον ἐκπτύσαντες, ἄλλῃ πῃ[1]
παρετράπησαν.

Τὴν δ᾽ ᾽Αλεξάνδρου παιδείαν ἂν ἐπιβλέπῃς,
Ὑρκανοὺς γαμεῖν ἐπαίδευσε καὶ γεωργεῖν ἐδίδαξεν
᾽Αραχωσίους, καὶ Σογδιανοὺς ἔπεισε πατέρας τρέ-
φειν καὶ μὴ φονεύειν, καὶ Πέρσας σέβεσθαι μητέρας
ἀλλὰ μὴ γαμεῖν. ὢ θαυμαστῆς φιλοσοφίας, δι᾽ ἣν
Ἰνδοὶ θεοὺς Ἑλληνικοὺς προσκυνοῦσι, Σκύθαι θά-
πτουσι τοὺς ἀποθανόντας οὐ κατεσθίουσι. θαυμά-
D ζομεν τὴν Καρνεάδου δύναμιν, εἰ Κλειτόμαχον,
᾽Ασδρούβαν καλούμενον πρότερον καὶ Καρχηδόνιον
τὸ γένος, ἑλληνίζειν ἐποίησε· θαυμάζομεν τὴν

---

[1] πῃ Abresch: που.

[a] It is interesting to note that dialogues bearing the
names of all these pupils have been handed down to us under
the name of Plato, although some of them are thought to be
spurious.

[b] Wyttenbach in sadness doubts whether these ethno-
logical remarks are the fruit of any research on the part of
Plutarch. But they probably derive from a hazy recollec-
tion of such passages as Herodotus, i. 216 (of the Massagetae).
Note, however, that Strabo supports Plutarch on this custom
of the Persians (xv. 3. 20), which is easily explained by the

manner of life which they led, or from the principles which they taught. By these criteria let Alexander also be judged! For from his words, from his deeds, and from the instruction which he imparted, it will be seen that he was indeed a philosopher.

5. And first, if you will, consider a matter entirely contrary to the general belief, and compare Alexander's pupils with those of Plato and Socrates. Plato and Socrates taught pupils of splendid natural endowment who spoke the same language ; so that, even if the pupils understood nothing else, at least they understood the Greek tongue. And even so, Plato and Socrates did not win over many. But their pupils, such as Critias and Alcibiades and Cleitophon,[a] were prone to spew the good word forth, as a horse the curbing bit, and turned them to other ways.

But if you examine the results of Alexander's instruction, you will see that he educated the Hyrcanians[b] to respect the marriage bond, and taught the Arachosians to till the soil, and persuaded the Sogdians to support their parents, not to kill them, and the Persians[b] to revere their mothers and not to take them in wedlock. O wondrous power of Philosophic Instruction, that brought the Indians to worship Greek gods, and the Scythians to bury their dead, not to devour them ! We admire Carneades' power, which made Cleitomachus,[c] formerly called Hasdrubal, and a Carthaginian by birth, adopt Greek ways. We admire the character of Zeno, which

fact that the young king inherited his father's harem as well as his father's stable, and that the father's younger wives furnished the beginning of the son's harem. *Cf.* also Sophocles, *Trachiniae*,1221-1251. For other pleasant customs of the Hyrcanians *cf. Moralia*, 499 D.

[c] *Cf.* Diogenes Laertius, iv. 67 ; Athenaeus, 402 c.

(328) διάθεσιν Ζήνωνος, εἰ Διογένη τὸν Βαβυλώνιον
ἔπεισε φιλοσοφεῖν. ἀλλ' Ἀλεξάνδρου τὴν Ἀσίαν
ἐξημεροῦντος Ὅμηρος ἦν ἀνάγνωσμα, καὶ Περσῶν
καὶ Σουσιανῶν καὶ Γεδρωσίων παῖδες τὰς Εὐριπίδου καὶ Σοφοκλέους τραγῳδίας ᾖδον. καὶ
Σωκράτης ὡς¹ μὲν ξένα παρεισάγων δαιμόνια δίκην
τοῖς Ἀθήνησιν ὠφλίσκανε συκοφάνταις· διὰ δ'
Ἀλέξανδρον τοὺς Ἑλλήνων θεοὺς Βάκτρα καὶ
Καύκασος προσεκύνησε. Πλάτων μὲν γὰρ μίαν
E γράψας πολιτείαν οὐδένα πέπεικεν αὐτῇ χρῆσθαι
διὰ τὸ αὐστηρόν· Ἀλέξανδρος δ' ὑπὲρ ἑβδομήκοντα
πόλεις βαρβάροις ἔθνεσιν ἐγκτίσας καὶ κατασπείρας
τὴν Ἀσίαν Ἑλληνικοῖς τέλεσι, τῆς ἀνημέρου καὶ
θηριώδους ἐκράτησε διαίτης. καὶ τοὺς μὲν Πλάτωνος ὀλίγοι νόμους ἀναγιγνώσκομεν, τοῖς δ'
Ἀλεξάνδρου μυριάδες ἀνθρώπων ἐχρήσαντο καὶ
χρῶνται· μακαριώτεροι τῶν διαφυγόντων Ἀλέξανδρον οἱ κρατηθέντες γενόμενοι· τοὺς μὲν γὰρ οὐδεὶς
ἔπαυσεν ἀθλίως ζῶντας, τοὺς δ' ἠνάγκασεν εὐδαι-
μονεῖν ὁ νικήσας. ὥσθ' ὅπερ εἶπε Θεμιστοκλῆς,
ὁπηνίκα φυγὼν ἔτυχε δωρεῶν μεγάλων παρὰ
F βασιλέως καὶ τρεῖς πόλεις ὑποφόρους ἔλαβε, τὴν
μὲν εἰς σῖτον τὴν δ' εἰς οἶνον τὴν δ' εἰς ὄψον, " ὦ
παῖδες ἀπωλόμεθ' ἂν εἰ μὴ ἀπωλόμεθα "· τοῦτο
περὶ τῶν ἁλόντων ὑπ' Ἀλεξάνδρου δικαιότερόν
ἐστιν εἰπεῖν. οὐκ ἂν ἡμερώθησαν, εἰ μὴ ἐκρατή-

---

¹ ὡς added by van Herwerden (after μὲν).

ᵃ Diogenes, from Seleucia in Mesopotamia (Strabo, xvi.
1. 16; Diogenes Laertius, vi. 81), was said to have been a
pupil of Chrysippus, and thus was converted to the inheritance of Zeno, Stoicism.

ᵇ Cf. Life of Alexander, chap. viii. (p. 668 E).

persuaded Diogenes [a] the Babylonian to be a philosopher. But when Alexander was civilizing Asia, Homer was commonly read, and the children of the Persians, of the Susianians, and of the Gedrosians learned to chant the tragedies of Sophocles and Euripides.[b] And although Socrates, when tried on the charge of introducing foreign deities,[c] lost his cause to the informers who infested Athens, yet through Alexander Bactria and the Caucasus learned to revere the gods of the Greeks. Plato wrote a book on the One Ideal Constitution, but because of its forbidding character he could not persuade anyone to adopt it; but Alexander established more than seventy cities among savage tribes, and sowed all Asia with Grecian magistracies, and thus overcame its uncivilized and brutish manner of living. Although few of us read Plato's *Laws*, yet hundreds of thousands have made use of Alexander's laws, and continue to use them. Those who were vanquished by Alexander are happier than those who escaped his hand; for these had no one to put an end to the wretchedness of their existence, while the victor compelled those others to lead a happy life. Therefore it is even more just to apply Themistocles' saying [d] to the nations conquered by Alexander. For, when Themistocles in exile had obtained great gifts from Artaxerxes, and had received three cities to pay him tribute, one to supply his bread, another his wine, and a third his meat, he exclaimed, " My children, we should be ruined now, had we not been ruined before." Thus Alexander's new subjects would not have been civilized, had they not been vanquished; Egypt

---

[c] *Cf.* Plato, *Apology*, 24 B ; Xenophon, *Memorabilia*, i. 1. 1.
        [d] *Cf. Moralia*, 185 F, and the note there.

θησαν· οὐκ ἂν εἶχεν Ἀλεξάνδρειαν Αἴγυπτος, οὐδὲ
Μεσοποταμία Σελεύκειαν οὐδὲ Προφθασίαν Σογ-
διανὴ οὐδ' Ἰνδία Βουκεφαλίαν, οὐδὲ πόλιν Ἑλλάδα
329 Καυκάσος παροικοῦσαν,[1] οἷς[2] ἐμπολισθεῖσιν[3] ἐσ-
βέσθη τὸ ἄγριον καὶ μετέβαλε τὸ χεῖρον ὑπὸ τοῦ
κρείττονος ἐθιζόμενον. εἰ τοίνυν μέγιστον μὲν οἱ
φιλόσοφοι φρονοῦσιν ἐπὶ τῷ τὰ σκληρὰ καὶ ἀπαί-
δευτα τῶν ἠθῶν ἐξημεροῦν καὶ μεθαρμόζειν, μυρία
δὲ φαίνεται γένη καὶ φύσεις θηριώδεις μεταβαλὼν
Ἀλέξανδρος, εἰκότως ἂν φιλοσοφώτατος νομίζοιτο.

6. Καὶ μὴν ἡ πολὺ θαυμαζομένη Πολιτεία τοῦ
τὴν Στωικῶν αἵρεσιν καταβαλομένου Ζήνωνος εἰς
ἓν τοῦτο συντείνει κεφάλαιον, ἵνα μὴ κατὰ πόλεις
μηδὲ κατὰ δήμους οἰκῶμεν ἰδίοις ἕκαστοι διωρι-
B σμένοι δικαίοις, ἀλλὰ πάντας ἀνθρώπους ἡγώμεθα
δημότας καὶ πολίτας, εἷς δὲ βίος ᾖ καὶ κόσμος,
ὥσπερ ἀγέλης συννόμου νομῷ[4] κοινῷ συντρεφο-
μένης. τοῦτο Ζήνων μὲν ἔγραψεν ὥσπερ ὄναρ ἢ
εἴδωλον εὐνομίας φιλοσόφου καὶ πολιτείας ἀνα-
τυπωσάμενος, Ἀλέξανδρος δὲ τῷ λόγῳ τὸ ἔργον
παρέσχεν. οὐ γάρ, ὡς Ἀριστοτέλης συνεβούλευεν
αὐτῷ, τοῖς μὲν Ἕλλησιν ἡγεμονικῶς τοῖς δὲ βαρβάροις δεσποτικῶς χρώμενος, καὶ τῶν μὲν ὡς

---

[1] παροικοῦσαν Reiske: περιοικοῦσαν.
[2] οἷς F.C.B.: αἷς.
[3] ἐμπολισθεῖσιν F.C.B.; ἐμπολισθείσαις Reiske: ἐμποδισθεῖσα.
[4] νομῷ Helmbold: νόμῳ.

---

[a] Alexandria-in-the-Caucasus: cf. Arrian, Anabasis, iii.
28. 4; iv. 22. 4; v. 1. 5; Curtius, vii. 3. 23; Diodorus,
xvii. 83. 1.
[b] Cf. Cambridge Ancient History, vol. vii. p. 225; Moralia, 653 E; Life of Lycurgus, xxxi. (59 A); Cicero, De

would not have its Alexandria, nor Mesopotamia its Seleuceia, nor Sogdiana its Prophthasia, nor India its Bucephalia, nor the Caucasus a Greek city [a] hard by; for by the founding of cities in these places savagery was extinguished and the worse element, gaining familiarity with the better, changed under its influence. If, then, philosophers take the greatest pride in civilizing and rendering adaptable the intractable and untutored elements in human character, and if Alexander has been shown to have changed the savage natures of countless tribes, it is with good reason that he should be regarded as a very great philosopher.

6. Moreover, the much-admired *Republic* [b] of Zeno, the founder of the Stoic sect, may be summed up in this one main principle : that all the inhabitants of this world of ours should not live differentiated by their respective rules of justice into separate cities and communities, but that we should consider all men to be of one community and one polity, and that we should have a common life and an order common to us all, even as a herd that feeds together and shares the pasturage of a common field. This Zeno wrote, giving shape to a dream or, as it were, shadowy picture of a well-ordered and philosophic commonwealth ; but it was Alexander who gave effect to the idea. For Alexander did not follow Aristotle's [c] advice to treat the Greeks as if he were their leader, and other peoples as if he were their master ; to have regard for the Greeks as for friends and kindred, but

Legibus, i. 7-11 (21-32): *De Officiis*, i. 7 (22); Diogenes Laertius, vii. 32-34, 121, 129, 131.

[c] Aristotle's name is not elsewhere linked with this advice: *cf.* Strabo, i. 4. 9 (p. 66), or Aristotle, Frag. 658 (ed. V. Rose).

(329) φίλων καὶ οἰκείων ἐπιμελούμενος τοῖς δ' ὡς ζῴοις
ἢ φυτοῖς προσφερόμενος,[1] πολέμων πολλῶν καὶ[2]
φυγῶν ἐνέπλησε καὶ στάσεων ὑπούλων τὴν ἡγε-
C μονίαν· ἀλλὰ κοινὸς ἥκειν θεόθεν ἁρμοστὴς καὶ
διαλλακτὴς τῶν ὅλων νομίζων, οὓς τῷ λόγῳ μὴ
συνῆγε τοῖς ὅπλοις βιαζόμενος, εἰς τὸ αὐτὸ συν-
ενεγκὼν τὰ πανταχόθεν, ὥσπερ ἐν κρατῆρι φιλο-
τησίῳ μείξας τοὺς βίους καὶ τὰ ἤθη καὶ τοὺς γάμους
καὶ τὰς[3] διαίτας, πατρίδα μὲν τὴν οἰκουμένην
προσέταξεν ἡγεῖσθαι πάντας, ἀκρόπολιν δὲ καὶ
φρουρὰν τὸ στρατόπεδον, συγγενεῖς δὲ τοὺς ἀγα-
θούς, ἀλλοφύλους δὲ τοὺς πονηρούς· τὸ δ' Ἑλληνικὸν καὶ βαρβαρικὸν μὴ χλαμύδι μηδὲ πέλτῃ
μηδ' ἀκινάκῃ μηδὲ κάνδυϊ διορίζειν, ἀλλὰ τὸ μὲν
D Ἑλληνικὸν ἀρετῇ τὸ δὲ βαρβαρικὸν κακίᾳ τεκ-
μαίρεσθαι· κοινὰς δ' ἐσθῆτας ἡγεῖσθαι καὶ τραπέζας
καὶ γάμους καὶ διαίτας, δι' αἵματος καὶ τέκνων
ἀνακεραννυμένους.

7. Δημάρατος μὲν οὖν ὁ Κορίνθιος εἷς ὢν τῶν
Φιλίππου ξένων καὶ φίλων, ὅτ' Ἀλέξανδρον εἶδεν
ἐν Σούσοις, περιχαρὴς γενόμενος καὶ δακρύσας
μεγάλης ἔφη χαρᾶς ἐστερῆσθαι τοὺς ἔμπροσθεν
τεθνηκότας Ἕλληνας, ὅτι Ἀλέξανδρον οὐκ εἶδον ἐν
τῷ Δαρείου θρόνῳ καθεζόμενον. ἐγὼ δ' οὐδὲ τούτου
μὰ Δία τοῦ θεάματος ζηλῶ τοὺς ἰδόντας, ὃ καὶ

[1] χρώμενος . . . ἐπιμελούμενος . . . προσφερόμενος Reiske,
confirmed by a few mss. : χρώμενον . . . ἐπιμελούμενον . . .
προσφερόμενον.
[2] πολέμων πολλῶν καὶ Bernardakis : πολέμῳ πολλῶν or
πολεμοποιῶν.   [3] τὰς added by Reiske.

to conduct himself toward other peoples as though they were plants or animals ; for to do so would have been to cumber his leadership with numerous battles and banishments and festering seditions. But, as he believed that he came as a heaven-sent governor to all, and as a mediator for the whole world, those whom he could not persuade to unite with him, he conquered by force of arms, and he brought together into one body all men everywhere, uniting and mixing in one great loving-cup, as it were, men's lives, their characters, their marriages, their very habits of life.[a] He bade them all consider as their fatherland the whole inhabited earth, as their stronghold and protection his camp, as akin to them all good men, and as foreigners only the wicked ; they should not distinguish between Grecian and foreigner by Grecian cloak and targe, or scimitar and jacket ; but the distinguishing mark of the Grecian should be seen in virtue, and that of the foreigner in iniquity ; clothing and food, marriage and manner of life they should regard as common to all, being blended into one by ties of blood and children.

7. Now Demaratus the Corinthian, one of Philip's intimate friends,[b] when he had seen Alexander in Susa, exclaimed with tears of joy[c] that all the Greeks who had died before that hour had been deprived of a great joy, since they had not seen Alexander seated on the throne of Darius. But I swear that for my part I feel no envy because of this spectacle toward them that saw it, for it was but the

[a] Cf. Arrian, Anabasis, vii. 11. 8-9.
[b] Cf. Moralia, 70 c ; Life of Alexander, chap. ix. (669 c).
[c] Ibid. chaps. xxxvii. (687 A), lvi. (696 F) ; Life of Agesilaüs, chap. xv. (604 A).

Τύχης ἦν καὶ κοινὸν ἑτέρων[1] βασιλέων· ἀλλ' ἐκείνης
ἡδέως ἄν μοι δοκῶ γενέσθαι τῆς καλῆς καὶ ἱερᾶς
νυμφαγωγίας θεατής, ὅτε μιᾷ σκηνῇ χρυσωρόφῳ
E περιλαβών, ἐφ' ἑστίας κοινῆς καὶ τραπέζης, ἑκατὸν
Περσίδας νύμφας, ἑκατὸν νυμφίους Μακεδόνας καὶ
Ἕλληνας, αὐτὸς ἐστεφανωμένος πρῶτος ἀναμέλπων
τὸν ὑμέναιον, ὥσπερ φιλοτήσιον ἐπᾴδων μέλος, εἰς
κοινωνίαν συνιοῦσι τοῖς μεγίστοις καὶ δυνατω-
τάτοις γένεσι, μιᾶς νυμφίος, πασῶν δὲ νυμφαγωγὸς
ἅμα καὶ πατὴρ καὶ ἁρμοστὴς κατὰ ζυγὰ συνῆπτεν.
ἡδέως γὰρ ἂν εἶπον,[2] " ὦ βάρβαρε Ξέρξη καὶ ἀνόητε
καὶ μάτην πολλὰ περὶ τὴν Ἑλλησποντίαν πονηθεὶς
γέφυραν, οὕτως ἔμφρονες βασιλεῖς Ἀσίαν Εὐρώπῃ
συνάπτουσιν, οὐ ξύλοις οὐδὲ σχεδίαις οὐδ' ἀψύχοις
F καὶ ἀσυμπαθέσι δεσμοῖς, ἀλλ' ἔρωτι νομίμῳ καὶ
γάμοις σώφροσι καὶ κοινωνίαις παίδων τὰ γένη
συνάπτοντες."

8. Πρὸς τοῦτον ἀποβλέπων τὸν κόσμον Ἀλέξανδρος οὐ τὴν ἐσθῆτα προσήκατο τὴν Μηδικήν, ἀλλὰ
τὴν Περσικὴν πολλῷ τῆς Μηδικῆς εὐτελεστέραν
οὖσαν. τὰ γὰρ ἔξαλλα καὶ τραγικὰ τοῦ βαρβαρι-
330 κοῦ κόσμου παραιτησάμενος, οἷον τιάραν καὶ κάνδυν
καὶ ἀναξυρίδας, ἐκ τοῦ Περσικοῦ καὶ Μακεδονικοῦ
τρόπου μεμειγμένην τινὰ στολὴν ἐφόρει, καθάπερ
Ἐρατοσθένης ἱστόρηκεν, ὡς μὲν φιλόσοφος τοῖς

---

[1] κοινὸν ἑτέρων Wyttenbach : κοινοτέρων.
[2] εἶπον Basel ed. of 1542 and Budaeus : εἶπεν.

---

[a] Cf. *Life of Alexander*, chap. lxx. (703 E) ; Arrian, *Anabasis*, vii. 4 ; Diodorus, xvii. 107. 6 ; Athenaeus, 538 B-E ;
Aelian, *Varia Historia*, viii. 7 ; but the number is not
elsewhere given as 100.

handiwork of Fortune, and the lot of other kings as well. But methinks I would gladly have been a witness of that fair and holy marriage-rite, when he brought together in one golden-canopied tent an hundred Persian brides and an hundred Macedonian and Greek bridegrooms, united at a common hearth and board.[a] He himself, crowned with garlands, was the first to raise the marriage hymn as though he were singing a song of truest friendship over the union of the two greatest and most mighty peoples ; for he, of one maid the bridegroom, and at the same time of all the brides the escort, as a father and sponsor united them in the bonds of wedlock. Indeed at this sight I should have cried out for joy, " O dullard Xerxes, stupid fool that spent so much fruitless toil to bridge the Hellespont ! This is the way that wise kings join Asia with Europe ; it is not by beams nor rafts, nor by lifeless and unfeeling bonds, but by the ties of lawful love and chaste nuptials and mutual joy in children that they join the nations together."

8. Considering carefully this order of affairs, Alexander did not favour the Median raiment, but preferred the Persian, for it was much more simple than the Median. Since he deprecated the unusual and theatrical varieties of foreign adornment, such as the tiara and the full-sleeved jacket and trousers, he wore a composite dress adapted from both Persian and Macedonian fashion,[b] as Eratosthenes[c] has recorded. As a philosopher what he wore was

---

[b] Cf. *Life of Alexander*, chap. xlv. (690 E–691 A) ; Diodorus, xvii. 77.

[c] Presumably in the treatise referred to by Strabo, i. 4. 9 (p. 66).

(330) ἀδιαφόροις[1] χρώμενος, ὡς δ' ἡγεμὼν κοινὸς καὶ
βασιλεὺς φιλάνθρωπος τῇ περὶ τὴν ἐσθῆτα τιμῇ
τὴν τῶν κεκρατημένων ἀνακτώμενος εὔνοιαν, ἵνα
βεβαίως παραμένωσιν ἀγαπῶντες ὡς ἄρχοντας
Μακεδόνας, μὴ μισοῦντες ὡς πολεμίους. τοὐναντίον γὰρ ἦν ἀσόφου καὶ τετυφωμένης ψυχῆς τὴν μὲν
αὐτόχρουν χλαμύδα θαυμάζειν, τὸν δὲ περιπόρφυρον
χιτῶνα δυσχεραίνειν, ἢ πάλιν ἐκεῖνα μὲν ἀτιμάζειν,
B τούτοις δ' ἐκπεπλῆχθαι, δίκην νηπίου παιδὸς
φυλάττοντα τὴν περιβολήν, ἣν ἡ πάτριος αὐτῷ
συνήθεια καθάπερ τίτθη περιέθηκε. ζῷα θηρεύον-
τες ἄνθρωποι δορὰς ἐλάφων περιτίθενται, καὶ
πτερωτοῖς ἀμπέχονται χιτωνίσκοις ἄγραις ἐπι-
χειροῦντες ὀρνίθων, καὶ φυλάττονται ταύροις
ὀφθῆναι φοινικίδας ἔχοντες, ἐλέφασι δὲ λευκοὺς
χιτῶνας· ἐρεθίζεται γὰρ ὑπὸ τῶν χρωμάτων τὰ
ζῷα τούτων καὶ διαθηριοῦται. εἰ δὲ βασιλεὺς
μέγας ἔθνη δυσκάθεκτα καὶ μαχόμενα καθάπερ
ζῷα τιθασεύων καὶ μειλισσόμενος ἐσθῆσιν οἰκείαις
C καὶ συνήθεσιν ἐξεπράυνε διαίταις καὶ κατέστελλεν,
οἰκειούμενος αὐτῶν τὸ δύσθυμον καὶ παρηγορῶν
τὸ σκυθρωπόν, ἐγκαλοῦσιν; οὐχὶ θαυμάζουσι τὴν
σοφίαν, ὅτι τῷ τυχόντι μετασχηματισμῷ τὴν
Ἀσίαν ἐδημαγώγησε, τοῖς μὲν ὅπλοις τῶν σωμάτων ἐπικρατήσας, τῇ δ' ἐσθῆτι τὰς ψυχὰς προσ-
αγαγόμενος[2]; καίτοι γ' Ἀρίστιππον θαυμάζουσι
τὸν Σωκρατικόν, ὅτι καὶ τρίβωνι λιτῷ καὶ Μιλησίᾳ

---

[1] τοῖς ἀδιαφόροις] τούτοις ἀδιαφόρως?
[2] προσαγαγόμενος] προσαγόμενος in some mss.

---

[a] Cf. Moralia, 144 D.
[b] Cf. Horace, Epistles, i. 17. 23-29 "personamque feret
non inconcinnus utramque."

a matter of indifference, but as sovereign of both nations and benevolent king he strove to acquire the goodwill of the conquered by showing respect for their apparel, so that they might continue constant in loving the Macedonians as rulers, and might not feel hate toward them as enemies. Conversely it were the mark of an unwise and vainglorious mind to admire greatly a cloak of uniform colour and to be displeased by a tunic with a purple border, or again to disdain those things and to be struck with admiration for these, holding stubbornly, in the manner of an unreasoning child, to the raiment in which the custom of his country, like a nurse, had attired him. When men hunt wild animals, they put on the skins of deer, and when they go to catch birds, they dress in tunics adorned with plumes and feathers; they are careful not to be seen by bulls when they have on red garments, nor by elephants when dressed in white; [a] for these animals are provoked and made savage by the sight of these particular colours. But if a great king, in taming and mollifying headstrong and warring nations, just as in dealing with animals, succeeded in soothing and stilling them by wearing a garb familiar to them and by following their wonted manner of life, thereby conciliating their rough natures and smoothing their sullen brows, can men impeach him? Must they not rather wonder at his wisdom, since by but a slight alteration of his apparel he made himself the popular leader of all Asia, conquering their bodies by his arms, but winning over their souls by his apparel? And yet men marvel at the disciple of Socrates, Aristippus, [b] that whether he wore a threadbare

(330) χλαμύδι[1] χρώμενος δι' ἀμφοτέρων ἐτήρει τὸ
εὔσχημον· Ἀλεξάνδρῳ δ' ἐγκαλοῦσιν, ὅτι τὴν
πάτριον ἐσθῆτα κοσμῶν οὐδὲ τὴν δορίκτητον
ὑπερεῖδε, μεγάλων πραγμάτων καταβαλλόμενος
D ἀρχάς. οὐ γὰρ λῃστρικῶς τὴν Ἀσίαν καταδραμὼν
οὐδ' ὥσπερ ἅρπαγμα καὶ λάφυρον εὐτυχίας ἀνελπίστου σπαράξαι καὶ ἀνασύρασθαι διανοηθείς,
καθάπερ ὕστερον μὲν Ἀννίβας Ἰταλίαν, πρότερον
δὲ Τρῆρες Ἰωνίαν καὶ Σκύθαι Μηδίαν ἐπῆλθον·
ἀλλ' ἑνὸς ὑπήκοα λόγου τὰ ἐπὶ γῆς καὶ μιᾶς
πολιτείας, ἕνα δῆμον ἀνθρώπους ἅπαντας ἀποφῆναι
βουλόμενος, οὕτως ἑαυτὸν ἐσχημάτιζεν· εἰ δὲ μὴ
ταχέως ὁ δεῦρο καταπέμψας τὴν Ἀλεξάνδρου
ψυχὴν ἀνεκαλέσατο δαίμων, εἷς ἂν νόμος ἅπαντας
ἀνθρώπους διῳκεῖτο καὶ πρὸς ἓν δίκαιον ὡς πρὸς
κοινὸν ἐπέβλεπον[2] φῶς. νῦν δὲ τῆς γῆς ἀνήλιον
E μέρος ἔμεινεν, ὅσον Ἀλέξανδρον οὐκ εἶδεν.

9. Οὐκοῦν πρώτη μὲν ἡ τῆς στρατείας ὑπόθεσις
φιλόσοφον τὸν ἄνδρα συνίστησιν, οὐχ ἑαυτῷ τρυφὴν
καὶ πολυτέλειαν ἀλλὰ πᾶσιν ἀνθρώποις ὁμόνοιαν
καὶ εἰρήνην καὶ κοινωνίαν πρὸς ἀλλήλους παρα-
σκευάσαι διανοηθέντα.

Δεύτερον δ' αὐτοῦ καὶ τὰς φωνὰς ἴδωμεν, ἐπεὶ
καὶ τὰ τῶν ἄλλων ἤθη βασιλέων καὶ δυναστῶν
μάλιστα ταῖς φωναῖς αἱ ψυχαὶ προβάλλουσιν.
Ἀντίγονος ὁ γέρων, σοφιστοῦ τινος αὐτῷ σύγγραμμα προσδιδόντος[3] περὶ δικαιοσύνης, "ἀβέλ-

---

[1] χλαμύδι] χλανίδι Cobet.
[2] διῳκεῖτο . . . ἐπέβλεπον Nachstädt: ἐπέβλεπε . . . διῳκεῖτο.
[3] προσδιδόντος S. A. Naber, is made fairly certain by προσ-
ᾴδοντος in some mss. and προσδόντος in most of the others.

404

cloak or a fine Milesian robe he retained his gentility in either ; but they impeach Alexander because, although paying due respect to his own national dress, he did not disdain that of his conquered subjects in establishing the beginnings of a vast empire. For he did not overrun Asia like a robber nor was he minded to tear and rend it, as if it were booty and plunder bestowed by unexpected good fortune, after the manner in which Hannibal later descended upon Italy, or as earlier the Treres[a] descended upon Ionia and the Scythians[b] upon Media. But Alexander desired to render all upon earth subject to one law of reason and one form of government and to reveal all men as one people, and to this purpose he made himself conform. But if the deity that sent down Alexander's soul into this world of ours had not recalled him quickly, one law would govern all mankind, and they all would look toward one rule of justice as though toward a common source of light. But as it is, that part of the world which has not looked upon Alexander has remained without sunlight.

9. Therefore, in the first place, the very plan and design of Alexander's expedition commends the man as a philosopher in his purpose not to win for himself luxury and extravagant living, but to win for all men concord and peace and community of interests.

And, in the second place, let us examine his sayings too, since it is by their utterances[c] that the souls of other kings and potentates also best reveal their characters. The elder Antigonus remarked to a certain sophist who put in his hands a treatise on

---

[a] Cf. Strabo, i. 3. 21 ; xi. 8. 4.
[b] Cf. Herodotus, i. 15, 103-106.   [c] Cf. Moralia, 172 D.

τερος εἶ," εἶπεν, " ὃς ὁρῶν με τὰς ἀλλοτρίας
πόλεις τύπτοντα λέγεις περὶ δικαιοσύνης." Διονύ-
F σιος δ' ὁ τύραννος ἐκέλευε τοὺς μὲν παῖδας ἀστρα-
γάλοις τοὺς δ' ἄνδρας ὅρκοις ἐξαπατᾶν. τοῖς δὲ
Σαρδαναπάλλου μνημείοις ἐπιγέγραπται

ταῦτ' ἔχω ὅσσ' ἔφαγον καὶ ἐφύβρισα.

τίς οὐκ ἂν εἴποι τῶν ἀποφθεγμάτων τούτων τῷ
μὲν ἀποφαίνεσθαι φιληδονίαν, τῷ δ' ἀθεότητα, τῷ
δ' ἀδικίαν καὶ πλεονεξίαν; τῶν δ' Ἀλεξάνδρου
φωνῶν ἂν ἀφέλῃς τὸ διάδημα καὶ τὸν Ἄμμωνα
331 καὶ τὴν εὐγένειαν, Σωκράτους ἢ Πλάτωνος ἢ
Πυθαγόρου σοι φανοῦνται. μὴ γὰρ ἃς οἱ ποιηταὶ
ταῖς εἰκόσιν αὐτοῦ καὶ τοῖς ἀνδριᾶσι μεγαληγορίας
ἐπεχάραττον, οὐ τῆς μετριότητος ἀλλὰ τῆς δυνάμεως τῆς Ἀλεξάνδρου στοχαζόμενοι, σκοπῶμεν·

αὐδασοῦντι δ' ἔοικεν ὁ χάλκεος εἰς Δία λεύσσων,
Γᾶν ὑπ' ἐμοὶ τίθεμαι· Ζεῦ, σὺ δ' Ὄλυμπον ἔχε.

καὶ ἄλλου ἀνδρός,[1] " ἐγὼ Διὸς μὲν υἱός." ταῦτα
μὲν οὖν, ὡς ἔφην, οἱ ποιηταὶ κολακεύοντες αὐτοῦ
τὴν τύχην προσεῖπον.

Τῶν δ' ἀληθινῶν ἀποφθεγμάτων Ἀλεξάνδρου
B πρῶτον ἄν τις τὰ παιδικὰ διέλθοι. ποδωκέστατος
γὰρ τῶν ἐφ' ἡλικίας νέων γενόμενος καὶ τῶν

---

[1] ἄλλου ἀνδρός F.C.B. : ἀλέξανδρος.

---

[a] Attributed elsewhere to Lysander : cf. Moralia, 229 B,
and the note (Vol. III. p. 373).

[b] Cf. Palatine Anthology, vii. 325 ; xvi. 27 : a full list
of citations portraying Sardanapalus in ancient popular
philosophy is given by W. Capelle, Hermes, lx. p. 394 ;
see also W. Headlam, Journal of Philosophy, xxvi. p. 98.

[c] Cf. 335 B, infra ; T. Preger, Inscriptiones Graecae

justice, " You are a fool to say anything about justice when you see me smiting other people's cities." The despot Dionysius remarked that one should trick children with dice, but men with oaths.[a] Upon the tomb of Sardanapalus [b] is written,

> These are still mine—what I ate, and my wanton love-frolics.

Who would not own that by these several sayings are revealed Sardanapalus's love of pleasure, Dionysius's impiety, and Antigonus's injustice and greed ? But if you subtract from Alexander's sayings his crown, his relationship with Ammon, and his noble birth, they will appear to you as the utterances of a Socrates or a Plato or a Pythagoras. Let us, then, pay no heed to the proud boasts which the poets inscribed upon his portraits and statues, studying, as they were, to portray, not Alexander's moderation, but his power :

> Eager to speak seems the statue of bronze, up to Zeus as it gazes :
> " Earth I have set under foot; Zeus, keep Olympus yourself." [c]

And another man makes Alexander say, " I am the son of Zeus." [d] These expressions, then, as I have said, the poets addressed to Alexander in flattery of his good fortune.

But of the genuine sayings of Alexander we might first review those of his youth. Since he was the swiftest of foot of all the young men of his age,[e] his

---

Metricae (1891), pp. 183-187. The epigram is more completely given in the *Anthology*, xvi. 120, where it is attributed to Archelaüs or Asclepiades. Probably, as Ouvré has seen, it belongs to the latter.

[d] *Cf. Life of Alexander*, chap. xxvii. (680 F).
[e] *Cf. Moralia*, 179 D ; *Life of Alexander*, chap. iv. (666 D).

(331) ἑταίρων αὐτὸν ἐπ᾽ Ὀλύμπια παρορμώντων, ἠρώ-
τησεν, εἰ βασιλεῖς ἀγωνίζονται· τῶν δ᾽ οὐ φαμένων,
ἄδικον εἶπεν εἶναι τὴν ἅμιλλαν, ἐν ᾗ νικήσει μὲν
ἰδιώτας, νικηθήσεται δὲ βασιλεύς.

Τοῦ δὲ πατρὸς Φιλίππου λόγχῃ τὸν μηρὸν ἐν
Τριβαλλοῖς διαπαρέντος, καὶ τὸν μὲν κίνδυνον
διαφυγόντος, ἀχθομένου δὲ τῇ χωλότητι, "θάρρει,
πάτερ," ἔφη, " καὶ πρόιθι φαιδρῶς,[1] ἵνα τῆς ἀρετῆς
κατὰ βῆμα μνημονεύῃς." ταῦτ᾽ οὐκ ἔστι διανοίας
Ο φιλοσόφου καὶ διὰ τὸν ἐπὶ τοῖς καλοῖς ἐνθουσιασμὸν
ἤδη τῶν τοῦ σώματος ἐλαττωμάτων κατεξανιστα-
μένης; πῶς γὰρ αὐτὸν οἴει[2] τοῖς ἰδίοις ἀγάλλεσθαι
τραύμασι, καθ᾽ ἕκαστον μέρος ἔθνους μνημονεύοντα
καὶ νίκης καὶ πόλεων ἁλισκομένων καὶ βασιλέων[3]
παραδιδόντων, οὐκ ἐγκαλυπτόμενον οὐδὲ κατα-
κρύπτοντα τὰς οὐλάς, ἀλλ᾽ ὥσπερ εἰκόνας ἐγ-
κεχαραγμένας ἀρετῆς καὶ ἀνδραγαθίας περιφέροντα;
10. Καὶ μὴν εἴ ποτε γένοιτο τῶν Ὁμήρου σύγκρισις ἐπῶν ἐν ταῖς διατριβαῖς ἢ παρὰ τὰ συμπόσια,
ἄλλον ἄλλου στίχον προκρίνοντος, αὐτὸς ὡς διαφέροντα πάντων ἐνέκρινε τοῦτον,

ἀμφότερον βασιλεύς τ᾽ ἀγαθὸς κρατερός τ᾽
αἰχμητής,

Δ ὃν ἄλλος ἔπαινον τῷ χρόνῳ προέλαβε, τοῦτον αὐτῷ
νόμον κεῖσθαι λογιζόμενος, ὥστ᾽ εἰπεῖν Ὅμηρον
ὅτι τῷ αὐτῷ μέτρῳ τὴν μὲν Ἀγαμέμνονος ἀνδρα-

---

[1] φαιδρῶς Reiske: φανερῶς (but cf. Philologus xc. p. 121,
note 2).
[2] οἴει Xylander and marginal variant in E: ἐπί.
[3] βασιλέων] Reiske would add ἑαυτούς.

[a] Attributed to a Spartan woman in Moralia, 241 E, where
see the note.

comrades urged him to enter the Olympic games. He asked if the competitors were kings, and when his friends replied that they were not, he said that the contest was unfair, for it was one in which a victory would be over commoners, but a defeat would be the defeat of a king.

When the thigh of his father Philip had been pierced by a spear in battle with the Triballians, and Philip, although he escaped with his life, was vexed with his lameness, Alexander said, " Be of good cheer, father, and go on your way rejoicing, that at each step you may recall your valour."[a] Are not these the words of a truly philosophic spirit which, because of its rapture for noble things, already revolts against mere physical encumbrances ? How, then, think you, did he glory in his own wounds, remembering by each part of his body affected a nation overcome, a victory won, the capture of cities, the surrender of kings ? He did not cover over nor hide his scars, but bore them with him openly as symbolic representations, graven on his body, of virtue and manly courage.

10. And in the same spirit if ever there chanced to be in hours of ease or at a banquet a comparison of the verses of Homer, each man choosing his favourite line, Alexander always judged this verse to be the greatest of all :

> Both things is he: both a goodly king and a warrior mighty.[b]

This praise, which at the time it was written another had received, Alexander conceived to be a law for himself, so that he said of Homer that in this same verse he had honoured the manly courage of Aga-

---

[b] *Iliad*, iii. 179 ; *cf.* Xenophon, *Memorabilia*, iii. 2. 2.

(331) γαθίαν κεκόσμηκε, τὴν δ ᾽Αλεξάνδρου μεμάν-
τευται. διαβὰς τοίνυν τὸν ῾Ελλήσποντον ἐθεᾶτο
τὴν Τροίαν ἀνατυπούμενος τὰς ἡρωικὰς πράξεις·
καί τινος αὐτῷ τῶν ἐγχωρίων ὑποσχομένου τὴν
Πάριδος λύραν, εἰ βούλοιτο, δώσειν, " οὐδέν,"
ἔφη, " τῆς ἐκείνου δέομαι· τὴν γὰρ ᾽Αχιλλέως
κέκτημαι, πρὸς ἢν ἐκεῖνος ἀνεπαύετο

  ἄειδε δ᾽ ἄρα κλέα ἀνδρῶν·

ἡ δὲ Πάριδος πάντως μαλακήν τινα καὶ θήλειαν
E ἁρμονίαν ἐρωτικοῖς ἔψαλλε μέλεσι." φιλοσόφου
τοίνυν ἐστὶ ψυχῆς σοφίας ἐρᾶν καὶ σοφοὺς ἄνδρας
θαυμάζειν μάλιστα· τοῦτο δ᾽ ᾽Αλεξάνδρῳ προσῆν
ὡς οὐδενὶ τῶν βασιλέων. καὶ πῶς μὲν εἶχε πρὸς
᾽Αριστοτέλην εἴρηται· καὶ ὅτι τὸν μὲν ἁρμονικὸν[1]
᾽Ανάξαρχον ἐντιμότατον τῶν φίλων ἐνόμιζε, Πύρ-
ρωνι δὲ τῷ ᾽Ηλείῳ πρῶτον ἐντυχόντι μυρίους
χρυσοῦς ἔδωκε, Ξενοκράτει δὲ τῷ Πλάτωνος
συνήθει πεντήκοντα τάλαντα δωρεὰν ἔπεμψεν, ᾽Ονη-
σίκριτον δὲ τὸν Διογένους τοῦ Κυνὸς μαθητὴν ὅτι
ἄρχοντα τῶν κυβερνητῶν κατέστησεν ὑπὸ πλειόνων
ἱστόρηται.

Διογένει δ᾽ αὐτῷ περὶ Κόρινθον εἰς λόγους
F ἐλθὼν οὕτως ἔφριξε καὶ κατεπλάγη τὸν βίον καὶ
τὸ ἀξίωμα τοῦ ἀνδρός, ὥστε πολλάκις αὐτοῦ

  [1] ἁρμονικὸν] εὐδαιμονικὸν suggested by Ménage from
Diogenes Laertius, ix. 60.

-----

  [a] Cf. Life of Alexander, chap. xv. (672 B); Aelian, Varia
Historia, ix. 38.
  [b] Homer, Il. ix. 189.
  [c] 327 F, supra; cf. Life of Alexander, chaps. vii., viii.
(668 A-F).

memnon and prophesied that of Alexander. Accordingly when he had crossed the Hellespont, he went to see the site of Troy,[a] imagining to himself the heroic deeds enacted there ; and when one of the natives of the country promised to give him the lyre of Paris, if he wished it, Alexander said, " Of his lyre I have no need ; for I already possess Achilles' lyre to the accompaniment of which, as he rested from his labours,

> he sang the famed deeds of heroes.[b]

But the lyre of Paris gave forth an altogether weak and womanish strain to accompany his love songs." Thus it is the mark of a truly philosophic soul to be in love with wisdom and to admire wise men most of all, and this was more characteristic of Alexander than of any other king. His attitude toward Aristotle has already been stated[c] ; and it is recorded by several authors that he considered the musician Anaxarchus the most valuable of all his friends, that he gave ten thousand gold pieces to Pyrrhon[d] of Elis the first time he met him, that he sent to Xenocrates,[e] the friend of Plato, fifty talents as a gift, and that he made Onesicritus,[f] the pupil of Diogenes the Cynic, chief pilot of his fleet.

But when he came to talk with Diogenes[g] himself in Corinth, he was so awed and astounded with the life and the worth of the man that often, when remembrance of the philosopher came to him, he would

---

[d] Cf. Sextus Empiricus, *Adversus Mathematicos*, i. 282.

[e] Cf. 333 B, *infra*, and *Moralia*, 181 E.

[f] Cf. *Life of Alexander*, chaps. lxv., lxvi. (701 c, 702 A); Arrian, *Anabasis*, vi. 2. 3, vii. 5. 6 ; Diogenes Laertius, vi. 84.

[g] Cf. *Life of Alexander*, chap. xiv. (671 D); Diogenes Laertius, vi. 32 ; Valerius Maximus, iv. 3. 4 ; Juvenal, xiv. 311-314. *Cf.* also *Moralia*, 782 A-B.

μνημονεύων λέγειν, " εἰ μὴ Ἀλέξανδρος ἤμην,
Διογένης ἂν ἤμην," τουτέστιν " ἠσχολούμην ἂν
περὶ λόγους, εἰ μὴ δι' ἔργων ἐφιλοσόφουν." οὐκ
εἶπεν, " εἰ μὴ βασιλεὺς ἤμην, Διογένης ἂν ἤμην,"
οὐδ', " εἰ μὴ πλούσιος καὶ Ἀργεάδης "· οὐ γὰρ
332 προέκρινε τὴν τύχην τῆς σοφίας οὐδὲ τὴν πορφύραν
καὶ τὸ διάδημα τῆς πήρας καὶ τοῦ τρίβωνος· ἀλλ'
εἶπεν, " εἰ μὴ Ἀλέξανδρος ἤμην, Διογένης ἂν
ἤμην," τουτέστιν " εἰ μὴ τὰ βαρβαρικὰ τοῖς
Ἑλληνικοῖς κεράσαι διενοούμην καὶ πᾶσαν ἤπειρον
ἐπιὼν ἐξημερῶσαι, καὶ πέρατα γῆς ἀνερευνῶν[1] καὶ
θαλάττης ὠκεανῷ προσερεῖσαι[2] Μακεδονίαν, καὶ
τὴν Ἑλλάδος[3] σπεῖραι καὶ καταχέασθαι γένους
παντὸς εὐδικίαν καὶ εἰρήνην, οὐκ ἂν ἐν ἀπράκτῳ
τρυφῶν ἐξουσίᾳ καθήμην, ἀλλ' ἐζήλουν ἂν τὴν
Διογένους εὐτέλειαν. νῦν δὲ σύγγνωθι, Διόγενες,
Ἡρακλέα μιμοῦμαι καὶ Περσέα ζηλῶ, καὶ τὰ
Β Διονύσου μετιὼν ἴχνη, θεοῦ γενάρχου καὶ προ-
πάτορος, βούλομαι πάλιν ἐν Ἰνδίᾳ νικῶντας
Ἕλληνας ἐγχορεῦσαι καὶ τοὺς ὑπὲρ Καύκασον
ὀρείους καὶ ἀγρίους τῶν βακχικῶν κώμων ἀνα-
μνῆσαι. κἀκεῖ τινες εἶναι λέγονται στερρᾶς καὶ
γυμνήτιδος σοφίας ἐθάδες ἄνδρες ἱεροὶ καὶ αὐτό-
νομοι, θεῷ σχολάζοντες, εὐτελέστεροι Διογένους,
οὐδὲν πήρας δεόμενοι· τροφὴν γὰρ οὐκ ἀποτίθενται,
πρόσφατον ἀεὶ καὶ νέαν ἀπὸ γῆς ἔχοντες· ποτὸν δὲ
ποταμοὶ ῥέουσι· φύλλα δ' αὐτοῖς δένδρων ἀπο-

---

[1] ἀνερευνῶν] ἀνευρὼν in most mss.
[2] προσερεῖσαι] προσορίσαι van Herwerden.
[3] Ἑλλάδος E. Capps: Ἑλλάδα.

---

[a] Cf. Arrian, Anabasis, iv. 10. 6; Rhein. Mus. liv. 470.
[b] Cf. 326 B, supra.

say, "If I were not Alexander, I should be Diogenes," that is to say : " If I did not actively practise philosophy, I should apply myself to its theoretical pursuit." He did not say, " If I were not a king, I should be Diogenes," nor " If I were not rich and an Argead " ; for he did not rank Fortune above Wisdom, nor a crown and royal purple above the philosopher's wallet and threadbare gown. But he said, " If I were not Alexander, I should be Diogenes"; that is to say : " If it were not my purpose to combine foreign things with things Greek, to traverse and civilize every continent, to search out the uttermost parts of land and sea, to push the bounds of Macedonia to the farthest Ocean, and to disseminate and shower the blessings of Greek justice and peace over every nation, I should not be content to sit quietly in the luxury of idle power, but I should emulate the frugality of Diogenes. But as things are, forgive me, Diogenes, that I imitate Heracles, and emulate Perseus, and follow in the footsteps of Dionysus,[a] the divine author and progenitor of my family,[b] and desire that victorious Greeks should dance again in India and revive the memory of the Bacchic revels among the savage mountain tribes beyond the Caucasus. Even there it is said that there are certain holy men, a law unto themselves, who follow a rigid gymnosophy [c] and give all their time to God ; they are more frugal than Diogenes since they have no need of a wallet. For they do not store up food, since they have it ever fresh and green from the earth ; the flowing rivers give them drink and they have fallen leaves and grassy

---

[c] Cf. Life of Alexander, chaps. lxiv., lxv. (700 F-701 F) for Alexander's dealings with the Gymnosophists.

413

(332) χυθέντα[1] καὶ πόα γῆς ἐγκατακλιθῆναι. δι' ἐμὲ
κἀκεῖνοι Διογένη γνώσονται καὶ Διογένης ἐκείνους.
C δεῖ κἀμὲ νόμισμα παρακόψαι καὶ παραχαράξαι τὸ
βαρβαρικὸν[2] Ἑλληνικῇ πολιτείᾳ.''

11. Εἶεν· αἱ δὴ πράξεις αὐτοῦ πότερον αὐτομα-
τισμὸν ἐπιφαίνουσι τύχης καὶ βίαν πολεμικὴν καὶ
χειροκρατίαν,[3] ἢ πολλὴν μὲν ἀνδρείαν καὶ δικαιοσύνην, πολλὴν δὲ σωφροσύνην καὶ πραότητα μετὰ
κόσμου καὶ συνέσεως, νήφοντι καὶ πεπνυμένῳ τῷ
λογισμῷ πάντα πράττοντος; οὐ γὰρ ἔστιν εἰπεῖν
διακρίναντά με μὰ τοὺς θεούς, ὅτι τοῦτο μὲν
ἀνδρείας, τοῦτο δὲ φιλανθρωπίας, τοῦτο δ' ἐγ-
κρατείας· ἀλλὰ πᾶν ἔργον ἐκ πασῶν ἔοικε τῶν
ἀρετῶν μεμεῖχθαι· βεβαιοῦντος αὐτοῦ τὸν Στωικὸν
D ἐκεῖνον λόγον ὅτι πᾶν ὃ ἂν δρᾷ ὁ σοφὸς κατὰ πᾶσαν
ἀρετὴν ἐνεργεῖ, καὶ μία μέν, ὡς ἔοικεν, ἀρετὴ
πρωταγωνιστεῖ πράξεως ἑκάστης, παρακαλεῖ δὲ
τὰς ἄλλας καὶ συντείνει πρὸς τὸ τέλος. ἰδεῖν γοῦν
ἔστιν ἐν Ἀλεξάνδρῳ τὸ μὲν πολεμικὸν φιλάνθρωπον,
τὸ δὲ πρᾶον ἀνδρῶδες, τὸ δὲ χαριστικὸν οἰκονο-
μικόν, τὸ δὲ θυμικὸν εὐδιάλλακτον, τὸ δ' ἐρωτικὸν
σῶφρον, τὸ δ' ἀνειμένον οὐκ ἀργόν, τὸ δ' ἐπίπονον
οὐκ ἀπαραμύθητον. τίς ἔμειξε πολέμοις ἑορτάς;
τίς δὲ κώμοις στρατείας; τίς δὲ πολιορκίαις καὶ
παρατάξεσι[4] βακχείας καὶ γάμους καὶ ὑμεναίους;
τίς ἀδικοῦσιν ἐχθρότερος ἢ δυστυχοῦσιν ἡμερώ-
E τερος; τίς μαχομένοις βαρύτερος ἢ δεομένοις
εὐγνωμονέστερος;

---

[1] ἀποχυθέντα Reiske ; ὑποχυθέντα Meziriacus : ἀποχυθέντων.
[2] τὸ βαρβαρικόν] τὸ βαρβαρικῇ θέσει κατεσκευασμένον in
some mss.
[3] χειροκρατίαν Reiske : χειροκρασίαν.
[4] παρατάξεσι Wyttenbach : πράξεσι.

earth to lie upon. Because of me even those far-away sages shall come to know of Diogenes, and he of them. And I also, like Diogenes, must alter the standard of coinage[a] and stamp foreign states with the impress of Greek government."

11. Very well. Do Alexander's actions, then, reveal the caprice of Fortune, the violence of war, the might of conquest, or do they rather reveal the great courage and justice, the great restraint and mildness together with the decorous behaviour and intelligence, of one who did all things with sober and sane judgement? For, by Heaven, it is impossible for me to distinguish his several actions and say that this betokens his courage, this his humanity, this his self-control, but everything he did seems the combined product of all the virtues; for he confirms the truth of that principle of the Stoïcs which declares that every act which the wise man performs is an activity in accord with every virtue; and although, as it appears, one particular virtue performs the chief rôle in every act, yet it but heartens on the other virtues and directs them toward the goal. Certainly one may observe that in Alexander the warlike is also humane, the mild also manly, the liberal provident, the irascible placable, the amatory temperate, his relaxation not idle, and his labours not without recreation. Who but he combined festivals with wars, campaigns with revels, Bacchic rites and weddings and nuptial songs with sieges and battle-fields? Who was ever more hostile to wrongdoers or kinder to the unfortunate? Who more stern to his opponents or more indulgent to petitioners?

[a] *Cf.* Diogenes Laertius, vi. 20, 21.

*Ἔπεισί μοι τὸ τοῦ Πώρου δεῦρο μετενεγκεῖν. ἐκεῖνος γὰρ ὡς ἤχθη πρὸς Ἀλέξανδρον αἰχμάλωτος, πυθομένου πῶς αὐτῷ χρήσεται, " βασιλικῶς," εἶπεν, " ὦ Ἀλέξανδρε." πάλιν δ' ἐπερομένου, " μή τι ἄλλο; " " οὐδέν," εἶπε, " πάντα γάρ ἐστιν ἐν τῷ βασιλικῶς." κἀμοὶ δὴ ταῖς Ἀλεξάνδρου πράξεσιν ἔπεισιν ἐπιφωνεῖν ἀεὶ " φιλοσόφως "· ἐν τούτῳ γὰρ πάντ' ἔνεστι. Ῥωξάνης ἐρασθεὶς τῆς Ὀξυάρτου θυγατρὸς ἐν ταῖς αἰχμαλωτίσι χορευούσης οὐχ ὕβρισεν ἀλλ' ἔγημε· φιλο-
F σόφως. Δαρεῖον ἰδὼν κατηκοντισμένον οὐκ ἔθυσεν οὐδ' ἐπαιάνισεν ὡς τοῦ μακροῦ πολέμου τέλος ἔχοντος, ἀλλὰ τὴν χλαμύδα τὴν ἑαυτοῦ περιελὼν ἐπέρριψε τῷ νεκρῷ καθάπερ τὴν[1] νέμεσιν[2] τύχης βασιλικῆς συγκαλύπτων· φιλοσόφως. ἐπιστολὴν δέ ποτε τῆς μητρὸς ἀπόρρητον διερχόμενος, Ἡφαιστίωνος, ὡς ἔτυχε, παρακαθημένου καὶ ἁπλῶς
333 συναναγιγνώσκοντος, οὐκ ἐκώλυσεν, ἀλλὰ τὸν δακτύλιον αὐτοῦ τῷ στόματι προσέθηκεν αὐτοῦ, κατασφραγισάμενος φιλικῇ πίστει τὴν σιωπήν· φιλοσόφως. εἰ γὰρ ταῦτ' οὐκ ἔστι φιλοσόφως, τίν' ἐστὶν ἄλλα;

12. Παραθῶμεν τὰ τῶν ὁμολογουμένων φιλοσόφων. Σωκράτης ἠνέσχετο συγκοιμηθέντος Ἀλκι-

---

[1] τὴν Helmbold : τινά.　　[2] νέμεσιν Reiske : γένεσιν.

---

[a] Cf. Moralia, 181 E, and 458 B ; Life of Alexander, chap. lx. (669 c) ; Arrian, Anabasis, v. 19. 2.
[b] Cf. 338 D, infra ; Life of Alexander, chap. xlvii. (691 E) ; Arrian, iv. 19 ; Curtius, viii. 4.
[c] Cf. Life of Alexander, chap. xliii. (690 B).

It occurs to me to introduce here an incident touching Porus.[a] For when Porus was brought as a captive before Alexander, the conqueror asked how he should treat him. "Like a king, Alexander," said Porus. When Alexander asked again if there were nothing else, "No," said he, "for everything is included in that word." And it naturally occurs to me also to exclaim over each of Alexander's deeds, "Like a philosopher!" For in this is included everything. He became enamoured of Roxanê,[b] the daughter of Oxyartes, as she danced among the captive maidens; yet he did not offer any violence to her, but made her his wife. "Like a philosopher!" When he saw Darius[c] pierced through by javelins, he did not offer sacrifice nor raise the paean of victory to indicate that the long war had come to an end; but he took off his own cloak and threw it over the corpse as though to conceal the divine retribution that waits upon the lot of kings. "Like a philosopher!" Once when he was reading a confidential letter from his mother, and Hephaestion,[d] who, as it happened, was sitting beside him, was quite openly reading it too, Alexander did not stop him, but merely placed his own signet-ring on Hephaestion's lips, sealing them to silence with a friend's confidence. "Like a philosopher!" For if these actions be not those of a philosopher, what others are?

12. But let us compare the actions of men who are admitted to be philosophers. Socrates forbore when Alcibiades[e] spent the night with him. But when

[a] Cf. Moralia, 180 D, and the note.
[e] Cf. Plato, Symposium, 218 c; Diogenes Laertius, ii. 31.

417

(333) βιάδου· Ἀλέξανδρος δέ, Φιλοξένου τοῦ τῆς
παραλίας ὑπάρχου γράψαντος, ὅτι παῖς ἐν Ἰωνίᾳ
γέγονεν οἷος οὐκ ἄλλος ὥραν καὶ εἶδος, καὶ πυνθανομένου διὰ τῶν γραμμάτων εἰ ἀναπέμψοι,[1]
πικρῶς ἀντέγραψεν, " ὦ κάκιστ' ἀνθρώπων, τί μοι
πώποτε τοιοῦτο συνέγνως, ἵνα τοιαύταις με κολα-
B κεύσῃς ἡδοναῖς; " Ξενοκράτην, πεντήκοντα τάλαντα δωρεὰν Ἀλεξάνδρου πέμψαντος, ὅτι οὐκ
ἔλαβε θαυμάζομεν· τὸ δὲ δοῦναι, οὔ; ἢ οὐχ
ὁμοίως καταφρονεῖν χρημάτων δοκοῦμεν τὸν μὴ
προσιέμενον καὶ τὸν χαριζόμενον; οὐκ ἐδεῖτο
πλούτου Ξενοκράτης διὰ φιλοσοφίαν, Ἀλέξανδρος
δ' ἐδεῖτο διὰ φιλοσοφίαν, ἵνα τοιούτοις χαρίζηται.[2]
τοῦτο ποσάκις Ἀλέξανδρος εἶπε βαλλόμενος,
εἰσβιαζόμενος[3]; καίτοι κρίσεις μὲν ὀρθὰς πᾶσιν
ἐνυπάρχειν ἀνθρώποις νομίζομεν· ἡ γὰρ φύσις
ἀγωγός ἐστιν ἀφ' ἑαυτῆς πρὸς τὸ καλόν· οἱ δὲ
φιλόσοφοι τῶν πολλῶν διαφέρουσι τῷ τὰς κρίσεις
C ἔχειν ἐρρωμένας παρὰ τὰ δεινὰ καὶ πεπηγυίας,
ἐπεὶ οὐ μετὰ τοιούτων προλήψεων " εἷς οἰωνὸς

---

[1] ἀναπέμψοι] ἀναπέμψει most mss.; ἀναπέμψῃ Cobet.
[2] Dübner assumes a lacuna after χαρίζηται.
[3] εἰσβιαζόμενος F.C.B.: ἐκβιαζόμενος.

[a] Cf. *Moralia*, 1099 D; *Life of Alexander*, chap. xxii.
(676 F).

Philoxenus,[a] the governor of the coast-lands of Asia Minor, wrote to Alexander that there was in Ionia a youth, the like of whom for bloom and beauty did not exist, and inquired in his letter whether he should send the boy on to him, Alexander wrote bitterly in reply, " Vilest of men, what deed of this sort have you ever been privy to in my past that now you would flatter me with the offer of such pleasures ? " We admire Xenocrates[b] because he would not accept the gift of fifty talents which Alexander sent him. But shall we not admire the giving of it ? Or do we think that he who does not welcome a gift and he who bestows it are not at one in their contempt for money ? Because of philosophy Xenocrates had no need of wealth and because of philosophy Alexander had need of wealth that he might lavish it upon such men. How many times has Alexander said this when forcing an attack amid a shower of missiles ?[c] And yet we believe that all men are endowed with the capacity to form right judgements. For Nature of herself is prone to lead men toward the Good. But philosophers differ from common persons in having their powers of judgement strong and firm to face danger, since the common man is not fortified by conceptions such as these : " Best is one omen "[d] and

---

[b] Cf. 331 E, supra.

[c] Alexander's remark that he needed money to give to others may be compared to the remark which Plutarch quotes in his *Life of Alexander*, chap. lx. (698 E), when Alexander was risking his life in crossing the swollen Hydaspes : " O Athenians, can you possibly believe what dangers I undergo to win good repute among you ? " Others think that the remark has been lost from the MSS.

[d] Homer, *Il.* xii. 243 εἷς οἰωνὸς ἄριστος ἀμύνεσθαι περὶ πάτρης.

(333) ἄριστος '' καὶ ''πέρας μέν ἐστιν ἅπασιν ἀνθρώποις
ὁ θάνατος.'' ἀλλὰ θραύουσιν οἱ καιροὶ παρὰ τὰ
δεινὰ τοὺς λογισμούς, καὶ τὰς κρίσεις ἐκκρούουσιν
αἱ φαντασίαι τῶν κινδύνων ἐγγὺς γενομένων.
''φόβος γὰρ '' οὐ μόνον ''μνήμην ἐκπλήττει,''
κατὰ τὸν Θουκυδίδην, ἀλλὰ καὶ προαίρεσιν πᾶσαν
καὶ φιλοτιμίαν καὶ ὁρμήν, εἰ μὴ[1] μηρίνθους φιλοσοφία περιτέθεικεν.

[1] εἰ μὴ added by Emperius.

---

[a] Cf. *Moralia*, 166 F; Demosthenes, *De Corona*, 97.
W. Crönert, in a review of Bell-Crum, *A Greek-Coptic
Glossary* (*Gnomon*, ii. p. 657), reconstructs, from the words of

" Death is the end for all men " ;[a] but crises destroy all his calculations in the face of danger, and the fantastic imaginings of perils close at hand dispel his powers of judgement. For not only does " fear," as Thucydides[b] says, " drive out memory," but it also drives out every purpose and ambition and impulse, unless philosophy has drawn her cords about them.

the Testament of the High Priest Fl. Phoebammon, trimeters of an Euripidean flavour :

πέρας δὲ παντὸς τοῦ βροτησίου γένους
ὁ θάνατος οὐδὲ δυνατόν ἐστιν ἐκφυγεῖν.

More likely here, however, would be such a line as

ὁ θάνατός ἐσθ' ἅπασιν ἀνθρώποις πέρας.

Plutarch and Demosthenes may both be quoting from something of the sort.

[b] Thucydides, ii. 87.

ΠΕΡΙ
D ΤΗΣ ΑΛΕΞΑΝΔΡΟΥ ΤΥΧΗΣ Η ΑΡΕΤΗΣ

ΛΟΓΟΣ Β

1. Διέφυγεν ἡμᾶς, ὡς ἔοικε, χθὲς εἰπεῖν ὅτι καὶ
τέχνας πολλὰς καὶ φύσεις μεγάλας ὁ κατ᾽ Ἀλέξανδρον χρόνος ἐνεγκεῖν εὐτύχησεν· ἢ τοῦτο μὲν οὐ
E τῆς Ἀλεξάνδρου τύχης γέγονεν ἀλλὰ τῆς ἐκείνων,
μάρτυρα λαβεῖν καὶ θεατὴν τὸν ἄριστα κρῖναι τὸ
κατορθούμενον καὶ μάλιστ᾽ ἀμείψασθαι δυνάμενον.
λέγεται γοῦν ὅτι χρόνοις ὕστερον Ἀρχεστράτου
γενομένου ποιητοῦ χαρίεντος, ἐν δὲ πενίᾳ καὶ
ἀδοξίᾳ διάγοντος εἶπέ τις πρὸς αὐτόν, “ ἀλλ᾽ εἰ
κατ᾽ Ἀλέξανδρον ἐγένου, κατὰ στίχον ἄν σοι
Κύπρον ἢ Φοινίκην ἔδωκεν.” οἶμαι δὲ καὶ τῶν
τότε τεχνιτῶν οὐ κατ᾽ Ἀλέξανδρον ἀλλὰ δι᾽
Ἀλέξανδρον τοὺς πρώτους γενέσθαι. καρπῶν μὲν
γὰρ εὐφορίαν εὐκρασία ποιεῖ καὶ λεπτότης τοῦ
περιέχοντος ἀέρος, τεχνῶν δὲ καὶ φύσεων ἀγαθῶν
αὔξησιν εὐμένεια καὶ τιμὴ καὶ φιλανθρωπία βασι-
F λέως ἐκκαλεῖται· καὶ τοὐναντίον ὑπὸ φθόνου καὶ

ON THE FORTUNE OR THE VIRTUE
OF ALEXANDER

II

1. YESTERDAY we forgot, it seems, to remark that the age of Alexander had the good fortune to produce both many artistic achievements and many men of great talent. Perhaps, however, this was not part of Alexander's good fortune, but rather that of the artists, to have obtained as witness and spectator of their achievements the man who was both best able to judge of their success and to reward them most liberally. At any rate, it is said that, when Archestratus, a poet of a later age, who, though an accomplished writer, was passing his days in poverty and neglect, someone remarked to him, " If you had been born in Alexander's time, for every verse he would have given you a Cyprus or a Phoenicia." And I think that the foremost of the artists of that age became so, not because they lived in Alexander's day, but through what Alexander did for them. For a good climate and a lightness of the surrounding air produces a bountiful harvest ; and likewise the favour, esteem, and benignity shown by a king evokes a rich increase in the arts and in men of talent. And, conversely, through jealousy

423

σμικρολογίας ἢ φιλονεικίας τῶν κρατούντων σβέν-
νυται καὶ φθίνει πᾶν τὸ τοιοῦτο.

Διονύσιος γοῦν ὁ τύραννος, ὥς φασι, κιθαρῳδοῦ
τινος εὐδοκιμοῦντος ἀκούων ἐπηγγείλατο δωρεὰν
αὐτῷ τάλαντον· τῇ δ' ὑστεραίᾳ τοῦ ἀνθρώπου τὴν
ὑπόσχεσιν ἀπαιτοῦντος, " χθές," εἶπεν, " εὐφραινό-
334 μενος ὑπὸ σοῦ παρ' ὃν ᾖδες χρόνον εὔφρανα κἀγώ
σε ταῖς ἐλπίσιν· ὥστε τὸν μισθὸν ὧν ἔτερπες
ἀπελάμβανες εὐθὺς ἀντιτερπόμενος."

Ἀλέξανδρος δ' ὁ Φεραίων τύραννος (ἔδει δὲ τοῦτο
μόνον αὐτὸν καλεῖσθαι καὶ μὴ καταισχύνειν τὴν
ἐπωνυμίαν), θεώμενος τραγῳδὸν ἐμπαθέστερον ὑφ'
ἡδονῆς διετέθη πρὸς τὸν οἶκτον. ἀναπηδήσας οὖν
ἐκ τοῦ θεάτρου θᾶττον ἢ βάδην ἀπῄει, δεινὸν εἶναι
λέγων, εἰ τοσούτους ἀποσφάττων πολίτας ὀφθήσεται τοῖς Ἑκάβης καὶ Πολυξένης πάθεσιν ἐπι-
δακρύων. οὗτος μὲν οὖν μικροῦ καὶ δίκην ἐπράξατο
Β τὸν τραγῳδόν, ὅτι τὴν ψυχὴν αὐτοῦ καθάπερ
σίδηρον ἐμάλαξεν.

Ἀρχελάῳ δὲ δοκοῦντι γλισχροτέρῳ περὶ τὰς
δωρεὰς εἶναι Τιμόθεος ᾄδων ἐνεσήμαινε[1] πολλάκις
τουτὶ τὸ κομμάτιον[2]

σὺ δὲ[3] τὸν γηγενέταν ἄργυρον αἰνεῖς.

ὁ δ' Ἀρχέλαος οὐκ ἀμούσως ἀντεφώνησε,

σὺ δέ γ' αἰτεῖς.

---

[1] ἐνεσήμαινε] ἐσήμαινε some mss.
[2] κομμάτιον Meziriacus, as in *Moralia*, 177 B: σκωμμάτιον.
[3] δὲ Bernardakis, as in *Moralia*, 177 B: δὴ.

---

[a] Cf. *Moralia*, 41 D-E.   [b] £200, or $1000.

and parsimony or emulous rivalry on the part of monarchs all artistic production is quenched and perishes.

Thus the despot Dionysius,[a] as the story goes, while listening to a celebrated harper, engaged to give him a talent.[b] Next day, when the man asked for the fulfilment of the promise, Dionysius said, "Yesterday I was delighted with your performance, and during the time that you were singing I also delighted you with hopes! The result is that at that very time you were receiving full pay for the pleasure you gave by having your pleasure too!"

Alexander,[c] the tyrant of Pherae (this last should be his only appellation; he should not be permitted to disgrace the name of Alexander), as he watched a tragic actor, felt himself much moved to pity through enjoyment of the acting. He jumped up, therefore, and left the theatre at a rapid pace, exclaiming that it would be a dreadful thing, if, when he was slaughtering so many citizens, he should be seen to weep over the sufferings of Hecuba and Polyxena. And he came near visiting punishment upon the actor because the man had softened his heart, as iron in the fire.

Archelaüs[d] was thought to be somewhat niggardly in his favours, and Timotheüs liked to hint at this by often chanting this refrain:

> Over the earth-born silver you rave.

But Archelaüs, with some wit, chanted in reply:

> That, however, is what you crave.

---

[c] Cf. *Life of Pelopidas*, xxix. (293 F); Aelian, *Varia Historia*, xiv. 40.
[d] Cf. *Moralia*, 177 B, and the note.

(334) Ὁ δὲ τῶν Σκυθῶν βασιλεὺς Ἀτέας[1] Ἰσμηνίαν
τὸν αὐλητὴν λαβὼν αἰχμάλωτον, ἐκέλευσε παρὰ
πότον αὐλῆσαι. θαυμαζόντων δὲ τῶν ἄλλων καὶ
κροτούντων, αὐτὸς ὤμοσεν ἀκροᾶσθαι τοῦ ἵππου
χρεμετίζοντος ἥδιον. οὕτω μακρὰν ἀπεσκηνώκει
τὰ ὦτα τῶν Μουσῶν, καὶ τὴν ψυχὴν ἐν ταῖς
φάτναις εἶχεν, οὐχ ἵππων ἀλλ' ὄνων ἐπιτηδειοτέραν
C ἀκούειν. τίς ἂν οὖν παρὰ τοιούτοις βασιλεῦσιν
αὔξησις ἢ τιμὴ τέχνης γένοιτο καὶ Μούσης τοιαύτης; ἀλλ' οὐδὲ παρὰ τοῖς ἀντιτέχνοις ἐθέλουσιν
εἶναι, καὶ διὰ τοῦτο βασκανίᾳ καὶ δυσμενείᾳ τοὺς
ἀληθῶς τεχνίτας καθαιροῦσιν. οἷος ἦν πάλιν αὖ
Διονύσιος ὁ τὸν ποιητὴν Φιλόξενον εἰς τὰς λατομίας
ἐμβαλών, ὅτι τραγῳδίαν αὐτοῦ διορθῶσαι κελευ-
σθεὶς εὐθὺς ἀπὸ τῆς ἀρχῆς ὅλην μέχρι τῆς κορωνίδος
περιέγραψεν.

Ἦν δὲ καὶ Φίλιππος ἐν τούτοις ὑπ' ὀψιμαθίας
ἑαυτοῦ μικρότερος καὶ[2] νεοπρεπέστερος· ὅθεν καί
φασι πρός τινα ψάλτην περὶ κρουμάτων αὐτοῦ
D διαφερομένου καὶ δοκοῦντος ἐξελέγχειν, ἠρέμα[3]
μειδιάσαντα τὸν ἄνθρωπον εἰπεῖν, " μὴ γένοιτό σοι,
βασιλεῦ, ἀθλίως οὕτως, ἵνα ταῦτ' ἐμοῦ βέλτιον
εἰδῇς."

2. Ἀλλ' Ἀλέξανδρος εἰδὼς τίνων δεῖ θεατὴν
εἶναι καὶ ἀκροατὴν καὶ τίνων ἀγωνιστὴν καὶ

---

[1] Ἀτέας Basel ed. of 1542: ἀντέας or -αιας.
[2] μικρότερος καὶ omitted in some mss.; καινοπρεπέστερος in
others.   [3] ἠρέμα F.C.B.: ἀτρέμα.

---

[a] Cf. Moralia, 174 f, and the note.

Ateas, the Scythian king, took the flute-player Ismenias captive, and ordered him to play at a banquet. The rest were delighted, and applauded, but Ateas swore his horse's neighing was sweeter to his ear.[a] So far from the Muses' habitation did he allow his ears to dwell, and his soul he kept in the mangers, better attuned to hear, not horses' neigh, but asses' bray ! At the court of monarchs such as these what advancement or esteem could there be for Art, or for Poetry and Music of excellence ? Nor, again, could artistic endeavour flourish at the court of those who wish to be rival performers in these arts, and thus through malice and ill-will suppress the true artists. Such a prince was Dionysius (to use him again as an example), who threw the poet Philoxenus [b] into the stone-quarries ; for when Dionysius ordered him to correct a tragedy of his, Philoxenus cancelled the whole piece from the very beginning to the final flourish.[c]

Philip also was in these matters somewhat more petty and childish than became him, since he had acquired his knowledge late in life. Thus they tell the tale that Philip [d] once argued with a certain harp-player about the technique of his instrument, and even thought he was confuting the man ; but the harp-player smiled gently and said, " God forbid, your Majesty, that you should ever fall so low as to know more of these matters than I."

2. But Alexander, knowing well in what matters he should be merely a spectator and listener, and in what he should play the chief rôle, trained himself

[b] *Ibid.* 471 E; Cicero, *Tusculan Disputations*, v. 22 (63); Aelian, *Varia Historia*, xii. 44 ; Diodorus, xv. 6.
[c] The *coronis* at the end of the roll.
[d] *Cf. Moralia*, 67 F, 179 B, 634 D.

427

(334) αὐτουργόν, ἤσκει μὲν ἀεὶ διὰ τῶν ὅπλων δεινὸς εἶναι καὶ κατὰ τὸν Αἰσχύλον

βριθὺς ὁπλιτοπάλας, δάιος ἀντιπάλοις.[1]

ταύτην ἔχων τέχνην προγονικὴν ἀπ' Αἰακιδῶν, ἀφ' Ἡρακλέους, ταῖς δ' ἄλλαις τέχναις τὸ τιμᾶν ἄνευ τοῦ ζηλοῦν ἀπεδίδου κατὰ[2] τὸ ἔνδοξον αὐτῶν καὶ χαρίεν, τῷ τέρπειν[3] δ' οὐκ ἦν εὐάλωτος εἰς τὸ μιμεῖσθαι. γεγόνασι δὲ κατ' αὐτὸν τραγῳδοὶ μὲν
E οἱ περὶ Θετταλὸν καὶ Ἀθηνόδωρον, ὧν ἀνταγωνιζομένων ἀλλήλοις, ἐχορήγουν μὲν οἱ Κύπριοι βασιλεῖς, ἔκρινον δ' οἱ δοκιμώτατοι τῶν στρατηγῶν. ἐπεὶ δ' ἐνίκησεν Ἀθηνόδωρος, " ἐβουλόμην ἄν," ἔφη, " μᾶλλον ἀπολωλεκέναι[4] μέρος τῆς βασιλείας ἢ Θετταλὸν ἐπιδεῖν ἡττημένον." ἀλλ' οὔτ' ἐνέτυχε τοῖς κριταῖς οὔτε τὴν κρίσιν ἐμέμψατο, πάντων[5] οἰόμενος δεῖν περιεῖναι, τοῦ δικαίου δ' ἡττᾶσθαι.

Κωμῳδοὶ δ' ἦσαν οἱ περὶ Λύκωνα τὸν Σκαρφέα· τούτῳ δ' εἴς τινα κωμῳδίαν ἐμβαλόντι στίχον αἰτητικὸν γελάσας ἔδωκε δέκα τάλαντα.

Κιθαρῳδοὶ δ' ἄλλοι τε καὶ Ἀριστόνικος, ὃς ἐν
F μάχῃ τινὶ προσβοηθήσας ἔπεσε λαμπρῶς ἀγωνισάμενος. ἐκέλευσεν οὖν αὐτοῦ γενέσθαι καὶ σταθῆναι χαλκοῦν ἀνδριάντα Πυθοῖ, κιθάραν ἔχοντα καὶ δόρυ προβεβλημένον, οὐ τὸν ἄνδρα τιμῶν

---

[1] ἀντιπάλοις Stephanus : ἀντιπάλοισι.
[2] κατὰ Emperius : καὶ.
[3] τῷ τέρπειν] τὸ τέρπειν some mss. ; τέρποντι Reiske ; τερπνῷ van Herwerden.
[4] ἀπολωλεκέναι Bernardakis and H. Richards : ἀπολωλέναι.
[5] πάντων] H. Richards would add ὅπλοις μὲν before πάντων or τῶν ἄλλων after it.

---

[a] *Cf.* 317 E, *supra*, and the note.

always to be formidable in arms, and, in the words of Aeschylus,[a]

Sturdy contender in arms, baleful to all that oppose.

This art he inherited from his ancestors, the Aeacidae, and from Heracles[b]; but upon the other arts he freely bestowed honour without jealousy according to their worth and artistic excellence; but he was not so easily carried away by the pleasure they give him as to try to imitate them. The tragic actors of his time were the group that centred about Thettalus and Athenodorus.[c] At the contest of these two, the kings of Cyprus defrayed the expenses of the performance and Alexander's most celebrated generals served as judges. When Athenodorus won, " I would rather," said Alexander, " have lost half my kingdom than see Thettalus defeated." However, he did not intercede with the judges nor find fault with the judgement, since he felt that, while he must be superior to all men, yet he must submit to Justice.

The comic actors of his time were the group that centred about Lycon of Scarpheia.[c] When Lycon inserted in one of his comedies a begging verse, Alexander laughed and gave him ten talents.

Various harp-players also were his friends, among them Aristonicus,[d] who came to Alexander's aid in a certain battle, and was slain, fighting gloriously. Therefore Alexander ordered to be made and set up at Delphi a bronze statue of him, with lyre in hand and spear advanced ; thereby he not only honoured

[b] *Cf. Life of Alexander*, chap. ii. (665 B).
[c] *Ibid.* chap. xxix. (681 D).
[d] *Cf.* Arrian, *Anabasis*, iv. 16. 7.

μόνον, ἀλλὰ καὶ μουσικὴν κοσμῶν ὡς ἀνδροποιὸν
καὶ μάλιστα δὴ πληροῦσαν ἐνθουσιασμοῦ καὶ
335 ὁρμῆς τοὺς γνησίως ἐντρεφομένους. καὶ γὰρ αὐτός,
Ἀντιγενίδου ποτὲ τὸν ἁρμάτειον αὐλοῦντος νόμον,
οὕτω παρέστη[1] καὶ διεφλέχθη τὸν θυμὸν ὑπὸ τῶν
μελῶν, ὥστε τοῖς ὅπλοις ἄξας[2] ἐπιβαλεῖν τὰς
χεῖρας ἐγγὺς παρακειμένοις καὶ μαρτυρῆσαι τοῖς
Σπαρτιάταις ᾄδουσιν

ῥέπει[3] γὰρ ἄντα τῷ σιδάρῳ[4] τὸ καλῶς κιθαρίδδειν.[5]

Ἦν δὲ καὶ Ἀπελλῆς ὁ ζωγράφος καὶ Λύσιππος
ὁ πλάστης κατ' Ἀλέξανδρον· ὧν ὁ μὲν ἔγραψε τὸν
κεραυνοφόρον οὕτως ἐναργῶς καὶ κεκραμένως, ὥστε
λέγειν ὅτι δυοῖν Ἀλεξάνδρων ὁ μὲν Φιλίππου γέγονεν ἀνίκητος, ὁ δ' Ἀπελλοῦ ἀμίμητος. Λυσίππου
Β δὲ τὸν πρῶτον[6] Ἀλέξανδρον πλάσαντος, ἄνω βλέ-
ποντα τῷ προσώπῳ πρὸς τὸν οὐρανόν (ὥσπερ αὐτὸς
εἰώθει βλέπειν Ἀλέξανδρος ἡσυχῇ παρεγκλίνων
τὸν τράχηλον) ἐπέγραψέ τις οὐκ ἀπιθάνως

αὐδασοῦντι δ' ἔοικεν ὁ χάλκεος εἰς Δία λεύσσων,
Γᾶν ὑπ' ἐμοὶ τίθεμαι· Ζεῦ, σὺ δ' Ὄλυμπον ἔχε.

[1] παρέστη] ἐξέστη Hartman ; παρεξέστη Pohlenz.
[2] ἄξας Wyttenbach : ἄϊξας.
[3] ῥέπει Scaliger : ἔρπει.
[4] τῷ σιδάρῳ Welcker : τῳ σιδάρῳ.
[5] κιθαρίδδειν some mss. here and in Life of Lycurgus, xxi.:
κιθαρίσδειν or -ζειν.
[6] πρῶτον] κριωτὸν Tucker.

---

[a] Cf. Moralia, 1133 ε (=Edmonds, Lyra Graeca, i. pp.
4-8). See also Dio Chrysostom, Oration i. 1-2, where
Timotheus is the flute-player and the tune the Orthian.

this particular man, but also paid tribute to Music herself, in the belief that she is a creator of true men and, in particular, that she fills with inspiration and impetuousness those who are truly her foster-children. For once upon a time, when Antigenides was playing on his flute the Chariot Song,[a] Alexander became so transported, and his spirit so inflamed by the strains, that he leapt up and laid hands upon the weapons that lay near, and thus confirmed the testimony of the Spartans who used to sing,[b]

The noble playing of the lyre is meet to match the sword.

Apelles the painter and Lysippus the sculptor also lived in the time of Alexander. The former painted "Alexander wielding the Thunderbolt"[c] so vividly and with so natural an expression, that men said that, of the two Alexanders, Alexander, son of Philip, was invincible, but the Alexander of Apelles was inimitable. And when Lysippus[d] modelled his first statue of Alexander which represented him looking up with his face turned towards the heavens (as indeed Alexander often did look, with a slight inclination of his head to one side[e]), someone engraved these verses[f] on the statue, not without some plausibility,

Eager to speak seems the statue of bronze, up to Zeus as it gazes :
   "Earth I have set under foot: Zeus, keep Olympus yourself!"

---

[b] Attributed to Alcman in *Life of Lycurgus*, chap. xxi. (53 D) : *cf.* Bergk, *Poet. Lyr. Graec.* iii. p. 51, or Edmonds, *Lyra Graeca*, i. p. 90.

[c] *Cf. Life of Alexander*, chap. iv. (666 B) ; Pliny, *Natural History*, xxxv. 10 (92).

[d] *Cf. Life of Alexander*, chap. iv. (666 B).

[e] *Cf. ibid.* and *Moralia*, 53 D.

[f] *Cf.* 331 A, *supra*, and the note.

(335) διὸ καὶ μόνον Ἀλέξανδρος ἐκέλευε Λύσιππον
εἰκόνας αὐτοῦ δημιουργεῖν. μόνος γὰρ οὗτος, ὡς
ἔοικε, κατεμήνυε[1] τῷ χαλκῷ τὸ ἦθος αὐτοῦ καὶ
συνεξέφερε[2] τῇ μορφῇ τὴν ἀρετήν· οἱ δ' ἄλλοι τὴν
ἀποστροφὴν τοῦ τραχήλου καὶ τῶν ὀμμάτων τὴν
διάχυσιν καὶ ὑγρότητα μιμεῖσθαι θέλοντες οὐ
διεφύλαττον αὐτοῦ τὸ ἀρρενωπὸν καὶ λεοντῶδες.

C   Ἐν δ' οὖν τοῖς ἄλλοις τεχνίταις καὶ Στασικράτης
ἦν ἀρχιτέκτων, οὐδὲν ἀνθηρὸν οὐδ' ἡδὺ καὶ πιθανὸν
τῇ ὄψει διώκων, ἀλλὰ καὶ χειρὶ μεγαλουργῷ καὶ
διαθέσει χορηγίας βασιλικῆς οὐκ ἀποδεούσῃ χρώμενος. οὗτος ἀναβὰς πρὸς Ἀλέξανδρον ἐμέμφετο
τὰς γραφομένας εἰκόνας αὐτοῦ καὶ γλυφομένας καὶ
πλαττομένας, ὡς ἔργα δειλῶν καὶ ἀγεννῶν τεχνι-
τῶν· "ἐγὼ δ'," εἶπεν, "εἰς ἄφθαρτον, ὦ βασιλεῦ, καὶ ζῶσαν ὕλην καὶ ῥίζας ἔχουσαν αἰδίους
καὶ βάρος ἀκίνητον καὶ ἀσάλευτον ἔγνωκά σου
D τὴν ὁμοιότητα καταθέσθαι τοῦ σώματος. ὁ γὰρ
Θρᾴκιος Ἄθως, ᾗ μέγιστος αὐτοῦ[3] καὶ περι-
φανέστατος ἐξανέστηκεν ἔχων ἑαυτῷ σύμμετρα
πλάτη καὶ ὕψη καὶ μέλη καὶ ἄρθρα καὶ διαστήματα
μορφοειδῆ, δύναται κατεργασθεὶς καὶ σχηματισθεὶς
εἰκὼν Ἀλεξάνδρου καλεῖσθαι καὶ εἶναι, ταῖς μὲν
βάσεσιν ἁπτομένου τῆς θαλάττης, τῶν δὲ χειρῶν
τῇ μὲν ἐναγκαλιζομένου καὶ φέροντος πόλιν ἐνοι-

---

[1] κατεμήνυε] ἐγκατεμήνυε Reiske.
[2] συνεξέφερε] συνεξέφαινε Abresch.
[3] αὐτοῦ] αὐτὸς αὐτοῦ van Herwerden.

432

Wherefore Alexander gave orders that Lysippus[a] only should make statues of him. For Lysippus was, it seemed, the only one that revealed in the bronze Alexander's character and in moulding his form portrayed also his virtues. The others wished to imitate the flexing of his neck and the melting and liquid softness of his eyes, but were unable to preserve his virile and leonine expression.

Among the other artists at his court was Stasicrates[b] the master-sculptor, not seeking to make something flowery or pleasant or lifelike to look upon, but employing a magnificence in workmanship and design worthy of a king's munificence. He followed Alexander into Asia and found fault with the paintings, sculptures, and moulded likenesses that had been made of him, on the ground that they were the works of timid and ignoble artists. "But I, your Majesty," said he, "have conceived the project of placing your likeness in living and imperishable material, with roots that are everlasting and weight immovable and unshakable. For Mount Athos in Thrace, in that part where is its highest and most conspicuous summit, has well-proportioned surfaces and heights, limbs and joints and proportions that suggest the human form. When it has been properly carved and worked into shape, it can be called Alexander's statue, and Alexander's statue it will be; with its base set in the sea, in its left hand it will encompass and hold a city peopled with ten thousand

[a] Cf. Pliny, *Natural History*, vii. 37 (125); Horace, *Epistles*, ii. 1. 240; Valerius Maximus, viii. 11. 2; Arrian, *Anabasis*, i. 16. 4.

[b] Cf. *Life of Alexander*, chap. lxxii. (705 A): the man is called Deinocrates by Vitruvius, ii. praef.; and Cheirocrates by the MSS. of Strabo, xiv. 1. 23.

κουμένην μυρίανδρον, τῇ δὲ δεξιᾷ ποταμὸν ἀέναον
ἐκ φιάλης σπένδοντος εἰς τὴν θάλατταν ἐκχεόμενον.
χρυσὸν δὲ καὶ χαλκὸν καὶ ἐλέφαντα καὶ ξύλα καὶ
E βαφάς, ἐκμαγεῖα[1] μικρὰ καὶ ὠνητὰ καὶ κλεπτόμενα
καὶ συγχεόμενα, καταβάλωμεν.'' ταῦτ' ἀκούσας
Ἀλέξανδρος τὸ μὲν φρόνημα τοῦ τεχνίτου καὶ τὸ
θάρσος ἀγασθεὶς ἐπήνεσεν, '' ἔα δὲ κατὰ χώραν,''
ἔφη, '' τὸν Ἄθω μένειν· ἀρκεῖ γὰρ ἑνὸς βασιλέως
ἐνυβρίσαντος εἶναι μνημεῖον· ἐμὲ δ' ὁ Καύκασος
δείξει καὶ τὰ Ἠμωδὰ καὶ Τάναϊς καὶ τὸ Κάσπιον
πέλαγος. αὗται τῶν ἐμῶν ἔργων εἰκόνες.''

3. Ἀλλὰ φέρε πρὸς θεῶν ἐκτελεσθῆναι καὶ
φανῆναι τοιοῦτον ἔργον· ἔσθ' ὅστις ἂν ἰδὼν ὑπέλαβε
κατὰ τύχην γεγονέναι καὶ αὐτομάτως τὸ σχῆμα
F καὶ τὴν διάθεσιν καὶ τὸ εἶδος; οὐδεὶς ἂν οἶμαι.
τί δὲ[2] τὸν κεραυνοφόρον; τί δὲ[2] τὸν ἐπὶ τῆς
αἰχμῆς προσαγορευόμενον; εἶτ' ἀνδριάντος μὲν
μέγεθος οὐκ ἂν ἄνευ τέχνης ὑπὸ τύχης γένοιτο
χρυσὸν καὶ χαλκὸν καὶ ἐλέφαντα καὶ πολλὴν καὶ
πλουσίαν ὕλην καταχεαμένης καὶ παραβαλούσης,
ἄνδρα δὲ μέγαν, μᾶλλον δὲ τῶν γεγονότων ἁπάντων μέγιστον, ἐνδέχεται χωρὶς ἀρετῆς ἀποτελε-
σθῆναι διὰ τύχην, ὅπλα καὶ χρήματα καὶ πεζοὺς[3]
336 καὶ ἵππους παρασκευάσασαν; ἃ τῷ μὴ μαθόντι
χρῆσθαι κίνδυνός ἐστιν, οὐ δύναμις οὐδὲ κόσμος,
ἀλλ' ἔλεγχος τῆς ἀσθενείας καὶ μικρότητος. ὀρθῶς

---

[1] ἐκμαγεῖα Reiske, confirmed by some mss.: καὶ ἐκμαγεῖα.
[2] τί δὲ] τί δέ; Stegmann.
[3] πεζοὺς F.C.B.; στόλους Kronenberg (cf. 344 E, infra):
πόλεις.

---

[a] The reference is to the chryselephantine statues of
Pheidias and his school with their inner frame-work of
timbers, and painted without.

inhabitants, and with its right pour from a bowl of libation an ever-flowing river down into the sea. But as for gold and bronze, ivory, wooden timbers, and dyes,[a] which make those paltry images that can be bought and sold, stolen, or melted down, let us reject them all ! '' Alexander listened to his words and admired but declined with thanks the lofty designs and the boldness of the artist. "But," said he, "let Athos remain as it is. It is enough that it be the memorial of the arrogance of one king[b]; but my imprint the Caucasus shall show and the Emodian[c] range and the Tanaïs and the Caspian Sea ; these will be the image of my deeds.

3. But imagine, pray, that such a work had been completed and made evident to men's eyes. Is there anyone who could look upon it and suppose that the form, the arrangement, and the appearance were created by Fortune and Accident ? No one, I think. What of Apelles' "Wielder of the Thunderbolt " ? [d] What of the statue which takes its name from the Spear ? [d] Shall we admit, then, that greatness in a statue cannot, without the help of Art,[e] be created by Fortune's profuse provision of gold and bronze and ivory and much rich material, but is it possible that a great man, or rather the greatest man of all that have ever lived, without the help of Virtue, was perfected through Fortune's supplying him with arms and money, foot and horse ? But for him who has not learned how to use these things they are a danger, not a strength and enrichment, but a means of proving his weakness and pettiness. For Antisthenes

[b] Xerxes' canal ; cf. 342 E, infra.
[c] A range of north-western India, the Prakrit Haimota ; cf. Arrian, Indica, 2. 3; 6. 4; Pliny, Natural History, vi. 17 (56).
[d] Cf. 335 A, supra, Moralia, 360 D.
[e] Cf. Moralia, 99 B-C.

(336) γὰρ Ἀντισθένης ἔλεγεν ὅτι '' πάντα δεῖ τοῖς
πολεμίοις εὔχεσθαι τἀγαθὰ πλὴν ἀνδρείας·
γίγνεται γὰρ οὕτως οὐ τῶν ἐχόντων, ἀλλὰ τῶν
κρατούντων.'' διὰ τοῦτό φασι καὶ τὴν φύσιν
ἀγεννεστάτῳ ζώῳ τῷ ἐλάφῳ κέρατα θαυμαστὰ τῷ
μεγέθει καὶ τραχύτητι πρὸς ἄμυναν ἐμφῦσαι, διδά-
σκουσαν ἡμᾶς ὡς οὐδὲν ὠφελεῖ τὸ ἰσχύειν καὶ
ὡπλίσθαι τοὺς μένειν καὶ θαρρεῖν μὴ δυναμένους.

B οὕτω καὶ ἡ τύχη πολλάκις ἀτόλμοις καὶ ἀνοήτοις
προσάπτουσα δυνάμεις καὶ ἀρχάς, αἷς ἐνασχη-
μονοῦσι, κοσμεῖ καὶ συνίστησι τὴν ἀρετὴν ὡς
μόνην μέγεθος ἀνδρὸς καὶ κάλλος οὖσαν. εἰ[1] μὲν
γάρ, ὥς φησιν Ἐπίχαρμος,

νοῦς ὁρῇ καὶ νοῦς ἀκούει, τἆλλα

δὲ

κωφὰ καὶ τυφλά,

τυγχάνει λόγου δεόμενα.[2] αἱ γὰρ αἰσθήσεις ἰδίας
ἔχειν ἀφορμὰς δοκοῦσιν· ὅτι δὲ νοῦς ὠφελεῖ καὶ
νοῦς κοσμεῖ καὶ νοῦς τὸ νικῶν καὶ κρατοῦν καὶ
βασιλεῦον, τὰ δ' ἄλλα τυφλὰ καὶ κωφὰ καὶ ἄψυχα
παρέλκει καὶ βαρύνει καὶ καταισχύνει χωρὶς
ἀρετῆς τοὺς ἔχοντας, ἀπὸ τῶν πραγμάτων λαβεῖν
ἔστι.

C Τῆς γὰρ αὐτῆς δυνάμεως ὑποκειμένης καὶ ἡγε-

---

[1] εἰ] εὖ Wyttenbach (and πως for ὡς); ὁ H. Richards;
ἔχει Wilamowitz-Möllendorff.
[2] δεόμενα] δεόμενον (demonstratione opus est) Reiske and
some mss.

---

[a] Cf. Stobaeus, Florilegium, lix. 41 (Hense, vol. iv. p. 362).
[b] An oft-quoted line. Cf. G. Kaibel, Comicorum Graec.
Frag. i. 137, Epicharmus, no. 249 ; Moralia, 98 c, with the

was right when he said,[a] "We should pray that our enemies be provided with all good things, except courage; for thus these good things will belong, not to their owners, but to those that conquer them." Therefore they say that Nature also for defence has caused horns, wonderful for their size and jagged points, to grow upon the deer, the most cowardly of all animals; and therein does Nature teach us that strength and arms are of no benefit to such as have not the courage to stand their ground. Thus also Fortune, by frequently bestowing on cowards and fools military forces and dominions, in which they disgrace themselves, emblazons and commends Virtue as the one quality that constitutes the greatness and beauty of man. For if indeed, as Epicharmus [b] says,

> Mind has sight and Mind has hearing;

but

> All things else are deaf and blind;

then it happens that these are really lacking in reason. For our perceptive faculties seem to respond to their own special stimuli; but the fact that it is mind which aids us and mind which emblazons our deeds, and it is mind that conquers and overpowers and plays the monarch, and that "all things else," since they are "blind and deaf" and soulless, mislead and burden and disgrace their possessors, if Virtue be not present,[c] is a truth which may be gleaned from history.

Now of the two monarchs Semiramis and Sardanapalus, in whose hands were placed the same power

note; also Cicero, *Tusculan Disp.* i. 20 (46); Maximus Tyrius, xi. 10.

[c] *Cf.* Plato, *Menexenus*, 246 E.

437

(336) μονίας, Σεμίραμις μὲν οὖσα γυνὴ στόλους ἐπλήρου
καὶ φάλαγγας ὥπλιζε καὶ Βαβυλῶνας ἔκτιζε, καὶ
περιέπλει τὴν Ἐρυθρὰν θάλατταν Αἰθίοπας κατα-
στρεφομένη καὶ Ἄραβας· Σαρδανάπαλλος δ' ἀνὴρ
πεφυκὼς ἔξαινεν οἴκοι πορφύραν, ἀναβάδην ἐν ταῖς
παλλακαῖς καθήμενος· ἀποθανόντος δ' αὐτοῦ,
λιθίνην εἰκόνα κατασκευάσαντες ἐπορχουμένην[1]
ἑαυτῇ βαρβαριστὶ καὶ τοῖς δακτύλοις ὑπὲρ κεφαλῆς
οἷον ὑποψοφοῦσαν,[2] ἐπέγραψαν, " ἔσθιε, πῖνε,
ἀφροδισίαζε· τἆλλα δ' οὐδέν."

Ὁ μὲν οὖν Κράτης ἰδὼν χρυσῆν εἰκόνα Φρύνης
D τῆς ἑταίρας ἑστῶσαν ἐν Δελφοῖς ἀνέκραγεν ὅτι
τοῦτο τῆς τῶν Ἑλλήνων ἀκρασίας τρόπαιον ἕστηκε·
τὸν δὲ Σαρδαναπάλλου βίον ἄν τις ἢ τάφον (οὐδὲν
γάρ, οἶμαι, διαφέρει) θεασάμενος εἴποι τοῦτο τῶν
τῆς Τύχης ἀγαθῶν τρόπαιον εἶναι. τί οὖν; ἐάσω-
μεν τὴν Τύχην Ἀλεξάνδρου μετὰ Σαρδανάπαλλον
ἅψασθαι καὶ τοῦ μεγέθους ἐκείνου καὶ τῆς δυνάμεως ἀντιποιεῖσθαι; τί γὰρ αὐτῷ πλέον ἔδωκεν
ὧν οἱ λοιποὶ βασιλεῖς ἔλαβον παρ' αὐτῆς; ὅπλων,
ἵππων, βελῶν, χρημάτων, δορυφόρων; ποιησάτω
τούτοις ἡ Τύχη μέγαν Ἀριδαῖον, εἰ δύναται·
ποιησάτω τούτοις μέγαν[3] Ὦχον ἢ Ὀάρσην
E ἢ Τιγράνην τὸν Ἀρμένιον ἢ τὸν Βιθυνὸν Νικο-

---

[1] ἐπορχουμένην] ἐποχουμένην Coraes.
[2] ἀποψοφοῦσαν Reiske.
[3] μέγαν Wyttenbach : μέγαν Ἄμασιν ἢ.

---

[a] Cf. Diodorus, ii. 4-20 ; Justin, i. 2.
[b] Cf. 326 F, supra ; Diodorus, ii. 21. 8 ff ; Athenaeus,
438

and dominion, Semiramis,[a] though a woman, equipped
great expeditions, armed her ranks, established the
Babylonian Empire, and sailed about the Persian
Gulf subduing the Ethiopians and Arabs. But
Sardanapalus,[b] though born a man, spent his days at
home carding purple wool, sitting with his knees drawn
up in front of him among his concubines ; and when
he died, they made a his stone statue of him dancing
in a barbaric fashion and apparently snapping its
fingers above its head. They engraved upon it :
" Eat, drink, and sport with love ; all else is naught."[c]

When Crates [d] saw a golden statue of Phrynê the
courtesan standing at Delphi, he cried out that it
stood there as a monument to Greek licentiousness ;
and thus if one examine either the life or the tomb
of Sardanapalus (for I think there is no difference
between them), one would say that they are a
monument to the bounty of Fortune. But if this
be so, shall we allow Fortune to lay hold upon
Alexander after Sardanapalus, and to lay claim to
Alexander's greatness and power ? For what greater
gift did she bestow on him than those which other
monarchs received at her hands : arms, horses,
missiles, money, guardsmen ? Let Fortune endeavour to make an Aridaeus [e] great by these, if
she can, or an Ochus or Oarses [f] or Tigranes the
Armenian, or the Bithynian Nicomedes. Of these

528 F ; W. K. Prentice, in *Trans. Amer. Phil. Assoc.* liv.
(1923) p. 79 : but the theory rightly set forth there, that
this description comes from Ctesias's *Persica*, is as old as
Hemsterhuys ; see Wyttenbach's note on this passage.

   [c] See the note on 330 F, *supra*.
   [d] Cf. *Moralia*, 401 A ; Athenaeus, 591 B ; Stobaeus,
Florilegium, vi. 39 (vol. iii. p. 296 Hense).
   [e] Cf. 337 D, *infra*.   [f] Cf. 337 E, *infra*.

μήδην· ὧν ὁ μὲν τὸ διάδημα τοῖς Πομπηίου
ποσὶν ὑπορρίψας αἰσχρῶς τὴν βασιλείαν ἀπέλαβε,[1]
λάφυρον γενομένην· Νικομήδης δὲ τὴν κεφαλὴν
ξυράμενος καὶ πιλίον ἐπιθέμενος ἀπελεύθερον ἑαυτὸν Ῥωμαίων ἀνηγόρευσεν.

4. Εἴπωμεν οὖν ὅτι μικροὺς ἡ Τύχη καὶ περι-
δεεῖς ποιεῖ καὶ ταπεινόφρονας; ἀλλ' οὐ δίκαιον
οὔτε κακίαν εἰς ἀτυχίαν οὔτ' ἀνδρείαν καὶ φρόνησιν
εἰς εὐτυχίαν τινὰ τίθεσθαι. μέγα[2] δὲ τῷ[3] ἄρχειν
Ἀλέξανδρον ἡ Τύχη· καὶ γὰρ ἔνδοξος ἐν ἐκείνῳ καὶ
ἀήττητος καὶ μεγαλόφρων καὶ ἀνύβριστος καὶ
F φιλάνθρωπος   εἶτ' ἐκλιπόντος εὐθὺς ὁ Λεωσθένης
ἔλεγε τὴν δύναμιν ἐμπλανωμένην ἑαυτῇ καὶ περι-
πίπτουσαν ἐοικέναι τῷ Κύκλωπι μετὰ τὴν τύφλωσιν
ἐκτείνοντι πανταχοῖ[5] τὰς χεῖρας ἐπ' οὐδένα σκοπὸν
φερομένας· οὕτως ἐρρέμβετο κενεμβατοῦν καὶ
σφαλλόμενον ὑπ' ἀναρχίας τὸ μέγεθος αὐτῆς. μᾶλλον δ' ὥσπερ τὰ νεκρὰ σώματα, τῆς ψυχῆς ἐκλι-
πούσης, οὐκέτι συνέστηκεν οὐδὲ συμπέφυκεν, ἀλλ'
ἐξίσταται καὶ διαλύεται ἀπ' ἀλλήλων καὶ ἄπεισι
καὶ φεύγει· οὕτως ἀφεῖσα τὸν Ἀλέξανδρον ἡ δύνα-
337 μις ἤσπαιρεν, ἐπάλλετο, ἐφλέγμαινε Περδίκκαις
καὶ Μελεάγροις καὶ Σελεύκοις καὶ Ἀντιγόνοις,
ὥσπερ πνεύμασι θερμοῖς ἔτι καὶ σφυγμοῖς διάτ-
τουσι καὶ διαφερομένοις· τέλος δ' ἀπομαραινομένη

---

[1] ἀπέλαβε (Gronovius) better accords with history : ἀπέβαλε.
[2] μέγα] μεγάλη (?) Meziriacus.
[3] τῷ] τὸ most mss.   [4] ἡ Τύχη] τῇ Τύχῃ Dübner.
[5] πανταχοῖ Abresch : πανταχοῦ.

---

[a] Cf. *Life of Pompey*, chap. xxxiii. (637 A) ; *Comp. of
Cimon and Lucullus*, iii. (522 E) ; Velleius Paterculus, ii.
37 ; Valerius Maximus, v. 1. 10 .

Tigranes[a] cast down his crown before the feet of Pompey and ignominiously received back his kingdom, which had become the spoil of war. But Nicomedes[b] shaved his head and put on the freedman's cap and proclaimed himself an emancipated slave of the Roman people.

4. Shall we say, then, that Fortune makes men petty, timid, and abject in spirit? Yet it is not right for anyone to charge baseness to misfortune, or courage and intelligence to good fortune; but Fortune was magnified by Alexander's reign, for in him she was illustrious, invincible, magnanimous, inoffensive, and humane. Then, immediately after Alexander's decease, Leosthenes[c] said that his forces, as they wandered here and there and fell foul of their own efforts, were like the Cyclops after his blinding, groping about everywhere with his hands, which were directed at no certain goal; even thus did that vast throng roam about with no safe footing, blundering through want of a leader. Or rather, in the manner of dead bodies, after the soul departs, when they are no longer held together by natural forces, but undergo dispersion and dissolution, and finally are dissipated and disappear altogether; even so Alexander's forces, having lost him, maintained a gasping, agitated, and fevered existence through men like Perdiccas, Meleager, Seleucus, and Antigonus, who, as it were, provided still a warm breath of life and blood that still pulsed and circulated. But at length the host wasted away and perished, generating

[b] Plutarch has confused Nicomedes with his father Prusias; cf. Polybius, xxx. 19; Livy, xlv. 44; Diodorus, xxxi. 15; Appian, *Mithridatica*, 2.

[c] The saying is elsewhere attributed to Demades; cf. *Moralia*, 181 F, and the note.

441

(337) καὶ φθίνουσα περὶ αὐτὴν οἷον εὐλάς τινας ἀνέζεσεν
ἀγεννῶν βασιλέων καὶ ἡγεμόνων ψυχορραγούντων.
αὐτὸς μὲν οὖν ταῦθ᾿, ὡς ἔοικεν, Ἡφαιστίωνι δι-
ενεχθέντι πρὸς Κρατερὸν ἐπιτιμῶν, " τίς δ᾿," εἶπεν,
" ἡ σὴ δύναμις ἢ πρᾶξις, ἄν σού τις ἀφέλῃ τὸν
Ἀλέξανδρον; " ἐγὼ δὲ τοῦτ᾿ εἰπεῖν πρὸς τὴν τότε
Τύχην οὐκ ὀκνήσω, " τί σου τὸ μέγεθος, τίς δ᾿ ἡ
δόξα, ποῦ δ᾿ ἡ δύναμις, ποῦ δὲ τὸ ἀνίκητον, ἄν
B σού τις ἀφέλῃ τὸν Ἀλέξανδρον; " τουτέστιν " ἄν
σού τις ἀφέλῃ τῶν ὅπλων τὴν ἐμπειρίαν, τοῦ πλούτου τὴν φιλοτιμίαν, τῆς πολυτελείας τὴν ἐγκράτειαν, ὧν ἀγωνίζῃ τὸ θάρσος, ἐν οἷς κρατεῖς τὴν
πραότητα; ποίησον ἄλλον εἰ δύνασαι μέγαν, τοῖς
χρήμασι μὴ χαριζόμενον, τοῖς στρατεύμασι μὴ
προκινδυνεύοντα, τοὺς φίλους μὴ τιμῶντα, τοὺς
αἰχμαλώτους μὴ ἐλεοῦντα, ταῖς ἡδοναῖς μὴ σωφρο-
νοῦντα, τοῖς καιροῖς μὴ ἀγρυπνοῦντα, ταῖς νίκαις[1]
μὴ εὐδιάλλακτον, τοῖς κατορθώμασι μὴ φιλάνθρωπον. τίς μέγας ἐν ἐξουσίαις μετ᾿ ἀβελτερίας καὶ
C μοχθηρίας; ἄφελε τὴν ἀρετὴν τοῦ εὐτυχοῦντος,
καὶ πανταχοῦ μικρός ἐστιν, ἐν χάρισι διὰ σμικρο-
λογίαν, ἐν πόνοις διὰ μαλακίαν, παρὰ θεοῖς διὰ
δεισιδαιμονίαν, πρὸς ἀγαθοὺς διὰ φθόνον, ἐν
ἀνδράσι διὰ φόβον, ἐν γυναιξὶ διὰ φιληδονίαν."
ὥσπερ γὰρ οἱ φαῦλοι τεχνῖται βάσεις[2] μεγάλας
μικροῖς ὑφιστάντες ἀναθήμασιν ἐλέγχουσιν αὐτῶν
καὶ τὰς μικρότητας, οὕτως ἡ Τύχη, ὅταν μικρὸν
ἦθος ἐξάρῃ πράγμασιν ἔχουσιν ὄγκον τινὰ καὶ περι-

---

[1] ταῖς νίκαις] τοῖς νείκεσι (?) Kaltwasser.
[2] βάσεις Wyttenbach: καὶ βάσεις.

about itself maggots, as it were, of ignoble kings and rulers in their last death-struggle. This, then, it is likely that Alexander himself meant when he rebuked Hephaestion[a] for quarrelling with Craterus : "What," said he, " will be your power and your achievements if someone deprive you of Alexander ? " But I, for my part, shall not hesitate to say this very thing to the Fortune that presided over Alexander's career : " What is your greatness or your repute ? Where is your power or your invincibility, if someone deprive you of Alexander ? " That is to say, " If someone deprive you of your skill in arms, your munificent use of riches, your self-restraint in expending them, your boldness against your foes in battle, your mildness toward the vanquished ? Make another great, if you can ; but one that shall not be generous with his substance, nor court danger in the front ranks, nor give honour to his friends, nor feel pity for his captives, nor be temperate in his pleasures, nor sleepless in crises, nor placable in his victories, nor humane amid his successes. What man is great in the exercise of power, if folly and wickedness attend him ? Take away virtue from the fortunate man and in everything he is petty ; in acts of generosity, through parsimony ; in hard tasks, through softness ; in religion, through superstition ; towards the good, through envy ; among men, through cowardice ; among women, through wantonness." Just as inexpert artisans, who construct large pedestals for petty offerings, make the smallness of the offerings noticeable, so Fortune, whenever she elevates a petty character by acts that have a certain pomp

---

[a] Cf. *Life of Alexander*, chap. xlvii. (691 F–692 A).

(337) φάνειαν, ἐπιδείκνυσι μᾶλλον καὶ καταισχύνει σφαλλόμενον καὶ σαλευόμενον ὑπὸ κουφότητος.

   5. Ὅθεν οὐκ ἐν τῇ κτήσει τῶν ἀγαθῶν ἀλλ' ἐν
D τῇ χρήσει τὸ μέγ' ἐστίν, ἐπεὶ καὶ νήπια βρέφη
κληρονομεῖ βασιλείας πατρῴας καὶ ἀρχάς, ὡς
Χάριλλος, ὃν Λυκοῦργος ἅμα τῷ σπαργάνῳ κομίσας
εἰς τὸ φιδίτιον¹ ἀνθ' ἑαυτοῦ βασιλέα τῆς Σπάρτης
ἀνηγόρευσε· καὶ οὐκ ἦν μέγας ὁ νήπιος, ἀλλ' ὁ τῷ
νηπίῳ τὸ πατρῷον ἀποδοὺς γέρας καὶ μὴ σφετερι-
σάμενος μηδ' ἀποστερήσας.

   Ἀριδαῖον δὲ τίς ἂν ἐποίησε μέγαν; ὃν οὐδὲν
νηπίου διαφέροντα μόνον δὲ σπαργανωθέντα²
πορφύρᾳ Μελέαγρος εἰς τὸν Ἀλεξάνδρου θρόνον
ἔθηκεν, εὖ γε ποιῶν, ἵν' ὀφθῇ παρ' ἡμέρας ὀλίγας
πῶς ἀρετῇ βασιλεύουσιν ἄνθρωποι καὶ πῶς τύχῃ.
ἀγωνιστῇ γὰρ ἡγεμονίας ὑποκριτὴν ἐπεισήγαγε,
E μᾶλλον δ' ὡς ἐπὶ σκηνῆς τὸ διάδημα κωφὸν δι-
εξῆλθε τῆς οἰκουμένης.

   καί κε γυνὴ φέροι ἄχθος, ἐπεί κεν ἀνὴρ ἀναθείη.³

τοὐναντίον μὲν οὖν εἴποι τις ἂν ὅτι ἀναλαβεῖν⁴ καὶ
ἀναθέσθαι δύναμιν καὶ πλοῦτον καὶ ἀρχὴν καὶ
γυναικός ἐστι καὶ παιδός· Ὀάρσῃ καὶ Δαρείῳ
Βαγώας ὁ εὐνοῦχος ἀράμενος ἐπέθηκε τὴν Περσῶν
βασιλείαν· τὸ δὲ λαβόντα μεγάλην ἐξουσίαν ἐν-

---

   ¹ φιδίτιον Stephanus : φιλίτιον.
   ² σπαργανωθέντα F.C.B. : σπαργανώσας τῇ (perhaps changed
from acc. to agree with Μελέαγρος).
   ³ ἀναθείη] ἀναθήῃ Hatzidakis ; probably the original reading in Aristophanes, but it is doubtful if Plutarch knew
it. Cf. φύει, 104 E.   ⁴ ἀναλαβεῖν E. Capps : λαβεῖν.

   ᵃ Cf. Life of Lycurgus, chap. iii. (41 A).
   ᵇ Cf. Moralia, 791 E.

and circumstance, makes the more conspicuous and disgraceful the blundering and instability that result from a shallow character.

5. Wherefore greatness lies, not in the possession of good things, but in our use of them, since even infant children inherit their fathers' kingdoms and dominions, even as Charillus,[a] whom Lycurgus carried in his swaddling-clothes into the common dining-hall and proclaimed king of Sparta in place of himself. Assuredly it was not the child who was great, but he who surrendered to the child its paternal rights, and did not keep them for himself nor take them away.

But who could have made Aridaeus[b] great, whom, differing no whit from a child, only that his swaddling-clothes were royal purple, Meleager set on the throne of Alexander ? And indeed it was well that he did so, that for a few days it might be observed how it is that men rule by right of virtue and how by gift of Fortune. For in succession to a real competitor for sovereignty Meleager introduced a mere actor, or rather, did a mute figure wearing a crown parade across the stage, as it were, of the inhabited world.

Even a woman can carry a burden if a man impose it upon her.[c]

Conversely, however, one might affirm that it lies within the strength of even a woman or a child to take up and impose the gifts of power and wealth and sovereignty. The eunuch Bagoas[d] took up the kingship of Persia and bestowed it upon Oarses and Darius.[e] But the ability to sustain and administer

<hr/>

[c] Aristophanes, *Knights*, 1056 : see Rogers's note *ad loc.*
[d] *Cf.* Arrian, *Anabasis*, ii. 14. 5 ; Aelian, *Varia Historia*, vi. 8 ; Diodorus, xvii. 5.
[e] *Cf.* 326 F, *supra.*

ἐγκεῖν καὶ μεταχειρίσασθαι καὶ μὴ συντριβῆναι
μηδὲ διαστραφῆναι τῷ βάρει καὶ μεγέθει τῶν πραγμάτων, ἀνδρός ἐστιν ἀρετὴν καὶ νοῦν καὶ φρόνημ'
F ἔχοντος· ἣν Ἀλέξανδρος ἔσχεν, ᾧ μέθην τινὲς
ἐγκαλοῦσι καὶ οἴνωσιν. ὁ δ' ἦν μέγας, ἐν τοῖς
πράγμασι νήφων καὶ μὴ μεθυσθεὶς μηδὲ βακχευ-
θεὶς ὑπ' ἐξουσίας καὶ δυνάμεως, ἧς μικρὸν ἕτεροι
μεταλαβόντες καὶ ἀπογευσάμενοι κρατεῖν ἑαυτῶν
οὐ δύνανται·

> κακοὶ γὰρ ἐμπλησθέντες ἢ νομίσματος,
> ἢ πόλεος ἐμπεσόντες εἰς τιμάς τινας,[1]
> σκιρτῶσιν, ἀδόκητ' εὐτυχησάντων δόμων.

338 Κλεῖτος ἐν Ἀμοργῷ τρεῖς ἢ τέτταρας Ἑλληνικὰς
ἀνατρέψας τριήρεις Ποσειδῶν ἀνηγορεύθη καὶ
τρίαιναν ἐφόρει. Δημήτριος δέ, ᾧ τῆς Ἀλεξάνδρου
δυνάμεως ἡ Τύχη σμικρὸν ἀποσπάσασα προσέθηκε,
Καταιβάτης καλούμενος ὑπήκουε,[2] καὶ πρέσβεις
πρὸς αὐτὸν οὐκ ἔπεμπον ἀλλὰ θεωροὺς αἱ πόλεις,
καὶ τὰς ἀποκρίσεις χρησμοὺς προσηγόρευον. Λυσί-
μαχος τὰ περὶ Θρᾴκην ὥσπερ ἐσχατιάς τινας τῆς
βασιλείας κατασχὼν εἰς τοσοῦτον ὑπεροψίας ἔ-
φθασε καὶ θρασύτητος, ὥστ' εἰπεῖν, "νῦν Βυζάντιοι
πρὸς ἐμὲ ἥκουσιν, ὅτε τῇ λόγχῃ τοῦ οὐρανοῦ
B ἅπτομαι." παρὼν δὲ Πασιάδης ὁ Βυζάντιος,
"ὑπάγωμεν," ἔφη "μὴ τῇ ἐπιδορατίδι τὸν οὐρανὸν
τρυπήσῃ."

---

[1] τιμάς τινας] ἀρχήν τινα Stobaeus.
[2] ὑπήκουε] ἐπήκουε some mss.

---

[a] From a much longer fragment of Euripides' *Erechtheus*;
Nauck, *Trag. Graec. Frag.* p. 471, Euripides, no. 362,
29-31.

great authority when one has once received it, and
not to be crushed or turned from one's purpose by
the weight and the magnitude of one's activities, is
the mark of a man who possesses virtue, sense, and
intelligence. This virtue Alexander possessed, whom
some accuse of drunkenness and a passion for wine !
But he was truly a great man, for in his conduct of
affairs he was sober, nor was he made drunk nor led to
revelling by authority and power ; but others, when
they get but a small portion, or even a taste, of power
are unable to control themselves :

> Bad men, when gorged with wealth, or chancing on
> Some honours in the State, caper and prance
> When luck, unhoped for, to their house has come.[a]

Cleitus,[b] when he had scuttled three or four Greek
triremes at Amorgos, caused himself to be proclaimed
Poseidon and carried a trident.   Demetrius, to whom
Fortune added the little that she was able to subtract
from Alexander's power, allowed himself to be called
" The Heaven-descended," [c] and the subject states
did not send ambassadors to him, but " Sacred
Deputies," and his replies they spoke of as " Oracles."
Lysimachus, who obtained possession of the regions
adjoining Thrace, the mere outskirts of the kingdom
of Alexander, as it were, reached such a pitch of
arrogance and boldness as to say, " The Byzantines
now come to me when I am touching Heaven with
my spear." But Pasiades of Byzantium, who was
present, said, " Let us be off, lest he make a hole
in the sky with his spear-point ! "

[b] *Cf.* Diodorus, xviii. 15. 9, 72.
[c] " Avatar," he that descends from Heaven (in thunder and
lightning), a common title of Zeus ; *cf. Life of Demetrius*,
chaps. x., xi. (893 D, E).

(338) Καίτοι[1] τί ἂν περὶ τούτων λέγοι τις, οἷς ἐξῆν δι'
'Αλέξανδρον μέγα φρονεῖν, ὅπου καὶ Κλέαρχος
'Ηρακλείας τύραννος γενόμενος σκηπτὸν[2] ἐφόρει,
καὶ τῶν υἱῶν ἕνα Κεραυνὸν ὠνόμασε; Διονύσιος
δὲ ὁ νεώτερος 'Απόλλωνος υἱὸν ἑαυτὸν ὠνόμασεν,
ἐπιγράψας

Δωρίδος ἐκ μητρὸς Φοίβου κοινώμασι βλαστών.

ὁ δὲ πατὴρ αὐτοῦ τῶν μὲν πολιτῶν μυρίους ἢ καὶ
πλείους ἀνελών, προδοὺς δὲ τὸν ἀδελφὸν ὑπὸ
φθόνου τοῖς πολεμίοις, οὐκ ἀναμείνας δὲ τὴν μη-
C τέρα γραῦν οὖσαν ὀλίγαις ἡμέραις ἀποθανεῖν
ὕστερον ἀλλ' ἀποπνίξας, ἐν δὲ τραγῳδίᾳ γράψας
αὐτὸς

ἡ γὰρ τυραννὶς ἀδικίας μήτηρ ἔφυ·

ὅμως τῶν θυγατέρων τὴν μὲν 'Αρετὴν τὴν δὲ
Σωφροσύνην ὠνόμασε τὴν δὲ Δικαιοσύνην. οἱ δ'
Εὐεργέτας οἱ δὲ Καλλινίκους οἱ δὲ Σωτῆρας οἱ δὲ
Μεγάλους ἀνηγόρευσαν ἑαυτούς. γάμους δ' αὐτῶν
ἐπαλλήλους ὥσπερ ἵππων ἢ ἀγέλαις γυναικῶν
ἀνέδην διημερευόντων, καὶ φθορὰς παίδων καὶ
τυμπανισμοὺς ἐν ἀνδρογύνοις καὶ κυβείας μεθη-
μερινὰς καὶ αὐλήσεις ἐν θεάτροις, καὶ νύκτα μὲν
ἐν δείπνοις ἡμέραν δ' ἐν ἀρίστοις ἐπιλείπουσαν,
οὐδεὶς ἂν ἐφίκοιτο τῷ λόγῳ διελθεῖν.
D 6. 'Αλλ' 'Αλέξανδρος ἠρίστα μὲν ὄρθρου καθ-

---

¹ καίτοι Reiske: καί.
² σκηπτὸν Meziriacus: σκῆπτρον.

ᵃ In Pontus : cf. Müller, *Frag. Hist. Graec.* iii. p. 526.
ᵇ *i.e.* a *skepton*, instead of *skeptron*, " sceptre."
ᶜ *Cf.* Bergk, *Poet. Lyr. Graec.* ii. p. 324.

And yet why should anyone mention these men who might have some legitimate ground for pride because of Alexander, when even Clearchus, after he became despot of Heracleia,[a] used to carry a thunderbolt,[b] and named one of his sons Thunderer? And Dionysius the younger styled himself the son of Apollo in the inscription:

> Sprung from a Dorian mother by union with Phoebus Apollo.[c]

And Dionysius's father killed ten thousand or more citizens, and, led on by envy, betrayed his brother to the enemy, nor could he wait for his already aged mother to die a few days later, but strangled her[d]; yet in one of his tragedies he wrote these words[e]:

> The mother of foul wrong is tyranny!

Notwithstanding, of his daughters he named one Virtue, another Temperance, a third Justice.[f] And yet other persons publicly styled themselves Benefactors,[g] Conquerors, Saviours, or The Great; but no one would be able to tell the tale of their marriages one after another, like the matings of horses, as they spent their days with no restraint amid herds of women, their corruption of boys, their beating of drums in the company of emasculated men, their daily dicing, their flute-playing in the public theatres, the night that was too short for them at their dinners, and the day at their breakfasts.

6. But Alexander took his breakfast at daybreak

---

[a] Cf. Aelian, *Varia Historia*, xiii. 45.

[e] Cf. Nauck, *Trag. Graec. Frag.* p. 797, Dionysius, no. 7.

[f] Cf. *Life of Dion*, chap. vi. (960 c).

[g] Probably Ptolemy Euergetes II. Physcon (*cf.* Athenaeus xii. 549 D), rather than Philopator (*cf. Moralia*, 56 E, Polybius v. 34), is alluded to.

(338) ἑζόμενος, ἐδείπνει δὲ πρὸς ἑσπέραν βαθεῖαν, ἔπινε
δὲ θύσας τοῖς θεοῖς, ἐκύβευε δὲ πρὸς Μήδιον
πυρέττων, ἔπαιζε δ' ὁδοιπορῶν ἅμα καὶ μανθάνων
τοξεύειν καὶ ἐπιβαίνειν[1] ἅρματος. ἔγημε δὲ Ῥω-
ξάνην ἑαυτῷ, μόνης[2] ἐρασθείς· τὴν δὲ Δαρείου
Στάτειραν τῇ βασιλείᾳ καὶ τοῖς πράγμασι (συνέφερε
γὰρ ἡ τῶν γενῶν ἀνάμειξις)· τῶν δ' ἄλλων Περ-
σίδων ἐκράτησε τοσοῦτον σωφροσύνῃ, ὅσον ἀνδρείᾳ
Περσῶν· ἄκουσαν μὲν γὰρ οὐδεμίαν εἶδεν, ἃς δ'
εἶδε μᾶλλον ἢ ἃς οὐκ εἶδε παρῆλθε. καὶ πᾶσιν ὧν
τοῖς ἄλλοις φιλάνθρωπος, μόνοις ὑπερηφάνως τοῖς
E καλοῖς ἐχρῆτο. περὶ δὲ τῆς Δαρείου γυναικός,
εὐπρεπεστάτης γενομένης, οὐδὲ φωνὴν ἐπαινοῦσαν
τὸ κάλλος ἤκουσεν· ἀποθανοῦσαν δ' οὕτω βασιλικῶς ἐκόσμησε καὶ συμπαθῶς ἐδάκρυσεν, ὥστ'
ἄπιστον αὐτοῦ τὸ σῶφρον ἐν[3] τῷ φιλανθρώπῳ
γενέσθαι καὶ λαβεῖν ἀδικίας ἔγκλημα τὴν χρηστό-
τητα. Δαρεῖος γὰρ ὑπόπτως[4] ἐκινήθη πρὸς τὴν
ἐξουσίαν αὐτοῦ καὶ τὴν ἡλικίαν· εἷς γὰρ ἦν καὶ
αὐτὸς ἔτι τῶν νομιζόντων διὰ Τύχην κρατεῖν Ἀλέ-
ξανδρον· ἐπεὶ δὲ τἀληθὲς ἔγνω βασανίσας πανταχόθεν, "οὐ πάντως,[5]" εἶπεν, "ἄρα φαύλως ἔχει
τὰ Περσῶν, οὐδέ τις ἐρεῖ παντάπασι κακοὺς ἡμᾶς

---

[1] ἐπιβαίνειν F.C.B. (cf. Life of Alexander, chap. xxiii. where
ἐπιβαίνειν comes first): ἀποβαίνειν.
[2] μόνης] most mss. have μόνην.   [3] Hartman would omit ἐν.
[4] ὑπόπτως Reiske (from Life of Alexander, chap. xxx.):
οὕτως.   [5] πάντως Xylander: πάντα.

---

[a] Cf. Life of Alexander, chap. xxiii. (677 D).
[b] Ibid. chap. lxxvi. (706 D).   [c] Cf. 332 E, supra.
[d] Cf. Life of Alexander, chap. lxx. (703 E); Diodorus,
xvii. 107; Justin, xii. 10.
[e] Cf. Moralia, 97 D, 522 A; Life of Alexander, chap. xxi.
(676 F).

seated[a]; he dined late in the evening; he drank only after sacrificing to the gods; he played dice with Medius when he had a fever[b]; he played games while travelling, at the same time also learning to wield a bow and mount a chariot.[a] For himself he married Roxanê,[c] the only woman he ever loved; but Stateira,[d] the daughter of Darius, he married for imperial and political reasons, since the union of the two races was highly advantageous. But as for the other Persian women, he was as much their superior in self-control as in valour he was superior to Persian men. For he looked at no woman against her will[e] and those that he looked at he passed by more readily than those that he did not look at; and although he bore himself humanely toward all other persons, it was toward fair youth alone that he conducted himself haughtily. He would not listen to a single word in praise of the beauty of the wife[f] of Darius, who was a very handsome woman; but when she died, he graced her funeral with such a royal pomp and bewailed her death so feelingly that his self-control was questioned amid his display of humanity, and his goodness incurred the charge of wrongdoing. For Darius[g] was disturbed by suspicion of Alexander's power and youth; for he also was still one of those who believed Alexander's victory to be through Fortune. But when he had tested the matter from every angle, and recognized the truth, "Then," said he, "the lot of the Persians is not so utterly wretched, nor will anyone say that we are altogether cowardly or unmanly in

[f] *Ibid.* chap. xxii. (677 A); Arrian, *Anabasis*, iv. 20; Athenaeus, xiii. 603 c; Quintus Curtius, *Hist. Alexandri*, iv. 10.
    [g] *Cf. Life of Alexander*, chap. xxx. (682 c-d).

F οὐδ' ἀνάνδρους ὑπὸ τοιούτου κρατηθέντας. ἐγὼ δ'
εὐτυχίαν μὲν εὔχομαι καὶ κράτος πολέμου παρὰ
θεῶν, ἵν' εὖ ποιῶν Ἀλέξανδρον ὑπερβάλωμαι· καὶ
μέ τις ἔχει φιλοτιμία καὶ ζῆλος ἡμερώτερον αὐτοῦ
φανῆναι· εἰ δ' οἴχεται τὰ ἐμά, Ζεῦ πατρῷε Περσῶν
καὶ βασίλειοι θεοί, μηδεὶς εἰς τὸν Κύρου θρόνον
ἄλλος ἢ Ἀλέξανδρος καθίσειε.'' τοῦτ' εἰσποίησις
ἦν Ἀλεξάνδρου διὰ θεῶν μαρτύρων.

339   7. Οὕτω νικῶσιν ἀρετῇ. πρόσγραψον, εἰ βούλει,
τῇ Τύχῃ τὰ Ἄρβηλα καὶ τὴν Κιλικίαν, καὶ τἄλλα,
ἃ γέγονε βίας ἔργα καὶ πολέμου· Τύχη τὴν Τύρον
ἔσεισεν αὐτῷ, καὶ Τύχη τὴν Αἴγυπτον ἀνέῳξε· διὰ
Τύχην Ἁλικαρνασσὸς ἔπεσε καὶ Μίλητος ἑάλω καὶ
Μαζαῖος Εὐφράτην ἔρημον ἀπέλιπε καὶ νεκρῶν τὸ
Βαβυλώνιον ἐπλήσθη πεδίον· ἀλλ' οὔτι[1] γε σώφρων
ἀπὸ Τύχης οὔτ' ἐγκρατὴς διὰ Τύχην, οὔτ' ἀνάλωτον
ὑφ' ἡδονῆς ἡ Τύχη καὶ ἄτρωτον ἐπιθυμίαις κατα-
κλείσασα τὴν ψυχὴν ἐφρούρει. καὶ μὴν ταῦτ' ἦν,
οἷς αὐτὸν ἐτρέψατο Δαρεῖον· τἄλλα δ' ὅπλων ἦσαν
B ἧτται καὶ ἵππων καὶ μάχαι καὶ φόνοι καὶ φυγαὶ
ἀνδρῶν. τὴν δὲ μεγάλην καὶ ἀναντίρρητον ἧτταν
ἡττήθη Δαρεῖος καὶ ἐνέκλινεν ἀρετῇ καὶ μεγαλο-
φροσύνῃ καὶ ἀνδρείᾳ καὶ δικαιοσύνῃ, θαυμάσας τὸ
ἐν ἡδονῇ καὶ πόνοις καὶ χάρισιν ἀνίκητον. ἐπεὶ ἔν
γε[2] πέλταις καὶ σαρίσσαις καὶ ἀλαλαγμοῖς καὶ

----

[1] οὔτι] οὔτοι Reiske ; οὔτε Bernardakis.
[2] ἔν γε] γ' ἐν Benseler.

----

[a] Cf. Life of Alexander, chap. xxv. (679 A) ; Arrian, Anabasis, ii. 23.
[b] Cf. 326 F, supra.
[c] Cf. Arrian, Anabasis, iii. 7. 2.

that we have been overcome by such a man. But for my part I pray the gods for fair fortune and for might in war, that I may surpass Alexander in bestowing favours ; and I am possessed by an ambitious and emulous desire to prove myself more humane than Alexander. But if my power be spent, do thou, O Zeus, ancestral god of the Persians, and ye other gods that guard our kingship, grant that none other than Alexander take his seat upon the throne of Cyrus." This was Darius's way of adopting Alexander, invoking the gods as witnesses.

7. Thus do men prevail through Virtue. Ascribe to Fortune, if you will, Arbela and the Cilician victory and his other deeds of violence and war : Fortune battered down the walls of Tyre [a] for him ; Fortune opened the way to Egypt [b] ; through Fortune Halicarnassus fell, and Miletus was captured, and Mazaeus [c] left the Euphrates unguarded, and the Babylonian plain was strewn with corpses. But at least it was not in any way Fortune's gift that he was temperate, nor was it because of Fortune that he was self-controlled, nor did Fortune lock his soul and keep it impregnable to pleasure and invulnerable to desire ; in fact, these were the qualities by which he defeated Darius himself. The rest were but defeats of arms and horses, battles, slaughters, and routs of men. But the truly great and indisputable defeat Darius suffered : he yielded in virtue and greatness of soul, in prowess and justice, and marvelled at Alexander's invincibility in pleasure, in toil, in the bestowal of favours. It is true that Tarrias,[d] son of

[d] Tarrias is elsewhere unknown : the stories here related of him are told of Antigenes in *Life of Alexander*, chap. lxx. (703 e-f).

(339) συρράξεσιν ὅπλων ἀνίκητος ἦν καὶ Ταρρίας¹ ὁ Δει-
νομένους καὶ 'Αντιγένης ὁ Πελληναῖος καὶ Φιλώτας ὁ Παρμενίωνος, ἀλλὰ πρὸς ἡδονὰς καὶ γύναια
καὶ χρυσίον καὶ ἀργύριον οὐδέν τι βελτίους τῶν
αἰχμαλώτων· ἀλλὰ Ταρρίας¹ μὲν ὅτε τῶν χρεῶν
ἠλευθέρου Μακεδόνας 'Αλέξανδρος καὶ διελύετο
C τοῖς δανείσασιν ὑπὲρ πάντων, ψευσάμενος ὀφείλειν
καὶ δανειστήν τινα φάσκοντα εἶναι τῇ τραπέζῃ
προσαγαγών· εἶτα φωραθεὶς ὀλίγου διέφθειρεν
αὐτὸς ἑαυτόν, εἰ μὴ γνοὺς 'Αλέξανδρος ἀφῆκε τῆς
αἰτίας αὐτὸν καὶ συνεχώρησεν ἔχειν τἀργύριον,
ἀναμνησθεὶς ὅτι Φιλίππου προσμαχομένου Περίνθῳ
βέλει πληγεὶς εἰς τὸν² ὀφθαλμόν, οὐ παρέσχεν οὐδ'
ὑπέμεινεν ἐξαιρεθῆναι τὸ βέλος αὐτοῦ πρὶν ἢ
τρέψασθαι τοὺς πολεμίους.

'Αντιγένης δὲ τοῖς ἀποπεμφθεῖσιν εἰς Μακεδονίαν
διὰ νόσον καὶ πήρωσιν ἀναμείξας ἑαυτὸν καὶ ἀπο-
γραψάμενος, ὡς ἐλήφθη μηδὲν κακὸν ἔχων, ἀλλὰ
προσποιούμενος ἀρρωστίαν τινά, ἀνὴρ πολεμικὸς
D καὶ τραυμάτων τὸ σῶμα μεστὸς ὀφθεὶς ἠνίασε τὸν
'Αλέξανδρον· πυνθανομένου δὲ τὴν αἰτίαν, ὡμο-
λόγησε Τελεσίππας ἐρᾶν καὶ συνακολουθεῖν ἐπὶ
θάλατταν ἀπιούσης³ μὴ δυνάμενος ἀπολειφθῆναι.
" καὶ τίνος," ἔφη, " τὸ γύναιόν ἐστιν," ὁ 'Αλέξανδρος, " καὶ πρὸς τίνα δεῖ διαλέγεσθαι; " τοῦ
δ' 'Αντιγένους εἰπόντος ὡς ἐλευθέρα ἐστίν, " οὐκ-

---

¹ Ταρρίας] 'Αταρρίας Nachstädt, cf. Quintus Curtius,
v. 2. 5.
² εἰς τὸν] τὸν Abresch.
³ ἀπιούσης F.C.B. (cf. the other versions of the story):
ἀπιούσῃ.

Deinomenes, and Antigenes of Pallenê, and Philotas, the son of Parmenion, were also invincible at least amid shields, pikes, battle-cries, and the clash of arms ; but towards pleasures and women and gold and silver they were no better than their captives. In fact, when Alexander was freeing the Macedonians from debt[a] and paying creditors for everybody, Tarrias said falsely that he was a debtor, and produced at the bank a person who asserted that he was Tarrias's creditor ; later, when he was detected, he was ready to commit suicide had not Alexander, coming to know of this, exculpated him, and allowed him to keep the money ; for the king remembered that when Philip was assaulting Perinthus, Tarrias, although his eye was pierced by a missile, would not submit nor suffer the shaft to be extracted until they had routed the enemy.

Antigenes[b] joined himself with those who were being sent back to Macedonia because of sickness or wounds,[c] and had himself enrolled among them ; but when, however, it was discovered that he had nothing wrong with him, but was feigning some infirmity, and it was seen that he was a stout fighting man whose body was covered with wounds, the matter vexed Alexander. When he asked the reason for such conduct, Antigenes confessed that he was in love with Telesippa, and was accompanying her to the sea, since he could not be left behind if she went away. " Whose is she ? " asked Alexander, " and to whom must we speak ? " Antigenes replied that she was

---

[a] Cf. 343 D, infra ; Arrian, Anabasis, vii. 5. 1-3.
[b] Repeated in Moralia, 181 A ; but told of Eurylochus in Life of Alexander, chap. xli. (689 B).
[c] Cf. Life of Alexander, chap. lxxi. (704 B).

(339) οὖν," εἶπε, "πείθωμεν αὐτὴν καταμένειν, ἐπαγ-
γελλόμενοι καὶ διδόντες." οὕτω παντὶ μᾶλλον
ἐρῶντι συγγνώμην εἶχεν ἢ αὑτῷ.

Καὶ μὴν καὶ Φιλώτας ὁ Παρμενίωνος τροφόν
E τινα[1] τῶν κακῶν εἶχε[2] τὴν ἀκρασίαν. Ἀντιγόνα
γὰρ ἦν Πελλαῖον γύναιον ἐν τοῖς περὶ Δαμασκὸν
αἰχμαλώτοις, ἡλώκει δ' ὑπ' Αὐτοφραδάτου πρότερον εἰς Σαμοθρᾴκην διαπλεύσασα, τὴν δ' ὄψιν ἦν
ἱκανή, καὶ τὸν Φιλώταν ἁψάμενον αὐτῆς εἶχε μάλα.
καὶ δὴ "ὁ σιδάρεος ἐκεῖνος[3]" πεπαινόμενος οὐκ
ἐκράτει τῶν λογισμῶν ἐν ταῖς ἡδοναῖς, ἀλλ' ἀνοι-
γόμενος[4] ἐξέφερε πολλὰ τῶν ἀπορρήτων πρὸς αὐτήν·
" τί γὰρ ἦν ἐκεῖνος ὁ Φίλιππος, εἰ μὴ Παρμενίων;
τί δ' Ἀλέξανδρος οὗτος, εἰ μὴ Φιλώτας; ποῦ δ'
ὁ Ἄμμων, ποῦ δ' οἱ δράκοντες, ἂν ἡμεῖς μὴ θέλω-
μεν;" τούτους τοὺς λόγους ἡ Ἀντιγόνα ἐξήνεγκε
F πρός τινα τῶν συνήθων γυναικῶν, ἐκείνη δὲ πρὸς
Κρατερόν· Κρατερὸς δὲ πρὸς Ἀλέξανδρον αὐτὴν
εἰσήγαγε τὴν Ἀντιγόναν κρύφα, καὶ τοῦ μὲν
σώματος οὐκ ἔθιγεν ἀλλ' ἀπέσχετο· τὸν δὲ Φιλώταν
ὑποικουρῶν δι' αὐτῆς ὅλον ἐφώρασε, καὶ πλέον ἢ
ἑπτὰ ἐτῶν διαγενομένων, οὐκ ἐν οἴνῳ ποτὲ τὴν
ὑπόνοιαν ταύτην ἐξέφηνεν ὁ μεθύων, οὐ δι' ὀργὴν

---

[1] τροφόν τινα Halm : τρόπον τινὰ or τρόπῳ τινί.
[2] εἶχε F.C.B. : ἔσχε.
[3] ἐκεῖνος Budaeus and Xylander : ἔκ τινος or ἐκείνη.
[4] ἀνοιγόμενος] οἰνωμένος, once suggested by Reiske, has
some support in σὺν οἴνῳ in *Life of Alexander*, chap. xlviii.

free-born. "Then," said Alexander, "let us persuade her with promises and presents to remain behind." So ready was he with an excuse for every lover rather than for himself.

And further, Philotas,[a] the son of Parmenion, had in his licentiousness the nurse, as it were, of all his ills. For among the captives taken at Damascus was a courtesan from Pella, by name Antigona. Ere this she had crossed over to Samothrace, and there had been taken captive by Autophradates. She was comely enough to look upon and, after Philotas had attached himself to her, she had complete possession of him. Indeed that man of iron[b] was so softened that he was not in control of his reasoning powers amid his pleasures, but unlocked and brought forth many of his secrets for the woman : " What was that famed Philip, were it not for Parmenion ? What was this Alexander, were it not for Philotas ? Where his Ammon, and where his serpents,[c] if we do not wish it so ? " These words Antigona reported to an intimate friend of hers among the women, and she reported them to Craterus ; Craterus brought Antigona herself secretly to Alexander, who did not touch her person, but restrained himself and, working secretly through her, he discovered the whole of Philotas's plans. And for a period of more than seven years Alexander never revealed his suspicion ; not in his cups, the reputed drunkard ! not in anger, this

---

[a] *Cf. Life of Alexander*, chaps. xlviii., xlix. (692 A–693 A).

[b] The Doric form suggests quotation from some poem or drama.

[c] A reference, perhaps, to Ammon (*i.e.* Zeus) in the form of a serpent, seen with Olympias, as told in *Life of Alexander*, chap. iii. (665 D); or perhaps to the expedition to the oracle of Ammon, *cf.* Arrian, *Anabasis*, iii. 3. 5.

ὁ θυμοειδής, οὐ πρὸς φίλον¹ ὁ πάντα πιστεύων
340 Ἡφαιστίωνι καὶ πάντων μεταδιδούς. λέγεται γὰρ
ὅτι καὶ τῆς μητρὸς ἀπόρρητον ἐπιστολὴν λύσαντος
αὐτοῦ καὶ σιωπῇ πρὸς ἑαυτὸν ἀναγιγνώσκοντος,
Ἡφαιστίων ἀτρέμα παραβάλλων τὴν κεφαλὴν
συνανεγίγνωσκεν· ὁ δὲ κωλῦσαι μὲν οὐχ ὑπέμεινεν,
ἐξελὼν δὲ τὸν δακτύλιον προσέθηκε τὴν σφραγῖδα
τῷ στόματι τοῦ Ἡφαιστίωνος.

8. Ἀλλὰ ταῦτα μὲν ἄν τις ἀπείποι λέγων, οἷς
ἀποδείκνυται κάλλιστα καὶ βασιλικώτατα τὴν ἐξουσίαν διατιθέμενος. καὶ γὰρ εἰ διὰ Τύχην μέγας
γέγονε, μείζων ἐστίν, ὅτι τῇ Τύχῃ καλῶς κέχρηται·
καὶ ὅσῳ τις ἂν μᾶλλον αὐτοῦ τὴν Τύχην ἐπαινῇ,
B τοσούτῳ μᾶλλον αὔξει τὴν ἀρετήν, δι' ἣν ἄξιος τῆς
Τύχης ἐγένετο.

Οὐ μὴν ἀλλ' ἤδη πρὸς τὰ πρῶτα τῆς αὐξήσεως
αὐτοῦ καὶ τὰς ἀρχὰς τῆς δυνάμεως βαδίζω,
καὶ σκοπῶ τί τὸ τῆς Τύχης ἔργον ἐν ἐκείνοις
γέγονε, δι' ὃ φασιν Ἀλέξανδρον ὑπὸ τῆς Τύχης
μέγαν γεγονέναι. πῶς γὰρ οὐχὶ τὸν ἄτρωτον, ὦ
Ζεῦ, τὸν ἀναίμακτον, τὸν ἀστράτευτον, ὃν χρε-
μετίσας ἵππος εἰς τὸν Κύρου θρόνον ἐκάθισεν, ὡς
Δαρεῖον τὸν Ὑστάσπου πρότερον; ἢ κολακευθεὶς
ἀνὴρ ὑπὸ τῆς γυναικός, ὡς Ξέρξην Δαρεῖος ὑπ'
Ἀτόσσης; ἐπὶ θύρας αὐτῷ τὸ διάδημα τῆς

¹ φίλον] φιλίαν Kronenberg.

man of fiery temper! not to a friend, this man who trusted Hephaestion in everything and shared everything with him! In fact it is recorded [a] that once, when he had broken the seal of a confidential letter from his mother and was reading it silently [b] to himself, Hephaestion quietly put his head beside Alexander's and read the letter with him; Alexander could not bear to stop him, but took off his ring and placed the seal on Hephaestion's lips.

8. But one might grow weary in the enumeration of these matters by which Alexander is shown to have made the most honourable and the most regal use of his authority. And even though he became great through Fortune, he is even greater in that he made good use of his Fortune. And the more we praise his Fortune the more shall we exalt his Virtue by reason of which he became worthy of his Fortune.

Now, however, I shall proceed at once to the first steps in his advancement and the beginnings of his power, and I shall examine in those matters the rôle played by Fortune, by reason of which men assert that Alexander became great through the instrumentality of Fortune. In Heaven's name! Why do they not assert this of one that never felt a wound nor lost a drop of blood nor ever served in war, whom the neighing of a horse [c] placed upon the throne of Cyrus, even as the first Darius, the son of Hystaspes? Or of Xerxes, whom a king, flattered by his wife, as Darius was flattered by Atossa, [d] set upon the throne? Did the royal diadem come to Alexander's doors, as

---

[a] Cf. 333 A, supra.
[b] "Silently," for reading was generally done aloud.
[c] Cf. Herodotus, iii. 84 ff.
[d] Ibid. vii. 3.

(340) βασιλείας[1] ἦλθεν, ὥσπερ Ὀάρσῃ[2] διὰ Βαγώαν, καὶ
C στολὴν ἐκδυσάμενος ἀστάνδου περιέθετο τὴν βασι-
λικὴν καὶ ὀρθοπαγῆ κίταριν; ἐξαίφνης καὶ ἀπροσδοκήτως κλήρῳ λαχὼν τῆς οἰκουμένης ἐβασίλευσεν,
ὡς Ἀθήνησι κλήρῳ θεσμοθετοῦσι καὶ ἄρχουσι;

Βούλει μαθεῖν πῶς βασιλεύουσιν ἄνθρωποι διὰ
Τύχην; ἐξέλιπέ ποτ' Ἀργείοις τὸ Ἡρακλειδῶν
γένος, ἐξ οὗ βασιλεύεσθαι πάτριον ἦν αὐτοῖς·
ζητοῦσι δὲ καὶ διαπυνθανομένοις ὁ θεὸς ἔχρησεν
ἀετὸν δείξειν· καὶ μεθ' ἡμέρας ὀλίγας ἀετὸς ὑπερ-
φανεὶς καὶ κατάρας ἐπὶ τὴν Αἴγωνος οἰκίαν ἐκά-
θισε, καὶ βασιλεὺς ᾑρέθη Αἴγων.

Πάλιν ἐν Πάφῳ, τοῦ βασιλεύοντος ἀδίκου καὶ
πονηροῦ φανέντος ἐκβαλὼν τοῦτον Ἀλέξανδρος
D ἕτερον ἐζήτει, τοῦ Κινυραδῶν γένους ἤδη φθίνειν
καὶ ἀπολείπειν δοκοῦντος. ἕνα δ' οὖν ἔφασαν
περιεῖναι πένητα καὶ ἄδοξον ἄνθρωπον ἐν κήπῳ
τινὶ παρημελημένως διατρεφόμενον. ἐπὶ τοῦτον οἱ
πεμφθέντες ἧκον, εὑρέθη δὲ πρασιαῖς ὕδωρ ἐπαν-
τλῶν· καὶ διεταράχθη τῶν στρατιωτῶν ἐπιλαμβανομένων αὐτοῦ καὶ βαδίζειν κελευόντων. ἀχθεὶς δὲ
πρὸς Ἀλέξανδρον ἐν εὐτελεῖ σινδονίσκῃ βασιλεὺς
ἀνηγορεύθη καὶ πορφύραν ἔλαβε, καὶ εἷς ἦν τῶν
ἑταίρων προσαγορευομένων· ἐκαλεῖτο δ' Ἀβδαλ-

---

[1] βασιλείας] Ἀσίας almost all mss.
[2] ὥσπερ Ὀάρσῃ (ὥσπερ Ἄρσῃ Reiske, cf. Diodorus, xvii. 5)
Bernardakis: ὡς Παρύσατις.

---

[a] Artaxerxes: cf. 336 E, 337 E, supra, Life of Artaxerxes,
chap. i. (1012 A): Reiske conjectured Ἄρσῃ from Diodorus,
xvii. 5, which may be right.   But Bagoas also put Darius III.
on the throne of Persia.   Cf. 326 F, supra.
[b] For the upright tiara cf. e.g. Xenophon, Anabasis, ii.

to Oarses[a] through the machinations of Bagoas, who stripped from him the garb of a courier and put upon him the royal raiment and the tiara that ever stands erect[b]? Was he suddenly and unexpectedly chosen by lot and thus came to rule the inhabited world, as at Athens the Thesmothetae and Archons attain their office?

Would you learn how it is that men come to the throne by choice of Fortune? Once upon a time among the Argives the family of Heracleidae became extinct, from which family it was their ancestral custom to select the Argive kings. When in their search they made inquiry of the god at Delphi, he replied that an eagle would show them; and a few days later an eagle appeared on high and, swooping down, alighted on the house of Aegon, and Aegon was chosen king.

Again in Paphos when the reigning king was seen to be unjust and wicked, Alexander expelled him and searched for another, since the family of Cinyradae appeared to be already passing away or extinct. However, they told him that there still survived one poor and obscure person, who eked out a forsaken existence in a certain garden. Men were sent to fetch him and, when they arrived, he was found watering his garden-plots; and he was much perturbed when the soldiers laid hands on him and ordered him to come with them. He was brought before Alexander and, dressed as he was in a single cheap garment, he was proclaimed king, and received the royal purple, and became one of those who are styled the king's "Companions." His name was

5. 23; *Life of Themistocles*, chap. xxix. (126 E); *Life of Artaxerxes*, chaps. xxvi., xxviii. (1024 E, 1025 E).

ώνυμος.¹ οὕτως αἱ τύχαι ποιοῦσι βασιλεῖς, μετ-
Ε αμφιέζουσι, μεταγράφουσι ταχὺ καὶ² ῥᾳδίως, μὴ
προσδεχομένους μηδ' ἐλπίζοντας.

9. Ἀλεξάνδρῳ δὲ τί παρ' ἀξίαν, τί ἀνιδρωτί, τί
ἀναιμωτί, τί προῖκα, τί μὴ πονήσαντι τῶν μεγάλων;
αἵματι κεκραμένους ποταμοὺς ἔπιε καὶ νεκροῖς
γεγεφυρωμένους διέβη, καὶ πόαν ἔφαγε διὰ λιμὸν
ἦν πρώτην³ εἶδε, καὶ βάθεσι χιόνων κατακεχωσμένα
ἔθνη καὶ πόλεις ὑπὸ γῆν ἐνδεδυκυίας διώρυξε,⁴ καὶ
θάλατταν μαχομένην ἔπλευσε, καὶ θῖνας ἀνύδρους
τὰς Γεδρωσίων⁵ καὶ Ἀραχωσίων ὁδεύων ἐν θαλάττῃ πρότερον ἢ ἐν γῇ φυτὸν εἶδεν.

Εἰ γὰρ ἦν ὡς πρὸς ἄνθρωπον ἀγαγεῖν Παρρησίαν
ὑπὲρ Ἀλεξάνδρου πρὸς τὴν Τύχην, οὐκ ἂν εἶπε,
F " ποῦ σὺ καὶ πότε ταῖς Ἀλεξάνδρου πράξεσιν ὁδὸν
ἔδωκας; ποίαν πέτραν ἀναιμωτὶ διὰ σὲ εἷλε;
ποίαν πόλιν ἀφρούρητον αὐτῷ παρέδωκας ἢ ποίαν
ἄνοπλον φάλαγγα; τίς εὑρέθη βασιλεὺς ῥάθυμος
ἢ στρατηγὸς ἀμελὴς ἢ κοιμώμενος πυλωρός; ἀλλ'
οὐδ' εὔβατος ποταμὸς οὐδὲ χειμὼν μέτριος οὐδὲ
341 θέρος ἄλυπον. ἄπιθι πρὸς Ἀντίοχον τὸν Σελεύκου,
πρὸς Ἀρταξέρξην τὸν Κύρου ἀδελφόν· ἄπελθε πρὸς
Πτολεμαῖον τὸν Φιλάδελφον. ἐκείνους ζῶντες οἱ

---

¹ Ἀβδαλώνυμος Cobet: ἄρα ἀλύνομος.
² καὶ added by Reiske.
³ πρώτην Abresch: πρῶτον.
⁴ ἐνδεδυκυίας διώρυξε] δεδυκυίας ἐξώρυξε Emperius.
⁵ Γεδρωσίων the usual spelling: γεδρουσίων or γεδροσίων.

ᵃ Cobet's conjecture (Abdalonymus for Aralynomus) is
only very partially supported by Diodorus, xvii. 46, 47.
But cf. the references ad loc. in Fischer's ed. (Leipzig 1906),
especially Quintus Curtius, Hist. Alexandri, iv. 1. 19.

Abdalonymus.[a] Thus does shifting Fortune create kings, change their raiment, and quickly and easily alter the status of men who expect nothing of the sort, and do not even hope for it.

9. But what greatness did Alexander acquire beyond his just merits, what without sweat, what without blood, what without a price, what without labour ? He drank rivers fouled with blood, crossed streams bridged by dead bodies, through hunger ate the first grass that he saw, dug through nations buried in deep snow [b] and cities built beneath the earth, sailed over a battling sea [c]; and as he traversed the parching strands of Gedrosia and Arachosia,[d] it was in the sea, not on the land, that first he saw a living plant.

If to Fortune, as to a human being, one might present Frankness in Alexander's behalf, would she not say, " When and where did you ever vouchsafe a way for the exploits of Alexander ? What fortress did he ever capture by your help without the shedding of blood ? What city unguarded or what regiment unarmed did you deliver into his hands ? What king was found to be indolent, or what general negligent, or what watchman asleep at the gate ? But no river was easy to cross, no storm was moderate, no summer's heat was without torment. Betake yourself to Antiochus, the son of Seleucus, or to Artaxerxes, the brother of Cyrus ; depart to Ptolemy Philadelphus ! Their fathers, while yet alive, pro-

[b] Cf. Diodorus, xvii. 82 ; Quintus Curtius, Hist. Alexandri, v. 3.
[c] Cf. Arrian, Anabasis, vi. 19 ; Quintus Curtius, Hist. Alexandri, ix. 9.
[d] Cf. Life of Alexander, chap. lxvi. (702 A) ; Arrian, Anabasis, vi. 22 ff ; Quintus Curtius, Hist. Alexandri, ix. 10.

(341) πατέρες βασιλεῖς ἀνηγόρευσαν, ἐκεῖνοι μάχας ἀ-
δακρύτους ἐνίκων, ἐκεῖνοι πανηγυρίζοντες ἐν πομπαῖς
καὶ θεάτροις διετέλεσαν, ἐκείνων ἕκαστος δι'
εὐτυχίαν βασιλεύων ἐγήρασεν.

" ' Ἀλεξάνδρου δ' εἰ μηδὲν ἄλλο, τὸ σῶμ' ἰδοὺ
κατατετρωμένον ἐξ ἄκρας κεφαλῆς ἄχρι ποδῶν
διακέκοπται καὶ περιτέθλασται τυπτόμενον ὑπὸ
τῶν πολεμίων

ἔγχεῖ τ' ἄορί τε μεγάλοισί τε χερμαδίοισιν·

B ἐπὶ Γρανίκου ξίφει διακοπεὶς τὸ κράνος ἄχρι τῶν
τριχῶν, ἐν Γάζῃ βέλει πληγεὶς τὸν ὦμον, ἐν Μαρακάνδοις[1] τοξεύματι τὴν κνήμην ὥστε τῆς κερκίδος
τὸ ὀστέον ἀποκλασθὲν ὑπὸ τῆς πληγῆς ἐξαλέσθαι·
περὶ τὴν Ὑρκανίαν λίθῳ τὸν τράχηλον, ἐξ οὗ καὶ[2]
τὰς ὄψεις ἀμαυρωθεὶς ἐφ' ἡμέρας πολλὰς ἐν φόβῳ
πηρώσεως ἐγένετο· πρὸς Ἀσσακηνοῖς[3] Ἰνδικῷ
βέλει τὸ σφυρόν, ὅτε καὶ πρὸς τοὺς κόλακας εἶπεν
ἐπιμειδιάσας, ' τουτὶ μὲν αἷμα, οὐκ

ἰχώρ, οἷός πέρ τε ῥέει μακάρεσσι θεοῖσιν· '

ἐν Ἰσσῷ ξίφει τὸν μηρόν, ὡς Χάρης φησίν, ὑπὸ
Δαρείου τοῦ βασιλέως εἰς χεῖρας αὐτῷ συνδραμόν-
C τος· αὐτὸς δ' Ἀλέξανδρος ἁπλῶς γράφων καὶ μετὰ
πάσης ἀληθείας πρὸς Ἀντίπατρον, ' συνέβη δέ
μοι,' φησί, ' καὶ αὐτῷ ἐγχειριδίῳ πληγῆναι εἰς τὸν[4]
μηρόν· ἀλλ' οὐδὲν ἄτοπον οὔτε παραχρῆμα οὔθ'

---

[1] Μαρακάνδοις Bernardakis: μαραγάνδοις.
[2] καὶ] κατὰ E. Capps.
[3] Ἀσσακηνοῖς Helmbold: Ἀσσακάνοις.
[4] εἰς τὸν] τὸν Abresch.

---

[a] For the wounds of Alexander see the note on 327 A, *supra*,
with the work of Nachstädt there referred to.

claimed them kings; they won battles that did not cost a tear; they made merry all their lives in processions and theatres; and every one of them, because of good fortune, grew old upon the throne.

"But in the case of Alexander, though I were to mention nothing else, behold his body gashed with wounds [a] from tip to toe, bruised all over, smitten at the hands of his enemies

> Now with the spear, now the sword, now with mighty masses of boulders.[b]

On the banks of the Granicus [c] his helmet was cleft through to his scalp by a sword; at Gaza his shoulder was wounded by a missile; at Maracanda his shin was so torn by an arrow that by the force of the blow the larger bone was broken and extruded. Somewhere in Hyrcania his neck was smitten by a stone, whereby his sight was dimmed, and for many days he was haunted by the fear of blindness. Among the Assacenians his ankle was wounded by an Indian arrow; that was the time when he smilingly said to his flatterers, 'this that you see is blood, not

> Ichor, that which flows from the wounds of the blessed immortals.' [d]

At Issus he was wounded in the thigh with a sword, as Chares [e] states, by Darius the king, who had come into hand-to-hand conflict with him. Alexander himself wrote of this simply, and with complete truth, in a letter to Antipater: 'I myself happened,' he writes, 'to be wounded in the thigh by a dagger. But nothing untoward resulted from the blow either

---

[b] Homer, *Il.* xi. 265, 541.
[c] *Cf.* 327 A, *supra*, and the notes.
[d] Homer, *Il.* v. 340; *cf. Moralia*, 180 E and the note.
[e] *Cf. Life of Alexander*, chap. xx. (675 E-F).

ὕστερον ἐκ τῆς πληγῆς ἀπήντησεν.' ἐν Μαλλοῖς
τοξεύματι διπήχει διὰ τοῦ θώρακος εἰς τὸ στῆθος·
ὑπελάσας δέ τις ἔβαλε[1] κατὰ τοῦ αὐχένος, ὡς
'Αριστόβουλος ἱστόρηκε. διαβὰς δὲ τὸν Τάναϊν
ἐπὶ τοὺς Σκύθας καὶ τρεψάμενος, ἐδίωξεν ἵππῳ
πεντήκοντα καὶ ἑκατὸν σταδίους, ὑπὸ διαρροίας
ἐνοχλούμενος.

10. "Εὖγ', ὦ Τύχη, τὸν 'Αλέξανδρον αὔξεις
καὶ μέγαν ποιεῖς, διορύττουσα πανταχόθεν, ὑπ-
D ερείπουσα,[2] πᾶν μέρος ἀνοίγουσα τοῦ σώματος·
οὐχ ὥσπερ ἡ 'Αθηνᾶ πρὸ τοῦ Μενελάου τὸ βέλος εἰς
τὰ καρτερώτατα τῶν ὅπλων ὑπάγουσα, θώρακι καὶ
μίτρᾳ καὶ ζωστῆρι τῆς πληγῆς τὸν τόνον ἀφεῖλε
θιγούσης τοῦ σώματος, ὅσον αἵματι πρόφασιν
ῥυῆναι, ἀλλὰ γυμνὰ παρέχουσα τοῖς βέλεσι τὰ
καίρια, καὶ δι' ὀστέων ἐλαύνουσα τὰς πληγάς, καὶ
περιτρέχουσα κύκλῳ τὸ σῶμα, καὶ πολιορκοῦσα
τὰς ὄψεις, τὰς βάσεις,[3] ἐμποδίζουσα τὰς διώξεις,
περισπῶσα τὰς νίκας, ἀνατρέπουσα τὰς ἐλπίδας."

'Εμοὶ μὲν οὐδεὶς βαρυτέρα δοκεῖ κεχρῆσθαι Τύχῃ
τῶν βασιλέων, καίτοι πολλοῖς ἐνέπεσε σκληρὰ καὶ
E βάσκανος· ἀλλ' ὡς σκηπτὸς ἀπέκοψε τοὺς ἄλλους
καὶ διέφθειρε, πρὸς δ' 'Αλέξανδρον αὐτῆς τὸ δυσ-
μενὲς γέγονε φιλόνεικον καὶ δύσερι καὶ δυσεκ-
βίαστον, ὥσπερ πρὸς τὸν 'Ηρακλέα. ποίους γὰρ

---

[1] ὑπελάσας δέ τις ἔβαλε F.C.B.; ὑπέρῳ δέ τις πελάσας ἔβαλε
Bernardakis: ὑπελάσας ἔλαβε.
[2] ὑπερείπουσα Reiske and Wyttenbach: ὑπερείδουσα.
[3] τὰς βάσεις] καὶ τὰς βάσεις Xylander.

---

[a] Cf. Life of Alexander, chap. xlv. (691 A); Arrian, Anabasis, iv. 4. 9; Quintus Curtius, Hist. Alexandri, vii. 9, 13.

immediately or later.' Among the Mallians he was wounded in the breast by an arrow three feet long, which penetrated his breastplate, and someone rode up under him, and struck him in the neck, as Aristobulus relates. When he had crossed the Tanaïs against the Scythians and had routed them, he pursued them on horseback an hundred and fifty stades, though he was grievously distressed with diarrhoea.[a]

10. " Well done, Fortune ! You exalt Alexander and make him great by running him through from every side, by making him lose his footing, by laying open every portion of his body. Not like Athena before Menelaüs [b] did you guide the missile to the stoutest parts of his armour, and by breastplate, belt, and kilt take away the intensity of the blow, which only grazed his body with force enough to cause blood to flow ; but you exposed to the missiles the vital portions of Alexander's body unprotected, you drove home the blows through his very bones, you circled about his body, you laid siege to his eyes and his feet, you hindered him in pursuing his foes, you endeavoured to strip him of his victories, you upset his expectations."

No other king seems to me to have felt the hand of Fortune more heavily upon him, even though on many it has fallen harshly and malignantly. But like a thunderbolt it cut down the other rulers, and destroyed them ; toward Alexander, however, Fortune's ill-will became but contentious and quarrelsome and hard to overpower, even as it was toward Heracles. For what manner of Typhons or monstrous

[b] *Cf.* Homer, *Il.* iv. 129.

Τυφῶνας ἢ πελωρίους γίγαντας οὐκ ἀνέστησεν
ἀνταγωνιστὰς ἐπ' αὐτόν; ἢ τίνας οὐκ ὠχύρωσε
τῶν πολεμίων πλήθεσιν ὅπλων ἢ βάθεσι ποταμῶν
ἢ τραχύτησι κρημνῶν ἢ θηρίων ἀλκαῖς ἀλλοφύλων;
εἰ δὲ μὴ μέγ' ἦν τὸ 'Αλεξάνδρου φρόνημα μηδ'
ἀπ' ἀρετῆς ὁρμώμενον μεγάλης ἐξανέφερε καὶ δι-
ηρείδετο πρὸς τὴν Τύχην, οὐκ ἂν ἔκαμε καὶ ἀπ-
ηγόρευσε παραττόμενος, ἐξοπλιζόμενος, πολιορ-
F κῶν, διώκων ἐν[1] ἀποστάσεσι μυρίαις, ἀποτροπαῖς,
σκιρτήσεσιν ἐθνῶν, βασιλέων ἀφηνιασμοῖς, πρὸς[2]
Βάκτρα Μαράκανδα Σογδιανούς, ἐν ἔθνεσιν ἀπίστοις
καὶ ἐπιβούλοις ὕδραν τέμνων ἀεί τισι πολέμοις
ἐπιβλαστάνουσαν;

11. Ἄτοπόν τι δόξω λέγειν, ἐρῶ δ' ἀληθές· παρὰ
μικρὸν[3] διὰ τὴν Τύχην 'Αλέξανδρος ἀπώλεσε τὸ
δοκεῖν Ἄμμωνος εἶναι. τίς γὰρ ἂν ἐκ θεῶν γεγονὼς ἐπισφαλεῖς οὕτω καὶ πολυπόνους καὶ τλή-
μονας ἐξεμόχθησεν ἄθλους πλὴν ὁ Διὸς Ἡρακλῆς;
342 ἀλλ' ἐκείνῳ μὲν εἷς ἀνὴρ ὑβριστὴς ἐπέτατε λέοντας
αἱρεῖν καὶ κάπρους διώκειν καὶ σοβεῖν ὄρνιθας ἵνα
μὴ σχολάζῃ τοῖς μείζοσι περιιών, 'Ανταίους κολά-
ζειν καὶ Βουσίριδας παύειν μιαιφονοῦντας· 'Αλε-
ξάνδρῳ δ' ἐπέτατε ἡ 'Αρετὴ τὸν βασιλικὸν καὶ
θεῖον ἆθλον, οὗ τέλος ἦν οὐ χρυσὸς ὑπὸ μυρίων
καμήλων περικομιζόμενος οὐδὲ τρυφαὶ Μηδικαὶ καὶ
τράπεζαι καὶ γυναῖκες οὐδὲ Χαλυβώνιος[4] οἶνος οὐδ'

---

[1] ἐν added by Wyttenbach.   [2] πρὸς added by E. Capps.
[3] παρὰ μικρὸν Wyttenbach: παρομικροῦ or προμικροῦ.
[4] Χαλυβώνιος Wyttenbach: χαλυδώνιος (καλ-).

giants did she not raise up to oppose him ? Whom of his foes did she not fortify with a vast supply of weapons or deep rivers or jagged cliffs or the might of beasts from foreign lands [a] ? But if Alexander's thought had not been set on high emprise, if it had not derived its impelling force from great Virtue, and had not refused to submit to defeat in its wrestling with Fortune, would he not have grown tired and weary of marshalling and arming his forces, weary of his sieges and pursuits amid unnumbered revolts, desertions, and riots of subject peoples, defections of kings, against Bactria, Maracanda, Sogdiana, as if he were cutting off the heads of a hydra which ever grew again in renewed wars among these faithless and conspiring peoples ?

11. I shall be thought to be making a strange statement, yet what I shall say is true : it was because of Fortune that Alexander all but lost the repute of being the son of Ammon ! For what offspring of the gods could have toiled through such hazardous, toilsome, and painful Labours save only Heracles, the son of Zeus ? But it was one arrogant man who imposed upon Heracles the task of capturing lions, of pursuing wild boars, of frightening off birds so that he might not have time to go about performing greater deeds, such as punishing men like Antaeus and stopping creatures like Busiris [b] from their abominable murders. But upon Alexander it was Virtue who laid the kingly and god-like Labour, the end and aim of which was not gold, carried about by countless camels, nor Persian luxury, banquets, and women, nor the wine

[a] Presumably elephants.
[b] Cf. 315 B, supra and Moralia 857 A.

(342) Ὑρκανικοὶ ἰχθύες, ἀλλ' ἐνὶ κόσμῳ κοσμήσαντα
πάντας ἀνθρώπους μιᾶς ὑπηκόους ἡγεμονίας καὶ
B μιᾶς ἐθάδας διαίτης καταστῆσαι. τοῦτον ἐκ παιδὸς
ἔμφυτον ἔχων ἔρωτα συντρεφόμενον καὶ συναυξα-
νόμενον, ὡς ἀφίκοντο πρέσβεις παρὰ τοῦ Περσῶν
βασιλέως πρὸς Φίλιππον, ὁ δ' οὐκ ἔνδημος ἦν, φιλοφρονούμενος καὶ ξενίζων αὐτοὺς Ἀλέξανδρος οὐδὲν
ἠρώτα παιδικόν, οἷον οἱ ἄλλοι, περὶ τῆς χρυσῆς
ἀναδενδράδος ἢ τῶν κρεμαστῶν κήπων ἢ πῶς ὁ
βασιλεὺς κεκόσμηται, ἀλλ' ὅλος ἐν τοῖς κυριωτά-
τοις ἦν τῆς ἡγεμονίας, διαπυνθανόμενος πόση
δύναμις ἡ Περσῶν, ποῦ τεταγμένος βασιλεὺς ἐν
ταῖς μάχαις διαγωνίζεται (καθάπερ Ὀδυσσεὺς
ἐκεῖνος,

  ποῦ δέ οἱ ἔντεα κεῖται ἀρήια, ποῦ δέ οἱ ἵπποι·),

C τίνες ὁδοὶ βραχύταται τοῖς ἄνω πορευομένοις ἀπὸ
θαλάττης· ὥστε τοὺς ξένους ἐκπεπλῆχθαι καὶ
λέγειν ὡς " ὁ παῖς οὗτος βασιλεὺς μέγας, ὁ δ'
ἡμέτερος πλούσιος." ἐπεὶ δὲ Φιλίππου τελευτήσαντος ὥρμητο διαβαλεῖν καὶ ταῖς ἐλπίσιν ἤδη καὶ
ταῖς παρασκευαῖς ἐμπεφυκὼς ἔσπευδεν ἅψασθαι τῆς
Ἀσίας, ἐνίστατο δὴ¹ ἡ Τύχη καὶ ἀπέστρεφε καὶ
ἀνθεῖλκεν ὀπίσω καὶ μυρίας περιέβαλλεν ἀσχολίας
καὶ διατριβὰς ἐπιλαμβανομένη· πρῶτον αὐτῷ τὰ
βαρβαρικὰ τῶν προσοίκων διετάραξεν, Ἰλλυρικοὺς
καὶ Τριβαλλικοὺς μηχανωμένη πολέμους. οἷς
μέχρι Σκυθίας τῆς παρ' Ἴστρον ἀποσπασθεὶς ἀπὸ

---

¹ δὴ Wyttenbach : δέ. Reiske would omit δέ.

ᵃ A city in Syria ; for the wine cf. Strabo, xv. 3. 22
(p. 735) ; Athenaeus, 28 D ; Suidas and Hesychius, s.v.

of Chalybon,[a] nor the fish of Hyrcania, but to order all men by one law and to render them submissive to one rule and accustomed to one manner of life. The desire which he cherished to accomplish this task was implanted in him from childhood, and was fostered and increased with the years that passed. Once, when ambassadors came from the Persian king to Philip, who was not at home, Alexander, while he entertained them hospitably,[b] asked no childish questions, as the others did, about the vine of gold,[c] or the Hanging Gardens, or how the Great King was arrayed ; but he was completely engrossed with the most vital concerns of the dominion, asking how large was the Persian army ; where the king stationed himself in battle (even as the famed Odysseus [d] asked

Where are his arms that he wields in the battle, and where are his horses?);

and which roads were the shortest for travellers going inland from the sea—so that the strangers were astounded and said, "This boy is a 'great king'; our king is only wealthy." But after Philip's end, when Alexander was eager to cross over and, already absorbed in his hopes and preparations, was hastening to gain a hold upon Asia, Fortune, seizing upon him, blocked his way, turned him about, dragged him back, and surrounded him with countless distractions and delays. First she threw into the utmost commotion the barbarian elements among his neighbours, and contrived wars with the Illyrians [e] and Triballians. By these wars he was drawn from his Asiatic projects as far away as the portion of Scythia that lies along

[b] Cf. *Life of Alexander*, chap. v. (666 E-F).
[c] Cf. Xenophon, *Hellenica*, vii. 1. 38 ; Diodorus, xix. 48.
[d] Homer, *Il.* x. 407. [e] Cf. 327 D, *supra*.

D τῶν ἄνω πράξεων καὶ περιδραμὼν[1] καὶ κατεργασά-
(342) μενος πάντα κινδύνοις καὶ ἀγῶσι μεγάλοις, αὖθις
ὥρμητο καὶ ἔσπευδε πρὸς τὴν διάβασιν· ἡ[2] δὲ
πάλιν αὐτῷ τὰς Θήβας ἐνέσεισε καὶ πόλεμον
Ἑλληνικὸν ἐμποδὼν κατέβαλε, καὶ δεινὴν πρὸς
ἄνδρας ὁμοφύλους καὶ συγγενεῖς διὰ φόνου καὶ
σιδήρου καὶ πυρὸς ἀνάγκην ἀμύνης, ἀτερπέστατον
τέλος ἔχουσαν.

Ἐκ τούτου διέβαινεν, ὡς μὲν Φύλαρχός φησιν,
ἡμερῶν τριάκοντ' ἔχων ἐφόδιον, ὡς δ' Ἀριστόβουλος, ἑβδομήκοντα τάλαντα· τῶν δ' οἴκοι κτη-
μάτων καὶ προσόδων βασιλικῶν διένειμε τὰς
πλείστας τοῖς ἑταίροις, μόνος δὲ Περδίκκας οὐδὲν
E ἔλαβε διδόντος, ἀλλ' ἠρώτησε, " σαυτῷ δὲ τί
καταλείπεις, Ἀλέξανδρε; " τοῦ δ' εἰπόντος ὅτι
τὰς ἐλπίδας, " οὐκοῦν," ἔφη, " καὶ ἡμεῖς τούτων
μεθέξομεν· οὐ γὰρ δίκαιον τὰ σὰ λαμβάνειν, ἀλλὰ
τὰ Δαρείου περιμένειν."

12. Τίνες οὖν ἦσαν αἱ[3] ἐλπίδες ἐφ' αἷς διέβαινεν
εἰς Ἀσίαν Ἀλέξανδρος; οὐ τείχεσι πόλεων μυρι-
άνδρων ἐκμετρουμένη δύναμις οὐδὲ στόλοι δι'
ὀρῶν πλέοντες, οὐδὲ μάστιγες οὐδὲ πέδαι, μανικὰ
καὶ βάρβαρα κολαστήρια θαλάττης, ἀλλὰ τὰ μὲν

---

[1] περιδραμὼν] ἐπιδραμὼν in Life of Alexander, chap. xi.
(cf. 212 D for the converse).
[2] ἡ Emperius : πάλιν ἡ.
[3] αἱ added by Bernardakis.

---

[a] Heracles, a reputed ancestor of the Macedonian kings,
was born in Thebes.

[b] The sack of Thebes and the enslaving of most of the
surviving inhabitants; cf. Life of Alexander, chap. xi.
(670 E), and Arrian, Anabasis, i. 8-9.

[c] Cited on the authority of Duris in 327 E, supra.

the Danube ; when, by sundry manœuvres, he had subjugated all this territory with much danger and great struggles, he was again eager and in haste for the crossing. Again, however, Fortune stirred up Thebes against him, and thrust in his pathway a war with Greeks, and the dread necessity of punishing, by means of slaughter and fire and sword, men that were his kith and kin,[a] a necessity which had a most unpleasant ending.[b]

After this he crossed with provision for thirty days, as Phylarchus [c] relates ; but Aristobulus says,[d] with seventy talents. He divided the greater part of his possessions at home and his royal revenues among his friends ; Perdiccas [e] alone would take nothing when Alexander offered, but asked, " What are you leaving for yourself, Alexander ? " And when Alexander replied, " High hopes ! ", " Then," said Perdiccas, " we also shall share in these ; for it is not right to take your possessions, but right to wait in expectation of those of Darius."

12. What, then, were the hopes on which Alexander relied when he crossed into Asia ? Not a force counted by means of a wall that would hold a city of 10,000 men,[f] nor fleets that sailed through mountains,[g] nor scourges or fetters, insane and barbaric implements for chastising the sea [h] ; but externally they

d Cf. 327 E, supra.

e Cf. Life of Alexander, chap. xv. (672 B).

f Xerxes counted his army, according to Herodotus vii. 60, by causing 10,000 men to fall in as compactly as possible ; then a low wall was built around them ; they then marched out, others marched in until the whole host (1,700,000 foot soldiers) had been counted.

g By Xerxes' canal through Athos : cf. 335 E, supra ; Herodotus, vii. 22, 23.

h Again referring to Xerxes ; cf. Herodotus, vii. 35.

ἐκτὸς ἐν ὀλίγοις ὅπλοις φιλοτιμία πολλὴ καὶ ζῆλος
ἡλικίας παραλλήλου καὶ ἅμιλλα περὶ δόξης καὶ
ἀρετῆς ἑταίρων· αὐτὸς δ' εἶχεν ἐν ἑαυτῷ τὰς
F μεγάλας ἐλπίδας· εὐσέβειαν περὶ θεούς, πίστιν πρὸς
φίλους, εὐτέλειαν, ἐγκράτειαν, ἐμπειρίαν,[1] ἀφοβίαν
πρὸς θάνατον, εὐψυχίαν, φιλανθρωπίαν, ὁμιλίαν
εὐάρμοστον, ἀψευδὲς ἦθος, εὐστάθειαν ἐν βουλαῖς,
τάχος ἐν πράξεσιν, πρῶτα[2] δόξης, προαίρεσιν ἐν
τῷ καλῷ τελεσιουργόν. Ὅμηρος μὲν γὰρ οὐ
πρεπόντως οὐδὲ πιθανῶς τὸ Ἀγαμέμνονος κάλλος
ἐκ τριῶν συνήρμοσεν εἰκόνων ὁμοιώσας,

343   ὄμματα καὶ κεφαλὴν ἴκελος Διὶ τερπικεραύνῳ,
      Ἄρεϊ δὲ ζώνην, στέρνον δὲ Ποσειδάωνι.

τὴν δ' Ἀλεξάνδρου φύσιν, εἴπερ ἐκ πολλῶν συν-
ήρμοσε καὶ συνέθηκεν ἀρετῶν ὁ γεννήσας θεός,
ἆρ' οὐκ ἂν εἴποιμεν ἔχειν φρόνημα μὲν τὸ Κύρου,
σωφροσύνην δὲ τὴν Ἀγησιλάου, σύνεσιν δὲ τὴν
Θεμιστοκλέους, ἐμπειρίαν δὲ τὴν Φιλίππου, τόλμαν
δὲ τὴν Βρασίδου, δεινότητα δὲ καὶ πολιτείαν τὴν
Περικλέους; τῶν δ' ἔτι παλαιοτέρων σωφρονέ-
στερος μὲν Ἀγαμέμνονος· ὁ μὲν γὰρ προέκρινε τῆς
γαμετῆς τὴν αἰχμάλωτον, ὁ δὲ καὶ πρὶν ἢ γῆμαι
B τῶν ἁλισκομένων ἀπείχετο. μεγαλοψυχότερος δ'
Ἀχιλλέως· ὁ μὲν γὰρ χρημάτων ὀλίγων τὸν
Ἕκτορος νεκρὸν ἀπελύτρωσεν, ὁ δὲ πολλοῖς χρήμασι Δαρεῖον ἔθαψε· καὶ ὁ μὲν παρὰ τῶν φίλων

---

[1] ἐμπειρίαν] εὐποιΐαν has slight ms. authority (but cf. 343 A,
infra ἐμπειρίαν . . . Φιλίππου).
[2] πρῶτα] ἔρωτα Reiske (τὰ πρῶτα?).

were the great ambition in his little army, mutual rivalry of hot youth, competition for repute and excellence among his Companions. And within himself he had his own high hopes, reverence for the gods, fidelity toward his friends, frugality, self-control, experience, fearlessness toward death, high courage, humanity, affability, integrity of character, constancy in counsel, quickness in execution, the height of good repute, and a disposition to gain his end in everything honourable. For not appropriately nor convincingly did Homer[a] employ a combination of three similes in his comparison describing the fair appearance of Agamemnon :

> Like in his eyes and his head unto Zeus who delighteth in thunder,
> Like unto Ares in waist, and in breadth of his chest to Poseidon.

But if the god who begat Alexander made his natural endowment an harmoniously joined combination of many virtues, may we not say that he possessed the high spirit of Cyrus, the discretion of Agesilaüs, the intelligence of Themistocles, the experience of Philip, the daring of Brasidas, the eloquence and statesmanship of Pericles ? And, to compare him with the men of still more ancient days, he was more self-restrained than Agamemnon ; for Agamemnon set a captive woman[b] above his wedded wife, but Alexander, even before his marriage, kept aloof from his captives. He was more magnanimous than Achilles ; for Achilles[c] gave back the body of Hector for a small ransom, but Alexander buried Darius at great expense ; Achilles,[d] when he had become reconciled,

---

[a] *Iliad*, ii. 478-479. [b] Chryseis : *Iliad*, i. 113.
[c] *Iliad*, xxiv. 552-600. [d] *Iliad*, xix. 140-147.

(343) δῶρα καὶ μισθὸν ἀντὶ τῆς ὀργῆς διαλλαγεὶς ἔλαβεν,
ὁ δὲ τοὺς πολεμίους κρατῶν ἐπλούτιζεν. εὐ-
σεβέστερος δὲ Διομήδους· ὁ μὲν γὰρ θεοῖς μάχεσθαι
ἦν ἕτοιμος, ὁ δὲ πάντα[1] τοὺς θεοὺς ἐνόμιζε κατ-
ορθοῦν. ποθεινότερος δὲ τοῖς προσήκουσιν Ὀδυσ-
σέως· ἐκείνου μὲν γὰρ ἡ τεκοῦσα διὰ λύπην
ἀπέθανε, τούτῳ δ' ἡ τοῦ πολεμίου μήτηρ ὑπ'
εὐνοίας συναπέθανε.

13 Τὸ δ' ὅλον, εἰ μὲν καὶ Σόλων διὰ Τύχην
C ἐπολιτεύσατο καὶ Μιλτιάδης διὰ Τύχην ἐστρατήγησε
καὶ Ἀριστείδης ἀπὸ Τύχης ἦν δίκαιος, οὐδὲν ἄρα
τῆς Ἀρετῆς ἔργον ἐστίν, ἀλλ' ὄνομα τοῦτο καὶ
λόγος ἔχων δόξαν ἄλλως διέξεισι τοῦ βίου, πλατ-
τόμενος ὑπὸ τῶν σοφιστῶν καὶ τῶν νομοθετῶν.
εἰ δὲ τούτων καὶ τῶν ὁμοίων ἀνδρῶν ἕκαστος
πένης μὲν ἢ πλούσιος ἢ ἀσθενὴς ἢ ἰσχυρὸς ἢ
ἄμορφος ἢ καλὸς ἢ εὔγηρως ἢ ὠκύμορος διὰ Τύχην
γέγονε, μέγαν δὲ στρατηγὸν καὶ μέγαν νομοθέτην
καὶ μέγαν ἐν ἀρχαῖς καὶ πολιτείαις ἕκαστος ἑαυτὸν
ἀρετῇ καὶ λόγῳ παρέσχηκε, φέρε θεῷ τὸν Ἀλέξανδρον ἅπασι παραβάλλων. Σόλων χρεῶν ἀπο-
D κοπὴν ἐν Ἀθήναις ἐποίησε, σεισάχθειαν προσ-
αγορεύσας· Ἀλέξανδρος δὲ τὰ χρέα τοῖς[2] δανείσασιν
ὑπὲρ τῶν ὀφειλόντων αὐτὸς ἐξέτισε. Περικλῆς
φορολογήσας τοὺς Ἕλληνας ἐκ τῶν χρημάτων

---

[1] Cobet would add διὰ after πάντα.
[2] τὰ χρέα τοῖς] τοῖς τὰ χρέα most mss.

---

[a] *Iliad*, v. 335-352, 855-861.
[b] *Odyssey*, xi. 202-203.
[c] Sisygambis, the mother of Darius : *cf.* Diodorus, xvii.

accepted gifts and recompense from his friends to requite him for ceasing from his Wrath, but Alexander enriched his enemies by conquering them. He was more reverent than Diomedes [a] ; for Diomedes was ready to fight with gods, but Alexander believed the gods to be the authors of all success. He was more deeply mourned by his relatives than was Odysseus ; for Odysseus' [b] mother died of grief, but the mother [c] of Alexander's foe, for the goodwill she bore him, shared his death.

13. In short, if Solon's statesmanship also was due to Fortune, and if Miltiades' generalship, and Aristeides' [d] justice were but the result of Fortune, then surely there is no work of Virtue in these men, but it is a name only, talk based on appearance, pervading their lives to no purpose, a figment of the sophists and legislators. But if every one of these men and of others like them became poor or rich, weak or strong, ugly or handsome, lived to a ripe old age or met an untimely death through Fortune, or if each one of them proved himself a great general, a great lawgiver, or great in government and statesmanship through Virtue and Reason, then consider Alexander and compare him with them all. Solon [e] brought about a cancellation of debts in Athens which he called the "Relief from Burdens" (Seisachtheia); but Alexander himself paid the debts which his men owed to their creditors.[f] Pericles collected tribute from the Greeks and with the money adorned the Acropolis

118. 3 ; Justin, xiii. 1 ; Quintus Curtius, *Hist. Alexandri*, x. 5. 21.

[d] Cf. *Moralia*, 97 c.

[e] Cf. *Moralia*, 828 F ; *Life of Solon*, chaps. xv., xvi. (86 D, 87 D) ; Aristotle, *Constitution of Athens*, 10. 1.

[f] Cf. 339 c, *supra*, and the note.

(343) ἐκόσμησεν ἱεροῖς τὴν ἀκρόπολιν· Ἀλέξανδρος δὲ
τὰ τῶν βαρβάρων χρήματα λαβὼν ἔπεμψεν εἰς τὴν
Ἑλλάδα, ναοὺς τοῖς θεοῖς ἀπὸ μυρίων ταλάντων[a]
οἰκοδομῆσαι κελεύσας. Βρασίδαν ἐν τῇ Ἑλλάδι
περιβόητον ἐποίησε τὸ πρὸς Μεθώνην διαδραμεῖν
τὸ στρατόπεδον τῶν πολεμίων βαλλόμενον παρὰ
τὴν θάλατταν· Ἀλεξάνδρου δ' ἐν Ὀξυδράκαις τὸ
δεινὸν ἐκεῖνο πήδημα καὶ ἄπιστον ἀκούουσι καὶ
θεωμένοις φοβερόν, ἐκ τειχῶν ἀφέντος ἑαυτὸν εἰς
E τοὺς πολεμίους δόρασι καὶ βέλεσι καὶ ξίφεσι
γυμνοῖς ἐκδεχομένους, τίνι ἄν τις εἰκάσειεν ἢ
πυρὶ κεραυνίῳ ῥαγέντι καὶ φερομένῳ μετὰ πνεύματος, οἷον[1] ἐπὶ γῆν κατέσκηψε φάσμα Φοίβου[2]
φλογοειδέσιν ὅπλοις περιλαμπόμενον; οἱ δὲ τὸ
πρῶτον ἐκπλαγέντες ἅμα φρίκῃ διέτρεσαν καὶ
ἀνεχώρησαν· εἶθ' ὡς ἑώρων ἄνθρωπον ἕνα πολλοῖς
ἐπιφερόμενον, ἀντέστησαν.

Ἐνταῦθ' ἄρ' ἡ Τύχη μεγάλα καὶ λαμπρὰ διέφηνεν
ἔργα τῆς πρὸς Ἀλέξανδρον εὐμενείας, ὅτ' αὐτὸν
μὲν εἰς χωρίον ἄσημον καὶ βάρβαρον ἐμβαλοῦσα
κατέκλεισε καὶ περιετείχισε, τοὺς δ' ὑπὸ σπουδῆς
F ἐπιβοηθοῦντας ἔξωθεν καὶ τῶν τειχῶν ἐφιεμένους,
κλάσασα καὶ συντρίψασα τὰς κλίμακας, ὑπεσκέλισε
καὶ κατεκρήμνισε. τριῶν δ' οἵπερ ἔφθησαν μόνοι
τοῦ τείχους λαβέσθαι καὶ καθέντες ἑαυτοὺς παρα-

---

[1] οἷον] ἢ οἷον Helmbold.
[2] Φοίβου omitted by all mss. except two; Φόβου Wyttenbach.

---

[a] £2,000,000 or $10,000,000.
[b] Cf. Diodorus, xviii. 4. 4.
[c] Cf. Thucydides, ii. 25. 2.

with temples ; but Alexander captured the riches of barbarians and sent them to Greece with orders that ten thousand talents [a] be used to construct temples for the gods.[b] Brasidas's [c] dash along the shore to Methonê through the armed host of the enemy amid showers of missiles made him renowned in Greece ; but that daring leap of Alexander in the country of the Oxydrachae,[d] incredible to them that hear of it and fearful to them that saw it, when he hurled himself down from the walls into the midst of the enemy, who received him with spears and arrows and naked swords—with what may one compare it, save with the levin bolt that breaks and flashes in the midst of a hurricane, like the apparition of Phoebus that darted down to earth,[e] gleaming round about with flaming armour. The enemy at first were amazed and affrighted and retired with trembling fear ; but a moment later, when they saw that he was but one man attacking many, they made a stand against him.

There indeed Fortune made manifest great and splendid results of her kindliness toward Alexander, when she cast him into an insignificant foreign town and shut him in and fenced him round about ! And when his men were earnestly trying to bring help from without and were attempting to scale the walls, Fortune, by breaking and shattering their ladders, took away their foothold and hurled them from the walls. And of the three [f] men who alone were quick enough to grasp the wall and, throwing themselves

---

[a] The Mallians : *cf.* 327 B, *supra.*

[e] *Cf.* perhaps Homer, *Il.* xv. 237 ; iv. 75-80.

[f] 327 B, *supra*, and *Life of Alexander*, chap. lxiii. (700 c) mention only two ; but Plutarch here seems to follow the authority used by Arrian, *Anabasis*, vi. 10, who gives the number as three ; *cf.* also 344 D, *infra.*

στῆναι[1] τῷ βασιλεῖ, τὸν μὲν εὐθὺς ἀνήρπασε καὶ
προανεῖλεν, ὁ δὲ τοξεύμασι πολλοῖς διαπεπαρμένος
ὅσον ὁρᾶν καὶ συναισθάνεσθαι μόνον ἀπεῖχε τοῦ
344 τεθνάναι· κεναὶ δ᾽ ἔξωθεν προσδρομαὶ καὶ ἀλα-
λαγμοὶ Μακεδόνων, οὐ μηχανῆς τινος οὐκ ὀργάνων
παρόντων, ἀλλ᾽ ὑπὸ σπουδῆς ξίφεσι τυπτόντων τὰ
τείχη καὶ χερσὶ γυμναῖς παραρρῆξαι καὶ μονονοὺ
διαφαγεῖν βιαζομένων.

Ὁ δ᾽ εὐτυχὴς βασιλεὺς καὶ ὑπὸ τῆς Τύχης
φυλαττόμενος ἀεὶ καὶ δορυφορούμενος, ὥσπερ
θηρίον ἄρκυσιν ἐνσχεθείς, ἔρημος καὶ ἀβοήθητος,
οὐχ ὑπὲρ Σούσων οὐδὲ Βαβυλῶνος οὐδὲ τοῦ[2]
Βάκτρα λαβεῖν οὐδὲ τοῦ μεγάλου[3] Πώρου κρατῆσαι·
τοῖς γὰρ ἐνδόξοις καὶ μεγάλοις ἀγῶσι, κἂν δυστυ-
χῶνται, τὸ γοῦν αἰσχρὸν οὐ πρόσεστιν. ἀλλ᾽ οὕτω
δύσερις ἦν καὶ βάσκανος ἡ Τύχη καὶ φιλοβάρβαρος
B καὶ μισαλέξανδρος, ὥστε μὴ τὸ σῶμα μόνον αὐτοῦ
μηδὲ τὸν βίον, ἀλλὰ καὶ τὴν δόξαν ἀνελεῖν ὅσον
ἐφ᾽ ἑαυτῇ καὶ διαφθεῖραι τὴν εὔκλειαν. οὐ γὰρ
παρ᾽ Εὐφράτην Ἀλέξανδρον ἢ Ὑδάσπην πεσόντα
κεῖσθαι δεινὸν ἦν, οὐδ᾽ ἀγεννὲς ἐν χερσὶ Δαρείου[4]
γενόμενον καὶ ἵπποις καὶ ξίφεσι καὶ κοπίσι Περσῶν
ἀμυνομένων ὑπὲρ τοῦ βασιλέως ἀποθανεῖν· οὐδὲ
τῶν Βαβυλῶνος ἐπιβαίνοντα τειχῶν σφαλῆναι καὶ
πεσεῖν ἀπ᾽ ἐλπίδος μεγάλης. οὕτω Πελοπίδας καὶ
Ἐπαμεινώνδας· ἀρετῆς ὁ τούτων θάνατος ἦν, οὐ
δυστυχίας ἐπὶ τηλικούτοις. τῆς δὲ νῦν ἐξεταζο-

---

[1] παραστῆναι] most mss. have περιστῆναι.
[2] τοῦ added by Reiske.
[3] τοῦ μεγάλου Meziriacus: τὸ μέγα τοῦ.
[4] Δαρείου] Δαρείῳ Abresch.

down inside, to take their stand beside the king, Fortune straightway snatched up one and made away with him before he could strike a blow ; and a second, pierced through by many arrows, was only so far from death that he could see and perceive his king's danger. But the charges and shouting of the Macedonians were unavailing for they had no machines nor siege engines with them ; but in their zeal they tried to hack the walls with their swords, and were forced to break them off with their bare hands, and all but bite their way through.

But the king, who was Fortune's favourite, and was always guarded and personally protected by her, was caught within like a wild beast in the toils, alone and without succour ; nor was he struggling for Susa or Babylon, nor to capture Bactria, nor to vanquish the great Porus ; for in great and glorious conflicts, even though men fail, disgrace, at least, can find no place. But so contentious and malicious was Fortune, so greatly did she favour barbarians and hate Alexander, that she tried to destroy not only his body and his life, but also, in so far as she could, to destroy his repute and to wipe out his fair fame. For it were not a terrible thing for Alexander to fall and lie buried beside the Euphrates or the Hydaspes, nor ignoble to meet death by coming into close combat with Darius or in confronting the horses and swords and battle-axes of the Persians as they fought to defend their king, nor to be overthrown while he bestrode the walls of Babylon and to fall from his high hope. Thus fell Pelopidas and Epameinondas ; their death was a death belonging to Virtue, not to misfortune, engaged as they were in such a high emprise. But of what sort was the deed of Fortune, who is now

C μένης Τύχης οἷον τὸ ἔργον; ἐν[1] ἐσχατιᾷ βαρβάρου
(344) παραποταμίας καὶ τείχεσιν ἀδόξου πολίχνης περι-
βαλούσης καὶ ἀποκρυψάσης τὸν τῆς οἰκουμένης
βασιλέα καὶ κύριον, ὅπλοις ἀτίμοις καὶ σκεύεσι
τοῖς παρατυχοῦσι τυπτόμενον καὶ βαλλόμενον
ἀπολέσθαι. καὶ γὰρ κοπίδι τὴν κεφαλὴν διὰ τοῦ
κράνους ἐπλήγη, καὶ βέλει τις ἀπὸ τόξου τὸν
θώρακα διέκοψεν, οὗ τοῖς περὶ τὸν μαστὸν ἐνερει-
σθέντος ὀστέοις καὶ καταπαγέντος ὁ μὲν καυλὸς
ἐξεῖχε βαρύνων, τῆς δ' ἀκίδος ὁ σίδηρος τεττάρων
δακτύλων εὖρος ἔσχε καὶ πέντε μῆκος. ἔσχατον
δὲ τῶν δεινῶν, ὁ μὲν ἠμύνετο τοὺς κατὰ στόμα καὶ
τὸν βαλόντα καὶ πελάσαι τολμήσαντα μετὰ ξίφους
D αὐτὸς τῷ ἐγχειριδίῳ φθάσας κατέβαλε καὶ ἀπ-
έκτεινεν· ἐν τούτῳ δέ τις δραμὼν ἐκ μυλῶνος ὑπέρῳ κατὰ τοῦ αὐχένος ὄπισθεν πληγὴν κατήνεγκεν,
ᾗ συνέχεε τὴν αἴσθησιν αὐτοῦ σκοτωθέντος· ἡ δ'
Ἀρετὴ παρῆν θάρσος μὲν αὐτῷ, ῥώμην δὲ καὶ
σπουδὴν τοῖς περὶ αὐτὸν ἐμποιοῦσα. Λιμναῖοι γὰρ
καὶ Πτολεμαῖοι καὶ Λεόννατοι[2] καὶ ὅσοι τὸ τεῖχος
ὑπερκαταβάντες[3] ἢ ῥήξαντες ἔστησαν πρὸ αὐτοῦ
τεῖχος ἀρετῆς ἦσαν, εὐνοίᾳ καὶ φιλίᾳ τοῦ βασιλέως τὰ σώματα κατὰ πρόσωπον[4] καὶ τὰς ψυχὰς
προβαλλόμενοι. οὐ γὰρ διὰ Τύχην ἀγαθῶν βασιλέων ἑταῖροι[5] προαποθνήσκουσιν ἑκουσίως καὶ προ-

---

[1] ἐν added by Wyttenbach.
[2] Λεόννατοι W. Schulze : Λεοννάτοι.
[3] ὑπερκαταβάντες] ὑπερβάντες Reiske.
[4] κατὰ πρόσωπον F.C.B. (cf. κατὰ στόμα a few lines above):
καὶ τὰ πρόσωπα, which Emperius would omit.
[5] ἑταῖροι Abresch : ἕτεροι.

---

[a] Plutarch the rhetorician increases by one finger's-breadth

under scrutiny ? Was it not that on the farthest out-
posts of a land beside a foreign river within the walls
of an obscure hamlet, which surrounded and hid away
from sight the lord and master of the inhabited world,
he should perish, smitten and stricken by ignominious
weapons and whatever else lay at hand ? For his head
was wounded through his helmet by an axe, and someone shot an arrow through his breastplate so that it
penetrated the bones of his breast and was lodged
there firmly, while the shaft protruded and hampered
him and the iron point was four fingers broad and five
fingers long.[a] But—the extreme of all the dangers
he confronted—while he was defending himself
against those who attacked him in front, the archer
who shot him had plucked up courage to approach
him with a sword, but Alexander with his dagger
was too quick for the man and knocked him down
and killed him ; but while he was thus occupied,
someone ran out from a mill, and gave him a blow
on the neck with a cudgel from behind ; this confused his senses, and his head swam. But Virtue
was by his side and in him she engendered daring,
and in his companions strength and zeal. For men
like Limnaeus and Ptolemy and Leonnatus and all
those who had surmounted the wall or had broken
through it took their stand before him and were a
bulwark of Virtue, exposing their bodies in the face
of the foe and even their lives for the goodwill and
love they bore their king. Surely it is not due to
Fortune that the companions of good kings risk their
lives and willingly die for them ; but this they do

the dimensions of the arrow-point which are given by
Plutarch the biographer in his *Life of Alexander*, chap.
lxiii. (700 E).

E κινδυνεύουσιν, ἀλλ' ἔρωτι τῆς Ἀρετῆς ὥσπερ
ὑπὸ φίλτρων μέλιτται τῷ ἄρχοντι προσέρχονται
καὶ προσπεφύκασι.

Τίς οὖν οὐκ ἂν εἶπε[1] τότε παρὼν ἀκίνδυνος
θεατὴς ὅτι Τύχης μέγαν ἀγῶνα καὶ Ἀρετῆς θεᾶται,
καὶ τὸ μὲν βάρβαρον παρ' ἀξίαν ἐπικρατεῖ διὰ
Τύχην, τὸ δ' Ἑλληνικὸν ἀντέχει παρὰ δύναμιν δι'
Ἀρετήν; κἂν μὲν ἐκεῖνοι περιγένωνται, Τύχης
καὶ δαίμονος φθονεροῦ καὶ νεμέσεως ἔσται τὸ
ἔργον· ἂν δ' οὗτοι κρατήσωσιν, Ἀρετὴ καὶ τόλμα
καὶ φιλία καὶ πίστις ἐξοίσεται τὸ νικητήριον;
ταῦτα γὰρ μόνα παρῆν Ἀλεξάνδρῳ, τῆς δ' ἄλλης
δυνάμεως καὶ παρασκευῆς καὶ στόλων καὶ ἵππων
F καὶ στρατοπέδων μέσον ἔθηκεν ἡ Τύχη τὸ τεῖχος.

Ἐτρέψαντο μὲν οὖν τοὺς βαρβάρους οἱ Μακεδόνες,
καὶ πεσοῦσιν αὐτοῖς ἐπικατέσκαψαν τὴν πόλιν.
Ἀλεξάνδρῳ δ' οὐδὲν ἦν ὄφελος· ἥρπαστο γὰρ μετὰ
τοῦ βέλους, καὶ τὸν κάλαμον[2] ἐν τοῖς σπλάγχνοις
εἶχε, καὶ δεσμὸς ἦν αὐτῷ καὶ ἧλος τὸ τόξευμα τοῦ
θώρακος πρὸς τὸ σῶμα. καὶ σπάσαι μὲν ὥσπερ
345 ἐκ ῥίζης τοῦ τραύματος βιαζομένοις οὐχ ὑπήκουεν
ὁ σίδηρος, ἕδραν ἔχων τὰ πρὸ τῆς καρδίας στερεὰ
τοῦ στήθους· ἐκπρῖσαι δὲ τοῦ δόνακος οὐκ ἐθάρρουν
τὸ προέχον, ἀλλ' ἐφοβοῦντο, μή πως σπαραγμῷ
σχιζόμενον τὸ ὀστέον ὑπερβολὰς ἀλγηδόνων παρ-
άσχῃ καὶ ῥῆξις αἵματος ἐκ βάθους γένηται.
πολλὴν δ' ἀπορίαν καὶ διατριβὴν ὁρῶν αὐτὸς
ἐπεχείρησεν ἐν χρῷ τοῦ θώρακος[3] ἀποτέμνειν τῷ

---

[1] εἶπε E. Kurtz: εἴποι.

[2] κάλαμον E. Kurtz (or καυλὸν) seems certain from the
account given in *Life of Alexander*, chap. lxiii. as well as
τοῦ δόνακος, 345 Α, *infra*: πόλεμον.

[3] θώρακος] some mss. have σώματος, perhaps rightly.

through a passion for Virtue, even as bees, as if under the spell of love-charms, approach and closely surround their sovereign.

What spectator, then, who might without danger to himself have been present at that scene, would not exclaim that he was witnessing the mighty contest of Fortune and Virtue ; that through Fortune the foreign host was prevailing beyond its deserts, but through Virtue the Greeks were holding out beyond their ability ? And if the enemy gains the upper hand, this will be the work of Fortune or of some jealous deity or of divine retribution ; but if the Greeks prevail, it will be Virtue and daring, friendship and fidelity, that will win the guerdon of victory ? These were, in fact, the only support that Alexander had with him at this time, since Fortune had put a barrier between him and the rest of his forces and equipment, fleets, horse, and camp.

Finally, the Macedonians routed the barbarians, and, when they had fallen, pulled down their city on their heads. But this was no help to Alexander ; for he had been hurried from the field, arrow and all, and he had the shaft in his vitals ; the arrow was as a bond or bolt holding his breastplate to his body. And when they tried forcibly to pull it out of the wound by the roots, as it were, the iron would not budge, since it was lodged in the bony part of the breast in front of the heart. They did not dare to saw off the protruding portion of the shaft, since they were afraid that the bone might be split by the jarring and cause excruciating pain, and that an internal haemorrhage might result. But when Alexander perceived their great perplexity and hesitation, he himself tried with his dagger to cut off the arrow

485

(345) ξιφιδίῳ τὸν οἰστόν· ἠτόνει δ᾽ ἡ χεὶρ καὶ βάρος
εἶχε ναρκῶδες ὑπὸ φλεγμονῆς τοῦ τραύματος.
ἐκέλευεν οὖν ἅπτεσθαι καὶ μὴ δεδιέναι τοὺς ἀτρώ-
B τους θαρρύνων· καὶ τοῖς μὲν ἐλοιδορεῖτο κλαίουσι
καὶ περιπαθοῦσι, τοὺς δὲ λιποτάκτας[1] ἀπεκάλει,
μὴ τολμῶντας αὐτῷ βοηθεῖν· ἐβόα δὲ πρὸς τοὺς
ἑταίρους, "μηδεὶς ἔστω μηδ᾽ ὑπὲρ ἐμοῦ δειλός·
ἀπιστοῦμαι μὴ φοβεῖσθαι θάνατον, εἰ τὸν ἐμὸν
φοβεῖσθ᾽ ὑμεῖς."

---

[1] λιποτάκτας Dübner : λειποτάκτας.

---

[a] Some think the narrative closes abruptly, and that it
should have been continued to include at least Alexander's

close to his breastplate ; but his hand was unsteady
and affected by a torpid languor from the inflamma-
tion of the wound.   Accordingly with encouraging
words he urged those that were unwounded to take
hold and not to be afraid ; and he railed at some
who were weeping and could not control themselves,
others he branded as deserters, since they had not
the courage to come to his assistance.   And he cried
aloud to his Companions, " Let no one be faint-
hearted even for my sake !   For it will not be believed
that I do not fear death, if you fear death for me ! " [a]

recovery, but the Greeks did not always insist on a happy
ending narrated in full.

WERE THE ATHENIANS MORE FAMOUS IN WAR OR IN WISDOM?

(BELLONE AN PACE CLARIORES FUERINT ATHENIENSES)

INTRODUCTION

PLUTARCH's discussion whether the Athenians were more famous in war or in wisdom, sometimes referred to by a briefer title, *De Gloria Atheniensium*, is an epideictic oration like the preceding essays ; we may perhaps infer from the words (345 F), " This city has been the mother and kindly nurse of many other arts," that it was delivered at Athens. Like the preceding essays, it closes abruptly, and again we do not know the reason therefor.

Ralph Waldo Emerson, in his introduction to the translation of Plutarch revised by Goodwin, says, " The vigor of his pen appears in the chapter ' Whether the Athenians were more Warlike or Learned . . .'" It is strange that this vigour should be devoted to glorifying the men of arms and vilifying the men of letters, and yet this is precisely what Plutarch attempts to do in this essay. It is true that he lived in an era of profound peace, when the horrors of war were remote, but it is somewhat surprising to find him arguing for this thesis, especially since he shows by incidental statements that he is thoroughly aware of the contributions that Athens has made to literature. We may, then, be justified in the inference that the essay is a *tour de force*, like other rhetorical discussions which were

490

ON THE FAME OF THE ATHENIANS

popular in Plutarch's day; it does not necessarily represent his own belief.

Many of the historical references will be found in an amplified form in the *Lives*.

The essay is no. 197 in Lamprias's list of Plutarch's works where it bears the simpler title, "In what were the Athenians famous?" (Κατὰ τί ἔνδοξοι Ἀθηναῖοι;).

ΠΟΤΕΡΟΝ ΑΘΗΝΑΙΟΙ ΚΑΤΑ ΠΟΛΕΜΟΝ Η ΚΑΤΑ ΣΟΦΙΑΝ ΕΝΔΟΞΟΤΕΡΟΙ

1. . . [1] Ταῦτ᾽ ὀρθῶς μὲν ἐκεῖνος εἶπε πρὸς τοὺς
μεθ᾽ ἑαυτὸν στρατηγούς, οἷς πάροδον ἐπὶ τὰς
ὕστερον πράξεις ἔδωκεν ἐξελάσας τὸν βάρβαρον
καὶ τὴν Ἑλλάδ᾽ ἐλευθερώσας· ὀρθῶς δ᾽ εἰρήσεται
καὶ πρὸς τοὺς ἐπὶ τοῖς λόγοις μέγα φρονοῦντας·
ἂν γὰρ ἀνέλῃς τοὺς πράττοντας, οὐχ ἕξεις τοὺς
γράφοντας. ἄνελε τὴν Περικλέους πολιτείαν καὶ
τὰ ναύμαχα πρὸς Ῥίῳ Φορμίωνος τρόπαια καὶ τὰς
περὶ Κύθηρα καὶ Μέγαρα καὶ Κόρινθον ἀνδραγαθίας
Νικίου καὶ τὴν Δημοσθένους Πύλον καὶ τοὺς
Κλέωνος τετρακοσίους αἰχμαλώτους καὶ Τολμίδαν[2]
Πελοπόννησον περιπλέοντα καὶ Μυρωνίδην νικῶντα
Βοιωτοὺς ἐν Οἰνοφύτοις, καὶ Θουκυδίδης σοι
διαγέγραπται. ἄνελε τὰ περὶ Ἑλλήσποντον Ἀλκιβιάδου νεανιεύματα καὶ τὰ πρὸς Λέσβῳ[3] Θρασύλλου
καὶ τὴν ὑπὸ Θηραμένους τῆς ὀλιγαρχίας κατάλυσιν
καὶ Θρασύβουλον καὶ Ἀρχῖνον[4] καὶ τοὺς ἀπὸ
Φυλῆς ἑβδομήκοντα κατὰ τῆς Σπαρτιατῶν ἡγεμονίας ἀνισταμένους καὶ Κόνωνα πάλιν ἐμβιβάζοντα

---

[1] Xylander was the first to suggest a lacuna at the
beginning.
[2] Τολμίδαν Xylander: Τολμίαν.
[3] Λέσβῳ F.C.B.: Λέσβον.
[4] Ἀρχῖνον Taylor, from 835 F: ἄρχιππον.

WERE THE ATHENIANS MORE FAMOUS IN WAR OR IN WISDOM?

1. . . . Thus [a] rightly spoke the great Themistocles to the generals who succeeded him, for whom he had opened a way for their subsequent exploits by driving out the barbarian host and making Greece free. And rightly will it be spoken also to those who pride themselves on their writings ; for if you take away the men of action, you will have no men of letters. Take away Pericles' statesmanship, and Phormio's trophies for his naval victories at Rhium, and Nicias's valiant deeds at Cythera and Megara and Corinth, Demosthenes' Pylos, and Cleon's four hundred captives, Tolmides' circumnavigation of the Peloponnesus, and Myronides' [b] victory over the Boeotians at Oenophyta—take these away and Thucydides is stricken from your list of writers. Take away Alcibiades' spirited exploits in the Hellespontine region, and those of Thrasyllus by Lesbos, and the overthrow by Theramenes of the oligarchy, Thrasybulus and Archinus and the uprising of the Seventy [c] from Phylê against the Spartan hegemony, and Conon's restoration of Athens to her

---

[a] Probably Plutarch began with his favourite tale of Themistocles' remark (dealing with the festival day and the day after) to the generals who came after him ; cf. 270 c, supra, and the note.　　　[b] Cf. Thucydides, i. 108 ; iv. 95.

[c] Cf. Xenophon, Hellenica, ii. 4. 2.

E τὰς Ἀθήνας εἰς τὴν θάλατταν, καὶ Κράτιππος
ἀνῄρηται.

Ξενοφῶν μὲν γὰρ αὐτὸς ἑαυτοῦ γέγονεν ἱστορία,
γράψας ἃ ἐστρατήγησε καὶ κατώρθωσε καὶ Θεμι-
στογένη περὶ τούτων συντετάχθαι τὸν Συρακόσιον,
ἵνα πιστότερος ᾖ διηγούμενος ἑαυτὸν ὡς ἄλλον,
ἑτέρῳ τὴν τῶν λόγων δόξαν χαριζόμενος. οἱ δ᾽
ἄλλοι πάντες ἱστορικοί, Κλειτόδημοι[1] Δίυλλοι
Φιλόχοροι Φύλαρχοι,[2] ἀλλοτρίων γεγόνασιν ἔργων[3]
ὥσπερ δραμάτων ὑποκριταί, τὰς τῶν στρατηγῶν
καὶ βασιλέων πράξεις διατιθέμενοι καὶ ταῖς ἐκείνων
ὑποδυόμενοι μνήμαις ἵν᾽ ὡς αὐγῆς τινος καὶ φωτὸς
F μετάσχωσιν. ἀνακλᾶται γὰρ ἀπὸ τῶν πραττόντων
ἐπὶ τοὺς γράφοντας καὶ ἀναλάμπει δόξης εἴδωλον
ἀλλοτρίας, ἐμφαινομένης διὰ τῶν λόγων τῆς
πράξεως ὡς ἐν ἐσόπτρῳ.

2. Πολλῶν μὲν δὴ καὶ ἄλλων ἡ πόλις ἥδε μήτηρ
καὶ τροφὸς εὐμενὴς τεχνῶν γέγονε, τὰς μὲν εὑρα-
μένη καὶ ἀναφήνασα πρώτη, ταῖς δὲ δύναμιν προσ-
θεῖσα καὶ τιμὴν καὶ αὔξησιν· οὐχ ἥκιστα δ᾽ ὑπ᾽
346 αὐτῆς ζωγραφία προῆκται καὶ κεκόσμηται. καὶ
γὰρ Ἀπολλόδωρος ὁ ζωγράφος, ἀνθρώπων πρῶτος
ἐξευρὼν φθορὰν καὶ ἀπόχρωσιν σκιᾶς, Ἀθηναῖος
ἦν· οὗ τοῖς ἔργοις ἐπιγέγραπται

μωμήσεταί τις μᾶλλον ἢ μιμήσεται.

[1] Κλειτόδημοι Wyttenbach: κλεινόδημοι.
[2] Φιλόχοροι Φύλαρχοι F.C.B. (Φύλαρχος Reiske): φιλόχορος
φίλαρχος.
[3] ἔργων Aldine ed., confirmed by one ms.: ἐρώτων.

[a] An historian who continued Thucydides, claiming to be
his contemporary (see E. Schwartz, *Hermes*, xliv. 496).

power on the sea—take these away and Cratippus [a] is no more.

Xenophon, to be sure, became his own history by writing of his generalship and his successes and recording that it was Themistogenes [b] the Syracusan who had compiled an account of them, his purpose being to win greater credence for his narrative by referring to himself in the third person, thus favouring another with the glory of the authorship. But all the other historians, men like Cleitodemus, Diyllus, [c] Philochorus, Phylarchus, have been for the exploits of others what actors are for plays, exhibiting the deeds of the generals and kings, and merging themselves with their characters as tradition records them, in order that they might share in a certain effulgence, so to speak, and splendour. For there is reflected from the men of action upon the men of letters an image of another's glory, which shines again there, since the deed is seen, as in a mirror, through the agency of their words.

2. This city, as we all know, has been the mother and kindly nurse of many other arts, some of which she was the first to discover and reveal, while to others she gave added strength and honour and advancement; not least of all, painting was enhanced and embellished by her. For Apollodorus the painter, the first man to discover the art of mixing colours and chiaroscuro, was an Athenian. Upon his productions is inscribed:

It were easier that you blame than try to make the same. [d]

[b] *Cf.* Xenophon, *Hellenica*, iii. 1. 2; M. MacLaren, *Trans. Amer. Phil. Assoc.* lxv. (1934) pp. 240-247.

[c] *Cf. Moralia*, 862 B; Müller, *Frag. Hist. Graec.* ii. 360-361.

[d] *Cf.* Pliny, *Natural History*, xxxv. 9. 62, where the verse is ascribed to Zeuxis; for other references see Edmonds, *Elegy and Iambus* (in the L.C.L.), ii. p. 24.

(346) καὶ Εὐφράνωρ καὶ Νικίας καὶ ᾿Ασκληπιόδωρος
καὶ Πάναινος[1] ὁ Φειδίου ἀδελφός, οἱ μὲν στρατηγοὺς
ἔγραψαν νικῶντας, οἱ δὲ μάχας, οἱ δ᾿ ἥρωας· ὥσπερ
Εὐφράνωρ τὸν Θησέα τὸν ἑαυτοῦ τῷ Παρρασίου
παρέβαλε, λέγων τὸν μὲν ἐκείνου ῥόδα βεβρωκέναι,
τὸν δ᾿ ἑαυτοῦ κρέα βόεια. τῷ γὰρ ὄντι γλαφυρῶς
ὁ Παρρασίου γέγραπται καὶ πεποίκιλται καί τι[2]
προσέοικε· τὸν δ᾿ Εὐφράνορος ἰδών τις εἶπεν οὐκ
ἀφυῶς[3]

B   δῆμον Ἐρεχθῆος μεγαλήτορος, ὅν ποτ᾿ Ἀθήνη
    θρέψε Διὸς θυγάτηρ.

Γέγραφε δὲ καὶ τὴν ἐν Μαντινείᾳ πρὸς Ἐπαμει-
νώνδαν ἱππομαχίαν οὐκ ἀνενθουσιάστως Εὐφράνωρ.
τὸ δ᾿ ἔργον ἔσχεν οὕτως· Ἐπαμεινώνδας Θηβαῖος
ἀπὸ[4] τῆς ἐν Λεύκτροις μάχης ἀρθεὶς μέγας ἐπεμ-
βῆναι τῇ Σπάρτῃ πεσούσῃ καὶ πατῆσαι τὸ φρόνημα
καὶ τὸ ἀξίωμα τῆς πόλεως ἠθέλησε. καὶ πρῶτα
μὲν ἐμβαλὼν ἑπτὰ μυριάσι στρατοῦ διεπόρθησε
τὴν χώραν καὶ τοὺς περιοίκους ἀπέστησεν αὐτῶν·
ἔπειτα περὶ Μαντίνειαν ἀντιτεταγμένους εἰς μάχην
C προυκαλεῖτο· μὴ βουλομένων δὲ μηδὲ τολμώντων,
ἀλλὰ τὴν Ἀθήνηθεν ἐπικουρίαν ἐκδεχομένων,
νυκτὸς ἄρας καὶ λαθὼν ἅπαντας εἰς τὴν Λακωνικὴν
κατέβη, καὶ μικροῦ ἔφθη τὴν πόλιν ἔρημον ἐξ

---

[1] Πάναινος O. Müller : Πλεισταίνετος.
[2] πεποίκιλται καί τι F.C.B. : πεποίηται καί τι.
[3] ἀφυῶς Reiske : ἀφυῶς τις.
[4] ἀπὸ] ὑπὸ Abresch.

Euphranor, Nicias, Asclepiodorus, and Panaenus, the brother of Pheidias, some of them painted conquering generals, others battles, and still others the heroes of old. As, for example, Euphranor compared his own Theseus with that of Parrhasius, saying that Parrhasius's Theseus [a] had fed on roses, but his on beef; for in truth Parrhasius's portrait has a certain delicacy and subtlety in its execution, and it does somewhat resemble Theseus; but someone, on seeing Euphranor's Theseus, exclaimed, not inaptly,

> Race of the great-hearted hero Erechtheus, whom once Athena
> Nurtured, the daughter of Zeus. [b]

Euphranor has painted also, not without some animation, the cavalry battle against Epameinondas at Mantineia. The action came about in this way : [c] Epameinondas the Theban, after the battle of Leuctra, was greatly elated, and conceived the desire to trample upon the prostrate Sparta, and grind her pride and self-esteem into the dust. And first he attacked with an army of seventy thousand, pillaged the Spartans' territory, and persuaded the Perioeci to revolt from them. Then he challenged to battle the forces that were drawn up in the vicinity of Mantineia; but when they did not wish or even dare to risk an engagement, but continued to await reinforcements from Athens, he broke camp by night and, without being observed by anybody, descended into Lacedaemon and almost succeeded, by a sudden

----

[a] Cf. Pliny, *Natural History*, xxxv. 9. 69.
[b] Homer, *Il.* ii. 547.
[c] Cf. *Life of Agesilaüs*, chaps. xxxiv.-xxxv. (615 c-616 a);
Xenophon, *Hellenica*, vii. 5 ; Diodorus, xv. 82-84.

(346) ἐφόδου λαβεῖν καὶ κατασχεῖν. αἰσθομένων δὲ τῶν
συμμάχων καὶ βοηθείας ταχείας[1] πρὸς τὴν πόλιν
γενομένης, ὑπεῖξε[2] μὲν ὡς αὖθις ἐπὶ λεηλασίαν
καὶ φθορὰν τῆς χώρας τρεψόμενος· ἐξαπατήσας δὲ
καὶ κατακοιμίσας οὕτω τοὺς πολεμίους ἀνέζευξε
νυκτὸς ἐκ τῆς Λακωνικῆς· καὶ διαδραμὼν τὴν[3]
μεταξὺ χώραν ἐπεφαίνετο τοῖς Μαντινεῦσιν ἀπροσ-
δόκητος διαβουλευομένοις καὶ[4] αὐτοῖς ἀκμὴν τοῦ
D πέμπειν τὴν εἰς Λακεδαίμονα βοήθειαν καὶ[5] εὐθέως
ὁπλίζεσθαι προσέταξε τοῖς Θηβαίοις. οἱ μὲν οὖν
Θηβαῖοι μέγα φρονοῦντες ἐν τοῖς ὅπλοις ἐπε-
φέροντο καὶ περιελάμβανον κύκλῳ τὰ τείχη. τῶν
δὲ Μαντινέων ἔκπληξις ἦν καὶ ἀλαλαγμὸς καὶ
διαδρομή, ὡς ῥεῦμα τὴν δύναμιν ἀθρόαν ἐμπίπ-
τουσαν ὤσασθαι μὴ δυναμένων μηδ' ἐπινοούντων
βοήθειαν. ἐν τούτῳ δὲ καιροῦ καὶ τύχης Ἀθηναῖοι
κατέβαινον ἀπὸ τῶν ἄκρων εἰς τὴν Μαντινικὴν οὐκ
εἰδότες τὴν ῥοπὴν οὐδὲ τὴν ὀξύτητα τοῦ ἀγῶνος,
ἀλλ' ὁδῷ πορευόμενοι καθ' ἡσυχίαν· ὡς δέ τις
E ἀστῶν[6] ἐκδραμὼν ἀπήγγειλε τὸν κίνδυνον, ὀλίγοι
μὲν ὄντες ὡς πρὸς τὸ πλῆθος τῶν πολεμίων, ἐξ
ὁδοῦ δὲ κεκμηκότες, οὐδενὸς δὲ τῶν ἄλλων συμμάχων παρόντος, ὅμως εὐθὺς εἰς τάξιν καθίσταντο
τοῖς πλείστοις[7]. οἱ δ' ἱππεῖς διασκευασάμενοι καὶ

[1] ταχείας F.C.B.; ταχέως Wyttenbach; διὰ τάχους may
also be read, and the ms. reading τάχος (often found in
poetry) may be right after all.
[2] ὑπεῖξε Wilamowitz-Möllendorff: ὑπέδειξε.
[3] τὴν Reiske: εἰς τήν.
[4] διαβουλευομένοις καὶ Helmbold: καὶ διαβουλευομένοις (-ος).
[5] καὶ added by Helmbold, after Pohlenz.

attack, in capturing and occupying the city, which was
without defenders. But when the Spartan allies perceived this, and aid for the city quickly arrived, he retired as though he were again about to turn to plundering and devastating the countryside. But when he
had thus deceived his enemies and quieted their
suspicions, he set forth by night from Laconia and,
rapidly traversing the intervening territory, appeared
to the Mantineans unexpectedly, while they also
were engaged in discussing the right moment for
sending aid to Sparta, and ordered the Thebans to
arm straightway for the attack. Accordingly the
Thebans, who took great pride in their skill at
arms, advanced to the attack and encircled the
city walls. There was consternation among the
Mantineans, and shouting and running hither and
thither, since they were unable to repulse this
assembled force which was bursting upon them like
a torrent, nor did any thought of possible succour
occur to their minds. At this crucial and fateful
moment the Athenians were descending from the
heights to the plain of Mantineia, with no knowledge
of this turn of fortune or of the keenness of the
struggle, but were proceeding leisurely on their
journey. However, when one of the Mantineans ran
out with report of the danger, although the Athenians
were few in comparison with the great numbers of
their enemy, and although they were weary from
their march, and none of their other allies was at
hand, nevertheless they straightway took their places
in battle-array with almost their whole number, while
the cavalry donned their armour and rode ahead of

---

[6] ἀστῶν F.C.B.: αὐτῶν.
[7] πλείστοις] ὁπλίταις Wyttenbach.

προεξελάσαντες,[1] ὑπὸ τὰς πύλας αὐτὰς καὶ τὸ
τεῖχος ἔθεντο καρτερὰν ἱππομαχίαν· καὶ κρατήσαντες ἐκ τῶν χειρῶν τοῦ Ἐπαμεινώνδα ἀφείλοντο
τὴν Μαντίνειαν.

Τοῦτο τὸ ἔργον Εὐφράνωρ ἔγραψε, καὶ πάρεστιν
ὁρᾶν ἐν εἰκόνι τῆς μάχης τὸ σύρρηγμα[2] καὶ τὴν
ἀντέρεισιν ἀλκῆς καὶ θυμοῦ καὶ πνεύματος γέμου-
F σαν. ἀλλ᾽ οὐκ ἂν οἶμαι τῷ ζωγράφῳ[3] κρίσιν
προθείητε[4] πρὸς τὸν στρατηγὸν οὐδ᾽ ἀνάσχοισθε
τῶν προτιμώντων τὸν πίνακα τοῦ τροπαίου καὶ τὸ
μίμημα τῆς ἀληθείας.

3. Πλὴν ὁ Σιμωνίδης τὴν μὲν ζωγραφίαν ποίησιν
σιωπῶσαν προσαγορεύει,[5] τὴν δὲ ποίησιν ζωγραφίαν λαλοῦσαν. ἃς γὰρ οἱ ζωγράφοι πράξεις
ὡς γιγνομένας δεικνύουσι, ταύτας οἱ λόγοι γεγενη-
347 μένας διηγοῦνται καὶ συγγράφουσι. εἰ δ᾽ οἱ μὲν
χρώμασι καὶ σχήμασι, οἱ δ᾽ ὀνόμασι καὶ λέξεσι
ταὐτὰ[6] δηλοῦσιν, ὕλῃ καὶ τρόποις μιμήσεως διαφέρουσι, τέλος δ᾽ ἀμφοτέροις ἓν ὑπόκειται, καὶ τῶν
ἱστορικῶν κράτιστος ὁ τὴν διήγησιν ὥσπερ γραφὴν
πάθεσι καὶ προσώποις εἰδωλοποιήσας. ὁ δ᾽ οὖν[7]
Θουκυδίδης ἀεὶ τῷ λόγῳ πρὸς ταύτην ἁμιλλᾶται
τὴν ἐνάργειαν, οἷον θεατὴν ποιῆσαι τὸν ἀκροατὴν
καὶ τὰ γιγνόμενα περὶ τοὺς ὁρῶντας ἐκπληκτικὰ
καὶ ταρακτικὰ πάθη τοῖς ἀναγιγνώσκουσιν ἐν-
εργάσασθαι λιχνευόμενος. ὁ γὰρ παρὰ τὴν ῥαχίαν

---

[1] προεξελάσαντες Reiske: προσεξελάσαντες.
[2] σύρρηγμα Meziriacus: σύγγραμμα.
[3] τῷ ζωγράφῳ Wyttenbach: τὴν ζωγράφου.
[4] προθείητε Wyttenbach: προσθείητε.
[5] προσαγορεύει] προσαγορεύων all mss. except E.
[6] ταὐτὰ Wyttenbach: ταῦτα.
[7] δ᾽ οὖν Helmbold: γοῦν.

the rest, and under the very gates and the wall of the city engaged in a sharp cavalry encounter; the Athenians prevailed and rescued Mantineia from the clutches of Epameinondas.

This was the action which Euphranor depicted, and in his portrayal of the battle one may see the clash of conflict and the stout resistance abounding in boldness and courage and spirit. But I do not think you would award judgement to the painter in comparison with the general, nor would you bear with those who prefer the picture to the trophy of victory, or the imitation to the actuality.

3. Simonides, however, calls painting inarticulate poetry and poetry articulate painting : [a] for the actions which painters portray as taking place at the moment literature narrates and records after they have taken place. Even though artists with colour and design, and writers with words and phrases, represent the same subjects, they differ in the material and the manner of their imitation ; and yet the underlying end and aim of both is one and the same; the most effective historian is he who, by a vivid representation of emotions and characters, makes his narration like a painting. Assuredly Thucydides [b] is always striving for this vividness in his writing, since it is his desire to make the reader a spectator, as it were, and to produce vividly in the minds of those who peruse his narrative the emotions of amazement and consternation which were experienced by those who beheld them. For he tells how Demosthenes [c] is

[a] Cf. *Moralia*, 18 A.
[b] Cf. *Life of Nicias*, chap. i. (523 c) ; Longinus, *On the Sublime*, chap. xxv.
[c] Cf. Thucydides, iv. 10-12.

B αὐτὴν[1] τῆς Πύλου παρατάττων τοὺς Ἀθηναίους
(347) Δημοσθένης, καὶ ὁ τὸν κυβερνήτην ἐπισπέρχων
Βρασίδας ἐξοκέλλειν καὶ χωρῶν ἐπὶ τὴν ἀποβάθραν[2]
καὶ τραυματιζόμενος καὶ λιποψυχῶν[3] καὶ ἀποκλίνων
εἰς τὴν παρεξειρεσίαν, καὶ οἱ πεζομαχοῦντες μὲν
ἐκ θαλάττης Λακεδαιμόνιοι, ναυμαχοῦντες δ' ἀπὸ
γῆς Ἀθηναῖοι· καὶ πάλιν " ὁ " ἐν τοῖς Σικελικοῖς
" ἐκ τῆς γῆς πεζὸς ἀμφοτέρων, ἰσορρόπου τῆς
ναυμαχίας καθεστηκυίας, ἄληκτον[4] ἀγῶνα καὶ ξύντασιν[5] τῆς γνώμης ἔχων " διὰ τὰς συντάξεις, καὶ[6]
" διὰ τὸ ἀκρίτως[7] συνεχὲς τῆς ἁμίλλης καὶ τοῖς
C σώμασιν αὐτοῖς ἴσα τῇ δόξῃ περιδεῶς συναπονεύων "[8] τῇ διαθέσει καὶ τῇ διατυπώσει τῶν
γιγνομένων γραφικῆς ἐναργείας ἐστίν.[9] ὥστ' εἰ
τοὺς ζῳγραφοῦντας οὐκ ἄξιον παραβάλλειν τοῖς
στρατηγοῖς, μηδὲ τοὺς ἱστοροῦντας παραβάλλωμεν.

Τὴν τοίνυν ἐν Μαραθῶνι μάχην ἀπήγγειλεν, ὡς
μὲν Ἡρακλείδης ὁ Ποντικὸς ἱστορεῖ, Θέρσιππος
ὁ Ἐροιεύς[10]· οἱ δὲ πλεῖστοι λέγουσιν Εὐκλέα,
δραμόντα σὺν τοῖς ὅπλοις[11] θερμὸν ἀπὸ τῆς μάχης
καὶ ταῖς θύραις ἐμπεσόντα τῶν πρώτων,[12] τοσοῦτο
μόνον εἰπεῖν, " χαίρετε· νικῶμεν,[13] " εἶτ' εὐθὺς

---

[1] αὐτὴν Reiske from Thucydides, iv. 10: αὐτῆς.
[2] ἀποβάθραν Bernardakis from Thucydides, iv. 12: βάθραν.
[3] λιποψυχῶν Dübner (as in Thucydides, iv. 12): λειποψυχῶν.
[4] ἄληκτον F.C.B.; πολὺν τὸν Thucydides, vii. 71; ἄπλετον
S. A. Naber; θαυμαστὸν H. Richards: ἄλαστον.
[5] ξύντασιν Reiske: σύνταξιν.
[6] καὶ added by F.C.B.
[7] διὰ τὸ ἀκρίτως added from Thucydides, vii. 71: ὡς.
[8] συναπονεύων Madvig, adapted from συναπονεύοντες *ibid.*:
συμπνέων.   [9] ἐστίν added by F.C.B.
[10] Ἐροιεύς Xylander; Ἐροιάδης Kirchner, *Prosopogr.
Attica*; Ἐρχιεύς Wilamowitz-Möllendorff: ἐρωεύς.

drawing up the Athenians at the very edge of the breakwater at Pylos, and Brasidas is urging on his pilot to beach the ship, and is hurrying to the landing-plank, and is wounded and falls fainting on the forward-deck; and the Spartans are fighting an infantry engagement from the sea, while the Athenians wage a naval battle from the land. Again, in his account of the Sicilian [a] expedition : " The armies of both sides on the land, as long as the fighting at sea is evenly balanced, are enduring an unceasing struggle and tension of mind " because of their battling forces ; and " because of the continued indecisiveness of the struggle they accompany it in an extremity of fear, with their very bodies swaying in sympathy with their opinion of the outcome." Such a description is characterized by pictorial vividness both in its arrangement and in its power of description ; so, if it be unworthy to compare painters with generals, let us not compare historians either.

Again, the news of the battle of Marathon Thersippus of Eroeadae brought back, as Heracleides Ponticus relates ; but most historians declare that it was Eucles who ran in full armour, hot from the battle, and, bursting in at the doors of the first men of the State, could only say, " Hail ! we are victorious ! " [b]

[a] *Cf.* Thucydides, vii. 71 ; in the next two sentences the text is very uncertain and can only be restored with great hesitation.

[b] *Cf.* Lucian, *Pro Lapsu inter Salutandum*, 3 ; and F. G. Allinson in the *Classical Weekly*, xxiv. p. 152.

---

[11] ὅπλοις Leonicus : ὁπλίταις.
[12] πρώτων] πρυτάνεων Cobet.
[13] νικῶμεν Cobet, from Lucian, *Pro lapsu inter salutandum*, 3 : καὶ χαίρομεν.

(347) ἐκπνεῦσαι. πλὴν οὗτος μὲν αὐτάγγελος ἧκε τῆς
μάχης ἀγωνιστὴς γενόμενος. φέρε δ' εἴ τις ὑπὲρ
D λόφου τινὸς ἢ σκοπῆς αἰπόλων ἢ βοτήρων τοῦ
ἀγῶνος ἄπωθεν γενόμενος θεατής, καὶ κατιδὼν
τὸ μέγα καὶ παντὸς λόγου μεῖζον ἐκεῖνο ἔργον
ἧκεν εἰς τὴν πόλιν ἄτρωτος ἄγγελος καὶ ἀναί-
μακτος, εἶτ' ἠξίου τιμὰς ἔχειν ἃς Κυνέγειρος[1]
ἔσχεν, ἃς Καλλίμαχος, ἃς Πολύζηλος, ὅτι τὰς
τούτων ἀριστείας καὶ τραύματα καὶ θανάτους
ἀπήγγειλεν· ἆρ' οὐκ ἂν ἐδόκει πᾶσαν ὑπερβάλλειν
ἀναίδειαν; ὅπου γε Λακεδαιμονίους φασὶ τῷ τὴν
ἐν Μαντινείᾳ φράσαντι νίκην, ἣν Θουκυδίδης
ἱστόρηκεν, εὐαγγέλιον ἐκ φιδιτίου κρέας ἀποστεῖλαι.[2] καὶ μὴν οἱ συγγράφοντες ἐξάγγελοί τινές
εἰσι τῶν πράξεων εὔφωνοι καὶ τῷ λόγῳ διὰ τὸ
κάλλος καὶ τὴν δύναμιν ἐξικνούμενοι, οἷς εὐαγ-
E γέλιον ὀφείλουσιν οἱ πρώτως ἐντυγχάνοντες καὶ
ἱστοροῦντες. ἀμέλει δὲ καὶ ἐγκωμιάζονται μνη-
μονευόμενοι καὶ ἀναγιγνωσκόμενοι διὰ τοὺς κατ-
ορθώσαντας· οὐ γὰρ οἱ λόγοι ποιοῦσι τὰς πράξεις
ἀλλὰ διὰ τὰς πράξεις[3] καὶ ἀκοῆς ἀξιοῦνται.

4. Καὶ γὰρ ἡ ποιητικὴ χάριν ἔσχε καὶ τιμὴν τῷ[4]
τοῖς πεπραγμένοις ἐοικότα λέγειν, ὡς Ὅμηρος ἔφη

ἴσκε[5] ψεύδεα πολλὰ λέγων ἐτύμοισιν ὁμοῖα.

[1] Κυνέγειρος Bernardakis and van Herwerden: κυναίγειρος.
[2] ἀποστεῖλαι Xylander: ἀπέστειλαν. In the *Life of
Agesilaüs*, chap. xxxiii., ἄλλο δ' οὐδέν is added at the end.
[3] ἀλλὰ διὰ τὰς πράξεις added by Madvig; Pohlenz would
add ἀλλ' αὐτοὶ γίνονται διὰ τὰς πράξεις.
[4] τῷ added by Reiske and Wyttenbach.
[5] ἴσκε Homer, *Od.* xix. 203 : ἴσχε or ἔσχε.

and straightway expired. Yet this man came as a self-sent messenger regarding a battle in which he himself had fought; but suppose that some goatherd or shepherd upon a hill or a height had been a distant spectator of the contest and had looked down upon that great event, too great for any tongue to tell, and had come to the city as a messenger, a man who had not felt a wound nor shed a drop of blood, and yet had insisted that he have such honours as Cynegeirus received, or Callimachus, or Polyzelus, because, forsooth, he had reported their deeds of valour, their wounds and death; would he not have been thought of surpassing impudence? Why, as we are told, the Spartans merely sent meat from the public commons to the man who brought glad tidings of the victory in Mantineia which Thucydides [a] describes! And indeed the compilers of histories are, as it were, reporters of great exploits who are gifted with the faculty of felicitous speech, and achieve success in their writing through the beauty and force of their narration; and to them those who first encountered and recorded the events are indebted for a pleasing retelling of them. We may be sure that such writers are lauded also merely through being remembered and read because of the men who won success; for the words do not create the deeds, but because of the deeds they are also deemed worthy of being read.

4. Poetry also has won favour and esteem because it utters words which match the deeds, as Homer [b] says,

Many the lies that he spoke, but he made them all to seem truthful.

[a] *Cf.* Thucydides, v. 65-73 ; *Life of Agesilaüs*, chap. xxxiii. (614 F).　　[b] Homer, *Od.* xix. 203 ; *cf. Moralia* 16 A.

λέγεται δὲ καὶ Μενάνδρῳ τῶν συνήθων τις εἰπεῖν,
" ἐγγὺς οὖν, Μένανδρε, τὰ Διονύσια, καὶ σὺ τὴν
κωμῳδίαν οὐ πεποίηκας; " τὸν δ' ἀποκρίνασθαι,
" νὴ τοὺς θεοὺς ἔγωγε πεποίηκα τὴν κωμῳδίαν·
F ᾠκονόμηται γὰρ ἡ διάθεσις· δεῖ δ' αὐτῇ τὰ στιχίδια
ἐπᾷσαι," ὅτι καὶ αὐτοὶ τὰ πράγματα τῶν λόγων
ἀναγκαιότερα καὶ κυριώτερα νομίζουσιν.

Ἡ δὲ Κόριννα τὸν Πίνδαρον, ὄντα νέον ἔτι καὶ
τῇ λογιότητι σοβαρῶς χρώμενον, ἐνουθέτησεν ὡς
ἄμουσον ὄντα καὶ[1] μὴ ποιοῦντα μύθους, ὃ τῆς
ποιητικῆς ἔργον εἶναι συμβέβηκε, γλώττας[2] δὲ καὶ
καταχρήσεις καὶ μεταφράσεις[3] καὶ μέλη καὶ ῥυθ-
348 μοὺς ἡδύσματα τοῖς πράγμασιν ὑποτιθέντα.[4] σφόδρ'
οὖν ὁ Πίνδαρος ἐπιστήσας τοῖς λεγομένοις ἐποίησεν
ἐκεῖνο τὸ μέλος

Ἰσμηνὸν ἢ χρυσαλάκατον Μελίαν,
ἢ Κάδμον ἢ σπαρτῶν ἱερὸν γένος ἀνδρῶν,
ἢ τὸ πάνυ[5] σθένος Ἡρακλέους
ἢ τὰν Διωνύσου πολυγαθέα τιμάν.[6]

δειξαμένου δὲ τῇ Κορίννῃ γελάσασα ἐκείνη τῇ
χειρὶ δεῖν ἔφη σπείρειν, ἀλλὰ μὴ ὅλῳ τῷ θυλάκῳ.
τῷ γὰρ ὄντι συγκεράσας καὶ συμφορήσας πανσπερ-
μίαν τινὰ μύθων ὁ Πίνδαρος εἰς τὸ μέλος ἐξέχεεν.
ἀλλ' ὅτι μὲν ἡ ποιητικὴ περὶ μυθοποιίαν ἐστὶ καὶ
Πλάτων εἴρηκεν. ὁ δὲ μῦθος εἶναι βούλεται λόγος

---

[1] Bernardakis would omit καί.
[2] γλώσσας Meziriacus: γλώσσαι, γλῶσσα, or γλῶσσαν.
[3] μεταφράσεις] μεταφορὰς Michael.
[4] ὑποτιθέντα Pohlenz: ὑποτίθεται.
[5] πάνυ] πάντολμον Lucian (Demosth. Encom. c. 19).
[6] ἢ τὰν Διωνύσου πολυγαθέα τιμάν ibid.: ἡττᾶν.

The story is also told that one of Menander's[a] intimate friends said to him, " The Dionysian Festival is almost here, Menander; haven't you composed your comedy ? " Menander answered, " By heaven, I have really composed the comedy : the plot's all in order. But I still have to fit the lines to it." For even poets consider the subject matter more necessary and vital than the words.

When Pindar was still young, and prided himself on his felicitous use of words, Corinna warned him that his writing lacked refinement, since he did not introduce myths, which are the proper business of poetry, but used as a foundation for his work unusual and obsolete words, extensions of meaning, paraphrases, lyrics and rhythms, which are mere embellishments of the subject matter.[b] So Pindar,[c] giving all heed to her words, composed the famous lyric :

> Ismenus, or Melia of the golden distaff,
> Or Cadmus, or the holy race of men that were sown,
> Or the mighty strength of Heracles,
> Or the gladsome worship of Dionysus.

He showed it to Corinna, but she laughed and said that one should sow with the hand, not with the whole sack. For in truth Pindar had confused and jumbled together a seed-mixture, as it were, of myths, and poured them into his poem.[d] That poetry concerns itself with the composition of mythological matters Plato[e] also has stated. A myth aims at being a false

[a] Cf. the Scholia Cruquiana on Horace, Ars Poetica, 311.
[b] Cf. Moralia, 769 c.
[c] Pindar, Frag. 29, ed. Christ; ed. Sandys (L.C.L.) p. 512 ; cf. Lucian, Demosthenis Encomium, 19.
[d] Edmonds's version (Lyra Graeca, iii. p. 7) of this famous passage is incomprehensible to me.
[e] Phaedo, 61 b ; cf. Moralia, 16 c.

(348) ψευδὴς ἐοικὼς ἀληθινῷ· διὸ καὶ πολὺ τῶν ἔργων
B ἀφέστηκεν, εἰ λόγος μὲν ἔργου, καὶ λόγου δὲ μῦθος
εἰκὼν καὶ εἴδωλόν ἐστι. καὶ τοσοῦτον τῶν ἱστο-
ρούντων οἱ πλάττοντες τὰς πράξεις ὑστεροῦσιν,
ὅσον ἀπολείπονται τῶν πραττόντων οἱ λέγοντες.

5. Ἐπικῆς[1] μὲν οὖν ποιήσεως ἡ πόλις οὐκ ἔσχη-
κεν ἔνδοξον δημιουργὸν οὐδὲ μελικῆς. ὁ γὰρ
Κινησίας ἀργαλέος ἔοικε ποιητὴς γεγονέναι διθυ-
ράμβων· καὶ αὐτὸς μὲν ἄγονος καὶ ἀκλεὴς γέγονε,
σκωπτόμενος δὲ καὶ χλευαζόμενος ὑπὸ τῶν κωμῳ-
διοποιῶν οὐκ εὐτυχοῦς δόξης μετέσθηκε. τῶν δὲ
δραματοποιῶν τὴν μὲν κωμῳδιοποιίαν οὕτως ἄσεμ-
νον ἡγοῦντο καὶ φορτικόν, ὥστε νόμος ἦν μηδένα
ποιεῖν κωμῳδίας Ἀρεοπαγίτην. ἤνθησε δ' ἡ
C τραγῳδία καὶ διεβοήθη, θαυμαστὸν ἀκρόαμα καὶ
θέαμα τῶν τότ' ἀνθρώπων γενομένη καὶ παρα-
σχοῦσα τοῖς μύθοις καὶ τοῖς πάθεσιν ἀπάτην, ὡς
Γοργίας φησίν, ἣν[2] ὅ τ' ἀπατήσας δικαιότερος τοῦ
μὴ ἀπατήσαντος, καὶ ὁ ἀπατηθεὶς σοφώτερος τοῦ
μὴ ἀπατηθέντος. ὁ μὲν γὰρ ἀπατήσας δικαιότερος,
ὅτι τοῦθ' ὑποσχόμενος πεποίηκεν· ὁ δ' ἀπατηθεὶς
σοφώτερος· εὐάλωτον γὰρ ὑφ' ἡδονῆς λόγων τὸ μὴ
ἀναίσθητον.

Τίν' οὖν αἱ καλαὶ τραγῳδίαι ταῖς Ἀθήναις ὄνησιν
ἤνεγκαν ὡς ἡ Θεμιστοκλέους δεινότης ἐτείχισε τὴν

---

[1] ἐπικῆς Reiske: τῆς.   [2] ἣν Stephanus: ἦν.

---

[a] Cf. Moralia, 1141 E; Aristophanes, Birds, 1373 ff.;
Frogs, 366; Ecclesiazusae, 327 ff.; Plato, Gorgias, 502 A.
Athenaeus, 551 D, quotes from an oration of Lysias against

tale, resembling a true one ; wherefore it is far removed from actual events, if a tale is but a picture and an image of actuality, and a myth is but a picture and image of a tale. And thus those who write of imaginative exploits lag as far behind historians as persons who tell of deeds come short of those that do them.

5. Athens, to be sure, possessed no famous writer of either epic or melic poetry ; for Cinesias [a] seems to have been an infelicitous dithyrambic poet. He was himself without family or fame but, jeered and mocked by the comic poets, he acquired his share in unfortunate notoriety. And for the dramatic poets, the Athenians considered the writing of comedy so undignified and vulgar a business that there was a law forbidding any member of the Areopagus to write comedies. But tragedy blossomed forth and won great acclaim, becoming a wondrous entertainment for the ears and eyes of the men of that age, and, by the mythological character of its plots, and the vicissitudes which its characters undergo, it effected a deception wherein, as Gorgias [b] remarks, " he who deceives is more honest than he who does not deceive, and he who is deceived is wiser than he who is not deceived." For he who deceives is more honest, because he has done what he promised to do ; and he who is deceived is wiser, because the mind which is not insensible to fine perceptions is easily enthralled by the delights of language.

What profit, then, did these fine tragedies bring to Athens to compare with the shrewdness of Themistocles which provided the city with a wall, with the

him ; but even though unpopular he was at least witty ; *cf. Moralia*, 22 A (170 A).   [b] *Cf. Moralia*, 15 D.

(348) πόλιν, ὡς ἡ Περικλέους ἐπιμέλεια τὴν ἄκραν[1]
D ἐκόσμησεν, ὡς Μιλτιάδης ἠλευθέρωσεν, ὡς Κίμων
προήγεν εἰς τὴν ἡγεμονίαν; εἰ οὕτως ἡ Εὐριπίδου
σοφία καὶ ἡ Σοφοκλέους λογιότης καὶ τὸ Αἰσχύλου
στόμα τι τῶν δυσχερῶν ἀπήλλαξεν ἤ τι τῶν λαμπρῶν περιεποίησεν, ἄξιόν γε τὰ δράματα τοῖς
τροπαίοις ἀντιπαραθεῖναι καὶ τῷ στρατηγίῳ τὸ
θέατρον ἀντανστῆσαι καὶ ταῖς ἀριστείαις τὰς
διδασκαλίας ἀντιπαραβαλεῖν.

6. Βούλεσθε τοὺς ἄνδρας εἰσάγωμεν αὐτοὺς τὰ
σύμβολα καὶ τὰ παράσημα τῶν ἔργων κομίζοντας,
ἰδίαν ἑκατέρῳ πάροδον ἀποδόντες; ἔνθεν μὲν δὴ
προσίτωσαν ὑπ' αὐλοῖς καὶ λύραις ποιηταὶ λέγοντες καὶ ᾄδοντες,

εὐφημεῖν χρὴ κἀξίστασθαι τοῖς ἡμετέροισι χο-
ροῖσιν[2]

ὅστις ἄπειρος τοιῶνδε λόγων ἢ γνώμην[3] μὴ
καθαρεύει,

ἢ γενναίων ὄργια Μουσῶν μήτ' ᾖσεν[4] μήτ'
ἐχόρευσε,

μηδὲ Κρατίνου τοῦ ταυροφάγου γλώττης βακχεῖ'
ἐτελέσθη,

καὶ σκευὰς καὶ προσωπεῖα καὶ βωμοὺς καὶ μηχανὰς
ἀπὸ σκηνῆς καὶ[5] περιάκτους καὶ τρίποδας ἐπι-
νικίους κομίζοντες[6]· τραγικοὶ[7] δ' αὐτοῖς ὑποκριταὶ
καὶ Νικόστρατοι καὶ Καλλιππίδαι καὶ Μυννίσκοι[8]

diligence of Pericles which adorned the Acropolis, with the liberty which Miltiades bestowed, with the supremacy to which Cimon advanced her ? If in this manner the wisdom of Euripides, the eloquence of Sophocles,[a] and the poetic magnificence of Aeschylus rid the city of any of its difficulties or gained for her any brilliant success, it is but right to compare their tragedies with trophies of victory, to let the theatre rival the War Office, and to compare the records of dramatic performances with the memorials of valour.

6. Is it, then, your pleasure that we introduce the men themselves bearing the emblems and badges of their achievements, and assign to each their proper entrance ? Then from this entrance let the poets approach, speaking and chanting to the accompaniment of flutes and lyres,

> Now speak not a word of evil sound, and keep clear the
>   way for our chorus,
> Whoever in words like these is unskilled and whose mind
>   is not free from uncleanness,
> Who never has sung and never has danced in the rites of
>   the noble Muses,
> Nor has ever been trained in the Bacchic rites of the tongue
>   of bull-eating Cratinus ! [b]

Let them bring with them their equipment, their masks and altars, their stage machinery, their revolving changes of scene, and the tripods that commemorate their victories. Let their tragic actors accompany them, men like Nicostratus and Callippides,

---

[a] Cf. Haigh, Tragic Drama of the Greeks, p. 166.

[b] Aristophanes, Frogs, 353-356 ; cf. Aulus Gellius, Praefatio, 20 f.

[8] Μυννίσκοι I.G. ii.² 2318. 119 (cf. Aristotle, Poetics, xxvi. (1461 b 34)) : μηνίσκοι.

καὶ Θεόδωροι καὶ Πῶλοι[1] συνίτωσαν, ὥσπερ γυναικὸς πολυτελοῦς τῆς τραγωδίας κομμωταὶ καὶ
διφροφόροι, μᾶλλον δ᾽ ὡς ἀγαλμάτων ἐγκαυταὶ[2] καὶ
F χρυσωταὶ καὶ βαφεῖς παρακολουθοῦντες· σκευῶν δὲ
καὶ προσώπων καὶ ξυστίδων ἁλουργῶν καὶ μη-
χανῶν ἀπὸ σκηνῆς καὶ χοροποιῶν καὶ δορυφόρων
δυσπραγμάτευτος λαὸς καὶ χορηγία πολυτελὴς
παρασκευαζέσθω. πρὸς ἃ Λάκων ἀνὴρ ἀποβλέψας
οὐ κακῶς εἶπεν ὡς ἁμαρτάνουσιν Ἀθηναῖοι μεγάλα
τὴν σπουδὴν εἰς τὴν παιδιὰν καταναλίσκοντες, τοῦτ-
έστι μεγάλων ἀποστόλων δαπάνας καὶ στρατευ-
μάτων ἐφόδια καταχορηγοῦντες εἰς τὸ θέατρον.
349 ἂν γὰρ ἐκλογισθῇ τῶν δραμάτων ἕκαστον ὅσου
κατέστη, πλέον ἀνηλωκὼς φανεῖται ὁ δῆμος εἰς
Βάκχας καὶ Φοινίσσας καὶ Οἰδίποδας καὶ Ἀντιγόνας[3] καὶ τὰ Μηδείας κακὰ καὶ Ἠλέκτρας, ὧν
ὑπὲρ τῆς ἡγεμονίας καὶ τῆς ἐλευθερίας πολεμῶν
τοὺς βαρβάρους[4] ἀνάλωσεν. οἱ μὲν γὰρ στρατηγοὶ
πολλάκις παραγγείλαντες ἄπυρα σιτία κομίζειν
ἐξῆγον ἐπὶ τὰς μάχας τοὺς ἄνδρας· καὶ νὴ Δί᾽ οἱ
τριήραρχοι τοῖς ἐλαύνουσιν ἄλφιτα παρασκευά-
σαντες, ὄψον δὲ κρόμμυα καὶ[5] τυρόν, ἐνεβίβαζον εἰς
τὰς τριήρεις· οἱ δὲ χορηγοὶ τοῖς χορευταῖς ἐγχέλεια
καὶ θριδάκια καὶ σκελίδας[6] καὶ μυελὸν παρατιθέντες,
εὔχουν ἐπὶ πολὺν χρόνον φωνασκουμένους καὶ
B τρυφῶντας. καὶ τούτων τοῖς μὲν ἡττηθεῖσι περιῆν

---

[1] Πῶλοι Stephanus : πολλοί.
[2] ἐγκαυταὶ Hatzidakis : ἐγκανσταί.
[3] Ἀντιγόνας Helmbold : ἀντιγόνην.
[4] τοὺς βαρβάρους] τοῖς βαρβάροις Meziriacus, but see
Wyttenbach's note.   [5] καὶ added by Turnebus.
[6] σκελίδας Reiske : σκελλίδας.

---

[a] That is, a tragedy is an unadorned statue. The actors

512

Mynniscus, Theodorus, and Polus, who robe Tragedy
and bear her litter, as though she were some woman
of wealth ; or rather, let them follow on as though
they were painters and gilders and dyers of statues.[a]
Let there be provided also a bounteous outlay for
stage furnishings, supernumeraries, sea-purple robes,
stage machinery, as well as dancing-masters and bodyguards, an intractable crowd. It was in reference to
all this that a Spartan [b] not ineptly remarked that the
Athenians were making a great mistake in wasting
their energies on amusements, that is to say, in lavish-
ing on the theatre what would pay for great fleets and
would support armies in the field. For, if we reckon up
the cost of each tragedy, the Athenian people will be
seen to have spent more on productions of *Bacchae*,
Phoenissae, *Oedipuses*, and *Antigones*, and the woes of
Medea and Electra, than they spent in fighting for
their supremacy and for their liberty against the
barbarians. For the generals often ordered their men
to bring along uncooked rations when they led them
forth to battle ; and the commanders, I can swear,
after providing barley-meal and a relish of onions and
cheese for the rowers, would embark them on the
triremes. But the men who paid for the choruses
gave the choristers eels and tender lettuces, roast-
beef and marrow, and pampered them for a long time
while they were training their voices and living in
luxury. The result for the defeated *choregoi* [c] was to

supply the decoration : encaustic paint, gold-leaf, and
dye.   [b] *Cf. Moralia*, 230 B and the note.
  [c] The *choregoi*, the men who trained the tragic choruses
at Athens, lavished their private resources on the festival
competitions ; but the victor had merely a tripod awarded
to him to show for all his vast expenditure, the loser worse
than nothing.

(349) προσυβρίσθαι καὶ γεγονέναι καταγελάστους· τοῖς
δὲ νικήσασιν τρίπους[1] ὑπῆρχεν, οὐκ ἀνάθημα τῆς
νίκης, ὡς Δημήτριός φησιν, ἀλλ' ἐπίσπεισμα τῶν
ἐκκεχυμένων βίων[2] καὶ τῶν ἐκλελοιπότων κενο-
τάφιον οἴκων.[3] τοιαῦτα γὰρ τὰ ποιητικῆς τέλη καὶ
λαμπρότερον οὐδὲν ἐξ αὐτῶν.

7. Τοὺς δὲ στρατηγοὺς αὖ πάλιν ἐνθένδε παριόντας σκοπῶμεν, ὧν παρερχομένων ὡς ἀληθῶς
" εὐφημεῖν χρὴ κἀξίστασθαι " τοὺς ἀπράκτους καὶ
ἀπολιτεύτους καὶ ἀστρατεύτους, " ὅστις " ἄτολμος[4]
πρὸς ἔργα τοιαῦτα " καὶ γνώμην[5] μὴ καθαρεύει,"
C μηδὲ Μιλτιάδου τοῦ μηδοφόνου μηδὲ τοῦ περσο-
κτόνου Θεμιστοκλέους χειρὸς " βακχεῖ ἐτελέσθη."
Ἀρήιος ὁ κῶμος οὗτος ἐκ γῆς ἅμα φάλαγγι καὶ
στόλοις ἐκ θαλάττης καὶ μεμειγμένοις[6] σκύλοις καὶ
τροπαίοις βεβριθώς.

κλῦθ'[7] Ἀλαλά,[8] Πολέμου θύγατερ,
ἐγχέων προοίμιον, ἇ θύεται[9]
ἄνδρες τὸν ἱρόθυτον[10] θάνατον,

ὡς ὁ Θηβαῖος Ἐπαμεινώνδας εἶπεν, ὑπὲρ πατρίδος
καὶ τάφων καὶ ἱερῶν ἐπιδιδόντες ἑαυτοὺς τοῖς
καλλίστοις καὶ λαμπροτάτοις ἀγῶσιν. ὧν τὰς
νίκας ὁρᾶν μοι δοκῶ προσερχομένας, οὐ βοῦν

---

[1] τρίπους E. Capps: οὐ τρίπους.
[2] ἐπίσπεισμα τῶν ἐκκεχυμένων βίων Reiske: ἐπὶ πεισμάτων ἐκκεχυμένον βίον. [3] οἴκων Reiske: οἶκον.
[4] ἄτολμος Turnebus: εὐτόλμως.
[5] γνώμην probably the preferable reading in Aristophanes: γνώμῃ. [6] μεμειγμένοις] ἡμαγμένοις Reiske.
[7] κλῦθ' 483 D: κλῦθι.
[8] Ἀλαλά Xylander from 483 D: ἄννα *** γώ.
[9] ἇ θύεται Haupt from scholium on Aesch. Pers. 49: ἀμφύετε.
[10] ἱρόθυτον Haupt: ἱεροθυτον.

be held in contumely and ridicule ; but to the victors belonged a tripod,[a] which was, as Demetrius says, not a votive offering to commemorate their victory, but a last oblation of their wasted livelihood, an empty memorial of their vanished estates. Such are the returns paid by the poetic art and nothing more splendid ever comes from it.

7. But let us now review the generals in their turn, as they make entrance from the other side ; and at their approach those who have had no part in deeds of valour or political life or campaigns must in very truth " speak not a word of evil sound and clear the way," whoever there be that lacks courage for such deeds as theirs and " whose mind is not free from uncleanness, nor has ever been trained in the Bacchic rites " that are the handiwork of Miltiades, bane of Medes, and Themistocles, slayer of Persians. This is the rebel-rout of the god of war, with battalions on land and squadrons on sea, laden with mingled spoils and trophies :

> Hearken, Alala, daughter of War,
>> Thou prelude of clashing spears, thou to whom are offered
> Heroes in the holy sacrifice of death,[b]

as Epameinondas the Theban cried, when he and his men were dedicating themselves to the noblest and most resplendent of struggles for their native land, the graves of their fathers, and their holy shrines. I seem to see their victories advancing, not dragging

---

[a] Cf. *Life of Aristeides*, chap. i. (318 E) ; *Life of Nicias*, chap. iii. (524 E).

[b] Pindar, Frag. 78 (ed. Christ); p. 558 ed. Sandys (in L.C.L.); cf. *Moralia*, 192 c (with Nachstädt's note *ad loc.*) and 483 D ; Athenaeus, 19 A.

(349) ἔπαθλον ἑλκούσας ἢ τράγον, οὐδ' ἀνεστεμμένας
κιττῷ καὶ Διονυσιακῆς τρυγὸς ὀδωδυίας· ἀλλ' ὅλαι
μὲν πόλεις αὐτῶν εἰσι καὶ νῆσοι καὶ ἤπειροι, καὶ
D ναοὶ χιλιοτάλαντοι[1] καὶ δήμων ἀποικισμοὶ μυρί-
ανδροι, τροπαίοις δὲ παντοδαποῖς ἀναστέφονται[2] καὶ
λαφύροις· ὧν ἀγάλματα καὶ σύμβολα παρθενῶνες
ἑκατόμπεδοι, νότια τείχη, νεώσοικοι,[3] προπύλαια,
Χερρόνησος, Ἀμφίπολις. Μαραθὼν τὴν Μιλτιάδου
νίκην προπέμπει, καὶ Σαλαμὶς τὴν Θεμιστοκλέους,
χιλίων σκαφῶν ναυαγίοις ἐπιβεβηκυῖαν. φέρει δ'
ἡ μὲν Κίμωνος τριήρεις ἑκατὸν Φοινίσσας ἀπ'
Εὐρυμέδοντος, ἡ δὲ Δημοσθένους καὶ Κλέωνος ἀπὸ
Σφακτηρίας τὴν Βρασίδου ἀσπίδ' αἰχμάλωτον καὶ
δεδεμένους στρατιώτας.[4] τειχίζει δὲ τὴν πόλιν ἡ
Κόνωνος, ἡ δὲ Θρασυβούλου κατάγει τὸν δῆμον ἀπὸ
E Φυλῆς ἐλεύθερον, αἱ[5] δ' Ἀλκιβιάδου περὶ Σικελίαν
ὀλισθοῦσαν τὴν πόλιν ἐγείρουσιν· ἐκ δὲ τῶν Νείλεω[6]
καὶ Ἀνδρόκλου περὶ Λυδίαν καὶ Καρίαν ἀγώνων
Ἰωνίαν ἀνισταμένην[7] ἐπεῖδεν ἡ Ἑλλάς. τῶν δ'
ἄλλων ἑκάστης ἂν πύθῃ τί τῇ πόλει γέγονεν ἐξ
αὐτῆς ἀγαθόν, ἡ μὲν ἐρεῖ Λέσβον, ἡ δὲ Σάμον, ἡ
δὲ Κύπρον, ἡ δὲ Πόντον Εὔξεινον, ἡ δὲ πεντακοσίας
τριήρεις, ἡ δὲ μύρια τάλαντα, προῖκα τῆς δόξης καὶ
τῶν τροπαίων. ταῦθ' ἡ πόλις ἑορτάζει καὶ ὑπὲρ

---

[1] ναοὶ χιλιοτάλαντοι Bryan: νηχοτάλαντοι. *Cf. Life of
Pericles*, chap. xii.
[2] ἀναστέφονται] ἀναστρέφονται most mss.
[3] νεώσοικοι Meziriacus: νεῶν οἶκοι.
[4] στρατιώτας] Σπαρτιάτας Wyttenbach.
[5] αἱ Meziriacus: ἡ or οἱ.
[6] Νείλεω (*cf.* 253 ℉ and 603 ʙ) Hatzidakis: Νειλέου.
[7] ἀνισταμένην] συνισταμένην Madvig.

along a bull or a goat as their prize, nor garlanded with ivy and redolent of the lees of Dionysus ; but whole cities are theirs, and islands, and even continents, temples costing a thousand talents,[a] and colonies of vast population ; and they are garlanded with all manner of trophies and spoils. Their ornaments and emblems are buildings like the Parthenon one hundred feet in length, southern Long Walls,[b] dockyards, Propylaea, Chersonese, and Amphipolis.[c] Marathon leads forward the Victory of Miltiades, and Salamis does the same for Themistocles' Victory, poised upon the wreckage of a thousand ships. Cimon's Victory brings an hundred Phoenician ships from the Eurymedon, and the Victory of Demosthenes and Cleon brings from Sphacteria the captive shield[d] of Brasidas and his soldiers in chains. Conon's Victory fortifies the city with new walls, while that of Thrasybulus leads back from Phylê the people restored to freedom. Alcibiades' Victories revive the city laid prostrate by her failure in Sicily. From the struggles of Neileus and Androclus[e] about Lydia and Caria Greece came to see that Ionia was rising. If you inquire of the other Victories in turn what good came to the State from each, one will reply Lesbos, another Samos, another Cyprus, another the Euxine, another five hundred triremes, another ten thousand talents, to say nothing of the glory and the trophies which they won. These are the things which the city

[a] £200,000 or $1,000,000. Cf. Life of Pericles, chap. xii. (158 F).
[b] The work of Cimon, according to the Life of Cimon, chap. xiii. (487 B).   [c] Cf. Thucydides, iv. 102.
[d] Cf. Thucydides, iv. 12, with Diodorus, xii. 62.
[e] Sons of Codrus, founders of Miletus and Ephesus respectively ; cf. Moralia, 253 F, 603 B.

τούτων θύει τοῖς θεοῖς, οὐκ ἐπὶ ταῖς Αἰσχύλου
νίκαις ἢ Σοφοκλέους· οὐδ' ὅτε Καρκίνος Ἀερόπῃ
εὐτύχει[1] ἢ Ἕκτορι Ἀστυδάμας, ἀλλ' ἕκτῃ μὲν
ἱσταμένου[2] Βοηδρομιῶνος ἐσέτι νῦν τὴν ἐν Μαραθῶνι νίκην ἡ πόλις ἑορτάζει· ἕκτῃ δ' ἐπὶ δέκα
F τοῦ[3] μηνὸς οἰνοχοεῖται τῆς Χαβρίου περὶ Νάξον
ἐπινίκια ναυμαχίας· τῇ δὲ δωδεκάτῃ χαριστήρια
ἔθυον ἐλευθερίας· ἐν ἐκείνῃ γὰρ οἱ ἀπὸ Φυλῆς
κατῆλθον. τρίτῃ δ' ἱσταμένου τὴν ἐν Πλαταιαῖς
μάχην ἐνίκων. τὴν δ' ἕκτην ἐπὶ δέκα τοῦ Μουνι-
χιῶνος Ἀρτέμιδι καθιέρωσαν, ἐν ᾗ τοῖς Ἕλλησι
περὶ Σαλαμῖνα νικῶσιν ἐπέλαμψεν ἡ θεὸς παν-
350 σέληνος. τὴν δὲ δωδεκάτην τοῦ Σκιρροφοριῶνος
ἱερωτέραν ἐποίησεν ὁ Μαντινειακὸς ἀγών, ἐν ᾧ τῶν
ἄλλων συμμάχων ἐκβιασθέντων καὶ τραπέντων,
μόνοι τὸ καθ' ἑαυτοὺς νικήσαντες ἔστησαν τρόπαιον
ἀπὸ τῶν νικώντων πολεμίων. ταῦτα τὴν πόλιν
ἦρεν[4] εἰς δόξαν, ταῦτ' εἰς μέγεθος· ἐπὶ[5] τούτοις
Πίνδαρος

ἔρεισμα τῆς Ἑλλάδος

προσεῖπε τὰς Ἀθήνας, οὐχ ὅτι ταῖς Φρυνίχου

---

[1] εὐτύχει F.C.B.; περιῆν Emperius; ἐνίκα H. Valesius;
εὐημέρει Porson and Wyttenbach: συνῆν.
[2] ἱσταμένου] ἱσταμένῃ most mss.
[3] ἐπὶ δέκα τοῦ [αὐτοῦ] added by Xylander from the *Life
of Phocion*, chap. vi.
[4] ἦρεν S. A. Naber: ἤγειρεν.
[5] ἐπὶ Emperius: ἐν.

---

[a] Nauck, *Trag. Graec. Frag.* p. 797.
[b] *Ibid.* p. 778.
[c] *Cf. Moralia*, 861 F, *Life of Camillus*, chap. xix.
(138 B), and How's note on Herodotus, vi. 106 (which,
however, misquotes Plutarch).

celebrates in her festivals, for these she sacrifices to the gods, not for the dramatic victories of Aeschylus and Sophocles. Nor is the day celebrated when Carcinus [a] was successful with his *Aërope*, or Astydamas [b] with his *Hector*, but even yet the State celebrates the victory at Marathon on the sixth of Boëdromion. [c] On the sixteenth of this month they pour a libation of wine in memory of Chabrias's victory at Naxos. [d] On the twelfth they used to sacrifice thank-offerings for the recovery of their liberty, for on that day the exiles returned from Phylê. [e] On the third they won the battle of Plataeae. [f] The sixteenth of Munichion they dedicated to Artemis, for on that day the goddess shone with full moon upon the Greeks as they were conquering at Salamis. The conflict at Mantineia [g] has made the twelfth of Scirophorion more sacred; for in this battle, when the other allies were overpowered and routed, it was the Athenians alone who defeated the force opposed to them and erected a trophy taken from the victorious enemy. These are the things which have uplifted Athens to heights of glory and greatness; it was for these that Pindar [h] addressed Athens as

The mainstay of Greece,

not because she had guided the Greeks aright with

---

[d] *Cf. Life of Phocion*, chap. vi. (744 D) ; *Life of Camillus*, chap. xix. (138 B) ; Diodorus, xv. 35.

[e] *Cf.* 345 E, 349 E, *supra*.

[f] *Cf. Life of Aristeides*, chap. xix. (330 F).

[g] *Cf.* 346 B-E, *supra*.

[h] Pindar, Fragg. 76 and 77 (ed. Christ): p. 556 ed. Sandys (L.C.L.) ; *cf.* also *Moralia*, 232 E, 552 B, 867 c ; *Life of Themistocles*, chap. viii. (115 F).

(350) τραγῳδίαις καὶ Θέσπιδος ὤρθουν[1] τοὺς Ἕλληνας,
ἀλλ᾽ ὅτι πρῶτον, ὥς φησιν αὐτός, ἐπ᾽ Ἀρτεμισίῳ

παῖδες Ἀθαναίων[2] ἐβάλοντο φαεννὰν[3] κρηπῖδ᾽
ἐλευθερίας·

B ἐπί τε Σαλαμῖνι καὶ Μυκάλῃ καὶ Πλαταιαῖς ὥσπερ
ἀδαμαντίνως[4] στηρίξαντες τὴν ἐλευθερίαν τῆς
Ἑλλάδος παρέδοσαν τοῖς ἄλλοις ἀνθρώποις.

8. Ἀλλὰ νὴ Δία παιδιὰ τὰ τῶν ποιητῶν· οἱ δὲ
ῥήτορες ἔχουσί τι παραβαλλόμενοι πρὸς τοὺς στρατηγούς, ἐξ ὧν εἰκότως[5] Αἰσχίνης σκώπτων τὸν
Δημοσθένην λέγειν φησὶν ὅτι γράψεται[6] τῷ βήματι
διαδικασίαν πρὸς τὸ στρατήγιον.[7] ἆρ᾽ οὖν ἄξιον
προκρῖναι τὸν Ὑπερείδου Πλαταϊκὸν τῆς Ἀρι-
στείδου Πλαταιᾶσι[8] νίκης; ἢ τὸν Λυσίου κατὰ
τῶν τριάκοντα τῆς Θρασυβούλου καὶ Ἀρχίνου[9]
τυραννοκτονίας; ἢ τὸν Αἰσχίνου κατὰ Τιμάρχου
C ἑταιρήσεως τῆς Φωκίωνος εἰς Βυζάντιον βοηθείας,
δι᾽ ἧς ἐκώλυσε τοὺς τῶν συμμάχων υἱοὺς ἐνύβρισμά
τε καὶ παροίνημα γενέσθαι Μακεδόνων; ἢ τοῖς
κοινοῖς[10] στεφάνοις, οὓς τὴν Ἑλλάδα ἐλευθερώσας

---

[1] ὤρθουν Reiske: ὤρθου.
[2] Ἀθαναίων Boeckh: ἀθηναίων.
[3] φαεννὰν Life of Themistocles, chap. viii.: φαεινήν.
[4] ἀδαμαντίνως E. Harrison, cf. Plato, Republic, 618 E
(-οις ἅλοις Hartung; κίοσι Schroeder; στήλαις van Herwerden):
ἀδαμάντινοι.
[5] εἰκότως Madvig: εἰκὸς ὡς (ὡς εἰκὸς ἐξ ὧν Emperius;
εἰκός, ὡς δῆλον ἐξ ὧν Pohlenz).
[6] γράψεται Pohlenz from Aeschines, Adv. Ctesiph. 146:
γράφεται.
[7] τὸ στρατήγιον Reiske: τὴν στρατηγίαν.
[8] Πλαταιᾶσι Cobet: παραγγελίας.
[9] Ἀρχίνου Reiske: ἀρχίου.
[10] κοινοῖς] Κόνωνος Madvig; Κονωνείοις Bernardakis.

the tragedies of Phrynichus and Thespis, but because, as he himself says, first at Artemisium

> Sons of the Athenians laid the far-shining foundation of freedom.[a]

And when at Salamis and Mycalê and Plataeae they had firmly established, as in adamant, the liberty of Greece, they handed it down to all mankind.

8. But the compositions of the poets we may affirm to be but a childish pastime ; orators, however, have some claim when compared with generals ; wherefore with good reason Aeschines[b] asserts derisively that Demosthenes declares that he will enter a suit for possession on behalf of the Speakers' Platform against the War Office. Is it, then, right to prefer Hypereides' Plataean oration to Aristeides' victory at Plataea ? Or Lysias's speech against the Thirty[c] to Thrasybulus's and Archinus's slaughter of those tyrants ? Or Aeschines' oration against Timarchus's wanton ways to Phocion's expedition to Byzantium,[d] by which he prevented the sons of Athenian allies from becoming victims of the wantonness and drunken lust of Macedonians ? Or with the crowns[e] which the Athenian people in common received when they had given freedom to Greece shall we compare

---

[a] Pindar, Fragg. 76 and 77 (ed. Christ) ; p. 556 ed Sandys (L.C.L.) ; *cf.* also *Moralia*, 232 E, 552 B, 867 C ; *Life of Themistocles*, chap. viii. (115 F).

[b] Aeschines, *Against Ctesiphon*, 146.

[c] The speech *Against Eratosthenes*.

[d] *Cf. Life of Phocion*, chap. xiv. (748 A) ; Diodorus, xvi. 77.

[e] Whether " the crowns of Conon " or " the crowns received by the Athenian people " should be read is hard to decide. In favour of Conon may be quoted Demosthenes, xx. 69-70 ; and in favour of the Athenian people (as well as Conon and Chabrias), Demosthenes, xxii. 616, and xxiv. 180.

(350) ἔλαβεν ὁ δῆμος,¹ τὸν Δημοσθένους περὶ τοῦ στεφά-
νου παραβάλωμεν, ἐν ᾧ τοῦτο λαμπρότατον καὶ
λογιώτατον ὁ ῥήτωρ πεποίηκεν, ὀμόσας "τοὺς ἐν
Μαραθῶνι προκινδυνεύσαντας τῶν προγόνων," οὐ²
τοὺς ἐν ταῖς σχολαῖς τὰ μειράκια προδιδάσκοντας.

Ἐφ' οἷς οὐ³ τοὺς Ἰσοκράτεις καὶ Ἀντιφῶντας
καὶ Ἰσαίους, ἀλλὰ τούτους ἡ πόλις δημοσίαις
ταφαῖς ἔθαψεν, ὑποδεξαμένη τὰ λείψανα τῶν
D σωμάτων, καὶ τούτους ἀπεθέωσε τοῖς ὅρκοις⁴ ὁ
ῥήτωρ ὀμνύων οὓς οὐκ ἐμιμεῖτο. Ἰσοκράτης δὲ
τοὺς ἐν Μαραθῶνι προκινδυνεύσαντας ὥσπερ ἀλ-
λοτρίαις ψυχαῖς φήσας ἐναγωνίσασθαι καὶ καθ-
υμνήσας τὴν τόλμαν αὐτῶν καὶ τὴν ὑπεροψίαν τοῦ
ζῆν, αὐτός, ὥς φασιν, ἤδη γέρων γεγονὼς πρὸς τὸν
πυθόμενον πῶς διάγει, "οὕτως," εἶπεν, "ὡς
ἄνθρωπος ὑπὲρ ἐνενήκοντα ἔτη γεγονὼς καὶ μέγιστον ἡγούμενος τῶν κακῶν τὸν θάνατον." οὐ
γὰρ ἀκονῶν ξίφος οὐδὲ λόγχην χαράττων οὐδὲ
λαμπρύνων κράνος οὐδὲ στρατευόμενος οὐδ' ἐρέτ-
των, ἀλλ' ἀντίθετα καὶ πάρισα καὶ ὁμοιόπτωτα
κολλῶν καὶ συντιθείς, μονονοῦ κολαπτῆρσι καὶ
E ξυστῆρσι τὰς περιόδους ἀπολεαίνων καὶ ῥυθμίζων
ἐγήρασε. πῶς οὖν οὐκ ἔμελλεν ἄνθρωπος ψόφον
ὅπλων φοβεῖσθαι καὶ σύρρηγμα φαλάγγων⁵ ὁ φοβού-
μενος φωνῆεν φωνήεντι συγκροῦσαι καὶ συλλαβῇ τὸ

---

¹ ὁ δῆμος, added by Helmbold, may have become absorbed
in Δημοσ-θένης.
² οὐ Stephanus: ἢ.   ³ οὐ added by Stephanus.
⁴ τοῖς ὅρκοις Meziriacus: τοὺς ὅρκους.
⁵ φαλάγγων Abresch: φάλαγγος.

ᵃ Quoted from De Corona, 208.
ᵇ Cf. Life of Demosthenes, chap. xiv. (852 c); Demosthenes
was an incompetent soldier.

Demosthenes' oration *On the Crown*? For in this speech the orator has made this matter exceedingly perspicuous and intelligible in taking his oath " by the memory of those of our ancestors who risked their lives for us at Marathon," [a] not by the teachers who in the schools gave them as youths their early training.

Wherefore the State has given public burial not to men like Isocrates, Antiphon, and Isaeus, but to these men, whose remains she has taken in her embrace ; and these men it was that the orator deified in his oath when he swore by men whose example he was not following.[b] But Isocrates, although he had declared [c] that those who had risked their lives at Marathon had fought as though their souls were not their own, and although he had hymned their daring and their contempt of life, himself (so they say), when he was already an old man,[d] replied to someone who asked him how he was getting on, " Even as does a man over ninety years of age who considers death the greatest of evils." For he had not grown old sharpening his sword nor whetting his spear-point nor polishing his helmet nor campaigning nor pulling at the oar, but in glueing together and arranging antitheses, balanced clauses, and inflexional similarities, all but smoothing off and proportioning his periods with chisel and file. How could this person do other than fear the clash of arms and the impact of phalanxes, he who feared to let vowel collide with vowel, or to

[c] Isocrates, *Panegyricus*, 86 ; *cf.* Thucydides' language in i. 70.

[d] Contrast Cicero's admiration for Isocrates' old age (*Cato Maior*, 5).

ἰσόκωλον ἐνδεὲς ἐξενεγκεῖν; Μιλτιάδης μὲν γὰρ
ἄρας[1] ἐς Μαραθῶνα τῇ ὑστεραίᾳ τὴν μάχην συνάψας
ἧκεν εἰς ἄστυ μετὰ τῆς στρατιᾶς νενικηκώς, καὶ
Περικλῆς ἐννέα μησὶ Σαμίους καταστρεψάμενος
ἐφρόνει τοῦ Ἀγαμέμνονος μεῖζον ἔτει δεκάτῳ τὴν
Τροίαν ἑλόντος· Ἰσοκράτης δὲ μικροῦ τρεῖς ὀλυμ-
πιάδας ἀνήλωσεν, ἵνα γράψῃ τὸν πανηγυρικὸν
λόγον, οὐ στρατευσάμενος ἐν τούτοις τοῖς χρόνοις
F οὐδὲ πρεσβεύσας οὐδὲ πόλιν κτίσας οὐδὲ ναύαρχος
ἐκπεμφθείς, καίτοι μυρίους τοῦ τότε χρόνου πολέμους ἐνέγκαντος· ἀλλ' ἐν ᾧ Τιμόθεος Εὔβοιαν
ἠλευθέρου καὶ Χαβρίας περὶ Νάξον ἐναυμάχει καὶ
περὶ Λέχαιον Ἰφικράτης κατέκοπτε τὴν Λακεδαιμονίων μόραν,[2] καὶ πᾶσαν ἐλευθερώσας πόλιν ὁ
351 δῆμος ἰσόψηφον αὐτοῖς[3] τὴν Ἑλλάδα κατέστησεν,
οἴκοι καθῆστο βιβλίον ἀναπλάττων τοῖς ὀνόμασιν,
ὅσῳ χρόνῳ τὰ προπύλαια Περικλῆς ἀνέστησε καὶ
τοὺς ἑκατομπέδους. καίτοι καὶ τοῦτον ὡς βραδέως
ἀνύοντα τοῖς ἔργοις ἐπισκώπτων Κρατῖνος οὕτω
πως λέγει περὶ τοῦ διὰ μέσου[4] τείχους,

> λόγοισι γὰρ αὐτὸ[5] προάγει Περικλέης,
> ἔργοισι δ' οὐδὲ κινεῖ.

σκόπει δὲ σοφιστικὴν μικροφροσύνην, τὸ ἔνατον

---

[1] ἄρας Emperius: αὐτός.   [2] μόραν Meziriacus: μοῖραν.
[3] αὐτοῖς Helmbold: αὐτοῖς.
[4] μέσου Wyttenbach: μέσον.
[5] λόγοισι γὰρ αὐτὸ] πάλαι γὰρ αὐτὸ λόγοισι *Life of Pericles*,
chap. xviii.; *cf.* Kock, i. p. 100.   αὐτὸ Reiske: αὐτὸν.

---

[a] A reference to Isocrates' avoidance of hiatus and his
attention to prose rhythm (Cicero, *Brutus*, 32).

utter a phrase whose balance was upset by the lack of a single syllable ? [a] For Miltiades set forth for Marathon, joined battle the next day, and returned victorious with his army to the city ; and Pericles,[b] when he had subdued the Samians in nine months, was prouder of his achievement than was Agamemnon, who captured Troy in the tenth year. But Isocrates consumed almost twelve years in writing his *Panegyric* [c] ; and during this period he took part in no campaigns, nor served on any embassy, nor founded any city, nor was dispatched as commander of a fleet, although this era brought forth countless wars. But while Timotheüs was freeing Euboea, and Chabrias [d] with his fleet was fighting at Naxos, and Iphicrates near Lechaeum was cutting to pieces the Spartan division,[e] and the Athenian people, having liberated every city, bestowed upon Greece equal suffrage with themselves, Isocrates sat at home remodelling a book with mere words, as long a time as sufficed for Pericles to erect the Propylaea and his temples a hundred feet long. Yet Cratinus [f] pokes fun even at Pericles for his slowness in accomplishing his undertakings, and remarks somewhat as follows about his Middle Wall : [g]

> Pericles in his talk makes the wall to advance,
> By his acts he does nothing to budge it.

But consider the petty spirit of this sophist, which

[b] Cf. *Life of Pericles*, chap. xxviii. (167 E) ; Thucydides, i. 117.
[c] Cf. *Moralia*, 837 F ; Quintilian, x. 4. 4 ; Longinus, *On the Sublime*, 4. 2.   [d] Cf. 348 F, *supra.*
[e] Cf. Demosthenes, *Oration* xxiii. 198.
[f] Kock, *Comic. Att. Frag.* i. p. 100, Cratinus, no. 300.
[g] Cf. *Life of Pericles*, chap. xiii. (160 A), where the quotation seems metrically and otherwise closer to the original.

(351) μέρος τοῦ βίου εἰς ἕνα λόγον καταναλίσκουσαν.
ἀλλὰ δὴ μέγα¹ τοὺς Δημοσθένους τοῦ ῥήτορος λόγους ἄξιόν ἐστι τοῖς τοῦ στρατηγοῦ ἔργοις² παραβάλλειν; τὸν κατὰ Κόνωνος αἰκίας³ τοῖς περὶ
B Πύλον τροπαίοις ἐκείνου⁴; τὸν⁵ πρὸς Ἀρεθούσιον⁶
περὶ ἀνδραπόδων τοῖς ἐξανδραποδισθεῖσιν ὑπ' ἐκείνου Σπαρτιάταις; ᾗ ἡλικίᾳ⁷ τοὺς ἐπιτροπικοὺς⁸
ἔγραψε, ταύτην Ἀλκιβιάδης ἔχων Μαντινεῖς καὶ
Ἠλείους ἐπὶ τὴν Λακεδαίμονα συνέστησε. καὶ μὴν
οἵ γε⁹ δημόσιοι λόγοι τοῦτ' ἔχουσι θαυμαστόν, ὅτι
τοῖς Φιλιππικοῖς ἐπὶ πράξεις προτρέπεται καὶ τὴν
Λεπτίνου πρᾶξιν ἐπαινεῖ.

¹ δὴ μέγα F.C.B.; νὴ Δία Madvig; μὰ τὸν Δία Wyttenbach:
δὴ μετά.
² τοῖς τοῦ στρατηγοῦ ἔργοις Wyttenbach: τοῖς στρατηγοῖς.
³ αἰκίας Xylander: ἀνοίας.
⁴ ἐκείνου Leonicus: ἔχειν.
⁵ τὸν added by Papabasileios.
⁶ Ἀρεθούσιον Cobet: ἀμαθούσιον.
⁷ ᾗ ἡλικίᾳ F.C.B.: ἢ ὅτι (ἢ ὅτι ὅτε τοὺς ἐπιτροπικοὺς ἔγραψε,
τὴν ἡλικίαν ταύτην Bernardakis; alii alia).
⁸ ἐπιτροπικοὺς Bernardakis: ἐποίκους.
⁹ γε van Herwerden: τε.

ᵃ Demosthenes, *Oration* liv.
ᵇ *Ibid.* liii.

caused the ninth part of his life to be spent on the composition of one speech. Is it, then, greatly worth our while to compare the speeches of the orator Demosthenes with the deeds of Demosthenes the general? To compare the speech *Against Conon*[a] for assault and battery with Demosthenes' trophies won at Pylos? To compare the speech directed at Arethusius[b] on the slaves with Demosthenes' reduction of the Spartans to slavery? The orator's age when he wrote his speeches against his guardians[c] was the same as that of Alcibiades when he united the Mantineans and Eleans against Sparta.[d] And indeed Demosthenes' public orations have this wonderful characteristic : in the *Philippics* he spurs his countrymen on to action and he praises the action of Leptines.[e]

[c] *Ibid.* xxvii., xxviii., xxix.
[d] *Cf.* Thucydides, v. 43.
[e] Wyttenbach is probably correct in regarding the text of this last paragraph as too corrupt and disjointed for any certain correction and interpretation. The statement concerning Leptines is certainly wrong (*cf.* Demosthenes, *Oration* xx.); but it may have been set right in the context, for the ending is surely missing.

INDEX

INDEX

Aesculapius, 141 : Roman name for Asclepius, god of medicine.

Aethicia, 189, 207 : a region of Thessaly.

Aetolian, 29, 315.

Africa, 365.

Agamemnon, 213, 311, 409, 475, 525 : commander-in-chief of the Greeks in the Trojan war.

Agatharchides, 259 : of Samos, historian.

Agathon, 313 : of Samos, an historian.

Agenor, 239 : king of Argos.

Agenor, 261 : an Argive.

Agesilaüs, 259 : brother of Themistocles.

Agesilaüs, 273 : called father of Pausanias.

Agesilaüs, 299 : an historian.

Agesilaüs, 475 ; king of Sparta 398–360 B.C. Plutarch wrote his life.

Agrigentum, 313 : a city in Sicily.

Agrionia, 167, 223 : a Greek festival, a sort of Feast of All Souls, or Ghosts' Assembly.

Aius Locutius, 338, note α.

Aix, 187 : son of the Python.

Ajax, 297 : son of Telamon and Eriboea, great hero of the Trojan war.

Alala, 515 : the " Battle - Cry," daughter of War.

Alalcomenae, 231 : a city of Ithaca.

Alalcomenium, 231 : the precinct of Athena in Alalcomenae in Boeotia.

Alba, 349 : Alba Longa, the chief city of Latium on Monte Cavo.

Albanians, 365 : a people of the eastern Caucasus.

Albans, 269, 283, 285, 355.

Alcathoë, 221 : daughter of Minyas.

Alcathoüs, 295 : father of Eriboea.

Alcibiades, 77, 393, 417, 493, 517, 527 : an Athenian general, son of Cleinias ; circa 451–404 B.C.

Alcippê, 315 : daughter of Oenomaüs.

Alcman, 333 ; quoted, 331, 431 : choral poet of the 2nd half of the 7th cent. B.C.

Alexander the Great, 275, 331, 377,

383, 387-419, 423, 427-485 : son of Philip, king of Macedon ; 356–323 B.C.

Alexander the Molossian, 377 : son of Neoptolemus and brother of Olympias, king of Epeirus from 342 till his death in 330 B.C.

Alexander of Pherae, 425 : tyrant of Thessaly from 369 till his assassination in 358 B.C.

Alexander Polyhistor, 157, 315 : an excerptor of much rare and curious information ; circa 100–40 B.C.

Alexandria, 231, 397 : a city in Egypt founded by Alexander the Great in 332 B.C.

Alexarchus, 269 : a Greek historian.

Alexida, 205 : daughter of Amphiaraüs.

Allia (Alliensis), 41, 43, 369 : a small tributary of the Tiber eleven miles from Rome, where the Romans were disastrously defeated by the Gauls in 387 (or 390 ?) B.C.

Alpheius, 179, 199 : a river of Arcadia.

Althaea, 295 : mother of Meleager.

Amazons, 243, 305.

Ameria, 295 : mother of Rhesus.

Ammon, 407, 457, 469 : the local god of the Egyptian Thebes, identified by the Greeks with Zeus.

Amorgos, 447 : an island in the Aegean east of Naxos.

Amphiaraüs, 205, 267 : an Argive prophet, killed in the expedition of the Seven against Thebes.

Amphictyon, 193 : father of Physcius.

Amphictyonic Assembly, 249, 261, 263 : council of the Sacred League which met twice yearly at Thermopylae.

Amphipolis, 517 : an Attic colony on the Strymon River in Thrace.

Amphissa, 195 : a town in Locris, near the borders of Phocis.

Amphithea, 297 : the wife of Aeolus, king of the Etruscans.

Amulius, 309 : tyrant of Alba, brother of Numitor.

530

INDEX

INDEX

INDEX

Asia Minor, 419.

Asiatic, 471.

Aspasians, 387 : a tribe in the north-west of the Punjab.

Assacenians, 465 : a tribe in the north-west of the Punjab.

Assyrians, 331.

Aster, 271 : a man of Olynthus.

Astydamas, 519 : an Attic tragic poet of the 4th cent. B.C.

Ateas (or Anteas), 427 : king of the Scythians, 4th cent. B.C.

Ateius Capito, 83 : a great Roman jurist, died A.D. 22.

Atepomarus, 301 : king of the Gauls.

Athena, 179, 273, 283, 467, 497.

Athenian, 45, 163, 365, 495, 513, 521, 525.

Athenians, 201, 217, 257, 259, 285, 301, 499-503, 509, 513, 519, 521.

Athenodorus, 429 : a tragic actor of the age of Alexander.

Athens, 77, 167, 217, 305, 347, 387, 395, 461, 477, 495, 497, 509, 519.

Athos, 433, 435 : a mountain on the peninsula of Actê.

Atilius, Gaius (C. Atilius Bubulcus), 355 : consul in 235 B.C.

Atilius Regulus, M., 291 : consul 267 and 256 B.C.; general in the 1st Punic war.

Atlantic Ocean, 365.

Atossa, 459 : daughter of Darius, wife successively of Cambyses, pseudo-Smerdis, and Darius I. ; mother of Xerxes.

Atreus, 303 : son of Pelops and Hippodameia.

Attica, 257.

Auas, 189 : a river of Thesprotia.

Augeas, 51 : an Argonaut, later king of Elis ; possessed great herds of cattle whose stables, which had not been cleaned for 30 years, it was Heracles' Labour to cleanse.

Augures, 109, 147, 149.

August, 65, 149.

Aulis, 279 : a port of Boeotia.

Auspices, 109.

Autophradate\s, 457 : a Persian admiral.

Auxiliaria, 275 : an epithet of Minerva.

Aventine, 11 : the southernmost of the hills of Rome.

BABYLON, 389, 481.

Babylonian, 395, 453 : Empire, 439.

Bacchae, 513 : plays of that name.

Bacchanalian, 285.

Bacchic, 169, 413, 415, 511, 515.

Bacchus, 51, 155.

Bactria, 395, 469, 481.

Bagoas, 445, 461 : an Egyptian eunuch at the court of Artaxerxes Ochus, whom he murdered, and placed successively Arses and Darius III. on the throne ; killed 335 B.C. by the latter.

Balearicus, see Caecilius.

Barrus, see Vetutius.

Bastarnian(s), 367 : an eastern German people living, *circa* 200–50 B.C., on the Black Sea and the lower Danube.

Beronicê, 183 : a Macedonian name.

Bias, 201 : of Prienê, one of the Seven Wise Men ; *circa* 550 B.C.

Bilip, 183 : Macedonian dialect for Philip.

Birdless Rock, see Aornos.

Bisaltia, 291 : daughter of the king of the Massylians.

Bithynia, 237 : a country in north-western Asia Minor.

Bithynian, 439.

Bithynians, 297.

Bletonesii, 125 : the inhabitants of Bletisa in Spain.

Boëdromion, 519 : Attic month (August-September).

Boeotia, 53, 157, 165, 195, 199, 221, 223, 229, 231, 279.

Boeotian, 277, 279.

Boeotians, 181, 221, 269, 493.

Bona Dea, 35 : the wife (sometimes the daughter) of Faunus.

Bottiaea(n), 217 : a city on the right bank of the river Axius in Macedonia.

Brasidas, 475, 479, 503, 517 : a distinguished Spartan commander in the Peloponnesian war. He was killed at Amphipolis in 422 B.C.

INDEX

Brauron, 201 : a town on the east coast of Attica.

Brennus, 279 : king of the Gauls.

Brundisium, 339 : a seaport of Calabria.

Bruttians, 377 : an Oscan people of south-eastern Italy.

Brutus, see Junius.

Bubulci, 73 : a cognomen of some members of the *gens Iunia.*

Bucephalia, 397 : a city on the Hydaspes, named by Alexander after his horse (*cf.* Aulus Gellius, v. 2. 5).

Bucolidae, 193 : a clan of Ithaca.

Bucolus, 227 : son of Colonus.

bulla(e), 87, 149.

Busiris, 313, 469 : a son of Poseidon ; king of Egypt.

Bysios, 181, 183 : a Delphian month.

Byzantines, 237, 447.

Byzantium, 309, 447, 521.

CABYÊ, 193 : mother of Opus.

Cadmus, 507 : a Phoenician adventurer, reputed founder of Thebes.

Caecilia, Gaia, 53 : see 52, note *c.*

Caecilius Metellus, M., 333 : son of Macedonicus, consul 115 B.C.

Caecilius Metellus Balearicus, Q., 333 : oldest son of Macedonicus, consul 123, censor 120 B.C.

Caecilius Metellus Caprarius, Q., 333 : son of Macedonicus, consul 113, censor 102 B.C.

Caecilius Metellus Diadematus, L., 333 : son of Macedonicus, consul 117 B.C.

Caecilius Metellus Macedonicus, Q., 333 : defeated the Achaeans in 165 ; consul 143, censor 131 ; died 115 B.C.

Caecilius Metellus Pius, Q., 65 : consul 80 ; consul 64 B.C.

Caedicius, Marcus, 339 : a Roman who heard the voice of Aius Locutius.

Caesar, see Julius.

Calaureia, 199 : an island in the Saronic Gulf, opposite Troezen.

Calligeneia, 213 : see 212, note *b.*

Callimachus, 257, 505 : the Athenian polemarch at the battle of Marathon.

Callippides, 511 : an Athenian tragic actor of the 2nd half of the 5th cent. B.C.

Callirrhoê, 291 : daughter of Lycus.

Callisthenes, 183 : of Olynthus, nephew of Aristotle ; historian of Alexander's exploits ; later fell into disfavour and died in prison.

Callisthenes, 267, 271, 301 ; a Greek historian, perhaps identical with the historian of Alexander.

Calpurnia, 287 : daughter of Marius.

Calpurnius, 297 : a Roman.

Calpurnius Crassus, 291 : a Roman commander.

Calvisius Sabinus, C., 339 : one of Caesar's generals ; consul 39 B.C.

Camilli, 329.

Camillus, see Furius.

Campania, 293.

Campanian, 293.

Candaules, 233 : king of Lydia.

Cantabri, 355 : an Iberian people of northern Spain.

Cantharion, 225 : an Arcadian.

Canulia, 297 : daughter of Papirius Tolucer.

Capitol, the, 147, 281, 367, 369 : at Rome.

Capitoline, the, 87, 137, 359, 369 : at Rome.

Caprarius, see Caecilius.

Capratine Nones, 345.

Carcinus, 519 : an Athenian tragic poet.

Caria, 233, 517.

Carmenta, 91-95 : a Roman goddess.

carmina, 91, 93.

Carneades, 391, 393 : of Cyrenê, *circa* 218-129 B.C. ; philosopher of the Third Academy.

Carthaginian, 365, 367, 393.

Carthaginians, 265, 279, 331, 365.

Carvilius, Spurius (Maximus Ruga), 27, 95 : consul 234 and 228 ; died 211 B.C.

Carvilius, Spurius, 89, 95 : freedman of Sp. Carvilius Maximus Ruga ; opened, between 254 and 234 B.C., the first school at Rome.

Caspian Sea, 365, 485.

INDEX

535

INDEX

INDEX

Cynosureis, 197 : division of the citizenry at Megara.

Cyprus, 241, 423, 429, 517.

Cyrus, 67, 385, 453, 459, 475 : called the Elder and the Great ; founder of the Persian Empire ; killed in 529 B.C.

Cyrus, 463 : the Younger, son of Darius II. ; revolted against his brother Artaxerxes II. ; fell at Cunaxa 401 B.C.

Cythera, 493 : an island opposite Cape Malea.

DAMASCUS, 457 : a city of Syria.

Damasenor, 213 : tyrant of Miletus.

Danaïs, 303 : a nymph, mother of Chrysippus.

Danube, 473.

Darius I., 459 : king of Persia 521–485 B.C.

Darius III., 275, 383, 399, 417, 445, 451, 453, 465, 473, 475, 481 : king of Persia 336–330 B.C.

Datis, 257 : Persian satrap who commanded at Marathon.

December, 33, 57, 59, 145.

decemviri, 89

Decii, 329.

Decimus, 155 : a Roman *praenomen*.

Decius Mus, P., 275, 285 : Roman general against the Latins (consul 340 B.C.).

Decius Mus, P., 285 : his son, consul 312, 308, 297, 295 B.C., immolated himself at the battle of Sentinum.

Deianeira, 95 : see 95, note *e*.

Deïmachus, 229 : son of Eleon.

Deinomenes, 455 : father of Tarrias.

Deinon, 229, 231 : general of the Tarentines.

Delos, 163 : an island in the middle of the Cyclades.

Delphi, 13, 39, 217, 237, 249, 317, 429, 439, 461.

Delphians, 181-187.

Delphus, 201, 203 : a Spartan.

Demaratus, 283 : a Greek historian.

Demaratus, 399 : a Corinthian.

Demetrius, 447 : called Poliorcetes, son of Antigonus the One-Eyed ; king of Macedon ; 337-283 B.C. Plutarch wrote his life.

Demetrius, 515 : probably Demetrius of Phalerum is meant.

Democritus quoted, 325 : philosopher of Abdera, the great exponent of the Atomic Theory ; *circa* 460-400 B.C.

Demodicê, 281 : daughter of Rheximachus.

Demodicus, 281 : son of Demostratus.

Demonicê, 279 : a maiden of Ephesus.

Demosthenes, 493, 501, 517, 527 : distinguished Athenian general ; killed at Syracuse 413 B.C.

Demosthenes, 521, 523, 527 ; quoted, 359, 523 : great Attic orator ; 385-322 B.C.

Demostratus, 281 : of Pheneüs, father of Demodicus.

Demostratus, 299 : of Ephesus, father of Aristonymus.

Demoteles, 243 : ruler of Samos.

Dercyllus, 283, 313 : a Greek historian.

Dexicreon, 241 : a man of Samos (?).

Diadematus, see Caecilius.

Dialis, see Flamen.

Diana, 9, 11.

Diocles, 229 : a Greek historian ; which writer of that name is here cited is quite uncertain.

Diogenes, 411-415 : of Sinopê, Cynic philosopher ; 4th cent.

Diogenes the Babylonian, 395 : of Seleuceia, Stoic philosopher ; died *circa* 150 B.C.

Diomedes, 21, 237, 291, 477 : son of Tydeus ; hero of the Trojan war.

Dion, 53.

Dionysiac, 159.

Dionysian Festival, 507 : at Athens.

Dionysius, 119 : of Halicarnassus ; historian, critic, and rhetorician of the 1st cent. B.C.

Dionysius the Elder, 407, 425, 427, 449 : born 430 ; tyrant of Syracuse 405-367 B.C.

Dionysius the Younger, 449 : tyrant of Syracuse until his expulsion by Timoleon 343 B.C.

Dionysius Siculus, 259 : a Greek historian.

Dionysus, 107, 155, 157, 217, 219, 223,

537

INDEX

Eumolpus, 287, 301 : son of Poseidon and Chionê ; king of Eleusis.

Eunosta, 227 : a nymph.

Eunostus, 227 : son of Elieus.

Euphranor, 497, 501 : of Corinth, a great painter ; early 4th cent. B.C.

Euphrates, 453, 481.

Euripides, 287, 293, 295, 395, 420, note a, 511 ; quoted, 133, 447 : Athenian tragic poet ; circa 485-406 B.C.

Euripus, 205 : the strait between Euboea and the mainland of Greece.

Europe, 401.

Eurotas, 331 : a river of Laconia.

Euryanassa, 303 : mother of Pelops.

Eurymedon, 517 : a river of Pamphylia where Cimon won a double victory over the Persians (circa 466 B.C.).

Euxine, 365, 517 : the Black Sea.

Evander, 57, 71, 91, 95, 115, 137 : an Arcadian ; according to some, son of Hermes ; founded a city in Italy near the future site of Rome.

Evenus, 315 : son of Ares and Steropê.

Fabia, 311 : wife of Fabius Fabricianus.

Fabia, 311 : daughter of Fabius Fabricianus.

Fabii Maximi, 329.

Fabius Fabricianus, 311 : a Roman commander.

Fabius Fabricianus, 311 : his son.

Fabius Maximus Gurges, Q., 263 : consul 292, 275 and 265 B.C. (cf. 263, note c).

Fabius Maximus Verrucosus, Q., 265, 311 : Cunctator ; consul 233, 228, 215, 214, 209 ; dictator 217 ; died 203 B.C. Plutarch wrote his life.

Fabricii, 329.

Fabricius Luscinus, C., 121 : consul 282 and 278 ; censor 275, commander against Pyrrhus 278 B.C.

Fabula, 61 : a name of the courtesan Larentia.

Falerii, 307 : a city of southern Etruria.

Fate, a, 93.

Faunus, 35, 313 : the seer (son of Mercury ?) ; god of fertility.

Faustus, 271 : son of Saturn.

Faustus, 311 : a shepherd.

Favorinus, 51 : of Arelatê (Arles), philosopher and sophist of the 1st cent. A.D.

February, 33, 57, 105.

Felix, 271 : son of Saturn.

Felix, 335 : a title adopted by Sulla.

Fenestella, 73 : an historian of the Early Empire.

Fenestella, Porta, 359.

fenestra, 63.

Feretrius, 263 : an epithet of Jupiter.

Fetiales, 97 : an ancient Roman priestly college.

Firmus, 305 : son of Ebius Tolieix.

flamen, 69, 83.

Flamen Dialis, 67, 75, 83, 161.

Flaminian, 103.

Flaminica, 133.

Flaminius, C., 103 ; consul 223 and 217, censor 220 B.C. ; fell at Trasimenê (217 B.C.).

Flavius Domitianus, T. 83 : son of Vespasian ; Emperor A.D. 81-96.

Florentia, 297 : daughter of Lucius Troscius.

Fornacalia, 135.

Fortuna (Fortuna), 63, 111, 113, 159, 323-377, 383-389, 401, 413, 415, 435-453, 459-485.

Forum, the, 121, 137, 267 : at Rome.

Forum Boarium, 125 : at Rome.

Fufetius, Mettius, 269 : king of Alba Longa.

Fulvius Stellus, 299 : a Roman.

furcifer(i), 107, 109.

Furies, 85.

Furius Camillus, M., 337, 369, 371, 375 : the conqueror of Veii and saviour of Rome after the battle of the Allia. Plutarch wrote his life.

Gabii, 347 : a town on the Via Praenestina.

Gaia, 53 : a Roman *praenomen*.

Gaius, 53, 155 : a Roman *praenomen*.

Gallic, 147, 281, 337, 339.

Gallus, see Sulpicius.

Gandridae, 387 : an Indian people of the Punjab.

INDEX

Garaetium, 291 : a fortress of the Massylians.

Gaul, 355.

Gauls, 41, 125, 129, 279, 285, 301, 367, 369, 375.

Gaza, 385, 465 : principal city of the Philistines.

Gedrosia, 463 : the south-eastern portion of the Iranian highlands.

Gedrosians, 395.

Gegania, 361 : wife of Servius Tullius.

Geneta Mana, 85.

Germans, 355.

Germany, 287.

Geryon, 31, 313 : giant son of Chrysaor and Callirrhoê.

Gestius, see Valerius.

Gidica, 307 : wife of Comminius Super.

Glaucia, 229 : daughter of Scamander.

Glaucia, 229 : a river of Boeotia.

Glauco, Lucius, 259 : a Roman patrician.

Gnaeus, 155 : a Roman *praenomen*.

Gorgias, 509 : of Leontini, a famous rhetorician ; *circa* 483–375 B.C.

Granicus, 275, 385, 465 : a river of the Troad.

Grecian, 391, 395, 399.

Greece, 27, 57, 169, 263, 273, 387, 479, 493, 517-521, 525.

Greek, 13, 37, 79, 97, 99, 103, 359, 393, 397, 401, 413, 415, 439, 447.

Greeks, 13, 29, 43, 55, 57, 63, 69, 85, 105, 125, 129, 141, 155, 181, 239, 247, 367, 395-399, 413, 473, 477, 485, 519.

Gyges, 233 : a Lydian.

Gyliphus, 309 : an Arcadian shepherd.

Gymnosophists, 413.

Habrotê, 195 : daughter of Onchestus.

Hades, 47.

Halicarnassus, 453 : a Dorian city of Asia Minor, opposite Rhodes.

Hanging Gardens, 471: of Babylon.

Hannibal, 265, 293, 367, 405 : the great Carthaginian general ; 247-183 B.C.

Harbingers, 273.

Harma, 267 : a town of Boeotia, near Tanagra.

Hasdrubal, 259 : a Carthaginian king.

Hasdrubal, 393 : Cleitomachus's Carthaginian name.

Hecatê, 85, 105, 165 : a Greek chthonic deity.

Hector, 475 : son of Priam, the Trojan hero.

Hector, 519 : a tragedy of Astydamas.

Hecuba, 293, 425 : wife of Priam.

Hegesistratus, 315 : of Ephesus.

Helen, 307 : daughter of Tyndareüs, wife of Menelaüs.

Hellespont, 401, 411 : the modern Dardanelles.

Hellespontine, 493.

Helvia, 127 : a Roman maiden.

Hephaestion, 417, 443, 459 : son of Amyntor, friend of Alexander ; died 324 B.C.

Hera, 9, 117, 167.

Heracleia, 449 : a city of Pontus.

Heracleidae, 461: descendants of Heracles.

Heracleides Ponticus, 503 : of Heracleia, pupil of Plato ; philosopher and historian of the 4th cent. B.C.

Heracleius, 269 : a river of Boeotia.

Heracles, 221, 229, 233, 245, 247, 269, 277, 313, 345, 377, 413, 429, 467, 469, 507 : see also Hercules.

Heraeïs, 195 : a division of the citizenry at Megara.

Hercules, 31, 51, 57, 61, 95, 137, 139, 313 : see also Heracles.

Hermes, 205, 241.

Herodorus, 139 : of Heracleia, logographer ; wrote a fanciful book on Heracles and on the Argonauts.

Herodotus, quoted, 47 : Greek historian of the 5th cent.

Herois, 185, 187 : a festival at Delphi.

Hesianax, 293 : a Greek historian.

Hesiod, 73 : of Ascra in Boeotia, didactic poet of the 8th cent. B.C.

Hippalcmas, 221 : father of Peneleös.

Hippasus, 221 : son of Leucippê.

Hippocoön, 137 : son of Oebalus of

INDEX

INDEX

INDEX

Maximus, C., 293 : a Roman.

Maximus Gurges, see Fabius.

May, 55, 131, 133.

Mazaeus, 453 : satrap of Babylon under Darius III.

Medea, 513 : daughter of Aeëtes, followed the Argonauts to Greece.

Medes, 515.

Media, 405.

Median, 401.

Medius, 451 : son of Oxythenus ; friend of Alexander.

Medullina, 287 : daughter of Aruntius.

Megara, 197, 225, 493.

Megareis, 197 : division of the citizenry at Megara.

Megareus, 195 : son of Onchestus.

Megarian, 195.

Megarians, 195, 197, 225, 243-249.

Megarid, 195, 247.

Melantheia, 199 : daughter of the Alpheius.

Meleager, 295 : son of Ares and Althaea.

Meleager, 441, 445 : a Macedonian general.

Meleager, 295 : a drama of Euripides.

Melia, 507 : daughter of Oceanus, mother of Ismenius.

Menander, 507 ; quoted, 335 : Athenian comic poet ; 342-291 B.C.

Menelaüs, 467 : husband of Helen, brother of Agamemnon.

Mens, 335.

Menyllus, 279, 295 : a Greek historian.

Mercury, 133, 313.

Meropes, 247 : Coans.

Mesopotamia, 397.

Messenians, 179.

Metella, 279 : daughter of Metellus.

Metellus, 259, 279 : a Roman general.

Metellus, see Caecilius.

Meteorology, 181 : a work of Theophrastus.

Methon, 185 : ancestor of Orpheus.

Methonê, 185, 269, 479 : city on the coast of Macedonia.

Mettius, see Fufetius.

Mezentius, 77, 119 : king of Caerê in Etruria.

Midas, 265 : king of Phrygia.

Middle Wall, 525 : at Athens.

Milesian, 259-265, 275, 277, 281-285, 291, 301, 311, 315, 405.

Milesians, 201, 213.

Miletus, 453 : chief city of Ionian Asia Minor.

Miltiades, 257, 477, 511, 515, 517, 525 : son of Cimon, in command of the Athenians at Marathon ; died soon after in disgrace.

Minerva, 275.

Minos, 217, 305 : son of Zeus and Europa, king of Crete.

Minyads, 223 : daughters of Minyas.

Minyae, 235 : a pre-Greek people of Boeotia and Asia Minor.

Minyan, 235.

Minyas, 221 : son of Poseidon.

Mithridates, 367 : Eupator, king of Pontus ; 132-63 B.C.

Mithridates, 385 : a Persian, son-in-law of Darius III.

Mithridatic wars, 335.

Mnasigeiton, 199 : a Greek historian.

Molossia, 189, 207 : district of Epeirus.

Molossian, 377.

Molpus, 209 : a flute-player.

Mucius Scaevola, 261, 329 : a Roman.

Munichion, 519 : Attic month (March-April).

Murcia, 35 : an epithet of Venus.

Muses, 95, 427, 511.

Muthias, 295 : brother of Silvia.

Mutilus, 353 : commander of the Samnites in the Social War.

Mycalê, 243, 521 : a mountain ridge near Miletus, where the Greeks routed the Persians in 479 B.C.

Mylasa, 233 : city of Caria.

Mynniscus, 513 : an Athenian tragic actor.

Myronides, 493 : son of Callias ; Athenian general ; routed the Boeotians at Oenophyta in 457/6 B.C.

Myrtia, 35 : an epithet of Venus.

Myrtis, 227 : of Anthedon, lyric poetess, teacher of Corinna.

Myson, 129, : of Chen, a sage ; *circa* 600 B.C.

544

INDEX

545

INDEX

Perillus, 313: bronze-founder of Agrigentum.

Perinthians, 243.

Perinthus, 455: Samian colony on the Propontis.

Perioeci, 497: the Achaean free population of Laconia, which had no citizen rights.

Perrhaebia, 37: a district of Thessaly.

Perseus, 333: son of Philip V.; last king of Macedonia 178–168 B.C.

Perseus, 413: son of Zeus and Danaë; slayer of the Medusa.

Persia, 385, 445.

Persian, 257, 259, 265, 275, 349, 365, 389, 401, 451, 469, 471; Gulf, 439.

Persians, 263, 273, 331, 393, 395, 451, 453, 481, 515.

Petronius Valentinus, 311: a Roman youth.

Phaedra, 305: daughter of Minos.

Phaenomena, 273: a poem of Aratus.

Phalaris, 313: tyrant of Agrigentum.

Phalion, 237: a place in Bithynia.

Pheidias, 497: Athenian sculptor of the 5th cent. B.C.

Phemius, 191: king of the Aenianians.

Pheneans, 281: the people of Pheneüs, a city of Arcadia.

Pherae, 199, 425: the chief city of the Thessalian Pelasgiotis.

Philarchus, 299: a man of Smyrna.

Philip, 269, 271, 387–391, 399, 400, 427, 431, 455, 457, 471, 475: of Macedon; conqueror of Greece, father of Alexander; king of Macedon 359–336 B.C.

Philip V.,'365, 367: king of Macedon, defeated by Flamininus at Cynocephalae, 197; 237–179 B.C.

Philippics, 527: orations of Demosthenes against Philip of Macedon.

Philochorus, 495: Athenian historian; killed soon after 216 B.C.

Philoetius, 193: the cowherd of Odysseus.

Philotas, 455, 457: son of Parmenion; prominent Companion of Alexander, executed for treason.

Philoxenus, 419: governor of the coast-lands of Asia Minor under Alexander.

Philoxenus, 427: of Cythera, poet at the court of Dionysius I. the Elder.

Phliasians, 225: people of Phlius, a city between Sicyon and Argolis.

Phloeum, 243: a place in Samos.

Phocion, 521: Athenian general and statesman; 402–317 B.C. Plutarch wrote his life.

Phocis, 69.

Phocus, 293: son of Aeacus and Psamathê.

Phoebus, 449, 479.

Phoenicia, 423.

Phoenician, 517.

Phoenissae, 513: dramas of that name.

Phormio, 493: distinguished Athenian admiral; died soon after 428 B.C.

Phrygia, 265.

Phrynê, 439: famous courtesan of Thespiae; 4th cent. B.C.

Phrynichus, 521; Athenian tragic poet, son of Polyphrasmon; early 5th cent. B.C.

Phylarchus, 473, 495: historian; opponent of Aratus of Sicyon; 3rd cent. B.C.

Phylê, 493, 517, 519: an Attic border fortress on Mt. Parnes.

Phyleus, 51: son of Augeas.

Phylonomê, 309: daughter of Nyctimus and Arcadia.

Physcius, 193: son of Amphictyon.

Physcus, 193: a city of the Ozolian Locrians.

Picus, 37: king of the Laurentians, turned by Circê into a woodpecker.

Pinarii, 95: a Roman family.

Pindar, 507; quoted, 331, 357, 507, 519: Greek choral poet, *circa* 522–442 B.C.

Piraeis, 195: a division of the citizenry at Megara.

Pisa, 303: a mountain of Arcadia.

Plataeae, 519, 521: a town in Boeotia near Attica, where the Greeks defeated the Persians under Mardonius in 479 B.C.

Plataean, 521.

547

INDEX

INDEX

549

INDEX

INDEX

INDEX

Printed in Great Britain by R. & R. CLARK, LIMITED, *Edinburgh*

THE LOEB CLASSICAL LIBRARY

VOLUMES ALREADY PUBLISHED

LATIN AUTHORS

AMMIANUS MARCELLINUS. J. C. Rolfe. 3 Vols.

APULEIUS: THE GOLDEN ASS (METAMORPHOSES). W. Adlington (1566). Revised by S. Gaselee.

ST. AUGUSTINE: CITY OF GOD. 7 Vols. Vol. I. G. E. McCracken. Vol. VI. W. C. Greene.

ST. AUGUSTINE, CONFESSIONS OF. W. Watts (1631). 2 Vols.

ST. AUGUSTINE: SELECT LETTERS. J. H. Baxter.

AUSONIUS. H. G. Evelyn White. 2 Vols.

BEDE. J. E. King. 2 Vols.

BOETHIUS: TRACTS AND DE CONSOLATIONE PHILOSOPHIAE. Rev. H. F. Stewart and E. K. Rand.

CAESAR: ALEXANDRIAN, AFRICAN AND SPANISH WARS. A. G. Way.

CAESAR: CIVIL WARS. A. G. Peskett.

CAESAR: GALLIC WAR. H. J. Edwards.

CATO AND VARRO: DE RE RUSTICA. H. B. Ash and W. D. Hooper.

CATULLUS. F. W. Cornish; TIBULLUS. J. B. Postgate; and PERVIGILIUM VENERIS. J. W. Mackail.

CELSUS: DE MEDICINA. W. G. Spencer. 3 Vols.

CICERO: BRUTUS AND ORATOR. G. L. Hendrickson and H. M. Hubbell.

CICERO: DE FINIBUS. H. Rackham.

CICERO: DE INVENTIONE, etc. H. M. Hubbell.

CICERO: DE NATURA DEORUM AND ACADEMICA. H. Rackham.

1

THE LOEB CLASSICAL LIBRARY

Livy. B. O. Foster, F. G. Moore, Evan T. Sage, A. C. Schlesinger and R. M. Geer (General Index). 14 Vols.

Lucan. J. D. Duff.

Lucretius. W. H. D. Rouse.

Martial. W. C. A. Ker. 2 Vols.

Minor Latin Poets: from Publilius Syrus to Rutilius Namatianus, including Grattius, Calpurnius Siculus, Nemesianus, Avianus, with "Aetna," "Phoenix" and other poems. J. Wight Duff and Arnold M. Duff.

Ovid: The Art of Love and other Poems. J. H. Mozley.

Ovid: Fasti. Sir James G. Frazer.

Ovid: Heroides and Amores. Grant Showerman.

Ovid: Metamorphoses. F. J. Miller. 2 Vols.

Ovid: Tristia and Ex Ponto. A. L. Wheeler.

Petronius. M. Heseltine; Seneca: Apocolocyntosis. W. H. D. Rouse.

Plautus. Paul Nixon. 5 Vols.

Pliny: Letters. Melmoth's translation revised by W. M. L. Hutchinson. 2 Vols.

Pliny: Natural History. 10 Vols. Vols. I-V and IX. H. Rackham. Vols. VI and VII. W. H. S. Jones. Vol. X. D. E. Eichholz.

Propertius. H. E. Butler.

Prudentius. H. J. Thomson. 2 Vols.

Quintilian. H. E. Butler. 4 Vols.

Remains of Old Latin. E. H. Warmington. 4 Vols. Vol. I (Ennius and Caecilius). Vol. II (Livius, Naevius, Pacuvius, Accius). Vol. III (Lucilius, Laws of the XII Tables). Vol. IV (Archaic Inscriptions).

Sallust. J. C. Rolfe.

Scriptores Historiae Augustae. D. Magie. 3 Vols.

Seneca: Apocolocyntosis. Cf. Petronius.

Seneca: Epistulae Morales. R. M. Gummere. 3 Vols.

Seneca: Moral Essays. J. W. Basore. 3 Vols.

Seneca: Tragedies. F. J. Miller. 2 Vols.

Sidonius: Poems and Letters. W. B. Anderson. 2 Vols.

Silius Italicus. J. D. Duff. 2 Vols.

Statius. J. H. Mozley. 2 Vols.

Suetonius. J. C. Rolfe. 2 Vols.

Tacitus: Dialogus. Sir Wm. Peterson; and Agricola and Germania. Maurice Hutton.

Tacitus: Histories and Annals. C. H. Moore and J. Jackson. 4 Vols.

3

THE LOEB CLASSICAL LIBRARY

TERENCE. John Sargeaunt. 2 Vols.
TERTULLIAN : APOLOGIA AND DE SPECTACULIS. T. R. Glover ;
  MINUCIUS FELIX. G. H. Rendall.
VALERIUS FLACCUS. J. H. Mozley.
VARRO : DE LINGUA LATINA. R. G. Kent. 2 Vols.
VELLEIUS PATERCULUS AND RES GESTAE DIVI AUGUSTI.
  F. W. Shipley.
VIRGIL. H. R. Fairclough. 2 Vols.
VITRUVIUS : DE ARCHITECTURA. F. Granger. 2 Vols.

GREEK AUTHORS

ACHILLES TATIUS. S. Gaselee.
AELIAN : ON THE NATURE OF ANIMALS. A. F. Scholfield.
  3 Vols.
AENEAS TACTICUS, ASCLEPIODOTUS AND ONASANDER. The
  Illinois Greek Club.
AESCHINES. C. D. Adams.
AESCHYLUS. H. Weir Smyth. 2 Vols.
ALCIPHRON, AELIAN AND PHILOSTRATUS : LETTERS. A. R.
  Benner and F. H. Fobes.
APOLLODORUS. Sir James G. Frazer. 2 Vols.
APOLLONIUS RHODIUS. R. C. Seaton.
THE APOSTOLIC FATHERS. Kirsopp Lake. 2 Vols.
APPIAN'S ROMAN HISTORY. Horace White. 4 Vols.
ARATUS. *Cf.* CALLIMACHUS.
ARISTOPHANES. Benjamin Bickley Rogers. 3 Vols. Verse
  trans.
ARISTOTLE : ART OF RHETORIC. J. H. Freese.
ARISTOTLE : ATHENIAN CONSTITUTION, EUDEMIAN ETHICS,
  VIRTUES AND VICES. H. Rackham.
ARISTOTLE : GENERATION OF ANIMALS. A. L. Peck.
ARISTOTLE : METAPHYSICS. H. Tredennick. 2 Vols.
ARISTOTLE : METEOROLOGICA. H. D. P. Lee.
ARISTOTLE : MINOR WORKS. W. S. Hett. " On Colours,"
  " On Things Heard," " Physiognomics," " On Plants,"
  " On Marvellous Things Heard," " Mechanical Problems,"
  " On Indivisible Lines," " Situations and Names of
  Winds," " On Melissus, Xenophanes, and Gorgias."
ARISTOTLE : NICOMACHEAN ETHICS. H. Rackham.

THE LOEB CLASSICAL LIBRARY

ARISTOTLE: OECONOMICA AND MAGNA MORALIA. G. C. Armstrong. (With Metaphysics, Vol. II.)

ARISTOTLE: ON THE HEAVENS. W. K. C. Guthrie.

ARISTOTLE: ON THE SOUL, PARVA NATURALIA, ON BREATH. W. S. Hett.

ARISTOTLE: THE CATEGORIES. ON INTERPRETATION. H. P. Cooke; PRIOR ANALYTICS. H. Tredennick.

ARISTOTLE: POSTERIOR ANALYTICS. H. Tredennick; TOPICS. E. S. Forster.

ARISTOTLE: SOPHISTICAL REFUTATIONS. COMING-TO-BE AND PASSING-AWAY. E. S. Forster. ON THE COSMOS. D. J. Furley.

ARISTOTLE: PARTS OF ANIMALS. A. L. Peck; MOTION AND PROGRESSION OF ANIMALS. E. S. Forster.

ARISTOTLE: PHYSICS. Rev. P. Wicksteed and F. M. Cornford. 2 Vols.

ARISTOTLE: POETICS; LONGINUS ON THE SUBLIME. W. Hamilton Fyfe; DEMETRIUS ON STYLE. W. Rhys Roberts.

ARISTOTLE: POLITICS. H. Rackham.

ARISTOTLE: PROBLEMS. W. S. Hett. 2 Vols.

ARISTOTLE: RHETORICA AD ALEXANDRUM. H. Rackham. (With Problems, Vol. II.)

ARRIAN: HISTORY OF ALEXANDER AND INDICA. Rev. E. Iliffe Robson. 2 Vols.

ATHENAEUS: DEIPNOSOPHISTAE. C. B. Gulick. 7 Vols.

ST. BASIL: LETTERS. R. J. Deferrari. 4 Vols.

CALLIMACHUS: FRAGMENTS. C. A. Trypanis.

CALLIMACHUS: HYMNS AND EPIGRAMS, AND LYCOPHRON. A. W. Mair; ARATUS. G. R. Mair.

CLEMENT OF ALEXANDRIA. Rev. G. W. Butterworth.

COLLUTHUS. Cf. OPPIAN.

DAPHNIS AND CHLOE. Cf. LONGUS.

DEMOSTHENES I: OLYNTHIACS, PHILIPPICS AND MINOR ORATIONS: I-XVII AND XX. J. H. Vince.

DEMOSTHENES II: DE CORONA AND DE FALSA LEGATIONE. C. A. Vince and J. H. Vince.

DEMOSTHENES III: MEIDIAS, ANDROTION, ARISTOCRATES, TIMOCRATES, ARISTOGEITON. J. H. Vince.

DEMOSTHENES IV-VI: PRIVATE ORATIONS AND IN NEAERAM. A. T. Murray.

DEMOSTHENES VII: FUNERAL SPEECH, EROTIC ESSAY, EXORDIA AND LETTERS. N. W. and N. J. DeWitt.

DIO CASSIUS: ROMAN HISTORY. E. Cary. 9 Vols.

THE LOEB CLASSICAL LIBRARY

DIO CHRYSOSTOM. 5 Vols. Vols. I and II. J. W. Cohoon. Vol. III. J. W. Cohoon and H. Lamar Crosby. Vols. IV and V. H. Lamar Crosby.

DIODORUS SICULUS. 12 Vols. Vols. I-VI. C. H. Oldfather. Vol. VII. C. L. Sherman. Vols. IX and X. Russel M. Geer. Vol. XI. F. R. Walton.

DIOGENES LAERTIUS. R. D. Hicks. 2 Vols.

DIONYSIUS OF HALICARNASSUS : ROMAN ANTIQUITIES. Spelman's translation revised by E. Cary. 7 Vols.

EPICTETUS. W. A. Oldfather. 2 Vols.

EURIPIDES. A. S. Way. 4 Vols. Verse trans.

EUSEBIUS : ECCLESIASTICAL HISTORY. Kirsopp Lake and J. E. L. Oulton. 2 Vols.

GALEN : ON THE NATURAL FACULTIES. A. J. Brock.

THE GREEK ANTHOLOGY. W. R. Paton. 5 Vols.

THE GREEK BUCOLIC POETS (THEOCRITUS, BION, MOSCHUS). J. M. Edmonds.

GREEK ELEGY AND IAMBUS WITH THE ANACREONTEA. J. M. Edmonds. 2 Vols.

GREEK MATHEMATICAL WORKS. Ivor Thomas. 2 Vols.

HERODES. Cf. THEOPHRASTUS : CHARACTERS.

HERODOTUS. A. D. Godley. 4 Vols.

HESIOD AND THE HOMERIC HYMNS. H. G. Evelyn White.

HIPPOCRATES AND THE FRAGMENTS OF HERACLEITUS. W. H. S. Jones and E. T. Withington. 4 Vols.

HOMER : ILIAD. A. T. Murray. 2 Vols.

HOMER : ODYSSEY. A. T. Murray. 2 Vols.

ISAEUS. E. S. Forster.

ISOCRATES. George Norlin and LaRue Van Hook. 3 Vols.

ST. JOHN DAMASCENE : BARLAAM AND IOASAPH. Rev. G. R. Woodward and Harold Mattingly.

JOSEPHUS. H. St. J. Thackeray and Ralph Marcus. 9 Vols. Vols. I-VII.

JULIAN. Wilmer Cave Wright. 3 Vols.

LONGUS : DAPHNIS AND CHLOE. Thornley's translation revised by J. M. Edmonds; and PARTHENIUS. S. Gaselee.

LUCIAN. 8 Vols. Vols. I-V. A. M. Harmon; Vol. VI. K. Kilburn; Vol. VII. M. D. Macleod.

LYCOPHRON. Cf. CALLIMACHUS.

LYRA GRAECA. J. M. Edmonds. 3 Vols.

LYSIAS. W. R. M. Lamb.

MANETHO. W. G. Waddell ; PTOLEMY : TETRABIBLOS. F. E. Robbins.

MARCUS AURELIUS. C. R. Haines.

MENANDER. F. G. Allinson.

MINOR ATTIC ORATORS. 2 Vols. K. J. Maidment and J. O. Burtt.

NONNOS: DIONYSIACA. W. H. D. Rouse. 3 Vols.

OPPIAN, COLLUTHUS, TRYPHIODORUS. A. W. Mair.

PAPYRI. NON-LITERARY SELECTIONS. A. S. Hunt and C. C. Edgar. 2 Vols. LITERARY SELECTIONS (Poetry). D. L. Page.

PARTHENIUS. *Cf.* LONGUS.

PAUSANIAS: DESCRIPTION OF GREECE. W. H. S. Jones. 5 Vols. and Companion Vol. arranged by R. E. Wycherley.

PHILO. 10 Vols. Vols. I-V. F. H. Colson and Rev. G. H. Whitaker; Vols. VI-X. F. H. Colson; General Index. Rev. J. W. Earp.

Two Supplementary Vols. Translation only from an Armenian Text. Ralph Marcus.

PHILOSTRATUS: IMAGINES; CALLISTRATUS: DESCRIPTIONS. A. Fairbanks.

PHILOSTRATUS: THE LIFE OF APOLLONIUS OF TYANA. F. C. Conybeare. 2 Vols.

PHILOSTRATUS AND EUNAPIUS: LIVES OF THE SOPHISTS. Wilmer Cave Wright.

PINDAR. Sir J. E. Sandys.

PLATO: CHARMIDES, ALCIBIADES, HIPPARCHUS, THE LOVERS, THEAGES, MINOS AND EPINOMIS. W. R. M. Lamb.

PLATO: CRATYLUS, PARMENIDES, GREATER HIPPIAS, LESSER HIPPIAS. H. N. Fowler.

PLATO: EUTHYPHRO, APOLOGY, CRITO, PHAEDO, PHAEDRUS. H. N. Fowler.

PLATO: LACHES, PROTAGORAS, MENO, EUTHYDEMUS. W. R. M. Lamb.

PLATO: LAWS. Rev. R. G. Bury. 2 Vols.

PLATO: LYSIS, SYMPOSIUM, GORGIAS. W. R. M. Lamb.

PLATO: REPUBLIC. Paul Shorey. 2 Vols.

PLATO: STATESMAN, PHILEBUS. H. N. Fowler; ION. W. R. M. Lamb.

PLATO: THEAETETUS AND SOPHIST. H. N. Fowler.

PLATO: TIMAEUS, CRITIAS, CLITOPHO, MENEXENUS, EPISTULAE. Rev. R. G. Bury.

PLUTARCH: MORALIA. 15 Vols. Vols. I-V. F. C. Babbitt; Vol. VI. W. C. Helmbold; Vol. VII. P. H. De Lacy and B. Einarson; Vol. IX. E. L. Minar, Jr., F. H. Sandbach,

THE LOEB CLASSICAL LIBRARY

W. C. Helmbold; Vol. X. H. N. Fowler; Vol. XII. H. Cherniss and W. C. Helmbold.

PLUTARCH: THE PARALLEL LIVES. B. Perrin. 11 Vols.

POLYBIUS. W. R. Paton. 6 Vols.

PROCOPIUS: HISTORY OF THE WARS. H. B. Dewing. 7 Vols.

PTOLEMY: TETRABIBLOS. *Cf.* MANETHO.

QUINTUS SMYRNAEUS. A. S. Way. Verse trans.

SEXTUS EMPIRICUS. Rev. R. G. Bury. 4 Vols.

SOPHOCLES. F. Storr. 2 Vols. Verse trans.

STRABO: GEOGRAPHY. Horace L. Jones. 8 Vols.

THEOPHRASTUS: CHARACTERS. J. M. Edmonds; HERODES, etc. A. D. Knox.

THEOPHRASTUS: ENQUIRY INTO PLANTS. Sir Arthur Hort. 2 Vols.

THUCYDIDES. C. F. Smith. 4 Vols.

TRYPHIODORUS. *Cf.* OPPIAN.

XENOPHON: CYROPAEDIA. Walter Miller. 2 Vols.

XENOPHON: HELLENICA, ANABASIS, APOLOGY, AND SYMPOSIUM. C. L. Brownson and O. J. Todd. 3 Vols.

XENOPHON: MEMORABILIA AND OECONOMICUS. E. C. Marchant.

XENOPHON: SCRIPTA MINORA. E. C. Marchant.

VOLUMES IN PREPARATION

GREEK AUTHORS

ARISTOTLE: HISTORY OF ANIMALS. A. L. Peck.

PLOTINUS. A. H. Armstrong.

LATIN AUTHORS

BABRIUS AND PHAEDRUS. B. E. Perry.

DESCRIPTIVE PROSPECTUS ON APPLICATION

CAMBRIDGE, MASS.   LONDON
HARVARD UNIV. PRESS   WILLIAM HEINEMANN LTD